Corporations, S Corporations, and Partnerships Practice Sets

West Federal Taxation
Corporations, Partnerships, Estates & Trusts
2006 EDITION

William H. Hoffman, Jr., J.D., Ph.D., CPA
University of Houston

William A. Raabe, Ph.D., CPA
The Ohio State University

James E. Smith, Ph.D., CPA
College of William and Mary

David M. Maloney, Ph.D., CPA
University of Virginia

Prepared by

Donald R. Trippeer
SUNY College at Oneonta

Australia · Brazil · Canada · Mexico · Singapore · Spain · United Kingdom · United States

Corporations, S Corporations, and Partnerships Practice Sets, 2006 Edition
William H. Hoffman, Jr., William A. Raabe, James E. Smith, David M. Maloney

VP/Editorial Director
Jack W. Calhoun

Acquisitions Editor
Dan S. Jones

Senior Developmental Editor
Craig Avery

Marketing Manager
Chris McNamee

Manager of Technology, Editorial
Vicky True

Technology Project Editor
Christine Wittmer

Web Coordinator
Scott Cook

Manufacturing Coordinator
Doug Wilke

Ancillary Coordinator
Erin M. Donohoe

Cover Images
© William J. Hebert/Getty Images, In

Production Artist
Patti Hudepohl

Printer
Globus
Minster, OH

Printed in the United States of America
1 2 3 4 5 08 07 06 05

ISBN 0-324-30492-7

For more information about our products, contact us at:

Thomson Learning Academic Resou Center

1-800-423-0563

Thomson Higher Education
5191 Natorp Boulevard
Mason, OH 45040
USA

TABLE OF CONTENTS

PREFACE

Although these practice sets are designed for use with West's Federal Taxation Series, they can be used effectively with most introductory textbooks on taxation. The practice sets should be assigned after coverage of the related materials, as they are comprehensive and require substantial text coverage for successful completion.

The practice sets include the common forms that would be used. Practice sets for corporation, S corporation, and partnership returns are enclosed. Practice sets for individual returns are published separately.

To facilitate completion of the returns, selected instructions for tax forms are provided.

All comments or suggestions will be appreciated.

Donald R. Trippeer
Colorado State University-Pueblo
donald.trippeer@colostate-pueblo.edu

CORPORATION PRACTICE SET

Keyboard, Inc.

Federal Tax Return

FACTS

Keyboard, Inc. is owned by Jared D. Cornwell and his wife, Louise A. Cornwell. The corporation manufactures computer keyboards that are ergonomically correct and designed to reduce carpal tunnel syndrome (business activity code number 334110), and has reported positive financial and taxable incomes since inception. The company is located at 4500 Industrial Blvd, Chicago, Illinois 45433. The company's employer identification number is 35-4576602, and the calendar year is used for tax purposes. The date of incorporation was March 6, 2002.

Jared D. Cornwell (social security number 333-43-5644) is an 80 percent shareholder and president of the company. Louise A. Cornwell (social security number 532-11-2311) is a 20 percent shareholder and vice president of the company. Both persons devote 100 percent of their time to the corporation. Jared's compensation is $156,816 per year, and Louise 's compensation is $87,120 per year.

The corporation is not a personal holding company. While the corporation is a 'closely-held C corporation,' it does not engage in activities to which the at-risk or passive activity loss limitations apply.

The corporation files its tax return on the accrual method. Inventory has been consistently valued at cost under the FIFO method using the full absorption procedure. Inventory capitalization rules of Internal Revenue Code Section 263A do not apply due to the 'small business exception' (average annual gross receipts for the three preceding taxable years do not exceed $10 million). The accounting records are computerized.

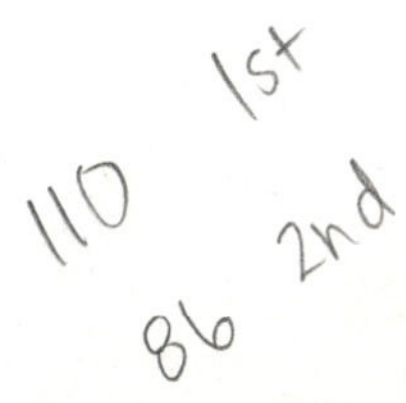

The corporation's audited income statement and balance sheet for the current year, prepared by the accounting firm of Jones & Jones, CPAs, follow:

KEYBOARD, INC.
INCOME STATEMENT
For the Year Ending December 31, 2004

Revenue:		
Sales (net)	$ 6,999,101	
Cost of goods sold	(5,831,301)	
Gross profit		$ 1,167,800
Operating expenses:		
Compensation of officers	$ 243,936	
Other salaries and wages	536,599	
Rental expense	36,764	
Interest expense	93,016	
Fines for improper disposal of waste	2,962	
Advertising	9,374	
Contributions	39,204	
Bad debt expense	3,485	
Depreciation expense	120,145	
Taxes	84,506	
Repairs and maintenance	7,852	
Miscellaneous expenses	21,216	
Total operating expenses		$(1,199,059)
Net Income from Operations		$ (31,259)
Other income and loss:		
Dividend income	$ 116,467	
Interest income	2,548	
Loss on sale of investment in stock	(2,787)	116,228
Net Income (Loss) before income tax		$ 84,969
Income tax expense		(3,485)
Net Income		$ 81,484

KEYBOARD, INC.
STATEMENT OF FINANCIAL POSITION
December 31, 2004

ASSETS	Beginning of Year	End of Year
Current Assets:		
Cash & Marketable Securities	$ 512,556	$ 497,498
Accounts receivable	247,508	279,285
Allowance for Doubtful Accounts	(15,682)	(17,207)
Inventory	567,116	686,549
Total current assets	$1,311,498	$1,446,125
Machinery, Building, and Land:		
Machinery	$ 339,768	$ 388,120
Less: Accumulated depreciation	(104,544)	(190,444)
Building	1,198,652	1,198,652
Less: Accumulated depreciation	(144,121)	(178,366)
Land	87,120	87,120
Total equipment, building, and land (net)	$1,376,875	$1,305,082
Other assets:		
Goodwill	–0–	25,483
Total Assets	$2,688,373	$2,776,690
LIABILITIES AND SHAREHOLDERS' EQUITY		
Current liabilities:		
Accounts payable	$ 223,378	$ 240,338
Notes payable (less than one year)	179,467	158,558
Total current liabilities	$ 402,845	$ 398,896
Notes payable (one year or more)	845,064	908,988
Total Liabilities	$1,247,909	$1,307,884
Common stock (11,000 shares authorized, 11,000 shares issued and outstanding, $10 par)	$ 110,000	$ 110,000
Additional paid-in capital	935,440	935,440
Retained earnings	395,024	423,366
Total Shareholders' Equity	$1,440,464	$1,468,806
Total Liabilities and Shareholders' Equity	$2,688,373	$2,776,690

STATEMENT OF RETAINED EARNINGS

Beginning Retained Earnings	$395,024
Net income for the year	81,484
Dividends paid in cash	(53,142)
Ending Retained Earnings	$423,366

ADDITIONAL INFORMATION

1. Keyboard, Inc. made estimated tax payments attributable to 2004 of $5,227. The corporation also had a credit from an overpayment of its prior year Federal income taxes of $471 that it elected to apply against its 2004 tax liability.

2. All notes payable were issued at par and provide market interest rates.

3. Ignore state income taxes.

4. Dividend income is from the following sources:

Computer Corp.	$68,551
Spam Corp.	26,136
Plastic Corp. (Keyboard, Inc. owns 85% of Plastic Corp.'s stock)	21,780
Total	$116,467

5. An analysis of the Allowance for Doubtful Accounts reveals:

Balance, 01/01/04	$15,682
2004 Transactions—	
Provision for bad debts	3,485
Recoveries on bad debts	(740)
Accounts written off as uncollectible	(1,220)
Balance, 12/31/04	$17,207

6. Goodwill of $25,483 arose on purchase of another business on 01/01/04. Amortization is not being taken for financial purposes.

7. Assume that deductions for tax depreciation (i.e., Modified Accelerated Cost Recovery) for the year total $142,317. For this practice set do not complete Form 4562 (Depreciation and Amortization).

8. Meals and entertainment costs of $1,742 included in Miscellaneous Expenses are subject to the 50% disallowance rule.

9. Contributions included:

PETA	$33,628
Government of Thailand	3,834
Community Soup Kitchen	1,742
Total	$39,204

All contributions were paid in cash during the year except for the Community Soup Kitchen contribution which was pledged by the corporation (i.e., approved by the Board of Directors) on December 16, 2004 and paid on May 1, 2005.

10. Included in interest income is $1,438 from $33,000 of Chicago, Illinois General Obligation Bonds held throughout the current year. These bonds are included in the marketable securities account.

11. On 05/19/04 the corporation sold 100 shares of Ink Corp. common stock for $9,583. The stock had been purchased on 07/23/01 for $12,370.

12. Plastic Corp. is a subsidiary of Keyboard, Inc., formed in 2002, and operated in Chicago, Illinois for the purpose of manufacturing specialty molds used in keyboard formation. Historically Plastic Corp. has been profitable and had a taxable income of $89,141 and an Alternative Minimum Taxable Income [Form 4626, Ln. 7] of $89,722. Keyboard, Inc. and Plastic Corp. have agreed to share equally any limitations on item(s) that the income tax law restricts across the corporations so long as the equal allocation results in utilization of maximum benefits available. However, if a corporation does not have sufficient investment, income, or tax to realize benefit of an item so allocated, any excess limitation shall be re-allocated to the other corporation to the extent that other corporation has sufficient investment, income, or tax liability to realize the benefit of the additional limitation. Sales by Plastic Corp. to Keyboard, Inc. are at "arms-length" prices (i.e., fair market values). Keyboard, Inc. has not elected to file a consolidated income tax return with Plastic Corp. Plastic Corp. (EIN 74-5555555) is located at 3000 St. Charles Way, Chicago, Illinois 45333.

13. Form 4626 (Alternative Minimum Tax—Corporations) must be included in the return. For that purpose, assume the adjustment for depreciation of tangible property placed in service after 1986 (Form 4626, Line 2a) is a $25,997 positive adjustment. Assume the Adjusted Current Earnings (ACE) Adjustment on Line 4e is $-0-. [This assumption removes the ACE adjustment from this practice set].

14. Disregard any penalty on underpayment of estimated tax.

REQUIRED

From the above information, prepare Keyboard, Inc.'s 2004 Federal income tax return (Form 1120), including all needed supporting statements, schedules, and forms. Unless otherwise noted, assume Keyboard, Inc. follows the policies of making all elections to minimize its current income taxes and, to the extent possible, of conforming procedures for financial and tax accounting. Round amounts to the nearest dollar. If additional information is needed, make realistic assumptions and fill in all required data.

CORPORATION PRACTICE SET

Keyboard, Inc.

FORMS

Form **1120**
Department of the Treasury
Internal Revenue Service

U.S. Corporation Income Tax Return

For calendar year 2004 or tax year beginning ...., 2004, ending ...., 20 ....
▶ See separate instructions.

OMB No. 1545-0123
2004

A Check if:
1 Consolidated return (attach Form 851) ☐
2 Personal holding co. (attach Sch. PH) ☐
3 Personal service corp. (see instructions) ☐
4 Schedule M-3 required (attach Sch. M-3) ☐

Use IRS label. Otherwise, print or type.
Name
Number, street, and room or suite no. If a P.O. box, see page 9 of instructions.
City or town, state, and ZIP code

B Employer identification number
C Date incorporated
D Total assets (see page 8 of instructions)
$

E Check if: (1) ☐ Initial return (2) ☐ Final return (3) ☐ Name change (4) ☐ Address change

Income

1a	Gross receipts or sales ____ b Less returns and allowances ____ c Bal ▶	1c	
2	Cost of goods sold (Schedule A, line 8)	2	
3	Gross profit. Subtract line 2 from line 1c	3	
4	Dividends (Schedule C, line 19)	4	
5	Interest	5	
6	Gross rents	6	
7	Gross royalties	7	
8	Capital gain net income (attach Schedule D (Form 1120))	8	
9	Net gain or (loss) from Form 4797, Part II, line 17 (attach Form 4797)	9	
10	Other income (see page 11 of instructions—attach schedule)	10	
11	**Total income.** Add lines 3 through 10 ▶	11	

Deductions (See instructions for limitations on deductions.)

12	Compensation of officers (Schedule E, line 4)	12	
13	Salaries and wages (less employment credits)	13	
14	Repairs and maintenance	14	
15	Bad debts	15	
16	Rents	16	
17	Taxes and licenses	17	
18	Interest	18	
19	Charitable contributions (see page 14 of instructions for 10% limitation)	19	
20	Depreciation (attach Form 4562) ... 20		
21	Less depreciation claimed on Schedule A and elsewhere on return ... 21a	21b	
22	Depletion	22	
23	Advertising	23	
24	Pension, profit-sharing, etc., plans	24	
25	Employee benefit programs	25	
26	Other deductions (attach schedule)	26	
27	**Total deductions.** Add lines 12 through 26 ▶	27	
28	Taxable income before net operating loss deduction and special deductions. Subtract line 27 from line 11	28	
29	**Less:** a Net operating loss deduction (see page 16 of instructions) ... 29a		
	b Special deductions (Schedule C, line 20) ... 29b	29c	

Tax and Payments

30	**Taxable income.** Subtract line 29c from line 28 (see instructions if Schedule C, line 12, was completed)	30	
31	**Total tax** (Schedule J, line 11)	31	
32	**Payments:** a 2003 overpayment credited to 2004 ... 32a		
b	2004 estimated tax payments ... 32b		
c	Less 2004 refund applied for on Form 4466 ... 32c ( ) d Bal ▶ 32d		
e	Tax deposited with Form 7004 ... 32e		
f	Credit for tax paid on undistributed capital gains (attach Form 2439) ... 32f		
g	Credit for Federal tax on fuels (attach Form 4136). See instructions ... 32g	32h	
33	Estimated tax penalty (see page 17 of instructions). Check if Form 2220 is attached ▶ ☐	33	
34	**Tax due.** If line 32h is smaller than the total of lines 31 and 33, enter amount owed	34	
35	**Overpayment.** If line 32h is larger than the total of lines 31 and 33, enter amount overpaid	35	
36	Enter amount of line 35 you want: **Credited to 2005 estimated tax** ▶ Refunded ▶	36	

Sign Here

Under penalties of perjury, I declare that I have examined this return, including accompanying schedules and statements, and to the best of my knowledge and belief, it is true, correct, and complete. Declaration of preparer (other than taxpayer) is based on all information of which preparer has any knowledge.

Signature of officer | Date | Title

May the IRS discuss this return with the preparer shown below (see instructions)? ☐ Yes ☐ No

Paid Preparer's Use Only

Preparer's signature | Date | Check if self-employed ☐ | Preparer's SSN or PTIN
Firm's name (or yours if self-employed), address, and ZIP code | EIN | Phone no. ( )

For Privacy Act and Paperwork Reduction Act Notice, see separate instructions. Cat. No. 11450Q Form **1120** (2004)

Schedule A Cost of Goods Sold (see page 17 of instructions)

1	Inventory at beginning of year	1	
2	Purchases	2	
3	Cost of labor	3	
4	Additional section 263A costs (attach schedule)	4	
5	Other costs (attach schedule)	5	
6	**Total.** Add lines 1 through 5	6	
7	Inventory at end of year	7	
8	**Cost of goods sold.** Subtract line 7 from line 6. Enter here and on page 1, line 2	8	

9a Check all methods used for valuing closing inventory:

(i) ☐ Cost as described in Regulations section 1.471-3

(ii) ☐ Lower of cost or market as described in Regulations section 1.471-4

(iii) ☐ Other (Specify method used and attach explanation.) ▶

b Check if there was a writedown of subnormal goods as described in Regulations section 1.471-2(c) ▶ ☐

c Check if the LIFO inventory method was adopted this tax year for any goods (if checked, attach Form 970) ▶ ☐

d If the LIFO inventory method was used for this tax year, enter percentage (or amounts) of closing inventory computed under LIFO . . . **9d**

e If property is produced or acquired for resale, do the rules of section 263A apply to the corporation? ☐ Yes ☐ No

f Was there any change in determining quantities, cost, or valuations between opening and closing inventory? If "Yes," attach explanation ☐ Yes ☐ No

Schedule C Dividends and Special Deductions (see page 18 of instructions)

		(a) Dividends received	(b) %	(c) Special deductions (a) × (b)
1	Dividends from less-than-20%-owned domestic corporations that are subject to the 70% deduction (other than debt-financed stock)		70	
2	Dividends from 20%-or-more-owned domestic corporations that are subject to the 80% deduction (other than debt-financed stock)		80	
3	Dividends on debt-financed stock of domestic and foreign corporations (section 246A)		see instructions	
4	Dividends on certain preferred stock of less-than-20%-owned public utilities		42	
5	Dividends on certain preferred stock of 20%-or-more-owned public utilities		48	
6	Dividends from less-than-20%-owned foreign corporations and certain FSCs that are subject to the 70% deduction		70	
7	Dividends from 20%-or-more-owned foreign corporations and certain FSCs that are subject to the 80% deduction		80	
8	Dividends from wholly owned foreign subsidiaries subject to the 100% deduction (section 245(b))		100	
9	**Total.** Add lines 1 through 8. See page 19 of instructions for limitation			
10	Dividends from domestic corporations received by a small business investment company operating under the Small Business Investment Act of 1958		100	
11	Dividends from affiliated group members and certain FSCs that are subject to the 100% deduction		100	
12	Dividends from controlled foreign corporations subject to the 85% deduction (attach Form 8895)		85	
13	Other dividends from foreign corporations not included on lines 3, 6, 7, 8, 11, or 12			
14	Income from controlled foreign corporations under subpart F (attach Form(s) 5471)			
15	Foreign dividend gross-up (section 78)			
16	IC-DISC and former DISC dividends not included on lines 1, 2, or 3 (section 246(d))			
17	Other dividends			
18	Deduction for dividends paid on certain preferred stock of public utilities			
19	**Total dividends.** Add lines 1 through 17. Enter here and on page 1, line 4 ▶			
20	**Total special deductions.** Add lines 9, 10, 11, 12, and 18. Enter here and on page 1, line 29b ▶			

Schedule E Compensation of Officers (see instructions for page 1, line 12, on page 13 of instructions)

Note: *Complete Schedule E only if total receipts (line 1a plus lines 4 through 10 on page 1) are $500,000 or more.*

	(a) Name of officer	(b) Social security number	(c) Percent of time devoted to business	Percent of corporation stock owned (d) Common	(e) Preferred	(f) Amount of compensation
1			%	%	%	
			%	%	%	
			%	%	%	
			%	%	%	
			%	%	%	

2	Total compensation of officers	
3	Compensation of officers claimed on Schedule A and elsewhere on return	
4	Subtract line 3 from line 2. Enter the result here and on page 1, line 12	

Form **1120** (2004)

Schedule J Tax Computation (see page 20 of instructions)

1 Check if the corporation is a member of a controlled group (see sections 1561 and 1563) . . . . . ▶ ☑

Important: Members of a controlled group, see page 20 of instructions.

2a If the box on line 1 is checked, enter the corporation's share of the $50,000, $25,000, and $9,925,000 taxable income brackets (in that order):

(1) $ (2) $ (3) $

b Enter the corporation's share of: (1) Additional 5% tax (not more than $11,750) $

(2) Additional 3% tax (not more than $100,000) $

3 Income tax. Check if a qualified personal service corporation under section 448(d)(2) (see page 21) . . ▶ ☐ | 3

4 Alternative minimum tax (attach Form 4626) | 4

5 Add lines 3 and 4 | 5

6a Foreign tax credit (attach Form 1118) | 6a

b Possessions tax credit (attach Form 5735) | 6b

c Check: ☐ Nonconventional source fuel credit ☐ QEV credit (attach Form 8834) | 6c

d General business credit. Check box(es) and indicate which forms are attached: ☐ Form 3800 ☐ Form(s) (specify) ▶ | 6d

e Credit for prior year minimum tax (attach Form 8827) | 6e

f Qualified zone academy bond credit (attach Form 8860) | 6f

7 **Total credits.** Add lines 6a through 6f | 7

8 Subtract line 7 from line 5 | 8

9 Personal holding company tax (attach Schedule PH (Form 1120)) | 9

10 Other taxes. Check if from: ☐ Form 4255 ☐ Form 8611 ☐ Form 8697 ☐ Form 8866 ☐ Other (attach schedule) | 10

11 **Total tax.** Add lines 8 through 10. Enter here and on page 1, line 31 | 11

Schedule K Other Information (see page 23 of instructions)

	Yes	No
1 Check accounting method: a ☐ Cash b ☑ Accrual c ☐ Other (specify) ▶		
2 See page 25 of the instructions and enter the:		
a Business activity code no. ▶		
b Business activity ▶		
c Product or service ▶		
3 At the end of the tax year, did the corporation own, directly or indirectly, 50% or more of the voting stock of a domestic corporation? (For rules of attribution, see section 267(c).)	✓	
If "Yes," attach a schedule showing: (a) name and employer identification number (EIN), (b) percentage owned, and (c) taxable income or (loss) before NOL and special deductions of such corporation for the tax year ending with or within your tax year.		
4 Is the corporation a subsidiary in an affiliated group or a parent-subsidiary controlled group?		✓
If "Yes," enter name and EIN of the parent corporation ▶		
5 At the end of the tax year, did any individual, partnership, corporation, estate, or trust own, directly or indirectly, 50% or more of the corporation's voting stock? (For rules of attribution, see section 267(c).)	✓	
If "Yes," attach a schedule showing name and identifying number. (Do not include any information already entered in 4 above.) Enter percentage owned ▶ 100%		
6 During this tax year, did the corporation pay dividends (other than stock dividends and distributions in exchange for stock) in excess of the corporation's current and accumulated earnings and profits? (See sections 301 and 316.)		
If "Yes," file **Form 5452,** Corporate Report of Nondividend Distributions.		
If this is a consolidated return, answer here for the parent corporation and on **Form 851,** Affiliations Schedule, for each subsidiary.		

	Yes	No
7 At any time during the tax year, did one foreign person own, directly or indirectly, at least 25% of (a) the total voting power of all classes of stock of the corporation entitled to vote or (b) the total value of all classes of stock of the corporation?		
If "Yes," enter: (a) Percentage owned ▶ and (b) Owner's country ▶		
c The corporation may have to file **Form 5472,** Information Return of a 25% Foreign-Owned U.S. Corporation or a Foreign Corporation Engaged in a U.S. Trade or Business. Enter number of Forms 5472 attached ▶		
8 Check this box if the corporation issued publicly offered debt instruments with original issue discount . ▶ ☐		
If checked, the corporation may have to file **Form 8281,** Information Return for Publicly Offered Original Issue Discount Instruments.		
9 Enter the amount of tax-exempt interest received or accrued during the tax year ▶ $		
10 Enter the number of shareholders at the end of the tax year (if 75 or fewer) ▶		
11 If the corporation has an NOL for the tax year and is electing to forego the carryback period, check here ▶ ☐		
If the corporation is filing a consolidated return, the statement required by Temporary Regulations section 1.1502-21T(b)(3)(i) or (ii) must be attached or the election will not be valid.		
12 Enter the available NOL carryover from prior tax years (Do not reduce it by any deduction on line 29a.) ▶ $		
13 Are the corporation's total receipts (line 1a plus lines 4 through 10 on page 1) for the tax year and its total assets at the end of the tax year less than $250,000?		
If "Yes," the corporation is not required to complete Schedules L, M-1, and M-2 on page 4. Instead, enter the total amount of cash distributions and the book value of property distributions (other than cash) made during the tax year. ▶ $		

Note: *If the corporation, at any time during the tax year, had assets or operated a business in a foreign country or U.S. possession, it may be required to attach* ***Schedule N (Form 1120),*** *Foreign Operations of U.S. Corporations, to this return. See Schedule N for details.*

Form **1120** (2004)

Note: *The corporation is not required to complete Schedules L, M-1, and M-2 if Question 13 on Schedule K is answered "Yes."*

Schedule L Balance Sheets per Books

	Beginning of tax year		End of tax year	
Assets	(a)	(b)	(c)	(d)
1 Cash				
2a Trade notes and accounts receivable				
b Less allowance for bad debts	( )		( )	
3 Inventories				
4 U.S. government obligations				
5 Tax-exempt securities (see instructions)				
6 Other current assets (attach schedule)				
7 Loans to shareholders				
8 Mortgage and real estate loans				
9 Other investments (attach schedule)				
10a Buildings and other depreciable assets				
b Less accumulated depreciation	( )		( )	
11a Depletable assets				
b Less accumulated depletion	( )		( )	
12 Land (net of any amortization)				
13a Intangible assets (amortizable only)				
b Less accumulated amortization	( )		( )	
14 Other assets (attach schedule)				
15 Total assets				
Liabilities and Shareholders' Equity				
16 Accounts payable				
17 Mortgages, notes, bonds payable in less than 1 year				
18 Other current liabilities (attach schedule)				
19 Loans from shareholders				
20 Mortgages, notes, bonds payable in 1 year or more				
21 Other liabilities (attach schedule)				
22 Capital stock: a Preferred stock				
b Common stock				
23 Additional paid-in capital				
24 Retained earnings—Appropriated (attach schedule)				
25 Retained earnings—Unappropriated				
26 Adjustments to shareholders' equity (attach schedule)				
27 Less cost of treasury stock		( )		( )
28 Total liabilities and shareholders' equity				

Schedule M-1 Reconciliation of Income (Loss) per Books With Income per Return (see page 24 of instructions)

1 Net income (loss) per books		7 Income recorded on books this year not included on this return (itemize):	
2 Federal income tax per books		Tax-exempt interest $	
3 Excess of capital losses over capital gains			
4 Income subject to tax not recorded on books this year (itemize):			
5 Expenses recorded on books this year not deducted on this return (itemize):		8 Deductions on this return not charged against book income this year (itemize):	
a Depreciation $		a Depreciation $	
b Charitable contributions $		b Charitable contributions $	
c Travel and entertainment $			
		9 Add lines 7 and 8	
6 Add lines 1 through 5		10 Income (page 1, line 28)—line 6 less line 9	

Schedule M-2 Analysis of Unappropriated Retained Earnings per Books (Line 25, Schedule L)

1 Balance at beginning of year		5 Distributions: a Cash	
2 Net income (loss) per books		b Stock	
3 Other increases (itemize):		c Property	
		6 Other decreases (itemize):	
		7 Add lines 5 and 6	
4 Add lines 1, 2, and 3		8 Balance at end of year (line 4 less line 7)	

Form **1120** (2004)

SCHEDULE D (Form 1120)

Department of the Treasury
Internal Revenue Service

Capital Gains and Losses

▶ **Attach to Form 1120, 1120-A, 1120-F, 1120-FSC, 1120-H, 1120-IC-DISC, 1120-L, 1120-ND, 1120-PC, 1120-POL, 1120-REIT, 1120-RIC, 1120-SF, 990-C, or certain Forms 990-T.**

OMB No. 1545-0123

2004

Name	Employer identification number

Part I — Short-Term Capital Gains and Losses—Assets Held One Year or Less

	(a) Description of property (Example: 100 shares of Z Co.)	(b) Date acquired (mo., day, yr.)	(c) Date sold (mo., day, yr.)	(d) Sales price (see instructions)	(e) Cost or other basis (see instructions)	(f) Gain or (loss) (Subtract (e) from (d))
1						

2	Short-term capital gain from installment sales from Form 6252, line 26 or 37	2	
3	Short-term gain or (loss) from like-kind exchanges from Form 8824	3	
4	Unused capital loss carryover (attach computation)	4	( )
5	Net short-term capital gain or (loss). Combine lines 1 through 4	5	

Part II — Long-Term Capital Gains and Losses—Assets Held More Than One Year

	(a)	(b)	(c)	(d)	(e)	(f)
6						

7	Enter gain from Form 4797, line 7 or 9	7	
8	Long-term capital gain from installment sales from Form 6252, line 26 or 37	8	
9	Long-term gain or (loss) from like-kind exchanges from Form 8824	9	
10	Capital gain distributions (see instructions)	10	
11	Net long-term capital gain or (loss). Combine lines 6 through 10	11	

Part III — Summary of Parts I and II

12	Enter excess of net short-term capital gain (line 5) over net long-term capital loss (line 11)	12	
13	Net capital gain. Enter excess of net long-term capital gain (line 11) over net short-term capital loss (line 5)	13	
14	Add lines 12 and 13. Enter here and on Form 1120, page 1, line 8, or the proper line on other returns	14	

Note: *If losses exceed gains, see **Capital losses** on page 2.*

General Instructions

Section references are to the Internal Revenue Code unless otherwise noted.

Purpose of Schedule

Use Schedule D to report sales and exchanges of capital assets and gains on distributions to shareholders of appreciated capital assets.

Note: *For more information, see Pub. 544, Sales and Other Dispositions of Assets.*

Other Forms the Corporation May Have To File

Use Form 4797, Sales of Business Property, to report the following:

- The sale or exchange of:

1. Property used in a trade or business;

2. Depreciable and amortizable property;

3. Oil, gas, geothermal, or other mineral property; and

4. Section 126 property.

- The involuntary conversion (other than from casualty or theft) of property and capital assets held for business or profit.
- The disposition of noncapital assets other than inventory or property held primarily for sale to customers in the ordinary course of the corporation's trade or business.
- The section 291 adjustment to section 1250 property.

Use Form 4684, Casualties and Thefts, to report involuntary conversions of property due to casualty or theft.

Use Form 6781, Gains and Losses From Section 1256 Contracts and Straddles, to report gains and losses from section 1256 contracts and straddles.

Use Form 8824, Like-Kind Exchanges, if the corporation made one or more "like-kind" exchanges. A like-kind exchange occurs when the corporation exchanges business or investment property for property of a like kind. For exchanges of capital assets, include the gain or (loss) from Form 8824, if any, on line 3 or line 9.

For Privacy Act and Paperwork Reduction Act Notice, see the Instructions for Forms 1120 and 1120-A. Cat. No. 11460M **Schedule D (Form 1120) 2004**

Capital Assets

Each item of property the corporation held (whether or not connected with its trade or business) is a capital asset except the following:

- Stock in trade or other property included in inventory or held mainly for sale to customers.
- Accounts or notes receivable acquired in the ordinary course of the trade or business for services rendered or from the sale of stock in trade or other property included in inventory or held mainly for sale to customers.
- Depreciable or real property used in the trade or business, even if it is fully depreciated.
- Certain copyrights; literary, musical, or artistic compositions; letters or memoranda; or similar property. See section 1221(a)(3).
- U.S. Government publications, including the Congressional Record, that the corporation received from the Government, other than by purchase at the normal sales price, or that the corporation got from another taxpayer who had received it in a similar way, if the corporation's basis is determined by reference to the previous owner's basis.
- Certain commodities derivative financial instruments held by a dealer. See section 1221(a)(6).
- Certain hedging transactions entered into in the normal course of the trade or business. See section 1221(a)(7).
- Supplies regularly used in the trade or business.

Capital losses. Capital losses are allowed only to the extent of capital gains. A net capital loss is carried back 3 years and forward up to 5 years as a short-term capital loss. Carry back a capital loss to the extent it does not increase or produce a net operating loss in the tax year to which it is carried. Foreign expropriation capital losses cannot be carried back, but are carried forward up to 10 years. A net capital loss of a regulated investment company (RIC) is carried forward up to 8 years.

Items for Special Treatment

Gain from installment sales. If the corporation sold property at a gain and it will receive a payment in a tax year after the year of sale, it generally must report the sale on the installment method unless it elects not to. However, the installment method may not be used to report sales of stock or securities traded on an established securities market.

Use Form 6252, Installment Sale Income, to report the sale on the installment method. Also use Form 6252 to report any payment received during the tax year from a sale made in an earlier year that was reported on the installment method. To elect out of the installment method, report the full amount of the gain on Schedule D for the year of the sale on a return filed by the due date (including extensions). If the original return was filed on time without making the election, the corporation may make the election on an amended return filed no later than 6 months after the original due date (excluding extensions). Write "Filed pursuant to section 301.9100-2" at the top of the amended return.

Rollover of gain from empowerment zone assets. If the corporation sold a qualifed empowerment zone asset held for more than 1 year, it may be able to elect to postpone part or all of the gain that would otherwise be included on Schedule D. If the corporation makes the election, the gain on the sale generally is recognized only to the extent, if any, that the amount realized on the sale exceeds the cost of qualified empowerment zone assets (replacement property) the corporation purchased during the 60-day period beginning on the date of the sale. The following rules apply.

- No portion of the cost of the replacement property may be taken into account to the extent the cost is taken into account to exclude gain on a different empowerment zone asset.
- The replacement property must qualify as an empowerment zone asset with respect to the same empowerment zone as the asset sold.
- The corporation must reduce the basis of the replacement property by the amount of postponed gain.
- This election does not apply to any gain (a) treated as ordinary income or (b) attributable to real property, or an intangible asset, which is not an integral part of an enterprise zone business.
- The District of Columbia enterprise zone is not treated as an empowerment zone for this purpose.
- The election is irrevocable without IRS consent.

See Pub. 954, Tax Incentives for Distressed Communities, for the definition of empowerment zone and enterprise zone business. The corporation can find out if its business is located within an empowerment zone by using the RC/EZ/EC Address Locator at *http://www.hud.gov/crlocator.*

Qualified empowerment zone assets are:

- Tangible property, if:

1. The corporation acquired the property after December 21, 2000,

2. The original use of the property in the empowerment zone began with the corporation, and

3. Substantially all of the use of the property, during substantially all of the time that the corporation held it, was in the corporation's enterprise zone business; and

- Stock in a domestic corporation or a capital or profits interest in a domestic partnership, if:

1. The corporation acquired the stock or partnership interest after December 21, 2000, solely in exchange for cash, from the corporation at its original issue (directly or through an underwriter) or from the partnership;

2. The business was an enterprise zone business (or a new business being organized as an enterprise zone business) as of the time the corporation acquired the stock or partnership interest; and

3. The business qualified as an enterprise zone business during substantially all of the time during which the corporation held the stock or partnership interest.

How to report. Report the entire gain realized from the sale as the corporation otherwise would, without regard to the election. On Schedule D, line 6, enter "Section 1397B Rollover" in column (a) and enter as a loss in column (f) the amount of gain included on Schedule D that the corporation is electing to postpone. If the corporation is reporting the sale directly on Schedule D, line 6, use the line directly below the line on which the sale is reported.

See section 1397B for more details.

Gain on distributions of appreciated property. Generally, gain (but not loss) is recognized on a nonliquidating distribution of appreciated property to the extent that the property's fair market value (FMV) exceeds its adjusted basis. See section 311.

Exclusion of Gain from DC Zone Assets. If the corporation sold or exchanged a District of Columbia Enterprise Zone (DC Zone) asset held for more than 5 years, it may be able to exclude any qualified capital gain. The exclusion applies to an interest in, or property of, certain businesses operating in the District of Columbia.

DC Zone asset. A DC Zone asset is any of the following.

- DC Zone business stock.
- DC Zone partnership interest.
- DC Zone business property.

Qualified capital gain. Qualified capital gain is any gain recognized on the sale or exchange of a DC Zone asset, but does not include any of the following.

- Gain treated as ordinary income under section 1245.
- Section 1250 gain figured as if section 1250 applied to all depreciation rather than the additional depreciation.
- Gain attributable to real property, or an intangible asset, that is not an integral part of a DC Zone business.
- Gain from a related-party transaction. See *Sales and Exchanges Between Related Persons* in chapter 2 of Pub. 544.

See Pub. 954 and section 1400B for more details on DC Zone assets and special rules.

How to report. Report the entire gain realized from the sale or exchange as the corporation otherwise would without regard to the exclusion. On Schedule D, line 6, enter "DC Zone Asset" in column (a) and enter as a loss in column (f) the amount of the allowable exclusion. If reporting the sale directly on Schedule D, line 6, use the line directly below the line on which the corporation is reporting the sale.

Gain on the constructive sale of certain appreciated financial positions. Generally, if the corporation holds an appreciated financial position in stock or certain other interests, it may have to recognize gain (but not loss) if it enters into a constructive sale (such as a "short sale against the box"). See Pub. 550, Investment Income and Expenses.

Gain from certain constructive ownership transactions. Gain in excess of the underlying net long-term capital gain the corporation would have recognized if it had held a financial asset directly during the term of a derivative contract must be treated as ordinary income. See section 1260. If any portion of the constructive ownership transaction was open in any prior year, the corporation may have to pay interest. See section 1260(b) for details, including how to figure the interest. Include the interest as an additional tax on Form 1120, Schedule J, line 10 (or the applicable line for other income tax returns). Write "Section 1260(b) interest" and the amount of the interest to the left of line 10, Schedule J.

Rollover of publicly traded securities gain into specialized small business investment companies (SSBICs). If the corporation sold publicly traded securities, it may elect under section 1044(a) to postpone all or part of the gain on that sale if it bought common stock or a partnership interest in an SSBIC during the 60-day period that began on the date of the sale. An SSBIC is any partnership or corporation licensed by the Small Business Administration under section 301(d) of the Small Business Investment Act of 1958. The corporation must recognize gain to the extent the sale proceeds exceed the cost (not taken into account previously) of its SSBIC stock or partnership interest purchased during the 60-day period that began on the date of the sale. The gain a corporation may postpone each tax year is limited to the smaller of (a) $1 million, reduced by the gain previously excluded under section 1044(a) or (b) $250,000. Reduce the basis of the SSBIC stock or partnership interest by any postponed gain.

To make the election, report the entire gain realized on the sale on line 1 or 6, whichever applies, in column (f). Directly below the line on which the gain is reported, enter in column (a), "SSBIC Rollover." Enter the amount of the postponed gain (in parentheses) in column (f). Also attach a schedule showing (a) how the postponed gain was figured, (b) the name of the SSBIC stock in which the common stock or partnership interest was purchased, (c) the date of that purchase, and (d) the new basis in that SSBIC stock or partnership interest. For more details, see section 1044 and Regulations section 1.1044(a)-1.

The corporation must make the election no later than the due date (including extensions) for filing its tax return for the year in which it sold the securities or partnership interest. If the original return was filed on time without making the election, the corporation may make the election on an amended return filed no later than 6 months after the original due date (excluding extensions). Write "Filed pursuant to section 301.9100-2" at the top of the amended return.

Gain on disposition of market discount bonds. See section 1276 for rules on the disposition of market discount bonds.

Gains on certain insurance property. Form 1120-L filers with gains on property held on December 31, 1958, and certain substituted property acquired after 1958, should see section 818(c).

Gains and losses from passive activities. A closely held or personal service corporation that has a gain or loss that relates to a passive activity (section 469) may be required to complete Form 8810, Corporate Passive Activity Loss and Credit Limitation, before completing Schedule D. A Schedule D loss may be limited under the passive activity rules. See Form 8810.

Gains and losses of foreign corporations from the disposition of investment in U.S. real property. Foreign corporations must report gains and losses from the disposition of U.S. real property interests. See section 897.

Gain or loss on distribution of property in complete liquidation. Generally, gain or loss is recognized on property distributed in a complete liquidation. Treat the property as if it had been sold at its FMV. An exception to this rule applies for liquidations of certain subsidiaries. See sections 336 and 337 for more information and other exceptions to the general rules.

Gain or loss on certain asset transfers to a tax-exempt entity. A taxable corporation that transfers all or substantially all of its assets to a tax-exempt entity or converts from a taxable corporation to a tax-exempt entity in a transaction other than a liquidation generally must recognize gain or loss as if it had sold the assets transferred at their FMV. For details, see Regulations section 1.337(d)-4.

Gain or loss on an option to buy or sell property. See sections 1032 and 1234 for the rules that apply to a purchaser or grantor of an option or a securities futures contract (as defined in section 1234B). See Pub. 550 for details.

Gain or loss from a short sale of property. Report the gain or loss to the extent that the property used to close the short sale is considered a capital asset in the hands of the taxpayer.

Gain or loss on certain short-term federal, state, and municipal obligations. These obligations are treated as capital assets in determining gain or loss. On any gain realized, a portion is treated as ordinary income and the balance as a short-term capital gain. See section 1271.

At-risk limitations (section 465). If the corporation sold or exchanged a capital asset used in an activity to which the at-risk rules apply, combine the gain or loss on the sale or exchange with the profit or loss from the activity. If the result is a net loss, complete Form 6198, At-Risk Limitations. Report any gain from the capital asset on Schedule D and on Form 6198.

Loss from a sale or exchange between the corporation and a related person. Except for distributions in complete liquidation of a corporation, no loss is allowed from the sale or exchange of property between the corporation and certain related persons. See section 267.

Loss from a wash sale. The corporation cannot deduct a loss from a wash sale of stock or securities (including contracts or options to acquire or sell stock or securities) unless the corporation is a dealer in stock or securities and the loss was sustained in a transaction made in the ordinary course of the corporation's trade or business. A wash sale occurs if the corporation acquires (by purchase or exchange), or has a contract or option to acquire, substantially identical stock or securities within 30 days before or after the date of the sale or exchange. See section 1091.

Loss from securities that are capital assets that become worthless during the year. Except for securities held by a bank, treat the loss as a capital loss as of the last day of the tax year. See section 582 for the rules on the treatment of securities held by a bank.

Losses limited after an ownership change or aquisition. If the corporation has undergone an "ownership change" as defined in section 382(g), section 383 may limit the amount of capital gains that may be offset by prechange capital losses. Also, if a corporation acquires control of another corporation (or acquires its assets in a reorganization), section 384 may limit the amount of recognized built-in capital gains that may be offset by preaquisition capital losses.

Loss from the sale or exchange of capital assets of an insurance company taxable under section 831. Capital losses of a casualty insurance company are deductible to the extent that the assets were sold to meet abnormal insurance losses or to provide for the payment of dividend and similar distributions to policyholders. See section 834(c)(6).

Gains and losses from partnerships. Report the corporation's share of capital gains and losses from investments in partnerships. Report a net short-term capital gain (loss) in Part I. On line 1, column (a), write "From Schedule K-1 (Form 1065)." Enter the amount of the gain (loss) in column (f). Report net long-term capital gains (losses) in Part II. On line 6, column (a), enter "From Schedule K-1 (Form 1065)." Enter the amount of the gain (loss) in column (f).

Specific Instructions

Parts I and II

Generally, report sales or exchanges (including like-kind exchanges) even if there is no gain or loss. In Part I, report the sale, exchange, or distribution of capital assets held 1 year or less. In Part II, report the sale, exchange, or distribution of capital assets held more than 1 year. Use the trade dates for the dates of acquisition and sale of stock and bonds traded on an exchange or over-the-counter market.

Column (b). Date acquired. A RIC or REIT's acquisition date for an asset it held on January 1, 2001, for which it made an election to recognize any gain under section 311 of the Taxpayer Relief Act of 1997, is the date of the deemed sale and reacquisition.

Column (d). Sales price. Enter either the gross sales price or the net sales price. If the net sales price is entered, do not increase the cost or other basis in column (e) by any expenses reflected in the net sales price.

Column (e). Cost or other basis. In general, the basis of property is its cost. See section 1012 and the related regulations. Special rules for determining basis are provided in sections in subchapters C, K, O, and P of the Code. These rules may apply to the:

- Receipt of certain distributions with respect to stock (section 301 or 1059),
- Liquidation of another corporation (section 334),
- Transfer to another corporation (section 358),
- Transfer from a shareholder or reorganization (section 362),
- Bequest (section 1014),
- Contribution or gift (section 1015),
- Tax-free exchange (section 1031),
- Involuntary conversion (section 1033),
- Certain asset acquisitions (section 1060), or
- Wash sale of stock (section 1091).

Attach an explanation if the corporation uses a basis other than actual cost of the property.

Before making an entry in column (e), increase the cost or other basis by any expense of sale, such as broker's fees, commissions, state and local transfer taxes, and option premiums, unless the net sales price was reported in column (d).

A RIC or REIT's basis in an asset it held on January 1, 2001, for which it made an election to recognize any gain under section 311 of the Taxpayer Relief Act of 1997, is the asset's closing market price or FMV, whichever applies, on the date of the deemed sale and reacquisition, whether the deemed sale resulted in a gain or unallowed loss.

If the corporation is allowed a charitable contribution deduction because it sold property in a bargain sale to a charitable organization, figure the adjusted basis for determining gain from the sale by dividing the amount realized by the FMV and multiplying that result by the adjusted basis. No loss is allowed in a bargain sale to a charity.

See section 852(f) for the treatment of certain load charges incurred in acquiring stock in a RIC with a reinvestment right.

Line 10. Enter the total capital gain distributions paid by a RIC or REIT during the year, regardless of how long the corporation owned stock in the RIC or REIT.

Also enter any amount received from a RIC or REIT that qualifies as a distribution in complete liquidation under section 332(b) and is designated by the RIC or REIT as a capital gain distribution. See section 332(c).

Form **4626**

Department of the Treasury
Internal Revenue Service

Alternative Minimum Tax—Corporations

► See separate instructions.
► Attach to the corporation's tax return.

OMB No. 1545-0175

2004

Name | Employer identification number

Note: *See page 1 of the instructions to find out if the corporation is a small corporation exempt from the alternative minimum tax (AMT) under section 55(e).*

1	Taxable income or (loss) before net operating loss deduction			1	
2	**Adjustments and preferences:**				
a	Depreciation of post-1986 property			2a	
b	Amortization of certified pollution control facilities			2b	
c	Amortization of mining exploration and development costs			2c	
d	Amortization of circulation expenditures (personal holding companies only)			2d	
e	Adjusted gain or loss			2e	
f	Long-term contracts			2f	
g	Merchant marine capital construction funds			2g	
h	Section 833(b) deduction (Blue Cross, Blue Shield, and similar type organizations only)			2h	
i	Tax shelter farm activities (personal service corporations only)			2i	
j	Passive activities (closely held corporations and personal service corporations only)			2j	
k	Loss limitations			2k	
l	Depletion			2l	
m	Tax-exempt interest income from specified private activity bonds			2m	
n	Intangible drilling costs			2n	
o	Other adjustments and preferences			2o	
3	Pre-adjustment alternative minimum taxable income (AMTI). Combine lines 1 through 2o			3	
4	**Adjusted current earnings (ACE) adjustment:**				
a	ACE from line 10 of the worksheet on page 11 of the instructions	4a			
b	Subtract line 3 from line 4a. If line 3 exceeds line 4a, enter the difference as a negative amount. See examples on page 6 of the instructions	4b			
c	Multiply line 4b by 75% (.75). Enter the result as a positive amount	4c			
d	Enter the excess, if any, of the corporation's total increases in AMTI from prior year ACE adjustments over its total reductions in AMTI from prior year ACE adjustments (see page 6 of the instructions). **Note:** *You **must** enter an amount on line 4d (even if line 4b is positive)*	4d			
e	ACE adjustment. • If line 4b is zero or more, enter the amount from line 4c • If line 4b is less than zero, enter the **smaller** of line 4c or line 4d as a negative amount			4e	
5	Combine lines 3 and 4e. If zero or less, stop here; the corporation does not owe any AMT			5	
6	Alternative tax net operating loss deduction (see page 7 of the instructions)			6	
7	**Alternative minimum taxable income.** Subtract line 6 from line 5. If the corporation held a residual interest in a REMIC, see page 7 of the instructions			7	
8	**Exemption phase-out** (if line 7 is $310,000 or more, skip lines 8a and 8b and enter -0- on line 8c):				
a	Subtract $150,000 from line 7 (if completing this line for a member of a controlled group, see page 7 of the instructions). If zero or less, enter -0-	8a			
b	Multiply line 8a by 25% (.25)	8b			
c	Exemption. Subtract line 8b from $40,000 (if completing this line for a member of a controlled group, see page 7 of the instructions). If zero or less, enter -0-			8c	
9	Subtract line 8c from line 7. If zero or less, enter -0-			9	
10	Multiply line 9 by 20% (.20)			10	
11	Alternative minimum tax foreign tax credit (AMTFTC) (see page 7 of the instructions)			11	
12	Tentative minimum tax. Subtract line 11 from line 10			12	
13	Regular tax liability before all credits except the foreign tax credit and possessions tax credit			13	
14	**Alternative minimum tax.** Subtract line 13 from line 12. If zero or less, enter -0-. Enter here and on Form 1120, Schedule J, line 4, or the appropriate line of the corporation's income tax return			14	

For Paperwork Reduction Act Notice, see page 10 of the instructions. Cat. No. 12955I Form **4626** (2004)

S CORPORATION PRACTICE SET

The Translator Corp.
Federal Tax Return

FACTS

Celine Morris, a graduate in computer engineering, developed and patented a small hand-held electronic device used for the translation of various languages. While working, Celine had traveled frequently to various countries in Europe and Asia. She often needed assistance or a translator when conducting business. The development of her translator enabled one to speak directly into the device and receive the message in the other language. Celine set up the Translator Corp. to manufacture and sell her product. The Translator Corp. is owned by the Morris family. The corporation is a small, closely-held manufacturer (the business code number is 334200, and the employer identification number is 26-5431478). The company is located at 300 Spanish Lane, Trenton, New Jersey 02311. The corporation, which uses a calendar year for tax purposes, has been an S corporation since its incorporation on July 1, 2001.

Celine Morris (social security number 433-22-3241) is president of the corporation. Celine owned 100% of the stock until September 13, 2002 when she sold 1% to Edgar Morris (Celine's uncle, social security number 123-33-4567), who serves as vice president for the company. Both officers devote 100 percent of their time to the corporation and live at 240 W. French Court, Trenton, New Jersey 03345. Annual compensation is $55,080 for Celine and $27,540 for Edgar. The corporation does not engage in activities to which the at-risk or passive activity loss limitations apply.

The corporation files its tax return on the accrual method. Inventory has been consistently valued at cost under the FIFO method using the full absorption procedure. Inventory capitalization rules of Internal Revenue Code Section 263A do not apply due to the 'small business exception' (average annual gross receipts for the three preceding taxable years do not exceed $10 million). The accounting records are computerized.

The corporation's audited income statement and balance sheet for the current year, prepared by the accounting firm of Wendell & Wendell, CPAs, follow:

THE TRANSLATOR CORP.
INCOME STATEMENT
For the Year Ending December 31, 2004

Revenue:		
Sales (net)	$1,731,211	
Cost of goods sold	(1,281,877)	
Gross profit		$ 449,334
Operating expenses:		
Compensation of officers	$ 82,620	
Other salaries and wages	187,881	
Employee benefits	8,418	
Rental expense	19,575	
Interest expense	10,447	
Advertising	5,357	
Key-person life insurance premiums	5,080	
Contributions	643	
Depreciation	25,046	
Taxes (other than income taxes)	17,762	
Repairs and maintenance	9,998	
Miscellaneous expenses	3,030	
Total operating expenses		$(375,857)
Net Income from Operations		$ 73,477
Other income and loss:		
Dividend Income	$ 2,178	
Interest Income	344	
Gain on sale of investment in stock	1,856	
Gain on sale of machine	6,656	
Casualty loss on machine	(459)	10,575
Net Income		$ 84,052

THE TRANSLATOR CORP.
STATEMENT OF FINANCIAL POSITION
December 31, 2004

ASSETS	Beginning of Year	End of Year
Current Assets:		
Cash & Marketable Securities	$ 8,586	$ 8,752
Accounts receivable	34,618	21,848
Inventory	147,544	142,140
Total current assets	$190,748	$172,740
Machinery and Equipment (M&E):		
Machinery and Equipment	$218,668	$257,938
Less: Accumulated depreciation	(17,778)	(33,414)
Total machinery and equipment (net)	$200,890	$224,524
Other assets:		
Life insurance cash surrender value	$ 13,203	$ 16,773
Total Assets	$404,841	$414,037
LIABILITIES AND SHAREHOLDERS' EQUITY		
Current liabilities:		
Accounts payable	$ 13,550	$ 15,898
Notes payable (less than one year)	16,434	17,260
Total current liabilities	$ 29,984	$ 33,158
Notes payable (one year or more)	55,080	25,900
Total Liabilities	$85,064	$ 59,058
Common stock (2,295 shares authorized, issued, and outstanding, $100 par)	$229,500	$229,500
Retained earnings	90,277	125,479
Total Shareholders' Equity	$319,777	$354,979
Total Liabilities and Shareholders' Equity	$404,841	$414,037

STATEMENT OF RETAINED EARNINGS

Beginning Retained Earnings	$90,277
Net income for the year	84,052
Dividends paid during the year	(48,850)
Ending Retained Earnings	$125,479

ADDITIONAL INFORMATION

1. Included in employee benefits expense are $418 and $298 premiums for $50,000 (face) group term life insurance premiums for Celine and Edgar, respectively. Family members are named beneficiaries in the policies.

2. All notes payable were issued at par and provide market interest rates.

3. Employees account to the company and are reimbursed by the exact amount of travel and entertainment expenses incurred on business. Included in Miscellaneous Expenses are $1,259 for transportation expenses, $230 for meals, and $138 for entertainment.

4. Dividend income is from minor investments in:

Wire Corp.	$1,534
American Insurance Company (a dividend on the key-person life insurance policy)	644
Total	$2,178

5. Contributions were paid in cash to:

Humane Society	$ 459
Republican Party	184
Total Contributions	$ 643

6. The key-person life insurance policy provides $500,000 coverage on Celine Morris. The company is the owner and beneficiary of the policy.

7. A schedule attached in the prior year's working papers reconciles Retained Earnings and Accumulated Adjustments Account balances at 12/31/04 as follows:

Balance per Schedule L (Balance Sheet)		$90,277
Accumulated depreciation for machinery and equipment (M&E) for tax		
M&E Acquired 07/01/02	$ 7,119	
M&E Acquired 02/01/03	28,615	
	$35,734	
Accumulated depreciation per books	17,778	
Excess of Accumulated Tax over Book Depreciation for M&E		(17,956)
Balance per Schedule M (Analysis of the Accumulated Adjustments Account)		$ 72,321

8. The balance in the "Other Adjustments Account" (Form 1120S, p. 4, Sch. M-2, col. (b)) at the beginning of the year was $-0-.

9. Depreciation information is attached.

10. Machine #9, purchased on 02/01/03 for $45,900, was sold to an unrelated party on 11/01/04 for $46,818.

11. Machine #13, purchased on 07/01/02 for $18,360, was totally destroyed by fire caused by a short in an electrical circuit on 04/01/04. Proceeds of $14,229 were received from the insurance company. On 08/01/04 $13,770 of the proceeds were invested in a replacement machine. Assume there will be no further qualified reinvestment of the proceeds.

12. Interest expense was on loans for the following purposes:

Purchase M&E	$4,945
Invest in stock of Wire Corp.	826
Invest in Trenton County, New Jersey water and sewer bonds	92
Cover shortage in working capital	4,584
Total	$10,447

13. On June 5, 2004, 450 shares of Wire Corp. common stock were sold. The company bought 1,800 shares of the stock on June 2, 2003 for $5,508. The stock was split 3-for-1 on February 21, 2004. (*Clue:* Use the book gain and basis to compute the proceeds.)

14. On May 15, 2003 The Translator Corp. purchased at par $8,500 of Trenton County, New Jersey water and sewer bonds. Interest of $344 was received on the bonds during the year.

REQUIRED

From the above information, prepare The Translator Corp.'s 2004 Federal income tax return (Form 1120S), including all supporting statements, schedules, and forms. Unless otherwise noted, assume the corporation makes all available elections to minimize the shareholders' current taxable incomes. Round amounts to the nearest dollar. If additional information is needed, make realistic assumptions and fill in all required data.

Even though the corporation may not be technically required to do so, Celine has expressed a desire that Schedule L (Balance Sheets), Schedule M-1 (Reconciliation of Income (Loss) per Books With Income (Loss) per Return), and Schedule M-2 (Analysis of Accumulated Adjustments Account, Other Adjustments Account, and Shareholders' Undistributed Taxable Income Previously Taxed) on Form 1120S, p. 4 be completed.

The Translator Corp.
Depreciation/Cost Recovery Information

Financial Depreciation Information	Balance 12/31/03	2004 Additions	2004 Retirements	Balance 12/31/04	Balance 12/31/03	2004 Provision	2004 Retirements	Balance 12/31/04
Machinery Acquired on:								
07/01/02	$ 18,360		($18,360)	$ 0	$ 2,754	$ 918	($3,672)	$ 0
02/01/03	200,308		(45,900)	154,408	15,024	17,736	(5,738)	27,022
05/01/04		$89,760		89,760		5,882		5,882
08/01/04		13,770		13,770		510		510
Total	$218,668	$103,530	($64,260)	$257,938	$17,778	$25,046	($9,410)	$33,414

TAX DEPRECIATION INFORMATION

MACRS (Modified Accelerated Cost Recovery System—For property placed is service after 1986)

Machinery and equipment (7-year statutory life, 200% declining balance switching to straight line, half-year convention). Statutory percentage for assets placed in service during a year are 14.29%, 24.49%, 17.49%, 12.49%, 8.93%, 8.92%, 8.93%, and 4.46% for recovery years 1–8, respectively. One-half of the normal MACRS amount is allowed for the year of disposition.

The corporation has elected not to take the additional 30% or 50% depreciation allowance on assets placed in service prior to 2004 and will make the same election for 2004.

The corporation has not elected Internal Revenue Code Sec. (IRC Sec.) 179 expense in the past; however, IRC Sec. 179 expense is to be claimed for machinery and equipment placed in service on 05/01/04.

ALTERNATIVE MINIMUM TAX (Tax Preferences and Adjustments)

For this practice set, ignore effects of the above cost recoveries on the Alternative Minimum Tax (i.e., leave the applicable spaces blank for these items in the 'Adjustments and Tax Preferences Items' section of Schedules K and K-1).

S CORPORATION PRACTICE SET

The Translator Corp.

FORMS

Form **1120S**

Department of the Treasury
Internal Revenue Service

U.S. Income Tax Return for an S Corporation

► Do not file this form unless the corporation has timely filed Form 2553 to elect to be an S corporation.

► See separate instructions.

OMB No. 1545-0130

2004

For calendar year 2004, or tax year beginning , 2004, and ending , 20

A Effective date of S election	Use the IRS label. Otherwise, print or type.	Name	C Employer identification number
		Number, street, and room or suite no. (If a P.O. box, see page 12 of the instructions.)	D Date incorporated
B Business code number (see pages 36–38 of the Insts.)		City or town, state, and ZIP code	E Total assets (see page 12 of instructions) $

F Check applicable boxes: (1) ☐ Initial return (2) ☐ Final return (3) ☐ Name change (4) ☐ Address change (5) ☐ Amended return

G Enter number of shareholders in the corporation at end of the tax year . . . . ►

Caution: *Include **only** trade or business income and expenses on lines 1a through 21. See page 13 of the instructions for more information.*

Income	1a	Gross receipts or sales ____ **b** Less returns and allowances ____ **c** Bal ►	1c	
	2	Cost of goods sold (Schedule A, line 8)	2	
	3	Gross profit. Subtract line 2 from line 1c	3	
	4	Net gain (loss) from Form 4797, Part II, line 17 *(attach Form 4797)*	4	
	5	Other income (loss) *(attach schedule)*	5	
	6	**Total income (loss).** Add lines 3 through 5 ►	6	
Deductions (see page 14 of the instructions for limitations)	7	Compensation of officers	7	
	8	Salaries and wages (less employment credits)	8	
	9	Repairs and maintenance	9	
	10	Bad debts	10	
	11	Rents	11	
	12	Taxes and licenses	12	
	13	Interest	13	
	14a	Depreciation *(attach Form 4562)* — 14a		
	b	Depreciation claimed on Schedule A and elsewhere on return — 14b		
	c	Subtract line 14b from line 14a	14c	
	15	Depletion **(Do not deduct oil and gas depletion.)**	15	
	16	Advertising	16	
	17	Pension, profit-sharing, etc., plans	17	
	18	Employee benefit programs	18	
	19	Other deductions *(attach schedule)*	19	
	20	**Total deductions.** Add the amounts shown in the far right column for lines 7 through 19 ►	20	
	21	Ordinary business income (loss). Subtract line 20 from line 6	21	
Tax and Payments	22	**Tax: a** Excess net passive income tax *(attach schedule)* — 22a		
	b	Tax from Schedule D (Form 1120S) — 22b		
	c	Add lines 22a and 22b (see page 18 of the instructions for additional taxes)	22c	
	23	**Payments: a** 2004 estimated tax payments and amount applied from 2003 return — 23a		
	b	Tax deposited with Form 7004 — 23b		
	c	Credit for Federal tax paid on fuels *(attach Form 4136)* — 23c		
	d	Add lines 23a through 23c	23d	
	24	Estimated tax penalty (see page 18 of instructions). Check if Form 2220 is attached ► ☐	24	
	25	**Tax due.** If line 23d is smaller than the total of lines 22c and 24, enter amount owed	25	
	26	**Overpayment.** If line 23d is larger than the total of lines 22c and 24, enter amount overpaid	26	
	27	Enter amount of line 26 you want: **Credited to 2005 estimated tax** ► ____ **Refunded** ►	27	

Sign Here

Under penalties of perjury, I declare that I have examined this return, including accompanying schedules and statements, and to the best of my knowledge and belief, it is true, correct, and complete. Declaration of preparer (other than taxpayer) is based on all information of which preparer has any knowledge.

► Signature of officer | Date | ► Title

May the IRS discuss this return with the preparer shown below (see instructions)? ☐ Yes ☐ No

Paid Preparer's Use Only

Preparer's signature ►	Date	Check if self-employed ☐	Preparer's SSN or PTIN
Firm's name (or yours if self-employed), address, and ZIP code ►		EIN	
		Phone no. ( )	

For Privacy Act and Paperwork Reduction Act Notice, see the separate instructions. Cat. No. 11510H Form **1120S** (2004)

Schedule A — Cost of Goods Sold (see page 18 of the instructions)

1	Inventory at beginning of year	1	
2	Purchases	2	
3	Cost of labor	3	
4	Additional section 263A costs *(attach schedule)*	4	
5	Other costs *(attach schedule)*	5	
6	**Total.** Add lines 1 through 5	6	
7	Inventory at end of year	7	
8	**Cost of goods sold.** Subtract line 7 from line 6. Enter here and on page 1, line 2	8	

9a Check all methods used for valuing closing inventory: *(i)* ☐ Cost as described in Regulations section 1.471-3
(ii) ☐ Lower of cost or market as described in Regulations section 1.471-4
(iii) ☐ Other (specify method used and attach explanation) ▶ ....

b Check if there was a writedown of subnormal goods as described in Regulations section 1.471-2(c) ▶ ☐

c Check if the LIFO inventory method was adopted this tax year for any goods (if checked, attach Form 970) ▶ ☐

d If the LIFO inventory method was used for this tax year, enter percentage (or amounts) of closing inventory computed under LIFO . . . **9d** ______

e If property is produced or acquired for resale, do the rules of Section 263A apply to the corporation? ☐ Yes ☐ No

f Was there any change in determining quantities, cost, or valuations between opening and closing inventory? ☐ Yes ☐ No
If "Yes," attach explanation.

Schedule B — Other Information (see page 19 of instructions)

		Yes	No
1	Check method of accounting: **(a)** ☐ Cash **(b)** ☐ Accrual **(c)** ☐ Other (specify) ▶..........		
2	See pages 36 through 38 of the instructions and enter the: **(a)** Business activity ▶.......... **(b)** Product or service ▶..........		
3	At the end of the tax year, did the corporation own, directly or indirectly, 50% or more of the voting stock of a domestic corporation? (For rules of attribution, see section 267(c).) If "Yes," attach a schedule showing: **(a)** name, address, and employer identification number and **(b)** percentage owned		
4	Was the corporation a member of a controlled group subject to the provisions of section 1561?		
5	Check this box if the corporation has filed or is required to file **Form 8264,** Application for Registration of a Tax Shelter ▶ ☐		
6	Check this box if the corporation issued publicly offered debt instruments with original issue discount ▶ ☐ If checked, the corporation may have to file **Form 8281,** Information Return for Publicly Offered Original Issue Discount Instruments.		
7	If the corporation: **(a)** was a C corporation before it elected to be an S corporation **or** the corporation acquired an asset with a basis determined by reference to its basis (or the basis of any other property) in the hands of a C corporation **and (b)** has net unrealized built-in gain (defined in section 1374(d)(1)) in excess of the net recognized built-in gain from prior years, enter the net unrealized built-in gain reduced by net recognized built-in gain from prior years ▶ $		
8	Check this box if the corporation had accumulated earnings and profits at the close of the tax year ▶ ☐		
9	Are the corporation's total receipts (see page 19 of the instructions) for the tax year **and** its total assets at the end of the tax year less than $250,000? If "Yes," the corporation is not required to complete Schedules L and M-1.		

Note: *If the corporation had assets or operated a business in a foreign country or U.S. possession, it may be required to attach* **Schedule N (Form 1120),** *Foreign Operations of U.S. Corporations, to this return. See Schedule N for details.*

Schedule K — Shareholders' Shares of Income, Deductions, Credits, etc.

	Shareholders' Pro Rata Share Items				Total amount
Income (Loss)	1 Ordinary business income (loss) (page 1, line 21)			1	
	2 Net rental real estate income (loss) *(attach Form 8825)*			2	
	3a Other gross rental income (loss)	3a			
	b Expenses from other rental activities *(attach schedule)*	3b			
	c Other net rental income (loss). Subtract line 3b from line 3a			3c	
	4 Interest income			4	
	5 Dividends: a Ordinary dividends			5a	
	b Qualified dividends	5b			
	6 Royalties			6	
	7 Net short-term capital gain (loss)			7	
	8a Net long-term capital gain (loss)			8a	
	b Collectibles (28%) gain (loss)	8b			
	c Unrecaptured section 1250 gain *(attach schedule)*	8c			
	9 Net section 1231 gain (loss) (attach Form 4797)			9	
	10 Other income (loss) *(attach schedule)*			10	

	Shareholders' Pro Rata Share Items (continued)		Total amount
Deductions	**11** Section 179 deduction *(attach Form 4562)*	**11**	
	12a Contributions	**12a**	
	b Deductions related to portfolio income *(attach schedule)*	**12b**	
	c Investment interest expense	**12c**	
	d Section 59(e)(2) expenditures **(1)** Type ▶ **(2)** Amount ▶	**12d(2)**	
	e Other deductions *(attach schedule)*	**12e**	
Credits & Credit Recapture	**13a** Low-income housing credit (section 42(j)(5))	**13a**	
	b Low-income housing credit (other)	**13b**	
	c Qualified rehabilitation expenditures (rental real estate) *(attach Form 3468)*	**13c**	
	d Other rental real estate credits	**13d**	
	e Other rental credits	**13e**	
	f Credit for alcohol used as fuel *(attach Form 6478)*	**13f**	
	g Other credits and credit recapture *(attach schedule)*	**13g**	
Foreign Transactions	**14a** Name of country or U.S. possession ▶		
	b Gross income from all sources	**14b**	
	c Gross income sourced at shareholder level	**14c**	
	Foreign gross income sourced at corporate level:		
	d Passive	**14d**	
	e Listed categories *(attach schedule)*	**14e**	
	f General limitation	**14f**	
	Deductions allocated and apportioned at shareholder level:		
	g Interest expense	**14g**	
	h Other	**14h**	
	Deductions allocated and apportioned at corporate level to foreign source income:		
	i Passive	**14i**	
	j Listed categories *(attach schedule)*	**14j**	
	k General limitation	**14k**	
	Other information:		
	l Foreign taxes paid	**14l**	
	m Foreign taxes accrued	**14m**	
	n Reduction in taxes available for credit *(attach schedule)*	**14n**	
Alternative Minimum Tax (AMT) Items	**15a** Post-1986 depreciation adjustment	**15a**	
	b Adjusted gain or loss	**15b**	
	c Depletion (other than oil and gas)	**15c**	
	d Oil, gas, and geothermal properties—gross income	**15d**	
	e Oil, gas, and geothermal properties—deductions	**15e**	
	f Other AMT items *(attach schedule)*	**15f**	
Items Affecting Shareholder Basis	**16a** Tax-exempt interest income	**16a**	
	b Other tax-exempt income	**16b**	
	c Nondeductible expenses	**16c**	
	d Property distributions	**16d**	
	e Repayment of loans from shareholders	**16e**	
Other Information	**17a** Investment income	**17a**	
	b Investment expenses	**17b**	
	c Dividend distributions paid from accumulated earnings and profits	**17c**	
	d Other items and amounts *(attach schedule)*		
	e Income/loss reconciliation. (Required only if Schedule M-1 must be completed.) Combine the amounts on lines 1 through 10 in the far right column. From the result, subtract the sum of the amounts on lines 11 through 12e and lines 14l or 14m, whichever applies	**17e**	

Form **1120S** (2004)

Note: The corporation is not required to complete Schedules L and M-1 if question 9 of Schedule B is answered "Yes."

Schedule L Balance Sheets per Books

Assets	Beginning of tax year (a)	(b)	End of tax year (c)	(d)
1 Cash				
2a Trade notes and accounts receivable				
b Less allowance for bad debts				
3 Inventories				
4 U.S. government obligations				
5 Tax-exempt securities				
6 Other current assets *(attach schedule)*				
7 Loans to shareholders				
8 Mortgage and real estate loans				
9 Other investments *(attach schedule)*				
10a Buildings and other depreciable assets				
b Less accumulated depreciation				
11a Depletable assets				
b Less accumulated depletion				
12 Land (net of any amortization)				
13a Intangible assets (amortizable only)				
b Less accumulated amortization				
14 Other assets *(attach schedule)*				
15 Total assets				
Liabilities and Shareholders' Equity				
16 Accounts payable				
17 Mortgages, notes, bonds payable in less than 1 year				
18 Other current liabilities *(attach schedule)*				
19 Loans from shareholders				
20 Mortgages, notes, bonds payable in 1 year or more				
21 Other liabilities *(attach schedule)*				
22 Capital stock				
23 Additional paid-in capital				
24 Retained earnings				
25 Adjustments to shareholders' equity *(attach schedule)*				
26 Less cost of treasury stock		( )		( )
27 Total liabilities and shareholders' equity				

Schedule M-1 Reconciliation of Income (Loss) per Books With Income (Loss) per Return

1 Net income (loss) per books		5 Income recorded on books this year not included on Schedule K, lines 1 through 10 (itemize): a Tax-exempt interest $	
2 Income included on Schedule K, lines 1, 2, 3c, 4, 5a, 6, 7, 8a, 9, and 10, not recorded on books this year (itemize):			
3 Expenses recorded on books this year not included on Schedule K, lines 1 through 12, and 14l or (14m) (itemize): a Depreciation $ b Travel and entertainment $		6 Deductions included on Schedule K, lines 1 through 12, and 14l or (14m), not charged against book income this year (itemize): a Depreciation $	
		7 Add lines 5 and 6	
4 Add lines 1 through 3		8 Income (loss) (Schedule K, line 17e). Line 4 less line 7	

Schedule M-2 Analysis of Accumulated Adjustments Account, Other Adjustments Account, and Shareholders' Undistributed Taxable Income Previously Taxed (see page 32 of the instructions)

	(a) Accumulated adjustments account	(b) Other adjustments account	(c) Shareholders' undistributed taxable income previously taxed
1 Balance at beginning of tax year			
2 Ordinary income from page 1, line 21			
3 Other additions			
4 Loss from page 1, line 21	( )		
5 Other reductions	( )	( )	
6 Combine lines 1 through 5			
7 Distributions other than dividend distributions			
8 Balance at end of tax year. Subtract line 7 from line 6			

Form **1120S** (2004)

SCHEDULE D (Form 1120S)

Department of the Treasury
Internal Revenue Service

Capital Gains and Losses and Built-In Gains

▶ Attach to Form 1120S.

▶ See separate instructions.

OMB No. 1545-0130

2004

Name | Employer identification number

Part I Short-Term Capital Gains and Losses—Assets Held One Year or Less

	(a) Description of property (Example, 100 shares of "Z" Co.)	(b) Date acquired (mo., day, yr.)	(c) Date sold (mo., day, yr.)	(d) Sales price	(e) Cost or other basis (see instructions)	(f) Gain or (loss) (Subtract (e) from (d))
1						

2	Short-term capital gain from installment sales from Form 6252, line 26 or 37	2	
3	Short-term capital gain or (loss) from like-kind exchanges from Form 8824	3	
4	Combine lines 1 through 3 in column (f)	4	
5	Tax on short-term capital gain included on line 21 below	5	( )
6	**Net short-term capital gain or (loss).** Combine lines 4 and 5. Enter here and on Form 1120S, Schedule K, line 7 or 10	6	

Part II Long-Term Capital Gains and Losses—Assets Held More Than One Year

	(a) Description of property (Example, 100 shares of "Z" Co.)	(b) Date acquired (mo., day, yr.)	(c) Date sold (mo., day, yr.)	(d) Sales price	(e) Cost or other basis (see instructions)	(f) Gain or (loss) (Subtract (e) from (d))
7						

8	Long-term capital gain from installment sales from Form 6252, line 26 or 37	8	
9	Long-term capital gain or (loss) from like-kind exchanges from Form 8824	9	
10	Capital gain distributions	10	
11	Combine lines 7 through 10 in column (f)	11	
12	Tax on long-term capital gain included on line 21 below	12	( )
13	**Net long-term capital gain or (loss).** Combine lines 11 and 12. Enter here and on Form 1120S, Schedule K, line 8a or 10	13	

Part III **Built-In Gains Tax** (See instructions **before** completing this part.)

14	Excess of recognized built-in gains over recognized built-in losses (attach computation schedule)	14	
15	Taxable income (attach computation schedule)	15	
16	Net recognized built-in gain. Enter the smallest of line 14, line 15, or line 7 of Schedule B	16	
17	Section 1374(b)(2) deduction	17	
18	Subtract line 17 from line 16. If zero or less, enter -0- here and on line 21	18	
19	Enter 35% of line 18	19	
20	Section 1374(b)(3) business credit and minimum tax credit carryforwards from C corporation years	20	
21	**Tax.** Subtract line 20 from line 19 (if zero or less, enter -0-). Enter here and on Form 1120S, page 1, line 22b	21	

For Privacy Act and Paperwork Reduction Act Notice, see the Instructions for Form 1120S. Cat. No. 11516V **Schedule D (Form 1120S) 2004**

6711

☐ Final K-1 ☐ Amended K-1 OMB No. 1545-0130

Schedule K-1 (Form 1120S) **2004**

Department of the Treasury
Internal Revenue Service

Tax year beginning 2004
and ending 2005

Shareholder's Share of Income, Deductions, Credits, etc.

▶ See back of form and separate instructions.

Part I Information About the Corporation

A Corporation's employer identification number

B Corporation's name, address, city, state, and ZIP code

C IRS Center where corporation filed return

D ☐ Tax shelter registration number, if any

E ☐ Check if Form 8271 is attached

Part II Information About the Shareholder

F Shareholder's identifying number

G Shareholder's name, address, city, state and ZIP code

H Shareholder's percentage of stock ownership for tax year . . . . ______ %

Part III Shareholder's Share of Current Year Income, Deductions, Credits, and Other Items

1 Ordinary business income (loss)

2 Net rental real estate income (loss)

3 Other net rental income (loss)

4 Interest income

5a Ordinary dividends

5b Qualified dividends

6 Royalties

7 Net short-term capital gain (loss)

8a Net long-term capital gain (loss)

8b Collectibles (28%) gain (loss)

8c Unrecaptured section 1250 gain

9 Net section 1231 gain (loss)

10 Other income (loss)

11 Section 179 deduction

12 Other deductions

13 Credits & credit recapture

14 Foreign transactions

15 Alternative minimum tax (AMT) items

16 Items affecting shareholder basis

17 Other information

* See attached statement for additional information.

For Privacy Act and Paperwork Reduction Act Notice, see Instructions for Form 1120S. Cat. No. 11520D Schedule K-1 (Form 1120S) 2004

This list identifies the codes used on Schedule K-1 for all shareholders and provides summarized reporting information for shareholders who file Form 1040. For detailed reporting and filing information, see the separate Shareholder's Instructions for Schedule K-1 and the instructions for your income tax return.

1. **Ordinary business income (loss).** You must first determine whether the income (loss) is passive or nonpassive. Then enter on your return as follows:

	Enter on
Passive loss	See the Shareholder's Instructions
Passive income	Schedule E, line 28, column (g)
Nonpassive loss	Schedule E, line 28, column (h)
Nonpassive income	Schedule E, line 28, column (j)

2. **Net rental real estate income (loss)**	See the Shareholder's Instructions
3. **Other net rental income (loss)**	
Net income	Schedule E, line 28, column (g)
Net loss	See the Shareholder's Instructions
4. **Interest income**	Form 1040, line 8a
5a. **Ordinary dividends**	Form 1040, line 9a
5b. **Qualified dividends**	Form 1040, line 9b
6. **Royalties**	Schedule E, line 4
7. **Net short-term capital gain (loss)**	Schedule D, line 5, column (f)
8a. **Net long-term capital gain (loss)**	Schedule D, line 12, column (f)
8b. **Collectibles (28%) gain (loss)**	28% Rate Gain Worksheet, line 4 (Schedule D instructions)
8c. **Unrecaptured section 1250 gain**	See the Shareholder's Instructions
9. **Net section 1231 gain (loss)**	See the Shareholder's Instructions

10. **Other income (loss)**

Code		
A	Other portfolio income (loss)	See the Shareholder's Instructions
B	Involuntary conversions	See the Shareholder's Instructions
C	1256 contracts & straddles	Form 6781, line 1
D	Mining exploration costs recapture	See Pub. 535, Chap. 8
E	Other income (loss)	See the Shareholder's Instructions

11. **Section 179 deduction**	See the Shareholder's Instructions

12. **Other deductions**

A	Cash contributions (50%)	Schedule A, line 15
B	Cash contributions (30%)	Schedule A, line 15
C	Noncash contributions (50%)	Schedule A, line 16
D	Noncash contributions (30%)	Schedule A, line 16
E	Capital gain property to a 50% organization (30%)	Schedule A, line 16
F	Capital gain property (20%)	Schedule A, line 16
G	Deductions—portfolio (2% floor)	Schedule A, line 22
H	Deductions—portfolio (other)	Schedule A, line 27
I	Investment interest expense	Form 4952, line 1
J	Deductions—royalty income	Schedule E, line 18
K	Section 59(e)(2) expenditures	See the Shareholder's Instructions
L	Reforestation expense deduction	See the Shareholder's Instructions
M	Preproductive period expenses	See the Shareholder's Instructions
N	Commercial revitalization deduction from rental real estate activities	See Form 8582 Instructions
O	Penalty on early withdrawal of savings	Form 1040, line 33
P	Other deductions	See the Shareholder's Instructions

13. **Credits & credit recapture**

Code		Enter on
A	Low-income housing credit (section 42(j)(5))	Form 8586, line 5
B	Low-income housing credit (other)	Form 8586, line 5
C	Qualified rehabilitation expenditures (rental real estate)	Form 3468, line 1
D	Qualified rehabilitation expenditures (other than rental real estate)	Form 3468, line 1
E	Basis of energy property	Form 3468, line 2
F	Qualified timber property	Form 3468, line 3
G	Other rental real estate credits	See the Shareholder's Instructions
H	Other rental credits	See the Shareholder's Instructions
I	Undistributed capital gains credit	Form 1040, line 69, box a
J	Work opportunity credit	Form 5884, line 3
K	Welfare-to-Work credit	Form 8861, line 3
L	Disabled access credit	Form 8826, line 7
M	Empowerment zone and renewal community employment credit	Form 8844, line 3
N	New York Liberty Zone business employee credit	Form 8884, line 3
O	New markets credit	Form 8874, line 2
P	Credit for employer social security and Medicare taxes	Form 8846, line 5
Q	Backup withholding	Form 1040, line 63
R	Credit for alcohol used as fuel	Form 6478, line 10
S	Recapture of low-income housing credit (section 42(j)(5))	Form 8611, line 8
T	Recapture of low-income housing credit (other)	Form 8611, line 8
U	Recapture of investment credit	See Form 4255
V	Other credits	See the Shareholder's Instructions
W	Recapture of other credits	See the Shareholder's Instructions

14. **Foreign transactions**

A	Name of country or U.S. possession	Form 1116, Part I
B	Gross income from all sources	Form 1116, Part I
C	Gross income sourced at shareholder level	Form 1116, Part I
	Foreign gross income sourced at corporate level	
D	Passive	Form 1116, Part I
E	Listed categories	Form 1116, Part I
F	General limitation	Form 1116, Part I
	Deductions allocated and apportioned at shareholder level	
G	Interest expense	Form 1116, Part I
H	Other	Form 1116, Part I
	Deductions allocated and apportioned at corporate level to foreign source income	
I	Passive	Form 1116, Part I
J	Listed categories	Form 1116, Part I
K	General limitation	Form 1116, Part I
	Other information	
L	Total foreign taxes paid	Form 1116, Part II
M	Total foreign taxes accrued	Form 1116, Part II
N	Reduction in taxes available for credit	Form 1116, line 12
O	Foreign trading gross receipts	Form 8873
P	Extraterritorial income exclusion	Form 8873
Q	Other foreign transactions	See the Shareholder's Instructions

15. **Alternative minimum tax (AMT) items**

A	Post-1986 depreciation adjustment	See the Shareholder's Instructions and the instructions for Form 6251
B	Adjusted gain or loss	
C	Depletion (other than oil & gas)	
D	Oil, gas, & geothermal properties—gross income	
E	Oil, gas, & geothermal properties—deductions	
F	Other AMT items	

16. **Items affecting shareholder basis**

A	Tax-exempt interest income	Form 1040, line 8b
B	Other tax-exempt income	See the Shareholder's Instructions
C	Nondeductible expenses	See the Shareholder's Instructions
D	Property distributions	See the Shareholder's Instructions
E	Repayment of loans from shareholders	See the Shareholder's Instructions

17. **Other information**

A	Investment income	Form 4952, line 4a
B	Investment expenses	Form 4952, line 5
C	Look-back interest—completed long-term contracts	See Form 8697
D	Look-back interest—income forecast method	See Form 8866
E	Dispositions of property with section 179 deductions	See the Shareholder's Instructions
F	Recapture of section 179 deduction	See the Shareholder's Instructions
G	Section 453(l)(3) information	See the Shareholder's Instructions
H	Section 453A(c) information	See the Shareholder's Instructions
I	Section 1260(b) information	See the Shareholder's Instructions
J	Interest allocable to production expenditures	See the Shareholder's Instructions
K	CCF nonqualified withdrawal	See the Shareholder's Instructions
L	Information needed to figure depletion—oil and gas	See the Shareholder's Instructions
M	Amortization of reforestation costs	See the Shareholder's Instructions
N	Other information	See the Shareholder's Instructions

6711

☐ Final K-1 ☐ Amended K-1 OMB No. 1545-0130

Schedule K-1 (Form 1120S) **2004**

Department of the Treasury
Internal Revenue Service

Tax year beginning 2004
and ending 2005

Shareholder's Share of Income, Deductions, Credits, etc.

▶ See back of form and separate instructions.

Part I Information About the Corporation

A Corporation's employer identification number

B Corporation's name, address, city, state, and ZIP code

C IRS Center where corporation filed return

D ☐ Tax shelter registration number, if any ______

E ☐ Check if Form 8271 is attached

Part II Information About the Shareholder

F Shareholder's identifying number

G Shareholder's name, address, city, state and ZIP code

H Shareholder's percentage of stock ownership for tax year . . . . ______ %

Part III Shareholder's Share of Current Year Income, Deductions, Credits, and Other Items

1	Ordinary business income (loss)	13	Credits & credit recapture
2	Net rental real estate income (loss)		
3	Other net rental income (loss)		
4	Interest income		
5a	Ordinary dividends		
5b	Qualified dividends	14	Foreign transactions
6	Royalties		
7	Net short-term capital gain (loss)		
8a	Net long-term capital gain (loss)		
8b	Collectibles (28%) gain (loss)		
8c	Unrecaptured section 1250 gain		
9	Net section 1231 gain (loss)		
10	Other income (loss)	15	Alternative minimum tax (AMT) items
11	Section 179 deduction	16	Items affecting shareholder basis
12	Other deductions		
		17	Other information

* See attached statement for additional information.

For Privacy Act and Paperwork Reduction Act Notice, see Instructions for Form 1120S. Cat. No. 11520D **Schedule K-1 (Form 1120S) 2004**

This list identifies the codes used on Schedule K-1 for all shareholders and provides summarized reporting information for shareholders who file Form 1040. For detailed reporting and filing information, see the separate Shareholder's Instructions for Schedule K-1 and the instructions for your income tax return.

1. Ordinary business income (loss). You must first determine whether the income (loss) is passive or nonpassive. Then enter on your return as follows:

	Enter on
Passive loss	See the Shareholder's Instructions
Passive income	Schedule E, line 28, column (g)
Nonpassive loss	Schedule E, line 28, column (h)
Nonpassive income	Schedule E, line 28, column (j)

2. Net rental real estate income (loss)	See the Shareholder's Instructions
3. Other net rental income (loss)	
Net income	Schedule E, line 28, column (g)
Net loss	See the Shareholder's Instructions
4. Interest income	Form 1040, line 8a
5a. Ordinary dividends	Form 1040, line 9a
5b. Qualified dividends	Form 1040, line 9b
6. Royalties	Schedule E, line 4
7. Net short-term capital gain (loss)	Schedule D, line 5, column (f)
8a. Net long-term capital gain (loss)	Schedule D, line 12, column (f)
8b. Collectibles (28%) gain (loss)	28% Rate Gain Worksheet, line 4 (Schedule D instructions)
8c. Unrecaptured section 1250 gain	See the Shareholder's Instructions
9. Net section 1231 gain (loss)	See the Shareholder's Instructions

10. Other income (loss)

Code	
A Other portfolio income (loss)	See the Shareholder's Instructions
B Involuntary conversions	See the Shareholder's Instructions
C 1256 contracts & straddles	Form 6781, line 1
D Mining exploration costs recapture	See Pub. 535, Chap. 8
E Other income (loss)	See the Shareholder's Instructions

11. Section 179 deduction	See the Shareholder's Instructions

12. Other deductions

A Cash contributions (50%)	Schedule A, line 15
B Cash contributions (30%)	Schedule A, line 15
C Noncash contributions (50%)	Schedule A, line 16
D Noncash contributions (30%)	Schedule A, line 16
E Capital gain property to a 50% organization (30%)	Schedule A, line 16
F Capital gain property (20%)	Schedule A, line 16
G Deductions—portfolio (2% floor)	Schedule A, line 22
H Deductions—portfolio (other)	Schedule A, line 27
I Investment interest expense	Form 4952, line 1
J Deductions—royalty income	Schedule E, line 18
K Section 59(e)(2) expenditures	See the Shareholder's Instructions
L Reforestation expense deduction	See the Shareholder's Instructions
M Preproductive period expenses	See the Shareholder's Instructions
N Commercial revitalization deduction from rental real estate activities	See Form 8582 Instructions
O Penalty on early withdrawal of savings	Form 1040, line 33
P Other deductions	See the Shareholder's Instructions

13. Credits & credit recapture

Code	Enter on
A Low-income housing credit (section 42(j)(5))	Form 8586, line 5
B Low-income housing credit (other)	Form 8586, line 5
C Qualified rehabilitation expenditures (rental real estate)	Form 3468, line 1
D Qualified rehabilitation expenditures (other than rental real estate)	Form 3468, line 1
E Basis of energy property	Form 3468, line 2
F Qualified timber property	Form 3468, line 3
G Other rental real estate credits	See the Shareholder's Instructions
H Other rental credits	See the Shareholder's Instructions
I Undistributed capital gains credit	Form 1040, line 69, box a
J Work opportunity credit	Form 5884, line 3
K Welfare-to-Work credit	Form 8861, line 3
L Disabled access credit	Form 8826, line 7
M Empowerment zone and renewal community employment credit	Form 8844, line 3
N New York Liberty Zone business employee credit	Form 8884, line 3
O New markets credit	Form 8874, line 2
P Credit for employer social security and Medicare taxes	Form 8846, line 5
Q Backup withholding	Form 1040, line 63
R Credit for alcohol used as fuel	Form 6478, line 10
S Recapture of low-income housing credit (section 42(j)(5))	Form 8611, line 8
T Recapture of low-income housing credit (other)	Form 8611, line 8
U Recapture of investment credit	See Form 4255
V Other credits	See the Shareholder's Instructions
W Recapture of other credits	See the Shareholder's Instructions

14. Foreign transactions

A Name of country or U.S. possession	Form 1116, Part I
B Gross income from all sources	Form 1116, Part I
C Gross income sourced at shareholder level	Form 1116, Part I
Foreign gross income sourced at corporate level	
D Passive	Form 1116, Part I
E Listed categories	Form 1116, Part I
F General limitation	Form 1116, Part I
Deductions allocated and apportioned at shareholder level	
G Interest expense	Form 1116, Part I
H Other	Form 1116, Part I
Deductions allocated and apportioned at corporate level to foreign source income	
I Passive	Form 1116, Part I
J Listed categories	Form 1116, Part I
K General limitation	Form 1116, Part I
Other information	
L Total foreign taxes paid	Form 1116, Part II
M Total foreign taxes accrued	Form 1116, Part II
N Reduction in taxes available for credit	Form 1116, line 12
O Foreign trading gross receipts	Form 8873
P Extraterritorial income exclusion	Form 8873
Q Other foreign transactions	See the Shareholder's Instructions

15. Alternative minimum tax (AMT) items

A Post-1986 depreciation adjustment	See the Shareholder's Instructions and the instructions for Form 6251
B Adjusted gain or loss	
C Depletion (other than oil & gas)	
D Oil, gas, & geothermal properties—gross income	
E Oil, gas, & geothermal properties—deductions	
F Other AMT items	

16. Items affecting shareholder basis

A Tax-exempt interest income	Form 1040, line 8b
B Other tax-exempt income	See the Shareholder's Instructions
C Nondeductible expenses	See the Shareholder's Instructions
D Property distributions	See the Shareholder's Instructions
E Repayment of loans from shareholders	See the Shareholder's Instructions

17. Other information

A Investment income	Form 4952, line 4a
B Investment expenses	Form 4952, line 5
C Look-back interest—completed long-term contracts	See Form 8697
D Look-back interest—income forecast method	See Form 8866
E Dispositions of property with section 179 deductions	See the Shareholder's Instructions
F Recapture of section 179 deduction	See the Shareholder's Instructions
G Section 453(l)(3) information	See the Shareholder's Instructions
H Section 453A(c) information	See the Shareholder's Instructions
I Section 1260(b) information	See the Shareholder's Instructions
J Interest allocable to production expenditures	See the Shareholder's Instructions
K CCF nonqualified withdrawal	See the Shareholder's Instructions
L Information needed to figure depletion—oil and gas	See the Shareholder's Instructions
M Amortization of reforestation costs	See the Shareholder's Instructions
N Other information	See the Shareholder's Instructions

Form **4562** Department of the Treasury Internal Revenue Service	**Depreciation and Amortization** **(Including Information on Listed Property)** ▶ See separate instructions. ▶ Attach to your tax return.	OMB No. 1545-0172 **2004** Attachment Sequence No. **67**
Name(s) shown on return	Business or activity to which this form relates	**Identifying number**

Part I Election To Expense Certain Property Under Section 179

Note: *If you have any listed property, complete Part V before you complete Part I.*

1	Maximum amount. See page 2 of the instructions for a higher limit for certain businesses	1	$102,000
2	Total cost of section 179 property placed in service (see page 3 of the instructions)	2	
3	Threshold cost of section 179 property before reduction in limitation	3	$410,000
4	Reduction in limitation. Subtract line 3 from line 2. If zero or less, enter -0-	4	
5	Dollar limitation for tax year. Subtract line 4 from line 1. If zero or less, enter -0-. If married filing separately, see page 3 of the instructions.	5	

	(a) Description of property	(b) Cost (business use only)	(c) Elected cost
6			
7	Listed property. Enter the amount from line 29	7	

8	Total elected cost of section 179 property. Add amounts in column (c), lines 6 and 7	8	
9	Tentative deduction. Enter the **smaller** of line 5 or line 8.	9	
10	Carryover of disallowed deduction from line 13 of your 2003 Form 4562	10	
11	Business income limitation. Enter the smaller of business income (not less than zero) or line 5 (see instructions)	11	
12	Section 179 expense deduction. Add lines 9 and 10, but do not enter more than line 11	12	
13	Carryover of disallowed deduction to 2005. Add lines 9 and 10, less line 12 ▶	13	

Note: *Do not use Part II or Part III below for listed property. Instead, use Part V.*

Part II Special Depreciation Allowance and Other Depreciation (Do not include listed property.)

14	Special depreciation allowance for qualified property (other than listed property) placed in service during the tax year (see page 3 of the instructions)	14	
15	Property subject to section 168(f)(1) election (see page 4 of the instructions)	15	
16	Other depreciation (including ACRS) (see page 4 of the instructions)	16	

Part III MACRS Depreciation (Do not include listed property.) (See page 5 of the instructions.)

Section A

17	MACRS deductions for assets placed in service in tax years beginning before 2004	17	
18	If you are electing under section 168(i)(4) to group any assets placed in service during the tax year into one or more general asset accounts, check here ▶ ☐		

Section B—Assets Placed in Service During 2004 Tax Year Using the General Depreciation System

(a) Classification of property	(b) Month and year placed in service	(c) Basis for depreciation (business/investment use only—see instructions)	(d) Recovery period	(e) Convention	(f) Method	(g) Depreciation deduction
19a 3-year property						
b 5-year property						
c 7-year property						
d 10-year property						
e 15-year property						
f 20-year property						
g 25-year property			25 yrs.		S/L	
h Residential rental property			27.5 yrs.	MM	S/L	
			27.5 yrs.	MM	S/L	
i Nonresidential real property			39 yrs.	MM	S/L	
				MM	S/L	

Section C—Assets Placed in Service During 2004 Tax Year Using the Alternative Depreciation System

(a) Classification of property	(b)	(c)	(d)	(e)	(f)	(g)
20a Class life					S/L	
b 12-year			12 yrs.		S/L	
c 40-year			40 yrs.	MM	S/L	

Part IV Summary (see page 8 of the instructions)

21	Listed property. Enter amount from line 28	21	
22	**Total.** Add amounts from line 12, lines 14 through 17, lines 19 and 20 in column (g), and line 21. Enter here and on the appropriate lines of your return. Partnerships and S corporations—see instr.	22	
23	For assets shown above and placed in service during the current year, enter the portion of the basis attributable to section 263A costs	23	

For Paperwork Reduction Act Notice, see separate instructions. Cat. No. 12906N Form **4562** (2004)

Part V **Listed Property** (Include automobiles, certain other vehicles, cellular telephones, certain computers, and property used for entertainment, recreation, or amusement.)

Note: *For any vehicle for which you are using the standard mileage rate or deducting lease expense, complete* ***only*** *24a, 24b, columns (a) through (c) of Section A, all of Section B, and Section C if applicable.*

Section A—Depreciation and Other Information (Caution: *See page 9 of the instructions for limits for passenger automobiles.*)

24a Do you have evidence to support the business/investment use claimed? ☐ Yes ☐ No 24b If "Yes," is the evidence written? ☐ Yes ☐ No

(a) Type of property (list vehicles first)	(b) Date placed in service	(c) Business/ investment use percentage	(d) Cost or other basis	(e) Basis for depreciation (business/investment use only)	(f) Recovery period	(g) Method/ Convention	(h) Depreciation deduction	(i) Elected section 179 cost
25 Special depreciation allowance for qualified listed property placed in service during the tax year and used more than 50% in a qualified business use (see page 8 of the instructions)						25		
26 Property used more than 50% in a qualified business use (see page 8 of the instructions):								
		%						
		%						
		%						
27 Property used 50% or less in a qualified business use (see page 8 of the instructions):								
		%				S/L –		
		%				S/L –		
		%				S/L –		
28 Add amounts in column (h), lines 25 through 27. Enter here and on line 21, page 1						28		
29 Add amounts in column (i), line 26. Enter here and on line 7, page 1							29	

Section B—Information on Use of Vehicles

Complete this section for vehicles used by a sole proprietor, partner, or other "more than 5% owner," or related person.
If you provided vehicles to your employees, first answer the questions in Section C to see if you meet an exception to completing this section for those vehicles.

	(a) Vehicle 1		(b) Vehicle 2		(c) Vehicle 3		(d) Vehicle 4		(e) Vehicle 5		(f) Vehicle 6	
30 Total business/investment miles driven during the year (**do not** include commuting miles—See page 2 of the instructions)												
31 Total commuting miles driven during the year												
32 Total other personal (noncommuting) miles driven												
33 Total miles driven during the year. Add lines 30 through 32												
	Yes	No	Yes	No	Yes	No	Yes	No	Yes	No	Yes	No
34 Was the vehicle available for personal use during off-duty hours?												
35 Was the vehicle used primarily by a more than 5% owner or related person?												
36 Is another vehicle available for personal use?												

Section C—Questions for Employers Who Provide Vehicles for Use by Their Employees

Answer these questions to determine if you meet an exception to completing Section B for vehicles used by employees who **are not** more than 5% owners or related persons (see page 10 of the instructions).

	Yes	No
37 Do you maintain a written policy statement that prohibits all personal use of vehicles, including commuting, by your employees?		
38 Do you maintain a written policy statement that prohibits personal use of vehicles, except commuting, by your employees? See page 10 of the instructions for vehicles used by corporate officers, directors, or 1% or more owners		
39 Do you treat all use of vehicles by employees as personal use?		
40 Do you provide more than five vehicles to your employees, obtain information from your employees about the use of the vehicles, and retain the information received?		
41 Do you meet the requirements concerning qualified automobile demonstration use? (See page 10 of the instructions.)		

Note: *If your answer to 37, 38, 39, 40, or 41 is "Yes," do not complete Section B for the covered vehicles.*

Part VI **Amortization**

(a) Description of costs	(b) Date amortization begins	(c) Amortizable amount	(d) Code section	(e) Amortization period or percentage	(f) Amortization for this year
42 Amortization of costs that begins during your 2004 tax year (see page 11 of the instructions):					
43 Amortization of costs that began before your 2004 tax year				43	
44 **Total.** Add amounts in column (f). See page 12 of the instructions for where to report				44	

Form **4562** (2004)

Form **4684**

Department of the Treasury
Internal Revenue Service

Casualties and Thefts

▶ See separate instructions.
▶ Attach to your tax return.
▶ Use a separate Form 4684 for each casualty or theft.

OMB No. 1545-0177

2004

Attachment
Sequence No. **26**

Name(s) shown on tax return | **Identifying number**

SECTION A—Personal Use Property (Use this section to report casualties and thefts of property **not** used in a trade or business or for income-producing purposes.)

1 Description of properties (show type, location, and date acquired for each property). Use a separate line for each property lost or damaged from the same casualty or theft.

Property **A** ____________________

Property **B** ____________________

Property **C** ____________________

Property **D** ____________________

		Properties			
		A	B	C	D
2 Cost or other basis of each property	2				
3 Insurance or other reimbursement (whether or not you filed a claim) (see instructions) **Note:** *If line 2 is* ***more*** *than line 3, skip line 4.*	3				
4 Gain from casualty or theft. If line 3 is **more** than line 2, enter the difference here and skip lines 5 through 9 for that column. See instructions if line 3 includes insurance or other reimbursement you did not claim, or you received payment for your loss in a later tax year	4				
5 Fair market value **before** casualty or theft	5				
6 Fair market value **after** casualty or theft	6				
7 Subtract line 6 from line 5	7				
8 Enter the **smaller** of line 2 or line 7	8				
9 Subtract line 3 from line 8. If zero or less, enter -0-	9				

10 Casualty or theft loss. Add the amounts on line 9 in columns A through D	10	
11 Enter the **smaller** of line 10 or $100	11	
12 Subtract line 11 from line 10 **Caution:** *Use only one Form 4684 for lines 13 through 18.*	12	
13 Add the amounts on line 12 of all Forms 4684	13	
14 Add the amounts on line 4 of all Forms 4684	14	
15 • If line 14 is **more** than line 13, enter the difference here and on Schedule D. **Do not** complete the rest of this section (see instructions). • If line 14 is **less** than line 13, enter -0- here and go to line 16. • If line 14 is **equal** to line 13, enter -0- here. **Do not** complete the rest of this section.	15	
16 If line 14 is **less** than line 13, enter the difference	16	
17 Enter 10% of your adjusted gross income from Form 1040, line 37. Estates and trusts, see instructions	17	
18 Subtract line 17 from line 16. If zero or less, enter -0-. Also enter the result on Schedule A (Form 1040), line 19. Estates and trusts, enter the result on the "Other deductions" line of your tax return	18	

For Paperwork Reduction Act Notice, see page 4 of the instructions. Cat. No. 12997O Form **4684** (2004)

Name(s) shown on tax return. Do not enter name and identifying number if shown on other side. | Identifying number

SECTION B—Business and Income-Producing Property

Part I Casualty or Theft Gain or Loss (Use a separate Part I for each casualty or theft.)

19 Description of properties (show type, location, and date acquired for each property). Use a separate line for each property lost or damaged from the same casualty or theft.

Property **A** ______

Property **B** ______

Property **C** ______

Property **D** ______

		Properties A		B		C		D	
20 Cost or adjusted basis of each property	20								
21 Insurance or other reimbursement (whether or not you filed a claim). See the instructions for line 3. **Note:** *If line 20 is* ***more*** *than line 21, skip line 22*	21								
22 Gain from casualty or theft. If line 21 is **more** than line 20, enter the difference here and on line 29 or line 34, column (c), except as provided in the instructions for line 33. Also, skip lines 23 through 27 for that column. See the instructions for line 4 if line 21 includes insurance or other reimbursement you did not claim, or you received payment for your loss in a later tax year	22								
23 Fair market value **before** casualty or theft	23								
24 Fair market value **after** casualty or theft	24								
25 Subtract line 24 from line 23	25								
26 Enter the **smaller** of line 20 or line 25. **Note:** *If the property was totally destroyed by casualty or lost from theft, enter on line 26 the amount from line 20.*	26								
27 Subtract line 21 from line 26. If zero or less, enter -0-	27								

28 Casualty or theft loss. Add the amounts on line 27. Enter the total here and on line 29 **or** line 34 (see instructions) | 28 |

Part II Summary of Gains and Losses (from separate Parts I)

(a) Identify casualty or theft		(b) Losses from casualties or thefts (i) Trade, business, rental or royalty property	(b) (ii) Income-producing and employee property		(c) Gains from casualties or thefts includible in income
Casualty or Theft of Property Held One Year or Less					
29		( )	( )		
		( )	( )		
30 Totals. Add the amounts on line 29	30	( )	( )		
31 Combine line 30, columns (b)(i) and (c). Enter the net gain or (loss) here and on Form 4797, line 14. If Form 4797 is not otherwise required, see instructions				31	
32 Enter the amount from line 30, column (b)(ii) here. Individuals, enter the amount from income-producing property on Schedule A (Form 1040), line 27, and enter the amount from property used as an employee on Schedule A (Form 1040), line 22. Estates and trusts, partnerships, and S corporations, see instructions				32	
Casualty or Theft of Property Held More Than One Year					
33 Casualty or theft gains from Form 4797, line 32				33	
34		( )	( )		
		( )	( )		
35 Total losses. Add amounts on line 34, columns (b)(i) and (b)(ii)	35	( )	( )		
36 Total gains. Add lines 33 and 34, column (c)				36	
37 Add amounts on line 35, columns (b)(i) and (b)(ii)				37	
38 If the loss on line 37 is **more** than the gain on line 36: a Combine line 35, column (b)(i) and line 36, and enter the net gain or (loss) here. Partnerships (except electing large partnerships) and S corporations, see the note below. All others, enter this amount on Form 4797, line 14. If Form 4797 is not otherwise required, see instructions				38a	
b Enter the amount from line 35, column (b)(ii) here. Individuals, enter the amount from income-producing property on Schedule A (Form 1040), line 27, and enter the amount from property used as an employee on Schedule A (Form 1040), line 22. Estates and trusts, enter on the "Other deductions" line of your tax return. Partnerships (except electing large partnerships) and S corporations, see the note below. Electing large partnerships, enter on Form 1065-B, Part II, line 11				38b	
39 If the loss on line 37 is **less** than or **equal** to the gain on line 36, combine lines 36 and 37 and enter here. Partnerships (except electing large partnerships), see the note below. All others, enter this amount on Form 4797, line 3				39	

Note: *Partnerships, enter the amount from line 38a, 38b, or line 39 on Form 1065, Schedule K, line 11. S corporations, enter the amount from line 38a or 38b on Form 1120S, Schedule K, line 10.*

Form **4797**

Department of the Treasury
Internal Revenue Service (99)

Sales of Business Property

(Also Involuntary Conversions and Recapture Amounts Under Sections 179 and 280F(b)(2))

▶Attach to your tax return. ▶See separate instructions.

OMB No. 1545-0184

2004

Attachment Sequence No. 27

Name(s) shown on return | Identifying number

1 Enter the gross proceeds from sales or exchanges reported to you for 2004 on Form(s) 1099-B or 1099-S (or substitute statement) that you are including on line 2, 10, or 20 (see instructions) 1

Part I Sales or Exchanges of Property Used in a Trade or Business and Involuntary Conversions From Other Than Casualty or Theft—Most Property Held More Than 1 Year (see instructions)

	(a) Description of property	(b) Date acquired (mo., day, yr.)	(c) Date sold (mo., day, yr.)	(d) Gross sales price	(e) Depreciation allowed or allowable since acquisition	(f) Cost or other basis, plus improvements and expense of sale	(g) Gain or (loss) Subtract (f) from the sum of (d) and (e)
2							

3	Gain, if any, from Form 4684, line 39	3	
4	Section 1231 gain from installment sales from Form 6252, line 26 or 37	4	
5	Section 1231 gain or (loss) from like-kind exchanges from Form 8824	5	
6	Gain, if any, from line 32, from other than casualty or theft	6	
7	Combine lines 2 through 6. Enter the gain or (loss) here and on the appropriate line as follows:	7	

Partnerships (except electing large partnerships) and S corporations. Report the gain or (loss) following the instructions for Form 1065, Schedule K, line 10, or Form 1120S, Schedule K, line 9. Skip lines 8, 9, 11, and 12 below.

All others. If line 7 is zero or a loss, enter the amount from line 7 on line 11 below and skip lines 8 and 9. If line 7 is a gain and you did not have any prior year section 1231 losses, or they were recaptured in an earlier year, enter the gain from line 7 as a long-term capital gain on Schedule D and skip lines 8, 9, 11, and 12 below.

8	Nonrecaptured net section 1231 losses from prior years (see instructions)	8	
9	Subtract line 8 from line 7. If zero or less, enter -0-. If line 9 is zero, enter the gain from line 7 on line 12 below. If line 9 is more than zero, enter the amount from line 8 on line 12 below and enter the gain from line 9 as a long-term capital gain on Schedule D (see instructions)	9	

Part II Ordinary Gains and Losses

10 Ordinary gains and losses not included on lines 11 through 16 (include property held 1 year or less):

11	Loss, if any, from line 7	11	( )
12	Gain, if any, from line 7 or amount from line 8, if applicable	12	
13	Gain, if any, from line 31	13	
14	Net gain or (loss) from Form 4684, lines 31 and 38a	14	
15	Ordinary gain from installment sales from Form 6252, line 25 or 36	15	
16	Ordinary gain or (loss) from like-kind exchanges from Form 8824	16	
17	Combine lines 10 through 16	17	
18	For all except individual returns, enter the amount from line 17 on the appropriate line of your return and skip lines a and b below. For individual returns, complete lines a and b below:		
a	If the loss on line 11 includes a loss from Form 4684, line 35, column (b)(ii), enter that part of the loss here. Enter the part of the loss from income-producing property on Schedule A (Form 1040), line 27, and the part of the loss from property used as an employee on Schedule A (Form 1040), line 22. Identify as from "Form 4797, line 18a." See instructions	18a	
b	Redetermine the gain or (loss) on line 17 excluding the loss, if any, on line 18a. Enter here and on Form 1040, line 14	18b	

For Paperwork Reduction Act Notice, see page 8 of the instructions. Cat. No. 13086I Form **4797** (2004)

Part III Gain From Disposition of Property Under Sections 1245, 1250, 1252, 1254, and 1255

19 (a) Description of section 1245, 1250, 1252, 1254, or 1255 property:	(b) Date acquired (mo., day, yr.)	(c) Date sold (mo., day, yr.)
A		
B		
C		
D		

These columns relate to the properties on lines 19A through 19D. ▶		Property A	Property B	Property C	Property D
20 Gross sales price (**Note:** *See line 1 before completing.*)	20				
21 Cost or other basis plus expense of sale	21				
22 Depreciation (or depletion) allowed or allowable	22				
23 Adjusted basis. Subtract line 22 from line 21	23				
24 Total gain. Subtract line 23 from line 20	24				
25 **If section 1245 property:**					
a Depreciation allowed or allowable from line 22	25a				
b Enter the **smaller** of line 24 or 25a	25b				
26 **If section 1250 property:** If straight line depreciation was used, enter -0- on line 26g, except for a corporation subject to section 291.					
a Additional depreciation after 1975 (see instructions)	26a				
b Applicable percentage multiplied by the **smaller** of line 24 or line 26a (see instructions)	26b				
c Subtract line 26a from line 24. If residential rental property **or** line 24 is not more than line 26a, skip lines 26d and 26e	26c				
d Additional depreciation after 1969 and before 1976	26d				
e Enter the **smaller** of line 26c or 26d	26e				
f Section 291 amount (corporations only)	26f				
g Add lines 26b, 26e, and 26f	26g				
27 **If section 1252 property:** Skip this section if you did not dispose of farmland or if this form is being completed for a partnership (other than an electing large partnership).					
a Soil, water, and land clearing expenses	27a				
b Line 27a multiplied by applicable percentage (see instructions)	27b				
c Enter the **smaller** of line 24 or 27b	27c				
28 **If section 1254 property:**					
a Intangible drilling and development costs, expenditures for development of mines and other natural deposits, and mining exploration costs (see instructions)	28a				
b Enter the **smaller** of line 24 or 28a	28b				
29 **If section 1255 property:**					
a Applicable percentage of payments excluded from income under section 126 (see instructions)	29a				
b Enter the **smaller** of line 24 or 29a (see instructions)	29b				

Summary of Part III Gains. Complete property columns A through D through line 29b before going to line 30.

30 Total gains for all properties. Add property columns A through D, line 24	30	
31 Add property columns A through D, lines 25b, 26g, 27c, 28b, and 29b. Enter here and on line 13	31	
32 Subtract line 31 from line 30. Enter the portion from casualty or theft on Form 4684, line 33. Enter the portion from other than casualty or theft on Form 4797, line 6	32	

Part IV Recapture Amounts Under Sections 179 and 280F(b)(2) When Business Use Drops to 50% or Less (see instructions)

		(a) Section 179	(b) Section 280F(b)(2)
33 Section 179 expense deduction or depreciation allowable in prior years	33		
34 Recomputed depreciation. See instructions	34		
35 Recapture amount. Subtract line 34 from line 33. See the instructions for where to report	35		

Form **4797** (2004)

Partnership Practice Set

The Location Company

Federal Tax Return

FACTS

The Location Company is a partnership owned and operated by Jerome Willard (social security number 433-22-3482) and Anika Willard (social security number 343-26-8178). The office is located at 300 W. Eastridge Lane, Little Rock, Arkansas 43566. The partnership's tax identification number is 37-3734061, and it uses a calendar year for tax purposes. The business was started on March 5, 1998 to manufacture handheld Global Positioning Systems. The partnership has prospered and sells its products throughout the United States on a wholesale basis to retail outlets. Both Jerome and Anika are active in the business. The business code number is 334500.

Jerome Willard is a 70 percent general partner, and Anika Willard is a 30 percent general partner who, among other duties, deals with tax matters for the partnership. Both Jerome and Anika devote 100 percent of their time to the business. Jerome lives at 610 Northern Way, Little Rock, Arkansas 43560 and Anika resides at 24 Western Edge Rd., Little Rock, Arkansas 43622. Both partners and the partnership file Federal income tax returns at the IRS Service Center in Ogden, Utah.

The partnership files its tax return on the accrual method. Inventory has been consistently valued at cost under the FIFO method using the full absorption procedure. Inventory capitalization rules of Internal Revenue Code Section 263A do not apply due to the 'small business exception' (average annual gross receipts for the three preceding taxable years do not exceed $10 million). The accounting records are computerized.

The income statement and balance sheet for the current year, prepared by the accounting firm of Here & There, CPAs, appear below:

THE LOCATION COMPANY
INCOME STATEMENT
For the Year Ending December 31, 2004

Revenue:		
Sales (net)	$ 972,622	
Cost of goods sold	(399,880)	
Gross profit		$ 572,742
Operating expenses:		
Wages to employees	$ 148,068	
Guaranteed payment to Anika Willard	43,472	
Rental expense	69,083	
Interest expense	26,106	
Advertising	45,906	
Contributions to United Way	4,347	
Depreciation expense	19,616	
Taxes	20,092	
Shipping	26,054	
Repairs and maintenance	6,449	
Total operating expenses		$(409,193)
Net Income from Operations		$ 163,549
Other incomes and expenses:		
Dividend income	$ 10,434	
Interest income	3,695	
Interest expense related to investments	(16,640)	
Net loss on sale of investments	(6,740)	
Net loss on sale of business assets	(18,204)	(27,455)
Net Income		$ 136,094

THE LOCATION COMPANY
STATEMENT OF FINANCIAL POSITION
December 31, 2004

ASSETS	Beginning of Year	End of Year
Current Assets:		
Cash & Marketable Securities	$161,163	$156,861
Accounts Receivable	23,475	33,835
Inventory	67,099	108,866
Total current assets	$251,737	$299,562
Depreciable Assets (Schedule attached)	$293,436	$294,523
Less: Accumulated depreciation	(39,578)	(36,100)
Total depreciable assets (net)	$253,858	$258,423
Other Assets:		
Land (used in the business)	$163,020	$108,680
Total Assets	$668,615	$666,665
LIABILITIES AND CAPITAL		
Current liabilities:		
Accounts payable	$ 46,607	$ 31,656
Notes payable (less than one year)	206,492	178,493
Total current liabilities	$253,099	$210,149
Capital:		
Jerome Willard	$290,862	$319,561
Anika Willard	124,654	136,955
Total capital	$415,516	$456,516
Total Liabilities and Capital	$668,615	$666,665

STATEMENT OF PARTNERS' CAPITAL

	Jerome Willard	Anika Willard	Total
Capital at beginning of year	$290,862	$124,654	$415,516
Net income for the year	95,266	40,828	136,094
Partners' Withdrawals	(66,567)	(28,527)	(95,094)
Capital at end of year	$319,561	$136,955	$456,516

ADDITIONAL INFORMATION

1. Dividend income is from the following sources:

Electro Corporation	$5,869
Bell Corp.	2,145
Mobile Corp.	2,420
Total	$10,434

Electro Corporation is located in Bath, England. You learn that English law requires an income tax withholding at the rate of 10% on such remittances outside that country. Assume that all of the dividends received are qualifying dividends for purposes of the 5%/15% tax rates.

2. Interest Income includes $1,956 received on City of Little Rock, Arkansas General Obligation bonds. The Location Company's employees have been unable to locate a Form 1099 for the interest.

3. Depreciation/Cost Recovery information is attached.

4. On April 5, 2004 a loss of $6,740 was suffered on the sale of 120 shares of common stock of Microchip, Inc. The stock, purchased on November 21, 1999 for $8,694, had been held for investment. After considering the sale, Jerome convinced himself that the sale had been premature because this company's record could only improve. Jerome had the partnership repurchase 30 shares of Microchip, Inc. common stock on May 11, 2004 for $3,022 and purchase 100 shares of Plastic, Inc. common stock on June 6, 2004 for $6,782.

5. Several business assets were sold during the year. A schedule attached to the partnership's financial statements provides these details:

Asset	Date Sold	Sales Price	Cost	Accumulated Depreciation	Financial Gain (Loss)
Land	* 03/12/04	$43,472	$54,340	$ -0-	$(10,868)
Buildings	* 03/12/04	29,357	32,604	5,162	1,915
M&E (Acq. 2000)	** 04/20/04	5,434	32,604	13,042	(14,128)
M&E (Acq. 2002)	** 04/20/04	21,722	21,736	4,891	4,877
Totals		$99,985	$141,284	$23,095	$(18,204)

* The land and buildings were sold to Jerome Willard for independently appraised fair market values. Both assets were acquired on 10/01/99.

** All machinery and equipment disposed of during the year was sold to an unrelated third party.

6. The partners wish to claim foreign tax credits for the English income tax withheld on the dividends from the English corporation.

7. Investment interest expense is for:

Loan to buy City of Little Rock, Arkansas bonds	$2,717
Loan to buy Yahoo Corp. stock	5,325
Loan to buy Citi Corp. stock	8,598
Total	$16,640

8. All liabilities of the partnership are recourse loans, and all notes payable were issued at par and provide market interest rates.

REQUIRED

From the above information, prepare The Location Company's 2004 Federal partnership return of income (Form 1065), including all supporting statements, schedules, and forms. Schedules K-1 for each of the partners should be in the return. Unless otherwise noted, assume the partnership makes all available elections to minimize the partners' current taxable incomes. Round amounts to the nearest dollar. If additional information is needed, make realistic assumptions and fill in all required data.

Even though the partnership may not be technically required to do so, Jerome has expressed a desire that Schedule L (Balance Sheets), Schedule M-1 (Reconciliation of Income (Loss) per Books With Income (Loss) per Return), and Schedule M-2 (Analysis of Partners' Capital Accounts) on Form 1065, p. 4 be completed.

The Location Company
Depreciation/Cost Recovery Information
2004

Financial Depreciation Information	Balance 12/31/03	2004 Additions	2004 Retirements	Balance 12/31/04	Balance 12/31/03	2004 Provision	2004 Retirements	Balance 12/31/04
Buildings Acquired on:								
10/01/99	$ 32,604		($32,604)	$ 0	$ 4,619	$ 543	($ 5,162)	$ 0
10/01/00	130,416			130,416	14,128	4,348		18,476
	$163,020	$ 0	($32,604)	$ 130,416	$18,747	$ 4,891	($ 5,162)	$18,476

Continued

Financial Depreciation Information	Balance 12/31/03	2004 Additions	2004 Retirements	Balance 12/31/04	Balance 12/31/03	2004 Provision	2004 Retirements	Balance 12/31/04
Machinery Acquired on:								
06/01/00	$ 32,604		($32,604)	$ 0	$ 11,411	$ 1,631	($ 13,042)	$ 0
03/01/02	43,472		(21,736)	21,736	7,608	3,260	(4,891)	5,977
08/01/03	54,340			54,340	1,812	5,434		7,246
04/01/04		88,031		88,031		4,401		4,401
	$ 130,416	$88,031	($54,340)	$164,107	$20,831	$14,726	($17,933)	$17,624
	$293,436	$88,031	($86,944)	$294,523	$39,578	$19,617	($23,095)	$36,100

TAX DEPRECIATION INFORMATION (Use 'general' statutory percentages below)

MACRS (Modified Accelerated Cost Recovery System—For property placed in service after 1986)

Nonresidential real property (39-year statutory life, straight line, mid-month convention). Statutory percentages for assets placed in service in October are .535% for recovery year 1, 2.564% for years 2–39, and 2.033% for year 40. (*Note:* The percentages are grouped for ease of presentation; the actual percentage for a year may differ by .001% from the rates shown.)

Machinery and equipment (7-year statutory life, 200% declining balance switching to straight line, half-year convention). Statutory percentage for assets placed in service during a year are 14.29%, 24.49%, 17.49%, 12.49%, 8.93%, 8.92%, 8.93%, and 4.46% for recovery years 1–8, respectively. One-half of the normal MACRS amount is allowed for the year of disposition. The partnership did not claim Internal Revenue Code Sec. (IRC Sec.) 179 expense for assets placed in service prior to 2004. The partnership elected not to take the additional 30% or 50% depreciation allowance for assets placed in service prior to 2004. The full allowable IRC Sec. 179 expense of $88,031 is claimed for machinery and equipment placed in service during 2004.

ALTERNATIVE MINIMUM TAX (Tax Preferences and Adjustments)

For this practice set, ignore effects of the above cost recoveries on the Alternative Minimum Tax (i.e., leave the applicable spaces blank for these items in the Adjustments and Tax Preferences Items section of Schedules K and K-1).

Total Tax Depreciation Provision 2004
including § 179

$ 112,015

Partnership Practice Set

The Location Company

FORMS

Page

1. For a short-term capital gain, report the full amount of the gain on Schedule K, line 8 or 11.

For a long-term capital gain, report the full amount of the gain on Schedule K, line 9a or 11. Report the collectibles (28%) gain (loss) on Schedule K, line 9b.

2. Enter each partner's share of the full amount of the gain on Schedule K-1, box 8 or 9a, or in box 11 using code E, whichever applies. Report the collectibles (28%) gain (loss) on Schedule K-1, box 9b.

If the partnership filed its original return on time without making the election, it may make the election on an amended return filed no later than 6 months after the due date of the return (excluding extensions). Write "Filed pursuant to section 301.9100-2" at the top of the amended return.

• A sale or other disposition of an interest in a partnership owning unrealized receivables or inventory items may result in ordinary gain or loss. See Pub. 541, Partnerships, for more details.

• Certain constructive ownership transactions. Gain in excess of the gain that would have been recognized if the partnership had held a financial asset directly during the term of a derivative contract must be treated as ordinary income. See section 1260 for details.

• Gain from the sale of collectibles. Report any collectibles (28%) gain (loss) included on lines 6 through 10 on line 9b of Schedule K (and each partner's share in box 9b of Schedule K-1). A collectibles (28%) gain (loss) is any long-term gain or deductible long-term loss from the sale or exchange of a collectible that is a capital asset.

Collectibles include works of art, rugs, antiques, metals (such as gold, silver, and platinum bullion), gems, stamps, coins, alcoholic beverages, and certain other tangible property.

Also include gain (but not loss) from the sale or exchange of an interest in a partnership or trust held more than 1 year and attributable to unrealized appreciation of collectibles. For details, see Regulations section 1.1(h)-1. Also, attach the statement reguired under Regulations section 1.1(h)-1(e).

Special rules for traders in securities. Traders in securities are engaged in the business of buying and selling securities for their own account. To be engaged in business as a trader in securities:

• The partnership must seek to profit from daily market movements in the prices of securities and not from dividends, interest, or capital appreciation.

• The partnership's trading activity must be substantial.

• The partnership must carry on the activity with continuity and regularity.

The following facts and circumstances should be considered in determining if a partnership's activity is a business:

• Typical holding periods for securities bought and sold.

• The frequency and dollar amount of the partnership's trades during the year.

• The extent to which the partners pursue the activity to produce income for a livelihood.

• The amount of time devoted to the activity.

Like an investor, a trader must report each sale of securities (taking into account commissions and any other costs of acquiring or disposing of the securities) on Schedule D or on an attached statement containing all the same information for each sale in a similar format. However, if a trader made the mark-to-market election (see page 5 of the *Instructions for Form 1065*), each transaction is reported in Part II of Form 4797 instead of Schedule D. Regardless of whether a trader reports its gains and losses on Schedule D or Form 4797, the gain or loss from the disposition of securities is not taken into account when figuring net earnings from self-employment on Schedules K and K-1. See section 1402(i) for an exception that applies to section 1256 contracts.

The limitation on investment interest expense that applies to investors does not apply to interest paid or incurred in a trading business. A trader reports interest expense and other expenses (excluding commissions and other costs of acquiring or disposing of securities) from a trading business on page 1 of Form 1065.

A trader also may hold securities for investment. The rules for investors generally will apply to those securities. Allocate interest and other expenses between the partnership's trading business and its investment securities. Investment interest expense is reported on line 13c of Schedule K and in box 13 of Schedule K-1 using code I.

Constructive sale treatment for certain appreciated positions. Generally, the partnership must recognize gain (but not loss) on the date it enters into a constructive sale of any appreciated position in stock, a partnership interest, or certain debt instruments as if the position were disposed of at FMV on that date.

The partnership is treated as making a constructive sale of an appreciated position when it (or a related person, in some cases) does one of the following:

• Enters into a short sale of the same or substantially identical property (that is, a "short sale against the box").

• Enters into an offsetting notional principal contract relating to the same or substantially identical property.

• Enters into a futures or forward contract to deliver the same or substantially identical property.

• Acquires the same or substantially identical property (if the appreciated position is a short sale, offsetting notional principal contract, or a futures or forward contract).

Exception. Generally, constructive sale treatment does not apply if:

• The partnership closed the transaction before the end of the 30th day after the end of the year in which it was entered into,

• The partnership held the appreciated position to which the transaction relates throughout the 60-day period starting on the date the transaction was closed, and

• At no time during that 60-day period was the partnership's risk of loss reduced by holding certain other positions.

For details and other exceptions to these rules, see Pub. 550.

Rollover of gain from qualified stock. If the partnership sold qualified small business stock (defined below) it held for more than 6 months, it may postpone gain if it purchased other qualified small business stock during the 60-day period that began on the date of the sale. The partnership must recognize gain to the extent the sale proceeds exceed the cost of the replacement stock. Reduce the basis of the replacement stock by any postponed gain.

If the partnership chooses to postpone gain, report the entire gain realized on the sale on line 1 or 6. Directly below the line on which the partnership reported the gain, enter in column (a) "Section 1045 Rollover" and enter as a (loss) in column (f) the amount of the postponed gain.

Caution. *The partnership also must separately state the amount of the gain rolled over on qualified stock under section 1045 on Form 1065, Schedule K, line 11, because each partner must determine if he or she qualifies for the rollover at the partner level. Also, the partnership must separately state on that line (and not on Schedule D) any gain that would qualify for the section 1045 rollover at the partner level instead of the partnership level (because a partner was entitled to purchase replacement stock) and any gain on qualified stock that could qualify for the partial exclusion under section 1202.*

To be qualified small business stock, the stock must meet all of the following tests:

• It must be stock in a C corporation (that is, not S corporation stock).

• It must have been originally issued after August 10, 1993.

• As of the date the stock was issued, the corporation was a qualified small business. A qualified small business is a domestic C corporation with total gross assets of $50 million or less (a) at all times after August 9, 1993, and before the stock was issued and (b) immediately after the stock was issued.

Gross assets include those of any predecessor of the corporation. All corporations that are members of the same parent-subsidiary controlled group are treated as one corporation.

• The partnership must have acquired the stock at its original issue (either directly or through an underwriter), either in exchange for money or other property or as pay for services (other than as an underwriter) to the corporation. In certain cases, the partnership may meet the test if it acquired the stock from another person who met this test (such as by gift or at death) or through a conversion or exchange of qualified business stock by the holder.

• During substantially all the time the partnership held the stock:

1. The corporation was a C corporation,

2. At least 80% of the value of the corporation's assets were used in the active conduct of one or more qualified businesses (defined below), and

3. The corporation was not a foreign corporation, domestic international sales corporation (DISC), former DISC, corporation that has made (or that has a subsidiary that has made) a section 936 election, regulated investment company (RIC), real estate investment trust (REIT), real estate mortgage investment conduit (REMIC), financial asset securitization investment trust (FASIT), or cooperative.

Note. *A specialized small business investment company (SSBIC) is treated as having met test 2 above.*

A qualified business is any business other than the following:

• One involving services performed in the fields of health, law, engineering, architecture, accounting, actuarial science, performing arts, consulting, athletics, financial services, or brokerage services.

• One whose principal asset is the reputation or skill of one or more employees.

• Any banking, insurance, financing, leasing, investing, or similar business.

• Any farming business (including the raising or harvesting of trees).

• Any business involving the production of products for which percentage depletion can be claimed.

• Any business of operating a hotel, motel, restaurant, or similar business.

Rollover of gain from empowerment zone assets. If the partnership sold a qualified empowerment zone asset it held for more than 1 year, it may be able to elect to postpone part or all of the gain. For details, see Pub. 954, Tax Incentives for Distressed Communities, and section 1397B.

Exclusion of gain from DC Zone assets. If the partnership sold or exchanged a District of Columbia Enterprise Zone (DC Zone) asset that it held for more than 5 years, it may be able to exclude the qualified capital gain. The sale or exchange of DC Zone capital assets reported on Schedule D include:

• Stock in a domestic corporation that was a DC Zone business.

• Interest in a partnership that was a DC Zone business.

Report the sale or exchange of property used in the partnership's DC Zone business on Form 4797.

Gains not qualified for exclusion. The following gains do not qualify for the exclusion of gain from DC Zone assets.

• Gain on the sale of an interest in a partnership, which is a DC Zone business, attributable to unrecaptured section 1250 gain. See the instructions for line 9c of Schedule K for information on how to report unrecaptured section 1250 gain.

• Gain on the sale of an interest in a partnership or S corporation attributable to real property or an intangible asset which is not an integral part of the DC Zone business.

• Gain from a related-party transaction. See *Sales and Exchanges Between Related Persons* in chapter 2 of Pub. 544.

See Pub. 954 and section 1400B for more details on DC Zone assets and special rules.

How to report. Report the entire gain realized from the sale or exchange as you otherwise would without regard to the exclusion. To report the exclusion, enter "DC Zone Asset Exclusion" on Schedule D, line 6, column (a) and enter as a (loss) in column (f) the amount of the exclusion.

Specific Instructions

Columns (b) and (c). Date Acquired and Date Sold

Use the trade dates for date acquired and date sold for stocks and bonds traded on an exchange or over-the-counter market. The acquisition date for an asset the partnership held on January 1, 2001, for which it made an election to recognize any gain on a deemed sale, is the date of the deemed sale and reacquisition.

Column (d). Sales Price

Enter in this column either the gross sales price or the net sales price from the sale. On sales of stocks and bonds, report the gross amount as reported to the partnership by the partnership's broker on Form 1099-B, Proceeds From Broker and Barter Exchange Transactions, or similar statement. However, if the broker advised the partnership that gross proceeds (gross sales price) less commissions and option premiums were reported to the IRS, enter that net amount in column (d).

Column (e). Cost or Other Basis

In general, the cost or other basis is the cost of the property plus purchase commissions and improvements and minus depreciation, amortization, and depletion. If the partnership got the property in a tax-free exchange, involuntary conversion, or wash sale of stock, it may not be able to use the actual cash cost as the basis. If the partnership does not use cash cost, attach an explanation of the basis.

If the partnership sold stock, adjust the basis by subtracting all the stock-related nontaxable distributions received before the sale. This includes nontaxable distributions from utility company stock and mutual funds. Also adjust the basis for any stock splits or stock dividends.

If the partnership elected to recognize gain on an asset held on January 1, 2001, its basis in the asset is its closing market price or FMV, whichever applies, on the date of the deemed sale and reacquisition, whether the deemed sale resulted in a gain or an unallowed loss.

If a charitable contribution deduction is passed through to a partner because of a bargain sale of property to a charitable organization, the adjusted basis for determining gain from the sale is an amount that has the same ratio to the adjusted basis as the amount realized has to the FMV.

See section 852(f) for the treatment of certain load charges incurred in acquiring stock in a mutual fund with a reinvestment right.

If the gross sales price is reported in column (d), increase the cost or other basis by any expense of sale, such as broker's fees, commissions, or option premiums, before making an entry in column (e).

For more details, see Pub. 551, Basis of Assets.

Column (f). Gain or (Loss)

Make a separate entry in this column for each transaction reported on lines 1 and 6 and any other line(s) that applies to the partnership. For lines 1 and 6, subtract the amount in column (e) from the amount in column (d). Enter negative amounts in parentheses.

Lines 4 and 9. Capital Gains (Losses) From Other Partnerships, Estates, and Trusts

See the Schedule K-1 or other information supplied to you by the other partnership, estate, or trust.

Line 10. Capital Gain Distributions

On line 10, column (f), report the total amount of (a) capital gain distributions and (b) the partnership's share of undistributed capital gains from a RIC or REIT. Report the partnership's share of taxes paid on undistributed capital gains by a RIC or REIT on a statement attached to Form 1065 for Schedule K, line 15f (and each partner's share in box 15 of Schedule K-1 using code I).

Instructions for Form 1065

U.S. Partnership Return of Income

2004

Instructions for Form 1065

U.S. Return of Partnership Income

Section references are to the Internal Revenue Code unless otherwise noted.

Contents	Page

What's New

1. The instructions for Schedules K and K-1 have been revised to reflect extensive changes to these schedules. See *General Reporting Requirements* on page 22 for new Schedule K-1 reporting requirements.

2. The American Jobs Creation Act of 2004 made several changes that affect partnerships and their partners. These changes include the following provisions. See Pub. 553, Highlights of 2004 Tax Changes, for more information.

- A new election to deduct a limited amount of business start-up and organizational expenses. For more information see *Business start-up and organizational costs* on page 16.
- Two new tax credits: the biodiesel fuels credit and the low sulfur diesel fuel production credit. The act also expanded the renewable electricity credit to include refined coal production. See the instructions for line 15f of Schedule K for more information.
- A new election to deduct up to $10,000 of reforestation expenses paid or incurred after October 22, 2004. The reforestation credit is repealed for expenses paid or incurred after this date. See the instructions for line 13e of Schedule K for more information.
- A new election to deduct certain costs of qualified film or television productions commencing after October 22, 2004. See section 181 for more information.

Photographs of Missing Children

The Internal Revenue Service is a proud partner with the National Center for Missing and Exploited Children. Photographs of missing children selected by the Center may appear in instructions on pages that would otherwise be blank. You can help bring these children home by looking at the photographs and calling 1-800-THE-LOST (1-800-843-5678) if you recognize a child.

Unresolved Tax Issues

If the partnership has attempted to deal with an IRS problem unsuccessfully, it should contact the Taxpayer Advocate. The Taxpayer Advocate independently represents the partnership's interests and concerns within the IRS by protecting its rights and resolving problems that have not been fixed through normal channels.

While the Taxpayer Advocates cannot change the tax law or make a technical tax decision, they can clear up problems that resulted from previous contacts and ensure that the partnership's case is given a complete and impartial review.

The partnership's assigned personal advocate will listen to its point of view and will work with the partnership to address its concerns. The partnership can expect the advocate to provide:

- A "fresh look" at a new or ongoing problem.
- Timely acknowledgement.
- The name and phone number of the individual assigned to its case.
- Updates on progress.
- Timeframes for action.
- Speedy resolution.
- Courteous service.

When contacting the Taxpayer Advocate, the partnership should provide the following information.

- The partnership's name, address, and employer identification number.
- The name and telephone number of an authorized contact person and the hours he or she can be reached.
- The type of tax return and year(s) involved.
- A detailed description of the problem.
- Previous attempts to solve the problem and the office that had been contacted.
- A description of the hardship the partnership is facing and verifying documentation (if applicable).

The partnership can contact a Taxpayer Advocate by calling a toll-free number,

Cat. No. 11392V

1-877-777-4778. Persons who have access to TTY/TDD equipment can call 1-800-829-4059 and ask for the Taxpayer Advocate. If the partnership prefers, it may call, write, or fax the Taxpayer Advocate office in its area. See Pub. 1546, The Taxpayer Advocate Service of the IRS, for a list of addresses and fax numbers.

How To Get Forms and Publications

Personal Computer

You can access the IRS website 24 hours a day, 7 days a week at *www.irs.gov* to:

- Order IRS products online.
- Download forms, instructions, and publications.
- See answers to frequently asked tax questions.
- Search publications online by topic or keyword.
- Send us comments or request help by email.
- Sign up to receive local and national tax news by email.

You can also reach us using file transfer protocol at *ftp.irs.gov*.

CD-ROM

Order Pub. 1796, 2004 Federal Tax Products CD-ROM, and get:

- Current year forms, instructions, and publications.
- Prior year forms, instructions, and publications.
- Frequently requested tax forms that can be filled in electronically, printed out for submission, and saved for recordkeeping.
- The Internal Revenue Bulletin.

Buy the CD-ROM on the Internet at *www.irs.gov/cdorders* from the National Technical Information Service (NTIS) for $22 (no handling fee), or call 1-877-CDFORMS (1-877-233-6767) toll free to buy the CD-ROM for $22 (plus a $5 handling fee).

By Phone and In Person

You can order forms and publications by calling 1-800-TAX-FORM (1-800-829-3676). You can also get most forms and publications at your local IRS office.

General Instructions

Purpose of Form

Form 1065 is an information return used to report the income, deductions, gains, losses, etc., from the operation of a partnership. A partnership does not pay tax on its income but "passes through" any profits or losses to its partners. Partners must include partnership items on their tax returns.

Definitions

Partnership

A partnership is the relationship between two or more persons who join to carry on a trade or business, with each person contributing money, property, labor, or skill and each expecting to share in the profits and losses of the business whether or not a formal partnership agreement is made.

The term "partnership" includes a limited partnership, syndicate, group, pool, joint venture, or other unincorporated organization, through or by which any business, financial operation, or venture is carried on, that is not, within the meaning of the regulations under section 7701, a corporation, trust, estate, or sole proprietorship.

A joint undertaking merely to share expenses is not a partnership. Mere co-ownership of property that is maintained and leased or rented is not a partnership. However, if the co-owners provide services to the tenants, a partnership exists.

Foreign Partnership

A foreign partnership is a partnership that is not created or organized in the United States or under the law of the United States or of any state.

General Partner

A general partner is a partner who is personally liable for partnership debts.

General Partnership

A general partnership is composed only of general partners.

Limited Partner

A limited partner is a partner in a partnership formed under a state limited partnership law, whose personal liability for partnership debts is limited to the amount of money or other property that the partner contributed or is required to contribute to the partnership. Some members of other entities, such as domestic or foreign business trusts or limited liability companies that are classified as partnerships, may be treated as limited partners for certain purposes. See, for example, Temporary Regulations section 1.469-5T(e)(3), which treats all members with limited liability as limited partners for purposes of section 469(h)(2).

Limited Partnership

A limited partnership is formed under a state limited partnership law and composed of at least one general partner and one or more limited partners.

Limited Liability Partnership

A limited liability partnership (LLP) is formed under a state limited liability partnership law. Generally, a partner in an LLP is not personally liable for the debts of the LLP or any other partner, nor is a partner liable for the acts or omissions of any other partner, solely by reason of being a partner.

Limited Liability Company

A limited liability company (LLC) is an entity formed under state law by filing articles of organization as an LLC. Unlike a partnership, none of the members of an LLC are personally liable for its debts. An LLC may be classified for federal income tax purposes as a partnership, a corporation, or an entity disregarded as an entity separate from its owner by applying the rules in Regulations section 301.7701-3. See Form 8832, Entity Classification Election, for more details.

Note. A domestic LLC with at least two members that does not file Form 8832 is classified as a partnership for federal income tax purposes.

Nonrecourse Loans

Nonrecourse loans are those liabilities of the partnership for which no partner bears the economic risk of loss.

Who Must File

Domestic Partnerships

Except as provided below, every domestic partnership must file Form 1065, unless it neither receives income nor incurs any expenditures treated as deductions or credits for federal income tax purposes.

Entities formed as LLCs that are classified as partnerships for federal income tax purposes must file Form 1065.

A religious or apostolic organization exempt from income tax under section 501(d) must file Form 1065 to report its taxable income, which must be allocated to its members as a dividend, whether distributed or not. Such an organization must figure its taxable income on an attachment to Form 1065 in the same manner as a corporation. The organization may use Form 1120, U.S. Corporation Income Tax Return, for this purpose. Enter the organization's taxable income, if any, on line 6a of Schedule K and each member's pro rata share in box 6a of Schedule K-1. Net operating losses are not deductible by the members but may be carried back or forward by the organization under the rules of section 172. The religious or apostolic organization also must make its annual information return available for public inspection. For this purpose, "annual information return" includes an exact copy of Form 1065 and all accompanying schedules and attachments, except Schedules K-1. For more details, see Regulations section 301.6104(d)-1.

A qualifying syndicate, pool, joint venture, or similar organization may elect under section 761(a) not to be treated as a partnership for federal income tax purposes and will not be required to file Form 1065 except for the year of election. For details, see section 761(a) and Regulations section 1.761-2.

An electing large partnership (as defined in section 775) must file Form 1065-B, U.S. Return of Income for Electing Large Partnerships.

Real estate mortgage investment conduits (REMICs) must file Form 1066, U.S. Real Estate Mortgage Investment Conduit (REMIC) Income Tax Return.

Certain publicly traded partnerships treated as corporations under section 7704 must file Form 1120.

Foreign Partnerships

Generally, a foreign partnership that has gross income effectively connected with the conduct of a trade or business within the United States or has gross income derived from sources in the United States must file Form 1065, even if its principal place of business is outside the United States or all its members are foreign persons. A foreign partnership required to file a return generally must report all of its foreign and U.S. source income.

A foreign partnership with U.S. source income is not required to file Form 1065 if it qualifies for either of the following two exceptions.

Exception for foreign partnerships with U.S. partners. A return is not required if:
- The partnership had no effectively connected income (ECI) during its tax year,
- The partnership had U.S. source income of $20,000 or less during its tax year,
- Less than 1% of any partnership item of income, gain, loss, deduction, or credit was allocable in the aggregate to direct U.S. partners at any time during its tax year, and
- The partnership is not a withholding foreign partnership as defined in Regulations section 1.1441-5(c)(2)(i).

Exception for foreign partnerships with no U.S. partners. A return is not required if:
- The partnership had no ECI during its tax year,
- The partnership had no U.S. partners at any time during its tax year,
- All required Forms 1042 and 1042-S were filed by the partnership or another withholding agent as required by Regulations section 1.1461-1(b) and (c),
- The tax liability of each partner for amounts reportable under Regulations sections 1.1461-1(b) and (c) has been fully satisfied by the withholding of tax at the source, and
- The partnership is not a withholding foreign partnership as defined in Regulations section 1.1441-5(c)(2)(i).

A foreign partnership filing Form 1065 solely to make an election (such as an election to amortize organization expenses) need only provide its name, address, and employer identification number (EIN) on page one of the form and attach a statement citing "Regulations section 1.6031(a)-1(b)(5)" and identifying the election being made. A foreign partnership filing Form 1065 solely to make an election must obtain an EIN if it does not already have one.

Termination of the Partnership

A partnership terminates when:

1. All its operations are discontinued and no part of any business, financial operation, or venture is continued by any of its partners in a partnership or
2. At least 50% of the total interest in partnership capital and profits is sold or exchanged within a 12-month period, including a sale or exchange to another partner. See Regulations section 1.708-1(b)(1) for more details.

The partnership's tax year ends on the date of termination. For purposes of 1 above, the date of termination is the date the partnership winds up its affairs. For purposes of 2 above, the date of termination is the date the partnership interest is sold or exchanged that, of itself or together with other sales or exchanges in the preceding 12 months, transfers an interest of 50% or more in both partnership capital and profits.

Special rules apply in the case of a merger, consolidation, or division of a partnership. See Regulations sections 1.708-1(c) and (d) for details.

Electronic Filing

Certain partnerships with more than 100 partners are required to file Form 1065, Schedules K-1, and related forms and schedules electronically. Other partnerships generally have the option to file electronically. Unless otherwise noted, this requirement or option does not apply to:
- Fiscal year returns with a tax period ending after June 30, 2005. Partnerships with any other fiscal year returns ending on or before June 30, 2005 (January 2005–June 2005) may voluntarily file their return electroncially.

Note: Fiscal year returns with an extended due date after October 15, 2005, may not file electronically.
- Returns filed for religious or apostolic organizations under section 501(d) or for organizations electing not to be treated as a partnership under section 761(a).
- Common trust fund returns. Common trust funds using Form 1065 to make a return of income may voluntarily file Form 1065 electronically.
- Returns filed on Form 1065-B.

For more details on electronic filing, see:

- Pub. 1524, Procedures for the 1065 e-file Program, U.S. Return of Partnership Income For Tax Year 2004;
- Pub. 1525, File Specifications, Validation Criteria and Record Layouts for the 1065 e-file Program, U.S. Return of Partnership Income for Tax Year 2004;
- Pub. 3416, 1065 e-file Program, U.S. Return of Partnership Income for Tax Year 2004 (Publication 1525 Supplement);
- Form 8453-P, U.S. Partnership Declaration and Signature for Electronic Filing; and
- Form 8633, Application to Participate in the IRS e-file Program.

For more information on filing electronically:

- Call the Electronic Filing Section at the Ogden Service Center at 866-255-0654 or
- Write to Internal Revenue Service, Ogden Submission Processing Center, 1065 e-file Team, Stop 1056, Ogden, UT 84201.

Electronic Filing Waiver

The IRS may waive the electronic filing rules if the partnership demonstrates that a hardship would result if it were required to file its return electronically. A partnership interested in requesting a waiver of the mandatory electronic filing requirement must file a written request, and request one in the manner prescribed by the Ogden Submission Processing Center (OSPC).
- All written requests for waivers should be mailed to:

Internal Revenue Service
Ogden Submission Processing Center
e-file Team, Stop 1057
Ogden, UT 84201
- Contact OSPC at 866-255-0654 for questions regarding the waiver procedures or process.

Visit *www.irs.gov/efile* for more information.

When To File

Generally, a domestic partnership must file Form 1065 by the 15th day of the 4th month following the date its tax year ended as shown at the top of Form 1065. For partnerships that keep their records and books of account outside the United States and Puerto Rico, an extension of time to file and pay is granted to the 15th day of the 6th month following the close of the tax year. If the due date falls on a Saturday, Sunday, or legal holiday, file by the next business day.

Private Delivery Services

The partnership can use certain private delivery services designated by the IRS to meet the "timely mailing as timely filing/paying" rule for Form 1065. These private delivery services include only the following.
- DHL Express (DHL): DHL Same Day Service, DHL Next Day 10:30 am, DHL Next Day 12:00 pm, DHL Next Day 3:00 pm, and DHL 2nd Day Service.
- Federal Express (FedEx): FedEx Priority Overnight, FedEx Standard Overnight, FedEx 2Day, FedEx International Priority, and FedEx International First.
- United Parcel Service (UPS): UPS Next Day Air, UPS Next Day Air Saver, UPS 2nd Day Air, UPS 2nd Day Air A.M., UPS Worldwide Express Plus, and UPS Worldwide Express.

The private delivery service can tell you how to get written proof of the mailing date.

Private delivery services cannot deliver items to P.O. boxes. You must use the U.S. Postal Service to mail any item to an IRS P.O. box address.

Extension

If you need more time to file a partnership return, file Form 8736, Application for Automatic Extension of Time To File U.S. Return for a Partnership, REMIC, or for Certain Trusts, for an automatic 3-month extension. File Form 8736 by the regular due date of the partnership return. The automatic 3-month extension period includes any 2-month extension granted to partnerships that keep their records and books of account outside the United States and Puerto Rico.

If, after you have filed Form 8736, you still need more time to file the partnership return, file Form 8800, Application for Additional Extension of Time To File U.S. Return for a Partnership, REMIC, or for Certain Trusts, for an additional extension of up to 3 months. The partnership must provide a full explanation of the reasons for requesting the extension in order to get this additional extension. Form 8800 must be filed by the extended due date of the partnership return.

Period Covered

Form 1065 is an information return for calendar year 2004 and fiscal years beginning in 2004 and ending in 2005. If the return is for a fiscal year or a short tax year, fill in the tax year space at the top of Form 1065 and each Schedule K-1.

The 2004 Form 1065 may also be used if:

1. The partnership has a tax year of less than 12 months that begins and ends in 2005 and
2. The 2005 Form 1065 is not available by the time the partnership is required to file its return.

However, the partnership must show its 2005 tax year on the 2004 Form 1065 and incorporate any tax law changes that are effective for tax years beginning after 2004.

Who Must Sign

General Partner or LLC Member Manager

Form 1065 is not considered to be a return unless it is signed. One general partner or LLC member manager must sign the return. Where a return is made for a partnership by a receiver, trustee or assignee, the fiduciary must sign the return, instead of the general partner or LLC member manager. Returns and forms signed by a receiver or trustee in bankruptcy on behalf of a partnership must be accompanied by a copy of the order or instructions of the court authorizing signing of the return or form.

Paid Preparer's Information

If a partner or an employee of the partnership completes Form 1065, the paid preparer's space should remain blank. In addition, anyone who prepares Form 1065 but does not charge the partnership should not complete this section.

Generally, anyone who is paid to prepare the partnership return must:

- Sign the return in the space provided for the preparer's signature.
- Fill in the other blanks in the "Paid Preparer's Use Only" area of the return.
- Give the partnership a copy of the return in addition to the copy to be filed with the IRS.

Note. A paid preparer may sign original returns, amended returns, or requests for filing extensions by rubber stamp, mechanical device, or computer software program.

Paid Preparer Authorization

If the partnership wants to allow the paid preparer to discuss its 2004 Form 1065 with the IRS, check the "Yes" box in the signature area of the return. The authorization applies only to the individual whose signature appears in the "Paid Preparer's Use Only" section of its return. It does not apply to the firm, if any, shown in the section.

If the "Yes" box is checked, the partnership is authorizing the IRS to call the paid preparer to answer any questions that may arise during the processing of its return. The partnership is also authorizing the paid preparer to:

- Give the IRS any information that is missing from its return,
- Call the IRS for information about the processing of its return, and
- Respond to certain IRS notices that the partnership has shared with the preparer about math errors and return preparation. The notices will not be sent to the preparer.

The partnership is not authorizing the paid preparer to bind the partnership to anything or otherwise represent the partnership before the IRS. If the partnership wants to expand the paid preparer's authorization, see Pub. 947, Practice Before the IRS and Power of Attorney.

The authorization cannot be revoked. However, the authorization will automatically end no later than the due date (excluding extensions) for filing the 2005 return.

Where To File

File Form 1065 at the applicable IRS address listed below.

If the partnership's principal business, office, or agency is located in:	And the total assets at the end of the tax year (Form 1065, page 1, item F) are:	Use the following Internal Revenue Service Center address:
Connecticut, Delaware, District of Columbia, Illinois, Indiana, Kentucky, Maine, Maryland, Massachusetts, Michigan, New Hampshire, New Jersey, New York, North Carolina, Ohio, Pennsylvania, Rhode Island, South Carolina, Vermont, Virginia, West Virginia, Wisconsin	Less than $10 million	Cincinnati, OH 45999-0011
	$10 million or more	Ogden, UT 84201-0011
Alabama, Alaska, Arizona, Arkansas, California, Colorado, Florida, Georgia, Hawaii, Idaho, Iowa, Kansas, Louisiana, Minnesota, Mississippi, Missouri, Montana, Nebraska, Nevada, New Mexico, North Dakota, Oklahoma, Oregon, South Dakota, Tennessee, Texas, Utah, Washington, Wyoming	Any amount	Ogden, UT 84201-0011
A foreign country or U.S. possession	Any amount	Philadelphia, PA 19255-0011

Penalties

Late Filing of Return

A penalty is assessed against the partnership if it is required to file a partnership return and it (a) fails to file the return by the due date, including extensions or (b) files a return that fails to show all the information required, unless such failure is due to reasonable cause. If the failure is due to reasonable cause, attach an explanation to the partnership return. The penalty is $50 for each month or part of a month (for a maximum of 5 months) the failure continues, multiplied by the total number of persons who were partners in the partnership during any part of the partnership's tax year for which the return is due.

Failure To Furnish Information Timely

For each failure to furnish Schedule K-1 to a partner when due and each failure to include on Schedule K-1 all the information required to be shown (or the inclusion of incorrect information), a $50 penalty may be imposed with respect to each Schedule K-1 for which a failure occurs. The maximum penalty is $100,000 for all such failures during a calendar year. If the requirement to report correct information is intentionally disregarded, each $50 penalty is increased to $100 or, if greater, 10% of the aggregate amount of items required to be reported, and the $100,000 maximum does not apply.

Trust Fund Recovery Penalty

This penalty may apply if certain excise, income, social security, and Medicare taxes that must be collected or withheld are not collected or withheld, or these taxes are not paid. These taxes are generally reported on:

- Form 720, Quarterly Federal Excise Tax Return;
- Form 941, Employer's Quarterly Federal Tax Return;
- Form 943, Employer's Annual Federal Tax Return for Agricultural Employees; or
- Form 945, Annual Return of Withheld Federal Income Tax.

The trust fund recovery penalty may be imposed on all persons who are determined by the IRS to have been responsible for collecting, accounting for, and paying over these taxes, and who acted willfully in not doing so. The penalty is equal to the unpaid trust fund tax. See the Instructions for Form 720, Pub. 15, Circular E, Employer's Tax Guide, or Pub. 51, Circular A, Agricultural Employer's Tax Guide, for more details, including the definition of a responsible person.

Accounting Methods

An accounting method is a set of rules used to determine when and how income and expenditures are reported. Figure ordinary business income using the method of accounting regularly used in keeping the partnership's books and records. In all cases, the method used must clearly show taxable income.

Generally, permissible methods include:

- Cash,
- Accrual, or
- Any other method authorized by the Internal Revenue Code.

Generally, a partnership may not use the cash method of accounting if (a) it has at least one corporate partner, average annual gross receipts of more than $5 million, and it is not a farming business or (b) it is a tax shelter (as defined in section 448(d)(3)). See section 448 for details.

Accrual method. If inventories are required, an accrual method of accounting must be used for sales and purchases of merchandise. However, qualifying taxpayers and eligible businesses of qualifying small business taxpayers are excepted from using an accrual method and may account for inventoriable items as materials and supplies that are not incidental. For more details, see *Schedule A. Cost of Goods Sold*, on page 19.

Under the accrual method, an amount is includible in income when:

1. All the events have occurred that fix the right to receive the income, which is the earliest of the date:
   - Payment is earned through the required performance,
   - Payment is due to the taxpayer, or
   - Payment is received by the taxpayer

and

2. The amount can be determined with reasonable accuracy.

See Regulations section 1.451-1(a) for details.

Generally, an accrual basis taxpayer can deduct accrued expenses in the tax year in which:

- All events that determine the liability have occurred,
- The amount of the liability can be figured with reasonable accuracy, and
- Economic performance takes place with respect to the expense.

For property and service liabilities, for example, economic performance occurs as the property or service is provided. There are special economic performance rules for certain items, including recurring expenses. See section 461(h) and the related regulations for the rules for determining when economic performance takes place.

Nonaccrual experience method. Accrual method partnerships are not required to accrue certain amounts to be received from the performance of services that, on the basis of their experience, will not be collected, if:

- The services are in the fields of health, law, engineering, architecture, accounting, actuarial science, performing arts, or consulting or
- The partnership's average annual gross receipts for the 3 prior tax years does not exceed $5 million.

This provision does not apply to any amount if interest is required to be paid on the amount or if there is any penalty for failure to timely pay the amount. For information, see section 448(d)(5) and Temporary Regulations section 1.448-2T. For reporting requirements, see the instructions for line 1a on page 15.

Percentage of completion method. Long-term contracts (except for certain real property construction contracts) must generally be accounted for using the percentage of completion method described in section 460. See section 460 and the underlying regulations for rules on long-term contracts.

Mark-to-market accounting method. Dealers in securities must use the mark-to-market accounting method described in section 475. Under this method, any security that is inventory to the dealer must be included in inventory at its fair market value (FMV). Any security that is not inventory and that is held at the close of the tax year is treated as sold at its FMV on the last business day of the tax year, and any gain or loss must be taken into account in determining gross income. The gain or loss taken into account is generally treated as ordinary gain or loss. For details, including exceptions, see section 475, the related regulations, and Rev. Rul. 94-7, 1994-1 C.B. 151.

Dealers in commodities and traders in securities and commodities can elect to use the mark-to-market accounting method. To make the election, the partnership must file a statement describing the election, the first tax year the election is to be effective, and, in the case of an election for traders in securities or commodities, the trade or business for which the election is made. Except for new taxpayers, the statement must be filed by the due date (not including extensions) of the income tax return for the tax year immediately preceding the election year and attached to that return, or, if applicable, to a request for an extension of time to file that return. For more details, see Rev. Proc. 99-17, 1999-1 I.R.B. 52, and sections 475(e) and (f).

Change in accounting method. Generally, the partnership must get IRS consent to change its method of accounting used to report income (for income as a whole or for any material item). To do so, it must file Form 3115, Application for Change in Accounting Method. See Form 3115 and Pub. 538, Accounting Periods and Methods.

Section 481(a) adjustment. The partnership may have to make an adjustment to prevent amounts of income or expenses from being duplicated. This is called a section 481(a) adjustment. The section 481(a) adjustment period is generally 1 year for a net negative adjustment and 4 years for a net positive adjustment. However, a partnership may elect to use a 1-year adjustment period for positive adjustments if the net section 481(a) adjustment for the accounting method change is less than $25,000. The partnership must complete the appropriate lines of Form 3115 to make the election.

Include any net positive section 481(a) adjustment on page 1, line 7. If the net section 481(a) adjustment is negative, report it on Form 1065, line 20.

Accounting Periods

A partnership is generally required to have one of the following tax years.

1. The tax year of a majority of its partners (majority tax year).
2. If there is no majority tax year, then the tax year common to all of the partnership's principal partners (partners with an interest of 5% or more in the partnership profits or capital).
3. If there is neither a majority tax year nor a tax year common to all principal partners, then the tax year that results in the least aggregate deferral of income.

Note. In determining the tax year of a partnership under 1, 2, or 3 above, the tax years of certain tax-exempt and foreign partners are disregarded. See Regulations section 1.706-1(b) for more details.

4. Some other tax year, if:
   - The partnership can establish that there is a business purpose for the tax year (see Pub. 538 for more information);
   - The partnership elects under section 444 to have a tax year other than a required tax year by filing Form 8716, Election to Have a Tax Year Other Than a Required Tax Year. For a partnership to have this election in effect, it must make the payments required by section 7519 and file Form 8752, Required Payment or Refund Under Section 7519.

   A section 444 election ends if a partnership changes its accounting period to its required tax year or some other permitted year or it is penalized for willfully failing to comply with the requirements of section 7519. If the termination results in a short tax year, type or legibly print at the top of the first page of Form 1065 for the short tax year, "SECTION 444 ELECTION TERMINATED"; or
   - The partnership elects to use a 52–53 week tax year that ends with reference to either its required tax year or a tax year elected under section 444 (see Pub. 538 for more information).

To change its tax year or to adopt or retain a tax year other than its required tax year, the partnership must file Form 1128, Application To Adopt, Change, or Retain a Tax Year, unless the partnership is making an election under section 444 (see Pub. 538).

If the partnership changes its tax year solely because its current tax year no longer qualifies as a natural business year, its partners may elect to take into account ratably over 4 tax years their distributive share of income attributable to the partnership's short tax year ending on or after May 10, 2002, but before June 1, 2004. See Rev. Proc. 2003-79, 2003-45 I.R.B. 1036, for details. If the partnership changes its tax year and the change falls within the scope of Rev. Proc. 2003-79, the partnership must attach a statement to Schedule K-1 that provides partners with the information they will need to make this election.

Note. The tax year of a common trust fund must be the calendar year.

Rounding Off to Whole Dollars

The partnership can round off cents to whole dollars on its return and schedules. If the partnership does round to whole dollars, it must round all amounts. To round, drop amounts under 50 cents and increase amounts from 50 to 99 cents to the next dollar (for example, $1.39 becomes $1 and $2.50 becomes $3).

If two or more amounts must be added to figure the amount to enter on a line, include cents when adding the amounts and round off only the total.

Recordkeeping

The partnership must keep its records as long as they may be needed for the administration of any provision of the Internal Revenue Code. If the consolidated audit procedures of sections 6221 through 6234 apply, the partnership usually must keep records that support an item of income, deduction, or credit on the partnership return for 3 years from the date the return is due or is filed, whichever is later. If the consolidated audit procedures do not apply, these records usually must be kept for 3 years from the date each partner's return is due or is filed, whichever is later. Keep records that verify the partnership's basis in property for as long as they are needed to figure the basis of the original or replacement property.

The partnership should also keep copies of all returns it has filed. They help in preparing future returns and in making computations when filing an amended return.

Amended Return

To correct an error on a Form 1065 already filed, file an amended Form 1065 and check box G(5) on page 1. Attach a statement that identifies the line number of each amended item, the corrected amount or treatment of the item, and an explanation of the reasons for each change. If the income, deductions, credits, or other information provided to any partner on Schedule K-1 are incorrect, file an amended Schedule K-1 (Form 1065) for that partner with the amended Form 1065. Also give a copy of the amended Schedule K-1 to that partner. Check the "Amended K-1" box at the top of the Schedule K-1 to indicate that it is an amended Schedule K-1.

Exception. If the partnership is filing an amended partnership return and the partnership is subject to the consolidated audit proceedings of sections 6221 through 6234, the tax matters partner must file Form 8082, Notice of Inconsistent Treatment or Administrative Adjustment Request (AAR).

A change to the partnership's federal return may affect its state return. This includes changes made as a result of an examination of the partnership return by the IRS. For more information, contact the state tax agency for the state in which the partnership return is filed.

Other Forms, Returns, And Statements That May Be Required

Form, Return or Statement	Use this to—
W-2 and W-3—Wage and Tax Statement; and Transmittal of Wage and Tax Statement	Report wages, tips, other compensation, and withheld income, social security and Medicare taxes for employees.
720—Quarterly Federal Excise Tax Return	Report and pay environmental excise taxes, communications and air transportation taxes, fuel taxes, manufacturers' taxes, ship passenger tax, and certain other excise taxes. Also see *Trust Fund Recovery Penalty* on page 4.
940 or 940-EZ—Employer's Annual Federal Unemployment (FUTA) Tax Return	Report and pay FUTA tax if the partnership either: 1. Paid wages of $1,500 or more in any calendar quarter during the calendar year (or the preceding calendar year) or 2. Had one or more employees working for the partnership for at least some part of a day in any 20 different weeks during the calendar year (or the preceding calendar year).
941—Employer's Quarterly Federal Tax Return	Report quarterly income tax withheld on wages and employer and employee social security and Medicare taxes. Also see *Trust Fund Recovery Penalty* on page 4.
943—Employer's Annual Federal Tax Return for Agricultural Employees	Report income tax withheld and employer and employee social security and Medicare taxes on farmworkers. Also see *Trust Fund Recovery Penalty* on page 4.
945—Annual Return of Withheld Federal Income Tax	Report income tax withheld from nonpayroll payments, including pensions, annuities, individual retirement accounts (IRAs), gambling winnings, and backup withholding. Also see *Trust Fund Recovery Penalty* on page 4.
1042 and 1042-S—Annual Withholding Tax Return for U.S. Source Income of Foreign Persons; and Foreign Person's U.S. Source Income Subject to Withholding	Report and send withheld tax on payments or distributions made to nonresident alien individuals, foreign partnerships, or foreign corporations to the extent these payments or distributions constitute gross income from sources within the United States that is not effectively connected with a U.S. trade or business. A domestic partnership must also withhold tax on a foreign partner's distributive share of such income, including amounts that are not actually distributed. Withholding on amounts not previously distributed to a foreign partner must be made and paid over by the earlier of: • The date on which Schedule K-1 is sent to that partner or • The 15th day of the 3rd month after the end of the partnership's tax year. For more details, see sections 1441 and 1442 and Pub. 515, Withholding of Tax on Nonresident Aliens and Foreign Entities.
1042-T—Annual Summary and Transmittal of Forms 1042-S	Transmit paper Forms 1042-S to the IRS.
1096—Annual Summary and Transmittal of U.S. Information Returns	Transmit paper Forms 1099, 1098, 5498, and W-2G to the IRS.
1098—Mortgage Interest Statement	Report the receipt from any individual of $600 or more of mortgage interest (including certain points) in the course of the partnership's trade or business.

Form, Return or Statement	Use this to—
1099-A, B, C, INT, LTC, MISC, OID, R, S, and **SA** **Important.** *Every partnership must file Forms 1099-MISC if, in the course of its trade or business, it makes payments of rents, commissions, or other fixed or determinable income (see section 6041) totaling $600 or more to any one person during the calendar year.*	Report the following: • Acquisitions or abandonments of secured property; • Proceeds from broker and barter exchange transactions; • Cancellation of debts; • Interest payments; • Payments of long-term care and accelerated death benefits; • Miscellaneous income payments; • Original issue discount; • Distributions from pensions, annuities, retirement or profit-sharing plans, IRAs, insurance contracts, etc.; • Proceeds from real estate transactions; and • Distributions from an HSA, Archer MSA, or Medicare Advantage MSA. Also use these returns to report amounts received as a nominee for another person. For more details, see the General Instructions for Forms 1099, 1098, 5498, and W-2G.
5471—Information Return of U.S. Persons With Respect to Certain Foreign Corporations	A partnership may have to file Form 5471 if it: • Controls a foreign corporation; or • Acquires, disposes of, or owns 5% or more in value of the outstanding stock of a foreign corporation; or • Owns stock in a corporation that is a controlled foreign corporation for an uninterrupted period of 30 days or more during any tax year of the foreign corporation, and it owned that stock on the last day of that year.
5713—International Boycott Report	Report operations in, or related to, a "boycotting" country, company, or national of a country and to figure the loss of certain tax benefits. The partnership must give each partner a copy of the Form 5713 filed by the partnership if there has been participation in, or cooperation with, an international boycott.
8264—Application for Registration of a Tax Shelter	Get a tax shelter registration number from the IRS. **Caution.** Until further guidance is issued, material advisors who provide material aid, assistance, or advice with respect to any reportable transaction after October 22, 2004, must use Form 8264 to disclose reportable transactions in accordance with interim guidance provided in Notice 2004-80, 2004-50 I.R.B. 963.
8271—Investor Reporting of Tax Shelter Registration Number	Report the registration number for a tax shelter that is required to be registered. Attach Form 8271 to any return on which a deduction, credit, loss, or other tax benefit attributable to a tax shelter is taken or any income attributable to a tax shelter is reported.
8275—Disclosure Statement	Disclose items or positions, except those contrary to a regulation, that are not otherwise adequately disclosed on a tax return. The disclosure is made to avoid the parts of the accuracy-related penalty imposed for disregard of rules or substantial understatement of tax. Also use Form 8275 for disclosures relating to preparer penalties for understatements due to unrealistic positions or disregard of rules.
8275-R—Regulation Disclosure Statement	Disclose any item on a tax return for which a position has been taken that is contrary to Treasury regulations.
8288 and **8288-A**—U.S. Withholding Tax Return for Dispositions by Foreign Persons of U.S. Real Property Interests; and Statement of Withholding on Dispositions by Foreign Persons of U.S. Real Property Interests	Report and send withheld tax on the sale of U.S. real property by a foreign person. See section 1445 and the related regulations for additional information.
8300—Report of Cash Payments Over $10,000 Received in a Trade or Business	Report the receipt of more than $10,000 in cash or foreign currency in one transaction or a series of related transactions.
8308—Report of a Sale or Exchange of Certain Partnership Interests	Report the sale or exchange by a partner of all or part of a partnership interest where any money or other property received in exchange for the interest is attributable to unrealized receivables or inventory items.
8594—Asset Acquisition Statement Under Section 1060	Report a sale of assets if goodwill or going concern value attaches, or could attach, to such assets. Both the seller and buyer of a group of assets that makes up a trade or business must use this form.
8697—Interest Computation Under the Look-Back Method for Completed Long-Term Contracts	Figure the interest due or to be refunded under the look-back method of section 460(b)(2) on certain long-term contracts that are accounted for under either the percentage of completion-capitalized cost method or the percentage of completion method. Partnerships that are not closely held use this form. Closely held partnerships should see the instructions on page 33 for line 20c, *Look-back interest—completed long-term contracts (code D)*, for details on the Form 8697 information they must provide to their partners.
8804, 8805, and **8813**—Annual Return for Partnership Withholding Tax (Section 1446); Foreign Partner's Information Statement of Section 1446 Withholding Tax; and Partnership Withholding Tax Payment (Section 1446)	Figure and report the withholding tax on the distributive shares of any effectively connected gross income for foreign partners. This is done on Forms 8804 and 8805. Use Form 8813 to send installment payments of withheld tax based on effectively connected taxable income allocable to foreign partners. **Exception.** *Publicly traded partnerships that do not elect to pay tax based on effectively connected taxable income do not file these forms. They must instead withhold tax on distributions to foreign partners and report and send payments using Forms 1042 and 1042-S. See Rev. Proc. 89-31, 1989-1 C.B. 895 and Rev. Proc. 92-66, 1992-2 C.B. 428 for more information.*

Form, Return or Statement	Use this to—
8832—Entity Classification Election	File an election to make a change in classification. Except for a business entity automatically classified as a corporation, a business entity with at least two members may choose to be classified either as a partnership or an association taxable as a corporation. A domestic eligible entity with at least two members that does not file Form 8832 is classified under the default rules as a partnership. However, a foreign eligible entity with at least two members is classified under the default rules as a partnership only if at least one member does not have limited liability. File Form 8832 only if the entity does not want to be classified under these default rules or if it wants to change its classification.
8865—Return of U.S. Person With Respect To Certain Foreign Partnerships	Report an interest in a foreign partnership. A domestic partnership may have to file Form 8865 if it: 1. Controlled a foreign partnership (that is, it owned more than 50% direct or indirect interest in the partnership). 2. Owned at least a 10% direct or indirect interest in a foreign partnership while U.S. persons controlled that partnership. 3. Had an acquisition, disposition, or change in proportional interest of a foreign partnership that: **a.** Increased its direct interest to at least 10% or reduced its direct interest of at least 10% to less than 10% or **b.** Changed its direct interest by at least a 10% interest. 4. Contributed property to a foreign partnership in exchange for a partnership interest if: **a.** Immediately after the contribution, the partnership directly or indirectly owned at least a 10% interest in the foreign partnership or **b.** The FMV of the property the partnership contributed to the foreign partnership in exchange for a partnership interest exceeds $100,000, when added to other contributions of property made to the foreign partnership (by the partnership or a related person) during the preceding 12-month period. Also, the domestic partnership may have to file Form 8865 to report certain dispositions by a foreign partnership of property it previously contributed to that partnership if it was a partner at the time of the disposition. For more details, including penalties for failing to file Form 8865, see Form 8865 and its separate instructions.
8866—Interest Computation Under the Look-Back Method for Property Depreciated Under the Income Forecast Method	Figure the interest due or to be refunded under the look-back method of section 167(g)(2) for certain property placed in service after September 13, 1995, depreciated under the income forecast method. Partnerships that are not closely held use this form. Closely held partnerships should see the instructions on page 33 for line 20c, *Look-back interest—income forecast method (code E)*, of Schedule K-1 for details on the Form 8866 information they must provide to their partners.
8876—Excise Tax on Structured Settlement Factoring Transactions	Report and pay the 40% excise tax imposed under section 5891.
Form 8886—Reportable Transaction Disclosure Statement	Disclose information for each reportable transaction in which the partnership participated. Form 8886 must be filed for each tax year that the federal income tax liability of the partnership is affected by its participation in the transaction. The partnership may have to pay a penalty if its required to file Form 8886 and does not do so. The following are reportable transactions. 1. Any listed transaction, which is a transaction that is the same as or substantially similar to tax avoidance transactions identified by the IRS. 2. Any transaction offered under conditions of confidentiality for which the partnership paid a minimum fee of at least $50,000 ($250,000 for partnerships if all partners are corporations). 3. Certain transactions for which the partnership has contractual protection against disallowance of the tax benefits. 4. Certain transactions resulting in a loss of at least $2 million in any single year or $4 million in any combination of years. 5. Certain transactions resulting in a book-tax difference of more than $10 million on a gross basis. 6. Certain transactions resulting in a tax credit of more than $250,000, it the partnership held the asset generating the credit for 45 days or less. See Regulations section 1.6011-4 and the instructions on page 34 for line 20c, *Other information (code Q)*, for more information.
Statement of section 743(b) basis adjustments	Report the adjustment of bases under section 743(b). If the partnership is required to adjust the bases of partnership properties under section 743(b) because of a section 754 election or because of a substantial built-in loss as defined in section 743(d) on the sale or exchange of a partnership interest or on the death of a partner, the partnership must attach a statement to its return for the year of the transfer. The statement must list: 1. The name and identifying number of the transferee partner, 2. The computation of the adjustment, and 3. The partnership properties to which the adjustment has been allocated. See section 743 and *Elections Made by the Partnership* on page 9 for more information.

Assembling the Return

When submitting Form 1065, organize the pages of the return in the following order:

- Pages 1–4,
- Schedule F (if required),
- Form 8825 (if required),
- Any other schedules in alphabetical order, and
- Any other forms in numerical order.

Complete every applicable entry space on Form 1065 and Schedule K-1. Do not enter "See attached" instead of completing the entry spaces. Penalties may be assessed if the partnership files an incomplete return. If you need more space on the forms or schedules, attach separate sheets and place them at the end of the return using the same size and format as on the printed forms. Show the totals on the printed forms. Also be sure to put the partnership's name and EIN on each supporting statement or attachment.

Separately Stated Items

Partners must take into account separately (under section 702(a)) their distributive shares of the following items (whether or not they are actually distributed):

1. Ordinary income (loss) from trade or business activities.
2. Net income (loss) from rental real estate activities.
3. Net income (loss) from other rental activities.
4. Gains and losses from sales or exchanges of capital assets.
5. Gains and losses from sales or exchanges of property described in section 1231.
6. Charitable contributions.
7. Dividends (passed through to corporate partners) that qualify for the dividends-received deduction.
8. Taxes described in section 901 paid or accrued to foreign countries and to possessions of the United States.
9. Other items of income, gain, loss, deduction, or credit, to the extent provided by regulations. Examples of such items include nonbusiness expenses, intangible drilling and development costs, amortizable basis of reforestation expenses, and soil and water conservation expenditures.

Elections Made by the Partnership

Generally, the partnership decides how to figure taxable income from its operations. For example, it chooses the accounting method and depreciation methods it will use. The partnership also makes elections under the following sections:

1. Section 179 (election to expense certain property).
2. Section 614 (definition of property—mines, wells, and other natural deposits). This election must be made before the partners figure their individual depletion allowances under section 613A(c)(7)(D).
3. Section 1033 (involuntary conversions).
4. Section 754 (manner of electing optional adjustment to basis of partnership property).

Under section 754, a partnership may elect to adjust the basis of partnership property when property is distributed or when a partnership interest is transferred. If the election is made with respect to a transfer of a partnership interest (section 743(b)) and the assets of the partnership constitute a trade or business for purposes of section 1060(c), then the value of any goodwill transferred must be determined in the manner provided in Regulations section 1.1060-1. Once an election is made under section 754, it applies both to all distributions and to all transfers made during the tax year and in all subsequent tax years unless the election is revoked. See Regulations section 1.754-1(c).

This election must be made in a statement that is filed with the partnership's timely filed return (including any extension) for the tax year during which the distribution or transfer occurs. The statement must include:

- The name and address of the partnership.
- A declaration that the partnership elects under section 754 to apply the provisions of section 734(b) and section 743(b).
- The signature of a partner authorized to sign the partnership return.

The partnership can get an automatic 12-month extension to make the section 754 election provided corrective action is taken within 12 months of the original deadline for making the election. For details, see Regulations section 301.9100-2.

See section 754 and the related regulations for more information.

If there is a distribution of property consisting of an interest in another partnership, see section 734(b).

The partnership is required to attach a statement for any section 743(b) basis adjustments. See page 8 for details.

5. Section 743(e) (electing investment partnership).

Elections Made by Each Partner

Elections under the following sections are made by each partner separately on the partner's tax return.

1. Section 59(e) (election to deduct ratably certain qualified expenditures such as intangible drilling costs, mining exploration expenses, or research and experimental expenditures).
2. Section 108 (income from discharge of indebtedness).
3. Section 617 (deduction and recapture of certain mining exploration expenditures paid or incurred).
4. Section 901 (foreign tax credit).

Partner's Dealings With Partnership

If a partner engages in a transaction with his or her partnership, other than in his or her capacity as a partner, the partner is treated as not being a member of the partnership for that transaction. Special rules apply to sales or exchanges of property between partnerships and certain persons, as explained in Pub. 541, Partnerships.

Contributions to the Partnership

Generally, no gain (loss) is recognized to the partnership or any of the partners when property is contributed to the partnership in exchange for an interest in the partnership. This rule does not apply to any gain realized on a transfer of property to a partnership that would be treated as an investment company (within the meaning of section 351) if the partnership were incorporated. If, as a result of a transfer of property to a partnership, there is a direct or indirect transfer of money or other property to the transferring partner, the partner may have to recognize gain on the exchange.

The basis to the partnership of property contributed by a partner is the adjusted basis in the hands of the partner at the time it was contributed, plus any gain recognized (under section 721(b)) by the partner at that time. See section 723 for more information.

Dispositions of Contributed Property

Generally, if the partnership disposes of property contributed to the partnership by a partner, income, gain, loss, and deductions from that property must be allocated among the partners to take into account the difference between the property's basis and its FMV at the time of the contribution. However, for contributions made after October 22, 2004, if the adjusted basis of the contributed property exceeds its fair market value at the time of the contribution, the built-in loss can only be taken into account by the contributing partner. For all other partners, the basis of the property in the hands of the partnership is treated as equal to its fair market value at the time of the contribution (see section 704(c)(1)(C)).

For property contributed to the partnership, the contributing partner must recognize gain or loss on a distribution of the property to another partner within 5 years of being contributed. For property contributed after June 8, 1997, the 5-year period is generally extended to 7 years. The gain or loss is equal to the amount that the contributing partner should have recognized if the property had been sold for its FMV when distributed, because of the difference between the property's basis and its FMV at the time of contribution.

See section 704(c) for details and other rules on dispositions of contributed property. See section 724 for the character of any gain or loss recognized on the disposition of unrealized receivables, inventory items, or capital loss property contributed to the partnership by a partner.

Recognition of Precontribution Gain on Certain Partnership Distributions

A partner who contributes appreciated property to the partnership must include in income any precontribution gain to the extent the FMV of other property (other than money) distributed to the partner by the partnership exceeds the adjusted basis of his or her partnership interest just before the distribution. Precontribution gain is the net gain, if any, that would have been recognized under section 704(c)(1)(B) if the partnership had distributed to another partner all the property that had been contributed to the partnership by the distributee partner within 5 years of the distribution and that was held by the partnership just before the distribution. For property contributed after June 8, 1997, the 5-year period is generally extended to 7 years.

Appropriate basis adjustments are to be made to the adjusted basis of the distributee partner's interest in the partnership and the partnership's basis in the contributed property to reflect the gain recognized by the partner.

For more details and exceptions, see Pub. 541.

Unrealized Receivables and Inventory Items

Generally, if a partner sells or exchanges a partnership interest where unrealized receivables or inventory items are involved, the transferor partner must notify the partnership, in writing, within 30 days of the exchange. The partnership must then file Form 8308, Report of a Sale or Exchange of Certain Partnership Interests.

If a partnership distributes unrealized receivables or substantially appreciated inventory items in exchange for all or part of a partner's interest in other partnership property (including money), treat the transaction as a sale or exchange between the partner and the partnership. Treat the partnership gain (loss) as ordinary business income (loss). The income (loss) is specially allocated only to partners other than the distributee partner.

If a partnership gives other property (including money) for all or part of that partner's interest in the partnership's unrealized receivables or substantially appreciated inventory items, treat the transaction as a sale or exchange of the property.

See Rev. Rul. 84-102, 1984-2 C.B. 119, for information on the tax consequences that result when a new partner joins a partnership that has liabilities and unrealized receivables. Also see Pub. 541 for more information on unrealized receivables and inventory items.

Passive Activity Limitations

In general, section 469 limits the amount of losses, deductions, and credits that partners may claim from "passive activities." The passive activity limitations do not apply to the partnership. Instead, they apply to each partner's share of any income or loss and credit attributable to a passive activity. Because the treatment of each partner's share of partnership income or loss and credit depends on the nature of the activity that generated it, the partnership must report income or loss and credits separately for each activity.

The following instructions and the instructions for Schedules K and K-1 (pages 21–34) explain the applicable passive activity limitation rules and specify the type of information the partnership must provide to its partners for each activity. If the partnership has more than one activity, it must report information for each activity on an attachment to Schedules K and K-1.

Generally, passive activities include (a) activities that involve the conduct of a trade or business if the partner does not materially participate in the activity; and (b) all rental activities (defined on page 11), regardless of the partner's participation. For exceptions, see *Activities That Are Not Passive Activities* below. The level of each partner's participation in an activity must be determined by the partner.

The passive activity rules provide that losses and credits from passive activities can generally be applied only against income and tax from passive activities. Thus, passive losses and credits cannot be applied against income from salaries, wages, professional fees, or a business in which the taxpayer materially participates; against "portfolio income" (defined on page 11); or against the tax related to any of these types of income.

Special provisions apply to certain activities. First, the passive activity limitations must be applied separately with respect to a net loss from passive activities held through a publicly traded partnership. Second, special rules require that net income from certain activities that would otherwise be treated as passive income must be recharacterized as nonpassive income for purposes of the passive activity limitations.

To allow each partner to correctly apply the passive activity limitations, the partnership must report income or loss and credits separately for each of the following types of activities and income: trade or business activities, rental real estate activities, rental activities other than rental real estate, and portfolio income.

Activities That Are Not Passive Activities

The following are not passive activities.

1. Trade or business activities in which the partner materially participated for the tax year.
2. Any rental real estate activity in which the partner materially participated if the partner met both of the following conditions for the tax year:

a. More than half of the personal services the partner performed in trades or businesses were performed in real property trades or businesses in which he or she materially participated and

b. The partner performed more than 750 hours of services in real property trades or businesses in which he or she materially participated.

Note. For a partner that is a closely held C corporation (defined in section 465(a)(1)(B)), the above conditions are treated as met if more than 50% of the corporation's gross receipts are from real property trades or businesses in which the corporation materially participated.

For purposes of this rule, each interest in rental real estate is a separate activity, unless the partner elects to treat all interests in rental real estate as one activity.

If the partner is married filing jointly, either the partner or his or her spouse must separately meet both of the above conditions, without taking into account services performed by the other spouse.

A real property trade or business is any real property development, redevelopment, construction, reconstruction, acquisition, conversion, rental, operation, management, leasing, or brokerage trade or business. Services the partner performed as an employee are not treated as performed in a real property trade or business unless he or she owned more than 5% of the stock (or more than 5% of the capital or profits interest) in the employer.

3. An interest in an oil or gas well drilled or operated under a working interest if at any time during the tax year the partner held the working interest directly or through an entity that did not limit the partner's liability (for example, an interest as a general partner). This exception applies regardless of whether the partner materially participated for the tax year.
4. The rental of a dwelling unit used by a partner for personal purposes during the year for more than the greater of 14 days or 10% of the number of days that the residence was rented at fair rental value.
5. An activity of trading personal property for the account of owners of interests in the activity. For purposes of this rule, personal property means property that is actively traded, such as stocks, bonds, and other securities. See Temporary Regulations section 1.469-1T(e)(6).

Trade or Business Activities

A trade or business activity is an activity (other than a rental activity or an activity treated as incidental to an activity of holding property for investment) that:

1. Involves the conduct of a trade or business (within the meaning of section 162),
2. Is conducted in anticipation of starting a trade or business, or
3. Involves research or experimental expenditures deductible under section 174 (or that would be if you chose to deduct rather than capitalize them).

If the partner does not materially participate in the activity, a trade or business activity held through a partnership is generally a passive activity of the partner.

Each partner must determine if they materially participated in an activity. As a result, while the partnership's overall trade or business income (loss) is reported on page 1 of Form 1065, the specific income and deductions from each separate trade or business activity must be reported on attachments to Form 1065. Similarly, while each partner's allocable share of the partnership's overall trade or business income (loss) is reported in box 1 of Schedule K-1, each partner's allocable share of the income and deductions from each trade or business activity must be reported on attachments to each Schedule K-1. See *Passive Activity Reporting Requirements* on page 13 for more information.

Rental Activities

Generally, except as noted below, if the gross income from an activity consists of amounts paid principally for the use of real or personal tangible property held by the partnership, the activity is a rental activity.

There are several exceptions to this general rule. Under these exceptions, an activity involving the use of real or personal tangible property is not a rental activity if any of the following apply.

- The average period of customer use (defined below) for such property is 7 days or less.
- The average period of customer use for such property is 30 days or less and significant personal services (defined below) are provided by or on behalf of the partnership.
- Extraordinary personal services (defined below) are provided by or on behalf of the partnership.
- The rental of such property is treated as incidental to a nonrental activity of the partnership under Temporary Regulations section 1.469-1T(e)(3)(vi) and Regulations section 1.469-1(e)(3)(vi).
- The partnership customarily makes the property available during defined business hours for nonexclusive use by various customers.
- The partnership provides property for use in a nonrental activity of a partnership or joint venture in its capacity as an owner of an interest in such partnership or joint venture. Whether the partnership provides property used in an activity of another partnership or of a joint venture in the partnership's capacity as an owner of an interest in the partnership or joint venture is determined on the basis of all the facts and circumstances.

In addition, a guaranteed payment described in section 707(c) is not income from a rental activity under any circumstances.

Average period of customer use. Figure the average period of customer use for a class of property by dividing the total number of days in all rental periods by the number of rentals during the tax year. If the activity involves renting more than one class of property, multiply the average period of customer use of each class by the ratio of the gross rental income from that class to the activity's total gross rental income. The activity's average period of customer use equals the sum of these class-by-class average periods weighted by gross income. See Regulations section 1.469-1(e)(3)(iii).

Significant personal services. Personal services include only services performed by individuals. To determine if personal services are significant personal services, consider all the relevant facts and circumstances. Relevant facts and circumstances include:

- How often the services are provided,
- The type and amount of labor required to perform the services, and
- The value of the services in relation to the amount charged for use of the property.

The following services are not considered in determining whether personal services are significant:

- Services necessary to permit the lawful use of the rental property.
- Services performed in connection with improvements or repairs to the rental property that extend the useful life of the property substantially beyond the average rental period.
- Services provided in connection with the use of any improved real property that are similar to those commonly provided in connection with long-term rentals of high-grade commercial or residential property. Examples include cleaning and maintenance of common areas, routine repairs, trash collection, elevator service, and security at entrances.

Extraordinary personal services. Services provided in connection with making rental property available for customer use are extraordinary personal services only if the services are performed by individuals and the customers' use of the rental property is incidental to their receipt of the services.

For example, a patient's use of a hospital room generally is incidental to the care received from the hospital's medical staff. Similarly, a student's use of a dormitory room in a boarding school is incidental to the personal services provided by the school's teaching staff.

Rental activity incidental to a nonrental activity. An activity is not a rental activity if the rental of the property is incidental to a nonrental activity, such as the activity of holding property for investment, a trade or business activity, or the activity of dealing in property.

Rental of property is incidental to an activity of holding property for investment if both of the following apply.

- The main purpose for holding the property is to realize a gain from the appreciation of the property.
- The gross rental income from such property for the tax year is less than 2% of the smaller of the property's unadjusted basis or its FMV.

Rental of property is incidental to a trade or business activity if all of the following apply:

- The partnership owns an interest in the trade or business at all times during the year.
- The rental property was mainly used in the trade or business activity during the tax year or during at least 2 of the 5 preceding tax years.
- The gross rental income from the property for the tax year is less than 2% of the smaller of the property's unadjusted basis or its FMV.

The sale or exchange of property that is both rented and sold or exchanged during the tax year (where the gain or loss is recognized) is treated as incidental to the activity of dealing in property if, at the time of the sale or exchange, the property was held primarily for sale to customers in the ordinary course of the partnership's trade or business.

See Temporary Regulations section 1.469-1T(e)(3) and Regulations section 1.469-1(e)(3) for more information on the definition of rental activities for purposes of the passive activity limitations.

Reporting of rental activities. In reporting the partnership's income or losses and credits from rental activities, the partnership must separately report rental real estate activities and rental activities other than rental real estate activities.

Partners who actively participate in a rental real estate activity may be able to deduct part or all of their rental real estate losses (and the deduction equivalent of rental real estate credits) against income (or tax) from nonpassive activities. The combined amount of rental real estate losses and the deduction equivalent of rental real estate credits from all sources (including rental real estate activities not held through the partnership) that may be claimed is limited to $25,000. This $25,000 amount is generally reduced for high-income partners.

Report rental real estate activity income (loss) on Form 8825, Rental Real Estate Income and Expenses of a Partnership or an S Corporation, and line 2 of Schedule K and box 2 of Schedule K-1, rather than on page 1 of Form 1065. Report credits related to rental real estate activities on lines 15c and 15d of Schedule K (box 15, codes C and G, of Schedule K-1) and low-income housing credits on lines 15a and 15b of Schedule K (box 15, codes A and B of Schedule K-1).

See the instructions on page 23 for *Line 3. Other Net Rental Income (Loss)* for reporting other net rental income (loss) other than rental real estate.

Portfolio Income

Generally, portfolio income includes all gross income, other than income derived in the ordinary course of a trade or business, that is attributable to interest; dividends; royalties; income from a real estate investment trust, a regulated investment company, a real estate mortgage investment conduit, a common trust fund, a controlled foreign corporation, a qualified electing fund, or a cooperative; income from the disposition of property that produces income of a type defined as portfolio income; and income from the disposition of property held for investment. See *Self-Charged Interest* on page 12 for an exception.

Solely for purposes of the preceding paragraph, gross income derived in the ordinary course of a trade or business includes (and portfolio income, therefore, does not include) only the following types of income:

- Interest income on loans and investments made in the ordinary course of a trade or business of lending money.
- Interest on accounts receivable arising from the performance of services or the sale of property in the ordinary course of a trade or business of performing such services or selling such property, but only if credit is customarily offered to customers of the business.
- Income from investments made in the ordinary course of a trade or business of furnishing insurance or annuity contracts or reinsuring risks underwritten by insurance companies.
- Income or gain derived in the ordinary course of an activity of trading or dealing in any property if such activity constitutes a trade or business (unless the dealer held the property for investment at any time before such income or gain is recognized).

• Royalties derived by the taxpayer in the ordinary course of a trade or business of licensing intangible property.
• Amounts included in the gross income of a patron of a cooperative by reason of any payment or allocation to the patron based on patronage occurring with respect to a trade or business of the patron.
• Other income identified by the IRS as income derived by the taxpayer in the ordinary course of a trade or business.

See Temporary Regulations section 1.469-2T(c)(3) for more information on portfolio income.

Report portfolio income and related deductions on Schedule K rather than on page 1 of Form 1065.

Self-Charged Interest

Certain self-charged interest income and deductions may be treated as passive activity gross income and passive activity deductions if the loan proceeds are used in a passive activity. Generally, self-charged interest income and deductions result from loans to and from the partnership and its partners. It also includes loans between the partnership and another partnership if each owner in the borrowing entity has the same proportional ownership interest in the lending entity. The self-charged interest rules do not apply to a partner's interest in a partnership if the partnership makes an election under Regulations section 1.469-7(g) to avoid the application of these rules. To make the election, the partnership must attach to its original or amended Form 1065, a statement that includes the name, address, and EIN of the partnership and a declaration that the election is being made under Regulations section 1.469-7(g). The election will apply to the tax year in which it was made and all subsequent tax years. Once made, the election may only be revoked with the consent of the IRS.

For more details on the self-charged interest rules, see Regulations section 1.469-7.

Grouping Activities

Generally, one or more trade or business activities or rental activities may be treated as a single activity if the activities make up an appropriate economic unit for the measurement of gain or loss under the passive activity rules. Whether activities make up an appropriate economic unit depends on all the relevant facts and circumstances. The factors given the greatest weight in determining whether activities make up an appropriate economic unit are:
• Similarities and differences in types of trades or businesses.
• The extent of common control.
• The extent of common ownership.
• Geographical location.
• Reliance between or among the activities.

Example. The partnership has a significant ownership interest in a bakery and a movie theater in Baltimore and a bakery and a movie theater in Philadelphia. Depending on the relevant facts and circumstances, there may be more than one reasonable method for grouping the partnership's activities. For instance, the following groupings may or may not be permissible.
• A single activity,
• A movie theater activity and a bakery activity,
• A Baltimore activity and a Philadelphia activity, or
• Four separate activities.

Once the partnership chooses a grouping under these rules, it must continue using that grouping in later tax years unless a material change in the facts and circumstances makes it clearly inappropriate.

The IRS may regroup the partnership's activities if the partnership's grouping fails to reflect one or more appropriate economic units and one of the primary purposes of the grouping is to avoid the passive activity limitations.

Limitation on grouping certain activities. The following activities may not be grouped together:

1. A rental activity with a trade or business activity unless the activities being grouped together make up an appropriate economic unit and

a. The rental activity is insubstantial relative to the trade or business activity or vice versa or

b. Each owner of the trade or business activity has the same proportionate ownership interest in the rental activity. If so, the portion of the rental activity involving the rental of property to be used in the trade or business activity may be grouped with the trade or business activity.

2. An activity involving the rental of real property with an activity involving the rental of personal property (except personal property provided in connection with the real property or vice versa).

3. Any activity with another activity in a different type of business and in which the partnership holds an interest as a limited partner or as a limited entrepreneur (as defined in section 464(e)(2)) if that other activity engages in holding, producing, or distributing motion picture films or videotapes; farming; leasing section 1245 property; or exploring for or exploiting oil and gas resources or geothermal deposits.

Activities conducted through other partnerships. Once a partnership determines its activities under these rules, the partnership as a partner may use these rules to group those activities with:
• Each other,
• Activities conducted directly by the partnership, or
• Activities conducted through other partnerships.

A partner may not treat as separate activities those activities grouped together by a partnership.

Recharacterization of Passive Income

Under Temporary Regulations section 1.469-2T(f) and Regulations section 1.469-2(f), net passive income from certain passive activities must be treated as nonpassive income. Net passive income is the excess of an activity's passive activity gross income over its passive activity deductions (current year deductions and prior year unallowed losses).

Income from the following six sources is subject to recharacterization.

Note. Any net passive income recharacterized as nonpassive income is treated as investment income for purposes of figuring investment interest expense limitations if it is from (a) an activity of renting substantially nondepreciable property from an equity-financed lending activity or (b) an activity related to an interest in a pass-through entity that licenses intangible property.

Significant participation passive activities. A significant participation passive activity is any trade or business activity in which the partner participated for more than 100 hours during the tax year but did not materially participate. Because each partner must determine the partner's level of participation, the partnership will not be able to identify significant participation passive activities.

Certain nondepreciable rental property activities. Net passive income from a rental activity is nonpassive income if less than 30% of the unadjusted basis of the property used or held for use by customers in the activity is subject to depreciation under section 167.

Passive equity-financed lending activities. If the partnership has net income from a passive equity-financed lending activity, the smaller of the net passive income or the equity-financed interest income from the activity is nonpassive income.

Note. The amount of income from the activities in paragraphs 1 through 3 that any partner will be required to recharacterize as nonpassive income may be limited under Temporary Regulations section 1.469-2T(f)(8). Because the partnership will not have information regarding all of a partner's activities, it must identify all partnership activities meeting the definitions in paragraphs 2 and 3 as activities that may be subject to recharacterization.

Rental of property incidental to a development activity. Net rental activity income is the excess of passive activity gross income from renting or disposing of property over passive activity deductions (current year deductions and prior year unallowed losses) that are reasonably allocable to the rented property. Net rental activity income is nonpassive income for a partner if all of the following apply.

• The partnership recognizes gain from the sale, exchange, or other disposition of the rental property during the tax year.
• The use of the item of property in the rental activity started less than 12 months before the date of disposition. The use of an item of rental property begins on the first day that (a) the partnership owns an interest in the property; (b) substantially all of the property is either rented or held out for rent and ready to be rented; and (c) no significant value-enhancing services remain to be performed.
• The partner materially or significantly participated for any tax year in an activity that involved performing services to enhance the value of the property (or any other item of property, if the basis of the property disposed of is determined in whole

or in part by reference to the basis of that item of property).

Because the partnership cannot determine a partner's level of participation, the partnership must identify net income from property described on page 12 (without regard to the partner's level of participation) as income that may be subject to recharacterization.

Rental of property to a nonpassive activity. If a taxpayer rents property to a trade or business activity in which the taxpayer materially participates, the taxpayer's net rental activity income from the property is nonpassive income.

Acquisition of an interest in a pass-through entity that licenses intangible property. Generally, net royalty income from intangible property is nonpassive income if the taxpayer acquired an interest in the pass-through entity after the pass-through entity created the intangible property or performed substantial services, or incurred substantial costs in developing or marketing the intangible property. "Net royalty income" means the excess of passive activity gross income from licensing or transferring any right in intangible property over passive activity deductions (current year deductions and prior year unallowed losses) that are reasonably allocable to the intangible property.

See Temporary Regulations section 1.469-2T(f)(7)(iii) for exceptions to this rule.

Passive Activity Reporting Requirements

To allow partners to correctly apply the passive activity loss and credit rules, any partnership that carries on more than one activity must:

1. Provide an attachment for each activity conducted through the partnership that identifies the type of activity conducted (trade or business, rental real estate, rental activity other than rental real estate, or investment).

2. On the attachment for each activity, provide a statement, using the same box numbers as shown on Schedule K-1, detailing the net income (loss), credits, and all items required to be separately stated under section 702(a) from each trade or business activity, from each rental real estate activity, from each rental activity other than a rental real estate activity, and from investments.

3. Identify the net income (loss) and credits from each oil or gas well drilled or operated under a working interest that any partner (other than a partner whose only interest in the partnership during the year is as a limited partner) holds through the partnership. Further, if any partner had an interest as a general partner in the partnership during less than the entire year, the partnership must identify both the disqualified deductions from each well that the partner must treat as passive activity deductions, and the ratable portion of the gross income from each well that the partner must treat as passive activity gross income.

4. Identify the net income (loss) and the partner's share of partnership interest expense from each activity of renting a dwelling unit that any partner uses for personal purposes during the year for more than the greater of 14 days or 10% of the number of days that the residence is rented at fair rental value.

5. Identify the net income (loss) and the partner's share of partnership interest expense from each activity of trading personal property conducted through the partnership.

6. For any gain (loss) from the disposition of an interest in an activity or of an interest in property used in an activity (including dispositions before 1987 from which gain is being recognized after 1986):

a. Identify the activity in which the property was used at the time of disposition.

b. If the property was used in more than one activity during the 12 months preceding the disposition, identify the activities in which the property was used and the adjusted basis allocated to each activity.

c. For gains only, if the property was substantially appreciated at the time of the disposition and the applicable holding period specified in Regulations section 1.469-2(c)(2)(iii)(A) was not satisfied, identify the amount of the nonpassive gain and indicate whether the gain is investment income under the provisions of Regulations section 1.469-2(c)(2)(iii)(F).

7. Specify the amount of gross portfolio income, the interest expense properly allocable to portfolio income, and expenses other than interest expense that are clearly and directly allocable to portfolio income.

8. Identify separately any of the following types of payments to partners.

a. Payments to a partner for services other than in the partner's capacity as a partner under section 707(a).

b. Guaranteed payments to a partner for services under section 707(c).

c. Guaranteed payments for use of capital.

d. If section 736(a)(2) payments are made for unrealized receivables or for goodwill, the amount of the payments and the activities to which the payments are attributable.

e. If section 736(b) payments are made, the amount of the payments and the activities to which the payments are attributable.

9. Identify the ratable portion of any section 481 adjustment (whether a net positive or a net negative adjustment) allocable to each partnership activity.

10. Identify the amount of gross income from each oil or gas property of the partnership.

11. Identify any gross income from sources that are specifically excluded from passive activity gross income, including:

a. Income from intangible property if the partner is an individual and the partner's personal efforts significantly contributed to the creation of the property.

b. Income from state, local, or foreign income tax refunds.

c. Income from a covenant not to compete (in the case of a partner who is an individual and who contributed the covenant to the partnership).

12. Identify any deductions that are not passive activity deductions.

13. If the partnership makes a full or partial disposition of its interest in another entity, identify the gain (loss) allocable to each activity conducted through the entity, and the gain allocable to a passive activity that would have been recharacterized as nonpassive gain had the partnership disposed of its interest in property used in the activity (because the property was substantially appreciated at the time of the disposition, and the gain represented more than 10% of the partner's total gain from the disposition).

14. Identify the following items from activities that may be subject to the recharacterization rules under Temporary Regulations section 1.469-2T(f) and Regulations section 1.469-2(f).

a. Net income from an activity of renting substantially nondepreciable property.

b. The smaller of equity-financed interest income or net passive income from an equity-financed lending activity.

c. Net rental activity income from property that was developed (by the partner or the partnership), rented, and sold within 12 months after the rental of the property commenced.

d. Net rental activity income from the rental of property by the partnership to a trade or business activity in which the partner had an interest (either directly or indirectly).

e. Net royalty income from intangible property if the partner acquired the partner's interest in the partnership after the partnership created the intangible property or performed substantial services, or incurred substantial costs in developing or marketing the intangible property.

15. Identify separately the credits from each activity conducted by or through the partnership.

16. Identify the partner's distributive share of the partnership's self-charged interest income or expense (see *Self-Charged Interest* on page 12).

a. **Loans between a partner and the partnership.** Identify the lending or borrowing partner's share of the self-charged interest income or expense. If the partner made the loan to the partnership, also identify the activity in which the loan proceeds were used. If the loan proceeds were used in more than one activity, allocate the interest to each activity based on the amount of the proceeds used in each activity.

b. **Loans between the partnership and another partnership or an S corporation.** If the partnership's partners have the same proportional ownership interest in the partnership and the other partnership or S corporation, identify each partner's share of the interest income or expense from the loan. If the partnership was the borrower, also identify the activity in which the loan proceeds were used. If the loan proceeds were used in more than one activity, allocate the interest to each activity based on the amount of the proceeds used in each activity.

Extraterritorial Income Exclusion

Generally, the partnership can exclude extraterritorial income to the extent of qualifying foreign trade income. However, the extraterritorial income exclusion is reduced by 20% for transactions after 2004, unless made under a binding contract with an unrelated person in effect on September 17, 2003, and at all times thereafter. For details and to figure the amount of the exclusion, see Form 8873, Extraterritorial Income Exclusion, and its separate instructions. The partnership must report the extraterritorial income exclusion on its return as follows.

1. If the partnership met the foreign economic process requirements explained in the Instructions for Form 8873, it can report the exclusion as a nonseparately stated item on whichever of the following lines apply to that activity.

- Form 1065, page 1, line 20;
- Form 8825, line 15; or
- Form 1065, Schedule K, line 3b.

In addition, the partnership must report as an item of information on Schedule K-1, box 16, using code O, the partner's distributive share of foreign trading gross receipts from Form 8873, line 15.

2. If the foreign trading gross receipts of the partnership for the tax year are $5 million or less and the partnership did not meet the foreign economic process requirements, it may not report the extraterritorial income exclusion as a nonseparately stated item on its return.

Instead, the partnership must report the following separately stated items to the partners on Schedule K-1, box 16.

- Foreign trading gross receipts (code O). Report each partner's distributive share of foreign trading gross receipts from line 15 of Form 8873 in box 16 using code O.
- Extraterritorial income exclusion (code P). Report each partner's distributive share of the extraterritorial income exclusion from Form 8873 in box 16 using code P and identify on an attached statement the activity to which the exclusion relates. If the partnership is required to complete more than one Form 8873 (for example, separate forms for transactions eligible for the 80% and 100% exclusions), combine the exclusions from lines 52a and 52b and report a single exclusion amount in box 16.

Note. Upon request of a partner, the partnership should furnish a copy of the partnership's Form 8873 if that partner has a reduction for international boycott operations, illegal bribes, kickbacks, etc.

Specific Instructions

These instructions follow the line numbers on the first page of Form 1065. The accompanying schedules are discussed separately. Specific instructions for most of the lines are provided. Lines that are not discussed are self-explanatory.

Fill in all applicable lines and schedules.

Enter any items specially allocated to the partners in the appropriate box of the applicable partner's Schedule K-1. Enter the total amount on the appropriate line of Schedule K. Do not enter separately stated amounts on the numbered lines on Form 1065, page 1, or on Schedule A or Schedule D.

File all four pages of Form 1065. However, if the answer to question 5 of Schedule B is "Yes," Schedules L, M-1, and M-2 on page 4 are optional. Also attach a Schedule K-1 to Form 1065 for each partner.

File only one Form 1065 for each partnership. Mark "Duplicate Copy" on any copy you give to a partner.

If a syndicate, pool, joint venture, or similar group files Form 1065, it must attach a copy of the agreement and all amendments to the return, unless a copy has previously been filed.

Note. A foreign partnership required to file a return generally must report all of its foreign and U.S. source income. For rules regarding whether a foreign partnership must file Form 1065, see *Who Must File* on page 2.

Name and Address

Use the label that was mailed to the partnership. Cross out any errors and print the correct information on the label.

Name. If the partnership did not receive a label, print or type the legal name of the partnership as it appears in the partnership agreement.

If the partnership has changed its name, check box G(3).

Address. Include the suite, room, or other unit number after the street address. If a preaddressed label is used, include this information on the label.

If the Post Office does not deliver mail to the street address and the partnership has a P.O. box, show the box number instead.

If the partnership receives its mail in care of a third party (such as an accountant or an attorney), enter on the street address line "C/O" followed by the third party's name and street address or P.O. box.

If the partnership's address is outside the United States or its possessions or territories, enter the information on the line for "City or town, state, and ZIP code" in the following order: city, province or state, and the foreign country. Follow the foreign country's practice in placing the postal code in the address. Do not abbreviate the country name.

If the partnership has changed its address since it last filed a return (including a change to an "in care of" address), check box G(4) for "Address change."

Note. If the partnership changes its mailing address after filing its return, it can notify the IRS by filing Form 8822, Change of Address, to notify the IRS of the new address.

Items A and C

Enter the applicable activity name and the code number from the list beginning on page 36.

For example, if, as its principal business activity, the partnership (a) purchases raw materials, (b) subcontracts out for labor to make a finished product from the raw materials, and (c) retains title to the goods, the partnership is considered to be a manufacturer and must enter "Manufacturer" in item A and enter in item C one of the codes (311110 through 339900) listed under "Manufacturing" beginning on page 36.

Item D. Employer Identification Number (EIN)

Show the correct EIN in item D on page 1 of Form 1065. If the partnership does not have an EIN, it must be applied for:

- Online—Click on the EIN link at *www.irs.gov/businesses/small*. The EIN is issued immediately once the application information is validated.
- By telephone at 1-800-829-4933, from 7:00 a.m. to 10:00 p.m. in the partnership's local time zone.
- By mailing or faxing Form SS-4, Application for Employer Identification Number.

A limited liability company must determine which type of federal tax entity it will be (that is, partnership, corporation, or disregarded entity) before applying for an EIN (see Form 8832, Entity Classification Election, for details). If the partnership has not received its EIN by the time the return is due, enter "Applied for" in the space for the EIN. For more details, see Pub. 583, Starting a Business and Keeping Records.

Note. The online application process is not yet available for the following types of entities: entities with addresses in foreign countries or Puerto Rico, REMICs, state and local governments, federal government/military entities, and Indian Tribal Government/Enterprise entities. Please call the toll-free Business and Specialty Tax Line at 1-800-829-4933 for assistance in applying for an EIN.

Do not request a new EIN for a partnership that terminated because of a sale or exchange of at least 50% of the total interests in partnership capital and profits.

Item F. Total Assets

You are not required to complete item F if the answer to question 5 of Schedule B is "Yes."

If you are required to complete this item, enter the partnership's total assets at the end of the tax year, as determined by the accounting method regularly used in keeping the partnership's books and records. If there were no assets at the end of the tax year, enter "0."

Item G

Do not check "Final return" (box G(2)) for a partnership that terminated because of a sale or exchange of at least 50% of the total interests in partnership capital and profits. However, be sure to file a return for the short year ending on the date of termination. See *Termination of the Partnership* on page 3.

For information on amended returns, see page 6.

Income

Report only trade or business activity income on lines 1a through 8. Do not report rental activity income or portfolio income on these lines. See the instructions on "Passive Activity Limitations" beginning on page 10 for definitions of rental income and portfolio income. Rental activity income and portfolio income are reported on Schedules K and K-1. Rental real estate activities are also reported on Form 8825.

Tax-exempt income. Do not include any tax-exempt income on lines 1a through 8. A partnership that receives any tax-exempt income other than interest, or holds any property or engages in any activity that produces tax-exempt income reports the amount of this income on line 18b of Schedule K and in box 18 of Schedule K-1 using code B.

Report tax-exempt interest income, including exempt-interest dividends received as a shareholder in a mutual fund or other regulated investment company, on line 18a of Schedule K and in box 18 of Schedule K-1 using code A.

See *Deductions* on page 16 for information on how to report expenses related to tax-exempt income.

Cancelled debt exclusion. If the partnership has had debt discharged resulting from a title 11 bankruptcy proceeding or while insolvent, see Form 982, Reduction of Tax Attributes Due to Discharge of Indebtedness, and Pub. 908, Bankruptcy Tax Guide.

Line 1a. Gross Receipts or Sales

Enter the gross receipts or sales from all trade or business operations except those that must be reported on lines 4 through 7. For example, do not include gross receipts from farming on this line. Instead, show the net profit (loss) from farming on line 5. Also, do not include on line 1a rental activity income or portfolio income.

In general, advance payments are reported in the year of receipt. To report income from long-term contracts, see section 460. For special rules for reporting certain advance payments for goods and long-term contracts, see Regulations section 1.451-5. For permissible methods for reporting advance payments for services and most goods by an accrual method partnership, see Rev. Proc. 2004-34, 2004-22 I.R.B. 991.

Installment sales. Generally, the installment method cannot be used for dealer dispositions of property. A "dealer disposition" is any disposition of:

1. Personal property by a person who regularly sells or otherwise disposes of personal property of the same type on the installment plan or
2. Real property held for sale to customers in the ordinary course of the taxpayer's trade or business.

Exception. These restrictions on using the installment method do not apply to dispositions of property used or produced in a farming business or sales of timeshares and residential lots. However, if the partnership elects to report dealer dispositions of timeshares and residential lots on the installment method, each partner's tax liability must be increased by the partner's allocable share of the interest payable under section 453(l)(3).

Enter on line 1a the gross profit on collections from installment sales for any of the following:

- Dealer dispositions of property before March 1, 1986.
- Dispositions of property used or produced in the trade or business of farming.
- Certain dispositions of timeshares and residential lots reported under the installment method.

Attach a statement showing the following information for the current year and the 3 preceding years:

- Gross sales.
- Cost of goods sold.
- Gross profits.
- Percentage of gross profits to gross sales.
- Amount collected.
- Gross profit on amount collected.

Nonaccrual experience method. Partnerships that qualify to use the nonaccrual experience method (described on page 5) should attach a statement showing total gross receipts, the amount not accrued as a result of the application of section 448(d)(5), and the net amount accrued. Enter the net amount on line 1a.

Line 2. Cost of Goods Sold

See the instructions for Schedule A on page 19.

Line 4. Ordinary Income (Loss) From Other Partnerships, Estates, and Trusts

Enter the ordinary income (loss) shown on Schedule K-1 (Form 1065) or Schedule K-1 (Form 1041), or other ordinary income (loss) from a foreign partnership, estate, or trust. Show the partnership's, estate's, or trust's name, address, and EIN on a separate statement attached to this return. If the amount entered is from more than one source, identify the amount from each source.

Do not include portfolio income or rental activity income (loss) from other partnerships, estates, or trusts on this line. Instead, report these amounts on Schedules K and K-1, or on line 20a of Form 8825 if the amount is from a rental real estate activity.

Ordinary income (loss) from another partnership that is a publicly traded partnership is not reported on this line. Instead, report the amount separately on line 11 of Schedule K and in box 11 of Schedule K-1 using code F.

Treat shares of other items separately reported on Schedule K-1 issued by the other entity as if the items were realized or incurred by this partnership.

If there is a loss from another partnership, the amount of the loss that may be claimed is subject to the at-risk and basis limitations as appropriate.

If the tax year of your partnership does not coincide with the tax year of the other partnership, estate, or trust, include the ordinary income (loss) from the other entity in the tax year in which the other entity's tax year ends.

Line 5. Net Farm Profit (Loss)

Enter the partnership's net farm profit (loss) from Schedule F (Form 1040), Profit or Loss From Farming. Attach Schedule F (Form 1040) to Form 1065. Do not include on this line any farm profit (loss) from other partnerships. Report those amounts on line 4. In figuring the partnership's net farm profit (loss), do not include any section 179 expense deduction; this amount must be separately stated.

Also report the partnership's fishing income on this line.

For a special rule concerning the method of accounting for a farming partnership with a corporate partner and for other tax information on farms, see Pub. 225, Farmer's Tax Guide.

Note. Because the election to deduct the expenses of raising any plant with a preproductive period of more than 2 years is made by the partner and not the partnership, farm partnerships that are not required to use an accrual method should not capitalize such expenses. Instead, state them separately on an attachment to Schedule K, line 13e, and in box 13 of Schedule K-1, using code O. See Regulations section 1.263A-4(d)(5) for more information.

Line 6. Net Gain (Loss) From Form 4797

Include only ordinary gains or losses from the sale, exchange, or involuntary conversion of assets used in a trade or business activity. Ordinary gains or losses from the sale, exchange, or involuntary conversion of rental activity assets are reported separately on line 19 of Form 8825 or line 3 of Schedule K and box 3 of Schedule K-1, generally as a part of the net income (loss) from the rental activity.

A partnership that is a partner in another partnership must include on Form 4797, Sales of Business Property, its share of ordinary gains (losses) from sales, exchanges, or involuntary conversions (other than casualties or thefts) of the other partnership's trade or business assets.

Partnerships should not use Form 4797 to report the sale or other disposition of property if a section 179 expense deduction was previously passed through to any of its partners for that property. Instead, report it in box 20 of Schedule K-1 using code F. See the instructions on page 33 for *Dispositions of property with section 179 deductions (code F)*, for details.

Line 7. Other Income (Loss)

Enter on line 7 trade or business income (loss) that is not included on lines 1a through 6. List the type and amount of income on an attached statement. Examples of such income include:

1. Interest income derived in the ordinary course of the partnership's trade or business, such as interest charged on receivable balances.
2. Recoveries of bad debts deducted in prior years under the specific charge-off method.

3. Taxable income from insurance proceeds.

4. The amount of credit figured on Form 6478, Credit for Alcohol Used as Fuel.

5. The amount of credit figured on Form 8864, Biodiesel Fuels Credit.

6. All section 481 income adjustments resulting from changes in accounting methods. Show the computation of the section 481 adjustments on an attached statement.

7. The amount of any deduction previously taken under section 179A that is subject to recapture. See Pub. 535, Business Expenses, for details, including how to figure the recapture.

8. The recapture amount for section 280F if the business use of listed property drops to 50% or less. To figure the recapture amount, the partnership must complete Part IV of Form 4797.

Do not include items requiring separate computations that must be reported on Schedules K and K-1. See the instructions for Schedules K and K-1 later in these instructions.

Do not report portfolio or rental activity income (loss) on this line.

Deductions

Report only trade or business activity deductions on lines 9 through 21.

Do not report the following expenses on lines 9 through 21:

- Rental activity expenses. Report these expenses on Form 8825 or line 3b of Schedule K.
- Deductions allocable to portfolio income. Report these deductions on line 13b of Schedule K and in box 13 of Schedule K-1 using code G, H, or J.
- Nondeductible expenses (for example, expenses connected with the production of tax-exempt income). Report nondeductible expenses on line 18c of Schedule K and in box 18 of Schedule K-1 using code C.
- Qualified expenditures to which an election under section 59(e) may apply. The instructions for line 13d of Schedule K and for Schedule K-1, code K, explain how to report these amounts.
- Items the partnership must state separately that require separate computations by the partners. Examples include expenses incurred for the production of income instead of in a trade or business, charitable contributions, foreign taxes paid, intangible drilling and development costs, soil and water conservation expenditures, amortizable basis of reforestation expenditures, and exploration expenditures. The distributive shares of these expenses are reported separately to each partner on Schedule K-1.

Limitations on Deductions

Section 263A uniform capitalization rules. The uniform capitalization rules of section 263A require partnerships to capitalize or include in inventory costs, certain costs incurred in connection with:

- The production of real and tangible personal property held in inventory or held for sale in the ordinary course of business.
- Real property or personal property (tangible and intangible) acquired for resale.
- The production of real property and tangible personal property by a partnership for use in its trade or business or in an activity engaged in for profit.

The costs required to be capitalized under section 263A are not deductible until the property to which the costs relate is sold, used, or otherwise disposed of by the partnership.

Exceptions. Section 263A does not apply to:

- Inventoriable items accounted for in the same manner as materials and supplies that are not incidental. See *Schedule A. Cost of Goods Sold* on page 19 for details.
- Personal property acquired for resale if the partnership's average annual gross receipts for the 3 prior tax years were $10 million or less.
- Timber.
- Most property produced under a long-term contract.
- Certain property produced in a farming business. See the note at the end of the instructions for line 5.

The partnership must report the following costs separately to the partners for purposes of determinations under section 59(e):

- Research and experimental costs under section 174.
- Intangible drilling costs for oil, gas, and geothermal property.
- Mining exploration and development costs.

Tangible personal property produced by a partnership includes a film, sound recording, videotape, book, or similar property.

Indirect costs. Partnerships subject to the uniform capitalization rules are required to capitalize not only direct costs but an allocable part of most indirect costs (including taxes) that benefit the assets produced or acquired for resale, or are incurred by reason of the performance of production or resale activities.

For inventory, some of the indirect costs that must be capitalized are:

- Administration expenses.
- Taxes.
- Depreciation.
- Insurance.
- Compensation paid to officers attributable to services.
- Rework labor.
- Contributions to pension, stock bonus, and certain profit-sharing, annuity, or deferred compensation plans.

Regulations section 1.263A-1(e)(3) specifies other indirect costs that relate to production or resale activities that must be capitalized and those that may be currently deductible.

Interest expense paid or incurred during the production period of designated property must be capitalized and is governed by special rules. For more details, see Regulations sections 1.263A-8 through 1.263A-15.

For more details on the uniform capitalization rules, see Regulations sections 1.263A-1 through 1.263A-3.

Transactions between related taxpayers. Generally, an accrual basis partnership can deduct business expenses and interest owed to a related party (including any partner) only in the tax year of the partnership that includes the day on which the payment is includible in the income of the related party. See section 267 for details.

Business start-up and organizational costs. Business start-up and organizational costs must be capitalized unless an election is made to deduct or amortize them. For costs paid or incurred before October 23, 2004, the partnership must capitalize them unless it elects to amortize these costs over a period of 60 months or more. For costs paid or incurred after October 22, 2004, the following rules apply separately to each category of costs.

- The partnership can elect to deduct up to $5,000 of such costs for the year the partnership begins business operations.
- The $5,000 deduction is reduced (but not below zero) by the amount the total costs exceed $50,000. If the total costs are $55,000 or more, the deduction is reduced to zero.
- If the election is made, any costs that are not deductible must be amortized ratably over a 180-month period beginning with the month the partnership begins business operations.

For more details on the election for business start-up costs, see section 195. To make the election, attach the statement required by Regulations section 1.195-1(b). For more details on the election for organizational costs, see section 248. To make the election, attach the statement required by Regulations section 1.248-1(c). Report the deductible amount of these costs and any amortization on line 20. For amortization that begins during the tax year, complete and attach Form 4562.

Syndication costs. Costs for issuing and marketing interests in the partnership, such as commissions, professional fees, and printing costs, must be capitalized. They cannot be depreciated or amortized. See the instructions for line 10 for the treatment of syndication fees paid to a partner.

Reducing certain expenses for which credits are allowable. For each of the following credits, the partnership must reduce the otherwise allowable deductions for expenses used to figure the credit by the amount of the current year credit.

1. The work opportunity credit.
2. The welfare-to-work credit.
3. The credit for increasing research activities.
4. The enhanced oil recovery credit.
5. The disabled access credit.
6. The empowerment zone and renewal community employment credit.
7. The Indian employment credit.
8. The credit for employer social security and Medicare taxes paid on certain employee tips.
9. The orphan drug credit.
10. Credit for small employer pension plan startup costs.
11. Credit for employer-provided childcare facilities and services.
12. The New York Liberty Zone business employee credit.
13. The low sulfur diesel fuel production credit.

If the partnership has any of these credits, figure each current year credit before figuring the deductions for expenses on which the credit is based.

Film and television production expenses. The partnership can elect to deduct certain costs of qualified film and television productions that begin after October 22, 2004. See section 181 for details.

Line 9. Salaries and Wages

Enter on line 9 the salaries and wages paid or incurred for the tax year, reduced by the current year credits claimed on:

- Form 5884, Work Opportunity Credit;
- Form 8844, Empowerment Zone and Renewal Community Employment Credit;
- Form 8845, Indian Employment Credit;
- Form 8861, Welfare-to-Work Credit; and
- Form 8884, New York Liberty Zone Business Employee Credit.

See the instructions for these forms for more information.

Do not include salaries and wages reported elsewhere on the return, such as amounts included in cost of goods sold, elective contributions to a section 401(k) cash or deferred arrangement, or amounts contributed under a salary reduction SEP agreement or a SIMPLE IRA plan.

Line 10. Guaranteed Payments to Partners

Deduct payments or credits to a partner for services or for the use of capital if the payments or credits are determined without regard to partnership income and are allocable to a trade or business activity. Also include on line 10 amounts paid during the tax year for insurance that constitutes medical care for a partner, a partner's spouse, or a partner's dependents.

Do not include any payments and credits that should be capitalized. For example, although payments or credits to a partner for services rendered in organizing or syndicating a partnership may be guaranteed payments, they are not deductible on line 10. They are capital expenditures. However, they should be separately reported on Schedule K, line 4 and on Schedule K-1, box 4.

Do not include distributive shares of partnership profits.

Report the guaranteed payments to the appropriate partners on Schedule K-1, box 4.

Line 11. Repairs and Maintenance

Enter the costs of incidental repairs and maintenance that do not add to the value of the property or appreciably prolong its life, but only to the extent that such costs relate to a trade or business activity and are not claimed elsewhere on the return.

The cost of new buildings, machinery, or permanent improvements that increase the value of the property are not deductible. They are chargeable to capital accounts and may be depreciated or amortized.

Line 12. Bad Debts

Enter the total debts that became worthless in whole or in part during the year, but only to the extent such debts relate to a trade or business activity. Report deductible nonbusiness bad debts as a short-term capital loss on Schedule D (Form 1065).

Cash method partnerships cannot take a bad debt deduction unless the amount was previously included in income.

Line 13. Rent

Enter rent paid on business property used in a trade or business activity. Do not deduct rent for a dwelling unit occupied by any partner for personal use.

If the partnership rented or leased a vehicle, enter the total annual rent or lease expense paid or incurred in the trade or business activities of the partnership. Also complete Part V of Form 4562, Depreciation and Amortization. If the partnership leased a vehicle for a term of 30 days or more, the deduction for vehicle lease expense may have to be reduced by an amount called the inclusion amount. You may have an inclusion amount if:

The lease term began:	And the vehicle's FMV on the first day of the lease exceeded:
After 12/31/03 but before 1/1/05	$17,500
After 12/31/02 but before 1/1/04	$18,000
After 12/31/98 but before 1/1/03	$15,500

If the lease term began before January 1, 1999, see Pub. 463, Travel, Entertainment, Gift, and Car Expenses, to find out if the partnership has an inclusion amount. The inclusion amount for lease terms beginning in 2005 will be published in the Internal Revenue Bulletin in early 2005.

See Pub. 463 for instructions on figuring the inclusion amount.

Line 14. Taxes and Licenses

Enter taxes and licenses paid or incurred in the trade or business activities of the partnership if not reflected in cost of goods sold. Federal import duties and federal excise and stamp taxes are deductible only if paid or incurred in carrying on the trade or business of the partnership.

Do not deduct the following taxes on line 14.

- Taxes not imposed on the partnership.
- Federal income taxes or taxes reported elsewhere on the return.
- Section 901 foreign taxes. Report these taxes separately on Schedule K, line 16l and on Schedule K-1, box 16, using codes L and M.
- Taxes allocable to a rental activity. Taxes allocable to a rental real estate activity are reported on Form 8825. Taxes allocable to a rental activity other than a rental real estate activity are reported on line 3b of Schedule K.
- Taxes allocable to portfolio income. These taxes are reported on line 13b of Schedule K and in box 13 of Schedule K-1 using code G.
- Taxes paid or incurred for the production or collection of income, or for the management, conservation, or maintenance of property held to produce income. Report these taxes separately on line 13e of Schedule K and in box 13 of Schedule K-1 using code T.

See section 263A(a) for rules on capitalization of allocable costs (including taxes) for any property.

- Taxes, including state or local sales taxes, that are paid or incurred in connection with an acquisition or disposition of property (these taxes must be treated as a part of the cost of the acquired property or, in the case of a disposition, as a reduction in the amount realized on the disposition).
- Taxes assessed against local benefits that increase the value of the property assessed (such as for paving, etc.).

See section 164(d) for apportionment of taxes on real property between seller and purchaser.

Line 15. Interest

Include only interest incurred in the trade or business activities of the partnership that is not claimed elsewhere on the return.

Do not deduct interest expense on debt required to be allocated to the production of designated property. Designated property includes real property, personal property that has a class life of 20 years or more, and other tangible property requiring more than 2 years (1 year in the case of property with a cost of more than $1 million) to produce or construct. Interest that is allocable to designated property produced by a partnership for its own use or for sale must be capitalized.

In addition, a partnership must also capitalize any interest on debt that is allocable to an asset used to produce designated property. A partner may be required to capitalize interest that was incurred by the partner for the partnership's production expenditures. Similarly, a partner may have to capitalize interest that was incurred by the partnership for the partner's own production expenditures. The information required by the partner to properly capitalize interest for this purpose must be provided by the partnership on an attachment for box 20 of Schedule K-1, using code L. See section 263A(f) and Regulations sections 1.263A-8 through 1.263A-15.

Do not include interest expense on debt used to purchase rental property or debt used in a rental activity. Interest allocable to a rental real estate activity is reported on Form 8825 and is used in arriving at net income (loss) from rental real estate activities on line 2 of Schedule K and in box 2 of Schedule K-1. Interest allocable to a rental activity other than a rental real estate activity is included on line 3b of Schedule K and is used in arriving at net income (loss) from a rental activity (other than a rental real estate activity). This net amount is reported on line 3c of Schedule K and box 3 of Schedule K-1.

Do not include interest expense on debt used to buy property held for investment. Do not include interest expense that is clearly and directly allocable to interest, dividend, royalty, or annuity income not derived in the ordinary course of a trade or business. Interest paid or incurred on debt used to purchase or carry investment property is reported on line 13c of Schedule K and in box 13 of Schedule K-1. See the instructions for line 13c of Schedule K, for box 13, code I of Schedule K-1, and Form 4952,

Investment Interest Expense Deduction, for more information on investment property.

Do not include interest on debt proceeds allocated to distributions made to partners during the tax year. Instead, report such interest on line 13e of Schedule K and in box 13 of Schedule K-1 using code S. To determine the amount to allocate to distributions to partners, see Notice 89-35, 1989-1 C.B. 675.

Temporary Regulations section 1.163-8T gives rules for allocating interest expense among activities so that the limitations on passive activity losses, investment interest, and personal interest can be properly figured. Generally, interest expense is allocated in the same manner that debt is allocated. Debt is allocated by tracing disbursements of the debt proceeds to specific expenditures, as provided in the regulations.

Interest paid by a partnership to a partner for the use of capital should be entered on line 10 as guaranteed payments.

Prepaid interest can only be deducted over the period to which the prepayment applies.

Note. Additional limitations on interest deductions apply when the partnership is a policyholder or beneficiary with respect to a life insurance, endowment, or annuity contract issued after June 8, 1997. For details, see section 264. Attach a statement showing the computation of the deduction disallowed under section 264.

Line 16. Depreciation

On line 16a, enter only the depreciation claimed on assets used in a trade or business activity. Enter on line 16b the depreciation reported elsewhere on the return (for example, on Schedule A) that is attributable to assets used in trade or business activities. See the Instructions for Form 4562 or Pub. 946, How To Depreciate Property, to figure the amount of depreciation to enter on this line.

Complete and attach Form 4562 only if the partnership placed property in service during the tax year or claims depreciation on any car or other listed property.

Do not include any section 179 expense deduction on this line. This amount is not deducted by the partnership. Instead, it is passed through to the partners in box 12 of Schedule K-1.

Line 17. Depletion

If the partnership claims a deduction for timber depletion, complete and attach Form T, Forest Activities Schedule.

Do not deduct depletion for oil and gas properties. Each partner figures depletion on oil and gas properties. See the instructions for Schedule K-1, box 20, "Information needed to figure depletion–oil and gas (code N)," for the information on oil and gas depletion that must be supplied to the partners by the partnership.

Line 18. Retirement Plans, etc.

Do not deduct payments for partners to retirement or deferred compensation plans including IRAs, qualified plans, and simplified employee pension (SEP) and SIMPLE IRA plans on this line. These amounts are reported on Schedule K-1, box 13, using code R, and are deducted by the partners on their own returns.

Enter the deductible contributions not claimed elsewhere on the return made by the partnership for its common-law employees under a qualified pension, profit-sharing, annuity, or SEP or SIMPLE IRA plan, and under any other deferred compensation plan.

If the partnership contributes to an individual retirement arrangement (IRA) for employees, include the contribution in salaries and wages on page 1, line 9, or Schedule A, line 3, and not on line 18.

Employers who maintain a pension, profit-sharing, or other funded deferred compensation plan (other than a SEP or SIMPLE IRA), whether or not the plan is qualified under the Internal Revenue Code and whether or not a deduction is claimed for the current year, generally must file the applicable form listed below.

- Form 5500, Annual Return/Report of Employee Benefit Plan. File this form for a plan that is not a one-participant plan (see below).
- Form 5500-EZ, Annual Return of One-Participant (Owners and Their Spouses) Retirement Plan. File this form for a plan that only covers one or more partners (or partners and their spouses).

There are penalties for not filing these forms on time.

Line 19. Employee Benefit Programs

Enter the partnership's contributions to employee benefit programs not claimed elsewhere on the return (for example, insurance, health, and welfare programs) that are not part of a pension, profit-sharing, etc., plan included on line 18.

Do not include amounts paid during the tax year for insurance that constitutes medical care for a partner, a partner's spouse, or a partner's dependents. Instead, include these amounts on line 10 as guaranteed payments and on Schedule K, line 4, and Schedule K-1, box 4, of each partner on whose behalf the amounts were paid. Also report these amounts on Schedule K, line 13e, and Schedule K-1, box 13, using code L, of each partner on whose behalf the amounts were paid.

Line 20. Other Deductions

Enter the total allowable trade or business deductions that are not deductible elsewhere on page 1 of Form 1065. Attach a statement listing by type and amount each deduction included on this line. Examples of other deductions include:

- Amortization (except as noted below). See the Instructions for Form 4562 for more information. Complete and attach Form 4562 if the partnership is claiming amortization of costs that began during the tax year.
- Insurance premiums.
- Legal and professional fees.
- Supplies used and consumed in the business.
- Utilities.
- Certain business start-up expenditures and organizational expenditures that the partnership has elected to amortize or deduct. See *Limitations on Deductions* beginning on page 16 for more details.

Also see *Special Rules* below for limits on certain other deductions.

Do not deduct on line 20:

- Items that must be reported separately on Schedules K and K-1.
- Qualified expenditures to which an election under section 59(e) may apply. See the instructions on page 26 for *Lines 13d(1) and 13d(2). Section 59(e)(2) Expenditures*, for details on treatment of these items.
- Reforestation expenditures. The partnership must separately state the reforestation expense deduction for expenditures paid or incurred after October 22, 2004, and the amortizable basis of expenditures paid or incurred before October 23, 2004. See the instructions for *Reforestation expense deduction (code S)* on page 27 and *Amortization of reforestation costs (code O)* on page 34. Deduct on line 20 only the amortization of reforestation expenditures paid or incurred after October 22, 2004. The amount the partnership can amortize is only the portion of such expenditures in excess of the separately-stated reforestation expense deduction.
- Fines or penalties paid to a government for violating any law. Report these expenses on Schedule K, line 18c.
- Expenses allocable to tax-exempt income. Report these expenses on Schedule K, line 18c.
- Net operating losses. Only individuals and corporations may claim a net operating loss deduction.
- Amounts paid or incurred to participate or intervene in any political campaign on behalf of a candidate for public office, or to influence the general public regarding legislative matters, elections, or referendums. Report these expenses on Schedule K, line 18c.
- Expenses paid or incurred to influence federal or state legislation, or to influence the actions or positions of certain federal executive branch officials. However, certain in-house lobbying expenditures that do not exceed $2,000 are deductible. See section 162(e) for more details.

Special Rules

Commercial revitalization deduction. If the partnership constructs, purchases, or substantially rehabilitates a qualified building in a renewal community it may qualify for a deduction of either (a) 50% of qualified capital expenditures in the year the building is placed in service or (b) amortization of 100% of the qualified capital expenditures over a 120-month period beginning with the month the building is placed in service. If the partnership elects to amortize these expenditures, complete and attach Form 4562. To qualify, the building must be nonresidential (as defined in section 168(e)(2)) and placed in service by the partnership. The partnership must be the original user of the building unless it is substantially rehabilitated. The amount of the qualified expenditures cannot exceed the lesser of $10 million or the amount allocated to the building by the commercial revitalization agency of the state in which the building is located. Any remaining expenditures are depreciated over the regular depreciation recovery period. See Pub. 954, Tax Incentives for Distressed Communities, and section 1400I for details.

Rental real estate. Do not report this deduction on line 20 if the building is placed in service as rental real estate. A commercial revitalization deduction for rental real estate is not deducted by the partnership but is passed through to the partners in box 13 of Schedule K-1, using code P.

Travel, meals, and entertainment. Subject to limitations and restrictions discussed below, a partnership can deduct ordinary and necessary travel, meals, and entertainment expenses paid or incurred in its trade or business. Also, special rules apply to deductions for gifts, skybox rentals, luxury water travel, convention expenses, and entertainment tickets. See section 274 and Pub. 463 for more details.

Travel. The partnership cannot deduct travel expenses of any individual accompanying a partner or partnership employee, including a spouse or dependent of the partner or employee, unless:

- That individual is an employee of the partnership and
- His or her travel is for a bona fide business purpose and would otherwise be deductible by that individual.

Meals and entertainment. Generally, the partnership can deduct only 50% of the amount otherwise allowable for meals and entertainment expenses paid or incurred in its trade or business. In addition (subject to exceptions under section 274(k)(2)):

- Meals must not be lavish or extravagant,
- A bona fide business discussion must occur during, immediately before, or immediately after the meal, and
- A partner or employee of the partnership must be present at the meal.

See section 274(n)(3) for a special rule that applies to expenses for meals consumed by individuals subject to the hours of service limits of the Department of Transportation.

Membership dues. The partnership may deduct amounts paid or incurred for membership dues in civic or public service organizations, professional organizations (such as bar and medical associations), business leagues, trade associations, chambers of commerce, boards of trade, and real estate boards. However, no deduction is allowed if a principal purpose of the organization is to entertain, or provide entertainment facilities for, members or their guests. In addition, the partnership may not deduct membership dues in any club organized for business, pleasure, recreation, or other social purpose. This includes country clubs, golf and athletic clubs, airline and hotel clubs, and clubs operated to provide meals under conditions favorable to business discussion.

Entertainment facilities. The partnership cannot deduct an expense paid or incurred for a facility (such as a yacht or hunting lodge) used for an activity usually considered entertainment, amusement, or recreation.

Generally, the partnership may be able to deduct otherwise nondeductible meals, travel, and entertainment expenses if the amounts are treated as compensation to the recipient and reported on Form W-2 for an employee or on Form 1099-MISC for an independent contractor.

Schedule A. Cost of Goods Sold

Cost of Goods Sold

Generally, inventories are required at the beginning and end of each tax year if the production, purchase, or sale of merchandise is an income-producing factor. See Regulations section 1.471-1.

However, if the partnership is a qualifying taxpayer or a qualifying small business taxpayer, it may adopt or change its accounting method to account for inventoriable items in the same manner as materials and supplies that are not incidental (unless its business is a tax shelter (as defined in section 448(d)(3))).

A **qualifying taxpayer** is a taxpayer that, with respect to each prior tax year ending after December 16, 1998, has average annual gross receipts of $1 million or less for the 3-tax-year period ending with that prior tax year. See Rev. Proc. 2001-10, 2001-2 I.R.B. 272 for details.

A **qualifying small business taxpayer** is a taxpayer (a) that, with respect to each prior tax year ending on or after December 31, 2000, has average annual gross receipts of $10 million or less for the 3-tax-year period ending with that prior tax year and (b) whose principal business activity is not an ineligible activity. See Rev. Proc. 2002-28, 2002-18 I.R.B. 815 for details.

Under this accounting method, inventory costs for raw materials purchased for use in producing finished goods and merchandise purchased for resale are deductible in the year the finished goods or merchandise are sold (but not before the year the partnership paid for the raw materials or merchandise if it is also using the cash method). For additional guidance on this method of accounting for inventoriable items, see Pub. 538.

Enter amounts paid for all raw materials and merchandise during the tax year on line 2. The amount the partnership can deduct for the tax year is figured on line 8.

All filers that have not elected to treat inventoriable items as materials and supplies that are not incidental should see *Section 263A uniform capitalization rules* on page 16 before completing Schedule A.

Line 1. Inventory at Beginning of Year

If the partnership is changing its method of accounting for the current tax year, it must refigure last year's closing inventory using its new method of accounting and enter the result on line 1. If there is a difference between last year's closing inventory and the refigured amount, attach an explanation and take it into account when figuring the partnership's section 481(a) adjustment (explained on page 5).

Line 2. Purchases

Reduce purchases by items withdrawn for personal use. The cost of these items should be shown on line 19b of Schedule K and in box 19 of Schedule K-1, using code B, as distributions to partners.

Line 4. Additional Section 263A Costs

An entry is required on this line only for partnerships that have elected a simplified method.

For partnerships that have elected the simplified production method, additional section 263A costs are generally those costs, other than interest, that were not capitalized under the partnership's method of accounting immediately prior to the effective date of section 263A that are required to be capitalized under section 263A. Interest must be accounted for separately. For new partnerships, additional section 263A costs are the costs, other than interest, that must be capitalized under section 263A, but which the partnership would not have been required to capitalize if it had existed before the effective date of section 263A. For more details, see Regulations section 1.263A-2(b).

For partnerships that have elected the simplified resale method, additional section 263A costs are generally those costs incurred with respect to the following categories.

- Off-site storage or warehousing;
- Purchasing;
- Handling, such as processing, assembly, repackaging, and transporting; and
- General and administrative costs (mixed service costs).

For details, see Regulations section 1.263A-3(d).

Enter on line 4 the balance of section 263A costs paid or incurred during the tax year not includable on lines 2, 3, and 5. Attach a statement listing these costs.

Line 5. Other Costs

Enter on line 5 any other inventoriable costs paid or incurred during the tax year not entered on lines 2 through 4. Attach a statement.

Line 7. Inventory at End of Year

See Regulations sections 1.263A-1 through 1.263A-3 for details on figuring the amount of additional section 263A costs to be included in ending inventory.

If the partnership accounts for inventoriable items in the same manner as materials and supplies that are not incidental, enter on line 7 the portion of its raw materials and merchandise purchased for resale that are included on line 6 and were not sold during the year.

Lines 9a through 9c. Inventory Valuation Methods

Inventories can be valued at:

- Cost,
- Cost or market value (whichever is lower), or
- Any other method approved by the IRS that conforms to the requirements of the applicable regulations cited below.

However, if the partnership is using the cash method of accounting, it is required to use cost.

Partnerships that account for inventoriable items in the same manner as materials and supplies that are not incidental may currently deduct expenditures for direct labor and all indirect costs that would otherwise be included in inventory costs. See Rev. Proc. 2001-10 and Rev. Proc. 2002-28 for more information.

The average cost (rolling average) method of valuing inventories generally does not conform to the requirements of the regulations. See Rev. Rul. 71-234, 1971-1 C.B. 148.

Partnerships that use erroneous valuation methods must change to a method permitted for federal tax purposes. To make this change, use Form 3115.

On line 9a, check the methods used for valuing inventories. Under lower of cost or market, the term "market" (for normal goods) means the current bid price prevailing on the inventory valuation date for the particular merchandise in the volume usually purchased by the taxpayer. For a manufacturer, market applies to the basic elements of cost—raw materials, labor, and burden. If section 263A applies to the taxpayer, the basic elements of cost must reflect the current bid price of all direct costs and all indirect costs properly allocable to goods on hand at the inventory date.

Inventory may be valued below cost when the merchandise is unsalable at normal prices or unusable in the normal way because the goods are subnormal due to damage, imperfections, shopwear, etc., within the meaning of Regulations section 1.471-2(c). These goods may be valued at the current bona fide selling price, minus the direct cost of disposition (but not less than scrap value) if such a price can be established.

If this is the first year the Last-in First-out (LIFO) inventory method was either adopted or extended to inventory goods not previously valued under the LIFO method, attach Form 970, Application To Use LIFO Inventory Method, or a statement with the information required by Form 970. Also check the box on line 9c.

If the partnership has changed or extended its inventory method to LIFO and has had to write up its opening inventory to cost in the year of election, report the effect of this write-up as income (line 7, page 1, Form 1065) proportionately over a 3-year period that begins in the tax year of the LIFO election.

For more information on inventory valuation methods, see Pub. 538, Accounting Periods and Methods.

Schedule B. Other Information

Question 1

Check box 1(f) for any other type of entity and state the type.

Question 3

The partnership must answer "Yes" to question 3, if during the tax year:

- It owned an interest in another partnership (foreign or domestic) or
- It was the "tax owner" of a foreign disregarded entity (FDE) under Regulations sections 301.7701-2 and 301.7701-3. The tax owner of an FDE is the person that is treated as owning the assets and liabilities of the FDE for purposes of U.S. income tax law.

If the partnership answered "Yes" to this question, it must:

1. Show each partnership's name, EIN (if any), and the country under whose laws the partnership was organized on an attached statement if the partnership directly or indirectly owned at least a 10% interest in any other foreign or domestic partnership (other than any partnership for which a Form 8865 is attached to the tax return).
2. Complete and attach Form 8858, Information Return of U.S. Persons With Respect to Foreign Disregarded Entities, for each FDE. For more information, see the instructions for Form 8858.

Note: Clearly indicate whether each entity in the attached schedule is a partnership or a disregarded entity.

Question 4

Generally, the tax treatment of partnership items is determined at the partnership level in a consolidated audit proceeding under sections 6221 and 6234, rather than in separate proceedings with individual partners. Small partnerships are not subject to the rules for consolidated audit proceedings. "Small partnerships" are defined as any partnership having 10 or fewer partners each of whom is an individual (other than a nonresident alien), a C corporation, or an estate of a deceased partner.

Small partnerships can elect to be subject to the rules for consolidated audit proceedings by attaching Form 8893, Election of Partnership Level Tax Treatment, or an election statement to the partnership return for the first taxable year for which the election is to be effective. This election must be signed by all persons who were partners of the partnership at any time during the partnership's taxable year. Once made, the election may not be revoked without IRS consent. See section 6231(a)(1)(B) and Form 8893 for more information.

CAUTION *The partnership does not make this election when it answers "Yes" to question 4. The election must be made separately.*

Question 5

Answer "Yes" to question 5 if the partnership meets all three of the requirements shown on the form. Total receipts is defined as the sum of gross receipts or sales (page 1, line 1a); all other income (page 1, lines 4 through 7); income reported on Schedule K, lines 3a, 5, 6a, and 7; income or net gain reported on Schedule K, lines 8, 9a, 10, and 11; and income or net gain reported on Form 8825, lines 2, 19, and 20a.

Question 6. Foreign Partners

Answer "Yes" to question 6 if the partnership had any foreign partners (for purposes of section 1446) at any time during the tax year. Otherwise, answer "No."

If the partnership had gross income effectively connected with a trade or business in the United States and foreign partners, it may be required to withhold tax under section 1446 on income allocable to foreign partners (without regard to distributions) and file Forms 8804, 8805, and 8813. See Rev. Proc. 89-31, 1989-1 C.B. 895 and Rev. Proc. 92-66, 1992-2 C.B. 428 for more information.

Question 7

Answer "Yes" to question 7 if interests in the partnership are traded on an established securities market or are readily tradable on a secondary market (or its substantial equivalent).

Question 8

Organizers of certain tax shelters are required to register the tax shelters by filing Form 8264, Application for Registration of a Tax Shelter, no later than the day on which an interest in the shelter is first offered for sale. Organizers filing a properly completed Form 8264 will receive a tax shelter registration number that they must furnish to their investors. See the Instructions for Form 8264 for the definition of a tax shelter and the investments exempted from tax shelter registration.

Question 9. Foreign Accounts

Answer "Yes" to question 9 if either 1 or 2 below applies to the partnership. Otherwise, check the "No" box.

1. At any time during calendar year 2004, the partnership had an interest in or signature or other authority over a bank account, securities account, or other financial account in a foreign country (see Form TD F 90-22.1, Report of Foreign Bank and Financial Accounts); and
   - The combined value of the accounts was more than $10,000 at any time during the calendar year; and
   - The accounts were not with a U.S. military banking facility operated by a U.S. financial institution.
2. The partnership owns more than 50% of the stock in any corporation that would answer the question "Yes" based on item 1 above.

If the "Yes" box is checked for the question:

- Enter the name of the foreign country or countries. Attach a separate sheet if more space is needed.
- File Form TD F 90-22.1 by June 30, 2005, with the Department of the Treasury at the

address shown on the form. Because Form TD F 90-22.1 is not a tax form, do not file it with Form 1065. You can order Form TD F 90-22.1 by calling 1-800-TAX-FORM (1-800-829-3676) or you can download it from the IRS website at *www.irs.gov*.

CAUTION *Failure to comply with these reporting requirements could result in a penalty of up to $10,000. Intentional disregard for these reporting requirements could result in a penalty equal to the greater of $100,000 or 50% of the amount of the transaction or account.*

Question 10

The partnership may be required to file Form 3520, Annual Return To Report Transactions With Foreign Trusts and Receipt of Certain Foreign Gifts, if:

- It directly or indirectly transferred property or money to a foreign trust. For this purpose, any U.S. person who created a foreign trust is considered a transferor.
- It is treated as the owner of any part of the assets of a foreign trust under the grantor trust rules.
- It received a distribution from a foreign trust.

For more information, see the Instructions for Form 3520.

Note. An owner of a foreign trust must ensure that the trust files an annual information return on Form 3520-A, Annual Information Return of Foreign Trust with a U.S. Owner.

Designation of Tax Matters Partner (TMP)

If the partnership is subject to the rules for consolidated audit proceedings in sections 6221 through 6234, the partnership can designate a partner as the TMP for the tax year for which the return is filed by completing the *Designation of Tax Matters Partner* section on page 2 of Form 1065. The designated TMP must be a general partner and, in most cases, must also be a U.S. person. For details, see Regulations section 301.6231(a)(7)-1.

For a limited liability company (LLC), only a member-manager of the LLC is treated as a general partner. A member-manager is any owner of an interest in the LLC who, alone or together with others, has the continuing exclusive authority to make the management decisions necessary to conduct the business for which the LLC was formed. If there are no elected or designated member-managers, each owner is treated as a member-manager. For details, see Regulations section 301.6231(a)(7)-2.

Schedules K and K-1. Partners' Distributive Share Items

Purpose of Schedules

Although the partnership is not subject to income tax, the partners are liable for tax on their shares of the partnership income, whether or not distributed, and must include their shares on their tax returns.

Schedule K (page 3 of Form 1065) is a summary schedule of all the partners' shares of the partnership's income, credits, deductions, etc. All partnerships must complete Schedule K. Rental activity income (loss) and portfolio income are not reported on page 1 of Form 1065. These amounts are not combined with trade or business activity income (loss). Schedule K is used to report the totals of these and other amounts.

Schedule K-1 (Form 1065) shows each partner's separate share. Attach a copy of each Schedule K-1 to the Form 1065 filed with the IRS; keep a copy with a copy of the partnership return as a part of the partnership's records; and furnish a copy to each partner. If a partnership interest is held by a nominee on behalf of another person, the partnership may be required to furnish Schedule K-1 to the nominee. See Temporary Regulations sections 1.6031(b)-1T and 1.6031(c)-1T for more information.

Give each partner a copy of either the Partner's Instructions for Schedule K-1 (Form 1065) or specific instructions for each item reported on the partner's Schedule K-1 (Form 1065).

Substitute Forms

The partnership does not need IRS approval to use a substitute Schedule K-1 if it is an exact copy of the IRS schedule. The boxes must use the same numbers and titles and must be in the same order and format as on the comparable IRS Schedule K-1. The substitute schedule must include the OMB number. The partnership must provide each partner with the Partner's Instructions for Schedule K-1 (Form 1065) or other prepared specific instructions for each item reported on the partner's Schedule K-1.

The partnership must request IRS approval to use other substitute Schedules K-1. To request approval, write to Internal Revenue Service, Attention: Substitute Forms Program, SE:W:CAR:MP:T:T:SP, 1111 Constitution Avenue, NW, IR-6406, Washington, DC 20224.

Each partner's information must be on a separate sheet of paper. Therefore, separate all continuously printed substitutes before you file them with the IRS.

The partnership may be subject to a penalty if it files Schedules K-1 that do not conform to the specifications of Rev. Proc. 2004-62, 2004-44 I.R.B. 728.

How Income Is Shared Among Partners

Allocate shares of income, gain, loss, deduction, or credit among the partners according to the partnership agreement for sharing income or loss generally. Partners may agree to allocate specific items in a ratio different from the ratio for sharing income or loss. For instance, if the net income exclusive of specially allocated items is divided evenly among three partners but some special items are allocated 50% to one, 30% to another, and 20% to the third partner, report the specially allocated items on the appropriate line of the applicable partner's Schedule K-1 and the total on the appropriate line of Schedule K, instead of on the numbered lines on page 1 of Form 1065 or Schedules A or D.

If a partner's interest changed during the year, see section 706(d) before determining each partner's distributive share of any item of income, gain, loss, deduction, etc. Income (loss) is allocated to a partner only for the part of the year in which that person is a member of the partnership. The partnership will either allocate on a daily basis or divide the partnership year into segments and allocate income, loss, or special items in each segment among the persons who were partners during that segment. Partnerships that report their income on the cash basis must allocate interest expense, taxes, and any payment for services or for the use of property on a daily basis if there is any change in any partner's interest during the year. See Pub. 541 for more details.

Special rules on the allocation of income, gain, loss, and deductions generally apply if a partner contributes property to the partnership and the FMV of that property at the time of contribution differs from the contributing partner's adjusted tax basis. Under these rules, the partnership must use a reasonable method of making allocations of income, gain, loss, and deductions from the property so that the contributing partner receives the tax burdens and benefits of any built-in gain or loss (that is, precontribution appreciation or diminution of value of the contributed property). See Regulations section 1.704-3 for details on how to make these allocations, including a description of specific allocation methods that are generally reasonable.

See *Dispositions of Contributed Property* on page 9 for special rules on the allocation of income, gain, loss, and deductions on the disposition of property contributed to the partnership by a partner.

If the partnership agreement does not provide for the partner's share of income, gain, loss, deduction, or credit, or if the allocation under the agreement does not have substantial economic effect, the partner's share is determined according to the partner's interest in the partnership. See Regulations section 1.704-1 for more information.

Specific Instructions (Schedule K-1 Only)

General Information

Generally, the partnership is required to prepare and give a Schedule K-1 to each person who was a partner in the partnership at any time during the year. Schedule K-1 must be provided to each partner on or before the day on which the partnership return is required to be filed.

However, if a foreign partnership meets each of the following four requirements, it is not required to file or provide Schedules K-1 for foreign partners (unless the foreign partner is a pass-through entity through which a U.S. person holds an interest in the foreign partnership).

- The partnership had no gross income effectively connected with the conduct of a

trade or business within the United States during its tax year.
• All required Forms 1042 and 1042-S were filed by the partnership or another withholding agent as required by Regulations section 1.1461-1(b) and (c).
• The tax liability for each foreign partner for amounts reportable under Regulations sections 1.1461-1(b) and (c) has been fully satisfied by the withholding of tax at the source.
• The partnership is not a withholding foreign partnership as defined in Regulations section 1.1441-5(c)(2)(i).

Generally, any person who holds an interest in a partnership as a nominee for another person must furnish to the partnership the name, address, etc., of the other person.

For an individual partner, enter the partner's social security number (SSN) or individual taxpayer identification number (ITIN). For all other partners, enter the partner's EIN. However, if a partner is an individual retirement arrangement (IRA), enter the identifying number of the custodian of the IRA. Do not enter the SSN of the person for whom the IRA is maintained.

Foreign partners without a U.S. taxpayer identifying number should be notified by the partnership of the necessity of obtaining a U.S. identifying number. Certain aliens who are not eligible to obtain SSNs can apply for an ITIN on Form W-7, Application for IRS Individual Taxpayer Identification Number.

If a husband and wife each had an interest in the partnership, prepare a separate Schedule K-1 for each of them. If a husband and wife held an interest together, prepare one Schedule K-1 if the two of them are considered to be one partner.

General Reporting Information

If the return is for a fiscal year or a short tax year, fill in the tax year space at the top of each Schedule K-1. On each Schedule K-1, enter the information about the partnership and the partner in Parts I and II (items A through N). In Part III, enter the partner's distributive share of each item of income, deduction, and credit and any other information the partner needs to file the partner's tax return.

Codes. In box 11 and boxes 13 through 20, identify each item by entering a code in the column to the left of the entry space for the dollar amount. These codes are identified in these instructions and on the back of the Schedule K-1.

Attached statements. Enter an asterisk (*) after the code, if any, in the column to the left of the dollar amount entry space for each item for which you have attached a statement providing additional information. For those informational items that cannot be reported as a single dollar amount, enter the code and asterisk in the left-hand column and enter "STMT" in the entry space to the right to indicate that the information is provided on an attached statement. More than one attached statement can be placed on the same sheet of paper and should be identified in alphanumeric order by box number followed by the letter code (if any). For example: "Box 20, Code N—Information Needed to Figure Depletion—Oil and Gas" (followed by the information the partner needs).

For electronically filed returns, the partnership must follow the instructions for attachments as described in Pub. 1525 when reporting the additional information that may be required for each respective box. See Pub. 1525 for more information.

Too few entry spaces on Schedule K-1? If the partnership has more coded items than the number of spaces in box 11 or boxes 13 through 20, do not enter a code or dollar amount in the last entry space of the box. In the last entry space, enter an asterisk in the left column and enter "STMT" in the entry space to the right. Report the additional items on an attached statement and provide the box number, the code, description, and dollar amount or information for each additional item. For example: "Box 15, Code J—Work Opportunity Credit—$1,000."

Part I. Information About the Partnership

On each Schedule K-1, enter the name, address, and identifying number of the partnership.

Item E. Tax Shelter Registration Number

If the partnership is a registration-required tax shelter, it must check this box and enter the tax shelter registration number in item E.

Item F

A partnership that has invested in a registration-required tax shelter must check this box and furnish a copy of its Form 8271 to its partners. See Form 8271 for more details.

Part II. Information About the Partner

Complete a Schedule K-1 for each partner. On each Schedule K-1, enter the partner's name, address, identifying number, and distributive share items.

Items G and H

If a single member limited liability company (LLC) owns an interest in the partnership, and the LLC is treated as a disregarded entity for federal income tax purposes, enter the owner's identifying number in item G and the owner's name and address in item H.

Item I

Complete item I on all Schedules K-1. If a partner holds interests as both a general and limited partner, check both boxes and attach a statement for each activity that shows the amounts allocable to the partner's interest as a limited partner.

Item J. Domestic/Foreign Partner

Check the foreign partner box if the partner is a nonresident alien individual, foreign partnership, foreign corporation, or a foreign estate or trust. Otherwise, check the domestic partner box.

Item K. What Type of Entity Is This Partner?

State on this line whether the partner is an individual, a corporation, an estate, a trust, a partnership, a disregarded entity, an exempt organization, or a nominee (custodian). If the entity is a limited liability company (LLC) and it is treated as other than a disregarded entity for federal income tax purposes, the partnership must enter the LLC's classification for federal income tax purposes (that is, a corporation or partnership). If the partner is a nominee, use one of the following codes after the word "nominee" to indicate the type of entity the nominee represents: I—Individual; C—Corporation; F—Estate or Trust; P—Partnership; DE—Disregarded Entity; E—Exempt Organization; or IRA—Individual Retirement Arrangement.

Item L. Partner's Profit, Loss, and Capital

On each line, enter the appropriate percentages at the beginning and the end of the year. However, if a partner's interest terminated during the year, enter in the *Beginning* column the percentages that existed immediately before the termination. When the profit or loss sharing percentage has changed during the year, show the percentage before the change in the *Beginning* column and the end-of-year percentage in the *Ending* column. If there are multiple changes in the profit and loss sharing percentage during the year, attach a statement giving the date and percentage before each change.

On the line for *Capital* enter the portion of the capital that the partner would receive if the partnership was liquidated by the distribution of undivided interests in partnership assets and liabilities.

Item M. Partner's Share of Liabilities

Enter each partner's share of nonrecourse liabilities, partnership-level qualified nonrecourse financing, and other recourse liabilities at the end of the year.

"Nonrecourse liabilities" are those liabilities of the partnership for which no partner bears the economic risk of loss. The extent to which a partner bears the economic risk of loss is determined under the rules of Regulations section 1.752-2. Do not include partnership-level qualified nonrecourse financing (defined on page 23) on the line for nonrecourse liabilities.

If the partner terminated his or her interest in the partnership during the year, enter the share that existed immediately before the total disposition. In all other cases, enter it as of the end of the year.

If the partnership is engaged in two or more different types of at-risk activities, or a combination of at-risk activities and any other activity, attach a statement showing the partner's share of nonrecourse liabilities, partnership-level qualified nonrecourse financing, and other recourse liabilities for each activity. See Pub. 925, Passive Activity and At-Risk Rules, to determine if the partnership is engaged in more than one at-risk activity.

The at-risk rules of section 465 generally apply to any activity carried on by the partnership as a trade or business or for the production of income. These rules generally limit the amount of loss and other deductions a partner can claim from any partnership activity to the amount for which that partner is considered at risk. However, for partners who acquired their partnership interests before 1987, the at-risk rules do not apply to losses from an activity of holding real property the partnership placed in service before 1987. The activity of holding mineral property does not qualify for this exception. Identify on an attachment to Schedule K-1 the amount of any losses that are not subject to the at-risk rules.

If a partnership is engaged in an activity subject to the limitations of section 465(c)(1) (such as, films or videotapes, leasing section 1245 property, farming, or oil and gas property), give each partner his or her share of the total pre-1976 losses from that activity for which there existed a corresponding amount of nonrecourse liability at the end of each year in which the losses occurred. See Form 6198, At-Risk Limitations, and related instructions for more information.

Qualified nonrecourse financing secured by real property used in an activity of holding real property that is subject to the at-risk rules is treated as an amount at risk. "Qualified nonrecourse financing" generally includes financing for which no one is personally liable for repayment that is borrowed for use in an activity of holding real property and that is loaned or guaranteed by a federal, state, or local government or that is borrowed from a "qualified" person. Qualified persons include any person actively and regularly engaged in the business of lending money, such as a bank or savings and loan association. Qualified persons generally do not include related parties (unless the nonrecourse financing is commercially reasonable and on substantially the same terms as loans involving unrelated persons), the seller of the property, or a person who receives a fee for the partnership's investment in the real property. See section 465 for more information on qualified nonrecourse financing.

The partner as well as the partnership must meet the qualified nonrecourse rules. Therefore, the partnership must enter on an attached statement any other information the partner needs to determine if the qualified nonrecourse rules are also met at the partner level.

Item N. Partner's Capital Account Analysis

You are not required to complete item N if the answer to question 5 of Schedule B is "Yes." If you are required to complete this item, see the instructions for Schedule M-2 on page 35. Check the appropriate box that describes the method of accounting used to compute the partner's capital account.

- Check the "tax basis" box if the method of accounting used to compute the partner's capital account is based on the partnership's income and deductions for federal tax purposes.
- Check the "GAAP" box if it is based on generally accepted accounting principles (GAAP).
- Check the "704(b) book" box if it is based on the capital accounting rules under Regulations section 1.704-1(b)(2)(iv).
- Check the "Other" box if any other method is used to compute the partner's capital account and attach a statement describing the method and showing how the partner's capital account was computed.

Specific Instructions (Schedules K and K-1, Part III, Except as Noted)

These instructions refer to the lines on Schedule K and the boxes on Schedule K-1.

Special Allocations

An item is specially allocated if it is allocated to a partner in a ratio different from the ratio for sharing income or loss generally.

Report specially allocated ordinary gain (loss) on Schedule K, line 11, and on Schedule K-1, box 11. Report other specially allocated items in the applicable boxes of the partner's Schedule K-1, with the total amount on the applicable line of Schedule K. See *How Income is Shared Among Partners* on page 21.

Example. A partnership has a long-term capital gain that is specially allocated to a partner and a net long-term capital gain reported on line 11, of Schedule D that must be reported on line 9a of Schedule K. Because specially allocated gains or losses are not reported on Schedule D, the partnership must report both the net long-term capital gain from Schedule D and the specially allocated gain on line 9a of Schedule K. Box 9a of the Schedule K-1 for the partners must include both the specially allocated gain and the partner's distributive share of the net long-term capital gain from Schedule D.

Income (Loss)

Line 1. Ordinary Business Income (Loss)

Enter the amount from page 1, line 22. Enter the income (loss) without reference to (a) the basis of the partners' interests in the partnership, (b) the partners' at-risk limitations, or (c) the passive activity limitations. These limitations, if applicable, are determined at the partner level.

Line 1 should not include rental activity income (loss) or portfolio income (loss).

Schedule K-1. Enter each partner's distributive share of ordinary business income (loss) in box 1 of Schedule K-1. If the partnership has more than one trade or business activity, identify on an attachment to Schedule K-1 the amount from each separate activity. See *Passive Activity Reporting Requirements* on page 13.

Line 2. Net Rental Real Estate Income (Loss)

Enter the net income (loss) from rental real estate activities of the partnership from Form 8825. Attach this form to Form 1065.

Schedule K-1. Enter each partner's distributive share of net rental real estate income (loss) in box 2 of Schedule K-1. If the partnership has more than one rental real estate activity, identify on an attachment to Schedule K-1 the amount attributable to each activity. See *Passive Activity Reporting Requirements* on page 13.

Line 3. Other Net Rental Income (Loss)

On Schedule K, line 3a, enter gross income from rental activities other than those reported on Form 8825. See page 11 of these instructions and Pub. 925 for the definition of rental activities. Include on line 3a, the gain (loss) from line 17 of Form 4797 that is attributable to the sale, exchange, or involuntary conversion of an asset used in a rental activity other than a rental real estate activity.

On line 3b of Schedule K, enter the deductible expenses of the activity. Attach a statement of these expenses to Form 1065.

Enter the net income (loss) on line 3c of Schedule K.

Schedule K-1. Enter each partner's distributive share of net income (loss) from rental activities other than rental real estate activities in box 3 of Schedule K-1. If the partnership has more than one rental activity reported in box 3, identify on an attachment to Schedule K-1 the amount from each activity. See *Passive Activity Reporting Requirements* on page 13.

Line 4. Guaranteed Payments to Partners

Guaranteed payments to partners include:

- Payments for salaries, health insurance, and interest deducted by the partnership and reported on Form 1065, page 1, line 10; Form 8825; or on Schedule K, line 3b; and
- Payments the partnership must capitalize. See the Instructions for Form 1065, line 10.

Generally, amounts reported on line 4 are not considered to be related to a passive activity. For example, guaranteed payments for personal services paid to a partner would not be passive activity income. Likewise, interest paid to any partner is not passive activity income.

Schedule K-1. Enter each partner's guaranteed payments in box 4 of Schedule K-1.

Portfolio Income

See page 11 of these instructions for a definition of portfolio income.

Do not reduce portfolio income by deductions allocated to it. Report such deductions (other than interest expense) on line 13b of Schedule K. Report each partner's distributive share of deductions (other than interest) allocable to portfolio income in box 13 of Schedule K-1, using codes G, H, and J.

Interest expense allocable to portfolio income is generally investment interest expense. It is reported on line 13c of Schedule K. Report each partner's distributive share of interest expense allocable to portfolio income in box 13 of Schedule K-1 using code I.

Line 5. Interest Income

Enter only taxable portfolio interest on this line. Taxable interest is interest from all sources except interest exempt from tax and interest on tax-free covenant bonds.

Schedule K-1. Enter each partner's distributive share of interest income in box 5 of Schedule K-1.

Line 6a. Ordinary Dividends

Enter only total taxable ordinary dividends on line 6a, including any qualified dividends reported on line 6b.

Schedule K-1. Enter each partner's distributive share of ordinary dividends in box 6a of Schedule K-1.

Line 6b. Qualified Dividends

Enter qualified dividends on line 6b. Except as provided below, qualified dividends are dividends received from domestic corporations and qualified foreign corporations.

Exceptions. The following dividends are not qualified dividends.

- Dividends the partnership received on any share of stock held for less than 61 days during the 121-day period that began 60 days before the ex-dividend date. When determining the number of days the partnership held the stock, it cannot count certain days during which the partnership's risk of loss was diminished. The ex-dividend date is the first date following the declaration of a dividend on which the purchaser of a stock is not entitled to receive the next dividend payment. When counting the number of days the partnership held the stock, include the day the partnership disposed of the stock but not the day the partnership acquired it.
- Dividends attributable to periods totaling more than 366 days that the partnership received on any share of preferred stock held for less than 91 days during the 181-day period that began 90 days before the ex-dividend date. When determining the number of days the partnership held the stock, do not count certain days during which the partnership's risk of loss was diminished. Preferred dividends attributable to periods totaling less than 367 days are subject to the 61-day holding period rule above.
- Dividends that relate to payments that the partnership is obligated to make with respect to short sales or positions in substantially similar or related property.
- Dividends paid by a regulated investment company that are not treated as qualified dividend income under section 854.
- Dividends paid by a real estate investment trust that are not treated as qualified dividend income under section 857(c).

See Pub. 550 for more details.

Qualified foreign corporation. A foreign corporation is a qualified foreign corporation if it is:

1. Incorporated in a possession of the United States or
2. Eligible for benefits of a comprehensive income tax treaty with the United States that the Secretary determines is satisfactory for this purpose and that includes an exchange of information program. See Notice 2003-69, 2003-42 I.R.B. 851, for details.

If the foreign corporation does not meet either 1 or 2, then it may be treated as a qualified foreign corporation for any dividend paid by the corporation if the stock associated with the dividend paid is readily tradable on an established securities market in the United States.

However, qualified dividends do not include dividends paid by the following foreign entities in either the tax year of the distribution or the preceding tax year.

- A foreign investment company (defined in section 1246(b)),
- A passive foreign investment company (defined in section 1297), or
- A foreign personal holding company (defined in section 552).

See Notice 2004-71, 2004-45 I.R.B. 793, for more details.

Schedule K-1. Enter each partner's distributive share of qualified dividends in box 6b of Schedule K-1.

Line 7. Royalties

Enter the royalties received by the partnership.

Schedule K-1. Enter each partner's distributive share of royalties in box 7 of Schedule K-1.

Line 8. Net Short-Term Capital Gain (Loss)

Enter the gain (loss) from line 5 of Schedule D (Form 1065).

Schedule K-1. Enter each partner's distributive share of net short-term capital gain (loss) in box 8 of Schedule K-1.

Line 9a. Net Long-Term Capital Gain (Loss)

Enter the gain or loss that is portfolio income (loss) from Schedule D (Form 1065), line 11.

Schedule K-1. Enter each partner's distributive share of net long-term capital gain (loss) in box 9a of Schedule K-1.

If any gain or loss from lines 5 or 11 of Schedule D is from the disposition of nondepreciable personal property used in a trade or business, it may not be treated as portfolio income. Instead, report it on line 11 of Schedule K and report each partner's distributive share in box 11 of Schedule K-1 using code F.

Line 9b. Collectibles (28%) Gain (Loss)

Figure the amount attributable to collectibles from the amount reported on Schedule D (Form 1065) line 11. A collectibles gain (loss) is any long-term gain or deductible long-term loss from the sale or exchange of a collectible that is a capital asset.

Collectibles include works of art, rugs, antiques, metal (such as gold, silver, platinum bullion), gems, stamps, coins, alcoholic beverages, and certain other tangible property.

Also, include gain (but not loss) from the sale or exchange of an interest in a partnership or trust held for more than 1 year and attributable to unrealized appreciation of collectibles. For details, see Regulations section 1.1(h)-1. Also attach the statement required under Regulations section 1.1(h)-1(e).

Schedule K-1. Report each partner's distributive share of the collectibles (28%) gain (loss) in box 9b of Schedule K-1.

Line 9c. Unrecaptured Section 1250 Gain

The three types of unrecaptured section 1250 gain must be reported separately on an attached statement to Form 1065.

From the sale or exchange of the partnership's business assets. Figure this amount for each section 1250 property in Part III of Form 4797 (except property for which gain is reported using the installment method on Form 6252) for which you had an entry in Part I of Form 4797 by subtracting line 26g of Form 4797 from the smaller of line 22 or line 24. Figure the total of these amounts for all section 1250 properties. Generally, the result is the partnership's unrecaptured section 1250 gain. However, if the partnership is reporting gain on the installment method for a section 1250 property held more than 1 year, see the next paragraph to figure the unrecaptured section 1250 gain on that property for this tax year.

The total unrecaptured section 1250 gain for an installment sale of section 1250 property held more than 1 year is figured in a manner similar to that used in the preceding paragraph. However, the total unrecaptured section 1250 gain must be allocated to the installment payments received from the sale. To do so, the partnership generally must treat the gain allocable to each installment payment as unrecaptured section 1250 gain until all such gain has been used in full. Figure the unrecaptured section 1250 gain for installment payments received during the tax year as the smaller of (a) the amount from line 26 or line 37 of Form 6252 (whichever applies) or (b) the total unrecaptured section 1250 gain for the sale reduced by all gain reported in prior years (excluding section 1250 ordinary income recapture).

CAUTION *If the partnership chose not to treat all of the gain from payments received after May 6, 1997, and before August 24, 1999, as unrecaptured section 1250 gain, use only the amount the partnership chose to treat as unrecaptured section 1250 gain for those payments to reduce the total unrecaptured section 1250 gain remaining to be reported for the sale.*

From the sale or exchange of an interest in a partnership. Also report as a separate amount any gain from the sale or exchange of an interest in a partnership attributable to unrecaptured section 1250 gain. See Regulations section 1.1(h)-1 and attach a statement required under Regulations section 1.1(h)-1(e).

From an estate, trust, REIT, or RIC. If the partnership received a Schedule K-1 or Form 1099-DIV from an estate, a trust, a real estate investment trust (REIT), or a regulated investment company (RIC) reporting "unrecaptured section 1250 gain," do not add it to the partnership's own unrecaptured section 1250 gain. Instead, report it as a separate amount. For example, if the partnership received a Form 1099-DIV from a REIT with unrecaptured section 1250 gain, report it as "Unrecaptured section 1250 gain from a REIT."

Schedule K-1. Report each partner's share of unrecaptured section 1250 gain from the sale or exchange of the partnership's business assets in box 9c of Schedule K-1.

If the partnership is reporting unrecaptured section 1250 gain from an estate, trust, REIT, or RIC or from the partnership's sale or exchange of an interest in another partnership (as explained on page 24), enter "STMT" in box 9c and an asterisk (*) in the left column of the box and attach a statement that separately identifies the amount of unrecaptured section 1250 gain from:

- The sale or exchange of the partnership's business assets.
- The sale or exchange of an interest in another partnership.
- An estate, trust, REIT, or RIC.

Line 10. Net Section 1231 Gain (Loss)

Enter the net section 1231 gain (loss) from Form 4797, line 7, column (g).

Do not include net gain or loss from involuntary conversions due to casualty or theft. Report net gain or loss from involuntary conversions due to casualty or theft on line 11 of Schedule K (box 11, code B, of Schedule K-1). See the instructions for line 11 on how to report net gain from involuntary conversions.

Schedule K-1. Report each partner's distributive share of net section 1231 gain (loss) in box 10 of Schedule K-1. If the partnership has more than one rental, trade, or business activity, identify on an attachment to Schedule K-1 the amount of section 1231 gain (loss) from each separate activity. See *Passive Activity Reporting Requirements* on page 13.

Line 11. Other Income (Loss)

Enter any other item of income or loss not included on lines 1 through 10. Attach a statement to Form 1065 that separately identifies each type and amount of income for each of the following six categories. The codes needed for Schedule K-1 reporting are provided for each category.

Other portfolio income (loss) (code A). Portfolio income not reported on lines 5 through 10.

Report and identify other portfolio income or loss on an attachment for line 11.

For example, income reported to the partnership from a real estate mortgage investment conduit (REMIC), in which the partnership is a residual interest holder, would be reported on an attachment for line 11. If the partnership holds a residual interest in a REMIC, report on the attachment for box 11 of Schedule K-1 of the partner's share of the following:

- Taxable income (net loss) from the REMIC (line 1b of Schedules Q (Form 1066)).
- "Excess inclusion" (line 2c of Schedules Q (Form 1066)).
- Section 212 expense (line 3b of Schedules Q (Form 1066)). Do not report these section 212 expense deductions related to portfolio income on Schedules K and K-1.

Because Schedule Q (Form 1066) is a quarterly statement, the partnership must follow the Schedule Q instructions to figure the amounts to report to the partner for the partnership's tax year.

Involuntary conversions (code B). Net gain (loss) from involuntary conversions due to casualty or theft. The amount for this line is shown on Form 4684, Casualties and Thefts, line 38a, 38b, or 39.

Each partner's share must be entered on Schedule K-1. Give each partner a schedule that shows the amounts to be reported on the partner's Form 4684, line 34, columns (b)(i), (b)(ii), and (c).

If there was a gain (loss) from a casualty or theft to property not used in a trade or business or for income-producing purposes, notify the partner. The partnership should not complete Form 4684 for this type of casualty or theft. Instead, each partner will complete his or her own Form 4684.

Section 1256 contracts and straddles (code C). Any net gain or loss from section 1256 contracts from Form 6781, Gains and Losses From Section 1256 Contracts and Straddles.

Mining exploration costs recapture (code D). Provide the information partners will need to recapture certain mining exploration expenditures. See Regulations section 1.617-3.

Cancellation of debt (code E). If cancellation of debt is reported to the partnership on Form 1099-C, report each partner's distributive share in box 11 using code E.

Note. Include the amount of income the partnership must recognize for a transfer of a partnership interest, after October 21, 2004, in satisfaction of a partnership debt when the debt relieved exceeds the FMV of the partnership interest. See section 108(e)(8) for more information.

Other income (loss) (code F). Include any other type of income, such as:

- Recoveries of tax benefit items (section 111).
- Gambling gains and losses subject to the limitations in section 165(d). Indicate on an attached statement whether or not the partnership is in the trade or business of gambling.
- Disposition of an interest in oil, gas, geothermal, or other mineral properties. Report the following information on an attached statement to Schedule K-1.
(a) Description of the property,
(b) The partner's share of the amount realized on the sale, exchange, or involuntary conversion of each property (fair market value of the property for any other disposition, such as a distribution),
(c) The partner's share of the partnership's adjusted basis in the property (except for oil or gas properties), and
(d) Total intangible drilling costs, development costs, and mining exploration costs (section 59(e) expenditures) passed through to partners for the property.
See Regulation section 1.1254-5 for more information.
- Gains from the disposition of farm recapture property (see Form 4797) and other items to which section 1252 applies.
- Any income, gain, or loss to the partnership under section 751(b).
- Specially allocated ordinary gain (loss).
- Gain from the sale or exchange of qualified small business stock (as defined in the instructions for Schedule D) that is eligible for the partial section 1202 exclusion. The section 1202 exclusion applies only to qualified small business stock held by the partnership for more than 5 years. Corporate partners are not eligible for the section 1202 exclusion. Additional limitations apply at the partner level. Report each partner's share of section 1202 gain on Schedule K-1. Each partner will determine if he or she qualifies for the section 1202 exclusion. Report on an attachment to Schedule K-1 for each sale or exchange the name of the corporation that issued the stock, the partner's share of the partnership's adjusted basis and sales price of the stock, and the dates the stock was bought and sold.
- Gain eligible for section 1045 rollover (replacement stock purchased by the partnership). Include only gain from the sale or exchange of qualified small business stock (as defined in the instructions for Schedule D) that was deferred by the partnership under section 1045 and reported on Schedule D. See the instructions for Schedule D for more details. Corporate partners are not eligible for the section 1045 rollover. Additional limitations apply at the partner level. Report each partner's share of the gain eligible for section 1045 rollover on Schedule K-1. Each partner will determine if he or she qualifies for the rollover. Report on an attachment to Schedule K-1 for each sale or exchange the name of the corporation that issued the stock, the partner's share of the partnership's adjusted basis and sales price of the stock, and the dates the stock was bought and sold.
- Gain eligible for section 1045 rollover (replacement stock not purchased by the partnership). Include only gain from the sale or exchange of qualified small business stock (as defined in the instructions for Schedule D) the partnership held for more than 6 months but that was not deferred by the partnership under section 1045. See the instructions for Schedule D for more details. A partner (other than a corporation) may be eligible to defer his or her distributive share of this gain under section 1045 if he or she purchases other qualified small business stock during the 60-day period that began on the date the stock was sold by the partnership. Additional limitations apply at the partner level. Report on an attachment to Schedule K-1 for each sale or exchange the name of the corporation that issued the stock, the partner's share of the partnership's adjusted basis and sales price of the stock, and the dates the stock was bought and sold.
- Any gain or loss from lines 5 or 11 of Schedule D that is not portfolio income (for example gain or loss from the disposition of nondepreciable personal property used in a trade or business).

Schedule K-1. Enter each partner's distributive share of the six other income categories listed above in box 11 of Schedule K-1. Enter the applicable code A, B, C, D, E, or F (as shown above).

If you are reporting each partner's distributive share of only one type of income under code F, enter the code with an asterisk (F*) and the dollar amount in the entry space in box 11 and attach a statement that shows "Box 11, Code F," and the type of income. If you are reporting multiple types of income under code F, enter the code with an asterisk (F*) and enter "STMT" in the entry space in box 11 and attach a statement that shows "Box 11, Code F," and the dollar amount of each type of income.

If the partnership has more than one trade or business or rental activity (for codes B through F), identify on an attachment to Schedule K-1 the amount from each separate activity. See *Passive Activity Reporting Requirements* on page 13.

Deductions

Line 12. Section 179 Deduction

A partnership can elect to expense part of the cost of certain property the partnership purchased this year for use in its trade or business or certain rental activities. See Pub. 946 for a definition of what kind of property qualifies for the section 179 expense deduction and the Instructions for Form 4562 for limitations on the amount of the section 179 expense deduction.

Complete Part I of Form 4562 to figure the partnership's section 179 expense deduction. The partnership does not claim the deduction itself but instead passes it through to the partners. Attach Form 4562 to Form 1065 and show the total section 179 expense deduction on Schedule K, line 12.

If the partnership is an enterprise zone business, also report on an attachment to Schedules K and K-1 the cost of section 179 property placed in service during the year that is qualified zone property.

See the instructions for line 20c of Schedule K for sales or other dispositions of property for which a section 179 deduction has passed through to partners and for the recapture rules if the business use of the property dropped to 50% or less.

Schedule K-1. Report each partner's distributive share of the section 179 expense deduction in box 12 of Schedule K-1. If the partnership has more than one rental, trade, or business activity, identify on an attachment to Schedule K-1 the amount of section 179 deduction from each separate activity. See *Passive Activity Reporting Requirements* on page 13.

Do not complete box 12 of Schedule K-1 for any partner that is an estate or trust; estates and trusts are not eligible for the section 179 expense deduction.

Line 13a. Contributions

Generally, no deduction is allowed for any contribution of $250 or more unless the partnership obtains a written acknowledgment from the charitable organization that shows the amount of cash contributed, describes any property contributed, and gives an estimate of the value of any goods or services provided in return for the contribution. The acknowledgment must be obtained by the due date (including extensions) of the partnership return or, if earlier, the date the partnership files its return. Do not attach the acknowledgment to the tax return, but keep it with the partnership's records. These rules apply in addition to the filing requirements for Form 8283 described below.

Enter the amount of charitable contributions made during the tax year. Attach a statement to Form 1065 that separately identifies the partnership's contributions for each of the following six categories. See *Limits on Deductions* in Publication 526, Charitable Contributions, for information on adjusted gross income (AGI) limitations on deductions for charitable contributions. The codes needed for Schedule K-1 reporting are provided for each category.

Cash contributions (50%) (code A). Enter the amount of cash contributions subject to the 50% AGI limitation.

Cash contributions (30%) (code B). Enter the amount of cash contributions subject to the 30% AGI limitation.

Noncash contributions (50%) (code C). Enter the amount of noncash contributions subject to the 50% AGI limitation.

Noncash contributions (30%) (code D). Enter the amount of noncash contributions subject to the 30% AGI limitation.

Capital gain property to a 50% organization (30%) (code E). Enter the amount of capital gain property contributions subject to the 30% AGI limitation.

Capital gain property (20%) (code F). Enter the amount of capital gain property contributions subject to the 20% AGI limitation.

Contributions of property. See *Contributions of Property* in Pub. 526 for information on noncash contributions and contributions of capital gain property. If the deduction claimed for noncash contributions exceeds $500, complete Form 8283, Noncash Charitable Contributions, and attach it to Form 1065.

If the partnership made a qualified conservation contribution under section 170(h), also include the fair market value of the underlying property before and after the donation, as well as the type of legal interest contributed, and describe the conservation purpose furthered by the donation. Give a copy of this information to each partner.

Nondeductible contributions. Certain contributions made to an organization conducting lobbying activities are not deductible. See section 170(f)(9) for more details. Also, see *Contributions You Cannot Deduct* in Publication 526 for more examples of nondeductible contributions.

Schedule K-1. Report each partner's distributive share of charitable contributions in box 13 of Schedule K-1 using codes A through F for each of the six contribution categories shown above. See the above instructions for *Contributions of property* for information on a statement concerning qualified conservation contributions that you may be required to attach to Schedule K-1. The partnership must attach a copy of its Form 8283 to the Schedule K-1 of each partner if the deduction for any item or group of similar items of contributed property exceeds $5,000, even if the amount allocated to any partner is $5,000 or less.

Line 13b. Deductions Related to Portfolio Income

Enter on line 13b the deductions clearly and directly allocable to portfolio income (other than interest expense and section 212 expenses from a REMIC). Attach a statement to Form 1065 that separately identifies the partnership's deduction related to portfolio income for each of the following categories. The codes needed for Schedule K-1 reporting are provided for each category.

Deductions—royalty income (code J). Enter the deductions related to royalty income.

Deductions—portfolio (2% floor) (code G). Enter the deductions related to portfolio income that are subject to the 2% of AGI floor (see the instructions for Schedule A (Form 1040)).

Deductions—portfolio (other) (code H). Enter the amount of any other deductions related to portfolio income.

No deduction is allowable under section 212 for expenses allocable to a convention, seminar, or similar meeting. Because these expenses are not deductible by partners, the partnership does not report these expenses on line 13b of Schedule K. The expenses are nondeductible and are reported as such on line 18c of Schedule K and in box 18 of Schedule K-1 using code C.

Schedule K-1. In box 13, report each partner's distributive share of deductions related to portfolio income that are reported on line 13b of Schedule K using code J (for deductions related to royalty income); G (for deductions related to portfolio income and subject to the 2% of AGI floor); or H (for other deductions related to portfolio income).

Line 13c. Investment Interest Expense

Include on this line the interest properly allocable to debt on property held for investment purposes. Property held for investment includes property that produces income (unless derived in the ordinary course of a trade or business) from interest, dividends, annuities, or royalties; and gains from the disposition of property that produces those types of income or is held for investment.

Investment interest expense does not include interest expense allocable to a passive activity.

Investment income and investment expenses other than interest are reported on lines 20a and 20b respectively. This information is needed by partners to determine the investment interest expense limitation (see Form 4952, Investment Interest Expense Deduction, for details).

Schedule K-1. Report each partner's distributive share of investment interest expense in box 13 of Schedule K-1 using code I.

Lines 13d(1) and 13d(2). Section 59(e)(2) Expenditures

Generally, section 59(e) allows each partner to make an election to deduct the partner's distributive share of the partnership's otherwise deductible qualified expenditures ratably over 10 years (3 years for circulation expenditures), beginning with the tax year in which the expenditures were made (or for intangible drilling and development costs, over the 60-month period beginning with the month in which such costs were paid or incurred).

The term "qualified expenditures" includes only the following types of expenditures paid or incurred during the tax year:

- Circulation expenditures.

• Research and experimental expenditures.
• Intangible drilling and development costs.
• Mining exploration and development costs.

If a partner makes the election, these items are not treated as tax preference items.

Because the partners are generally allowed to make this election, the partnership cannot deduct these amounts or include them as AMT items on Schedule K-1. Instead, the partnership passes through the information the partners need to figure their separate deductions.

On line 13d(1), enter the type of expenditures claimed on line 13d(2). Enter on line 13d(2) the qualified expenditures paid or incurred during the tax year to which an election under section 59(e) may apply. Enter this amount for all partners whether or not any partner makes an election under section 59(e).

On an attached statement, identify the property for which the expenditures were paid or incurred. If the expenditures were for intangible drilling costs or development costs for oil and gas properties, identify the month(s) in which the expenditures were paid or incurred. If there is more than one type of expenditure or more than one property, provide the amounts (and the months paid or incurred if required) for each type of expenditure separately for each property.

Schedule K-1. Report each partner's distributive share of section 59(e) expenditures in box 13 of Schedule K-1 using code K. On an attached statement, identify (a) the type of expenditure, (b) the property for which the expenditures are paid or incurred, and (c) for oil and gas properties only, the month in which intangible drilling costs and development costs were paid or incurred. If there is more than one type of expenditure or the expenditures are for more than one property, provide each partner's distributive share of the amounts (and the months paid or incurred for oil and gas properties) for each type of expenditure separately for each property.

Line 13e. Other Deductions

Enter deductions not included on lines 12, 13a, 13b, 13c, 13d(2), 16l(1), and 16l(2). Attach a statement to Form 1065 that separately identifies the type and amount of each deduction for the following nine categories. The codes needed for Schedule K-1 reporting are provided for each category.

Amounts paid for medical insurance (code L). Enter amounts paid during the tax year for insurance that constitutes medical care for the partner (including the partner's spouse and dependents.)

Educational assistance benefits (code M). Enter amounts paid during the tax year for educational assistance benefits paid to a partner.

Dependent care benefits (code N). Enter amounts paid during the tax year for dependent care benefits paid on behalf of each partner.

Preproductive period expenses (code O). If the partnership is required to use an accrual method of accounting under section 447 or 448(a)(3), it must capitalize these expenses. If the partnership is permitted to use the cash method, enter the amount of preproductive period expenses that qualify under Regulations section 1.263-4(d). An election not to capitalize these expenses must be made at the partner level. See *Uniform Capitalization Rules* in Publication 225, Farmer's Tax Guide.

Commercial revitalization deduction from rental real estate activities (code P). Enter the commercial revitalization deduction on line 13e only if it is for a rental real estate activity. If the deduction is for a nonrental building, it is deducted by the partnership on line 20 of Form 1065. See the instructions for line 20 on page 18 for more information.

Penalty on early withdrawal of savings (code Q). Enter the amount of any penalty on early withdrawal of savings not reported on line 13b because the partnership withdrew funds from its time savings deposit before its maturity.

Pensions and IRAs (code R). Enter the payments for a partner to an IRA, qualified plan, or simplified employee pension (SEP) or SIMPLE IRA plan. If a qualified plan is a defined benefit plan, a partner's distributive share of payments is determined in the same manner as his or her distributive share of partnership taxable income. For a defined benefit plan, attach to the Schedule K-1 for each partner a statement showing the amount of benefit accrued for the tax year.

Reforestation expense deduction (code S). The partnership can elect to deduct a limited amount of its reforestation expenditures paid or incurred after October 22, 2004. The amount the partnership may elect to deduct is limited to $10,000 for each qualified timber property. See section 194(c) for a definition of reforestation expenditures and qualified timber property. Provide a description of the qualified timber property on an attached statement to Form 1065 and Schedule K-1. If the partnership is electing to deduct amounts for more than one qualified timber property, provide a description and the amount for each property on the statement. The partnership must amortize over 84 months any amount not deducted. See the instructions for line 20 on page 18.

Other deductions (code T). Include any other deduction, such as:

• Amounts paid by the partnership that would be allowed as itemized deductions on any of the partners' income tax returns if they were paid directly by a partner for the same purpose. These amounts include, but are not limited to, expenses under section 212 for the production of income other than from the partnership's trade or business. However, do not enter expenses related to portfolio income or investment interest expense reported on line 13c of Schedule K on this line.
• Soil and water conservation expenditures (section 175).
• Expenditures paid or incurred for the removal of architectural and transportation barriers to the elderly and disabled that the partnership has elected to treat as a current expense. See section 190.
• Interest expense allocated to debt-financed distributions. See Notice 89-35, 1989-1 C.B. 675, or Publication 535, chapter 5, for more information.
• Interest paid or accrued on debt properly allocable to each general partner's share of a working interest in any oil or gas property (if the partner's liability is not limited). General partners that did not materially participate in the oil or gas activity treat this interest as investment interest; for other general partners, it is trade or business interest.
• Contributions to a capital construction fund.

Schedule K-1. Enter each partner's distributive share of the nine deduction categories listed above in box 13 of Schedule K-1. Enter the applicable code L, M, N, O, P, Q, R, S, or T (as shown above). If you are reporting only one type of deduction under code T, enter code T with an asterisk (T*) and the dollar amount in the entry space in box 13 and attach a statement that shows the box number, code, and type of deduction. If you are reporting multiple types of deductions under code T, enter the code with an asterisk (T*) and enter "STMT" in the dollar amount entry space in box 13 and attach a statement that shows the box number, code, and the dollar amount of each type of deductions. If the partnership has more than one trade or business activity, identify on an attachment to Schedule K-1 the amount for each separate activity. See *Passive Activity Reporting Requirements* on page 13.

Self-Employment

Note. If the partnership is an options dealer or a commodities dealer, see section 1402(i) before completing lines 14a, 14b, and 14c, to determine the amount of any adjustment that may have to be made to the amounts shown on the *Worksheet for Figuring Net Earnings (Loss) From Self-Employment* on page 28. If the partnership is engaged solely in the operation of a group investment program, earnings from the operation are not self-employment earnings for either general or limited partners.

General partners. General partners' net earnings (loss) from self-employment do not include:

• Dividends on any shares of stock and interest on any bonds, debentures, notes, etc., unless the dividends or interest are received in the course of a trade or business, such as a dealer in stocks or securities or interest on notes or accounts receivable.
• Rentals from real estate, except rentals of real estate held for sale to customers in the course of a trade or business as a real estate dealer or payments for rooms or space when significant services are provided.
• Royalty income, except royalty income received in the course of a trade or business.

See the instructions for Schedule SE (Form 1040), Self-Employment Tax, for more information.

Limited partners. Generally, a limited partner's share of partnership income (loss) is not included in net earnings (loss) from self-employment. Limited partners treat as self-employment earnings only guaranteed payments for services they actually rendered to, or on behalf of, the partnership to the extent that those payments are payment for those services.

Line 14a. Net Earnings (Loss) From Self-Employment

Schedule K. Enter on line 14a the amount from line 5 of the worksheet.

Schedule K-1. Do not complete this line for any partner that is an estate, trust, corporation, exempt organization, or individual retirement arrangement (IRA).

Enter in box 14 of Schedule K-1 each individual general partner's share of the amount shown on line 5 of the worksheet and each individual limited partner's share of the amount shown on line 4c of the worksheet, using code A.

Line 14b. Gross Farming or Fishing Income

Enter on line 14b the partnership's gross farming or fishing income from self-employment. Individual partners need this amount to figure net earnings from self-employment under the farm optional method in Section B, Part II of Schedule SE (Form 1040). Enter each individual partner's distributive share in box 14 of Schedule K-1 using code B.

Line 14c. Gross Nonfarm Income

Enter on line 14c the partnership's gross nonfarm income from self-employment. Individual partners need this amount to figure net earnings from self-employment under the nonfarm optional method in Section B, Part II of Schedule SE (Form 1040). Enter each individual partner's share in box 14 of Schedule K-1 using code C.

Worksheet Instructions

Line 1b. Include on line 1b any part of the net income (loss) from rental real estate activities from Schedule K, line 2, that is from:

1. Rentals of real estate held for sale to customers in the course of a trade or business as a real estate dealer or
2. Rentals for which services were rendered to the occupants (other than services usually or customarily rendered for the rental of space for occupancy only). The supplying of maid service is such a service; but the furnishing of heat and light, the cleaning of public entrances, exits, stairways and lobbies, trash collection, etc., are not considered services rendered to the occupants.

Lines 3b and 4b. Allocate the amounts on these lines in the same way Form 1065, page 1, line 22, is allocated to these particular partners.

Line 4a. Include in the amount on line 4a any guaranteed payments to partners reported on Schedule K, line 4, and Schedule K-1, box 4, and derived from a trade or business as defined in section 1402(c). Also include other ordinary business income and expense items (other than expense items subject to separate limitations at the partner level, such as the section 179 expense deduction) reported on Schedules K and K-1 that are used to figure self-employment earnings under section 1402.

Credits and Credit Recapture

Note. Do not attach Form 3800, General Business Credit, to Form 1065.

Low-Income Housing Credit

Section 42 provides a credit that can be claimed by owners of low-income residential rental buildings. If the partners are eligible to take the low-income housing credit, complete and attach Form 8586, Low-Income Housing Credit; Form 8609, Low-Income Housing Credit Allocation Certification; and Schedule A (Form 8609), Annual Statement, to Form 1065.

Note. If part or all of the credit reported on lines 15a or 15b is attributable to additions to qualified basis of property placed in service before 1990, report on an attachment to Schedules K and K-1 the amount of the credit on each line that is attributable to property placed in service (a) before 1990 and (b) after 1989.

Line 15a. Low-Income Housing Credit (Section 42(j)(5))

Enter on line 15a the total low-income housing credit for property with respect to which a partnership is to be treated under section 42(j)(5) as the taxpayer to which the low-income housing credit was allowed.

If the partnership invested in another partnership to which the provisions of section 42(j)(5) apply, report on line 15a the credit reported to the partnership on Schedule K-1 (Form 1065), box 15, code A.

Schedule K-1. Report in box 15 of Schedule K-1 each partner's distributive share of the low income housing credit reported on line 15a of Schedule K using code A. If the partnership has credits from more than one rental activity, identify on an attachment to Schedule K-1 the amount for each separate activity. See *Passive Activity Reporting Requirements* on page 13.

Line 15b. Low-Income Housing Credit (Other)

Enter on line 15b any low-income housing credit not reported on line 15a. This includes any credit reported to the partnership on Schedule K-1 (Form 1065), box 15, using code B.

Schedule K-1. Report in box 15 of Schedule K-1 each partner's distributive share of the low income housing credit reported on line 15b of Schedule K using code B. If the partnership has credits from more than one rental activity, identify on an attachment to Schedule K-1 the amount for each separate activity. See *Passive Activity Reporting Requirements* on page 13.

Line 15c. Qualified Rehabilitation Expenditures (Rental Real Estate)

Enter on line 15c the total qualified rehabilitation expenditures related to rental real estate activities of the partnership. Also complete the applicable lines of Form 3468, Investment Credit, that apply to qualified rehabilitation expenditures for property related to rental real estate activities of the

Worksheet for Figuring Net Earnings (Loss) From Self-Employment

1a	Ordinary business income (loss) (Schedule K, line 1)	1a	171257		
b	Net income (loss) from certain rental real estate activities (see instructions)	1b			
c	Other net rental income (loss) (Schedule K, line 3c)	1c			
d	Net loss from Form 4797, Part II, line 17, included on line 1a above. Enter as a positive amount	1d			
e	Combine lines 1a through 1d	1e	171257		
2	Net gain from Form 4797, Part II, line 17, included on line 1a above	2	8827		
3a	Subtract line 2 from line 1e. If line 1e is a loss, increase the loss on line 1e by the amount on line 2	3a	162430		
b	Part of line 3a allocated to limited partners, estates, trusts, corporations, exempt organizations, and IRAs	3b			
c	Subtract line 3b from line 3a. If line 3a is a loss, reduce the loss on line 3a by the amount on line 3b. Include each individual general partner's share in box 14 of Schedule K-1, using code A			3c	162430
4a	Guaranteed payments to partners (Schedule K, line 4) derived from a trade or business as defined in section 1402(c) (see instructions)	4a	43472		
b	Part of line 4a allocated to individual limited partners for other than services and to estates, trusts, corporations, exempt organizations, and IRAs	4b			
c	Subtract line 4b from line 4a. Include each individual general partner's share and each individual limited partner's share in box 14 of Schedule K-1, using code A			4c	43472
5	Net earnings (loss) from self-employment. Combine lines 3c and 4c. Enter here and on Schedule K, line 14a			5	205902

partnership for which income or loss is reported on line 2 of Schedule K. See Form 3468 for details on qualified rehabilitation expenditures. Attach Form 3468 to Form 1065.

Qualified rehabilitation expenditures for property not related to rental real estate activities must be reported on line 15f, "Other credits and credit recapture."

Schedule K-1. Report each partner's distributive share of qualified rehabilitation expenditures related to rental real estate activities in box 15 of Schedule K-1 using code C. Attach a statement to Schedule K-1 that separately identifies the partner's share of expenditures from pre-1936 buildings and from certified historic structures (lines 1b and 1c of Form 3468, respectively). If the partnership has expenditures from more than one rental real estate activity, identify on an attachment to Schedule K-1 the amount for each separate activity. See *Passive Activity Reporting Requirements* on page 13.

Line 15d. Other Rental Real Estate Credits

Enter on line 15d any other credit (other than credits reported on lines 15a through 15c) related to rental real estate activities. On the dotted line to the left of the entry space for line 15d, identify the type of credit. If there is more than one type of credit, attach a statement to Form 1065 that identifies the type and amount for each credit. These credits may include any type of credit listed in the instructions for line 15f.

Schedule K-1. Report in box 15 of Schedule K-1 each partner's distributive share of other rental real estate credits using code G. If you are reporting each partner's distributive share of only one type of rental real estate credit under code G, enter the code with an asterisk (G*) and the dollar amount in the entry space in box 15 and attach a statement that shows "Box 15, Code G," and type of credit. If you are reporting multiple types of rental real estate credit under code G, enter the code with an asterisk (G*) and enter a "STMT" in the entry space in box 15 and attach a statement that shows "Box 15, Code G, " and the type and dollar amount of the credits. If the partnership has credits from more than one rental real estate activity, identify on the attached statement the amount of each type of credit for each separate activity. See *Passive Activity Reporting Requirements* on page 13.

Line 15e. Other Rental Credits

Enter on line 15e any other credit (other than credits reported on lines 15a through 15d) related to rental activities. On the dotted line to the left of the entry space for line 15e, identify the type of credit. If there is more than one type of credit, attach a statement to Form 1065 that identifies the type and amount for each credit. These credits may include any type of credit listed in the instructions for line 15f.

Schedule K-1. Report in box 15 of Schedule K-1 each partner's distributive share of other rental credits using code H. If you are reporting each partner's distributive share of only one type of rental credit under code H, enter the code with an asterisk (H*) and the dollar amount in the entry space in box 15 and attach a statement that shows "Box 15, Code H," and type of credit. If you are reporting multiple types of rental credit under code H, enter the code with an asterisk (H*) and enter "STMT" in the entry space in box 15 and attach a statement that shows "Box 15, Code H," and the type and dollar amount of the credits. If the partnership has credits from more than one rental activity, identify on the attached statement the amount of each type of credit for each separate activity. See *Passive Activity Reporting Requirements* on page 13.

Line 15f. Other Credits and Credit Recapture

Enter on line 15f any other credit, except credits or expenditures shown or listed for lines 15a through 15e. Do not include any credit recapture amounts on line 15f, but provide credit recapture information on an attached statement of Schedule K-1 as explained below. On the dotted line to the left of the entry space for line 15f, identify the type of credit. If there is more than one type of credit or if there are any credits subject to recapture, attach a statement to Form 1065 that separately identifies each type and amount of credit and credit recapture information for the following categories. The codes needed for box 15 of Schedule K-1 are provided in the heading of each category.

Qualified rehabilitation expenditures (other than rental real estate) (code D). Enter total qualified rehabilitation expenditures from activities other than rental real estate activities. Complete line 1 of Form 3468, Investment Credit, for property not related to rental real estate activities of the partnership for which income or loss is reported on line 1 of Schedule K. See Form 3468 for details on qualified rehabilitation expenditures. Attach Form 3468 to Form 1065.

Note. Report qualified rehabilitation expenditures related to rental real estate activities on line 15c.

Schedule K-1. Report each partner's distributive share of qualified rehabilitation expenditures related to other than rental real estate activities in box 15 of Schedule K-1 using code D. Attach a statement to Schedule K-1 that separately identifies the partner's share of expenditures from pre-1936 buildings and from certified historic structures (lines 1b and 1c of Form 3468, respectively). If the partnership has expenditures from more than one activity, identify on a statement attached to Schedule K-1 the amount for each separate activity. See *Passive Activity Reporting Requirements* on page 13.

Basis of energy property (code E). Enter the basis of energy property placed in service during the tax year that qualifies for the energy credit. See the instructions for Form 3468 for details. Complete line 2 of Form 3468; attach Form 3468 to Form 1065.

Qualified timber property (code F). Enter the amortizable basis of timber property acquired before October 23, 2004, that qualifies for the reforestation credit. See the instructions for Form 3468 for details. Complete line 3 of Form 3468 and attach it to Form 1065.

Undistributed capital gains credit (code I). This credit represents taxes paid on undistributed capital gains by a regulated investment company (RIC) or a real estate investment trust (REIT). As a shareholder of a RIC or REIT, the partnership will receive notice of the amount of tax paid on undistributed capital gains on Form 2439, Notice to Shareholder of Undistributed Long-Term Capital Gains.

Work opportunity credit (code J). Complete Form 5884 to determine the amount of the credit. Attach it to Form 1065.

Welfare-to-work credit (code K). Complete Form 8861 to determine the amount of the credit. Attach it to Form 1065.

Disabled access credit (code L). Complete Form 8826 to determine the amount of the credit. Attach it to Form 1065.

Empowerment zone and renewal community employment credit (code M). Complete Form 8844 to determine the amount of the credit. Attach it to Form 1065.

New York Liberty Zone business employee credit (code N). Complete Form 8884 to determine the amount of the credit. Attach it to Form 1065.

New markets credit (code O). Complete Form 8874 to determine the amount of the credit. Attach it to Form 1065.

Credit for employer social security and Medicare taxes (code P). Complete Form 8846 to determine the amount of the credit. Attach it to Form 1065

Backup withholding (code Q). This credit is for backup withholding on dividends, interest, and other types of income of the partnership.

Recapture of low-income housing credit (codes R and S). If recapture of part or all of the low-income housing credit is required because (a) prior year qualified basis of a building decreased or (b) the partnership disposed of a building or part of its interest in a building, see Form 8611, Recapture of Low-Income Housing Credit. Complete lines 1 through 7 of Part I of Form 8611 to determine the amount of credit to recapture. Use code R on Schedule K-1 to report recapture of the low-income housing credit from a section 42(j)(5) partnership. Use code S to report recapture of any other low-income housing credit. See the instructions for lines 15a and 15b on page 28 for more information.

Note. If a partner's ownership interest in a building decreased because of a transaction at the partner level, the partnership must provide the necessary information to the partner to enable the partner to figure the recapture.

CAUTION *If the partnership filed Form 8693, Low-Income Housing Credit Disposition Bond, to avoid recapture of the low-income housing credit, no entry should be made on Schedule K-1.*

See Form 8586, Form 8611, and section 42 for more information.

Recapture of investment credit (code T). Complete and attach Form 4255, Recapture of Investment Credit, when investment credit property is disposed of, or it no longer qualifies for the credit, before the end of the recapture period or the useful life applicable to the property. State the type of property at the top of Form 4255, and complete lines 2,

4, and 5, whether or not any partner is subject to recapture of the credit.

Attach to each Schedule K-1 a separate statement providing the information the partnership is required to show on Form 4255, but list only the partner's distributive share of the cost of the property subject to recapture. Also indicate the lines of Form 4255 on which the partners should report these amounts.

Other credits (code U). Attach a statement to Form 1065 that identifies the type and amount of any other credits not reported elsewhere, such as:

- Nonconventional source fuel credit. The credit is figured at the partnership level and then is apportioned to the partners based on their distributive shares of partnership income attributable to sales of qualified fuels. Show the computation of this credit on a statement and attach it to Form 1065. See section 29 for more information.
- Qualified electric vehicle credit. Complete Form 8834 to determine the amount of the credit and attach it to Form 1065.
- Unused investment credit from cooperatives.
- Credit for alcohol used as fuel (Form 6478). This credit is apportioned to persons who were partners on the last day of the partnership's tax year. The credit must be included in income on page 1, line 7, of Form 1065. See section 40(f) for an election the partnership can make to not have the credit apply. If this credit includes the small ethanol producer credit, identify on a statement attached to each Schedule K-1 (a) the amount of the small producer credit included in the total credit allocated to the partner, (b) the number of gallons of qualified ethanol fuel production allocated to the partner, and (c) the partner's share in gallons of the partnership's productive capacity for alcohol.
- Credit for increasing research activities. Complete Form 6765 to determine the amount of the credit and attach it to Form 1065.
- Enhanced oil recovery credit. Complete Form 8830 to determine the amount of the credit and attach it to Form 1065.
- Renewable electricity and refined coal production credit. Complete Form 8835 to determine the amount of the credit. Attach a statement to Form 1065 and Schedule K-1 showing separately the amount of the credit from Section A and from Section B of Form 8835. Attach Form 8835 to Form 1065.
- Indian employment credit. Complete Form 8845 to determine the amount of the credit and attach it to Form 1065.
- Orphan drug credit. Complete Form 8820 to determine the amount of the credit and attach it to Form 1065.
- Credit for contributions to selected community development corporations. Complete Form 8847 to determine the amount of the credit and attach it to Form 1065.
- Credit for small employer pension start-up costs. Complete Form 8881 to determine the amount of the credit and attach it to Form 1065.
- Credit for employer-provided childcare facilities and services. Complete Form 8882 to determine the amount of the credit and attach it to Form 1065.
- Biodiesel fuels credit. Complete Form 8864 to determine the amount of the credit and attach it to Form 1065. The credit must be included in income on page 1, line 7 of Form 1065.
- Low sulfur diesel fuel production credit. Complete Form 8896 to determine the amount of the credit and attach it to Form 1065.
- General credits from an electing large partnership.

Recapture of other credits (code V). On an attached statement to Schedule K-1, provide any information partners will need to report recapture of credits (other than recapture of low-income housing credit and investment credit reported on Schedule K-1 using codes R, S, and T). Examples of credit recapture information reported using code V include:

- Any information needed by a partner to compute recapture of the qualified electric vehicle credit. See Pub. 535 for more information.
- Any information needed by a partner to compute recapture of the new markets credit. See Form 8874 for details on recapture.
- Any information needed by a partner to compute recapture of the Indian employment credit. Generally, if the partnership terminates a qualified employee less than 1 year after the date of initial employment, any Indian employment credit allowed for a prior tax year by reason of wages paid or incurred to that employee must be recaptured. For details, see section 45A(d).
- Any information needed by a partner to compute recapture of the credit for employer-provided childcare facilities and services. See section 45F(d) for details on recapture.

Schedule K-1. Enter in box 15 of Schedule K-1 each partner's distributive share of the credit and credit recapture categories listed above. See additional Schedule K-1 reporting information provided in the instructions above. Enter the applicable code D through V in the column to the left of the dollar amount entry space.

If you are reporting each partner's distributive share of only one type of credit under code U, enter the code with an asterisk (U*) and the dollar amount in the entry space in box 15 and attach a statement that shows "Box 15, Code U," and type of credit. If you are reporting multiple types of credit under code U, enter the code with an asterisk (U*) and enter "STMT" in the entry space in box 15 and attach a statement that shows "Box 15, Code U, " and the type and dollar amount of the credits. If the partnership has credits from more than one activity, identify on an attached statement to Schedule K-1 the amount of each type of credit for each separate activity. See *Passive Activity Reporting Requirements* on page 13.

Foreign Transactions

Lines 16a through 16m must be completed if the partnership has foreign income, deductions, or losses, or has paid or accrued foreign taxes.

The codes A through N for box 16 of Schedule K-1 correspond with the line numbers 16a through 16m. Codes O, P, and Q for box 16 are reported on line 20c of Schedule K. On Schedule K-1 for the items coded C, E, J, L, M, and N, enter the code followed by an asterisk and the partner's distributive share of the dollar amount. Attach a statement to Schedule K-1 for these coded items providing the information described below. If the partnership had income from, or paid or accrued taxes to, more than one country or U.S. possession, see the requirement for an attached statement in the instruction for line 16a below. See Pub. 514, Foreign Tax Credit for Individuals, and the Instructions for Form 1116, for more information.

Line 16a. Name of Country or U.S. Possession

Enter the name of the foreign country or U.S. possession from which the partnership had income or to which the partnership paid or accrued taxes. If the partnership had income from, or paid or accrued taxes to, more than one foreign country or U.S. possession, enter "See attached" and attach a statement for each country for lines 16a through 16m (codes A through N of Schedule K-1). On Schedule K-1, if there is more than one country enter code A followed by an asterisk (A*), enter "STMT," and attach a statement to Schedule K-1 for each country for the information and amounts coded A through N and code Q.

Line 16b. Gross Income From all Sources

Enter the partnership's gross income from all sources (both U.S. and foreign).

Line 16c. Gross Income Sourced at Partner Level

Enter the total gross income of the partnership that is required to be sourced at the partner level. This includes income from the sale of most personal property, other than inventory, depreciable property, and certain intangible property. See Pub. 514 and section 865 for details. Attach a statement to Form 1065 showing the following information.

- The amount of this gross income (without regard to its source) in each category identified in the instructions for lines 16d, 16e, and 16f, including each of the listed categories.
- Specifically identify gains on the sale of personal property other than inventory, depreciable property, and certain intangible property on which a foreign tax of 10% or more was paid or accrued. Also list losses on the sale of such property if the foreign country would have imposed a 10% or higher tax had the sale resulted in a gain. See *Sales or Exchanges of Certain Personal Property* in Pub. 514 and section 865.
- Specify foreign source capital gains or losses within each separate limitation category. Also separately identify foreign source gains or losses within each separate limitation category that are collectibles (28%) gains and losses or unrecaptured section 1250 gains.

Lines 16d–16f. Foreign Gross Income Sourced at Partnership Level

Separately report gross income from sources outside the United States by category of income as follows. See Pub. 514 for more information on the categories of income.

Line 16d. Passive foreign source income.

Line 16e. Listed categories of income. Attach a statement showing the amount of foreign source income included in each of the following listed categories.
- Financial services income;
- High withholding tax interest;
- Shipping income;
- Dividends from a domestic international sales corporation (DISC) or a former DISC;
- Distributions from a foreign sales corporation (FSC) or a former FSC;
- Section 901(j) income; and
- Certain income re-sourced by treaty.

Line 16f. General limitation foreign source income (all other foreign source income). Include all foreign income sourced at the partnership level that is not reported on lines 16d and 16e.

Lines 16g–16h. Deductions Allocated and Apportioned at Partner Level

Line 16g. Interest expense. Enter on line 16g the partnership's total interest expense (including interest equivalents under Temporary Regulations section 1.861-9T(b)). Do not include interest directly allocable under Temporary Regulations section 1.861-10T to income from a specific property. This type of interest is allocated and apportioned at the partnership level and is included on lines 16i through 16k.

Line 16h. Other. On line 16h, enter the total of all other deductions or losses that are required to be allocated at the partner level. For example, include on line 16h research and experimental expenditures (see Regulations section 1.861-17(f)).

Lines 16i–16k. Deductions Allocated and Apportioned at Partnership Level to Foreign Source Income

Separately report partnership deductions that are allocated and apportioned at the partnership level by category of income as follows. See Pub. 514 for more information.

Line 16i. Passive foreign source income.

Line 16j. Listed categories of income. Attach a statement showing the amount of deductions allocated and apportioned at the partnership level to each of the following listed categories.
- Financial services income;
- High withholding tax interest;
- Shipping income;
- Dividends from a domestic international sales corporation (DISC) or a former DISC;
- Distributions from a foreign sales corporation (FSC) or a former FSC;
- Section 901(j) income; and
- Certain income re-sourced by treaty.

Line 16k. General limitation foreign source income (all other foreign source income).

Line 16l. Total Foreign Taxes Paid or Accrued

Enter in U.S. dollars the total foreign taxes (described in section 901 or section 903) that were paid or accrued by the partnership (according to its method of accounting for such taxes). Enter the amount paid on line 16l(1) or enter the amount accrued on line 16l(2). Translate these amounts into U.S. dollars by using the applicable exchange rate (see Pub. 514).

Line 16l(1). Foreign taxes paid. If the partnership uses the cash method of accounting, enter foreign taxes paid during the tax year on line 16l(1). Report each partner's distributive share in box 16 of Schedule K-1 using code L.

Line 16l(2). Foreign taxes accrued. If the partnership uses the accrual method of accounting, enter foreign taxes accrued on line 16l(2). Report each partner's distributive share in box 16 of Schedule K-1 using code M.

A partnership reporting foreign taxes using the cash method can make an irrevocable election to report these taxes using the accrual method for the year of the election and all future years. Make this election by reporting all foreign taxes using the accrual method on line 16l(2) (see Regulations section 1.905-1).

Attach a statement reporting the following information.

1. The total amount of foreign taxes (including foreign taxes on income sourced at the partner level) relating to each category of income (see instructions for lines 16d–16f).
2. The dates on which the taxes were paid or accrued, the exchange rates used, and the amounts in both foreign currency and U.S. dollars, for:
   - Taxes withheld at source on interest.
   - Taxes withheld at source on dividends.
   - Taxes withheld at source on rents and royalties.
   - Other foreign taxes paid or accrued.

Line 16m. Reduction in Taxes Available for Credit

Enter the total reductions in taxes available for credit. Attach a statement showing the reductions for:
- Taxes on foreign mineral income (section 901(e)).
- Taxes on foreign oil and gas extraction income (section 907(a)).
- Taxes attributable to boycott operations (section 908).
- Failure to timely file (or furnish all of the information required on) Forms 5471 and 8865.
- Any other items (specify).

Alternative Minimum Tax (AMT) Items

Lines 17a through 17f must be completed for all partners except certain small corporations exempt from the alternative minimum tax (AMT) under section 55(e).

Enter items of income and deductions that are adjustments or tax preference items for the AMT. See Form 6251, Alternative Minimum Tax— Individuals; Form 4626, Alternative Minimum Tax—Corporations; or Schedule I of Form 1041, U.S. Income Tax Return for Estates and Trusts, to determine the amounts to enter and for other information.

Do not include as a tax preference item any qualified expenditures to which an election under section 59(e) may apply. Because these expenditures are subject to an election by each partner, the partnership cannot figure the amount of any tax preference related to them. Instead, the partnership must pass through to each partner in box 13, code K, of Schedule K-1 the information needed to figure the deduction.

Schedule K-1. Report each partner's distributive share of amounts reported on lines 17a through 17f (concerning alternative minimum tax items) in box 17 of Schedule K-1 using codes A through F, respectively. If the partnership is reporting items of income or deduction for oil, gas, and geothermal properties, you may be required to identify these items on a statement attached to Schedule K-1 (see the instructions for lines 17d and 17e for details). Also see the requirement for an attached statement in the instructions for line 17f.

Line 17a. Post-1986 Depreciation Adjustment

Figure the adjustment for line 17a based only on tangible property placed in service after 1986 (and tangible property placed in service after July 31, 1986, and before 1987 for which the partnership elected to use the general depreciation system). Do not make an adjustment for motion picture films, videotapes, sound recordings, certain public utility property (as defined in section 168(i)(10), property depreciated under the unit-of-production method (or any other method not expressed in a term of years), qualified Indian reservation property, property eligible for a special depreciation allowance, qualified revitalization expenditures, or the section 179 expense deduction.

For property placed in service before 1999, refigure depreciation for the AMT as follows (using the same convention used for the regular tax).
- For section 1250 property (generally, residential rental and nonresidential real property), use the straight line method over 40 years.
- For tangible property (other than section 1250 property) depreciated using the straight line method for the regular tax, use the straight line method over the property's class life. Use 12 years if the property has no class life.
- For any other tangible property, use the 150% declining balance method, switching to the straight line method the first tax year it gives a larger deduction, over the property's AMT class life. Use 12 years if the property has no class life.

Note. See Pub. 946 for a table of class lives.

For property placed in service after 1998, refigure depreciation for the AMT only for property depreciated for the regular tax using the 200% declining balance method. For the AMT, use the 150% declining balance method, switching to the straight line method the first tax year it gives a larger deduction, and the same convention and recovery period used for the regular tax.

Figure the adjustment by subtracting the AMT deduction for depreciation from the regular tax deduction and enter the result on line 17a. If the AMT deduction is more than the regular tax deduction, enter the difference as a negative amount. Depreciation capitalized to inventory must also be refigured using the AMT rules.

Include on this line the current year adjustment to income, if any, resulting from the difference.

Line 17b. Adjusted Gain (Loss)

If the partnership disposed of any tangible property placed in service after 1986 (or after July 31, 1986, if an election was made to use the General Depreciation System), or if it disposed of a certified pollution control facility placed in service after 1986, refigure the gain or loss from the disposition using the adjusted basis for the AMT. The property's adjusted basis for the AMT is its cost or other basis minus all depreciation or amortization deductions allowed or allowable for the AMT during the current tax year and previous tax years. Enter on this line the difference between the regular tax gain (loss) and the AMT gain (loss). If the AMT gain is less than the regular tax gain, or the AMT loss is more than the regular tax loss, or there is an AMT loss and a regular tax gain, enter the difference as a negative amount.

If any part of the adjustment is allocable to net short-term capital gain (loss), net long-term capital gain (loss), or net section 1231 gain (loss), attach a statement that identifies the amount of the adjustment allocable to each type of gain or loss.

For a net long-term capital gain (loss), also identify the amount of the adjustment that is collectibles (28%) gain (loss).

For a net section 1231 gain (loss), also identify the amount of adjustment that is unrecaptured section 1250 gain.

Line 17c. Depletion (Other Than Oil and Gas)

Do not include any depletion on oil and gas wells. The partners must figure their oil and gas depletion deductions and preference items separately under section 613A.

Refigure the depletion deduction under section 611 for mines, wells (other than oil and gas wells), and other natural deposits for the AMT. Percentage depletion is limited to 50% of the taxable income from the property as figured under section 613(a), using only income and deductions for the AMT. Also, the deduction is limited to the property's adjusted basis at the end of the year as figured for the AMT. Figure this limit separately for each property. When refiguring the property's adjusted basis, take into account any AMT adjustments made this year or in previous years that affect basis (other than the current year's depletion).

Enter the difference between the regular tax and AMT deduction. If the AMT deduction is greater, enter the difference as a negative amount.

Oil, Gas, and Geothermal Properties—Gross Income and Deductions

Generally, the amounts to be entered on lines 17d and 17e are only the income and deductions for oil, gas, and geothermal properties that are used to figure the partnership's ordinary income (loss) (line 22 of Form 1065).

If there are any items of income or deductions for oil, gas, and geothermal properties included in the amounts that are required to be passed through separately to the partners on Schedule K-1 (items not reported on line 1 of Schedule K-1), give each partner a statement that shows, for the box in which the income or deduction is included, the amount of income or deductions included in the total amount for that box. Do not include any of these direct pass-through amounts on line 17d or 17e. The partner is told in the Partner's Instructions for Schedule K-1 (Form 1065) to adjust the amounts in box 17, code D or E, for any other income or deductions from oil, gas, or geothermal properties included in boxes 2 through 13, and 19 or 20 of Schedule K-1 in order to determine the total income and deductions from oil, gas, and geothermal properties for the partnership.

Figure the amounts for lines 17d and 17e separately for oil and gas properties that are not geothermal deposits and for all properties that are geothermal deposits.

Give the partners a statement that shows the separate amounts included in the computation of the amounts on lines 17d and 17e of Schedule K.

Line 17d. Oil, Gas, and Geothermal Properties—Gross Income

Enter the total amount of gross income (within the meaning of section 613(a)) from all oil, gas, and geothermal properties received or accrued during the tax year and included on page 1, Form 1065.

Line 17e. Oil, Gas, and Geothermal Properties—Deductions

Enter the amount of any deductions allowed for the AMT that are allocable to oil, gas, and geothermal properties.

Line 17f. Other AMT Items

Attach a statement to Form 1065 and Schedule K-1 that shows other items not shown on lines 17a through 17e that are adjustments or tax preference items or that the partner needs to complete Form 6251, Form 4626, or Schedule I of Form 1041. See these forms and their instructions to determine the amount to enter.

Other AMT items include the following.

- Accelerated depreciation of real property under pre-1987 rules.
- Accelerated depreciation of leased personal property under pre-1987 rules.
- Long-term contracts entered into after February 28, 1986. Except for certain home construction contracts, the taxable income from these contracts must be figured using the percentage of completion method of accounting for the AMT.
- Losses from tax shelter farm activities. No loss from any tax shelter farm activity is allowed for the AMT.
- Any information needed by certain corporate partners to compute the adjusted current earnings (ACE) adjustment.

Schedule K-1. If you are reporting each partner's distributive share of only one type of AMT item under code F, enter the code with an asterisk (F*) and the dollar amount in the entry space in box 17 and attach a statement that shows the type of AMT item. If you are reporting multiple types of AMT items under code F, enter the code with an asterisk (F*) and enter "STMT" in the entry space in box 17 and attach a statement that shows the dollar amount of each type of AMT item.

Tax-Exempt Income and Nondeductible Expenses

Line 18a. Tax-exempt interest income. Enter on line 18a tax-exempt interest income, including any exempt-interest dividends received from a mutual fund or other regulated investment company. Individual partners must report this information on line 8b of Form 1040. The adjusted basis of the partner's interest is increased by the amount shown on this line under section 705(a)(1)(B).

Line 18b. Other tax-exempt income. Enter on line 18b all income of the partnership exempt from tax other than tax-exempt interest (for example, life insurance proceeds). The adjusted basis of the partner's interest is increased by the amount shown on this line under section 705(a)(1)(B).

Line 18c. Nondeductible expenses. Enter on line 18c nondeductible expenses paid or incurred by the partnership.

Do not include separately stated deductions shown elsewhere on Schedules K and K-1, capital expenditures, or items the deduction for which is deferred to a later tax year. The adjusted basis of the partner's interest is decreased by the amount shown on this line under section 705(a)(2)(B).

Schedule K-1. Report in box 18 of Schedule K-1 each partner's distributive share of amounts reported on lines 18a, 18b, and 18c of Schedule K (concerning items affecting partners' basis) using codes A through C, respectively.

Distributions

Line 19a. Distributions of cash and marketable securities. Enter on line 19a the total distributions to each partner of cash and marketable securities that are treated as money under section 731(c)(1). Generally, marketable securities are valued at FMV on the date of distribution. However, the value of marketable securities does not include the distributee partner's share of the gain on the securities distributed to that partner. See section 731(c)(3)(B) for details.

If the amount on line 19a includes marketable securities treated as money, state separately on an attachment to Schedules K and K-1 (a) the partnership's adjusted basis of those securities immediately before the distribution and (b) the FMV of those securities on the date of distribution (excluding the distributee partner's share of the gain on the securities distributed to that partner).

Line 19b. Distributions of other property. Enter on line 19b the total distributions to each partner of property not included on line 19a. In computing the amount of the distribution, use the adjusted basis of the property to the partnership immediately before the distribution. In addition, attach a statement showing the adjusted basis and FMV of each property distributed.

Schedule K-1. Report in box 19 each partner's distributive share of the amount on line 19a using code A and the amount on line 19b using code B. Attach a statement to Schedule K-1 that provides the information required in the instructions for lines 19a and 19b.

Other Information

Lines 20a and 20b. Investment Income and Expenses

Enter on line 20a the investment income included on lines 5, 6a, 7, and 11, of Schedule K. Do not include other portfolio gains or losses on this line.

Enter on line 20b the investment expense included on line 13b of Schedule K.

Investment income includes gross income from property held for investment, the excess of net gain attributable to the disposition of property held for investment over net capital gain from the disposition of property held for investment, and any net capital gain from the disposition of property held for investment that each partner elects to include in investment income under section 163(d)(4)(B)(iii). Generally, investment income and investment expenses do not include any income or expenses from a passive activity. See Regulations section 1.469-2(f)(10) for exceptions.

Property subject to a net lease is not treated as investment property because it is subject to the passive loss rules. Do not reduce investment income by losses from passive activities.

Investment expenses are deductible expenses (other than interest) directly connected with the production of investment income. See the Instructions for Form 4952 for more information.

Schedule K-1. Report each partner's distributive share of amounts reported on lines 20a and 20b (investment income and expenses) in box 20 of Schedule K-1 using codes A and B, respectively.

If there are other items of investment income or expense included in the amounts that are required to be passed through separately to the partners on Schedule K-1, such as net short-term capital gain or loss, net long-term capital gain or loss, and other portfolio gains or losses, give each partner a statement identifying these amounts.

Line 20c. Other Items and Amounts

Report the following information on a statement attached to Form 1065. On Schedule K-1 enter the appropriate code in box 20 for each information item followed by an asterisk in the left-hand column of the entry space (for example,"C*"). In the right-hand column, enter "STMT." The codes are provided for each information category.

Fuel tax credit information (code C). Report the number of gallons of each fuel sold or used during the tax year for a nontaxable use qualifying for the credit for taxes paid on fuel, type of use, and the applicable credit per gallon. See Form 4136, Credit for Federal Tax Paid on Fuels, for details.

Look-back interest—completed long-term contracts (code D). If the partnership is a closely held (defined in section 460(b)(4)) and it entered into any long-term contracts after February 28, 1986, that are accounted for under either the percentage of completion-capitalized cost method or the percentage of completion method, it must attach a statement to Form 1065 showing the information required in items (a) and (b) of the instructions for lines 1 and 3 of Part II of Form 8697. It must also report the amounts for Part II, lines 1 and 3, to its partners. See the Instructions for Form 8697 for more information.

Look-back interest—income forecast method (code E). If the partnership closely held (defined in section 460(b)(4)) and it depreciated certain property placed in service after September 13, 1995, under the income forecast method, it must attach to Form 1065 the information specified in the instructions for Form 8866, line 2, for the 3rd and 10th tax years beginning after the tax year the property was placed in service. It must also report the line 2 amounts to its partners. See the Instructions for Form 8866 for more details.

Dispositions of property with section 179 deductions (code F). This represents gain or loss on the sale, exchange, or other disposition of property for which a section 179 deduction has been passed through to partners. The partnership must provide all the following information with respect to such dispositions (see the instructions for line 6, on page 15).

- Description of the property.
- Date the property was acquired and placed in service.
- Date of the sale or other disposition of the property.
- The partner's share of the gross sales price or amount realized.
- The partner's share of the cost or other basis plus expense of sale (reduced as explained in the instructions for Form 4797, line 21).
- The partner's share of the depreciation allowed or allowable, determined as described in the instructions for Form 4797, line 22, but excluding the section 179 deduction.
- The partner's share of the section 179 deduction (if any) passed through for the property and the partnership's tax year(s) in which the amount was passed through.
- If the disposition is due to a casualty or theft, a statement indicating so, and any additional information needed by the partner.
- If the sale was an installment sale made during the partnership's tax year, any information the partner needs to complete Form 6252, Installment Sale Income. The partnership also must separately report the partner's share of all payments received for the property in the following tax years. (Installment payments received for sales made in prior tax years should be reported in the same manner used in the prior tax years.) See the instructions for Form 6252 for details.

Recapture of section 179 deduction (code G). This amount represents recapture of section 179 deduction if business use of the property dropped to 50% or less. If the business use of any property (placed in service after 1986) for which a section 179 deduction was passed through to partners dropped to 50% or less (for a reason other than disposition), the partnership must provide all the following information.

- The partner's distributive share of the original basis and depreciation allowed or allowable (not including the section 179 deduction).
- The partner's distributive share of the section 179 deduction (if any) passed through for the property and the partnership's tax year(s) in which the amount was passed through.

Special basis adjustments (code H). If the partnership holds oil and gas properties that are depleted at the partner level under section 613A(c)(7)(D) and is notified of a transfer of an interest in the partnership, it must attach a statement to the transferee partner's Schedule K-1 that identifies any section 743(b) basis adjustments to property, other than depletable oil and gas property, allocable to the partner.

Section 453(l)(3) information (code I). Supply any information needed by a partner to compute the interest due under section 453(l)(3). If the partnership elected to report the dispositions of certain timeshares and residential lots on the installment method, each partner's tax liability must be increased by the partner's distributive share of the interest on tax attributable to the installment payments received during the tax year.

Section 453A(c) information (code J). Supply any information needed by a partner to compute the interest due under section 453A(c). If an obligation arising from the disposition of property to which section 453A applies is outstanding at the close of the year, each partner's tax liability must be increased by the tax due under section 453A(c) on the partner's distributive share of the tax deferred under the installment method.

Section 1260(b) information (code K). Supply any information needed by a partner to figure the interest due under section 1260(b). If the partnership had gain from certain constructive ownership transactions, each partner's tax liability must be increased by the partner's distributive share of interest due on any deferral of gain recognition. See section 1260(b) for details, including how to figure the interest.

Interest allocable to production expenditures (code L). Supply any information needed by a partner to properly capitalize interest as required by section 263A(f). See *Section 263A uniform capitalization rules* on page 16 for more information.

CCF nonqualified withdrawal (code M). Report nonqualified withdrawals by the partnership from a capital construction fund to partners.

Information needed to figure depletion–oil and gas (code N). Report gross income and other information relating to oil and gas well properties to partners to allow them to figure the depletion deduction for oil and gas well properties. Allocate to each partner a proportionate share of the adjusted basis of each partnership oil or gas property. See section 613A(c)(7)(D) for details.

The partnership cannot deduct depletion on oil and gas wells. Each partner must determine the allowable amount to report on his or her return. See Pub. 535 for more information.

Amortization of reforestation costs (code O). Report the amortizable basis of reforestation expenditures paid or incurred before October 23, 2004, for which the partnership elected amortization, and the tax year the amortization began for the current tax year and the 7 preceding tax years. The amortizable basis cannot exceed $10,000 for each of those tax years.

Unrelated business taxable income (code P). Report any information a partner that is a tax-exempt organization may need to figure its share of unrelated business taxable income under section 512(a)(1) (but excluding any modifications required by paragraphs (8) through (15) of section 512(b)). Partners are required to notify the partnership of their tax-exempt status. See Form 990-T, Exempt Organization Business Income Tax Return, for more information.

Other information (code Q). Report to each partner:
• Any information a partner that is a publicly traded partnership may need to determine if it meets the 90% qualifying income test of section 7704(c)(2). Partners are required to notify the partnership of their status as a publicly traded partnership.
• Any information or statements the partners need to allow them to comply with the registration and disclosure requirements under section 6111 and section 6662(d)(2)(B)(ii) and the list keeping requirements of Regulations section 301.6112-1. See Form 8264 and Notice 2004-80, 2004-50 I.R.B. 963.
• If the partnership participates in a transaction that must be disclosed on Form 8886 (see page 8), both the partnership and its partners may be required to file Form 8886. The partnership must determine if any of its partners are required to disclose the transaction and provide those partners with information they will need to file Form 8886. This determination is based on the category(s) under which a transaction qualified for disclosures. See the instructions for Form 8886 for details.
• Any income or gain reported on lines 1 through 11 of Schedule K that qualify as inversion gain, if the partnership is an expatriated entity or is a partner in an expatriated entity. For details, see section 7874. Attach a statement to Form 1065 that shows the amount of each type of income or gain included in the inversion gain. The partnership must report each partner's distributive share of the inversion gain in box 20 of Schedule K-1 using code Q. Attach a statement to Schedule K-1 that shows the partner's distributive share of the amount of each type of income or gain included in the inversion gain.
• Any other information the partners need to prepare their tax returns.

Other Foreign Transactions (Box 16 of Schedule K-1, Codes O, P, and Q)

Do not report these amounts in box 20 of Schedule K-1. Instead, report them in Box 16 as explained below.

• **Foreign trading gross receipts (code O).** Report each partner's distributive share of foreign trading gross receipts from line 15 of Form 8873 in box 16 using code O. See *Extraterritorial Income Exclusion* on page 14.
• **Extraterritorial income exclusion (code P).** If the partnership is not permitted to deduct the extraterritorial income exclusion as a non-separately stated item, attach a statement to Schedule K-1 showing the partner's distributive share of the extraterritorial income exclusion reported on lines 52a and 52b of Form 8873. Also identify the activity to which the exclusion is related. See *Extraterritorial Income Exclusion* on page 14 for more information.
• **Other foreign transactions (code Q).** Report any other foreign transaction information the partners need to prepare their tax returns.

Analysis of Net Income (Loss)

For each type of partner shown, enter the portion of the amount shown on line 1 that was allocated to that type of partner. Report all amounts for LLC members on the line for limited partners. The sum of the amounts shown on line 2 must equal the amount shown on line 1. In addition, the amount on line 1 must equal the amount on line 9, Schedule M-1 (if the partnership is required to complete Schedule M-1).

In classifying partners who are individuals as "active" or "passive," the partnership should apply the rules below. In applying these rules, a partnership should classify each partner to the best of its knowledge and belief. It is assumed that in most cases the level of a particular partner's participation in an activity will be apparent.

1. If the partnership's principal activity is a trade or business, classify a general partner as "active" if the partner materially participated in all partnership trade or business activities; otherwise, classify a general partner as "passive."

2. If the partnership's principal activity consists of a working interest in an oil or gas well, classify a general partner as "active."

3. If the partnership's principal activity is a rental real estate activity, classify a general partner as "active" if the partner actively participated in all of the partnership's rental real estate activities; otherwise, classify a general partner as "passive."

4. Classify as "passive" all partners in a partnership whose principal activity is a rental activity other than a rental real estate activity.

5. If the partnership's principal activity is a portfolio activity, classify all partners as "active."

6. Classify as "passive" all limited partners and LLC members in a partnership whose principal activity is a trade or business or rental activity.

7. If the partnership cannot make a reasonable determination whether a partner's participation in a trade or business activity is material or whether a partner's participation in a rental real estate activity is active, classify the partner as "passive."

Schedule L. Balance Sheets per Books

Note. Schedules L, M-1, and M-2 are not required to be completed if the partnership answered "Yes" to question 5 of Schedule B.

The balance sheets should agree with the partnership's books and records. Attach a statement explaining any differences.

Partnerships reporting to the Interstate Commerce Commission (ICC) or to any national, state, municipal, or other public officer may send copies of their balance sheets prescribed by the ICC or national, state, or municipal authorities, as of the beginning and end of the tax year, instead of completing Schedule L. However, statements filed under this procedure must contain sufficient information to enable the IRS to reconstruct a balance sheet similar to that contained on Form 1065 without contacting the partnership during processing.

All amounts on the balance sheet should be reported in U.S. dollars. If the partnership's books and records are kept in a foreign currency, the balance sheet should be translated in accordance with U.S. generally accepted accounting principles (GAAP).

Exception. If the partnership or any qualified business unit of the partnership uses the U.S. dollar approximate separate transactions method, Schedule L should reflect the tax balance sheet prepared and translated into U.S. dollars according to Regulations section 1.985-3(d), and not a U.S. GAAP balance sheet.

Line 5. Tax-Exempt Securities

Include on this line:

1. State and local government obligations, the interest on which is excludable from gross income under section 103(a) and

2. Stock in a mutual fund or other regulated investment company that distributed exempt-interest dividends during the tax year of the partnership.

Line 18. All Nonrecourse Loans

Nonrecourse loans are those liabilities of the partnership for which no partner bears the economic risk of loss.

Schedule M-1. Reconciliation of Income (Loss) per Books With Income (Loss) per Return

Line 2

Report on this line income included on Schedule K, lines 1, 2, 3c, 5, 6a, 7, 8, 9a, 10, and 11 not recorded on the partnership's books this year. Describe each such item of income. Attach a statement if necessary.

Line 3. Guaranteed Payments

Include on this line guaranteed payments shown on Schedule K, line 4 (other than amounts paid for insurance that constitutes medical care for a partner, a partner's spouse, and a partner's dependents).

Line 4b. Travel and Entertainment

Include on this line:

- Meal and entertainment expenses not deductible under section 274(n).
- Expenses for the use of an entertainment facility.
- The part of business gifts over $25.
- Expenses of an individual allocable to conventions on cruise ships over $2,000.
- Employee achievement awards over $400.
- The part of the cost of entertainment tickets that exceeds face value (also subject to 50% limit).
- The part of the cost of skyboxes that exceeds the face value of nonluxury box seat tickets.
- The part of the cost of luxury water travel expenses not deductible under section 274(m).
- Expenses for travel as a form of education.
- Nondeductible club dues.
- Other nondeductible travel and entertainment expenses.

Schedule M-2. Analysis of Partners' Capital Accounts

Show what caused the changes during the tax year in the partners' capital accounts as reflected on the partnership's books and records. The amounts on Schedule M-2 should equal the total of the amounts reported in item N of all the partners' Schedules K-1.

The partnership may, but is not required to, use the rules in Regulations section 1.704-1(b)(2)(iv) to determine the partners' capital accounts in Schedule M-2 and item N of the partners' Schedules K-1. If the beginning and ending capital accounts reported under these rules differ from the amounts reported on Schedule L, attach a statement reconciling any differences.

Line 2. Capital Contributed During Year

Include on line 2a the amount of money contributed and on line 2b the amount of property contributed by each partner to the partnership as reflected on the partnership's books and records.

Line 3. Net Income (Loss) per Books

Enter on line 3 the net income (loss) shown on the partnership books from Schedule M-1, line 1.

Line 6. Distributions

Line 6a. Cash. Enter on line 6a the amount of money distributed to each partner by the partnership.

Line 6b. Property. Enter the amount of property distributed to each partner by the partnership as reflected on the partnership's books and records. Include withdrawals from inventory for the personal use of a partner.

Privacy Act and Paperwork Reduction Act Notice. We ask for the information on this form to carry out the Internal Revenue laws of the United States. You are required to give us the information. We need it to ensure that you are complying with these laws and to allow us to figure and collect the right amount of tax. Section 6109 requires return preparers to provide their identifying numbers on the return.

You are not required to provide the information requested on a form that is subject to the Paperwork Reduction Act unless the form displays a valid OMB control number. Books or records relating to a form or its instructions must be retained as long as their contents may become material in the administration of any Internal Revenue law. Generally, tax returns and return information are confidential, as required by section 6103.

The time needed to complete and file this form and related schedules will vary depending on individual circumstances. The estimated average times are:

Form	Recordkeeping	Learning about the law or the form	Preparing the form	Copying, assembling, and sending the form to the IRS
1065	44 hr., 20 min.	28 hr., 10 min.	48 hr., 54 min.	5 hr., 21 min.
Sch. D (Form 1065)	6 hr., 56 min.	2 hr., 34 min.	2 hr., 48 min.	
Sch. K-1 (Form 1065)	19 hr., 58 min.	12 hr., 28 min.	13 hr., 26 min.	
Sch. L (Form 1065)	15 hr., 32 min.	6 min.	21 min.	
Sch. M-1 (Form 1065)	3 hr., 21 min.	12 min.	15 min.	
Sch. M-2 (Form 1065)	3 hr., 6 min.	6 min.	9 min.	

If you have comments concerning the accuracy of these time estimates or suggestions for making these forms simpler, we would be happy to hear from you. You can write to the Internal Revenue Service, Tax Products Coordinating Committee, SE:W:CAR:MP:T:T:SP, 1111 Constitution Ave. NW, IR-6406, Washington, DC 20224. Do not send the tax form to this address. Instead, see *Where To File* on page 4.

Codes for Principal Business Activity and Principal Product or Service

This list of Principal Business Activities and their associated codes is designed to classify an enterprise by the type of activity in which it is engaged to facilitate the administration of the Internal Revenue Code. These Principal Business Activity Codes are based on the North American Industry Classification System.

Using the list of activities and codes below, determine from which activity the business derives the largest percentage of its "total receipts." Total receipts is defined as the sum of gross receipts or sales (page 1, line 1a); all other income (page 1, lines 4 through 7); income reported on Schedule K, lines 3a, 5, 6a, and 7; income or net gain reported on Schedule K, lines 8, 9a, 10, and 11; and income or net gain reported on Form 8825, lines 2, 19, and 20a. If the business purchases raw materials and supplies them to a subcontractor to produce the finished product, but retains title to the product, the business is considered a manufacturer and must use one of the manufacturing codes (311110–339900).

Once the Principal Business Activity is determined, enter the six-digit code from the list below on page 1, item C. Also enter a brief description of the business activity in item A and the principal product or service of the business in item B.

Code

Agriculture, Forestry, Fishing and Hunting

Crop Production

111100 Oilseed & Grain Farming
111210 Vegetable & Melon Farming (including potatoes & yams)
111300 Fruit & Tree Nut Farming
111400 Greenhouse, Nursery, & Floriculture Production
111900 Other Crop Farming (including tobacco, cotton, sugarcane, hay, peanut, sugar beet & all other crop farming)

Animal Production

112111 Beef Cattle Ranching & Farming
112112 Cattle Feedlots
112120 Dairy Cattle & Milk Production
112210 Hog & Pig Farming
112300 Poultry & Egg Production
112400 Sheep & Goat Farming
112510 Animal Aquaculture (including shellfish & finfish farms & hatcheries)
112900 Other Animal Production

Forestry and Logging

113110 Timber Tract Operations
113210 Forest Nurseries & Gathering of Forest Products
113310 Logging

Fishing, Hunting and Trapping

114110 Fishing
114210 Hunting & Trapping

Support Activities for Agriculture and Forestry

115110 Support Activities for Crop Production (including cotton ginning, soil preparation, planting, & cultivating)
115210 Support Activities for Animal Production
115310 Support Activities For Forestry

Mining

211110 Oil & Gas Extraction
212110 Coal Mining
212200 Metal Ore Mining
212310 Stone Mining & Quarrying
212320 Sand, Gravel, Clay, & Ceramic & Refractory Minerals Mining & Quarrying
212390 Other Nonmetallic Mineral Mining & Quarrying
213110 Support Activities for Mining

Utilities

221100 Electric Power Generation, Transmission & Distribution
221210 Natural Gas Distribution
221300 Water, Sewage & Other Systems

Construction

Construction of Buildings

236110 Residential Building Construction
236200 Nonresidential Building Construction

Code

Heavy and Civil Engineering Construction

237100 Utility System Construction
237210 Land Subdivision
237310 Highway, Street, & Bridge Construction
237990 Other Heavy & Civil Engineering Construction

Specialty Trade Contractors

238100 Foundation, Structure, & Building Exterior Contractors (including framing carpentry, masonry, glass, roofing, & siding)
238210 Electrical Contractors
238220 Plumbing, Heating, & Air-Conditioning Contractors
238290 Other Building Equipment Contractors
238300 Building Finishing Contractors (including drywall, insulation, painting, wallcovering, flooring, tile, & finish carpentry)
238900 Other Specialty Trade Contractors (including site preparation)

Manufacturing

Food Manufacturing

311110 Animal Food Mfg
311200 Grain & Oilseed Milling
311300 Sugar & Confectionery Product Mfg
311400 Fruit & Vegetable Preserving & Specialty Food Mfg
311500 Dairy Product Mfg
311610 Animal Slaughtering and Processing
311710 Seafood Product Preparation & Packaging
311800 Bakeries & Tortilla Mfg
311900 Other Food Mfg (including coffee, tea, flavorings & seasonings)

Beverage and Tobacco Product Manufacturing

312110 Soft Drink & Ice Mfg
312120 Breweries
312130 Wineries
312140 Distilleries
312200 Tobacco Manufacturing

Textile Mills and Textile Product Mills

313000 Textile Mills
314000 Textile Product Mills

Apparel Manufacturing

315100 Apparel Knitting Mills
315210 Cut & Sew Apparel Contractors
315220 Men's & Boys' Cut & Sew Apparel Mfg
315230 Women's & Girls' Cut & Sew Apparel Mfg
315290 Other Cut & Sew Apparel Mfg
315990 Apparel Accessories & Other Apparel Mfg

Leather and Allied Product Manufacturing

316110 Leather & Hide Tanning & Finishing
316210 Footwear Mfg (including rubber & plastics)

Code

316990 Other Leather & Allied Product Mfg

Wood Product Manufacturing

321110 Sawmills & Wood Preservation
321210 Veneer, Plywood, & Engineered Wood Product Mfg
321900 Other Wood Product Mfg

Paper Manufacturing

322100 Pulp, Paper, & Paperboard Mills
322200 Converted Paper Product Mfg

Printing and Related Support Activities

323100 Printing & Related Support Activities

Petroleum and Coal Products Manufacturing

324110 Petroleum Refineries (including integrated)
324120 Asphalt Paving, Roofing, & Saturated Materials Mfg
324190 Other Petroleum & Coal Products Mfg

Chemical Manufacturing

325100 Basic Chemical Mfg
325200 Resin, Synthetic Rubber, & Artificial & Synthetic Fibers & Filaments Mfg
325300 Pesticide, Fertilizer, & Other Agricultural Chemical Mfg
325410 Pharmaceutical & Medicine Mfg
325500 Paint, Coating, & Adhesive Mfg
325600 Soap, Cleaning Compound, & Toilet Preparation Mfg
325900 Other Chemical Product & Preparation Mfg

Plastics and Rubber Products Manufacturing

326100 Plastics Product Mfg
326200 Rubber Product Mfg

Nonmetallic Mineral Product Manufacturing

327100 Clay Product & Refractory Mfg
327210 Glass & Glass Product Mfg
327300 Cement & Concrete Product Mfg
327400 Lime & Gypsum Product Mfg
327900 Other Nonmetallic Mineral Product Mfg

Primary Metal Manufacturing

331110 Iron & Steel Mills & Ferroalloy Mfg
331200 Steel Product Mfg from Purchased Steel
331310 Alumina & Aluminum Production & Processing
331400 Nonferrous Metal (except Aluminum) Production & Processing
331500 Foundries

Fabricated Metal Product Manufacturing

332110 Forging & Stamping
332210 Cutlery & Handtool Mfg
332300 Architectural & Structural Metals Mfg
332400 Boiler, Tank, & Shipping Container Mfg
332510 Hardware Mfg

Code

332610 Spring & Wire Product Mfg
332700 Machine Shops; Turned Product; & Screw, Nut, & Bolt Mfg
332810 Coating, Engraving, Heat Treating, & Allied Activities
332900 Other Fabricated Metal Product Mfg

Machinery Manufacturing

333100 Agriculture, Construction, & Mining Machinery Mfg
333200 Industrial Machinery Mfg
333310 Commercial & Service Industry Machinery Mfg
333410 Ventilation, Heating, Air-Conditioning, & Commercial Refrigeration Equipment Mfg
333510 Metalworking Machinery Mfg
333610 Engine, Turbine & Power Transmission Equipment Mfg
333900 Other General Purpose Machinery Mfg

Computer and Electronic Product Manufacturing

334110 Computer & Peripheral Equipment Mfg
334200 Communications Equipment Mfg
334310 Audio & Video Equipment Mfg
334410 Semiconductor & Other Electronic Component Mfg
334500 Navigational, Measuring, Electromedical, & Control Instruments Mfg
334610 Manufacturing & Reproducing Magnetic & Optical Media

Electrical Equipment, Appliance, and Component Manufacturing

335100 Electric Lighting Equipment Mfg
335200 Household Appliance Mfg
335310 Electrical Equipment Mfg
335900 Other Electrical Equipment & Component Mfg

Transportation Equipment Manufacturing

336100 Motor Vehicle Mfg
336210 Motor Vehicle Body & Trailer Mfg
336300 Motor Vehicle Parts Mfg
336410 Aerospace Product & Parts Mfg
336510 Railroad Rolling Stock Mfg
336610 Ship & Boat Building
336990 Other Transportation Equipment Mfg

Furniture and Related Product Manufacturing

337000 Furniture & Related Product Manufacturing

Miscellaneous Manufacturing

339110 Medical Equipment & Supplies Mfg
339900 Other Miscellaneous Manufacturing

Codes for Principal Business Activity and Principal Product or Service *(continued)*

Code	
Wholesale Trade	
Merchant Wholesalers, Durable Goods	
423100	Motor Vehicle & Motor Vehicle Parts & Supplies
423200	Furniture & Home Furnishings
423300	Lumber & Other Construction Materials
423400	Professional & Commercial Equipment & Supplies
423500	Metal & Mineral (except Petroleum)
423600	Electrical & Electronic Goods
423700	Hardware, & Plumbing & Heating Equipment & Supplies
423800	Machinery, Equipment, & Supplies
423910	Sporting & Recreational Goods & Supplies
423920	Toy & Hobby Goods & Supplies
423930	Recyclable Materials
423940	Jewelry, Watch, Precious Stone, & Precious Metals
423990	Other Miscellaneous Durable Goods
Merchant Wholesalers, Nondurable Goods	
424100	Paper & Paper Products
424210	Drugs & Druggists' Sundries
424300	Apparel, Piece Goods, & Notions
424400	Grocery & Related Products
424500	Farm Product Raw Materials
424600	Chemical & Allied Products
424700	Petroleum & Petroleum Products
424800	Beer, Wine, & Distilled Alcoholic Beverages
424910	Farm Supplies
424920	Book, Periodical, & Newspapers
424930	Flower, Nursery Stock, & Florists' Supplies
424940	Tobacco & Tobacco Products
424950	Paint, Varnish, & Supplies
424990	Other Miscellaneous Nondurable Goods
Wholesale Electronic Markets and Agents and Brokers	
425110	Business to Business Electronic Markets
425120	Wholesale Trade Agents & Brokers
Retail Trade	
Motor Vehicle and Parts Dealers	
441110	New Car Dealers
441120	Used Car Dealers
441210	Recreational Vehicle Dealers
441221	Motorcycle Dealers
441222	Boat Dealers
441229	All Other Motor Vehicle Dealers
441300	Automotive Parts, Accessories, & Tire Stores
Furniture and Home Furnishings Stores	
442110	Furniture Stores
442210	Floor Covering Stores
442291	Window Treatment Stores
442299	All Other Home Furnishings Stores
Electronics and Appliance Stores	
443111	Household Appliance Stores
443112	Radio, Television, & Other Electronics Stores
443120	Computer & Software Stores
443130	Camera & Photographic Supplies Stores

Code	
Building Material and Garden Equipment and Supplies Dealers	
444110	Home Centers
444120	Paint & Wallpaper Stores
444130	Hardware Stores
444190	Other Building Material Dealers
444200	Lawn & Garden Equipment & Supplies Stores
Food and Beverage Stores	
445110	Supermarkets and Other Grocery (except Convenience) Stores
445120	Convenience Stores
445210	Meat Markets
445220	Fish & Seafood Markets
445230	Fruit & Vegetable Markets
445291	Baked Goods Stores
445292	Confectionery & Nut Stores
445299	All Other Specialty Food Stores
445310	Beer, Wine, & Liquor Stores
Health and Personal Care Stores	
446110	Pharmacies & Drug Stores
446120	Cosmetics, Beauty Supplies, & Perfume Stores
446130	Optical Goods Stores
446190	Other Health & Personal Care Stores
Gasoline Stations	
447100	Gasoline Stations (including convenience stores with gas)
Clothing and Clothing Accessories Stores	
448110	Men's Clothing Stores
448120	Women's Clothing Stores
448130	Children's & Infants' Clothing Stores
448140	Family Clothing Stores
448150	Clothing Accessories Stores
448190	Other Clothing Stores
448210	Shoe Stores
448310	Jewelry Stores
448320	Luggage & Leather Goods Stores
Sporting Goods, Hobby, Book, and Music Stores	
451110	Sporting Goods Stores
451120	Hobby, Toy, & Game Stores
451130	Sewing, Needlework, & Piece Goods Stores
451140	Musical Instrument & Supplies Stores
451211	Book Stores
451212	News Dealers & Newsstands
451220	Prerecorded Tape, Compact Disc, & Record Stores
General Merchandise Stores	
452110	Department Stores
452900	Other General Merchandise Stores
Miscellaneous Store Retailers	
453110	Florists
453210	Office Supplies & Stationery Stores
453220	Gift, Novelty, & Souvenir Stores
453310	Used Merchandise Stores
453910	Pet & Pet Supplies Stores
453920	Art Dealers
453930	Manufactured (Mobile) Home Dealers
453990	All Other Miscellaneous Store Retailers (including tobacco, candle, & trophy shops)
Nonstore Retailers	
454110	Electronic Shopping & Mail-Order Houses
454210	Vending Machine Operators
454311	Heating Oil Dealers
454312	Liquefied Petroleum Gas (Bottled Gas) Dealers
454319	Other Fuel Dealers

Code	
454390	Other Direct Selling Establishments (including door-to-door retailing, frozen food plan providers, party plan merchandisers, & coffee-break service providers)
Transportation and Warehousing	
Air, Rail, and Water Transportation	
481000	Air Transportation
482110	Rail Transportation
483000	Water Transportation
Truck Transportation	
484110	General Freight Trucking, Local
484120	General Freight Trucking, Long-distance
484200	Specialized Freight Trucking
Transit and Ground Passenger Transportation	
485110	Urban Transit Systems
485210	Interurban & Rural Bus Transportation
485310	Taxi Service
485320	Limousine Service
485410	School & Employee Bus Transportation
485510	Charter Bus Industry
485990	Other Transit & Ground Passenger Transportation
Pipeline Transportation	
486000	Pipeline Transportation
Scenic & Sightseeing Transportation	
487000	Scenic & Sightseeing Transportation
Support Activities for Transportation	
488100	Support Activities for Air Transportation
488210	Support Activities for Rail Transportation
488300	Support Activities for Water Transportation
488410	Motor Vehicle Towing
488490	Other Support Activities for Road Transportation
488510	Freight Transportation Arrangement
488990	Other Support Activities for Transportation
Couriers and Messengers	
492110	Couriers
492210	Local Messengers & Local Delivery
Warehousing and Storage	
493100	Warehousing & Storage (except lessors of miniwarehouses & self-storage units)
Information	
Publishing Industries (except Internet)	
511110	Newspaper Publishers
511120	Periodical Publishers
511130	Book Publishers
511140	Directory & Mailing List Publishers
511190	Other Publishers
511210	Software Publishers
Motion Picture and Sound Recording Industries	
512100	Motion Picture & Video Industries (except video rental)
512200	Sound Recording Industries
Broadcasting (except Internet)	
515100	Radio & Television Broadcasting
515210	Cable & Other Subscription Programming

Code	
Internet Publishing and Broadcasting	
516110	Internet Publishing & Broadcasting
Telecommunications	
517000	Telecommunications (including paging, cellular, satellite, cable & other program distribution, resellers, & other telecommunications)
Internet Service Providers, Web Search Portals, and Data Processing Services	
518111	Internet Service Providers
518112	Web Search Portals
518210	Data Processing, Hosting, & Related Services
Other Information Services	
519100	Other Information Services (including news syndicates & libraries)
Finance and Insurance	
Depository Credit Intermediation	
522110	Commercial Banking
522120	Savings Institutions
522130	Credit Unions
522190	Other Depository Credit Intermediation
Nondepository Credit Intermediation	
522210	Credit Card Issuing
522220	Sales Financing
522291	Consumer Lending
522292	Real Estate Credit (including mortgage bankers & originators)
522293	International Trade Financing
522294	Secondary Market Financing
522298	All Other Nondepository Credit Intermediation
Activities Related to Credit Intermediation	
522300	Activities Related to Credit Intermediation (including loan brokers, check clearing, & money transmitting)
Securities, Commodity Contracts, and Other Financial Investments and Related Activities	
523110	Investment Banking & Securities Dealing
523120	Securities Brokerage
523130	Commodity Contracts Dealing
523140	Commodity Contracts Brokerage
523210	Securities & Commodity Exchanges
523900	Other Financial Investment Activities (including portfolio management & investment advice)
Insurance Carriers and Related Activities	
524140	Direct Life, Health, & Medical Insurance & Reinsurance Carriers
524150	Direct Insurance & Reinsurance (except Life, Health & Medical) Carriers
524210	Insurance Agencies & Brokerages
524290	Other Insurance Related Activities (including third-party administration of insurance and pension funds)
Funds, Trusts, and Other Financial Vehicles	
525100	Insurance & Employee Benefit Funds
525910	Open-End Investment Funds (Form 1120-RIC)
525920	Trusts, Estates, & Agency Accounts

Codes for Principal Business Activity and Principal Product or Service *(continued)*

Code

525930 Real Estate Investment Trusts (Form 1120-REIT)
525990 Other Financial Vehicles (including closed-end investment funds)

"Offices of Bank Holding Companies" and "Offices of Other Holding Companies" are located under *Management of Companies (Holding Companies)* below.

Real Estate and Rental and Leasing

Real Estate

531110 Lessors of Residential Buildings & Dwellings
531114 Cooperative Housing
531120 Lessors of Nonresidential Buildings (except Miniwarehouses)
531130 Lessors of Miniwarehouses & Self-Storage Units
531190 Lessors of Other Real Estate Property
531210 Offices of Real Estate Agents & Brokers
531310 Real Estate Property Managers
531320 Offices of Real Estate Appraisers
531390 Other Activities Related to Real Estate

Rental and Leasing Services

532100 Automotive Equipment Rental & Leasing
532210 Consumer Electronics & Appliances Rental
532220 Formal Wear & Costume Rental
532230 Video Tape & Disc Rental
532290 Other Consumer Goods Rental
532310 General Rental Centers
532400 Commercial & Industrial Machinery & Equipment Rental & Leasing

Lessors of Nonfinancial Intangible Assets (except copyrighted works)

533110 Lessors of Nonfinancial Intangible Assets (except copyrighted works)

Professional, Scientific, and Technical Services

Legal Services

541110 Offices of Lawyers
541190 Other Legal Services

Accounting, Tax Preparation, Bookkeeping, and Payroll Services

541211 Offices of Certified Public Accountants
541213 Tax Preparation Services
541214 Payroll Services
541219 Other Accounting Services

Architectural, Engineering, and Related Services

541310 Architectural Services
541320 Landscape Architecture Services
541330 Engineering Services
541340 Drafting Services
541350 Building Inspection Services
541360 Geophysical Surveying & Mapping Services
541370 Surveying & Mapping (except Geophysical) Services
541380 Testing Laboratories

Specialized Design Services

541400 Specialized Design Services (including interior, industrial, graphic, & fashion design)

Computer Systems Design and Related Services

541511 Custom Computer Programming Services

Code

541512 Computer Systems Design Services
541513 Computer Facilities Management Services
541519 Other Computer Related Services

Other Professional, Scientific, and Technical Services

541600 Management, Scientific, & Technical Consulting Services
541700 Scientific Research & Development Services
541800 Advertising & Related Services
541910 Marketing Research & Public Opinion Polling
541920 Photographic Services
541930 Translation & Interpretation Services
541930 Translation & Interpretation Services
541940 Veterinary Services
541990 All Other Professional, Scientific, & Technical Services

Management of Companies (Holding Companies)

551111 Offices of Bank Holding Companies
551112 Offices of Other Holding Companies

Administrative and Support and Waste Management and Remediation Services

Administrative and Support Services

561110 Office Administrative Services
561210 Facilities Support Services
561300 Employment Services
561410 Document Preparation Services
561420 Telephone Call Centers
561430 Business Service Centers (including private mail centers & copy shops)
561440 Collection Agencies
561450 Credit Bureaus
561490 Other Business Support Services (including repossession services, court reporting, & stenotype services)
561500 Travel Arrangement & Reservation Services
561600 Investigation & Security Services
561710 Exterminating & Pest Control Services
561720 Janitorial Services
561730 Landscaping Services
561740 Carpet & Upholstery Cleaning Services
561790 Other Services to Buildings & Dwellings
561900 Other Support Services (including packaging & labeling services, & convention & trade show organizers)

Waste Management and Remediation Services

562000 Waste Management & Remediation Services

Educational Services

611000 Educational Services (including schools, colleges, & universities)

Code

Health Care and Social Assistance

Offices of Physicians and Dentists

621111 Offices of Physicians (except mental health specialists)
621112 Offices of Physicians, Mental Health Specialists
621210 Offices of Dentists

Offices of Other Health Practitioners

621310 Offices of Chiropractors
621320 Offices of Optometrists
621330 Offices of Mental Health Practitioners (except Physicians)
621340 Offices of Physical, Occupational & Speech Therapists, & Audiologists
621391 Offices of Podiatrists
621399 Offices of All Other Miscellaneous Health Practitioners

Outpatient Care Centers

621410 Family Planning Centers
621420 Outpatient Mental Health & Substance Abuse Centers
621491 HMO Medical Centers
621492 Kidney Dialysis Centers
621493 Freestanding Ambulatory Surgical & Emergency Centers
621498 All Other Outpatient Care Centers

Medical and Diagnostic Laboratories

621510 Medical & Diagnostic Laboratories

Home Health Care Services

621610 Home Health Care Services

Other Ambulatory Health Care Services

621900 Other Ambulatory Health Care Services (including ambulance services & blood & organ banks)

Hospitals

622000 Hospitals

Nursing and Residential Care Facilities

623000 Nursing & Residential Care Facilities

Social Assistance

624100 Individual & Family Services
624200 Community Food & Housing, & Emergency & Other Relief Services
624310 Vocational Rehabilitation Services
624410 Child Day Care Services

Arts, Entertainment, and Recreation

Performing Arts, Spectator Sports, and Related Industries

711100 Performing Arts Companies
711210 Spectator Sports (including sports clubs & racetracks)
711300 Promoters of Performing Arts, Sports, & Similar Events
711410 Agents & Managers for Artists, Athletes, Entertainers, & Other Public Figures
711510 Independent Artists, Writers, & Performers

Museums, Historical Sites, and Similar Institutions

712100 Museums, Historical Sites, & Similar Institutions

Amusement, Gambling, and Recreation Industries

713100 Amusement Parks & Arcades
713200 Gambling Industries Code

Code

713900 Other Amusement & Recreation Industries (including golf courses, skiing facilities, marinas, fitness centers, & bowling centers)

Accommodation and Food Services

Accommodation

721110 Hotels (except Casino Hotels) & Motels
721120 Casino Hotels
721191 Bed & Breakfast Inns
721199 All Other Traveler Accommodation
721210 RV (Recreational Vehicle) Parks & Recreational Camps
721310 Rooming & Boarding Houses

Food Services and Drinking Places

722110 Full-Service Restaurants
722210 Limited-Service Eating Places
722300 Special Food Services (including food service contractors & caterers)
722410 Drinking Places (Alcoholic Beverages)

Other Services

Repair and Maintenance

811110 Automotive Mechanical & Electrical Repair & Maintenance
811120 Automotive Body, Paint, Interior, & Glass Repair
811190 Other Automotive Repair & Maintenance (including oil change & lubrication shops & car washes)
811210 Electronic & Precision Equipment Repair & Maintenance
811310 Commercial & Industrial Machinery & Equipment (except Automotive & Electronic) Repair & Maintenance
811410 Home & Garden Equipment & Appliance Repair & Maintenance
811420 Reupholstery & Furniture Repair
811430 Footwear & Leather Goods Repair
811490 Other Personal & Household Goods Repair & Maintenance

Personal and Laundry Services

812111 Barber Shops
812112 Beauty Salon's
812113 Nail Salons
812190 Other Personal Care Services (including diet & weight reducing centers)
812210 Funeral Homes & Funeral Services
812220 Cemeteries & Crematories
812310 Coin-Operated Laundries & Drycleaners
812320 Drycleaning & Laundry Services (except Coin-Operated)
812330 Linen & Uniform Supply
812910 Pet Care (except Veterinary) Services
812920 Photofinishing
812930 Parking Lots & Garages
812990 All Other Personal Services

Religious, Grantmaking, Civic, Professional, and Similar Organizations

813000 Religious, Grantmaking, Civic, Professional, & Similiar Organizations (including condominium and homeowners associations)

■

INSTRUCTIONS FOR SCHEDULE D (FORM1065)

Capital Gains and Losses

General Instructions

Section references are to the Internal Revenue Code.

Purpose of Schedule

Use Schedule D (Form 1065) to report sales or exchanges of capital assets, capital gain distributions, and nonbusiness bad debts. Do not report on Schedule D capital gains (losses) specially allocated to any partners.

Enter capital gains (losses) specially allocated to the partnership as a partner in other partnerships and from estates and trusts on Schedule D, line 4 or 9, whichever applies. Enter capital gains (losses) of the partnership that are specially allocated to partners directly on line 8, 9a, or 11 of Schedule K. See *How Income Is Shared Among Partners* in the Instructions for Form 1065 for more information.

Note. *For more information, see Pub. 544, Sales and Other Dispositions of Assets.*

Other Forms The Partnership May Have To File

Use Form 4797, Sales of Business Property, to report:

- Sales or exchanges of property used in a trade or business.
- Sales or exchanges of depreciable or amortizable property.
- Sales or other dispositions of securities or commodities held in connection with a trading business, if the partnership made a mark-to-market election (see page 5 of the instructions for Form 1065).
- Involuntary conversions (other than from casualties or thefts).
- The disposition of noncapital assets (other than inventory or property held primarily for sale to customers in the ordinary course of a trade or business).

Use Form 4684, Casualties and Thefts, to report involuntary conversions of property due to casualty or theft.

Use Form 6781, Gains and Losses From Section 1256 Contracts and Straddles, to report gains and losses from section 1256 contracts and straddles. If there are limited partners, see section 1256(e)(4) for the limitation on losses from hedging transactions.

Use Form 8824, Like-Kind Exchanges, if the partnership made one or more like-kind exchanges. A "like-kind exchange" occurs when business or investment property is exchanged for property of a like kind.

What Are Capital Assets?

Each item of property the partnership held (whether or not connected with its trade or business) is a capital asset except:

- Stock in trade or other property included in inventory or held mainly for sale to customers.
- Accounts or notes receivable acquired in the ordinary course of the trade or business for services rendered or from the sale of stock in trade or other property held mainly for sale to customers.
- Depreciable or real property used in the trade or business, even if it is fully depreciated.
- Certain copyrights; literary, musical, or artistic compositions; letters or memoranda; or similar property. See section 1221(a)(3).
- U.S. Government publications, including the Congressional Record, that the partnership received from the Government, other than by purchase at the normal sales price, or that the partnership got from another taxpayer who had received it in a similar way, if the partnership's basis is determined by reference to the previous owner.
- Certain commodities derivative financial instruments held by a dealer. See section 1221(a)(6).
- Certain hedging transactions entered into in the normal course of the trade or business. See section 1221(a)(7).
- Supplies regularly used in the trade or business.

Items for Special Treatment

- Transactions by a securities dealer. See section 1236.
- Bonds and other debt instruments. See Pub. 550, Investment Income and Expenses.
- Certain real estate subdivided for sale that may be considered a capital asset. See section 1237.
- Gain on the sale of depreciable property to a more than 50%-owned entity, or to a trust in which the partnership is a beneficiary, is treated as ordinary gain.
- Liquidating distributions from a corporation. See Pub. 550 for details.
- Gain on the sale or exchange of stock in certain foreign corporations. See section 1248.
- Gain or loss on options to buy or sell, including closing transactions. See Pub. 550 for details.
- Gain or loss from a short sale of property. See Pub. 550 for details.
- Transfer of property to a political organization if the fair market value (FMV) of the property exceeds the partnership's adjusted basis in such property. See section 84.
- Any loss on the disposition of converted wetland or highly erodible cropland that is first used for farming after March 1, 1986, is reported as a long-term capital loss on Schedule D, but any gain on such a disposition is reported as ordinary income on Form 4797. See section 1257 for details.
- Transfer of partnership assets and liabilities to a newly formed corporation in exchange for all of its stock. See Rev. Rul. 84-111, 1984-2 C.B. 88.
- Disposition of foreign investment in a U.S. real property interest. See section 897.
- Any loss from a sale or exchange of property between the partnership and certain related persons is not allowed, except for distributions in complete liquidation of a corporation. See sections 267 and 707(b) for details.
- Any loss from securities that are capital assets that become worthless during the year is treated as a loss from the sale or exchange of a capital asset on the last day of the tax year.
- Gain from the sale or exchange of stock in a collapsible corporation is not a capital gain. See section 341.
- Nonrecognition of gain on sale of stock to an employee stock ownership plan (ESOP) or an eligible cooperative. See section 1042 and Temporary Regulations section 1.1042-1T for rules under which the partnership may elect not to recognize gain from the sale of certain stock to an ESOP or an eligible cooperative.
- A nonbusiness bad debt must be treated as a short-term capital loss and can be deducted only in the year the debt becomes totally worthless. For each bad debt, enter the name of the debtor and "schedule attached" in column (a) of line 1 and the amount of the bad debt as a loss in column (f). Also attach a statement of facts to support each bad debt deduction.
- Any loss from a wash sale of stock or securities (including contracts or options to acquire or sell stock or securities) cannot be deducted unless the partnership is a dealer in stock or securities and the loss was sustained in a transaction made in the ordinary course of the partnership's trade or business. A wash sale occurs if the partnership acquires (by purchase or exchange), or has a contract or option to acquire, substantially identical stock or securities within 30 days before or after the date of the sale or exchange. See section 1091 for more information.
- If the partnership sold property at a gain and it will receive a payment in a tax year after the year of sale, it generally must report the sale on the installment method unless it elects not to. However, the installment method may not be used to report sales of stock or securities traded on an established securities market. Use Form 6252, Installment Sale Income, to report the sale on the installment method. Also use Form 6252 to report any payment received during the tax year from a sale made in an earlier year that was reported on the installment method.

If the partnership wants to elect out of the installment method for installment gain that is not specially allocated among the partners, it must report the full amount of the gain on a timely filed return (including extensions).

If the partnership wants to elect out of the installment method for installment gain that is specially allocated among the partners, it must do the following on a timely filed return (including extensions):

1. For a short-term capital gain, report the full amount of the gain on Schedule K, line 8 or 11.

For a long-term capital gain, report the full amount of the gain on Schedule K, line 9a or 11. Report the collectibles (28%) gain (loss) on Schedule K, line 9b.

2. Enter each partner's share of the full amount of the gain on Schedule K-1, box 8 or 9a, or in box 11 using code E, whichever applies. Report the collectibles (28%) gain (loss) on Schedule K-1, box 9b.

If the partnership filed its original return on time without making the election, it may make the election on an amended return filed no later than 6 months after the due date of the return (excluding extensions). Write "Filed pursuant to section 301.9100-2" at the top of the amended return.

- A sale or other disposition of an interest in a partnership owning unrealized receivables or inventory items may result in ordinary gain or loss. See Pub. 541, Partnerships, for more details.

- Certain constructive ownership transactions. Gain in excess of the gain that would have been recognized if the partnership had held a financial asset directly during the term of a derivative contract must be treated as ordinary income. See section 1260 for details.

- Gain from the sale of collectibles. Report any collectibles (28%) gain (loss) included on lines 6 through 10 on line 9b of Schedule K (and each partner's share in box 9b of Schedule K-1). A collectibles (28%) gain (loss) is any long-term gain or deductible long-term loss from the sale or exchange of a collectible that is a capital asset.

Collectibles include works of art, rugs, antiques, metals (such as gold, silver, and platinum bullion), gems, stamps, coins, alcoholic beverages, and certain other tangible property.

Also include gain (but not loss) from the sale or exchange of an interest in a partnership or trust held more than 1 year and attributable to unrealized appreciation of collectibles. For details, see Regulations section 1.1(h)-1. Also, attach the statement required under Regulations section 1.1(h)-1(e).

Special rules for traders in securities. Traders in securities are engaged in the business of buying and selling securities for their own account. To be engaged in business as a trader in securities:

- The partnership must seek to profit from daily market movements in the prices of securities and not from dividends, interest, or capital appreciation.

- The partnership's trading activity must be substantial.

- The partnership must carry on the activity with continuity and regularity.

The following facts and circumstances should be considered in determining if a partnership's activity is a business:

- Typical holding periods for securities bought and sold.

- The frequency and dollar amount of the partnership's trades during the year.

- The extent to which the partners pursue the activity to produce income for a livelihood.

- The amount of time devoted to the activity.

Like an investor, a trader must report each sale of securities (taking into account commissions and any other costs of acquiring or disposing of the securities) on Schedule D or on an attached statement containing all the same information for each sale in a similar format. However, if a trader made the mark-to-market election (see page 5 of the *Instructions for Form 1065*), each transaction is reported in Part II of Form 4797 instead of Schedule D. Regardless of whether a trader reports its gains and losses on Schedule D or Form 4797, the gain or loss from the disposition of securities is not taken into account when figuring net earnings from self-employment on Schedules K and K-1. See section 1402(i) for an exception that applies to section 1256 contracts.

The limitation on investment interest expense that applies to investors does not apply to interest paid or incurred in a trading business. A trader reports interest expense and other expenses (excluding commissions and other costs of acquiring or disposing of securities) from a trading business on page 1 of Form 1065.

A trader also may hold securities for investment. The rules for investors generally will apply to those securities. Allocate interest and other expenses between the partnership's trading business and its investment securities. Investment interest expense is reported on line 13c of Schedule K and in box 13 of Schedule K-1 using code I.

Constructive sale treatment for certain appreciated positions. Generally, the partnership must recognize gain (but not loss) on the date it enters into a constructive sale of any appreciated position in stock, a partnership interest, or certain debt instruments as if the position were disposed of at FMV on that date.

The partnership is treated as making a constructive sale of an appreciated position when it (or a related person, in some cases) does one of the following:

- Enters into a short sale of the same or substantially identical property (that is, a "short sale against the box").

- Enters into an offsetting notional principal contract relating to the same or substantially identical property.

- Enters into a futures or forward contract to deliver the same or substantially identical property.

- Acquires the same or substantially identical property (if the appreciated position is a short sale, offsetting notional principal contract, or a futures or forward contract).

Exception. Generally, constructive sale treatment does not apply if:

- The partnership closed the transaction before the end of the 30th day after the end of the year in which it was entered into,

- The partnership held the appreciated position to which the transaction relates throughout the 60-day period starting on the date the transaction was closed, and

- At no time during that 60-day period was the partnership's risk of loss reduced by holding certain other positions.

For details and other exceptions to these rules, see Pub. 550.

Rollover of gain from qualified stock. If the partnership sold qualified small business stock (defined below) it held for more than 6 months, it may postpone gain if it purchased other qualified small business stock during the 60-day period that began on the date of the sale. The partnership must recognize gain to the extent the sale proceeds exceed the cost of the replacement stock. Reduce the basis of the replacement stock by any postponed gain.

If the partnership chooses to postpone gain, report the entire gain realized on the sale on line 1 or 6. Directly below the line on which the partnership reported the gain, enter in column (a) "Section 1045 Rollover" and enter as a (loss) in column (f) the amount of the postponed gain.

Caution. *The partnership also must separately state the amount of the gain rolled over on qualified stock under section 1045 on Form 1065, Schedule K, line 11, because each partner must determine if he or she qualifies for the rollover at the partner level. Also, the partnership must separately state on that line (and not on Schedule D) any gain that would qualify for the section 1045 rollover at the partner level instead of the partnership level (because a partner was entitled to purchase replacement stock) and any gain on qualified stock that could qualify for the partial exclusion under section 1202.*

To be qualified small business stock, the stock must meet all of the following tests:

- It must be stock in a C corporation (that is, not S corporation stock).

- It must have been originally issued after August 10, 1993.

- As of the date the stock was issued, the corporation was a qualified small business. A qualified small business is a domestic C corporation with total gross assets of $50 million or less (a) at all times after August 9, 1993, and before the stock was issued and (b) immediately after the stock was issued.

Gross assets include those of any predecessor of the corporation. All corporations that are members of the same parent-subsidiary controlled group are treated as one corporation.

• The partnership must have acquired the stock at its original issue (either directly or through an underwriter), either in exchange for money or other property or as pay for services (other than as an underwriter) to the corporation. In certain cases, the partnership may meet the test if it acquired the stock from another person who met this test (such as by gift or at death) or through a conversion or exchange of qualified business stock by the holder.

• During substantially all the time the partnership held the stock:

1. The corporation was a C corporation,

2. At least 80% of the value of the corporation's assets were used in the active conduct of one or more qualified businesses (defined below), and

3. The corporation was not a foreign corporation, domestic international sales corporation (DISC), former DISC, corporation that has made (or that has a subsidiary that has made) a section 936 election, regulated investment company (RIC), real estate investment trust (REIT), real estate mortgage investment conduit (REMIC), financial asset securitization investment trust (FASIT), or cooperative.

Note. *A specialized small business investment company (SSBIC) is treated as having met test 2 above.*

A qualified business is any business other than the following:

• One involving services performed in the fields of health, law, engineering, architecture, accounting, actuarial science, performing arts, consulting, athletics, financial services, or brokerage services.

• One whose principal asset is the reputation or skill of one or more employees.

• Any banking, insurance, financing, leasing, investing, or similar business.

• Any farming business (including the raising or harvesting of trees).

• Any business involving the production of products for which percentage depletion can be claimed.

• Any business of operating a hotel, motel, restaurant, or similar business.

Rollover of gain from empowerment zone assets. If the partnership sold a qualified empowerment zone asset it held for more than 1 year, it may be able to elect to postpone part or all of the gain. For details, see Pub. 954, Tax Incentives for Distressed Communities, and section 1397B.

Exclusion of gain from DC Zone assets. If the partnership sold or exchanged a District of Columbia Enterprise Zone (DC Zone) asset that it held for more than 5 years, it may be able to exclude the qualified capital gain. The sale or exchange of DC Zone capital assets reported on Schedule D include:

• Stock in a domestic corporation that was a DC Zone business.

• Interest in a partnership that was a DC Zone business.

Report the sale or exchange of property used in the partnership's DC Zone business on Form 4797.

Gains not qualified for exclusion. The following gains do not qualify for the exclusion of gain from DC Zone assets.

• Gain on the sale of an interest in a partnership, which is a DC Zone business, attributable to unrecaptured section 1250 gain. See the instructions for line 9c of Schedule K for information on how to report unrecaptured section 1250 gain.

• Gain on the sale of an interest in a partnership or S corporation attributable to real property or an intangible asset which is not an integral part of the DC Zone business.

• Gain from a related-party transaction. See *Sales and Exchanges Between Related Persons* in chapter 2 of Pub. 544.

See Pub. 954 and section 1400B for more details on DC Zone assets and special rules.

How to report. Report the entire gain realized from the sale or exchange as you otherwise would without regard to the exclusion. To report the exclusion, enter "DC Zone Asset Exclusion" on Schedule D, line 6, column (a) and enter as a (loss) in column (f) the amount of the exclusion.

Specific Instructions

Columns (b) and (c). Date Acquired and Date Sold

Use the trade dates for date acquired and date sold for stocks and bonds traded on an exchange or over-the-counter market. The acquisition date for an asset the partnership held on January 1, 2001, for which it made an election to recognize any gain on a deemed sale, is the date of the deemed sale and reacquisition.

Column (d). Sales Price

Enter in this column either the gross sales price or the net sales price from the sale. On sales of stocks and bonds, report the gross amount as reported to the partnership by the partnership's broker on Form 1099-B, Proceeds From Broker and Barter Exchange Transactions, or similar statement. However, if the broker advised the partnership that gross proceeds (gross sales price) less commissions and option premiums were reported to the IRS, enter that net amount in column (d).

Column (e). Cost or Other Basis

In general, the cost or other basis is the cost of the property plus purchase commissions and improvements and minus depreciation, amortization, and depletion. If the partnership got the property in a tax-free exchange, involuntary conversion, or wash sale of stock, it may not be able to use the actual cash cost as the basis. If the partnership does not use cash cost, attach an explanation of the basis.

If the partnership sold stock, adjust the basis by subtracting all the stock-related nontaxable distributions received before the sale. This includes nontaxable distributions from utility company stock and mutual funds. Also adjust the basis for any stock splits or stock dividends.

If the partnership elected to recognize gain on an asset held on January 1, 2001, its basis in the asset is its closing market price or FMV, whichever applies, on the date of the deemed sale and reacquisition, whether the deemed sale resulted in a gain or an unallowed loss.

If a charitable contribution deduction is passed through to a partner because of a bargain sale of property to a charitable organization, the adjusted basis for determining gain from the sale is an amount that has the same ratio to the adjusted basis as the amount realized has to the FMV.

See section 852(f) for the treatment of certain load charges incurred in acquiring stock in a mutual fund with a reinvestment right.

If the gross sales price is reported in column (d), increase the cost or other basis by any expense of sale, such as broker's fees, commissions, or option premiums, before making an entry in column (e).

For more details, see Pub. 551, Basis of Assets.

Column (f). Gain or (Loss)

Make a separate entry in this column for each transaction reported on lines 1 and 6 and any other line(s) that applies to the partnership. For lines 1 and 6, subtract the amount in column (e) from the amount in column (d). Enter negative amounts in parentheses.

Lines 4 and 9. Capital Gains (Losses) From Other Partnerships, Estates, and Trusts

See the Schedule K-1 or other information supplied to you by the other partnership, estate, or trust.

Line 10. Capital Gain Distributions

On line 10, column (f), report the total amount of (a) capital gain distributions and (b) the partnership's share of undistributed capital gains from a RIC or REIT. Report the partnership's share of taxes paid on undistributed capital gains by a RIC or REIT on a statement attached to Form 1065 for Schedule K, line 15f (and each partner's share in box 15 of Schedule K-1 using code I).

INSTRUCTIONS FOR FORM 1120

U.S. Corporation Income Tax Return

2004

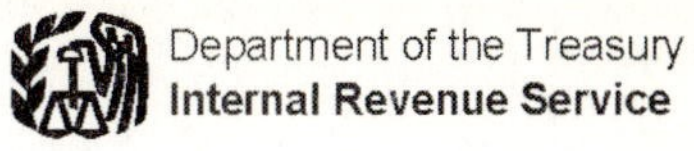

Instructions for Forms 1120 and 1120-A

Section references are to the Internal Revenue Code unless otherwise noted.

Contents Page

Contents Page

What's New

- Corporations can now use Form 1120-A to file a final return. A "Final return" box is added to the return.
- Corporations claiming the credit for prior year minimum tax must now file Form 1120.
- Corporations with total assets of $10 million or more on the last day of the tax year must complete new Schedule M-3, Net Income (Loss) Reconciliation for Corporations With Total Assets of $10 Million or More, instead of Schedule M-1.
- The special rules for FASITs generally do not apply after 2004. See page 3.
- Corporations can file new Form 8895, Section 965(f) Election for Corporations that are U.S. Shareholders of a Controlled Foreign Corporation, to elect the 85% dividends-received deduction on repatriated dividends received under section 965. Changes are made to Form 1120, Schedule C, lines 11 and 12.
- For tax years beginning after October 22, 2004, corporations can elect to be taxed on income from qualifying shipping activities using an alternative tax method. See page 10.
- Corporations can elect to deduct a limited amount of business start-up and organizational costs paid or incurred after October 22, 2004. See page 12.
- Corporations cannot deduct certain interest paid or incurred in tax years beginning after October 22, 2004, on an underpayment of tax from certain undisclosed transactions. See page 14.
- For charitable contributions of certain property made after June 3, 2004, a corporation must file Form 8283 and obtain a qualified appraisal if claiming a deduction of more than $5,000. See page 14.
- For charitable contributions of patents and certain other intellectual property made after June 3, 2004, corporations will receive a reduced deduction but can deduct certain qualified donee income. See page 14.
- Special rules apply to charitable contributions after 2004 of used motor vehicles, boats, or airplanes with a claimed value of more than $500. See section 170(f)(12).
- Corporations can deduct certain costs of qualified film or television productions commencing after October 22, 2004. See section 181.
- Corporations can elect to deduct up to $10,000 of reforestation costs paid or incurred after October 22, 2004. The reforestation credit (see Form 3468) is repealed for expenses paid or incurred after this date. See *Other Deductions* on page 15.
- The deduction for certain travel, meals, and entertainment expenses incurred after October 22, 2004, is limited to the amount treated as compensation to officers, directors, and more-than-10% shareholders. See section 274(e)(2).
- If the corporation is an expatriated entity or a partner in an expatriated entity, the corporation's taxable income cannot be less than its inversion gain for the tax year. See section 7874.

Photographs of Missing Children

The Internal Revenue Service is a proud partner with the National Center for Missing and Exploited Children. Photographs of missing children selected by the Center may appear in instructions on pages that would otherwise be blank. You can help bring these children home by looking at the photographs and calling 1-800-THE-LOST (1-800-843-5678) if you recognize a child.

Unresolved Tax Issues

If the corporation has attempted to deal with an IRS problem unsuccessfully, it should contact the Taxpayer Advocate. The Taxpayer Advocate independently represents the corporation's interests and concerns within the IRS by protecting its rights and resolving problems that have not been fixed through normal channels.

While Taxpayer Advocates cannot change the tax law or make a technical tax decision, they can clear up problems that resulted from previous contacts and ensure that the corporation's case is given a complete and impartial review.

The corporation's assigned personal advocate will listen to its point of view and will work with the corporation to address its concerns. The corporation can expect the advocate to provide:

- A "fresh look" at a new or ongoing problem.
- Timely acknowledgment.

Cat. No. 11455T

• The name and phone number of the individual assigned to its case.
• Updates on progress.
• Timeframes for action.
• Speedy resolution.
• Courteous service.

When contacting the Taxpayer Advocate, the corporation should be prepared to provide the following information.
• The corporation's name, address, and employer identification number (EIN).
• The name and telephone number of an authorized contact person and the hours he or she can be reached.
• The type of tax return and year(s) involved.
• A detailed description of the problem.
• Previous attempts to solve the problem and the office that was contacted.
• A description of the hardship the corporation is facing and verifying documentation (if applicable).

The corporation can contact a Taxpayer Advocate by calling 1-877-777-4778 (toll free). Persons who have access to TTY/TDD equipment can call 1-800-829-4059 and ask for Taxpayer Advocate assistance. If the corporation prefers, it can call, write, or fax the Taxpayer Advocate office in its area. See Pub. 1546 for a list of addresses and fax numbers.

Direct Deposit of Refund

To request a direct deposit of the corporation's income tax refund into an account at a U.S. bank or other financial institution, attach Form 8050, Direct Deposit of Corporate Tax Refund (see page 17).

How To Make a Contribution To Reduce Debt Held by the Public

To help reduce debt held by the public, make a check payable to "Bureau of the Public Debt." Send it to Bureau of the Public Debt, Department G, P.O. Box 2188, Parkersburg, WV 26106-2188. Or, enclose a check with the income tax return. Contributions to reduce debt held by the public are deductible subject to the rules and limitations for charitable contributions.

How To Get Forms and Publications

Personal computer. You can access the IRS website 24 hours a day, 7 days a week, at *www.irs.gov* to:
• Order IRS products online.
• Download forms, instructions, and publications.
• See answers to frequently asked tax questions.
• Search publications online by topic or keyword.
• Send us comments or request help by email.
• Sign up to receive local and national tax news by email.

You can also reach us using file transfer protocol at *ftp.irs.gov*.

CD-ROM. Order Pub. 1796, Federal Tax Products on CD-ROM, and get:
• Current year forms, instructions, and publications.
• Prior year forms, instructions, and publications.
• Frequently requested tax forms that can be filled in electronically, printed out for submission, and saved for recordkeeping.
• The Internal Revenue Bulletin.

Buy the CD-ROM on the Internet at *www.irs.gov/cdorders* from the National Technical Information Service (NTIS) for $22 (no handling fee) or call 1-877-CDFORMS (1-877-233-6767) toll free to buy the CD-ROM for $22 (plus a $5 handling fee).

By phone and in person. You can order forms and publications by calling 1-800-TAX-FORM (1-800-829-3676). You can also get most forms and publications at your local IRS office.

IRS E-Services Make Taxes Easier

Now more than ever before, businesses can enjoy the benefits of filing and paying their federal taxes electronically. Whether you rely on a tax professional or handle your own taxes, the IRS offers you convenient programs to make taxes easier.
• You can *e-file* your Form 1120; Form 940 and 941 employment tax returns; Form 1099 and other information returns. Visit *www.irs.gov/efile* for more information.
• You can pay taxes online or by phone using the free Electronic Federal Tax Payment System (EFTPS). Visit *www.eftps.gov* or call 1-800-555-4477 for more information.

Use these electronic options to make filing and paying taxes easier.

General Instructions

Purpose of Form

Use Form 1120, U.S. Corporation Income Tax Return, or Form 1120-A, U.S. Corporation Short-Form Income Tax Return, to report the income, gains, losses, deductions, credits, and to figure the income tax liability of a corporation. Also see Pub. 542, Corporations, for more information.

Who Must File

Unless exempt under section 501, all domestic corporations (including corporations in bankruptcy) must file an income tax return whether or not they have taxable income. Domestic corporations must file Form 1120 or, if they qualify, Form 1120-A, unless they are required to file a special return (see *Special Returns for Certain Organizations* on page 3).

Limited liability companies. If an entity with more than one owner was formed as a limited liability company (LLC) under state law, it generally is treated as a partnership for federal income tax purposes and files Form 1065, U.S. Return of Partnership Income. Generally, a single-member LLC is disregarded as an entity separate from its owner and reports its income and deductions on its owner's federal income tax return. The LLC can file a Form 1120 or Form 1120-A only if it has filed Form 8832, Entity Classification Election, to elect to be treated as an association taxable as a corporation. For more information about LLCs, see Pub. 3402, Tax Issues for Limited Liability Companies.

Corporations engaged in farming. Any corporation that engages in farming should use Form 1120 or, if they qualify, Form 1120-A, to report the income (loss) from such activities. Enter the income and deductions of the corporation according to the instructions for lines 1 through 10 and 12 through 29.

Who May File Form 1120-A

Form 1120-A may be filed by a corporation if it met all of the following requirements during the tax year.

1. Its gross receipts (line 1a on page 1) are under $500,000.
2. Its total income (line 11 on page 1) is under $500,000.
3. Its total assets (Item D on page 1) are under $500,000.
4. Its only dividend income is from domestic corporations and those dividends (a) qualify for the 70% dividends-received deduction and (b) are not from debt-financed securities. Subchapter T cooperatives can include patronage dividends on Form 1120-A.
5. It does not owe alternative minimum tax.
6. It does not have any of the "write-in" additions to tax listed in the instructions for Schedule J, line 3 (see page 20) or line 11 (see page 22).
7. It has no nonrefundable tax credits other than the general business credit.
8. It is not:

a. Dissolving or liquidating,
b. A member of a controlled group,
c. A personal holding company,
d. Filing a consolidated return,
e. Electing to forego the entire carryback period for any NOL, or
f. Required to file one of the returns listed under *Special Returns for Certain Organizations* on page 3.

9. It does not have:

a. Any ownership in a foreign corporation or foreign partnership,
b. Foreign shareholders that directly or indirectly own 25% or more of its stock, or
c. Any ownership in, or transactions with, a foreign trust.

Special Returns for Certain Organizations

Instead of filing Form 1120 or Form 1120-A, certain organizations, as shown below, have to file special returns.

If the organization is a:	File Form
Farmers' cooperative (sec. 1381)	990-C
Exempt organization with unrelated trade or business income	990-T
Religious or apostolic organization exempt under section 501(d)	1065
Entity formed as a limited liability company under state law and treated as a partnership for federal income tax purposes	1065
Entity that elects to be treated as a real estate mortgage investment conduit (REMIC) under section 860D	1066
Interest charge domestic international sales corporation (section 992)	1120-IC-DISC
Foreign corporation (other than life and property and casualty insurance company filing Form 1120-L or Form 1120-PC)	1120-F
Foreign sales corporation (section 922)	1120-FSC
Condominium management, residential real estate management, or timeshare association that elects to be treated as a homeowners association under section 528	1120-H
Life insurance company (section 801)	1120-L
Fund set up to pay for nuclear decommissioning costs (section 468A)	1120-ND
Property and casualty insurance company (section 831)	1120-PC
Political organization (section 527)	1120-POL
Real estate investment trust (section 856)	1120-REIT
Regulated investment company (section 851)	1120-RIC
S corporation (section 1361)	1120S
Settlement fund (section 468B)	1120-SF

Ownership Interest in a Financial Asset Securitization Investment Trust (FASIT)

If a corporation holds an ownership interest in a FASIT, it must report all items of income, gain, deductions, losses, and credits on the corporation's income tax return (except as provided in section 860H). Show a breakdown of the items on an attached schedule. For more information, see sections 860H and 860L.

The special rules for FASITs generally do not apply after 2004. However, the rules do apply to any FASIT in existence on October 22, 2004, to the extent that regular interests issued by the FASIT before October 22, 2004, continue to remain outstanding in accordance with their original terms.

Electronic Filing

Corporations can generally file Form 1120 and related forms, schedules, and attachments electronically. However, the option to file electronically does not apply to certain returns, including:

- Amended returns,
- Bankruptcy returns,
- Final returns,
- Returns with a name change,
- Returns with precomputed penalty and interest,
- Returns with reasonable cause for failing to file timely,
- Returns with reasonable cause for failing to pay timely,
- Returns with request for overpayment to be applied to another account,
- Short-year returns, and
- 52-53 week tax year returns.

Visit *www.irs.gov/efile* for details.

When To File

Generally, a corporation must file its income tax return by the 15th day of the 3rd month after the end of its tax year. A new corporation filing a short-period return must generally file by the 15th day of the 3rd month after the short period ends. A corporation that has dissolved

Where To File

File the corporation's return at the applicable IRS address listed below.

If the corporation's principal business, office, or agency is located in:	And the total assets at the end of the tax year (Form 1120, page 1, item D) are:	Use the following Internal Revenue Service Center address:
Connecticut, Delaware, District of Columbia, Illinois, Indiana, Kentucky, Maine, Maryland, Massachusetts, Michigan, New Hampshire, New Jersey, New York, North Carolina, Ohio, Pennsylvania, Rhode Island, South Carolina, Vermont, Virginia, West Virginia, Wisconsin	Less than $10 million	Cincinnati, OH 45999-0012
	$10 million or more	Ogden, UT 84201-0012
Alabama, Alaska, Arizona, Arkansas, California, Colorado, Florida, Georgia, Hawaii, Idaho, Iowa, Kansas, Louisiana, Minnesota, Mississippi, Missouri, Montana, Nebraska, Nevada, New Mexico, North Dakota, Oklahoma, Oregon, South Dakota, Tennessee, Texas, Utah, Washington, Wyoming	Any amount	Ogden, UT 84201-0012
A foreign country or U.S. possession (or the corporation is claiming the possessions corporation tax credit under sections 30A and 936)	Any amount	Philadelphia, PA 19255-0012

A group of corporations with members located in more than one service center area will often keep all the books and records at the principal office of the managing corporation. In this case, the tax returns of the corporations may be filed with the service center for the area in which the principal office of the managing corporation is located.

must generally file by the 15th day of the 3rd month after the date it dissolved.

If the due date falls on a Saturday, Sunday, or legal holiday, the corporation can file on the next business day.

Private delivery services. Corporations can use certain private delivery services designated by the IRS to meet the "timely mailing as timely filing/paying" rule for tax returns and payments. These private delivery services include only the following.

- DHL Express (DHL): DHL Same Day Service, DHL Next Day 10:30 am, DHL Next Day 12:00 pm, DHL Next Day 3:00 pm, and DHL 2nd Day Service.
- Federal Express (FedEx): FedEx Priority Overnight, FedEx Standard Overnight, FedEx 2Day, FedEx International Priority, and FedEx International First.
- United Parcel Service (UPS): UPS Next Day Air, UPS Next Day Air Saver, UPS 2nd Day Air, UPS 2nd Day Air A.M., UPS Worldwide Express Plus, and UPS Worldwide Express.

The private delivery service can tell you how to get written proof of the mailing date.

Private delivery services cannot deliver items to P.O. boxes. You must use the U.S. Postal Service to mail any item to an IRS P.O. box address.

Extension. File Form 7004, Application for Automatic Extension of Time To File Corporation Income Tax Return, to request a 6-month extension of time to file.

Who Must Sign

The return must be signed and dated by:

- The president, vice president, treasurer, assistant treasurer, chief accounting officer or
- Any other corporate officer (such as tax officer) authorized to sign.

If a return is filed on behalf of a corporation by a receiver, trustee or assignee, the fiduciary must sign the return, instead of the corporate officer. Returns and forms signed by a receiver or trustee in bankruptcy on behalf of a corporation must be accompanied by a copy of the order or instructions of the court authorizing signing of the return or form.

If an employee of the corporation completes Form 1120 or Form 1120-A, the paid preparer's space should remain blank. Anyone who prepares Form 1120 or Form 1120-A but does not charge the corporation should not complete that section. Generally, anyone who is paid to prepare the return must sign it and fill in the "Paid Preparer's Use Only" area.

The **paid preparer** must complete the required preparer information and—

- Sign the return in the space provided for the preparer's signature.
- Give a copy of the return to the taxpayer.

Note. A paid preparer may sign original returns, amended returns, or requests for filing extensions by rubber stamp, mechanical device, or computer software program.

Paid Preparer Authorization

If the corporation wants to allow the IRS to discuss its 2004 tax return with the paid preparer who signed it, check the "Yes" box in the signature area of the return. This authorization applies only to the individual whose signature appears in the "Paid Preparer's Use Only" section of the corporation's return. It does not apply to the firm, if any, shown in that section.

If the "Yes" box is checked, the corporation is authorizing the IRS to call the paid preparer to answer any questions that may arise during the processing of its return. The corporation is also authorizing the paid preparer to:

- Give the IRS any information that is missing from the return,
- Call the IRS for information about the processing of the return or the status of any related refund or payment(s), and
- Respond to certain IRS notices that the corporation has shared with the preparer about math errors, offsets, and return preparation. The notices will not be sent to the preparer.

The corporation is not authorizing the paid preparer to receive any refund check, bind the corporation to anything (including any additional tax liability), or otherwise represent the corporation before the IRS. If the corporation wants to expand the paid preparer's authorization, see Pub. 947, Practice Before the IRS and Power of Attorney.

The authorization cannot be revoked. However, the authorization will automatically end no later than the due date (excluding extensions) for filing the corporation's 2005 tax return.

Statements

Consolidated returns. File supporting statements for each corporation included in the consolidated return. Do not use Form 1120 as a supporting statement. On the supporting statement, use columns to show the following, both before and after adjustments.

1. Items of gross income and deductions.
2. A computation of taxable income.
3. Balance sheets as of the beginning and end of the tax year.
4. A reconciliation of income per books with income per return.
5. A reconciliation of retained earnings.

TIP *The corporation does not have to complete (3), (4), and (5) above, if its total receipts (line 1a plus lines 4 through 10 on page 1 of the return) and its total assets at the end of the tax year are less than $250,000.*

Enter the totals for the consolidated group on Form 1120. Attach consolidated balance sheets and a reconciliation of consolidated retained earnings. For more information on consolidated returns, see the regulations under section 1502.

Stock ownership in foreign personal holding companies (FPHC). Attach the statement required by section 551(c) if:

- The corporation owned 5% or more in value of the outstanding stock of a FPHC and
- The corporation was required to include in its gross income any undistributed FPHC income from a FPHC.

Transfers to a corporation controlled by the transferor. If a person receives stock of a corporation in exchange for property, and no gain or loss is recognized under section 351, the person (transferor) and the transferee must each attach to their tax returns the information required by Regulations section 1.351-3.

Dual consolidated losses. If a domestic corporation incurs a dual consolidated loss (as defined in Regulations section 1.1503-2(c)(5)), the corporation (or consolidated group) may need to attach an elective relief agreement and/or an annual certification as provided in Temporary Regulations section 1.1503-2T(g)(2).

Amended Return

Use Form 1120X, Amended U.S. Corporation Income Tax Return, to correct a previously filed Form 1120 or Form 1120-A.

Assembling the Return

To ensure that the corporation's tax return is correctly processed, attach all schedules and other forms after page 4, Form 1120 (or page 2, Form 1120-A), and in the following order.

1. Schedule N (Form 1120).
2. Form 8050.
3. Form 4136.
4. Form 4626.
5. Form 851.
6. Additional schedules in alphabetical order.
7. Additional forms in numerical order.

Complete every applicable entry space on Form 1120 or Form 1120-A. Do not enter "See Attached" instead of completing the entry spaces. If more space is needed on the forms or schedules, attach separate sheets using the same size and format as the printed forms. If there are supporting statements and attachments, arrange them in the same order as the schedules or forms they support and attach them last. Show the totals on the printed forms. Also be sure to enter the corporation's name and EIN on each supporting statement or attachment.

Accounting Methods

An accounting method is a set of rules used to determine when and how income and expenses are reported. Figure taxable income using the method of accounting regularly used in keeping the corporation's books and records. In all cases, the method used must clearly show taxable income.

Generally, permissible methods include:

- Cash,
- Accrual, or
- Any other method authorized by the Internal Revenue Code.

Accrual method. Generally, a corporation (other than a qualified personal service corporation) must use the accrual method of accounting if its average annual gross receipts exceed $5 million. See section 448(c). A corporation engaged in farming operations also must use the accrual method. For exceptions, see section 447.

If inventories are required, the accrual method generally must be used for sales and purchases of merchandise. However, qualifying taxpayers and eligible businesses of qualifying small business taxpayers are excepted from using the accrual method for eligible trades or businesses and may account for inventoriable items as materials and supplies that are not incidental. For details, see *Cost of Goods Sold* on page 17.

Under the accrual method, an amount is includible in income when:

1. All the events have occurred that fix the right to receive the income, which is the earliest of the date:

a. The required performance takes place,

b. Payment is due, or

c. Payment is received and

2. The amount can be determined with reasonable accuracy.

See Regulations section 1.451-1(a) for details.

Generally, an accrual basis taxpayer can deduct accrued expenses in the tax year when:

- All events that determine the liability have occurred,
- The amount of the liability can be figured with reasonable accuracy, and
- Economic performance takes place with respect to the expense.

There are exceptions to the economic performance rule for certain items, including recurring expenses. See section 461(h) and the related regulations for the rules for determining when economic performance takes place.

Nonaccrual experience method. Accrual method corporations are not required to accrue certain amounts to be received from the performance of services that, on the basis of their experience, will not be collected, if:

- The services are in the fields of health, law, engineering, architecture, accounting, actuarial science, performing arts, or consulting or
- The corporation's average annual gross receipts for the 3 prior tax years does not exceed $5 million.

This provision does not apply to any amount if interest is required to be paid on the amount or if there is any penalty for failure to timely pay the amount. For more information, see section 448(d)(5) and Temporary Regulations section 1.448-2T. For reporting requirements, see the instructions for line 1 on page 11.

Percentage-of-completion method. Long-term contracts (except for certain real property construction contracts) must generally be accounted for using the percentage of completion method described in section 460. See section 460 and the related regulations for rules on long-term contracts.

Mark-to-market accounting method. Generally, dealers in securities must use the mark-to-market accounting method described in section 475. Under this method, any security that is inventory to the dealer must be included in inventory at its FMV. Any security held by a dealer that is not inventory and that is held at the close of the tax year is treated as sold at its FMV on the last business day of the tax year. Any gain or loss must be taken into account in determining gross income. The gain or loss taken into account is generally treated as ordinary gain or loss. For details, including exceptions, see section 475, the related regulations, and Rev. Rul. 94-7, 1994-1 C.B. 151.

Dealers in commodities and traders in securities and commodities can elect to use the mark-to-market accounting method. To make the election, the corporation must file a statement describing the election, the first tax year the election is to be effective, and, for an election for traders in securities or commodities, the trade or business for which the election is made. Except for new taxpayers, the statement must be filed by the due date (not including extensions) of the income tax return for the tax year immediately preceding the election year and attached to that return, or if applicable, to a request for an extension of time to file that return. For more details, see sections 475(e) and (f) and Rev. Proc. 99-17, 1999-7 I.R.B. 52.

Change in accounting method. To change its method of accounting used to report taxable income (for income as a whole or for the treatment of any material item), the corporation must file Form 3115, Application for Change in Accounting Method. For more information, see Form 3115 and Pub. 538, Accounting Periods and Methods.

Section 481(a) adjustment. The corporation may have to make an adjustment under section 481(a) to prevent amounts of income or expense from being duplicated or omitted. The section 481(a) adjustment period is generally 1 year for a net negative adjustment and 4 years for a net positive adjustment. However, a corporation can elect to use a 1-year adjustment period if the net section 481(a) adjustment for the change is less than $25,000. The corporation must complete the appropriate lines of Form 3115 to make the election.

Include any net positive section 481(a) adjustment on page 1, line 10. If the net section 481(a) adjustment is negative, report it on Form 1120, line 26 (Form 1120-A, line 22).

Accounting Periods

A corporation must figure its taxable income on the basis of a tax year. A tax year is the annual accounting period a corporation uses to keep its records and report its income and expenses. Generally, corporations can use a calendar year or a fiscal year. Personal service corporations, however, must use a calendar year unless they meet one of the exceptions discussed under *Accounting period* on page 10.

For more information about accounting periods, see Regulations sections 1.441-1 and 1.441-2 and Pub. 538.

Calendar year. If the calendar year is adopted as the annual accounting period, the corporation must maintain its books and records and report its income and expenses for the period from January 1 through December 31 of each year.

Fiscal year. A fiscal year is 12 consecutive months ending on the last day of any month except December. A 52-53-week year is a fiscal year that varies from 52 to 53 weeks.

Adoption of tax year. A corporation adopts a tax year when it files its first income tax return. It must adopt a tax year by the due date (not including extensions) of its first income tax return.

Change of tax year. Generally, a corporation must get the consent of the IRS before changing its tax year by filing Form 1128, Application To Adopt, Change, or Retain a Tax Year. However, under certain conditions, a corporation can change its tax year without getting the consent.

For more information on change of tax year, see Form 1128, Regulations section 1.442-1, and Pub. 538. Personal service corporations should also see *Accounting period* on page 10.

Rounding Off to Whole Dollars

The corporation can round off cents to whole dollars on its return and schedules. If the corporation does round to whole dollars, it must round all amounts. To round, drop amounts under 50 cents and increase amounts from 50 to 99 cents to the next dollar (for example, $1.39 becomes $1 and $2.50 becomes $3).

If two or more amounts must be added to figure the amount to enter on a line, include cents when adding the amounts and round off only the total.

Recordkeeping

Keep the corporation's records for as long as they may be needed for the administration of any provision of the Internal Revenue Code. Usually, records that support an item of income, deduction, or credit on the return must be kept for 3 years from the date the return is due or filed, whichever is later. Keep records that verify the corporation's basis in property for as long as they are needed to figure the basis of the original or replacement property.

The corporation should keep copies of all filed returns. They help in preparing future and amended returns.

Depository Methods of Tax Payment

The corporation must pay the tax due in full no later than the 15th day of the 3rd month after the end of the tax year. The two methods of depositing corporate income taxes are discussed below.

Electronic Deposit Requirement

The corporation must make electronic deposits of all depository taxes (such as employment tax, excise tax, and corporate income tax) using the Electronic Federal Tax Payment System (EFTPS) in 2005 if:

- The total deposits of such taxes in 2003 were more than $200,000 or
- The corporation was required to use EFTPS in 2004.

If the corporation is required to use EFTPS and fails to do so, it may be subject to a 10% penalty. If the corporation is not required to use EFTPS, it can participate voluntarily. To enroll in or get more information about EFTPS, call 1-800-555-4477 or 1-800-945-8400. To enroll online, visit *www.eftps.gov*.

Depositing on time. For EFTPS deposits to be made timely, the corporation must initiate the transaction at least 1 business day before the date the deposit is due.

Deposits With Form 8109

If the corporation does not use EFTPS, deposit corporation income tax payments (and estimated tax payments) with Form 8109, Federal Tax Deposit Coupon. If you do not have a preprinted Form 8109, use Form 8109-B to make deposits. You can get this form by calling 1-800-829-4933. Be sure to have your EIN ready when you call.

Do not send deposits directly to an IRS office; otherwise, the corporation may have to pay a penalty. Mail or deliver the completed Form 8109 with the payment to an authorized depositary (a commercial bank or other financial institution authorized to accept federal tax deposits). Make checks or money orders payable to the depositary.

If the corporation prefers, it can mail the coupon and payment to Financial Agent, Federal Tax Deposit Processing, P.O. Box 970030, St. Louis, MO 63197. Make the check or money order payable to "Financial Agent."

To help ensure proper crediting, enter the corporation's EIN, the tax period to which the deposit applies, and "Form 1120" on the check or money order. Be sure to darken the "1120" box under "Type of Tax" and the appropriate "Quarter" box under "Tax Period" on the coupon. Records of these deposits will be sent to the IRS. For more information, see "Marking the Proper Tax Period" in the instructions for Form 8109.

For more information on deposits, see the instructions in the coupon booklet (Form 8109) and Pub. 583, Starting a Business and Keeping Records.

If the corporation owes tax when it files Form 1120 or Form 1120-A, do not include the payment with the tax return. Instead, mail or deliver the payment with Form 8109 to an authorized depositary, or use EFTPS, if applicable.

Estimated Tax Payments

Generally, the following rules apply to the corporation's payments of estimated tax.

- The corporation must make installment payments of estimated tax if it expects its total tax for the year (less applicable credits) to be $500 or more.
- The installments are due by the 15th day of the 4th, 6th, 9th, and 12th months of the tax year. If any date falls on a Saturday, Sunday, or legal holiday, the installment is due on the next regular business day.
- Use Form 1120-W, Estimated Tax for Corporations, as a worksheet to compute estimated tax.
- If the corporation does not use EFTPS, use the deposit coupons (Forms 8109) to make deposits of estimated tax.

For more information on estimated tax payments, including penalties that apply if the corporation fails to make required payments, see the instructions for line 33 on page 17.

Overpaid estimated tax. If the corporation overpaid estimated tax, it may be able to get a quick refund by filing Form 4466, Corporation Application for Quick Refund of Overpayment of Estimated Tax. The overpayment must be at least 10% of the corporation's expected income tax liability and at least $500. File Form 4466 after the end of the corporation's tax year, and no later than the 15th day of the third month after the end of the tax year. Form 4466 must be filed before the corporation files its tax return.

Interest and Penalties

Interest. Interest is charged on taxes paid late even if an extension of time to file is granted. Interest is also charged on penalties imposed for failure to file, negligence, fraud, substantial valuation misstatements, and substantial understatements of tax from the due date (including extensions) to the date of payment. The interest charge is figured at a rate determined under section 6621.

Penalty for late filing of return. A corporation that does not file its tax return by the due date, including extensions, may be penalized 5% of the unpaid tax for each month or part of a month the return is late, up to a maximum of 25% of the unpaid tax. The minimum penalty for a return that is over 60 days late is the smaller of the tax due or $100. The penalty will not be imposed if the corporation can show that the failure to file on time was due to reasonable cause. Corporations that file late should attach a statement explaining the reasonable cause.

Penalty for late payment of tax. A corporation that does not pay the tax when due generally may be penalized ½ of 1% of the unpaid tax for each month or part of a month the tax is not paid, up to a maximum of 25% of the unpaid tax. The penalty will not be imposed if the corporation can show that the failure to pay on time was due to reasonable cause.

Trust fund recovery penalty. This penalty may apply if certain excise, income, social security, and Medicare taxes that must be collected or withheld are not collected or withheld, or these taxes are not paid. These taxes are generally reported on Form 720, Quarterly Federal Excise Tax Return; Form 941, Employer's Quarterly Federal Tax Return; Form 943, Employers Annual Federal Tax Return for Agricultural Employees; or Form 945, Annual Return of Withheld Federal Income Tax. The trust fund recovery penalty may be imposed on all persons who are determined by the IRS to have been responsible for collecting, accounting for, and paying over these taxes, and who acted willfully in not doing so. The penalty is equal to the unpaid trust fund tax. See the Instructions for Form 720, Pub. 15 (Circular E), Employer's Tax Guide, or Pub. 51 (Circular A), Agricultural Employer's Tax Guide, for details, including the definition of responsible persons.

Other penalties. Other penalties can be imposed for negligence, substantial understatement of tax, and fraud. See sections 6662 and 6663.

Other Forms That May Be Required

Form	**Use this to—**
W-2 and **W-3**—Wage and Tax Statement; and Transmittal of Wage and Tax Statements	Report wages, tips, and other compensation, and withheld income, social security, and Medicare taxes for employees.
W-2G—Certain Gambling Winnings	Report gambling winnings from horse racing, dog racing, jai alai, lotteries, keno, bingo, slot machines, sweepstakes, wagering pools, etc.
926—Return by a U.S. Transferor of Property to a Foreign Corporation	Report certain transfers to foreign corporations under section 6038B.
940 or **940-EZ**—Employer's Annual Federal Unemployment (FUTA) Tax Return	Report and pay FUTA tax if the corporation either: 1. Paid wages of $1,500 or more in any calendar quarter during the calendar year (or the preceding calendar year), or 2. Had one or more employees working for the corporation for at least some part of a day in any 20 different weeks during the calendar year (or the preceding calendar year).
952—Consent To Extend the Time To Assess Tax Under Section 332(b)	Extend the period of assessment of all income taxes of the receiving corporation on the complete liquidation of a subsidiary under section 332.
966—Corporate Dissolution or Liquidation	Report the adoption of a resolution or plan to dissolve the corporation or liquidate any of its stock.
1042 and **1042-S**—Annual Withholding Tax Return for U.S. Source Income of Foreign Persons; and Foreign Person's U.S. Source Income Subject to Withholding	Report withheld tax on payments or distributions made to nonresident alien individuals, foreign partnerships, or foreign corporations to the extent these payments or distributions constitute gross income from sources within the United States that is not effectively connected with a U.S. trade or business. See Pub. 515, Withholding of Tax on Nonresident Aliens and Foreign Entities.
1042-T—Annual Summary and Transmittal of Forms 1042-S	Transmit paper Forms 1042-S to the IRS.
1096—Annual Summary and Transmittal of U.S. Information Returns	Transmit paper Forms 1099, 1098, 5498, and W-2G to the IRS.
1098—Mortgage Interest Statement	Report the receipt from any individual of $600 or more of mortgage interest (including certain points) in the course of the corporation's trade or business.
1098-E—Student Loan Interest Statement	Report the receipt of $600 or more of student loan interest in the course of the corporation's trade or business.
1099-A, B, C, CAP, DIV, INT, LTC, MISC, OID, PATR, R, S and **SA** **Important:** *Every corporation must file Forms 1099-MISC if, in the course of its trade or business, it makes payments of rents, commissions, or other fixed or determinable income (see section 6041) totaling $600 or more to any one person during the calendar year.*	Report the following: • Acquisitions or abandonments of secured property; • Proceeds from broker and barter exchange transactions; • Cancellation of debts; • Changes in corporate control and capital structure; • Dividends and distributions; • Interest payments; • Payments of long-term care and accelerated death benefits; • Miscellaneous income payments to certain fishing boat crew members, to providers of health and medical services, of rent or royalties, of nonemployee compensation, etc.; • Original issue discount; • Taxable distributions received from cooperatives; • Distributions from pensions, annuities, retirement or profit-sharing plans, IRAs, insurance contracts, etc.; • Proceeds from real estate transactions; and • Distributions from an HSA, Archer MSA, or Medicare Advantage MSA. Also use these returns to report amounts received as a nominee for another person. For more details, see the General Instructions for Forms 1099, 1098, 5498, and W-2G.
1122—Authorization and Consent of Subsidiary Corporation To Be Included in a Consolidated Income Tax Return	For the first year a subsidiary corporation is being included in a consolidated return, attach this form to the parent's consolidated return. Attach a separate Form 1122 for each subsidiary being included in the consolidated return.
3520—Annual Return To Report Transactions With Foreign Trusts and Receipt of Certain Foreign Gifts	Report a distribution received from a foreign trust; or, if the corporation was the grantor of, transferor of, or transferor to, a foreign trust that existed during the tax year. See Question 5 of Schedule N (Form 1120).
3520-A—Annual Information Return of Foreign Trust With a U.S. Owner	Report information about the foreign trust, its U.S. beneficiaries, and any U.S. person who is treated as an owner of any portion of the foreign trust.
5452—Corporate Report of Nondividend Distributions	Report nondividend distributions.

Form	Use this to—
5471—Information Return of U.S. Persons With Respect to Certain Foreign Corporations	A corporation may have to file Form 5471 if it: • Controls a foreign corporation; or • Acquires, disposes of, or owns 10% or more in value or vote of the outstanding stock of a foreign corporation; or • Owns stock in a corporation that is a controlled foreign corporation for an uninterrupted period of 30 days or more during any tax year of the foreign corporation, and it owned that stock on the last day of that year. See Question 4 of Schedule N (Form 1120).
5498—IRA Contribution Information	Report contributions (including rollover contributions) to any IRA, including a SEP, SIMPLE, or Roth IRA, and to report Roth IRA conversions, IRA recharacterizations, and the fair market value (FMV) of the account.
5498-ESA—Coverdell ESA Contribution Information	Report contributions (including rollover contributions) to and the FMV of a Coverdell education savings account (ESA).
5498-SA—HSA, Archer MSA, or Medicare Advantage MSA Information	Report contributions to an HSA or Archer MSA and the FMV of an HSA, Archer MSA, or Medicare Advantage MSA. For more information, see the general and specific instructions for Forms 1099, 1098, 5498, and W-2G.
5713—International Boycott Report	Report operations in, or related to, a "boycotting" country, company, or national of a country and to figure the loss of certain tax benefits.
8023—Elections Under Section 338 for Corporations Making Qualified Stock Purchases	Make elections under section 338 for a "target" corporation if the purchasing corporation has made a qualified stock purchase of the target corporation.
8027—Employer's Annual Information Return of Tip Income and Allocated Tips	Report receipts from large food or beverage operations, tips reported by employees, and allocated tips.
8264—Application for Registration of a Tax Shelter	Get a tax shelter registration number from the IRS. Until further guidance is issued, material advisors who provide material aid, assistance, or advice with respect to any reportable transaction after October 22, 2004, must use Form 8264 to disclose reportable transactions in accordance with interim guidance provided in Notice 2004-80, 2004-50 I.R.B. 963.
8271—Investor Reporting of Tax Shelter Registration Number	Report the registration number for a tax shelter that is required to be registered. Attach Form 8271 to any tax return (including Forms 1139 and 1120X) on which a deduction, credit, loss, or other tax benefit attributable to a tax shelter is taken or any income attributable to a tax shelter is reported.
8275—Disclosure Statement	Disclose items or positions, except those contrary to a regulation, that are not otherwise adequately disclosed on a tax return. The disclosure is made to avoid the parts of the accuracy-related penalty imposed for disregard of rules or substantial understatement of tax. Also use Form 8275 for disclosures relating to preparer penalties for understatements due to unrealistic positions or disregard of rules.
8275-R—Regulation Disclosure Statement	Disclose any item on a tax return for which a position has been taken that is contrary to Treasury regulations.
8281—Information Return for Publicly Offered Original Issue Discount Instruments	Report the issuance of public offerings of debt instruments (obligations).
8288 and 8288-A—U.S. Withholding Tax Return for Dispositions by Foreign Persons of U.S. Real Property Interests; and Statement of Withholding on Dispositions by Foreign Persons of U.S. Real Property Interests	Report and send withheld tax on the purchase of U.S. real property from a foreign person. See section 1445 and the related regulations for more information.
8300—Report of Cash Payments Over $10,000 Received in a Trade or Business	Report the receipt of more than $10,000 in cash or foreign currency in one transaction or a series of related transactions.
8594—Asset Acquisition Statement Under Section 1060	Report a sale of assets that make up a trade or business if goodwill or going concern value attaches, or could attach, to such assets and if the buyer's basis is determined only by the amount paid for the assets. Both the seller and buyer must use this form.
8806—Information Return for Acquisition of Control or Substantial Change in Capital Structure	Report an acquisition of control or a substantial change in the capital structure of a domestic corporation.
8817—Allocation of Patronage and Nonpatronage Income and Deductions	Figure and report patronage and nonpatronage income and deductions (used by taxable cooperatives).
8842—Election To Use Different Annualization Periods for Corporate Estimated Tax	Elect one of the annualization periods in section 6655(e)(2) for figuring estimated tax payments under the annualized income installment method.
8849—Claim for Refund of Excise Taxes	Claim a refund of certain excise taxes.
8858—Information Return of U.S. Persons With Respect To Foreign Disregarded Entities	This form is required if the corporation directly or indirectly owns a foreign disregarded entity. See Question 1 of Schedule N (Form 1120).

Form	Use this to—
8865—Return of U.S. Person With Respect To Certain Foreign Partnerships	Report an interest in a foreign partnership. A domestic corporation may have to file Form 8865 if it: 1. Controlled a foreign partnership (owned more than a 50% direct or indirect interest in the partnership). 2. Owned at least a 10% direct or indirect interest in a foreign partnership while U.S. persons controlled that partnership. 3. Had an acquisition, disposition, or change in proportional interest of a foreign partnership that: a. Increased its direct interest to at least 10% or reduced its direct interest of at least 10% to less than 10% or b. Changed its direct interest by at least a 10% interest. 4. Contributed property to a foreign partnership in exchange for a partnership interest if: a. Immediately after the contribution, the corporation directly or indirectly owned at least a 10% interest in the foreign partnership or b. The FMV of the property the corporation contributed to the foreign partnership in exchange for a partnership interest exceeds $100,000 when added to other contributions of property made to the foreign partnership during the preceding 12-month period. The domestic corporation may also have to file Form 8865 to report certain dispositions by a foreign partnership of property it previously contributed to that partnership if it was a partner at the time of the disposition. For more details, including penalties for failing to file Form 8865, see Form 8865 and its separate instructions.
8876—Excise Tax on Structured Settlement Factoring Transactions	Report and pay the 40% excise tax imposed under section 5891.
8883—Asset Allocation Statement Under Section 338	Report information about transactions involving the deemed sale of corporate assets under section 338.
8886—Reportable Transaction Disclosure Statement	Disclose information for each reportable transaction in which the corporation participated. Form 8886 must be filed for each tax year that the federal income tax liability of the corporation is affected by its participation in the transaction. The corporation may have to pay a penalty if it is required to file Form 8886 and does not do so. The following are reportable transactions. 1. Any listed transaction, which is a transaction that is the same as or substantially similar to tax avoidance transactions identified by the IRS. 2. Any transaction offered under conditions of confidentiality for which the corporation paid an advisor a fee of at least $250,000. 3. Certain transactions for which the corporation has contractual protection against disallowance of the tax benefits. 4. Certain transactions resulting in a loss of at least $10 million in any single year or $20 million in any combination of years. 5. Certain transactions resulting in a book-tax difference of more than $10 million on a gross basis. 6. Certain transactions resulting in a tax credit of more than $250,000, if the corporation held the asset generating the credit for 45 days or less.
8895—Section 965(f) Election for Corporations that are U.S. Shareholders of a Controlled Foreign Corporation	Elect the 85% dividends-received deduction on repatriated dividends under section 965.

Specific Instructions

Subchapter T Cooperative

To ensure that Form 1120 or Form 1120-A is timely and properly processed, a corporation that is a cooperative should write "SUBCHAPTER T COOPERATIVE" at the top of page 1 of the form.

Period Covered

File the 2004 return for calendar year 2004 and fiscal years that begin in 2004 and end in 2005. For a fiscal year return, fill in the tax year space at the top of the form.

Note. The 2004 Form 1120 can also be used if:

- The corporation has a tax year of less than 12 months that begins and ends in 2005 and
- The 2005 Form 1120 is not available at the time the corporation is required to file its return.

The corporation must show its 2005 tax year on the 2004 Form 1120 and take into account any tax law changes that are effective for tax years beginning after December 31, 2004.

Name and Address

Use the preprinted label on the tax package information form (Form 8160-A) or the Form 1120 package that was mailed to the corporation. Cross out any errors and print the correct information on the label. If the corporation did not receive a label, print or type the corporation's true name (as set forth in the charter or other legal document creating it), address, and EIN on the appropriate lines.

Include the suite, room, or other unit number after the street address. If the Post Office does not deliver mail to the street address and the corporation has a P.O. box, show the box number instead.

If the corporation receives its mail in care of a third party (such as an accountant or an attorney), enter on the street address line "C/O" followed by the third party's name and street address or P.O. box.

Item A

Consolidated Return (Form 1120 Only)

Corporations filing a consolidated return must attach Form 851, Affiliations Schedule, and other supporting statements to the return. For details, see *Other Forms That May Be Required* on page 7, and *Statements* on page 4.

Personal Holding Company (Form 1120 Only)

A personal holding company must attach to Form 1120 a Schedule PH (Form 1120), U.S. Personal Holding Company (PHC) Tax. See the instructions for that form for details.

Personal Service Corporation

A personal service corporation is a corporation whose principal activity (defined below) for the testing period for the tax year is the performance of personal services. The services must be substantially performed by employee-owners. Employee-owners must own more than 10% of the FMV of the corporation's outstanding stock on the last day of the testing period.

Testing period. Generally, the testing period for a tax year is the prior tax year. The testing period for a new corporation starts with the first day of its first tax year and ends on the earlier of:

- The last day of its first tax year or
- The last day of the calendar year in which the first tax year began.

Principal activity. The principal activity of a corporation is considered to be the performance of personal services if, during the testing period, the corporation's compensation costs for the performance of personal services (defined below) are more than 50% of its total compensation costs.

Performance of personal services. The term "performance of personal services" includes any activity involving the performance of personal services in the field of health, law, engineering, architecture, accounting, actuarial science, performing arts, or consulting (as defined in Temporary Regulations section 1.448-1T(e)).

Substantial performance by employee-owners. Personal services are substantially performed by employee-owners if, for the testing period, more than 20% of the corporation's compensation costs for the performance of personal services are for services performed by employee-owners.

Employee-owner. A person is considered to be an employee-owner if the person:

- Is an employee of the corporation on any day of the testing period and
- Owns any outstanding stock of the corporation on any day of the testing period.

Stock ownership is determined under the attribution rules of section 318, except that "any" is substituted for "50% or more in value" in section 318(a)(2)(C).

Accounting period. A personal service corporation must use a calendar tax year unless:

- It elects to use a 52-53-week tax year that ends with reference to the calendar year or tax year elected under section 444;
- It can establish a business purpose for a different tax year and obtains the approval of the IRS (see Form 1128 and Pub. 538); or
- It elects under section 444 to have a tax year other than a calendar year. To make the election, use Form 8716, Election To Have a Tax Year Other Than a Required Tax Year.

If a corporation makes the section 444 election, its deduction for certain amounts paid to employee-owners may be limited. See Schedule H (Form 1120), Section 280H Limitations for a Personal Service Corporation (PSC), to figure the maximum deduction.

If a section 444 election is terminated and the termination results in a short tax year, type or print at the top of the first page of Form 1120 or Form 1120-A for the short tax year "SECTION 444 ELECTION TERMINATED." See Temporary Regulations section 1.444-1T(a)(5) for more information.

Personal service corporations that want to change their tax year must file Form 1128 to get IRS consent. For rules and procedures on adopting, changing, or retaining an accounting period for a personal service corporation, see Form 1128 and Pub. 538.

Other rules. For other rules that apply to personal service corporations, see *Passive activity limitations* on page 12 and *Contributions of property other than cash* on page 14.

Schedule M-3

A corporation with total assets (consolidated for all corporations included within the tax consolidation group) of $10 million or more on the last day of the tax year must complete new Schedule M-3 instead of Schedule M-1.

Item B. Employer Identification Number (EIN)

Enter the corporation's EIN. If the corporation does not have an EIN, it must apply for one. An EIN can be applied for:

- Online—Click on the EIN link at *www.irs.gov/businesses/small*. The EIN is issued immediately once the application information is validated.
- By telephone at 1-800-829-4933 from 7:00 a.m. to 10:00 p.m. in the corporation's local time zone.
- By mailing or faxing Form SS-4, Application for Employer Identification Number.

If the corporation has not received its EIN by the time the return is due, enter "Applied for" in the space for the EIN. For more details, see Pub. 583.

Note. The online application process is not yet available for corporations with addresses in foreign countries or Puerto Rico.

Item D. Total Assets

Enter the corporation's total assets (as determined by the accounting method regularly used in keeping the corporation's books and records) at the end of the tax year. If there are no assets at the end of the tax year, enter -0-.

If the corporation is required to complete Schedule L, enter total assets from Schedule L, line 15, column (d) on page 1, item D. If filing a consolidated return, report total consolidated assets for all corporations joining in the return. See *Consolidated returns* on page 4.

Item E. Initial Return, Final Return, Name Change, or Address Change

- If this is the corporation's first return, check the "Initial return" box.
- If the corporation ceases to exist, check the "Final return" box.
- If the corporation changed its name since it last filed a return, check the box for "Name change." Generally, a corporation also must have amended its articles of incorporation and filed the amendment with the state in which it was incorporated.
- If the corporation has changed its address since it last filed a return (including a change to an "in care of" address), check the box for "Address change."

Note. If a change in address occurs after the return is filed, use Form 8822, Change of Address, to notify the IRS of the new address.

Income

Except as otherwise provided in the Internal Revenue Code, gross income includes all income from whatever source derived.

Extraterritorial income. Gross income generally does not include extraterritorial income that is qualifying foreign trade income. However, the extraterritorial income exclusion is reduced by 20% for transactions after 2004, unless made under a binding contract with an unrelated person in effect on September 17, 2003, and at all times thereafter. Use Form 8873, Extraterritorial Income Exclusion, to figure the exclusion. Include the exclusion in the total for "Other deductions" on line 26, Form 1120 (line 22, Form 1120-A).

Income from qualifying shipping activities. For tax years beginning after October 22, 2004, the corporation's gross income does not include income from qualifying shipping activities (as defined in section 1356) if the corporation makes an election under section 1354 to be taxed on its notional shipping income (as defined in section 1353) at the highest corporate tax rate (35%). If the election is made, the corporation generally may not claim any loss, deduction, or credit with respect to qualifying shipping activities. A corporation making this election also may elect to defer gain on the disposition of a qualifying vessel under section 1359.

Report the section 1352(1) tax on Schedule J, line 3, and report the section 1352(2) tax on Schedule J, line 10. For Schedule J, line 10, check the "Other" box and attach a schedule that shows the computation of the section 1352(2) amount.

Line 1. Gross Receipts or Sales

Enter gross receipts or sales from all business operations except those that must be reported on lines 4 through 10. In general, advance payments are reported in the year of receipt. To report income from long-term contracts, see section 460. For special rules for reporting certain advance payments for goods and long-term contracts, see Regulations section 1.451-5. For permissible methods for reporting advance payments for services by an accrual method corporation, see Rev. Proc. 2004-34, 2004-22 I.R.B. 991.

Installment sales. Generally, the installment method cannot be used for dealer dispositions of property. A "dealer disposition" is: (a) any disposition of personal property by a person who regularly sells or otherwise disposes of personal property of the same type on the installment plan or (b) any disposition of real property held for sale to customers in the ordinary course of the taxpayer's trade or business.

These restrictions on using the installment method do not apply to dispositions of property used or produced in a farming business or sales of timeshares and residential lots for which the corporation elects to pay interest under section 453(l)(3).

For sales of timeshares and residential lots reported under the installment method, the corporation's income tax is increased by the interest payable under section 453(l)(3). To report this addition to the tax, see the instructions for line 10, Schedule J, Form 1120.

Enter on line 1 (and carry to line 3), the gross profit on collections from installment sales for any of the following.

- Dealer dispositions of property before March 1, 1986.
- Dispositions of property used or produced in the trade or business of farming.
- Certain dispositions of timeshares and residential lots reported under the installment method.

Attach a schedule showing the following information for the current and the 3 preceding years: (a) gross sales, (b) cost of goods sold, (c) gross profits, (d) percentage of gross profits to gross sales, (e) amount collected, and (f) gross profit on the amount collected.

Nonaccrual experience method. Corporations that qualify to use the nonaccrual experience method (described on page 5) should attach a schedule showing total gross receipts, the amount not accrued as a result of the application of section 448(d)(5), and the net amount accrued. Enter the net amount on line 1a.

Line 2. Cost of Goods Sold

Enter the cost of goods sold on line 2, page 1. Before making this entry, a Form 1120 filer must complete Schedule A on page 2 of Form 1120. See the Schedule A instructions on page 17. Form 1120-A filers can use the worksheet on page 17 to figure the amount to enter on line 2.

Line 4. Dividends

Form 1120 filers. See the instructions for Schedule C on page 18. Then, complete Schedule C and enter on line 4 the amount from Schedule C, line 19.

Form 1120-A filers. Enter the total dividends received (that are not from debt-financed stock) from domestic corporations that qualify for the 70% dividends-received deduction.

Line 5. Interest

Enter taxable interest on U.S. obligations and on loans, notes, mortgages, bonds, bank deposits, corporate bonds, tax refunds, etc. Do not offset interest expense against interest income. Special rules apply to interest income from certain below-market-rate loans. See section 7872 for details.

Note. Report tax-exempt interest income on Form 1120, Schedule K, item 9 (Form 1120-A, Part II, item 3). Also, if required, include the same amount on Schedule M-1, line 7; Form 1120-A, Part IV, line 6; or Schedule M-3, Part II, line 13.

Line 6. Gross Rents

Enter the gross amount received for the rental of property. Deduct expenses such as repairs, interest, taxes, and depreciation on the proper lines for deductions. A rental activity held by a closely held corporation or a personal service corporation may be subject to the passive activity loss rules. See *Passive activity limitations* on page 12.

Line 8. Capital Gain Net Income

Every sale or exchange of a capital asset must be reported in detail on Schedule D (Form 1120), Capital Gains and Losses, even if there is no gain or loss.

Line 9. Net Gain or (Loss)

Enter the net gain or (loss) from line 17, Part II, Form 4797, Sales of Business Property.

Line 10. Other Income

Enter any other taxable income not reported on lines 1 through 9. List the type and amount of income on an attached schedule. If the corporation has only one item of other income, describe it in parentheses on line 10. Examples of other income to report on line 10 are:

1. Recoveries of bad debts deducted in prior years under the specific charge-off method.
2. The amount included in income from Form 6478, Credit for Alcohol Used as Fuel.
3. The amount included in income from Form 8864, Biodiesel Fuels Credit.
4. Refunds of taxes deducted in prior years to the extent they reduced income subject to tax in the year deducted (see section 111). Do not offset current year taxes against tax refunds.
5. The amount of any deduction previously taken under section 179A that is subject to recapture. The corporation must recapture the benefit of any allowable deduction for clean-fuel vehicle property (or clean-fuel vehicle refueling property) if the property later ceases to qualify. See Regulations section 1.179A-1 for details.
6. Ordinary income from trade or business activities of a partnership (from Schedule K-1 (Form 1065 or 1065-B)). Do not offset ordinary losses against ordinary income. Instead, include the losses on line 26, Form 1120 (line 22, Form 1120-A). Show the partnership's name, address, and EIN on a separate statement attached to this return. If the amount entered is from more than one partnership, identify the amount from each partnership.
7. Any **LIFO recapture** amount under section 1363(d). The corporation may have to include a LIFO recapture amount in income if it:

a. Used the LIFO inventory method for its last tax year before the first tax year for which it elected to become an S corporation or

b. Transferred LIFO inventory assets to an S corporation in a nonrecognition transaction in which those assets were transferred basis property.

The LIFO recapture amount is the amount by which the C corporation's inventory under the FIFO method exceeds the inventory amount under the LIFO method at the close of the corporation's last tax year as a C corporation (or for the year of the transfer, if (b) above applies). For more information, see Regulations section 1.1363-2 and Rev. Proc. 94-61, 1994-2 C.B. 775. Also see the instructions for Schedule J, line 11.

Deductions

Limitations on Deductions

Section 263A uniform capitalization rules. The uniform capitalization rules of section 263A generally require corporations to capitalize, or include in inventory, certain costs incurred in connection with:

- The production of real property and tangible personal property held in inventory or held for sale in the ordinary course of business.
- Real property or personal property (tangible and intangible) acquired for resale.
- The production of real property and tangible personal property by a corporation for use in its trade or business or in an activity engaged in for profit.

Tangible personal property produced by a corporation includes a film, sound recording, videotape, book, or similar property.

Corporations subject to the section 263A uniform capitalization rules are required to capitalize:

1. Direct costs and
2. An allocable part of most indirect costs (including taxes) that (a) benefit the assets produced or acquired for resale or (b) are incurred by reason of the performance of production or resale activities.

For inventory, some of the indirect expenses that must be capitalized are:

- Administration expenses.
- Taxes.
- Depreciation.
- Insurance.
- Compensation paid to officers attributable to services.
- Rework labor.
- Contributions to pension, stock bonus, and certain profit-sharing, annuity, or deferred compensation plans.

Regulations section 1.263A-1(e)(3) specifies other indirect costs that relate to production or resale activities that must be capitalized and those that may be currently deductible.

Interest expense paid or incurred during the production period of designated property must be capitalized and is governed by special rules. For more details, see Regulations sections 1.263A-8 through 1.263A-15.

The costs required to be capitalized under section 263A are not deductible until the property (to which the costs relate) is sold, used, or otherwise disposed of by the corporation.

Exceptions. Section 263A does not apply to:

- Personal property acquired for resale if the corporation's average annual gross receipts for the 3 prior tax years were $10 million or less.
- Timber.
- Most property produced under a long-term contract.
- Certain property produced in a farming business.
- Research and experimental costs under section 174.
- Intangible drilling costs for oil, gas, and geothermal property.
- Mining exploration and development costs.
- Inventoriable items accounted for in the same manner as materials and supplies that are not incidental. See *Cost of Goods Sold* on page 17 for details.

For more details on the uniform capitalization rules, see Regulations sections 1.263A-1 through 1.263A-3. See Regulations section 1.263A-4 for rules for property produced in a farming business.

Transactions between related taxpayers. Generally, an accrual basis taxpayer can only deduct business expenses and interest owed to a related party in the year the payment is included in the income of the related party. See sections 163(e)(3),163(j), and 267 for limitations on deductions for unpaid interest and expenses.

Section 291 limitations. Corporations may be required to adjust deductions for depletion of iron ore and coal, intangible drilling and exploration and development costs, certain deductions for financial institutions, and the amortizable basis of pollution control facilities. See section 291 to determine the amount of the adjustment. Also see section 43.

Golden parachute payments. A portion of the payments made by a corporation to key personnel that exceeds their usual compensation may not be deductible. This occurs when the corporation has an agreement (golden parachute) with these key employees to pay them these excess amounts if control of the corporation changes. See section 280G and Regulations section 1.280G-1.

Business start-up and organizational costs. Business start-up and organizational costs must be capitalized unless an election is made to deduct or amortize them. For costs paid or incurred before October 23, 2004, the corporation must capitalize them unless it elects to amortize these costs over a period of 60 months or more. For costs paid or incurred after October 22, 2004, the following rules apply separately to each category of costs.

- The corporation can elect to deduct up to $5,000 of such costs for the year the corporation begins business operations.
- The $5,000 deduction is reduced (but not below zero) by the amount the total costs exceed $50,000. If the total costs are $55,000 or more, the deduction is reduced to zero.
- If the election is made, any costs that are not deductible must be amortized ratably over a 180-month period beginning with the month the corporation begins business operations.

For more details on the election for business start-up costs, see section 195 and attach the statement required by Regulations section 1.195-1(b). For more details on the election for organizational costs, see section 248 and attach the statement required by Regulations section 1.248-1(c). Report the deductible amount of these costs and any amortization on line 26 (line 22 of Form 1120-A). For amortization that begins during the 2004 tax year, complete and attach Form 4562.

Passive activity limitations. Limitations on passive activity losses and credits under section 469 apply to personal service corporations (see *Personal Service Corporation* on page 10) and closely held corporations (see below).

Generally, the two kinds of passive activities are:

- Trade or business activities in which the corporation did not materially participate for the tax year and
- Rental activities, regardless of its participation.

For exceptions, see Form 8810, Corporate Passive Activity Loss and Credit Limitations.

An activity is a trade or business activity if it is not a rental activity and:

- The activity involves the conduct of a trade or business (deductions from the activity would be allowable under section 162 if other limitations, such as the passive loss rules, did not apply) or
- The activity involves research and experimental costs that are deductible under section 174 (or would be deductible if the corporation chose to deduct rather than capitalize them).

Corporations subject to the passive activity limitations must complete Form 8810 to compute their allowable passive activity loss and credit. Before completing Form 8810, see Temporary Regulations section 1.163-8T, which provides rules for allocating interest expense among activities. If a passive activity is also subject to the earnings stripping rules of section 163(j) or the at-risk rules of section 465, those rules apply before the passive loss rules. For more information, see section 469, the related regulations, and Pub. 925, Passive Activity and At-Risk Rules.

Closely held corporations. A corporation is a closely held corporation if:

- At any time during the last half of the tax year more than 50% in value of its outstanding stock is directly or indirectly owned by or for not more than five individuals and
- The corporation is not a personal service corporation.

Certain organizations are treated as individuals for purposes of this test. See section 542(a)(2). For rules for determining stock ownership, see section 544 (as modified by section 465(a)(3)).

Reducing certain expenses for which credits are allowable. For each credit listed below, the corporation must reduce the otherwise allowable deductions for expenses used to figure the credit by the amount of the current year credit.

- Work opportunity credit.
- Research credit.
- Orphan drug credit.
- Disabled access credit.
- Enhanced oil recovery credit.
- Empowerment zone and renewal community employment credit.
- Indian employment credit.
- Employer credit for social security and Medicare taxes paid on certain employee tips.
- Welfare-to-work credit.
- Credit for small employer pension plan startup costs.
- Credit for employer-provided childcare facilities and services.
- New York Liberty Zone business employee credit.
- Low sulfur diesel fuel production credit.

If the corporation has any of these credits, figure each current year credit before figuring the deduction for expenses on which the credit is based.

Line 12. Compensation of Officers

Enter deductible officers' compensation on line 12. Form 1120 filers must complete Schedule E if their total receipts (line 1a, plus lines 4 through 10) are $500,000 or more. Do not include compensation deductible elsewhere on the return, such as amounts included in cost of goods sold, elective contributions to a section 401(k) cash or deferred arrangement, or amounts contributed under a salary reduction SEP agreement or a SIMPLE IRA plan.

Include only the deductible part of each officer's compensation on Schedule E. See *Disallowance of deduction for employee compensation in excess of $1 million* below. Complete Schedule E, line 1, columns (a) through (f), for all officers. The corporation determines who is an officer under the laws of the state where it is incorporated.

If a consolidated return is filed, each member of an affiliated group must furnish this information.

Disallowance of deduction for employee compensation in excess of $1 million. Publicly held corporations cannot deduct compensation to a "covered employee" to the extent that the compensation exceeds $1 million. Generally, a covered employee is:

- The chief executive officer of the corporation (or an individual acting in that capacity) as of the end of the tax year or
- An employee whose total compensation must be reported to shareholders under the Securities Exchange Act of 1934 because the employee is among the four highest compensated officers for that tax year (other than the chief executive officer).

For this purpose, compensation does not include the following.

- Income from certain employee trusts, annuity plans, or pensions.
- Any benefit paid to an employee that is excluded from the employee's income.

The deduction limit does not apply to:

- Commissions based on individual performance,
- Qualified performance-based compensation, and
- Income payable under a written, binding contract in effect on February 17, 1993.

The $1 million limit is reduced by amounts disallowed as excess parachute payments under section 280G.

For details, see section 162(m) and Regulations section 1.162-27.

Line 13. Salaries and Wages

Enter the total salaries and wages paid for the tax year, reduced by the amount claimed on:

- Form 5884, Work Opportunity Credit, line 2,
- Form 8844, Empowerment Zone and Renewal Community Employment Credit, line 2,
- Form 8845, Indian Employment Credit, line 4,
- Form 8861, Welfare-to-Work Credit, line 2, and
- Form 8884, New York Liberty Zone Business Employee Credit, line 2.

Do not include salaries and wages deductible elsewhere on the return, such as amounts included in cost of goods sold, elective contributions to a section 401(k) cash or deferred arrangement, or amounts contributed under a salary reduction SEP agreement or a SIMPLE IRA plan.

CAUTION *If the corporation provided taxable fringe benefits to its employees, such as personal use of a car, do not deduct as wages the amount allocated for depreciation and other expenses claimed on lines 20 and 26, Form 1120 (lines 20 and 22, Form 1120-A).*

Line 14. Repairs and Maintenance

Enter the cost of incidental repairs and maintenance not claimed elsewhere on the return, such as labor and supplies, that do not add to the value of the property or appreciably prolong its life. New buildings, machinery, or permanent improvements that increase the value of the property are not deductible. They must be depreciated or amortized.

Line 15. Bad Debts

Enter the total debts that became worthless in whole or in part during the tax year. A small bank or thrift institution using the reserve method of section 585 should attach a schedule showing how it figured the current year's provision. A cash basis taxpayer cannot claim a bad debt deduction unless the amount was previously included in income.

Line 16. Rents

If the corporation rented or leased a vehicle, enter the total annual rent or lease expense paid or incurred during the year. Also complete Part V of Form 4562, Depreciation and Amortization. If the corporation leased a vehicle for a term of 30 days or more, the deduction for vehicle lease expense may have to be reduced by an amount called the inclusion amount. The corporation may have an inclusion amount if:

The lease term began:	And the vehicle's FMV on the first day of the lease exceeded:
After 12/31/03 and before 1/1/05 . . .	$17,500
After 12/31/02 but before 1/1/04	$18,000
After 12/31/98 but before 1/1/03	$15,500

If the lease term began before January 1, 1999, see Pub. 463, Travel, Entertainment, Gift, and Car Expenses, to find out if the corporation has an inclusion amount. The inclusion amount for lease terms beginning in 2005 will be published in the Internal Revenue Bulletin in early 2005.

See Pub. 463 for instructions on figuring the inclusion amount.

Line 17. Taxes and Licenses

Enter taxes paid or accrued during the tax year, but do not include the following.

- Federal income taxes.
- Foreign or U.S. possession income taxes if a tax credit is claimed (however, see the Instructions for Form 5735 for special rules for possession income taxes).
- Taxes not imposed on the corporation.
- Taxes, including state or local sales taxes, that are paid or incurred in connection with an acquisition or disposition of property (these taxes must be treated as a part of the cost of the acquired property or, in the case of a disposition, as a reduction in the amount realized on the disposition).
- Taxes assessed against local benefits that increase the value of the property assessed (such as for paving, etc.).
- Taxes deducted elsewhere on the return, such as those reflected in cost of goods sold.

See section 164(d) for apportionment of taxes on real property between seller and purchaser.

Line 18. Interest

Note. Do not offset interest income against interest expense.

The corporation must make an interest allocation if the proceeds of a loan were used for more than one purpose (for example, to purchase a portfolio investment and to acquire an interest in a passive activity). See Temporary Regulations section 1.163-8T for the interest allocation rules.

Mutual savings banks, building and loan associations, and cooperative banks can deduct the amounts paid or credited to the accounts of depositors as dividends, interest, or earnings. See section 591.

Do not deduct the following interest.

- Interest on indebtedness incurred or continued to purchase or carry obligations if the interest is wholly exempt from income tax. For exceptions, see section 265(b).
- For cash basis taxpayers, prepaid interest allocable to years following the current tax year (for example, a cash basis calendar year taxpayer who in 2004 prepaid interest allocable to any period after 2004 can deduct only the amount allocable to 2004).
- Interest and carrying charges on straddles. Generally, these amounts must be capitalized. See section 263(g).
- Interest on debt allocable to the production of designated property by a corporation for its own use or for sale. The corporation must capitalize this interest. Also capitalize any interest on debt allocable to an asset used to produce the property. See section 263A(f) and Regulations sections 1.263A-8 through 1.263A-15 for definitions and more information.

• Interest paid or incurred on any portion of an underpayment of tax that is attributable to an understatement arising from an undisclosed listed transaction or an undisclosed reportable avoidance transaction (other than a listed transaction) entered into in tax years beginning after October 22, 2004.

Special rules apply to:
• Interest on which no tax is imposed (see section 163(j)).
• Foregone interest on certain below-market-rate loans (see section 7872).
• Original issue discount on certain high-yield discount obligations. (See section 163(e) to figure the disqualified portion.)
• Interest which is allocable to unborrowed policy cash values of life insurance, endowment, or annuity contracts issued after June 8, 1997. See section 264(f). Attach a statement showing the computation of the deduction.

Line 19. Charitable Contributions

Enter contributions or gifts actually paid within the tax year to or for the use of charitable and governmental organizations described in section 170(c) and any unused contributions carried over from prior years.

Corporations reporting taxable income on the accrual method can elect to treat as paid during the tax year any contributions paid by the 15th day of the 3rd month after the end of the tax year if the contributions were authorized by the board of directors during the tax year. Attach a declaration to the return stating that the resolution authorizing the contributions was adopted by the board of directors during the tax year. The declaration must include the date the resolution was adopted.

Limitation on deduction. The total amount claimed cannot be more than 10% of taxable income (line 30, Form 1120, or line 26, Form 1120-A) computed without regard to the following.
• Any deduction for contributions.
• The special deductions on line 29b, Form 1120 (line 25b, Form 1120-A).
• The deduction allowed under section 249.
• Any net operating loss (NOL) carryback to the tax year under section 172.
• Any capital loss carryback to the tax year under section 1212(a)(1).

Carryover. Charitable contributions over the 10% limitation cannot be deducted for the tax year but can be carried over to the next 5 tax years.

Special rules apply if the corporation has an NOL carryover to the tax year. In figuring the charitable contributions deduction for the tax year, the 10% limit is applied using the taxable income after taking into account any deduction for the NOL.

To figure the amount of any remaining NOL carryover to later years, taxable income must be modified (see section 172(b)). To the extent that contributions are used to reduce taxable income for this purpose and increase an NOL carryover, a contributions carryover is not allowed. See section 170(d)(2)(B).

Substantiation requirements. Generally, no deduction is allowed for any contribution of $250 or more unless the corporation gets a written acknowledgment from the donee organization that shows the amount of cash contributed, describes any property contributed, and, either gives a description and a good faith estimate of the value of any goods or services provided in return for the contribution or states that no goods or services were provided in return for the contribution. The acknowledgment must be obtained by the due date (including extensions) of the corporation's return, or, if earlier, the date the return is filed. Do not attach the acknowledgment to the tax return, but keep it with the corporation's records. These rules apply in addition to the filing requirements for Form 8283, Noncash Charitable Contributions, discussed below.

For more information on charitable contributions, including substantiation and recordkeeping requirements, see section 170 and the related regulations and Pub. 526, Charitable Contributions.

Contributions of property other than cash. If a corporation (other than a closely held or personal service corporation) contributes property other than cash and claims over a $500 deduction for the property, it must attach a schedule to the return describing the kind of property contributed and the method used to determine its fair market value (FMV). Closely held corporations and personal service corporations must complete Form 8283 and attach it to their returns. All other corporations generally must complete and attach Form 8283 to their returns for contributions of property (other than money) if the total claimed deduction for all property contributed was more than $5,000.

If the corporation made a "qualified conservation contribution" under section 170(h), also include the FMV of the underlying property before and after the donation, as well as the type of legal interest contributed, and describe the conservation purpose benefited by the donation. If a contribution carryover is included, show the amount and how it was determined.

Contributions after June 3, 2004. For contributions of certain property made after June 3, 2004, a corporation must file Form 8283 and get a qualified appraisal if claiming a deduction of more than $5,000. Do not attach the appraisal to the tax return unless claiming a deduction of more than $500,000 or, for art, a deduction of $20,000 or more. See Form 8283.

Contributions of used vehicles. Special rules apply to contributions after 2004 of used motor vehicles, boats, or airplanes with a claimed value of more than $500. See section 170(f)(12).

Reduced deduction for contributions of certain property. For a charitable contribution of property, the corporation must reduce the contribution by the sum of:
• The ordinary income and short-term capital gain that would have resulted if the property were sold at its FMV and
• For certain contributions, the long-term capital gain that would have resulted if the property were sold at its FMV.

The reduction for the long-term capital gain applies to:
• Contributions of tangible personal property for use by an exempt organization for a purpose or function unrelated to the basis for its exemption,
• Contributions of any property to or for the use of certain private foundations except for stock for which market quotations are readily available (section 170(e)(5)), and
• Any patent or certain other intellectual property contributed after June 3, 2004. See section 170(e)(1)(B). However, the corporation can deduct certain qualified donee income from this property. See section 170(m).

Larger deduction. A larger deduction is allowed for certain contributions of:
• Inventory and other property to certain organizations for use in the care of the ill, needy, or infants (see section 170(e)(3) and Regulations section 1.170A-4A);
• Scientific equipment used for research to institutions of higher learning or to certain scientific research organizations (other than by personal holding companies and service organizations) (see section 170(e)(4)); and
• Computer technology and equipment for educational purposes. See section 170(e)(6).

Line 20. Depreciation

Include on line 20 depreciation and the part of the cost of certain property that the corporation elected to expense under section 179. See Form 4562 and its instructions.

Line 22. Depletion (Form 1120 Only)

See sections 613 and 613A for percentage depletion rates applicable to natural deposits. Also see section 291 for the limitation on the depletion deduction for iron ore and coal (including lignite).

Attach Form T (Timber), Forest Activities Schedule, if a deduction for depletion of timber is taken.

Foreign intangible drilling costs and foreign exploration and development costs must either be added to the corporation's basis for cost depletion purposes or be deducted ratably over a 10-year period. See sections 263(i), 616, and 617 for details.

See Pub. 535 for more information on depletion.

Line 24. Pension, Profit-Sharing, etc., Plans (Form 1120 Only)

Enter the deduction for contributions to qualified pension, profit-sharing, or other funded deferred compensation plans. Employers who maintain such a plan generally must file one of the forms listed below, even if the plan is not a qualified plan under the Internal Revenue Code. The filing requirement applies even if the corporation does not claim a deduction for the current tax year. There are penalties for failure to file these forms on time and for overstating the pension plan deduction. See sections 6652(e) and 6662(f).

Form 5500, Annual Return/Report of Employee Benefit Plan. File this form for a plan that is not a one-participant plan (see below).

Form 5500-EZ, Annual Return of One-Participant (Owners and Their Spouses) Retirement Plan. File this form for a plan that only covers the owner (or the owner and his or her spouse) but only if the owner (or the owner and his or her spouse) owns the entire business.

Line 25. Employee Benefit Programs (Form 1120 Only)

Enter contributions to employee benefit programs not claimed elsewhere on the return (for example, insurance, health and welfare programs, etc.) that are not an incidental part of a pension, profit-sharing, etc., plan included on line 24.

Line 26, Form 1120 (Line 22, Form 1120-A). Other Deductions

Attach a schedule, listing by type and amount, all allowable deductions that are not deductible elsewhere on Form 1120 or Form 1120-A. Form 1120-A filers should include amounts described in the instructions above for lines 22, 24, and 25 of Form 1120. Enter the total of other deductions on line 26, Form 1120 (line 22, Form 1120-A).

Examples of other deductions include:

- Amortization (see Form 4562).
- Certain costs of qualified film or television productions commencing after October 22, 2004. See section 181 for details.
- Certain business start-up and organizational costs that the corporation elects to deduct. See page 12.
- Reforestation costs. The corporation can elect to deduct up to $10,000 of qualified reforestation expenses paid or incurred after October 22, 2004, for each qualifying timber property. The corporation can elect to amortize over 84 months any amount not deducted.
- Insurance premiums.
- Legal and professional fees.
- Supplies used and consumed in the business.
- Utilities.
- Ordinary losses from trade or business activities of a partnership (from Schedule K-1 (Form 1065 or 1065-B)). Do not offset ordinary income against ordinary losses. Instead, include the income on line 10. Show the partnership's name, address, and EIN on a separate statement attached to this return. If the amount is from more than one partnership, identify the amount from each partnership.
- Extraterritorial income exclusion (from Form 8873, line 52a or 52b).
- Deduction for clean-fuel vehicle and certain refueling property (see Pub. 535).
- Dividends paid in cash on stock held by an employee stock ownership plan. However, a deduction can only be taken for the dividends above if, according to the plan, the dividends are:

1. Paid in cash directly to the plan participants or beneficiaries;
2. Paid to the plan, which distributes them in cash to the plan participants or their beneficiaries no later than 90 days after the end of the plan year in which the dividends are paid;
3. At the election of such participants or their beneficiaries (a) payable as provided under 1or 2 above or (b) paid to the plan and reinvested in qualifying employer securities; or
4. Used to make payments on a loan described in section 404(a)(9).

See section 404(k) for more details and the limitation on certain dividends.

See *Special rules* below for limits on certain other deductions.

Do not deduct:

- Fines or penalties paid to a government for violating any law.
- Any amount that is allocable to a class of exempt income. See section 265(b) for exceptions.

Special rules apply to the following expenses.

Travel, meals, and entertainment. Subject to limitations and restrictions discussed below, a corporation can deduct ordinary and necessary travel, meals, and entertainment expenses paid or incurred in its trade or business. Also, special rules apply to deductions for gifts, skybox rentals, luxury water travel, convention expenses, and entertainment tickets. See section 274 and Pub. 463 for more details.

Travel. The corporation cannot deduct travel expenses of any individual accompanying a corporate officer or employee, including a spouse or dependent of the officer or employee, unless:

- That individual is an employee of the corporation and
- His or her travel is for a bona fide business purpose and would otherwise be deductible by that individual.

Meals and entertainment. Generally, the corporation can deduct only 50% of the amount otherwise allowable for meals and entertainment expenses paid or incurred in its trade or business. In addition (subject to exceptions under section 274(k)(2)):

- Meals must not be lavish or extravagant;
- A bona fide business discussion must occur during, immediately before, or immediately after the meal; and
- An employee of the corporation must be present at the meal.

See section 274(n)(3) for a special rule that applies to expenses for meals consumed by individuals subject to the hours of service limits of the Department of Transportation.

Membership dues. The corporation can deduct amounts paid or incurred for membership dues in civic or public service organizations, professional organizations (such as bar and medical associations), business leagues, trade associations, chambers of commerce, boards of trade, and real estate boards. However, no deduction is allowed if a principal purpose of the organization is to entertain, or provide entertainment facilities for, members or their guests. In addition, corporations cannot deduct membership dues in any club organized for business, pleasure, recreation, or other social purpose. This includes country clubs, golf and athletic clubs, airline and hotel clubs, and clubs operated to provide meals under conditions favorable to business discussion.

Entertainment facilities. The corporation cannot deduct an expense paid or incurred for a facility (such as a yacht or hunting lodge) used for an activity usually considered entertainment, amusement, or recreation.

Amounts treated as compensation. Generally, the corporation may be able to deduct otherwise nondeductible meals, travel, and entertainment expenses if the amounts are treated as compensation to the recipient and reported on Form W-2 for an employee or on Form 1099-MISC for an independent contractor.

However, if the recipient is an officer, director, or beneficial owner (directly or indirectly) of more than 10% of any class of stock, the deduction for otherwise nondeductible meals, travel, and entertainment expenses incurred after October 22, 2004, is limited to the amount treated as compensation. See section 274(e)(2).

Lobbying expenses. Generally, lobbying expenses are not deductible. These expenses include:

- Amounts paid or incurred in connection with influencing federal or state legislation (but not local legislation) or
- Amounts paid or incurred in connection with any communication with certain federal executive branch officials in an attempt to influence the official actions or positions of the officials. See Regulations section 1.162-29 for the definition of "influencing legislation."

Dues and other similar amounts paid to certain tax-exempt organizations may not be deductible. See section 162(e)(3). If certain in-house lobbying expenditures do not exceed $2,000, they are deductible. For information on contributions to charitable organizations that conduct lobbying activities, see section 170(f)(9).

For more information on other deductions that may apply to corporations, see Pub. 535.

Line 28, Form 1120 (Line 24, Form 1120-A). Taxable Income Before NOL Deduction and Special Deductions

At-risk rules. Generally, special at-risk rules under section 465 apply to closely held corporations (see *Passive activity limitations* on page 12) engaged in any activity as a trade or business or for the production of income. These corporations may have to adjust the amount on line 28, Form 1120, or line 24, Form 1120-A. (See below.)

The at-risk rules do not apply to:

- Holding real property placed in service by the taxpayer before 1987;
- Equipment leasing under sections 465(c)(4), (5), and (6); or
- Any qualifying business of a qualified corporation under section 465(c)(7).

However, the at-risk rules do apply to the holding of mineral property.

If the at-risk rules apply, adjust the amount on this line for any section 465(d) losses. These losses are limited to the amount for which the corporation is at risk for each separate activity at the close of the tax year. If the corporation is involved in one or more activities, any of which incurs a loss for the year, report the losses for each activity separately. Attach Form 6198, At-Risk Limitations, showing the amount at risk and gross income and deductions for the activities with the losses.

If the corporation sells or otherwise disposes of an asset or its interest (either total or partial) in an activity to which the at-risk rules apply, determine the net profit or loss from the activity by combining the gain or loss on the sale or disposition with the profit or loss from the activity. If the corporation has a net loss, it may be limited because of the at-risk rules.

Treat any loss from an activity not allowed for the tax year as a deduction allocable to the activity in the next tax year.

Line 29a, Form 1120 (Line 25a, Form 1120-A). Net Operating Loss Deduction

A corporation can use the NOL incurred in one tax year to reduce its taxable income in another tax year. Enter on line 29a (line 25a, Form 1120-A), the total NOL carryovers from other tax years, but do not enter more than the corporation's taxable income (after special deductions). Attach a schedule showing the computation of the NOL deduction. Form 1120 filers must also complete item 12 on Schedule K.

The following special rules apply.

- A personal service corporation may not carry back an NOL to or from any tax year to which an election under section 444 to have a tax year other than a required tax year applies.
- A corporate equity reduction interest loss may not be carried back to a tax year preceding the year of the equity reduction transaction (see section 172(b)(1)(E)).
- If an ownership change occurs, the amount of the taxable income of a loss corporation that may be offset by the pre-change NOL carryovers may be limited (see section 382 and the related regulations). A loss corporation must file an information statement with its income tax return for each tax year that certain ownership shifts occur (see Temporary Regulations section 1.382-2T(a)(2)(ii) for details). See Regulations section 1.382-6(b) for details on how to make the closing-of-the-books election.
- If a corporation acquires control of another corporation (or acquires its assets in a reorganization), the amount of pre-acquisition losses that may offset recognized built-in gain may be limited (see section 384).

For details on the NOL deduction, see Pub. 542, section 172, and Form 1139, Corporation Application for Tentative Refund.

Line 29b, Form 1120 (Line 25b, Form 1120-A). Special Deductions

Form 1120 filers. See the instructions for Schedule C on page 18.

Form 1120-A filers. Generally, enter 70% of line 4, page 1, on line 25b. However, this deduction cannot be more than 70% of line 24, page 1. Compute line 24 without regard to any adjustment under section 1059 and without regard to any capital loss carryback to the tax year under section 1212(a)(1).

In a year in which an NOL occurs, this 70% limitation does not apply even if the loss is created by the dividends-received deduction. See sections 172(d) and 246(b).

Line 30, Form 1120 (Line 26, Form 1120-A). Taxable Income

Minimum taxable income. The corporation's taxable income cannot be less than the largest of the following amounts.

- The amount of nondeductible CFC dividends under section 965. This amount is equal to the difference between columns (a) and (c) of Form 1120, Schedule C, line 12.
- The inversion gain of the corporation for the tax year, if the corporation is an expatriated entity or a partner in an expatriated entity. For details, see section 7874.
- The sum of the corporation's excess inclusions from Schedules Q (1066), line 2c, and the corporation's taxable income determined solely with respect to its ownership and high-yield interests in FASITs. For details, see sections 860E(a) and 860J.

Net operating loss (NOL). If line 30 (figured without regard to the **minimum taxable income** rule stated above) is zero or less, the corporation may have an NOL that can be carried back or forward as a deduction to other tax years. Generally, a corporation first carries back an NOL 2 tax years. However, the corporation can elect to waive the carryback period and instead carry the NOL forward to future tax years. To make the election, see the instructions for Schedule K, item 11 on page 23.

See Form 1139 for details, including other elections that may be available, which must be made no later than 6 months after the due date (excluding extensions) of the corporation's tax return.

Capital construction fund. To take a deduction for amounts contributed to a capital construction fund (CCF), reduce the amount that would otherwise be entered on line 30 (line 26, Form 1120-A) by the amount of the deduction. On the dotted line next to the entry space, enter "CCF" and the amount of the deduction. For more information, see Pub. 595, Tax Highlights for Commercial Fishermen.

Line 32b, Form 1120 (Line 28b, Form 1120-A). Estimated Tax Payments

Enter any estimated tax payments the corporation made for the tax year.

Beneficiaries of trusts. If the corporation is the beneficiary of a trust, and the trust makes a section 643(g) election to credit its estimated tax payments to its beneficiaries, include the corporation's share of the payment in the total for line 32b, Form 1120 (line 28b, Form 1120-A). Enter "T" and the amount on the dotted line next to the entry space.

Special estimated tax payments for certain life insurance companies. If the corporation is required to make or apply special estimated tax payments (SETP) under section 847 in addition to its regular estimated tax payments, enter on line 32b (line 28b, Form 1120-A), the corporation's total estimated tax payments. In the margin near line 32b, enter "Form 8816" and the amount. Attach a schedule showing your computation of estimated tax payments. See sections 847(2) and 847(8) and Form 8816, Special Loss Discount Account and Special Estimated Tax Payments for Insurance Companies, for more information.

Line 32f, Form 1120 (Line 28f, Form 1120-A)

Enter the credit (from Form 2439, Notice to Shareholder of Undistributed Long-Term Capital Gains) for the corporation's share of the tax paid by a regulated investment company (RIC) or a real estate investment trust (REIT) on undistributed long-term capital gains included in the corporation's income. Attach Form 2439 to Form 1120 or Form 1120-A.

Line 32g, Form 1120 (Line 28g, Form 1120-A)

Credit for Federal Tax on Fuels

Enter any credit from Form 4136, Credit for Federal Tax Paid on Fuels. Attach Form 4136 to Form 1120 or Form 1120-A.

Credit for tax on ozone-depleting chemicals. Include on line 32g (line 28g, Form 1120-A) any credit the corporation is claiming under section 4682(g)(2) for tax on ozone-depleting chemicals. Enter "ODC" to the left of the entry space.

Line 32h, Form 1120 (Line 28h, Form 1120-A). Total Payments

On Form 1120, add the amounts on lines 32d through 32g and enter the total on line 32h. On Form 1120-A, add the amounts on lines 28d through 28g and enter the total on line 28h.

Backup withholding. If the corporation had federal income tax withheld from any payments it received because, for example, it failed to give the payer its correct EIN, include the amount withheld in the total for line 32h, Form 1120 (line 28h, Form 1120-A). On Form 1120, enter the amount withheld and the words "Backup Withholding" in the blank space above line 32h. On Form 1120-A, show the amount withheld on the dotted line to the left of line 28h, and enter "Backup Withholding."

Line 33, Form 1120 (Line 29, Form 1120-A). Estimated Tax Penalty

A corporation that does not make estimated tax payments when due may be subject to an underpayment penalty for the period of underpayment. Generally, a corporation is subject to the penalty if its tax liability is $500 or more and it did not timely pay the smaller of:

- Its tax liability for 2004 or
- Its prior year's tax.

See section 6655 for details and exceptions, including special rules for large corporations.

Use Form 2220, Underpayment of Estimated Tax by Corporations, to see if the corporation owes a penalty and to figure the amount of the penalty. Generally, the corporation does not have to file this form because the IRS can figure the amount of any penalty and bill the corporation for it. However, even if the corporation does not owe the penalty, complete and attach Form 2220 if:

- The annualized income or adjusted seasonal installment method is used or
- The corporation is a large corporation computing its first required installment based on the prior year's tax. (See the Instructions for Form 2220 for the definition of a large corporation.)

If Form 2220 is attached, check the box on line 33, Form 1120 (line 29, Form 1120-A), and enter the amount of any penalty on this line.

Line 36, Form 1120 (Line 32, Form 1120-A). Direct Deposit of Refund

If the corporation wants its refund directly deposited into its checking or savings account at any U.S. bank or other financial institution instead of having a check sent to the corporation, complete Form 8050 and attach it to the corporation's tax return.

Schedule A, Form 1120 (Worksheet, Form 1120-A)

Cost of Goods Sold

Generally, inventories are required at the beginning and end of each tax year if the production, purchase, or sale of merchandise is an income-producing factor. See Regulations section 1.471-1.

However, if the corporation is a qualifying taxpayer or a qualifying small business taxpayer, it can adopt or change its accounting method to account for inventoriable items in the same manner as materials and supplies that are not incidental (unless its business is a tax shelter (as defined in section 448(d)(3))).

A qualifying taxpayer is a taxpayer that, for each prior tax year ending after December 16, 1998, has average annual gross receipts of $1 million or less for the 3-tax-year period ending with that prior tax year.

A qualifying small business taxpayer is a taxpayer (a) that, for each prior tax year ending on or after December 31, 2000, has average annual gross receipts of $10 million or less for the 3-tax-year period ending with that prior tax year and (b) whose principal business activity is not an ineligible activity.

Under this accounting method, inventory costs for raw materials purchased for use in producing finished goods and merchandise purchased for resale are deductible in the year the finished goods or merchandise are sold (but not before the year the corporation paid for the raw materials or merchandise, if it is also using the cash method). For additional guidance on this method of accounting for inventoriable items, see Pub. 538 and the instructions for Form 3115.

Enter amounts paid for all raw materials and merchandise during the tax year on line 2. The amount the corporation can deduct for the tax year is figured on line 8.

All filers not using the cash method of accounting should see *Section 263A uniform capitalization rules* on page 11 before completing Schedule A or the worksheet. The instructions for lines 1 through 7 that follow apply to Schedule A (Form 1120) and the worksheet for Form 1120-A below.

Line 1. Inventory at Beginning of Year

If the corporation is changing its method of accounting for the current tax year, it must refigure last year's closing inventory using its new method of accounting and enter the result on line 1. If there is a difference between last year's closing inventory and the refigured amount, attach an explanation and take it into account when figuring the corporation's section 481(a) adjustment (explained on page 5).

Line 4. Additional Section 263A Costs

An entry is required on this line only for corporations that have elected a simplified method of accounting.

For corporations that have elected the simplified production method, additional section 263A costs are generally those costs, other than interest, that were not capitalized under the corporation's method of accounting immediately prior to the effective date of section 263A but are

Cost of Goods Sold Worksheet
(Form 1120-A)
(keep for your records)

1. Inventory at beginning of year. Enter here and in Part III, line 3, column (a), Form 1120-A	1.	
2. Purchases. Enter here and in Part II, line 5a(1), Form 1120-A	2.	
3. Cost of labor. Enter here and include in total in Part II, line 5a(3), Form 1120-A	3.	
4. Additional section 263A costs. Enter here and in Part II, line 5a(2), Form 1120-A (see instruction for line 4)	4.	
5. Other costs. Enter here and include in Part II, line 5a(3), Form 1120-A	5.	
6. **Total.** Add lines 1 through 5	6.	
7. Inventory at end of year. Enter here and in Part III, line 3, column (b), Form 1120-A	7.	
8. **Cost of goods sold.** Subtract line 7 from line 6. Enter the result here and on page 1, line 2, Form 1120-A	8.	

now required to be capitalized under section 263A. For details, see Regulations section 1.263A-2(b).

For corporations that have elected the simplified resale method, additional section 263A costs are generally those costs incurred with respect to the following categories.

- Off-site storage or warehousing.
- Purchasing; handling, such as processing, assembling, repackaging, and transporting.
- General and administrative costs (mixed service costs).

For details, see Regulations section 1.263A-3(d).

Enter on line 4 the balance of section 263A costs paid or incurred during the tax year not includible on lines 2, 3, and 5.

Line 5. Other Costs

Enter on line 5 any costs paid or incurred during the tax year not entered on lines 2 through 4.

Line 7. Inventory at End of Year

See Regulations sections 1.263A-1 through 1.263A-3 for details on figuring the amount of additional section 263A costs to be included in ending inventory. If the corporation accounts for inventoriable items in the same manner as materials and supplies that are not incidental, enter on line 7 the portion of its raw materials and merchandise purchased for resale that is included on line 6 and was not sold during the year.

Lines 9a Through 9f. Inventory Valuation Methods

Inventories can be valued at:

- Cost;
- Cost or market value (whichever is lower); or
- Any other method approved by the IRS that conforms to the requirements of the applicable regulations cited below.

However, if the corporation is using the cash method of accounting, it is required to use cost.

Corporations that account for inventoriable items in the same manner as materials and supplies that are not incidental can currently deduct expenditures for direct labor and all indirect costs that would otherwise be included in inventory costs.

The average cost (rolling average) method of valuing inventories generally does not conform to the requirements of the regulations. See Rev. Rul. 71-234, 1971-1 C.B. 148.

Corporations that use erroneous valuation methods must change to a method permitted for federal income tax purposes. Use Form 3115 to make this change.

On line 9a, check the method(s) used for valuing inventories. Under lower of cost or market, the term "market" (for normal goods) means the current bid price prevailing on the inventory valuation date for the particular merchandise in the volume usually purchased by the taxpayer. For a manufacturer, market applies to the basic elements of cost—raw materials, labor, and burden. If section 263A applies to the taxpayer, the basic elements of cost must reflect the current bid price of all direct costs and all indirect costs properly allocable to goods on hand at the inventory date.

Inventory may be valued below cost when the merchandise is unsalable at normal prices or unusable in the normal way because the goods are subnormal due to damage, imperfections, shopwear, etc., within the meaning of Regulations section 1.471-2(c). The goods may be valued at the current bona fide selling price, minus direct cost of disposition (but not less than scrap value) if such a price can be established.

If this is the first year the Last-in, First-out (LIFO) inventory method was either adopted or extended to inventory goods not previously valued under the LIFO method provided in section 472, attach Form 970, Application To Use LIFO Inventory Method, or a statement with the information required by Form 970. Also check the LIFO box on line 9c. On line 9d, enter the amount or the percent of total closing inventories covered under section 472. Estimates are acceptable.

If the corporation changed or extended its inventory method to LIFO and had to write up the opening inventory to cost in the year of election, report the effect of the write-up as other income (line 10, page 1), proportionately over a 3-year period that begins with the year of the LIFO election (section 472(d)).

Note. Corporations using the LIFO method that make an S corporation election or transfer LIFO inventory to an S corporation in a nonrecognition transaction may be subject to an additional tax attributable to the LIFO recapture amount. See the instructions for line 11, Schedule J, on page 22, and line 10, *Other Income*, on page 11.

For more information on inventory valuation methods, see Pub. 538.

Schedule C (Form 1120 Only)

For purposes of the 20% ownership test on lines 1 through 7, the percentage of stock owned by the corporation is based on voting power and value of the stock. Preferred stock described in section 1504(a)(4) is not taken into account. Corporations filing a consolidated return should see Regulations sections 1.1502-13, 1.1502-26, and 1.1502-27 before completing Schedule C.

Corporations filing a consolidated return must not report as dividends on Schedule C any amounts received from corporations within the tax consolidation group. Such dividends are eliminated in consolidation rather than offset by the dividends-received deduction.

Line 1, Column (a)

Enter dividends (except those received on debt-financed stock acquired after July 18, 1984–see section 246A) that:

- Are received from less-than-20%-owned domestic corporations subject to income tax and
- Qualify for the 70% deduction under section 243(a)(1).

Also include on line 1:

- Taxable distributions from an IC-DISC or former DISC that are designated as eligible for the 70% deduction and certain dividends of Federal Home Loan Banks. See section 246(a)(2).
- Dividends (except those received on debt-financed stock acquired after July 18, 1984) from a regulated investment company (RIC). The amount of dividends eligible for the dividends-received deduction under section 243 is limited by section 854(b). The corporation should receive a notice from the RIC specifying the amount of dividends that qualify for the deduction.

Report so-called dividends or earnings received from mutual savings banks, etc., as interest. Do not treat them as dividends.

Line 2, Column (a)

Enter on line 2:

- Dividends (except those received on debt-financed stock acquired after July 18, 1984) that are received from 20%-or-more-owned domestic corporations subject to income tax and that are subject to the 80% deduction under section 243(c) and
- Taxable distributions from an IC-DISC or former DISC that are considered eligible for the 80% deduction.

Line 3, Column (a)

Enter dividends that are:

- Received on debt-financed stock acquired after July 18, 1984, from domestic and foreign corporations subject to income tax that would otherwise be subject to the dividends-received deduction under section 243(a)(1), 243(c), or 245(a). Generally, debt-financed stock is stock that the corporation acquired by incurring a debt (for example, it borrowed money to buy the stock).
- Received from a RIC on debt-financed stock. The amount of dividends eligible for the dividends-received deduction is limited by section 854(b). The corporation should receive a notice from the RIC specifying the amount of dividends that qualify for the deduction.

Line 3, Columns (b) and (c)

Dividends received on debt-financed stock acquired after July 18, 1984, are not entitled to the full 70% or 80% dividends-received deduction. The 70% or 80% deduction is reduced by a percentage that is related to the amount of debt incurred to acquire the stock. See section 246A. Also see section 245(a) before making this computation for an additional limitation that applies to dividends received from foreign corporations. Attach a schedule to Form 1120 showing how the amount on line 3, column (c), was figured.

Line 4, Column (a)

Enter dividends received on preferred stock of a less-than-20%-owned public utility that is subject to income tax and is allowed the deduction provided in section 247 for dividends paid.

Line 5, Column (a)

Enter dividends received on preferred stock of a 20%-or-more-owned public utility that is subject to income tax and is allowed the deduction provided in section 247 for dividends paid.

Line 6, Column (a)

Enter the U.S.-source portion of dividends that:

- Are received from less-than-20%-owned foreign corporations and
- Qualify for the 70% deduction under section 245(a). To qualify for the 70% deduction, the corporation must own at least 10% of the stock of the foreign corporation by vote and value.

Also include dividends received from a less-than-20%-owned FSC that:

- Are attributable to income treated as effectively connected with the conduct of a trade or business within the United States (excluding foreign trade income) and
- Qualify for the 70% deduction under section 245(c)(1)(B).

Line 7, Column (a)

Enter the U.S.-source portion of dividends that:

- Are received from 20%-or-more-owned foreign corporations and
- Qualify for the 80% deduction under section 245(a).

Also include dividends received from a 20%-or-more-owned FSC that:

- Are attributable to income treated as effectively connected with the conduct of a trade or business within the United States (excluding foreign trade income) and
- Qualify for the 80% deduction under section 245(c)(1)(B).

Line 8, Column (a)

Enter dividends received from wholly owned foreign subsidiaries that are eligible for the 100% deduction under section 245(b).

In general, the deduction under section 245(b) applies to dividends paid out of the earnings and profits of a foreign corporation for a tax year during which:

- All of its outstanding stock is directly or indirectly owned by the domestic corporation receiving the dividends and
- All of its gross income from all sources is effectively connected with the conduct of a trade or business within the United States.

Line 9, Column (c)

Generally, line 9, column (c), cannot exceed the amount from the worksheet below. However, in a year in which an NOL occurs, this limitation does not apply even if the loss is created by the dividends-received deduction. See sections 172(d) and 246(b).

Line 10, Columns (a) and (c)

Small business investment companies operating under the Small Business Investment Act of 1958 (see 15 U.S.C. 661 and following) must enter dividends that are received from domestic corporations subject to income tax even though a deduction is allowed for the entire amount of those dividends. To claim the 100% deduction on line 10, column (c), the company must file with its return a statement that it was a federal licensee under the Small Business Investment Act of 1958 at the time it received the dividends.

Line 11, Columns (a) and (c)

Enter dividends from FSCs that are attributable to foreign trade income and that are eligible for the 100% deduction provided in section 245(c)(1)(A).

Also, enter dividends that qualify under section 243(b) for the 100% dividends-received deduction described in section 243(a)(3). Corporations taking this deduction are subject to the provisions of section 1561.

The 100% deduction does not apply to affiliated group members that are joining in the filing of a consolidated return.

Line 12, Column (a)

Enter qualifying dividends from Form 8895.

Line 13, Column (a)

Enter foreign dividends not reportable on lines 3, 6, 7, 8, 11 or 12 of column (a). Include on line 13 the corporation's share of the ordinary earnings of a qualified electing fund from line 1c of Form 8621, Return by a Shareholder of a Passive Foreign Investment Company or Qualifying Electing Fund. Exclude distributions of amounts constructively taxed in the current year or in prior years under subpart F (sections 951 through 964).

Line 14, Column (a)

Include income constructively received from CFCs under subpart F. This amount should equal the total subpart F income reported on Schedule I, Form 5471.

Line 15, Column (a)

Include gross-up for taxes deemed paid under sections 902 and 960.

Line 16, Column (a)

Enter taxable distributions from an IC-DISC or former DISC that are designated as not eligible for a dividends-received deduction.

No deduction is allowed under section 243 for a dividend from an IC-DISC or former DISC (as defined in section 992(a)) to the extent the dividend:

- Is paid out of the corporation's accumulated IC-DISC income or previously taxed income or
- Is a deemed distribution under section 995(b)(1).

Line 17, Column (a)

Include the following:

1. Dividends (other than capital gain distributions reported on Schedule D (Form 1120) and exempt-interest dividends) that are received from RICs and that are not subject to the 70% deduction.

Worksheet for Schedule C, line 9
(keep for your records)

1.	Refigure line 28, page 1, Form 1120, without any adjustment under section 1059 and without any capital loss carryback to the tax year under section 1212(a)(1)	1.	
2.	Complete line 10 and 11, column (c), and enter the total here	2.	21,780
3.	Subtract line 2 from line 1	3.	
4.	Multiply line 3 by 80%	4.	
5.	Add lines 2, 5, 7, and 8, column (c), and the part of the deduction on line 3, column (c), that is attributable to dividends from 20%-or-more-owned corporations	5.	—
6.	Enter the smaller of line 4 or 5. If line 5 is greater than line 4, stop here; enter the amount from line 6 on line 9, column (c), and do not complete the rest of this worksheet	6.	
7.	Enter the total amount of dividends from 20%-or-more-owned corporations that are included on lines 2, 3, 5, 7, and 8, column (a)	7.	
8.	Subtract line 7 from line 3	8.	
9.	Multiply line 8 by 70%	9.	
10.	Subtract line 5 above from line 9, column (c)	10.	
11.	Enter the smaller of line 9 or line 10	11.	
12.	**Dividends-received deduction after limitation** (sec. 246(b)). Add lines 6 and 11. Enter the result here and on line 9, column (c) . . .	12.	

2. Dividends from tax-exempt organizations.

3. Dividends (other than capital gain distributions) received from a REIT that, for the tax year of the trust in which the dividends are paid, qualifies under sections 856 through 860.

4. Dividends not eligible for a dividends-received deduction, which include the following.

a. Dividends received on any share of stock held for less than 46 days during the 91-day period beginning 45 days before the ex-dividend date. When counting the number of days the corporation held the stock, you cannot count certain days during which the corporation's risk of loss was diminished. See section 246(c)(4) and Regulations section 1.246-5 for more details.

b. Dividends attributable to periods totaling more than 366 days that the corporation received on any share of preferred stock held for less than 91 days during the 181-day period that began 90 days before the ex-dividend date. When counting the number of days the corporation held the stock, you cannot count certain days during which the corporation's risk of loss was diminished. See section 246(c)(4) and Regulations section 1.246-5 for more details. Preferred dividends attributable to periods totaling less than 367 days are subject to the 46-day holding period rule above.

c. Dividends on any share of stock to the extent the corporation is under an obligation (including a short sale) to make related payments with respect to positions in substantially similar or related property.

5. Any other taxable dividend income not properly reported above (including distributions under section 936(h)(4)).

If patronage dividends or per-unit retain allocations are included on line 17, identify the total of these amounts in a schedule attached to Form 1120.

Line 18, Column (c)

Section 247 allows public utilities a deduction of 40% of the smaller of (a) dividends paid on their preferred stock during the tax year or (b) taxable income computed without regard to this deduction. In a year in which an NOL occurs, compute the deduction without regard to section 247(a)(1)(B). See section 172(d).

Schedule J, Form 1120 (Part I, Form 1120-A)

Lines 1 and 2 (Form 1120 Only)

Members of a controlled group. A member of a controlled group must check the box on line 1 and complete lines 2a and 2b of Schedule J, Form 1120. The term "controlled group" means any parent-subsidiary group, brother-sister group, or combined group. See the definitions below.

Parent-subsidiary group. A parent-subsidiary group is one or more chains of corporations connected through stock ownership with a common parent corporation if:

- Stock possessing at least 80% of the total combined voting power of all classes of stock entitled to vote or at least 80% of the total value of shares of all classes of stock of each of the corporations, except the common parent corporation, is directly or indirectly owned by one or more of the other corporations; and
- The common parent corporation directly or indirectly owns stock possessing at least 80% of the total combined voting power of all classes of stock entitled to vote or at least 80% of the total value of shares of all classes of stock of at least one of the other corporations, excluding, in computing such voting power or value, stock owned directly by such other corporations.

Brother-sister group. A brother-sister group is two or more corporations if 5 or fewer persons who are individuals, estates, or trusts directly or indirectly own stock possessing:

1. At least 80% of the total combined voting power of all classes of stock entitled to vote or at least 80% of the total value of shares of all classes of the stock of each corporation, and
2. More than 50% of the total combined voting power of all classes of stock entitled to vote or more than 50% of the total value of shares of all classes of stock of each corporation, taking into account the stock ownership of each such person only to the extent such stock ownership is identical with respect to each such corporation.

For tax years beginning after October 22, 2004, the definition of brother-sister group does not include (1) above, but only for purposes of the taxable income brackets, alternative minimum tax exemption amounts, and accumulated earnings credit.

Combined group. A combined group is three or more corporations each of which is a member of a parent-subsidiary group or a brother-sister group, and one of which is:

- A common parent corporation included in a group of corporations in a parent-subsidiary group, and also
- Included in a group of corporations in a brother-sister group.

For more details on controlled groups, see section 1563.

Line 2a. Members of a controlled group are entitled to one $50,000, one $25,000, and one $9,925,000 taxable income bracket amount (in that order) on line 2a.

When a controlled group adopts or later amends an apportionment plan, each member must attach to its tax return a copy of its consent to this plan. The copy (or an attached statement) must show the part of the amount in each taxable income bracket apportioned to that member. See Regulations section 1.1561-3(b) for other requirements and for the time and manner of making the consent.

Unequal apportionment plan. Members of a controlled group can elect an unequal apportionment plan and divide the taxable income brackets as they want. There is no need for consistency among taxable income brackets. Any member may be entitled to all, some, or none of the taxable income bracket. However, the total amount for all members cannot be more than the total amount in each taxable income bracket.

Equal apportionment plan. If no apportionment plan is adopted, members of a controlled group must divide the amount in each taxable income bracket equally among themselves. For example, Controlled Group AB consists of Corporation A and Corporation B. They do not elect an apportionment plan. Therefore, each corporation is entitled to:

- $25,000 (one-half of $50,000) on line 2a(1),
- $12,500 (one-half of $25,000) on line 2a(2), and
- $4,962,500 (one-half of $9,925,000) on line 2a(3).

Line 2b. Members of a controlled group are treated as one group to figure the applicability of the additional 5% tax and the additional 3% tax. If an additional tax applies, each member will pay that tax based on the part of the amount used in each taxable income bracket to reduce that member's tax. See section 1561(a). If an additional tax applies, attach a schedule showing the taxable income of the entire group and how the corporation figured its share of the additional tax.

Line 2b(1). Enter the corporation's share of the additional 5% tax on line 2b(1).

Line 2b(2). Enter the corporation's share of the additional 3% tax on line 2b(2).

Line 3, Form 1120 (Line 1, Form 1120-A)

Members of a controlled group should use the worksheet on page 21 to figure the tax for the group. In addition, members of a controlled group must attach to Form 1120 a statement showing the computation of the tax entered on line 3.

Most corporations not filing a consolidated return figure their tax by using the Tax Rate Schedule on page 21. Qualified personal service corporations should see the instructions on page 21.

Tax Rate Schedule

If taxable income (line 30, Form 1120, or line 26, Form 1120-A) on page 1 is:

Over—	But not over—	Tax is:	Of the amount over—
$0	$50,000	15%	$0
50,000	75,000	$ 7,500 + 25%	50,000
75,000	100,000	13,750 + 34%	75,000
100,000	335,000	22,250 + 39%	100,000
335,000	10,000,000	113,900 + 34%	335,000
10,000,000	15,000,000	3,400,000 + 35%	10,000,000
15,000,000	18,333,333	5,150,000 + 38%	15,000,000
18,333,333	-----	35%	0

Qualified personal service corporation. A qualified personal service corporation is taxed at a flat rate of 35% on taxable income. If the corporation is a qualified personal service corporation, check the box on line 3, Schedule J, Form 1120 (line 1, Part I, Form 1120-A) even if the corporation has no tax liability.

A corporation is a qualified personal service corporation if it meets both of the following tests.

1. Substantially all of the corporation's activities involve the performance of services in the fields of health, law, engineering, architecture, accounting, actuarial science, performing arts, or consulting.

2. At least 95% of the corporation's stock, by value, is directly or indirectly owned by

a. Employees performing the services,

b. Retired employees who had performed the services listed above,

c. Any estate of an employee or retiree described above, or

d. Any person who acquired the stock of the corporation as a result of the death of an employee or retiree (but only for the 2-year period beginning on the date of the employee or retiree's death).

Mutual savings bank conducting life insurance business. The tax under section 594 consists of the sum of (a) a partial tax computed on Form 1120 on the taxable income of the bank determined without regard to income or deductions allocable to the life insurance department and (b) a partial tax on the taxable income computed on Form 1120-L of the life insurance department. Enter the combined tax on line 3 of Schedule J, Form 1120. Attach Form 1120-L as a schedule (and identify it as such) or a statement showing the computation of the taxable income of the life insurance department.

Deferred tax under section 1291. If the corporation was a shareholder in a passive foreign investment company (PFIC) and received an excess distribution or disposed of its investment in the PFIC during the year, it must include the increase in taxes due under section 1291(c)(2) in the total for line 3, Schedule J, Form 1120. On the dotted line next to line 3, enter "Section 1291" and the amount.

Do not include on line 3 any interest due under section 1291(c)(3). Instead, show the amount of interest owed in the bottom margin of page 1, Form 1120, and enter "Section 1291 interest." For details, see Form 8621.

Tax Computation Worksheet for Members of a Controlled Group (keep for your records)

Note. Each member of a controlled group (except a qualified personal service corporation) must compute the tax using this worksheet.

1.	Enter taxable income (Form 1120, page 1, line 30)	1.	23,217
2.	Enter line 1 or the corporation's share of the $50,000 taxable income bracket, whichever is less	2.	23,217
3.	Subtract line 2 from line 1	3.	0
4.	Enter line 3 or the corporation's share of the $25,000 taxable income bracket, whichever is less	4.	
5.	Subtract line 4 from line 3	5.	
6.	Enter line 5 or the corporation's share of the $9,925,000 taxable income bracket, whichever is less	6.	
7.	Subtract line 6 from line 5	7.	
8.	Multiply line 2 by 15%	8.	
9.	Multiply line 4 by 25%	9.	
10.	Multiply line 6 by 34%	10.	
11.	Multiply line 7 by 35%	11.	
12.	If the taxable income of the controlled group exceeds $100,000, enter this member's share of the smaller of: 5% of the taxable income in excess of $100,000, or $11,750 (see the instructions for Schedule J, line 2b)	12.	
13.	If the taxable income of the controlled group exceeds $15 million, enter this member's share of the smaller of: 3% of the taxable income in excess of $15 million, or $100,000 (see the instructions for Schedule J, line 2b)	13.	
14.	**Total.** Add lines 8 through 13. Enter here and on line 3, Schedule J, Form 1120	14.	

Additional tax under section 197(f). A corporation that elects to pay tax on the gain from the sale of an intangible under the related person exception to the anti-churning rules should include any additional tax due under section 197(f)(9)(B) in the total for line 3. On the dotted line next to line 3, enter "Section 197" and the amount. For more information, see Pub. 535.

Line 4 (Form 1120 Only)

A corporation that is not a small corporation exempt from the AMT (see below) may be required to file Form 4626 if it claims certain credits, even though it does not owe any AMT. See Form 4626 for details.

Unless the corporation is treated as a small corporation exempt from the AMT, it may owe the AMT if it has any of the adjustments and tax preference items listed on Form 4626. The corporation must file Form 4626 if its taxable income (or loss) before the NOL deduction, combined with these adjustments and tax preference items is more than the smaller of $40,000 or the corporation's allowable exemption amount (from Form 4626). For this purpose, taxable income does not include the NOL deduction. See Form 4626 for details.

Exemption for small corporations. A corporation is treated as a small corporation exempt from the AMT for its tax year beginning in 2004 if that year is the corporation's first tax year in existence (regardless of its gross receipts) or:

1. It was treated as a small corporation exempt from the AMT for all prior tax years beginning after 1997 and

2. Its average annual gross receipts for the 3-tax-year period (or portion thereof during which the corporation was in existence) ending before its tax year beginning in 2004 did not exceed $7.5 million ($5 million if the corporation had only 1 prior tax year).

Line 6a (Form 1120 Only)

To find out when a corporation can take the credit for payment of income tax to a foreign country or U.S. possession, see Form 1118, Foreign Tax Credit—Corporations.

Line 6b (Form 1120 Only)

The Small Business Job Protection Act of 1996 repealed the possessions credit. However, existing credit claimants may qualify for a credit under the transitional rules. See Form 5735, Possessions Corporation Tax Credit (Under Sections 936 and 30A).

Line 6c (Form 1120 Only)

If the corporation can take either of the following credits, check the appropriate box(es) and include the amount of the credits in the total for line 6c.

Nonconventional source fuel credit. A credit is allowed for the sale of qualified fuels produced from a nonconventional source. Section 29 contains a definition of qualified fuels, provisions for figuring the credit, and other special rules. Attach a separate schedule to the return showing the computation of the credit.

Qualified electric vehicle (QEV) credit. Use Form 8834, Qualified Electric Vehicle Credit, if the corporation can claim a credit for the purchase of a new qualified electric vehicle. Vehicles that qualify for this credit are not eligible for the deduction for clean-fuel vehicles under section 179A.

Line 6d, Form 1120 (Line 2, Form 1120-A)

Enter on line 6d (line 2 of Form 1120-A) the corporation's total general business credit.

If the corporation is filing Form 8844 (Empowerment Zone and Renewal Community Employment Credit), Form 8884 (New York Liberty Zone Business Employee Credit), or Form 8835 (see list below) with a credit from Section B, check the "Form(s)" box, enter the form number in the space provided, and include the allowable credit on line 6d (line 2 of Form 1120-A).

If the corporation is required to file Form 3800, General Business Credit, check the "Form 3800" box and include the allowable credit on line 6d (line 2 of Form 1120-A).

If the corporation is not required to file Form 3800, check the "Form(s)" box, enter the form number in the space provided, and include on line 6d (line 2 of Form 1120-A) the allowable credit from the applicable form listed below.

- Investment Credit (Form 3468).
- Work Opportunity Credit (Form 5884).
- Credit for Alcohol Used as Fuel (Form 6478).
- Credit for Increasing Research Activities (Form 6765).
- Low-Income Housing Credit (Form 8586).
- Orphan Drug Credit (Form 8820).
- Disabled Access Credit (Form 8826).
- Enhanced Oil Recovery Credit (Form 8830).
- Renewable Electricity and Refined Coal Production Credit (Form 8835).
- Indian Employment Credit (Form 8845).
- Credit for Employer Social Security and Medicare Taxes Paid on Certain Employee Tips (Form 8846).
- Credit for Contributions to Selected Community Development Corporations (Form 8847).
- Welfare-to-Work Credit (Form 8861).
- Biodiesel Fuels Credit (Form 8864).
- New Markets Credit (Form 8874).
- Credit for Small Employer Pension Plan Startup Costs (Form 8881).
- Credit for Employer-Provided Childcare Facilities and Services (Form 8882).
- Low Sulfur Diesel Fuel Production Credit (Form 8896).

Line 6e (Form 1120 Only)

To figure the minimum tax credit and any carryforward of that credit, use Form 8827, Credit for Prior Year Minimum Tax—Corporations. Also see Form 8827 if any of the corporation's 2003 nonconventional source fuel credit or qualified electric vehicle credit was disallowed solely because of the tentative minimum tax limitation. See section 53(d).

Line 6f (Form 1120 Only)

Enter the amount of any credit from Form 8860, Qualified Zone Academy Bond Credit.

Line 9 (Form 1120 Only)

A corporation is taxed as a personal holding company under section 542 if:

- At least 60% of its adjusted ordinary gross income for the tax year is personal holding company income and
- At any time during the last half of the tax year more than 50% in value of its outstanding stock is directly or indirectly owned by five or fewer individuals.

See Schedule PH (Form 1120) for definitions and details on how to figure the tax.

Line 10, Form 1120 (Line 4, Form 1120-A)

Include any of the following taxes and interest in the total on line 10 (Form 1120-A, Part I, line 4). Check the appropriate box(es) for the form, if any, used to compute the total.

Recapture of investment credit. If the corporation disposed of investment credit property or changed its use before the end of its useful life or recovery period, it may owe a tax. See Form 4255, Recapture of Investment Credit.

Recapture of low-income housing credit. If the corporation disposed of property (or there was a reduction in the qualified basis of the property) for which it took the low-income housing credit, it may owe a tax. See Form 8611, Recapture of Low-Income Housing Credit.

Interest due under the look-back methods. If the corporation used the look-back method for certain long-term contracts, see Form 8697, Interest Computation Under the Look-Back Method for Completed Long-Term Contracts, for information on figuring the interest the corporation may have to include. The corporation may also have to include interest due under the look-back method for property depreciated under the income forecast method. See Form 8866, Interest Computation Under the Look-Back Method for Property Depreciated Under the Income Forecast Method.

Other. Additional taxes and interest amounts can be included in the total entered on line 10 (Form 1120-A, Part I, line 4). Check the box for "Other" if the corporation includes any additional taxes and interest such as the items discussed below. See *How to report* below for details on reporting these amounts on an attached schedule.

- Recapture of qualified electric vehicle (QEV) credit. The corporation must recapture part of the QEV credit it claimed in a prior year if, within 3 years of the date the vehicle was placed in service, it ceases to qualify for the credit. See Regulations section 1.30-1 for details on how to figure the recapture.
- Recapture of Indian employment credit. Generally, if an employer terminates the employment of a qualified employee less than 1 year after the date of initial employment, any Indian employment credit allowed for a prior tax year because of wages paid or incurred to that employee must be recaptured. For details, see Form 8845 and section 45A.
- Recapture of new markets credit (see Form 8874).
- Recapture of employer-provided childcare facilities and services credit (see Form 8882).
- Tax and interest on a nonqualified withdrawal from a capital construction fund (section 7518).
- Interest on deferred tax attributable to (a) installment sales of certain timeshares and residential lots (section 453(l)(3)) and (b) certain nondealer installment obligations (section 453A(c)).
- Interest due on deferred gain (section 1260(b)).
- For tax years beginning after October 22, 2004, tax on notional shipping income. See *Income from qualifying shipping activities* on page 10.

How to report. If the corporation checked the "Other" box, attach a schedule showing the computation of each item included in the total for line 10 (Form 1120-A, Part I, line 4) and identify the applicable Code section and the type of tax or interest.

Line 11 (Form 1120 Only)

Include any deferred tax on the termination of a section 1294 election applicable to shareholders in a qualified electing fund in the amount entered on line 11. See Form 8621, Part V, and *How to report,* on page 23.

Subtract the following amounts from the total for line 11.

- Deferred tax on the corporation's share of undistributed earnings of a qualified electing fund (see Form 8621, Part II).
- Deferred LIFO recapture tax (section 1363(d)). This tax is the part of the LIFO recapture tax that will be deferred and paid with Form 1120S in the future. To figure the deferred tax, first figure the total LIFO recapture tax. Follow the steps below to figure the total LIFO recapture tax and the deferred amount. Also see the instructions regarding LIFO recapture amount under *Line 10. Other Income,* on page 11.

Step 1. Figure the tax on the corporation's income including the LIFO recapture amount. (Complete Schedule J through line 10, but do not enter a total on line 11 yet.)

Step 2. Using a separate worksheet, complete Schedule J again, but do not include the LIFO recapture amount in the corporation's taxable income.

Step 3. Compare the tax in Step 2 to the tax in Step 1. (The difference between the two is the LIFO recapture tax.)

Step 4. Multiply the amount figured in Step 3 by 75%. (The result is the deferred LIFO recapture tax.)

How to report. Attach a schedule showing the computation of each item included in, or subtracted from, the total for line 11. On the dotted line next to line 11, specify (a) the applicable Code section, (b) the type of tax, and (c) enter the amount of tax. For example, if the corporation is deferring a $100 LIFO recapture tax, subtract this amount from the total on line 11, then enter "Section 1363-Deferred Tax-$100" on the dotted line next to line 11.

Schedule K, Form 1120 (Part II, Form 1120-A)

The following instructions apply to Form 1120, page 3, Schedule K, or Form 1120-A, page 2, Part II. Be sure to complete all the items that apply to the corporation.

Question 4 (Form 1120 Only)

Check the "Yes" box for question 4 if:

- The corporation is a subsidiary in an affiliated group (defined below), but is not filing a consolidated return for the tax year with that group or
- The corporation is a subsidiary in a parent-subsidiary controlled group (defined on page 20).

Any corporation that meets either of the requirements above should check the "Yes" box. This applies even if the corporation is a subsidiary member of one group and the parent corporation of another.

Note. If the corporation is an "excluded member" of a controlled group (see section 1563(b)(2)), it is still considered a member of a controlled group for this purpose.

Affiliated group. An affiliated group is one or more chains of includible corporations (section 1504(a)) connected through stock ownership with a common parent corporation. The common parent must be an includible corporation and the following requirements must be met.

1. The common parent must own directly stock that represents at least 80% of the total voting power and at least 80% of the total value of the stock of at least one of the other includible corporations.

2. Stock that represents at least 80% of the total voting power and at least 80% of the total value of the stock of each of the other corporations (except for the common parent) must be owned directly by one or more of the other includible corporations.

For this purpose, the term "stock" generally does not include any stock that (a) is nonvoting, (b) is nonconvertible, (c) is limited and preferred as to dividends and does not participate significantly in corporate growth, and (d) has redemption and liquidation rights that do not exceed the issue price of the stock (except for a reasonable redemption or liquidation premium). See section 1504(a)(4). See section 1563(d)(1) for the definition of stock for purposes of determining stock ownership above.

Question 6 (Form 1120-A Only)

Foreign financial accounts. Check the "Yes" box for question 6 if either 1 or 2 below applies to the corporation. Otherwise, check the "No" box.

1. At any time during the 2004 calendar year, the corporation had an interest in or signature or other authority over a bank, securities, or other financial account in a foreign country (see Form TD F 90-22.1, Report of Foreign Bank and Financial Accounts); and

   a. The combined value of the accounts was more than $10,000 at any time during the calendar year and

   b. The account was not with a U.S. military banking facility operated by a U.S. financial institution.

2. The corporation owns more than 50% of the stock in any corporation that would answer "Yes" to item 1 above.

If the "Yes" box is checked:

- Enter the name of the foreign country or countries. Attach a separate sheet if more space is needed.
- File Form TD F 90-22.1 by June 30, 2005, with the Department of the Treasury at the address shown on the form. Because Form TD F 90-22.1 is not a tax form, do not file it with Form 1120-A. You can order Form TD F 90-22.1 by calling 1-800-TAX-FORM (1-800-829-3676) or you can download it from the IRS website at *www.irs.gov.*

Question 7 (Form 1120 Only)

Check the "Yes" box if one foreign person owned at least 25% of (a) the total voting power of all classes of stock of the corporation entitled to vote or (b) the total value of all classes of stock of the corporation.

The constructive ownership rules of section 318 apply in determining if a corporation is foreign owned. See section 6038A(c)(5) and the related regulations.

Enter on line 7a the percentage owned by the foreign person specified in question 7. On line 7b, enter the name of the owner's country.

Note. If there is more than one 25%-or-more foreign owner, complete lines 7a and 7b for the foreign person with the highest percentage of ownership.

Foreign person. The term "foreign person" means:

- A foreign citizen or nonresident alien.
- An individual who is a citizen of a U.S. possession (but who is not a U.S. citizen or resident).
- A foreign partnership.
- A foreign corporation.
- Any foreign estate or trust within the meaning of section 7701(a)(31).
- A foreign government (or one of its agencies or instrumentalities) to the extent that it is engaged in the conduct of a commercial activity as described in section 892.

Owner's country. For individuals, the term "owner's country" means the country of residence. For all others, it is the country where incorporated, organized, created, or administered.

Requirement to file Form 5472. If the corporation checked "Yes," it may have to file Form 5472, Information Return of a 25% Foreign Owned U.S. Corporation or a Foreign Corporation Engaged in a U.S. Trade or Business. Generally, a 25% foreign-owned corporation that had a reportable transaction with a foreign or domestic related party during the tax year must file Form 5472. See Form 5472 for filing instructions and penalties for failure to file.

Item 9, Form 1120 (Item 3, Form 1120-A)

Show any tax-exempt interest received or accrued. Including any exempt-interest dividends received as a shareholder in a mutual fund or other RIC. Also, if required, include the same amount on Schedule M-1, line 7; Form 1120-A, Part IV, line 6; or Schedule M-3, Part II, line 13.

Item 11 (Form 1120 Only)

If the corporation has an NOL for its 2004 tax year, it can elect to waive the entire carryback period for the NOL and instead carry the NOL forward to future tax years. To do so, check the box on line 11 and file the tax return by its due date, including extensions (do not attach the statement described in Temporary Regulations section 301.9100-12T). Once made, the election is irrevocable. See Pub. 542 and Form 1139 for more details.

Corporations filing a consolidated return must also attach the statement required by Temporary Regulations section 1.1502-21T(b)(3)(i) or (ii).

Item 12 (Form 1120 Only)

Enter the amount of the NOL carryover to the tax year from prior years, even if some of the loss is used to offset income on this return. The amount to enter is the total of all NOLs generated in prior years but not used to offset income (either as a carryback or carryover) to a tax year prior to 2004. Do not reduce the amount by any NOL deduction reported on line 29a.

Schedule L, Form 1120 (Part III, Form 1120-A)

The balance sheet should agree with the corporation's books and records.

Corporations with total receipts (line 1a plus lines 4 through 10 on page 1) and total assets at the end of the tax year less than $250,000 are not required to complete Schedules L, M-1, and M-2 if the "Yes" box on Schedule K, question 13, is checked. If the corporation is required to complete Schedule L, include total assets reported on Schedule L, line 15, column (d), on page 1, item D.

If filing a consolidated return, report total consolidated assets, liabilities, and shareholder's equity for all corporations joining in the return. See *Consolidated returns* on page 4 of these instructions.

Corporations with total assets (consolidated for all corporations included within the tax consolidation group) of $10 million or more on the last day of the tax year must complete Schedule M-3 instead of Schedule M-1. See the separate instructions for Schedule M-3 for provisions also affecting Schedule L.

Line 1

Include certificates of deposit as cash on this line.

Line 5

Include on this line:

- State and local government obligations, the interest on which is excludable from gross income under section 103(a) and
- Stock in a mutual fund or other RIC that distributed exempt-interest dividends during the tax year of the corporation.

Line 26, Form 1120 (Line 21, Form 1120-A)

Some examples of adjustments to report on this line include:

- Unrealized gains and losses on securities held "available for sale."
- Foreign currency translation adjustments.
- The excess of additional pension liability over unrecognized prior service cost.
- Guarantees of employee stock (ESOP) debt.
- Compensation related to employee stock award plans.

If the total adjustment to be entered on line 26 (line 21, Form 1120-A) is a negative amount, enter the amount in parentheses.

Schedule M-1, Form 1120 (Part IV, Form 1120-A)

Corporations with total receipts (line 1a plus lines 4 through 10 on page 1) and total assets at the end of the tax year less than $250,000 are not required to complete Schedules L, M-1, and M-2 if the "Yes" box on Schedule K, question 13, is checked.

Corporations with total assets (consolidated for all corporations included within the tax consolidation group) of $10 million or more on the last day of the tax year must complete Schedule M-3 instead of Schedule M-1. See the separate instructions for Schedule M-3.

Line 5c, Form 1120 (Line 5, Form 1120-A)

Include any of the following.

- Meal and entertainment expenses not deductible under section 274(n).
- Expenses for the use of an entertainment facility.
- The part of business gifts over $25.
- Expenses of an individual over $2,000, which are allocable to conventions on cruise ships.
- Employee achievement awards over $400.
- The cost of entertainment tickets over face value (also subject to 50% limit under section 274(n)).
- The cost of skyboxes over the face value of nonluxury box seat tickets.
- The part of luxury water travel expenses not deductible under section 274(m).
- Expenses for travel as a form of education.
- Other nondeductible travel and entertainment expenses.

For more information, see Pub. 542.

Line 7, Form 1120 (Line 6, Form 1120-A)

Report any tax exempt interest received or accrued, including any exempt-interest dividends received as a shareholder in a mutual fund or other RIC. Also report this same amount on Schedule K, item 9 (item 3, Form 1120-A).

Privacy Act and Paperwork Reduction Act Notice. We ask for the information on these forms to carry out the Internal Revenue laws of the United States. You are required to give us the information. We need it to ensure that you are complying with these laws and to allow us to figure and collect the right amount of tax. Section 6109 requires return preparers to provide their identifying numbers on the return.

You are not required to provide the information requested on a form that is subject to the Paperwork Reduction Act unless the form displays a valid OMB control number. Books or records relating to a form or its instructions must be retained as long as their contents may become material in the administration of any Internal Revenue law. Generally, tax returns and return information are confidential, as required by section 6103.

The time needed to complete and file the following forms will vary depending on individual circumstances. The estimated average times are:

Form	Recordkeeping	Learning about the law or the form	Preparing the form	Copying, assembling, and sending the form to the IRS
1120	70 hr., 47 min.	42 hr., 1 min.	72 hr., 56 min.	8 hr., 2 min.
1120-A	43 hr., 30 min.	24 hr., 13 min.	42 hr., 33 min.	4 hr., 49 min.
Sch. D (1120)	6 hr., 56 min.	3 hr., 55 min.	6 hr., 3 min.	32 min.
Sch. H (1120)	5 hr., 58 min.	35 min.	43 min.	-----
Sch. M-3	76 hr., 3 min.	3 hr., 40 min.	5 hr., 4 min.	-----
Sch. N (1120)	3 hr., 49 min.	1 hr., 30 min.	4 hr., 25 min.	48 min.
Sch. PH (1120)	15 hr., 18 min.	6 hr., 12 min.	8 hr., 35 min.	32 min.

If you have comments concerning the accuracy of these time estimates or suggestions for making this form and related schedules simpler, we would be happy to hear from you. You can write to Internal Revenue Service, Tax Products Coordinating Committee, SE:W:CAR:MP:T:T:SP, 1111 Constitution Ave. NW, IR-6406, Washington, DC 20224. Do not send the tax form to this address. Instead, see *Where To File* on page 3.

Forms 1120 and 1120-A

Principal Business Activity Codes

This list of principal business activities and their associated codes is designed to classify an enterprise by the type of activity in which it is engaged to facilitate the administration of the Internal Revenue Code. These principal business activity codes are based on the North American Industry Classification System.

Using the list of activities and codes below, determine from which activity the company derives the largest percentage of its "total receipts." Total receipts is defined as the sum of gross receipts or sales (page 1, line 1a) plus all other income (page 1, lines 4 through 10). If the company purchases raw materials and supplies them to a subcontractor to produce the finished product, but retains title to the product, the company is considered a manufacturer and must use one of the manufacturing codes (311110-339900).

Once the principal business activity is determined, entries must be made on Form 1120, Schedule K, lines 2a, 2b, and 2c, or on Form 1120-A, Part II, lines 1a, 1b, and 1c. For the business activity code number, enter the six digit code selected from the list below. On the next line (Form 1120, Schedule K, line 2b, or Form 1120-A, Part II, line 1b), enter a brief description of the company's business activity. Finally, enter a description of the principal product or service of the company on Form 1120, Schedule K, line 2c, or Form 1120-A, Part II, line 1c.

Code

Agriculture, Forestry, Fishing and Hunting

Crop Production

111100 Oilseed & Grain Farming
111210 Vegetable & Melon Farming (including potatoes & yams)
111300 Fruit & Tree Nut Farming
111400 Greenhouse, Nursery, & Floriculture Production
111900 Other Crop Farming (including tobacco, cotton, sugarcane, hay, peanut, sugar beet & all other crop farming)

Animal Production

112111 Beef Cattle Ranching & Farming
112112 Cattle Feedlots
112120 Dairy Cattle & Milk Production
112210 Hog & Pig Farming
112300 Poultry & Egg Production
112400 Sheep & Goat Farming
112510 Animal Aquaculture (including shellfish & finfish farms & hatcheries)
112900 Other Animal Production

Forestry and Logging

113110 Timber Tract Operations
113210 Forest Nurseries & Gathering of Forest Products
113310 Logging

Fishing, Hunting and Trapping

114110 Fishing
114210 Hunting & Trapping

Support Activities for Agriculture and Forestry

115110 Support Activities for Crop Production (including cotton ginning, soil preparation, planting, & cultivating)
115210 Support Activities for Animal Production
115310 Support Activities For Forestry

Mining

211110 Oil & Gas Extraction
212110 Coal Mining
212200 Metal Ore Mining
212310 Stone Mining & Quarrying
212320 Sand, Gravel, Clay, & Ceramic & Refractory Minerals Mining & Quarrying
212390 Other Nonmetallic Mineral Mining & Quarrying
213110 Support Activities for Mining

Utilities

221100 Electric Power Generation, Transmission & Distribution
221210 Natural Gas Distribution
221300 Water, Sewage & Other Systems

Construction

Construction of Buildings

236110 Residential Building Construction
236200 Nonresidential Building Construction

Heavy and Civil Engineering Construction

237100 Utility System Construction
237210 Land Subdivision

Code

237310 Highway, Street, & Bridge Construction
237990 Other Heavy & Civil Engineering Construction

Specialty Trade Contractors

238100 Foundation, Structure, & Building Exterior Contractors (including framing carpentry, masonry, glass, roofing, & siding)
238210 Electrical Contractors
238220 Plumbing, Heating, & Air-Conditioning Contractors
238290 Other Building Equipment Contractors
238300 Building Finishing Contractors (including drywall, insulation, painting, wallcovering, flooring, tile, & finish carpentry)
238900 Other Specialty Trade Contractors (including site preparation)

Manufacturing

Food Manufacturing

311110 Animal Food Mfg
311200 Grain & Oilseed Milling
311300 Sugar & Confectionery Product Mfg
311400 Fruit & Vegetable Preserving & Specialty Food Mfg
311500 Dairy Product Mfg
311610 Animal Slaughtering and Processing
311710 Seafood Product Preparation & Packaging
311800 Bakeries & Tortilla Mfg
311900 Other Food Mfg (including coffee, tea, flavorings & seasonings)

Beverage and Tobacco Product Manufacturing

312110 Soft Drink & Ice Mfg
312120 Breweries
312130 Wineries
312140 Distilleries
312200 Tobacco Manufacturing

Textile Mills and Textile Product Mills

313000 Textile Mills
314000 Textile Product Mills

Apparel Manufacturing

315100 Apparel Knitting Mills
315210 Cut & Sew Apparel Contractors
315220 Men's & Boys' Cut & Sew Apparel Mfg
315230 Women's & Girls' Cut & Sew Apparel Mfg
315290 Other Cut & Sew Apparel Mfg
315990 Apparel Accessories & Other Apparel Mfg

Leather and Allied Product Manufacturing

316110 Leather & Hide Tanning & Finishing
316210 Footwear Mfg (including rubber & plastics)
316990 Other Leather & Allied Product Mfg

Wood Product Manufacturing

321110 Sawmills & Wood Preservation

Code

321210 Veneer, Plywood, & Engineered Wood Product Mfg
321900 Other Wood Product Mfg

Paper Manufacturing

322100 Pulp, Paper, & Paperboard Mills
322200 Converted Paper Product Mfg

Printing and Related Support Activities

323100 Printing & Related Support Activities

Petroleum and Coal Products Manufacturing

324110 Petroleum Refineries (including integrated)
324120 Asphalt Paving, Roofing, & Saturated Materials Mfg
324190 Other Petroleum & Coal Products Mfg

Chemical Manufacturing

325100 Basic Chemical Mfg
325200 Resin, Synthetic Rubber, & Artificial & Synthetic Fibers & Filaments Mfg
325300 Pesticide, Fertilizer, & Other Agricultural Chemical Mfg
325410 Pharmaceutical & Medicine Mfg
325500 Paint, Coating, & Adhesive Mfg
325600 Soap, Cleaning Compound, & Toilet Preparation Mfg
325900 Other Chemical Product & Preparation Mfg

Plastics and Rubber Products Manufacturing

326100 Plastics Product Mfg
326200 Rubber Product Mfg

Nonmetallic Mineral Product Manufacturing

327100 Clay Product & Refractory Mfg
327210 Glass & Glass Product Mfg
327300 Cement & Concrete Product Mfg
327400 Lime & Gypsum Product Mfg
327900 Other Nonmetallic Mineral Product Mfg

Primary Metal Manufacturing

331110 Iron & Steel Mills & Ferroalloy Mfg
331200 Steel Product Mfg from Purchased Steel
331310 Alumina & Aluminum Production & Processing
331400 Nonferrous Metal (except Aluminum) Production & Processing
331500 Foundries

Fabricated Metal Product Manufacturing

332110 Forging & Stamping
332210 Cutlery & Handtool Mfg
332300 Architectural & Structural Metals Mfg
332400 Boiler, Tank, & Shipping Container Mfg
332510 Hardware Mfg
332610 Spring & Wire Product Mfg
332700 Machine Shops; Turned Product; & Screw, Nut, & Bolt Mfg
332810 Coating, Engraving, Heat Treating, & Allied Activities

Code

332900 Other Fabricated Metal Product Mfg

Machinery Manufacturing

333100 Agriculture, Construction, & Mining Machinery Mfg
333200 Industrial Machinery Mfg
333310 Commercial & Service Industry Machinery Mfg
333410 Ventilation, Heating, Air-Conditioning, & Commercial Refrigeration Equipment Mfg
333510 Metalworking Machinery Mfg
333610 Engine, Turbine & Power Transmission Equipment Mfg
333900 Other General Purpose Machinery Mfg

Computer and Electronic Product Manufacturing

334110 Computer & Peripheral Equipment Mfg
334200 Communications Equipment Mfg
334310 Audio & Video Equipment Mfg
334410 Semiconductor & Other Electronic Component Mfg
334500 Navigational, Measuring, Electromedical, & Control Instruments Mfg
334610 Manufacturing & Reproducing Magnetic & Optical Media

Electrical Equipment, Appliance, and Component Manufacturing

335100 Electric Lighting Equipment Mfg
335200 Household Appliance Mfg
335310 Electrical Equipment Mfg
335900 Other Electrical Equipment & Component Mfg

Transportation Equipment Manufacturing

336100 Motor Vehicle Mfg
336210 Motor Vehicle Body & Trailer Mfg
336300 Motor Vehicle Parts Mfg
336410 Aerospace Product & Parts Mfg
336510 Railroad Rolling Stock Mfg
336610 Ship & Boat Building
336990 Other Transportation Equipment Mfg

Furniture and Related Product Manufacturing

337000 Furniture & Related Product Manufacturing

Miscellaneous Manufacturing

339110 Medical Equipment & Supplies Mfg
339900 Other Miscellaneous Manufacturing

Wholesale Trade

Merchant Wholesalers, Durable Goods

423100 Motor Vehicle & Motor Vehicle Parts & Supplies
423200 Furniture & Home Furnishings
423300 Lumber & Other Construction Materials
423400 Professional & Commercial Equipment & Supplies
423500 Metal & Mineral (except Petroleum)

Code

423600 Electrical & Electronic Goods
423700 Hardware, & Plumbing & Heating Equipment & Supplies
423800 Machinery, Equipment, & Supplies
423910 Sporting & Recreational Goods & Supplies
423920 Toy & Hobby Goods & Supplies
423930 Recyclable Materials
423940 Jewelry, Watch, Precious Stone, & Precious Metals
423990 Other Miscellaneous Durable Goods

Merchant Wholesalers, Nondurable Goods

424100 Paper & Paper Products
424210 Drugs & Druggists' Sundries
424300 Apparel, Piece Goods, & Notions
424400 Grocery & Related Products
424500 Farm Product Raw Materials
424600 Chemical & Allied Products
424700 Petroleum & Petroleum Products
424800 Beer, Wine, & Distilled Alcoholic Beverages
424910 Farm Supplies
424920 Book, Periodical, & Newspapers
424930 Flower, Nursery Stock, & Florists' Supplies
424940 Tobacco & Tobacco Products
424950 Paint, Varnish, & Supplies
424990 Other Miscellaneous Nondurable Goods

Wholesale Electronic Markets and Agents and Brokers

425110 Business to Business Electronic Markets
425120 Wholesale Trade Agents & Brokers

Retail Trade

Motor Vehicle and Parts Dealers

441110 New Car Dealers
441120 Used Car Dealers
441210 Recreational Vehicle Dealers
441221 Motorcycle Dealers
441222 Boat Dealers
441229 All Other Motor Vehicle Dealers
441300 Automotive Parts, Accessories, & Tire Stores

Furniture and Home Furnishings Stores

442110 Furniture Stores
442210 Floor Covering Stores
442291 Window Treatment Stores
442299 All Other Home Furnishings Stores

Electronics and Appliance Stores

443111 Household Appliance Stores
443112 Radio, Television, & Other Electronics Stores
443120 Computer & Software Stores
443130 Camera & Photographic Supplies Stores

Building Material and Garden Equipment and Supplies Dealers

444110 Home Centers
444120 Paint & Wallpaper Stores
444130 Hardware Stores
444190 Other Building Material Dealers
444200 Lawn & Garden Equipment & Supplies Stores

Food and Beverage Stores

445110 Supermarkets and Other Grocery (except Convenience) Stores
445120 Convenience Stores
445210 Meat Markets

Code

445220 Fish & Seafood Markets
445230 Fruit & Vegetable Markets
445291 Baked Goods Stores
445292 Confectionery & Nut Stores
445299 All Other Specialty Food Stores
445310 Beer, Wine, & Liquor Stores

Health and Personal Care Stores

446110 Pharmacies & Drug Stores
446120 Cosmetics, Beauty Supplies, & Perfume Stores
446130 Optical Goods Stores
446190 Other Health & Personal Care Stores

Gasoline Stations

447100 Gasoline Stations (including convenience stores with gas)

Clothing and Clothing Accessories Stores

448110 Men's Clothing Stores
448120 Women's Clothing Stores
448130 Children's & Infants' Clothing Stores
448140 Family Clothing Stores
448150 Clothing Accessories Stores
448190 Other Clothing Stores
448210 Shoe Stores
448310 Jewelry Stores
448320 Luggage & Leather Goods Stores

Sporting Goods, Hobby, Book, and Music Stores

451110 Sporting Goods Stores
451120 Hobby, Toy, & Game Stores
451130 Sewing, Needlework, & Piece Goods Stores
451140 Musical Instrument & Supplies Stores
451211 Book Stores
451212 News Dealers & Newsstands
451220 Prerecorded Tape, Compact Disc, & Record Stores

General Merchandise Stores

452110 Department Stores
452900 Other General Merchandise Stores

Miscellaneous Store Retailers

453110 Florists
453210 Office Supplies & Stationery Stores
453220 Gift, Novelty, & Souvenir Stores
453310 Used Merchandise Stores
453910 Pet & Pet Supplies Stores
453920 Art Dealers
453930 Manufactured (Mobile) Home Dealers
453990 All Other Miscellaneous Store Retailers (including tobacco, candle, & trophy shops)

Nonstore Retailers

454110 Electronic Shopping & Mail-Order Houses
454210 Vending Machine Operators
454311 Heating Oil Dealers
454312 Liquefied Petroleum Gas (Bottled Gas) Dealers
454319 Other Fuel Dealers
454390 Other Direct Selling Establishments (including door-to-door retailing, frozen food plan providers, party plan merchandisers, & coffee-break service providers)

Transportation and Warehousing

Air, Rail, and Water Transportation

481000 Air Transportation
482110 Rail Transportation
483000 Water Transportation

Code

Truck Transportation

484110 General Freight Trucking, Local
484120 General Freight Trucking, Long-distance
484200 Specialized Freight Trucking

Transit and Ground Passenger Transportation

485110 Urban Transit Systems
485210 Interurban & Rural Bus Transportation
485310 Taxi Service
485320 Limousine Service
485410 School & Employee Bus Transportation
485510 Charter Bus Industry
485990 Other Transit & Ground Passenger Transportation

Pipeline Transportation

486000 Pipeline Transportation

Scenic & Sightseeing Transportation

487000 Scenic & Sightseeing Transportation

Support Activities for Transportation

488100 Support Activities for Air Transportation
488210 Support Activities for Rail Transportation
488300 Support Activities for Water Transportation
488410 Motor Vehicle Towing
488490 Other Support Activities for Road Transportation
488510 Freight Transportation Arrangement
488990 Other Support Activities for Transportation

Couriers and Messengers

492110 Couriers
492210 Local Messengers & Local Delivery

Warehousing and Storage

493100 Warehousing & Storage (except lessors of miniwarehouses & self-storage units)

Information

Publishing Industries (except Internet)

511110 Newspaper Publishers
511120 Periodical Publishers
511130 Book Publishers
511140 Directory & Mailing List Publishers
511190 Other Publishers
511210 Software Publishers

Motion Picture and Sound Recording Industries

512100 Motion Picture & Video Industries (except video rental)
512200 Sound Recording Industries

Broadcasting (except Internet)

515100 Radio & Television Broadcasting
515210 Cable & Other Subscription Programming

Internet Publishing and Broadcasting

516110 Internet Publishing & Broadcasting

Telecommunications

517000 Telecommunications (including paging, cellular, satellite, cable & other program distribution, resellers, & other telecommunications)

Internet Service Providers, Web Search Portals, and Data Processing Services

518111 Internet Service Providers
518112 Web Search Portals

Code

518210 Data Processing, Hosting, & Related Services

Other Information Services

519100 Other Information Services (including news syndicates & libraries)

Finance and Insurance

Depository Credit Intermediation

522110 Commercial Banking
522120 Savings Institutions
522130 Credit Unions
522190 Other Depository Credit Intermediation

Nondepository Credit Intermediation

522210 Credit Card Issuing
522220 Sales Financing
522291 Consumer Lending
522292 Real Estate Credit (including mortgage bankers & originators)
522293 International Trade Financing
522294 Secondary Market Financing
522298 All Other Nondepository Credit Intermediation

Activities Related to Credit Intermediation

522300 Activities Related to Credit Intermediation (including loan brokers, check clearing, & money transmitting)

Securities, Commodity Contracts, and Other Financial Investments and Related Activities

523110 Investment Banking & Securities Dealing
523120 Securities Brokerage
523130 Commodity Contracts Dealing
523140 Commodity Contracts Brokerage
523210 Securities & Commodity Exchanges
523900 Other Financial Investment Activities (including portfolio management & investment advice)

Insurance Carriers and Related Activities

524140 Direct Life, Health, & Medical Insurance & Reinsurance Carriers
524150 Direct Insurance & Reinsurance (except Life, Health & Medical) Carriers
524210 Insurance Agencies & Brokerages
524290 Other Insurance Related Activities (including third-party administration of insurance and pension funds)

Funds, Trusts, and Other Financial Vehicles

525100 Insurance & Employee Benefit Funds
525910 Open-End Investment Funds (Form 1120-RIC)
525920 Trusts, Estates, & Agency Accounts
525930 Real Estate Investment Trusts (Form 1120-REIT)
525990 Other Financial Vehicles (including closed-end investment funds)

"Offices of Bank Holding Companies" and "Offices of Other Holding Companies" are located under **Management of Companies (Holding Companies)** on page 27.

Real Estate and Rental and Leasing

Real Estate

531110 Lessors of Residential Buildings & Dwellings
531114 Cooperative Housing

Code	
531120	Lessors of Nonresidential Buildings (except Miniwarehouses)
531130	Lessors of Miniwarehouses & Self-Storage Units
531190	Lessors of Other Real Estate Property
531210	Offices of Real Estate Agents & Brokers
531310	Real Estate Property Managers
531320	Offices of Real Estate Appraisers
531390	Other Activities Related to Real Estate
Rental and Leasing Services	
532100	Automotive Equipment Rental & Leasing
532210	Consumer Electronics & Appliances Rental
532220	Formal Wear & Costume Rental
532230	Video Tape & Disc Rental
532290	Other Consumer Goods Rental
532310	General Rental Centers
532400	Commercial & Industrial Machinery & Equipment Rental & Leasing
Lessors of Nonfinancial Intangible Assets (except copyrighted works)	
533110	Lessors of Nonfinancial Intangible Assets (except copyrighted works)

Professional, Scientific, and Technical Services

Code	
Legal Services	
541110	Offices of Lawyers
541190	Other Legal Services
Accounting, Tax Preparation, Bookkeeping, and Payroll Services	
541211	Offices of Certified Public Accountants
541213	Tax Preparation Services
541214	Payroll Services
541219	Other Accounting Services
Architectural, Engineering, and Related Services	
541310	Architectural Services
541320	Landscape Architecture Services
541330	Engineering Services
541340	Drafting Services
541350	Building Inspection Services
541360	Geophysical Surveying & Mapping Services
541370	Surveying & Mapping (except Geophysical) Services
541380	Testing Laboratories
Specialized Design Services	
541400	Specialized Design Services (including interior, industrial, graphic, & fashion design)
Computer Systems Design and Related Services	
541511	Custom Computer Programming Services
541512	Computer Systems Design Services
541513	Computer Facilities Management Services
541519	Other Computer Related Services
Other Professional, Scientific, and Technical Services	
541600	Management, Scientific, & Technical Consulting Services
541700	Scientific Research & Development Services
541800	Advertising & Related Services
541910	Marketing Research & Public Opinion Polling
541920	Photographic Services
541930	Translation & Interpretation Services
541940	Veterinary Services
541990	All Other Professional, Scientific, & Technical Services

Management of Companies (Holding Companies)

Code	
551111	Offices of Bank Holding Companies
551112	Offices of Other Holding Companies

Administrative and Support and Waste Management and Remediation Services

Code	
Administrative and Support Services	
561110	Office Administrative Services
561210	Facilities Support Services
561300	Employment Services
561410	Document Preparation Services
561420	Telephone Call Centers
561430	Business Service Centers (including private mail centers & copy shops)
561440	Collection Agencies
561450	Credit Bureaus
561490	Other Business Support Services (including repossession services, court reporting, & stenotype services)
561500	Travel Arrangement & Reservation Services
561600	Investigation & Security Services
561710	Exterminating & Pest Control Services
561720	Janitorial Services
561730	Landscaping Services
561740	Carpet & Upholstery Cleaning Services
561790	Other Services to Buildings & Dwellings
561900	Other Support Services (including packaging & labeling services, & convention & trade show organizers)
Waste Management and Remediation Services	
562000	Waste Management & Remediation Services

Educational Services

Code	
611000	Educational Services (including schools, colleges, & universities)

Health Care and Social Assistance

Code	
Offices of Physicians and Dentists	
621111	Offices of Physicians (except mental health specialists)
621112	Offices of Physicians, Mental Health Specialists
621210	Offices of Dentists
Offices of Other Health Practitioners	
621310	Offices of Chiropractors
621320	Offices of Optometrists
621330	Offices of Mental Health Practitioners (except Physicians)
621340	Offices of Physical, Occupational & Speech Therapists, & Audiologists
621391	Offices of Podiatrists
621399	Offices of All Other Miscellaneous Health Practitioners
Outpatient Care Centers	
621410	Family Planning Centers
621420	Outpatient Mental Health & Substance Abuse Centers
621491	HMO Medical Centers
621492	Kidney Dialysis Centers
621493	Freestanding Ambulatory Surgical & Emergency Centers
621498	All Other Outpatient Care Centers
Medical and Diagnostic Laboratories	
621510	Medical & Diagnostic Laboratories
Home Health Care Services	
621610	Home Health Care Services
Other Ambulatory Health Care Services	
621900	Other Ambulatory Health Care Services (including ambulance services & blood & organ banks)
Hospitals	
622000	Hospitals
Nursing and Residential Care Facilities	
623000	Nursing & Residential Care Facilities
Social Assistance	
624100	Individual & Family Services
624200	Community Food & Housing, & Emergency & Other Relief Services
624310	Vocational Rehabilitation Services
624410	Child Day Care Services

Arts, Entertainment, and Recreation

Code	
Performing Arts, Spectator Sports, and Related Industries	
711100	Performing Arts Companies
711210	Spectator Sports (including sports clubs & racetracks)
711300	Promoters of Performing Arts, Sports, & Similar Events
711410	Agents & Managers for Artists, Athletes, Entertainers, & Other Public Figures
711510	Independent Artists, Writers, & Performers
Museums, Historical Sites, and Similar Institutions	
712100	Museums, Historical Sites, & Similar Institutions
Amusement, Gambling, and Recreation Industries	
713100	Amusement Parks & Arcades
713200	Gambling Industries
713900	Other Amusement & Recreation Industries (including golf courses, skiing facilities, marinas, fitness centers, & bowling centers)

Accommodation and Food Services

Code	
Accommodation	
721110	Hotels (except Casino Hotels) & Motels
721120	Casino Hotels
721191	Bed & Breakfast Inns
721199	All Other Traveler Accommodation
721210	RV (Recreational Vehicle) Parks & Recreational Camps
721310	Rooming & Boarding Houses
Food Services and Drinking Places	
722110	Full-Service Restaurants
722210	Limited-Service Eating Places
722300	Special Food Services (including food service contractors & caterers)
722410	Drinking Places (Alcoholic Beverages)

Other Services

Code	
Repair and Maintenance	
811110	Automotive Mechanical & Electrical Repair & Maintenance
811120	Automotive Body, Paint, Interior, & Glass Repair
811190	Other Automotive Repair & Maintenance (including oil change & lubrication shops & car washes)
811210	Electronic & Precision Equipment Repair & Maintenance
811310	Commercial & Industrial Machinery & Equipment (except Automotive & Electronic) Repair & Maintenance
811410	Home & Garden Equipment & Appliance Repair & Maintenance
811420	Reupholstery & Furniture Repair
811430	Footwear & Leather Goods Repair
811490	Other Personal & Household Goods Repair & Maintenance
Personal and Laundry Services	
812111	Barber Shops
812112	Beauty Salons
812113	Nail Salons
812190	Other Personal Care Services (including diet & weight reducing centers)
812210	Funeral Homes & Funeral Services
812220	Cemeteries & Crematories
812310	Coin-Operated Laundries & Drycleaners
812320	Drycleaning & Laundry Services (except Coin-Operated)
812330	Linen & Uniform Supply
812910	Pet Care (except Veterinary) Services
812920	Photofinishing
812930	Parking Lots & Garages
812990	All Other Personal Services
Religious, Grantmaking, Civic, Professional, and Similar Organizations	
813000	Religious, Grantmaking, Civic, Professional, & Similar Organizations (including condominium and homeowners associations)

Index

■

INSTRUCTIONS FOR FORM 1120S

U.S. Income Tax Return for an S Corporation

2004

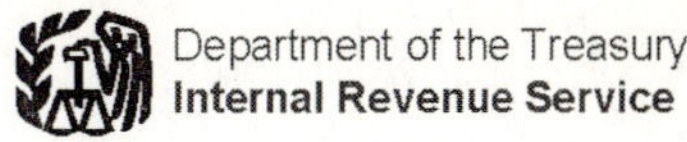

Department of the Treasury
Internal Revenue Service

Instructions for Form 1120S

U.S. Income Tax Return for an S Corporation

Section references are to the Internal Revenue Code unless otherwise noted.

Contents Page

Contents Page

What's New

1. The instructions for Schedules K and K-1 have been revised to reflect extensive changes to these schedules. See *General Reporting Information* on page 20 for new Schedule K-1 reporting requirements.

2. The American Jobs Creation Act of 2004 made several changes that affect S corporations and their shareholders. These changes include the following provisions. See Pub. 553, Highlights of 2004 Tax Changes, for more information.

- A new election to deduct a limited amount of business start-up and organizational expenses. For more information, see *Business start-up and organizational costs* on page 14.
- Two new tax credits: the biodiesel fuels credit and the low sulfur diesel fuel production credit. The act also expanded the renewable electricity credit to include refined coal production. See the instructions for line 13g of Schedule K for more information.
- A new election to deduct up to $10,000 of reforestation expenses paid or incurred after October 22, 2004. The reforestation credit is repealed for expenses paid or incurred after this date. See the instructions for line 12e of Schedule K for more information.
- A new election to deduct certain costs of qualified film or television productions commencing after October 22, 2004. See section 181 for more information.
- The deduction for certain travel, meals, and entertainment expenses incurred after October 22, 2004, is limited to the amount treated as compensation to officers, directors, and more-than-10% shareholders. See section 274(e)(2).

Photographs of Missing Children

The Internal Revenue Service is a proud partner with the National Center for Missing and Exploited Children. Photographs of missing children selected by the Center may appear in instructions on pages that would otherwise be blank. You can help bring these children home by looking at the photographs and calling 1-800-THE-LOST (1-800-843-5678) if you recognize a child.

Unresolved Tax Issues

If the corporation has attempted to deal with an IRS problem unsuccessfully, it should contact the Taxpayer Advocate. The Taxpayer Advocate independently represents the corporation's interests and concerns within the IRS by protecting its rights and resolving problems that have not been fixed through normal channels.

While Taxpayer Advocates cannot change the tax law or make a technical tax decision, they can clear up problems that resulted from previous contacts and ensure that the corporation's case is given a complete and impartial review.

The corporation's assigned personal advocate will listen to its point of view and will work with the corporation to address its concerns. The corporation can expect the advocate to provide:

- A "fresh look" at a new or ongoing problem.
- Timely acknowledgment.
- The name and phone number of the individual assigned to its case.
- Updates on progress.
- Timeframes for action.

Cat. No. 11515K

• Speedy resolution.
• Courteous service.

When contacting the Taxpayer Advocate, the corporation should provide the following information:
• The corporation's name, address, and employer identification number (EIN).
• The name and telephone number of an authorized contact person and the hours he or she can be reached.
• The type of tax return and year(s) involved.
• A detailed description of the problem.
• Previous attempts to solve the problem and the office that had been contacted.
• A description of the hardship the corporation is facing and verifying documentation (if applicable).

The corporation may contact a Taxpayer Advocate by calling a toll-free number, 1-877-777-4778 or by visiting the IRS website at *www.irs.gov/advocate*. Persons who have access to TTY/TDD equipment may call 1-800-829-4059 and ask for Taxpayer Advocate assistance. If the corporation prefers, it may call, write, or fax the Taxpayer Advocate office in its area. See Pub. 1546, The Taxpayer Advocate Service of the IRS, for a list of addresses and fax numbers.

Direct Deposit of Refund

To request a direct deposit of the corporation's income tax refund, attach Form 8050, Direct Deposit of Corporate Tax Refund (see page 18).

How To Make a Contribution To Reduce the Public Debt

To make a contribution to reduce the public debt, send a check made payable to the "Bureau of the Public Debt" to Bureau of the Public Debt, Department G, P.O. Box 2188, Parkersburg, WV 26106-2188. Or, enclose a check with Form 1120S. Contributions to reduce the public debt are deductible, subject to the rules and limitations for charitable contributions.

How To Get Forms and Publications

Personal computer. You can access the IRS website 24 hours a day, 7 days a week at www.irs.gov to:
• Order IRS products online.
• Download forms, instructions, and publications.
• See answers to frequently asked tax questions.
• Search publications online by topic or keyword.
• Send us comments or request help by email.
• Sign up to receive local and national tax news by email.

You can also reach us using file transfer protocol at *ftp.irs.gov*.

CD-ROM. Order Pub. 1796, Federal Tax Products on CD-ROM, and get:
• Current year forms, instructions, and publications.
• Prior year forms, instructions, and publications.
• Frequently requested tax forms that may be filled in electronically, printed out for submission, and saved for recordkeeping.
• The Internal Revenue Bulletin.

Buy the CD-ROM on the Internet at *www.irs.gov/cdorders* from the National Technical Information Service (NTIS) for $22 (no handling fee) or call 1-877-CDFORMS (1-877-233-6767) toll free to buy the CD-ROM for $22 (plus a $5 handling fee).

By phone and in person. You can order forms and publications by calling 1-800-TAX-FORM (1-800-829-3676). You can also get most forms and publications at your local IRS office.

IRS E-Services Make Taxes Easier

Now more than ever before businesses can enjoy the benefits of filing and paying their federal taxes electronically. Whether you rely on a tax professional or handle your own taxes, the IRS offers you convenient programs to make taxes easier.
• You can *e-file* your Form 1120S tax return; Form 940 and 941 employment tax returns; Form 1099 and other information returns. Visit *www.irs.gov/efile* for more information.
• You can pay taxes online or by phone using the free Electronic Federal Tax Payment System (EFTPS). Visit *www.eftps.gov* or call 1-800-555-4477 for more information.

Use these electronic options to make filing and paying taxes easier.

General Instructions

Purpose of Form

Form 1120S is used to report the income, deductions, gains, losses, etc., of a domestic corporation that has elected to be an S corporation by filing Form 2553, Election by a Small Business Corporation, and whose election is in effect for the tax year.

Who Must File

A corporation must file Form 1120S if (a) it elected to be an S corporation by filing Form 2553, (b) the IRS accepted the election, and (c) the election remains in effect. Do not file Form 1120S for any tax year before the year the election takes effect.

You cannot file Form 1120S unless you have previously filed a properly completed Form 2553. After filing Form 2553 you should have received confirmation that Form 2553 was accepted. If you did not receive notification of acceptance or nonacceptance of the election within 3 months of filing Form 2553 (6 months if you checked box Q1 to request a letter ruling), you should contact the service center where the form was filed to make sure the IRS received the election. If you have not filed Form 2553, or did not file Form 2553 on time, you may be entitled to relief for a late filed election to be an S corporation. See the Instructions for Form 2553 for details.

Termination of Election

Once the election is made, it stays in effect until it is terminated. If the election is terminated, the corporation (or a successor corporation) can make another election on Form 2553 only with IRS consent for any tax year before the 5th tax year after the first tax year in which the termination took effect. See Regulations section 1.1362-5 for more details.

An election terminates automatically in any of the following cases:

1. The corporation is no longer a small business corporation as defined in section 1361(b). This kind of termination of an election is effective as of the day the corporation no longer meets the definition of a small business corporation. Attach to Form 1120S for the final year of the S corporation a statement notifying the IRS of the termination and the date it occurred.

2. The corporation, for each of three consecutive tax years, (a) has accumulated earnings and profits and (b) derives more than 25% of its gross receipts from passive investment income as defined in section 1362(d)(3)(C). The election terminates on the first day of the first tax year beginning after the third consecutive tax year. The corporation must pay a tax for each year it has excess net passive income. See the instructions for line 22a on page 18 for details on how to figure the tax.

3. The election is revoked. An election may be revoked only with the consent of shareholders who, at the time the revocation is made, hold more than 50% of the number of issued and outstanding shares of stock (including non-voting stock). The revocation may specify an effective revocation date that is on or after the day the revocation is filed. If no date is specified, the revocation is effective at the start of a tax year if the revocation is made on or before the 15th day of the 3rd month of that tax year. If no date is specified and the revocation is made after the 15th day of the 3rd month of the tax year, the revocation is effective at the start of the next tax year.

To revoke the election, the corporation must file a statement with the service center where it filed its election to be an S corporation. In the statement, the corporation must notify the IRS that it is revoking its election to be an S corporation. The statement must be signed by each shareholder who consents to the revocation and contain the information required by Regulations section 1.1362-6(a)(3).

A revocation may be rescinded before it takes effect. See Regulations section 1.1362-6(a)(4) for details.

For rules on allocating income and deductions between an S short year and a C short year and other special rules that apply when an election is terminated, see section 1362(e) and Regulations section 1.1362-3.

If an election was terminated under 1 or 2 above, and the corporation believes the termination was inadvertent, the corporation may request permission from the IRS to continue to be treated as an S corporation. See Regulations section 1.1362-4 for the specific requirements that must be met to qualify for inadvertent termination relief.

Electronic Filing

S corporations have the option to file Form 1120S and related forms, schedules, and attachments electronically. However, the option to file electronically does not apply to certain returns, including:

- Amended returns,
- Bankruptcy returns,
- Final returns,
- Returns with a name change,
- Returns with precomputed penalty and interest,
- Returns with reasonable cause for failing to file timely,
- Returns with reasonable cause for failing to pay timely,
- Returns with request for overpayment to be applied to another account,
- Short-year returns, and
- 52–53 week tax year returns.

Visit *www.irs.gov/efile* for more information.

When To File

In general, file Form 1120S by the 15th day of the 3rd month following the date the corporation's tax year ended as shown at the top of Form 1120S. For calendar year corporations, the due date is March 15, 2005. If the due date falls on a Saturday, Sunday, or legal holiday, file on the next business day. A corporation that has dissolved must generally file by the 15th day of the 3rd month after the date of dissolution.

If the S corporation election was terminated during the tax year and the corporation reverts to a C corporation, file Form 1120S for the S corporation's short year by the due date (including extensions) of the C corporation's short year return.

Private delivery services. Corporations can use certain private delivery services designated by the IRS to meet the "timely mailing as timely filing/paying" rule for tax returns and payments. These private delivery services include only the following:

- DHL Express (DHL): DHL Same Day Service; DHL Next Day 10:30 am; DHL Next Day 12:00 pm; DHL Next Day 3:00 pm; and DHL 2nd Day Service.
- Federal Express (FedEx): FedEx Priority Overnight, FedEx Standard Overnight, FedEx 2Day, FedEx International Priority, FedEx International First.
- United Parcel Service (UPS): UPS Next Day Air, UPS Next Day Air Saver, UPS 2nd Day Air, UPS 2nd Day Air A.M., UPS Worldwide Express Plus, UPS Worldwide Express.

The private delivery service can tell you how to get written proof of the mailing date.

Private delivery services cannot deliver items to P.O. boxes. You must use the U.S. Postal Service to mail any item to an IRS P.O. box address.

Most private delivery services will not accept your return without a street address in addition to the city, state, and ZIP code. You can get the street address of your service center by calling 1-800-829-4933.

Extension. Use Form 7004 to request a 6-month extension of time to file.

Period Covered

File the 2004 return for calendar year 2004 and fiscal years beginning in 2004 and ending in 2005. If the return is for a fiscal year or a short tax year, fill in the tax year space at the top of the form.

Note. The 2004 Form 1120S may also be used if:

- *The corporation has a tax year of less than 12 months that begins and ends in 2005 and*
- *The 2005 Form 1120S is not available by the time the corporation is required to file its return.*

The corporation must show its 2005 tax year on the 2004 Form 1120S and take into account any tax law changes that are effective for tax years beginning after December 31, 2004.

Who Must Sign

The return must be signed and dated by:

- The president, vice president, treasurer, assistant treasurer, chief accounting officer, or
- Any other corporate officer (such as tax officer) authorized to sign.
- Where a return is made for a corporation by a receiver, trustee or assignee, the fiduciary must sign the return, instead of the corporate officer. Returns and forms signed by a receiver or trustee in bankruptcy on behalf of a corporation must be accompanied by a copy of the order or instructions of the court authorizing signing of the return or form.

If an employee of the corporation completes Form 1120S, the paid preparer's space should remain blank. In addition, anyone who prepares Form 1120S, but does not charge the corporation, should not complete that section. Generally, anyone who is paid to prepare the return must sign it and fill in the "Paid Preparer's Use Only" area.

The paid preparer must complete the required preparer information and:

- Sign the return in the space provided for the preparer's signature.
- Give a copy of the return to the taxpayer.

Note. A paid preparer may sign original returns, amended returns, or requests for filing extensions by rubber stamp, mechanical device, or computer software program.

Where To File

File your return at the applicable IRS address listed below.

If the corporation's principal business, office, or agency is located in:	And the total assets at the end of the tax year (Form 1120S, page 1, item E) are:	Use the following Internal Revenue Service Center address:
Connecticut, Delaware, District of Columbia, Illinois, Indiana, Kentucky, Maine, Maryland, Massachusetts, Michigan, New Hampshire, New Jersey, New York, North Carolina, Ohio, Pennsylvania, Rhode Island, South Carolina, Vermont, Virginia, West Virginia, Wisconsin	Less than $10 million	Cincinnati, OH 45999-0013
	$10 million or more	Ogden, UT 84201-0013
Alabama, Alaska, Arizona, Arkansas, California, Colorado, Florida, Georgia, Hawaii, Idaho, Iowa, Kansas, Louisiana, Minnesota, Mississippi, Missouri, Montana, Nebraska, Nevada, New Mexico, North Dakota, Oklahoma, Oregon, South Dakota, Tennessee, Texas, Utah, Washington, Wyoming	Any amount	Ogden, UT 84201-0013
A foreign country or U.S. possession	Any amount	Philadelphia, PA 19255-0013

Paid Preparer Authorization

If the corporation wants to allow the IRS to discuss its 2004 tax return with the paid preparer who signed it, check the "Yes" box in the signature area of the return. This authorization applies only to the individual whose signature appears in the "Paid Preparer's Use Only" section of the return. It does not apply to the firm, if any, shown in that section.

If the "Yes" box is checked, the corporation is authorizing the IRS to call the paid preparer to answer any questions that may arise during the processing of its return. The corporation is also authorizing the paid preparer to:

- Give the IRS any information that is missing from its return,
- Call the IRS for information about the processing of its return or the status of its refund or payment(s), and
- Respond to certain IRS notices that the corporation has shared with the preparer about math errors, offsets, and return preparation. The notices will not be sent to the preparer.

The corporation is not authorizing the paid preparer to receive any refund check, bind the corporation to anything (including any additional tax liability), or otherwise represent the corporation before the IRS. If the corporation wants to expand the paid preparer's authorization, see Pub. 947, Practice Before the IRS and Power of Attorney.

The authorization cannot be revoked. However, the authorization will automatically end no later than the due date (excluding extensions) for filing the 2005 tax return.

Accounting Methods

An accounting method is a set of rules used to determine when and how income and expenditures are reported.

Figure ordinary income using the method of accounting regularly used in keeping the corporation's books and records. The method used must clearly reflect income.

Generally, permissible methods include:

- Cash,
- Accrual, or
- Any other method authorized by the Internal Revenue Code.

Generally, a corporation may not use the cash method of accounting if it is a tax shelter (as defined in section 448(d)(3)). See section 448 for details.

If inventories are required, the accrual method generally must be used for sales and purchases of merchandise. However, qualifying taxpayers and eligible businesses of qualifying small business taxpayers are excepted from using the accrual method and may account for inventoriable items as materials and supplies that are not incidental. For details, see *Schedule A. Cost of Goods Sold* on page 18.

Accrual method. Under the accrual method, an amount is includible in income when

- All the events have occurred that fix the right to receive the income, which is the earliest of the date (a) the required performance takes place, (b) payment is due, or (c) payment is received, and
- The amount can be determined with reasonable accuracy.

See Regulations section 1.451-1(a) for details.

Generally, an accrual basis taxpayer can deduct accrued expenses in the tax year in which:

- All events that determine the liability have occurred,
- The amount of the liability can be figured with reasonable accuracy, and
- Economic performance takes place with respect to the expense.

There are exceptions for certain items, including recurring expenses. See section 461(h) and the related regulations for the rules for determining when economic performance takes place.

Percentage-of-completion method. Long-term contracts (except for certain real property construction contracts) must generally be accounted for using the percentage of completion method. For rules on long-term contracts, see section 460 and the underlying regulations.

Mark-to-market accounting method. Generally, dealers in securities must use the mark-to-market accounting method described in section 475. Under this method, any security that is inventory to the dealer must be included in inventory at its fair market value (FMV). Any security held by a dealer that is not inventory and that is held at the close of the tax year is treated as sold at its FMV on the last business day of the tax year. Any gain or loss must be taken into account in determining gross income. The gain or loss taken into account is generally treated as ordinary gain or loss. For details, including exceptions, see section 475, the related regulations, and Rev. Rul. 94-7, 1994-1 C.B. 151.

Dealers in commodities and traders in securities and commodities may elect to use the mark-to-market accounting method. To make the election, the corporation must file a statement: describing the election, the first tax year the election is to be effective, and, in the case of an election for traders in securities or commodities, the trade or business for which the election is made. Except for new taxpayers, the statement must be filed by the due date (not including extensions) of the income tax return for the tax year immediately preceding the election year and attached to that return, or, if applicable, to a request for an extension of time to file that return. For more details, see sections 475(e) and (f) and Rev. Proc. 99-17, 1999-7 I.R.B. 52.

Change in accounting method. Generally, the corporation must get IRS consent to change its method of accounting used to report taxable income (for income as a whole or for any material item). To do so, it must file Form 3115, Application for Change in Accounting Method. For more information, see Pub. 538, Accounting Periods and Methods.

Section 481(a) adjustment. The corporation may have to make an adjustment under section 481(a) to prevent amounts of income or expense from being duplicated or omitted. The section 481(a) adjustment period is generally 1 year for a net negative adjustment and 4 years for a net positive adjustment. However, a corporation may elect to use a 1-year adjustment period for positive adjustments if the net section 481(a) adjustment for the accounting method change is less than $25,000. For more details on the section 481(a) adjustment, see Form 3115.

Include any net positive section 481(a) adjustment on page 1, line 5. If the net section 481(a) adjustment is negative, report it on page 1, line 19.

Accounting Periods

A corporation must figure its taxable income on the basis of a tax year. A tax year is the annual accounting period a corporation uses to keep its records and report its income and expenses.

Generally, an S corporation tax year is required to be:

- A calendar year.
- A 52-53 week tax year that ends with reference to a calendar year or a tax year elected under section 444.
- A tax year elected under section 444.
- Any other tax year for which the corporation establishes a business purpose by filing Form 1128.

A new S corporation must use Form 2553 to adopt a tax year other than a calendar year. To change the corporation's tax year, see Pub. 538 and Form 1128, Application To Adopt, Change, or Retain a Tax Year, (unless the corporation is making an election under section 444, discussed below).

Establish a business purpose. To establish a business purpose for changing or retaining its tax year on Form 1128, the corporation must establish that:

- The requested tax year is the corporation's natural business year or ownership tax year under the automatic approval request provisions of Rev. Proc. 2002-38, 2002-2 I.R.B. 1037, or
- There is a business purpose for the requested tax year under the ruling request provisions of Rev. Proc. 2002-39, 2002-2 I.R.B. 1046 (a user fee is required).

If the corporation changes its tax year solely because its current tax year no longer qualifies as a natural business year (or, for certain corporations, an ownership tax year), its shareholders may elect to take into account ratably over 4 tax years their pro rata share of income attributable to the corporation's short tax year ending on or after May 10, 2002, but before June 1, 2004. See Rev. Proc. 2003-79, 2003-45 I.R.B. 1036, for details. If the corporation changes its tax year and the change falls within the scope of Rev. Proc. 2003-79, the corporation must attach a statement to Schedule K-1 that provides shareholders with the information they will need to make this election.

Electing a tax year under section 444. Under the provisions of section 444, an S corporation may elect to have a tax year other than a permitted year, but only if the deferral period of the tax year is not longer than the shorter of 3 months or the deferral period of the tax year being changed. This election is made by filing Form 8716, Election To Have a Tax Year Other Than a Required Tax Year.

An S corporation may not make or continue an election under section 444 if it is a member of a tiered structure, other than a tiered structure that consists entirely of partnerships and S corporations that have the same tax year. For the S corporation to have a section 444 election in effect, it must make the payments required by section 7519. See Form 8752, Required Payment or Refund Under Section 7519.

A section 444 election ends if: an S corporation changes its accounting period to a calendar year or some other permitted year; it is penalized for willfully failing to comply with the requirements of section 7519; or its S election is terminated (unless it immediately becomes a personal service corporation). If the termination results in a short tax year, type or legibly print at the top of the first page of Form 1120S for the short tax year, "SECTION 444 ELECTION TERMINATED."

Rounding Off to Whole Dollars

The corporation may round off cents to whole dollars on its return and schedules. If the corporation does round to whole dollars, it must round all amounts. To round, drop amounts under 50 cents and increase amounts from 50 to 99 cents to the next dollar (for example, $1.39 becomes $1 and $2.50 becomes $3).

If two or more amounts must be added to figure the amount to enter on a line, include cents when adding the amounts and round off only the total.

Recordkeeping

Keep the corporation's records for as long as they may be needed for the administration of any provision of the Internal Revenue Code. Usually, records that support an item of income, deduction, or credit on the return must be kept for 3 years from the date each shareholder's return is due or is filed, whichever is later. Keep records that verify the corporation's basis in property for as long as they are needed to figure the basis of the original or replacement property.

The corporation should keep copies of all returns filed. They may help in preparing future returns and in making amended returns.

Depository Method of Tax Payment

The corporation must pay the tax due in full no later than the 15th day of the 3rd month after the end of the tax year. The two methods of depositing corporate income taxes are discussed below.

Electronic Deposit Requirement

The corporation must make electronic deposits of all depository taxes (such as employment tax, excise tax, and corporate income tax) using the Electronic Federal Tax Payment System (EFTPS) in 2005 if:

- The total deposits of such taxes in 2003 were more than $200,000 or
- The corporation was required to use EFTPS in 2004.

If the corporation is required to use EFTPS and fails to do so, it may be subject to a 10% penalty. If the corporation is not required to use EFTPS, it may participate voluntarily. To enroll in or get more information about EFTPS, call 1-800-555-4477 or 1-800-945-8400. To enroll online, visit *www.eftps.gov*.

Depositing on time. For EFTPS deposits to be made timely, the corporation must initiate the transaction at least 1 business day before the date the deposit is due.

Deposits With Form 8109

If the corporation does not use EFTPS, deposit corporation income tax payments (and estimated tax payments) with Form 8109, Federal Tax Deposit Coupon. If you do not have a preprinted Form 8109, use Form 8109-B to make deposits. You can get this form only by calling 1-800-829-4933. Be sure to have your EIN ready when you call.

Do not send deposits directly to an IRS office; otherwise, the corporation may have to pay a penalty. Mail or deliver the completed Form 8109 with the payment to an authorized depositary, i.e., a commercial bank or other financial institution authorized to accept federal tax deposits.

Make checks or money orders payable to the depositary. To help ensure proper crediting, enter the corporation's EIN, the tax period to which the deposit applies, and "Form 1120S" on the check or money order. Be sure to darken the "1120" box under "Type of Tax" and the appropriate "Quarter" box under "Tax Period" on the coupon. Records of these deposits will be sent to the IRS. For more information, See "Marking the Proper Tax Period" in the instructions for Form 8109.

If the corporation prefers, it may mail the coupon and payment to: Financial Agent, Federal Tax Deposit Processing, P.O. Box 970030, St. Louis, MO 63197. Make the check or money order payable to "Financial Agent."

For more information on deposits, see the instructions in the coupon booklet (Form 8109) and Pub. 583, Starting a Business and Keeping Records.

Estimated Tax Payments

Generally, the corporation must make installment payments of estimated tax for the following taxes if the total of these taxes is $500 or more: (a) the tax on built-in gains, (b) the excess net passive income tax, and (c) the investment credit recapture tax.

The amount of estimated tax required to be paid annually is the smaller of: (a) the total of the above taxes shown on the return for the tax year (or if no return is filed, the total of these taxes for the year) or (b) the sum of *(i)* the investment credit recapture tax and the built-in gains tax shown on the return for the tax year (or if no return is filed, the total of these taxes for the tax year) and *(ii)* any excess net passive income tax shown on the corporation's return for the preceding tax year. If the preceding tax year was less than 12 months, the estimated tax must be determined under (a).

The estimated tax is generally payable in four equal installments. However, the corporation may be able to lower the amount of one or more installments by using the annualized income installment method or adjusted seasonal installment method under section 6655(e).

For a calendar year corporation, the payments are due for 2004 by April 15, June 15, September 15, and December 15. For a fiscal year corporation, they are due by the 15th day of the 4th, 6th, 9th, and 12th months of the fiscal year. If any date falls on a Saturday, Sunday, or legal holiday, the installment is due on the next regular business day.

The corporation must make the payments using the depository method described above.

For more information on estimated tax payments, including penalties that apply if the corporation fails to make required payments, see the instructions for line 24 on page 18.

Interest and Penalties

Interest. Interest is charged on taxes paid late even if an extension of time to file is granted. Interest is also charged on penalties imposed for failure to file, negligence, fraud, substantial valuation misstatements, and substantial understatements of tax from the due date (including extensions) to the date of payment. The interest charge is figured at a rate determined under section 6621.

Late filing of return. A corporation that does not file its tax return by the due date, including extensions, may have to pay a penalty of 5% a month, or part of a month, up to a maximum of 25%, for each month the return is not filed. The penalty is imposed on the net amount due. The minimum penalty for filing a return more than 60 days late is the smaller of the tax due or $100. The penalty will not be imposed if the corporation can show that the failure to file on time was due to reasonable cause. If the failure is due to reasonable cause, attach an explanation to the return.

Late payment of tax. A corporation that does not pay the tax when due generally may have to pay a penalty of ½ of 1% a month or part of a month, up to a maximum of 25%, for each month the tax is not paid. The penalty is imposed on the net amount due.

The penalty will not be imposed if the corporation can show that failure to pay on time was due to reasonable cause.

Failure to furnish information timely. Section 6037(b) requires an S corporation to furnish to each shareholder a copy of the information shown on Schedule K-1 (Form 1120S) that is attached to Form 1120S. Provide Schedule K-1 to each shareholder on or before the day on which the corporation files Form 1120S.

For each failure to furnish Schedule K-1 to a shareholder when due and each failure to include on Schedule K-1 all the information required to be shown (or the inclusion of incorrect information), a $50 penalty may be imposed with regard to each Schedule K-1 for which a failure occurs. If the requirement to report correct information is intentionally disregarded, each $50 penalty is increased to $100 or, if greater, 10% of the aggregate amount of items required to be reported. See sections 6722 and 6724 for more information.

The penalty will not be imposed if the corporation can show that not furnishing information timely was due to reasonable cause and not due to willful neglect.

Trust fund recovery penalty. This penalty may apply if certain excise, income, social security, and Medicare taxes that must be collected or withheld are not collected or withheld, or these taxes are not paid. These taxes are generally reported on Forms 720, 941, 943, or 945 (see *Other Forms, Returns, and Statements That May Be Required* below). The trust fund recovery penalty may be imposed on all persons who are determined by the IRS to have been responsible for collecting, accounting for, and paying over these taxes, and who acted willfully in not doing so. The penalty is equal to the unpaid trust fund tax. See the instructions for Form 720, Pub. 15 (Circular E), Employer's Tax Guide, or Pub. 51 (Circular A), Agricultural Employer's Tax Guide, for more details, including the definition of responsible persons.

Other Forms, Returns, and Statements That May Be Required

• Schedule N (Form 1120), Foreign Operations of U.S. Corporations. The corporation may have to file this schedule if it had assets in or operated a business in a foreign country or a U.S. possession.
• Forms W-2, Wage and Tax Statement, and W-3, Transmittal of Wage and Tax Statements. Use these forms to report wages, tips, other compensation, and withheld income, social security, and Medicare taxes for employees.
• Form 720, Quarterly Federal Excise Tax Return. Use Form 720 to report environmental taxes, communications and air transportation taxes, fuel taxes, manufacturers taxes, ship passenger tax, and certain other excise taxes.
• Form 926, Information Return of a U.S. Transferor of Property to a Foreign Corporation. Use this form to report certain information required under section 6038B.
• Form 940 or Form 940-EZ, Employer's Annual Federal Unemployment (FUTA) Tax Return. The corporation may be liable for FUTA tax and may have to file Form 940 or 940-EZ if it either:

1. Paid wages of $1,500 or more in any calendar quarter in 2003 or 2004 or
2. Had one or more employees who worked for the corporation for at least some part of a day in any 20 or more different weeks in 2003 or 20 or more different weeks in 2004.

A corporate officer who performs substantial services is considered an employee. Except as provided in section 3306(a), reasonable compensation for these services is subject to FUTA tax, no matter what the corporation calls the payments.

• Form 941, Employer's Quarterly Federal Tax Return or Form 943, Employer's Annual Tax Return for Agricultural Employees. Employers must file these forms to report income tax withheld, and employer and employee social security and Medicare taxes. Also, see *Trust Fund Recovery Penalty* above. A corporate officer who performs substantial services is considered an employee. Distributions and other payments by an S corporation to a corporate officer must be treated as wages to the extent the amounts are reasonable compensation for services to the corporation.
• Form 945, Annual Return of Withheld Federal Income Tax. File Form 945 to report income tax withheld from nonpayroll distributions or payments, including pensions, annuities, IRAs, gambling winnings, and backup withholding. Also, see *Trust Fund Recovery Penalty* above.
• Form 966, Corporate Dissolution or Liquidation.
• Forms 1042 and 1042-S, Annual Withholding Tax Return for U.S. Source Income of Foreign Persons; and Foreign Person's U.S. Source Income Subject to Withholding. Use these forms to report and send withheld tax on payments made to nonresident alien individuals, foreign partnerships, or foreign corporations to the extent those payments constitute gross income from sources within the United States (see sections 861 through 865). For more details, see sections 1441 and 1442, and Pub. 515, Withholding of Tax on Nonresident Aliens and Foreign Entities.
• Form 1042-T, Annual Summary and Transmittal of Forms 1042-S. Use Form 1042-T to transmit paper Forms 1042-S to the IRS.
• Form 1096, Annual Summary and Transmittal of U.S. Information Returns.
• Form 1098, Mortgage Interest Statement. Use this form to report the receipt from any individual of $600 or more of mortgage interest (including points) in the course of the corporation's trade or business and reimbursements of overpaid interest.
• Forms 1099. Use these information returns to report the following.

1. 1099-A, Acquisition or Abandonment of Secured Property.
2. 1099-B, Proceeds From Broker and Barter Exchange Transactions.
3. 1099-C, Cancellation of Debt.
4. 1099-DIV, Dividends and Distributions. Use Form 1099-DIV to report actual dividends paid by the corporation. Only distributions from accumulated earnings and profits are classified as dividends from an S corporation. Do not issue Form 1099-DIV for dividends received by the corporation that are allocated to shareholders in boxes 5a or 5b of Schedule K-1.
5. 1099-INT, Interest Income.
6. 1099-LTC, Long-Term Care and Accelerated Death Benefits.
7. 1099-MISC, Miscellaneous Income. Use this form to report payments: to certain fishing boat crew members, to providers of health and medical services, of rent or royalties, of nonemployee compensation, etc.

Note. Every corporation must file Form 1099-MISC if it makes payments of rents, commissions, or other fixed or determinable income (see section 6041) totaling $600 or more to any one person in the course of its trade or business during the calendar year.

8. 1099-OID, Original Issue Discount.
9. 1099-PATR, Taxable Distributions Received From Cooperatives.
10. 1099-R, Distributions From Pensions, Annuities, Retirement or Profit-Sharing Plans, IRAs, Insurance Contracts, etc.
11. 1099-S, Proceeds From Real Estate Transactions.
12. 1099-SA, Distributions From an HSA, Archer MSA, or Medicare Advantage MSA.

• Form 3520, Annual Return to Report Transactions With Foreign Trusts and Receipt of Certain Foreign Gifts. The corporation may have to file this form if it:

1. Directly or indirectly transferred property or money to a foreign trust. For this purpose, any U.S. person who created a foreign trust is considered a transferor.
2. Is treated as the owner of any part of the assets of a foreign trust under the grantor trust rules.
3. Received a distribution from a foreign trust.

For more information, see the Instructions for Form 3520.

Note. An owner of a foreign trust must ensure that the trust files an annual information return on Form 3520-A, Annual Information Return of Foreign Trust With a U.S. Owner.

• Form 5471, Information Return of U.S. Persons With Respect to Certain Foreign Corporations. This form is required if the corporation controls a foreign corporation; acquires, disposes of, or owns 10% or more in value or vote of the outstanding stock of a foreign corporation; or had control of a foreign corporation for an uninterrupted period of at least 30 days during the annual accounting period of the foreign corporation. See Question 4 of Schedule N (Form 1120).

• Form 5498, IRA Contribution Information. Use this form to report contributions (including rollover contributions) to any IRA, including a SEP, SIMPLE, or Roth IRA, and to report Roth IRA conversions, IRA recharacterizations, and the fair market value of the account.

• Form 5498-ESA, Coverdell ESA Contribution Information. Use this form to report contributions (including rollover contributions) to, and the fair market value of, a Coverdell education savings account (ESA).

• Form 5498-SA, HSA, Archer MSA, or Medicare Advantage MSA Information. Use this form to report contributions to an HSA, Archer MSA and the fair market value of an HSA, Archer MSA, or Medicare Advantage MSA.

For more information, see the general and specific Instructions for Forms 1099, 1098, 5498, and W-2G.

• Form 5713, International Boycott Report. Corporations that had operations in, or related to, certain "boycotting" countries file Form 5713.

• Form 8023, Elections Under Section 338 for Corporations Making Qualified Stock Purchases. Corporations file this form to make elections under section 338 for a "target" corporation if the purchasing corporation has made a qualified stock purchase of the target corporation.

• Form 8050, Direct Deposit of Corporate Tax Refund. File Form 8050 to request that the IRS deposit a corporate tax refund (including a refund of $1 million or more) directly into an account at any U.S. bank or other financial institution (such as a mutual fund or brokerage firm) that accepts direct deposits.

• Form 8264, Application for Registration of a Tax Shelter. Tax shelter organizers must use this form to register tax shelters with the IRS to receive a tax shelter registration number. **Caution:** Until further guidance is issued, material advisors who provide material aid, assistance, or advice with respect to any reportable transaction after October 22, 2004, must use Form 8264 to disclose reportable transactions in accordance with interim guidance provided in Notice 2004-80, 2004-50 I.R.B. 963.

• Form 8271, Investor Reporting of Tax Shelter Registration Number. Corporations, which have acquired an interest in a tax shelter that is required to be registered, use this form to report the tax shelter's registration number. Attach Form 8271 to any return (including an amended return) on which a deduction, credit, loss, or other tax benefit attributable to a tax shelter is taken or any income attributable to a tax shelter is reported.

• Form 8275, Disclosure Statement. File Form 8275 to disclose items or positions, except those contrary to a regulation, that are not otherwise adequately disclosed on a tax return. The disclosure is made to avoid the parts of the accuracy-related penalty imposed for disregard of rules or substantial understatement of tax. Form 8275 is also used for disclosures relating to preparer penalties for understatements due to unrealistic positions or disregard of rules.

• Form 8275-R, Regulation Disclosure Statement, is used to disclose any item on a tax return for which a position has been taken that is contrary to Treasury regulations.

• Form 8281, Information Return for Publicly Offered Original Issue Discount Instruments (OID). This form is used by issuers of publicly offered debt instruments having OID to provide the information required by section 1275(c).

• Forms 8288 and 8288-A, U.S. Withholding Tax Return for Dispositions by Foreign Persons of U.S. Real Property Interests; and Statement of Withholding on Dispositions by Foreign Persons of U.S. Real Property Interests. Use these forms to report and transmit withheld tax on the sale of U.S. real property by a foreign person. See section 1445 and the related regulations for additional information.

• Form 8300, Report of Cash Payments Over $10,000 Received in a Trade or Business. Use this form to report the receipt of more than $10,000 in cash or foreign currency in one transaction or a series of related transactions.

• Form 8594, Asset Acquisition Statement Under Section 1060. Corporations file this form to report the purchase or sale of a group of assets that make up a trade or business if goodwill or going concern value could attach to the assets, and if the buyer's basis is determined only by the amount paid for the assets.

• Form 8697, Interest Computation Under the Look-Back Method for Completed Long-Term Contracts. Certain S corporations that are not closely held may have to file Form 8697 to figure the interest due or to be refunded under the look-back method of section 460(b)(2). The look-back method applies to certain long-term contracts accounted for under either the percentage of completion method or the percentage of completion-capitalized cost method. Closely held corporations should see the Schedule K instructions on page 30 for code C for details on the Form 8697 information they must provide to their shareholders.

• Form 8865, Return of U.S. Persons With Respect To Certain Foreign Partnerships. A corporation may have to file Form 8865 if it:

1. Controlled a foreign partnership (i.e., owned more than a 50% direct or indirect interest in the partnership).

2. Owned at least a 10% direct or indirect interest in a foreign partnership while U.S. persons controlled that partnership.

3. Had an acquisition, disposition, or change in proportional interest of a foreign partnership that:

a. Increased its direct interest to at least 10% or reduced its direct interest of at least 10% to less than 10%.

b. Changed its direct interest by at least a 10% interest.

4. Contributed property to a foreign partnership in exchange for a partnership interest if:

a. Immediately after the contribution, the corporation owned, directly or indirectly, at least a 10% interest in the foreign partnership or

b. The fair market value of the property the corporation contributed to the foreign partnership, when added to other contributions of property made to the foreign partnership (by the corporation or a related person) during the preceding 12-month period, exceeded $100,000.

Also, the corporation may have to file Form 8865 to report certain dispositions by a foreign partnership of property it previously contributed to that foreign partnership if it was a partner at the time of the disposition.

For more details, including penalties for failing to file Form 8865, see Form 8865 and its separate instructions.

• Form 8866, Interest Computation Under the Look-Back Method for Property Depreciated Under the Income Forecast Method. Certain S corporations that are not closely held may have to file Form 8866. Figure the interest due or to be refunded under the look-back method of section 167(g)(2) for certain property placed in service after September 13, 1995, that is depreciated under the income forecast method. Closely held corporations should see the Schedule K instructions on page 30 for line 17d, code D, for details on the Form 8866 information they must provide to their shareholders.

• Form 8873, Extraterritorial Income Exclusion. Use this form to report the amount of extraterritorial income excluded from the corporation's gross income for the tax year.

• Form 8876, Excise Tax on Structured Settlement Factoring Transactions. Use Form 8876 to report and pay the 40% excise tax imposed under section 5891.

• Form 8883, Asset Allocation Statement Under Section 338. Corporations use this form to report information about transactions involving the deemed sale of assets under section 338.

• Form 8886, Reportable Transaction Disclosure Statement. Use this form to disclose information for each reportable transaction in which the corporation participated. Form 8886 must be filed for each tax year the corporation participated in the transaction. You may have to pay a penalty if you are required to file Form 8886 but do not do so. The following are reportable transactions.

1. Any listed transaction, which is a transaction that is the same as or substantially similar to tax avoidance transactions identified by the IRS.

2. Any transaction offered under conditions of confidentiality for which the corporation paid a minimum fee of at least $50,000.

3. Certain transactions for which the corporation has contractual protection against disallowance of the tax benefits.

4. Certain transactions resulting in a loss of at least $2 million in any single year or $4 million in any combination of years.

5. Certain transactions resulting in a book-tax difference of more than $10 million on a gross basis.

6. Any transaction resulting in a tax credit of more than $250,000, if the corporation held the asset generating the credit for 45 days or less.

Statements

Stock ownership in foreign corporations. If the corporation owned at least 5% in value of the outstanding stock of a foreign personal holding company, and the corporation was required to include in its gross income any undistributed foreign personal holding company income, attach the statement required by section 551(c).

Transfers to a corporation controlled by the transferor. If a person receives stock of a corporation in exchange for property, and no gain or loss is recognized under section 351, the transferor and transferee must each attach to their tax returns the information required by Regulations section 1.351-3.

Assembling the Return

To ensure that the corporation's tax return is correctly processed, attach all schedules and forms after page 4, Form 1120S, in the following order:

1. Schedule N (Form 1120).
2. Form 8050.
3. Form 4136, Credit for Federal Tax Paid on Fuels.
4. Additional schedules in alphabetical order.
5. Additional forms in numerical order.

Complete every applicable entry space on Form 1120S and Schedule K-1. Do not write "See Attached" instead of completing the entry spaces. If more space is needed on the forms or schedules, attach separate sheets using the same size and format as the printed forms. If there are supporting statements and attachments, arrange them in the same order as the forms or schedules they support and attach them last. Show the totals on the printed forms. Also, be sure to enter the corporation's name and EIN on each supporting statement or attachment.

Amended Return

To correct an error on a Form 1120S already filed, file an amended Form 1120S and check box F(5) on page 1 of the return. Attach a statement that identifies the line number of each amended item, the corrected amount or treatment of the item, and an explanation of the reasons for each change.

If the amended return results in a change to income, or a change in the distribution of any income or other information provided any shareholder, an amended Schedule K-1 (Form 1120S) must also be filed with the amended Form 1120S and given to that shareholder. Be sure to check the "amended K-1" box on each Schedule K-1 to indicate that it is an amended Schedule K-1.

A change to the corporation's federal return may affect its state return. This includes changes made as the result of an IRS examination. For more information, contact the state tax agency for the state(s) in which the corporation's return was filed.

Passive Activity Limitations

In general, section 469 limits the amount of losses, deductions, and credits that shareholders may claim from "passive activities." The passive activity limitations do not apply to the corporation. Instead, they apply to each shareholder's share of any income or loss and credit attributable to a passive activity. Because the treatment of each shareholder's share of corporate income or loss and credit depends upon the nature of the activity that generated it, the corporation must report income or loss and credits separately for each activity.

The instructions below (pages 8 through 11) and the instructions for Schedules K and K-1 (pages 19 through 31) explain the applicable passive activity limitation rules and specify the type of information the corporation must provide to its shareholders for each activity. If the corporation had more than one activity, it must report information for each activity on an attachment to Schedules K and K-1.

Generally, passive activities include: (a) activities that involve the conduct of a trade or business in which the shareholder does not materially participate and (b) any rental activity (defined below) even if the shareholder materially participates. For exceptions, see *Activities That Are Not Passive Activities.* The level of each shareholder's participation in an activity must be determined by the shareholder.

The passive activity rules provide that losses and credits from passive activities can generally be applied only against income and tax from passive activities. Thus, passive losses and credits cannot be applied against income from salaries, wages, professional fees, or a business in which the shareholder materially participates; against "portfolio income" (defined on page 10); or against the tax related to any of these types of income.

Special rules require that net income from certain activities that would otherwise be treated as passive income must be recharacterized as nonpassive income for purposes of the passive activity limitations. See *Recharacterization of Passive Income* on page 10.

To allow each shareholder to apply the passive activity limitations at their level, the corporation must report income or loss and credits separately for each of the following: trade or business activities, rental real estate activities, rental activities other than rental real estate, and portfolio income.

Activities That Are Not Passive Activities

The following are not passive activities:

1. Trade or business activities in which the shareholder materially participated for the tax year.

2. Any rental real estate activity in which the shareholder materially participated if the shareholder met both of the following conditions for the tax year:

a. More than half of the personal services the shareholder performed in trades or businesses were performed in real property trades or businesses in which he or she materially participated, and

b. The shareholder performed more than 750 hours of services in real property trades or businesses in which he or she materially participated.

For purposes of this rule, each interest in rental real estate is a separate activity unless the shareholder elects to treat all interests in rental real estate as one activity.

If the shareholder is married filing jointly, either the shareholder or his or her spouse must separately meet both conditions 2a and b above, without taking into account services performed by the other spouse.

A real property trade or business is any real property development, redevelopment, construction, reconstruction, acquisition, conversion, rental, operation, management, leasing, or brokerage trade or business. Services the shareholder performed as an employee are not treated as performed in a real property trade or business unless he or she owned more than 5% of the stock in the employer.

3. The rental of a dwelling unit used by a shareholder for personal purposes during the year for more than the greater of 14 days or 10% of the number of days that the residence was rented at fair rental value.

4. An activity of trading personal property for the account of owners of interests in the activity. For purposes of this rule, personal property means property that is actively traded, such as stocks, bonds, and other securities. See Temporary Regulations section 1.469-1T(e)(6) for more details.

Note. The section 469(c)(3) exception for a working interest in oil and gas properties does not apply to an S corporation because state law generally limits the liability of shareholders.

Trade or Business Activities

A trade or business activity is an activity (other than a rental activity or an activity treated as incidental to an activity of holding property for investment) that:

1. Involves the conduct of a trade or business (within the meaning of section 162),
2. Is conducted in anticipation of starting a trade or business, or
3. Involves research or experimental expenditures deductible under section 174 (or that would be if you chose to deduct rather than capitalize them).

If the shareholder does not materially participate in the activity, a trade or business activity of the corporation is a passive activity for the shareholder.

Each shareholder must determine if they materially participated in an activity. As a result, while the corporation's ordinary business income (loss) is reported on page 1 of Form 1120S, the specific income and deductions from each separate trade or business activity must be reported on attachments to Form 1120S. Similarly, while each shareholder's allocable share of the corporation's ordinary business income (loss) is reported in box 1 of Schedule K-1, each shareholder's allocable share of the income and deductions from each trade or business activity must be reported on attachments to each Schedule K-1. See *Passive Activity Reporting Requirements* on page 11 for more information.

Rental Activities

Generally, except as noted below, if the gross income from an activity consists of amounts paid principally for the use of real or personal tangible property held by the corporation, the activity is a rental activity.

There are several exceptions to this general rule. Under these exceptions, an activity involving the use of real or personal tangible property is not a rental activity if any of the following apply:

- The average period of customer use (defined below) for such property is 7 days or less.
- The average period of customer use for such property is 30 days or less and significant personal services (defined below) are provided by or on behalf of the corporation.
- Extraordinary personal services (defined below) are provided by or on behalf of the corporation.
- Rental of the property is treated as incidental to a nonrental activity of the corporation under Temporary Regulations section 1.469-1T(e)(3)(vi) and Regulations section 1.469-1(e)(3)(vi).
- The corporation customarily makes the property available during defined business hours for nonexclusive use by various customers.
- The corporation provides property for use in a nonrental activity of a partnership in its capacity as an owner of an interest in such partnership. Whether the corporation provides property used in an activity of a partnership in the corporation's capacity as an owner of an interest in the partnership is based on all the facts and circumstances.

In addition, a guaranteed payment described in section 707(c) is never income from a rental activity.

Average period of customer use. Figure the average period of customer use for a class of property by dividing the total number of days in all rental periods by the number of rentals during the tax year. If the activity involves renting more than one class of property, multiply the average period of customer use of each class by the ratio of the gross rental income from that class to the activity's total gross rental income. The activity's average period of customer use equals the sum of these class-by-class average periods weighted by gross income. See Regulations section 1.469-1(e)(3)(iii).

Significant personal services. Personal services include only services performed by individuals. To determine if personal services are significant personal services, consider all of the relevant facts and circumstances. Relevant facts and circumstances include:

- How often the services are provided,
- The type and amount of labor required to perform the services, and
- The value of the services in relation to the amount charged for the use of the property.

The following services are not considered in determining whether personal services are significant:

- Services necessary to permit the lawful use of the rental property.
- Services performed in connection with improvements or repairs to the rental property that extend the useful life of the property substantially beyond the average rental period.
- Services provided in connection with the use of any improved real property that are similar to those commonly provided in connection with long-term rentals of high-grade commercial or residential property. Examples include cleaning and maintenance of common areas, routine repairs, trash collection, elevator service, and security at entrances.

Extraordinary personal services. Services provided in connection with making rental property available for customer use are extraordinary personal services only if the services are performed by individuals and the customers' use of the rental property is incidental to their receipt of the services. For example, a patient's use of a hospital room generally is incidental to the care that the patient receives from the hospital's medical staff. Similarly, a student's use of a dormitory room in a boarding school is incidental to the personal services provided by the school's teaching staff.

Rental property incidental to a nonrental activity. An activity is not a rental activity if the rental of the property is incidental to a nonrental activity, such as the activity of holding property for investment, a trade or business activity, or the activity of dealing in property.

Rental of property is incidental to an activity of holding property for investment if both of the following apply:

- The main purpose for holding the property is to realize a gain from the appreciation of the property.
- The gross rental income from such property for the tax year is less than 2% of the smaller of the property's unadjusted basis or its fair market value.

Rental of property is incidental to a trade or business activity if all of the following apply:

- The corporation owns an interest in the trade or business at all times during the year.
- The rental property was mainly used in the trade or business activity during the tax year or during at least 2 of the 5 preceding tax years.
- The gross rental income from the property is less than 2% of the smaller of the property's unadjusted basis or its fair market value.

The sale or exchange of property that is also rented during the tax year (in which the gain or loss is recognized) is treated as incidental to the activity of dealing in property if, at the time of the sale or exchange, the property was held primarily for sale to customers in the ordinary course of the corporation's trade or business.

See Temporary Regulations section 1.469-1T(e)(3) and Regulations section 1.469-1(e)(3) for more information on the definition of rental activities for purposes of the passive activity limitations.

Reporting of rental activities. In reporting the corporation's income or losses and credits from rental activities, the corporation must separately report (a) rental real estate activities and (b) rental activities other than rental real estate activities.

Shareholders who actively participate in a rental real estate activity may be able to deduct part or all of their rental real estate losses (and the deduction equivalent of rental real estate credits) against income (or tax) from nonpassive activities. Generally, the combined amount of rental real estate losses and the deduction equivalent of rental real estate credits from all sources (including rental real estate activities not held through the corporation) that may be claimed is limited to $25,000.

Report rental real estate activity income (loss) on Form 8825, Rental Real Estate Income and Expenses of a Partnership or an S Corporation, and on line 2 of Schedule K and in box 2 of Schedule K-1, rather than on page 1 of Form 1120S. Report credits related to rental real estate activities on lines 13c and 13d of Schedule K (box 13, codes C and G, of Schedule K-1) and low-income housing credits on lines 13a and 13b of Schedule K (box 13, codes A and B, of Schedule K-1).

Report income (loss) from rental activities other than rental real estate on line 3 and credits related to rental activities other than rental real estate on line 13e of Schedule K and in box 13, code H, of Schedule K-1.

Portfolio Income

Generally, portfolio income includes all gross income, other than income derived in the ordinary course of a trade or business, that is attributable to interest; dividends; royalties; income from a real estate investment trust, a regulated investment company, a real estate mortgage investment conduit, a common trust fund, a controlled foreign corporation, a qualified electing fund, or a cooperative; income from the disposition of property that produces income of a type defined as portfolio income; and income from the disposition of property held for investment. See *Self-Charged Interest* below for an exception.

Solely for purposes of the preceding paragraph, gross income derived in the ordinary course of a trade or business includes (and portfolio income, therefore, does not include) only the following types of income:

- Interest income on loans and investments made in the ordinary course of a trade or business of lending money.
- Interest on accounts receivable arising from the performance of services or the sale of property in the ordinary course of a trade or business of performing such services or selling such property, but only if credit is customarily offered to customers of the business.
- Income from investments made in the ordinary course of a trade or business of furnishing insurance or annuity contracts or reinsuring risks underwritten by insurance companies.
- Income or gain derived in the ordinary course of an activity of trading or dealing in any property if such activity constitutes a trade or business (unless the dealer held the property for investment at any time before such income or gain is recognized).
- Royalties derived by the taxpayer in the ordinary course of a trade or business of licensing intangible property.
- Amounts included in the gross income of a patron of a cooperative by reason of any payment or allocation to the patron based on patronage occurring with respect to a trade or business of the patron.
- Other income identified by the IRS as income derived by the taxpayer in the ordinary course of a trade or business.

See Temporary Regulations section 1.469-2T(c)(3) for more information on portfolio income.

Report portfolio income and related deductions on Schedule K rather than on page 1 of Form 1120S.

Self-Charged Interest

Certain self-charged interest income and deductions may be treated as passive activity gross income and passive activity deductions if the loan proceeds are used in a passive activity. Generally, self-charged interest income and deductions result from loans between the corporation and its shareholders. Self-charged interest also occurs in loans between the corporation and another S corporation or partnership if each owner in the borrowing entity has the same proportional ownership interest in the lending entity.

The self-charged interest rules do not apply to a shareholder's interest in an S corporation if the S corporation makes an election under Regulations section 1.469-7(g) to avoid the application of these rules. To make the election, the S corporation must attach to its original or amended Form 1120S a statement that includes the name, address, and EIN of the S corporation and a declaration that the election is being made under Regulations section 1.469-7(g). The election will apply to the tax year for which it was made and all subsequent tax years. Once made, the election may only be revoked with the consent of the IRS.

For more details on the self-charged interest rules, see Regulations section 1.469-7.

Grouping of Activities

Generally, one or more trade or business or rental activities may be treated as a single activity if the activities make up an appropriate economic unit for measurement of gain or loss under the passive activity rules. Whether activities make up an appropriate economic unit depends on all the relevant facts and circumstances. The factors given the greatest weight in determining whether activities make up an appropriate economic unit are:

1. Similarities and differences in types of trades or businesses,
2. The extent of common control,
3. The extent of common ownership,
4. Geographical location, and
5. Reliance between or among the activities.

Example. The corporation has a significant ownership interest in a bakery and a movie theater in Baltimore and in a bakery and a movie theater in Philadelphia. Depending on the relevant facts and circumstances, there may be more than one reasonable method for grouping the corporation's activities. For instance, the following groupings may or may not be permissible:

- A single activity,
- A movie theater activity and a bakery activity,
- A Baltimore activity and a Philadelphia activity, or
- Four separate activities.

Once the corporation chooses a grouping under these rules, it must continue using that grouping in later tax years unless a material change in the facts and circumstances makes it clearly inappropriate.

The IRS may regroup the corporation's activities if the corporation's grouping fails to reflect one or more appropriate economic units and one of the primary purposes for the grouping is to avoid the passive activity limitations.

Limitation on grouping certain activities. The following activities may not be grouped together:

1. A rental activity with a trade or business activity unless the activities being grouped together make up an appropriate economic unit and

a. The rental activity is insubstantial relative to the trade or business activity or vice versa or

b. Each owner of the trade or business activity has the same proportionate ownership interest in the rental activity. If so, the portion of the rental activity involving the rental of property to be used in the trade or business activity may be grouped with the trade or business activity.

2. An activity involving the rental of real property with an activity involving the rental of personal property (except for personal property provided in connection with real property or vice versa).

3. Any activity with another activity in a different type of business and in which the corporation holds an interest as a limited partner or as a limited entrepreneur (as defined in section 464(e)(2)) if that other activity engages in holding, producing, or distributing motion picture films or videotapes; farming; leasing section 1245 property; or exploring for, or exploiting, oil and gas resources, or geothermal deposits.

Activities conducted through partnerships. Once a partnership determines its activities under these rules, the corporation as a partner may use these rules to group those activities with:

- Each other,
- Activities conducted directly by the corporation, or
- Activities conducted through other partnerships.

The corporation may not treat as separate activities those activities grouped together by the partnership.

Recharacterization of Passive Income

Under Temporary Regulations section 1.469-2T(f) and Regulations section 1.469-2(f), net passive income from certain passive activities must be treated as nonpassive income. Net passive income is the excess of an activity's passive activity gross income over its passive activity deductions (current year deductions and prior year unallowed losses).

Income from the following six sources is subject to recharacterization.

Note. Any net passive income recharacterized as nonpassive income is treated as investment income for purposes of figuring investment interest expense limitations if it is from (a) an activity of renting substantially nondepreciable property from an equity-financed lending activity or (b) an activity related to an interest in a pass-through entity that licenses intangible property.

1. **Significant participation passive activities.** A significant participation passive activity is any trade or business activity in which the shareholder participated for more than 100 hours during the tax year but did not materially participate. Because each shareholder must determine his or her level of participation, the corporation will not be able to identify significant participation passive activities.

2. **Certain nondepreciable rental property activities.** Net passive income from a rental activity is nonpassive income if less than 30% of the unadjusted basis of the property used or held for use by customers in the activity is subject to depreciation under section 167.

3. **Passive equity-financed lending activities.** If the corporation has net income from a passive equity-financed lending activity, the smaller of the net passive income or equity-financed interest income from the activity is nonpassive income.

Note. The amount of income from the activities in items 1 through 3 above that any shareholder will be required to recharacterize as nonpassive income may be limited under Temporary Regulations section 1.469-2T(f)(8). Because the corporation will not have information regarding all of a shareholder's activities, it must identify all corporate activities meeting the definitions in items 2 and 3 as activities that may be subject to recharacterization.

4. **Rental of property incidental to a development activity.** Net rental activity income is the excess of passive activity gross income from renting or disposing of property over passive activity deductions (current year deductions and prior year unallowed losses) that are reasonably allocable to the rented property. Net rental activity income is nonpassive income for a shareholder if all of the following apply:

- The corporation recognizes gain from the sale, exchange, or other disposition of the rental property during the tax year.
- The use of the item of property in the rental activity started less than 12 months before the date of disposition. The use of an item of rental property begins on the first day on which (a) the corporation owns an interest in the property, (b) substantially all of the property is either rented or held out for rent and ready to be rented, and (c) no significant value-enhancing services remain to be performed.
- The shareholder materially participated or significantly participated for any tax year in an activity that involved the performing of services to enhance the value of the property (or any other item of property, if the basis of the property disposed of is determined in whole or in part by reference to the basis of that item of property).

Because the corporation cannot determine a shareholder's level of participation, the corporation must identify net income from property described above (without regard to the shareholder's level of participation) as income that may be subject to recharacterization.

5. **Rental of property to a nonpassive activity.** If a taxpayer rents property to a trade or business activity in which the taxpayer materially participates, the taxpayer's net rental activity income (defined in item 4) from the property is nonpassive income.

6. **Acquisition of an interest in a pass-through entity that licenses intangible property.** Generally, net royalty income from intangible property is nonpassive income if the taxpayer acquired an interest in the pass-through entity after it created the intangible property or performed substantial services or incurred substantial costs in developing or marketing the intangible property. Net royalty income is the excess of passive activity gross income from licensing or transferring any right in intangible property over passive activity deductions (current year deductions and prior year unallowed losses) that are reasonably allocable to the intangible property. See Temporary Regulations section 1.469-2T(f)(7)(iii) for exceptions to this rule.

Passive Activity Reporting Requirements

To allow shareholders to correctly apply the passive activity loss and credit limitation rules, any corporation that carries on more than one activity must:

1. Provide an attachment for each activity conducted through the corporation that identifies the type of activity conducted (trade or business, rental real estate, rental activity other than rental real estate, or investment).

2. On the attachment for each activity, provide a schedule, using the same box numbers as shown on Schedule K-1, detailing the net income (loss), credits, and all items required to be separately stated under section 1366(a)(1) from each trade or business activity, from each rental real estate activity, from each rental activity other than a rental real estate activity, and from investments.

3. Identify the net income (loss) and the shareholder's share of corporation interest expense from each activity of renting a dwelling unit that any shareholder uses for personal purposes during the year for more than the greater of 14 days or 10% of the number of days that the residence is rented at fair rental value.

4. Identify the net income (loss) and the shareholder's share of interest expense from each activity of trading personal property conducted through the corporation.

5. For any gain (loss) from the disposition of an interest in an activity or of an interest in property used in an activity (including dispositions before 1987 from which gain is being recognized after 1986):

a. Identify the activity in which the property was used at the time of disposition;

b. If the property was used in more than one activity during the 12 months preceding the disposition, identify the activities in which the property was used and the adjusted basis allocated to each activity; and

c. For gains only, if the property was substantially appreciated at the time of the disposition and the applicable holding period specified in Regulations section 1.469-2(c)(2)(iii)(A) was not satisfied, identify the amount of the nonpassive gain and indicate whether or not the gain is investment income under Regulations section 1.469-2(c)(2)(iii)(F).

6. Identify the shareholder's pro rata share of the corporation's self-charged interest income or expense (see *Self-Charged Interest* on page 10).

a. **Loans between a shareholder and the corporation.** Identify the lending or borrowing shareholder's share of the self-charged interest income or expense. If the shareholder made the loan to the corporation, also identify the activity in which the loan proceeds were used. If the proceeds were used in more than one activity, allocate the interest to each activity based on the amount of the proceeds used in each activity.

b. **Loans between the corporation and another S corporation or partnership.** If the corporation's shareholders have the same proportional ownership interest in this corporation as in the other S corporation or partnership, identify each shareholder's share of the interest income or expense from the loan. If the corporation was the borrower, also identify the activity in which the loan proceeds were used. If the proceeds were used in more than one activity, allocate the interest to each activity based on the amount of the proceeds used in each activity.

7. Specify the amount of gross portfolio income, the interest expense properly allocable to portfolio income, and expenses other than interest expense that are clearly and directly allocable to portfolio income.

8. Identify the ratable portion of any section 481 adjustment (whether a net positive or a net negative adjustment) allocable to each corporate activity.

9. Identify any gross income from sources specifically excluded from passive activity gross income, including:

a. Income from intangible property, if the shareholder is an individual whose personal efforts significantly contributed to the creation of the property;

b. Income from state, local, or foreign income tax refunds; and

c. Income from a covenant not to compete, if the shareholder is an individual who contributed the covenant to the corporation.

10. Identify any deductions that are not passive activity deductions.

11. If the corporation makes a full or partial disposition of its interest in another entity, identify the gain (loss) allocable to each activity conducted through the entity, and the gain allocable to a passive activity that would have been recharacterized as nonpassive gain had the corporation disposed of its interest in property used in the activity (because the property was substantially appreciated at the time of the disposition, and the gain represented more than 10% of the shareholder's total gain from the disposition).

12. Identify the following items from activities that may be subject to the recharacterization rules under Temporary Regulations section 1.469-2T(f) and Regulations section 1.469-2(f):

a. Net income from an activity of renting substantially nondepreciable property;

b. The smaller of equity-financed interest income or net passive income from an equity-financed lending activity;

c. Net rental activity income from property developed (by the shareholder or the corporation), rented, and sold within 12 months after the rental of the property commenced;

d. Net rental activity income from the rental of property by the corporation to a trade or business activity in which the shareholder had an interest (either directly or indirectly); and

e. Net royalty income from intangible property if the shareholder acquired the shareholder's interest in the corporation after the corporation created the intangible property or performed substantial services or incurred substantial costs in developing or marketing the intangible property.

13. Identify separately the credits from each activity conducted by or through the corporation.

Extraterritorial Income Exclusion

The corporation may exclude extraterritorial income to the extent of qualifying foreign trade income. However, the extraterritorial income exclusion is reduced by 20% for transactions after 2004, unless made under a binding contract with an unrelated person in effect on September 17, 2003, and at all times thereafter. For details and to figure the amount of the exclusion, see Form 8873 and its separate instructions. The corporation must report the extraterritorial income exclusion on its return as follows:

1. If the corporation met the foreign economic process requirements explained in the Instructions for Form 8873, it may report the exclusion as a non-separately stated item on whichever of the following lines apply to that activity:

- Form 1120S, page 1, line 19;
- Form 8825, line 15; or
- Form 1120S, Schedule K, line 3b.

In addition, the corporation must report as an item of information on Schedule K-1, box 14, code O, the shareholder's pro rata share of foreign trading gross receipts from Form 8873, line 15.

2. If the foreign trading gross receipts of the corporation for the tax year are $5 million or less and the corporation did not meet the foreign economic process requirements, it may not report the extraterritorial income exclusion as a non-separately stated item on its return. Instead, it must report the following two separately-stated items to the shareholders on Schedule K-1, box 14, codes O and P, respectively:

- Foreign trading gross receipts (code O). Report each shareholder's pro rata share of foreign trading gross receipts from line 15 of Form 8873 in box 14 using code O.
- Extraterritorial income exclusion (code P). Report each shareholder's pro rata share of the extraterritorial income exclusion from Form 8873 in box 14 using code P and identify on an attached statement the activity to which the exclusion relates. If the corporation is required to complete more than one Form 8873 (e.g. separate forms for transactions eligible for the 80% and 100% exclusions), combine the exclusions from lines 52a and 52b and report a single exclusion amount in box 14.

Note. Upon request of a shareholder, the corporation should furnish a copy of the corporation's Form 8873 if that shareholder has a reduction for international boycott operations, illegal bribes, kickbacks, etc.

Specific Instructions

These instructions follow the line numbers on the first page of Form 1120S. The accompanying schedules are discussed separately. Specific instructions for most of the lines are provided. Lines that are not discussed are self-explanatory.

Fill in all applicable lines and schedules.

File all four pages of Form 1120S. However, if the answer to Question 9 of Schedule B is "Yes", Schedules L and M-1 on page 4 are optional.

Attach a Schedule K-1 to Form 1120S for each shareholder.

Name

Use the label mailed to the corporation. If the corporation did not receive a label, print or type the corporation's true name (as set forth in the corporate charter or other legal document creating it).

Address

Include the suite, room, or other unit number after the street address. If a preaddressed label is used, cross out any errors and print the correct information. Add any missing items, such as the suite or room number. If the Post Office does not deliver to the street address and the corporation has a P.O. box, show the box number instead of the street address.

If the corporation receives its mail in care of a third party (such as an accountant or an attorney), enter on the street address line "C/O" followed by the third party's name and street address or P.O. box.

Item B. Business Code No.

See the Codes for Principal Business Activity on pages 35 through 37 of these instructions.

Item C. Employer Identification Number (EIN)

Enter the corporation's EIN. If the corporation does not have an EIN, it must apply for one. An EIN may be applied for:

- Online–Click on the EIN link at *www.irs.gov/businesses/small.* The EIN is issued immediately once the application information is validated.
- By telephone at 1-800-829-4933 from 7:00 am to 10:00 pm in the corporation's local time zone.
- By mailing or faxing Form SS-4, Application for Employer Identification Number.

If the corporation has not received its EIN by the time the return is due, write "Applied for" in the space for the EIN. For more details, see Pub. 583.

For assistance in applying for an EIN, call the toll-free Business and Specialty Tax Line at 1-800-829-4933.

Item E. Total Assets

Enter the corporation's total assets at the end of the tax year, as determined by the accounting method regularly used in maintaining the corporation's books and records. If there were no assets at the end of the tax year, enter "0". If the S election terminated during the tax year, see the instructions for Schedule L on page 31 for special rules that may apply when figuring the corporation's year-end assets.

Item F. Initial Return, Final Return, Name Change, Address Change, and Amended Return

- If this is the corporation's first return, check the "Initial return" box.
- If the corporation has ceased to exist, file Form 1120S and check the "Final return" box. Also check the "Final K-1" box on each Schedule K-1 to indicate that it is a final Schedule K-1.
- If the corporation changed its name since it last filed a return, check the box for "Name change." Generally, a corporation must also have amended its articles of incorporation and filed the amendment with the state in which it is incorporated.
- If the corporation has changed its address since it last filed a return, (including a change to an "in care of"

address), check the box for "Address change."

Note. If a change in address occurs after the return is filed, use Form 8822, Change of Address, to notify the IRS of the new address.

• If this amends a previously filed return, check the box for "Amended return." If Schedules K-1 are also being amended, check the "Amended K-1" box on each Schedule K-1.

Income

CAUTION *Report only trade or business activity income or loss on lines 1a through 6. Do not report rental activity income or portfolio income or loss on these lines. (See Passive Activity Limitations beginning on page 8 for definitions of rental income and portfolio income.) Rental activity income and portfolio income are reported on Schedules K and K-1 (rental real estate activities are also reported on Form 8825).*

Tax-exempt income. Do not include any tax-exempt income on lines 1 through 5. A corporation that receives any exempt income other than interest, or holds any property or engages in an activity that produces exempt income, reports this income on line 16b of Schedule K and in box 16, code B, of Schedule K-1.

Report tax-exempt interest income, including exempt-interest dividends received as a shareholder in a mutual fund or other regulated investment company, on line 16a of Schedule K and in box 16, code A, of Schedule K-1.

See *Deductions* beginning on page 14 for information on how to report expenses related to tax-exempt income.

Cancelled debt exclusion. If the S corporation has had debt discharged resulting from a title 11 bankruptcy proceeding, or while insolvent, see Form 982, Reduction of Tax Attributes Due to Discharge of Indebtedness, and Pub. 908, Bankruptcy Tax Guide.

Line 1. Gross Receipts or Sales

Enter gross receipts or sales from all trade or business operations except those that must be reported on lines 4 and 5. In general, advance payments are reported in the year of receipt.

• To report income from long-term contracts, see section 460.

• For special rules for reporting certain advance payments for goods and long-term contracts, see Regulations section 1.451-5.

• For permissible methods for reporting certain advance payments for services and most goods by an accrual method corporation, see Rev. Proc. 2004-34, 2004-22 I.R.B. 991.

Installment sales. Generally, the installment method cannot be used for dealer dispositions of property. A "dealer disposition" is any disposition of (a) personal property by a person who regularly sells or otherwise disposes of personal property of the same type on the installment plan or (b) real property held for sale to customers in the ordinary course of the taxpayer's trade or business.

Exception. These restrictions on using the installment method do not apply to dispositions of property used or produced in a farming business or sales of timeshares and residential lots for which the corporation elects to pay interest under section 453(l)(3).

Enter on line 1a the gross profit on collections from installment sales for any of the following:

• Dealer dispositions of property before March 1, 1986.

• Dispositions of property used or produced in the trade or business of farming.

• Certain dispositions of timeshares and residential lots reported under the installment method.

Attach a schedule showing the following information for the current and the 3 preceding years:

• Gross sales.
• Cost of goods sold.
• Gross profits.
• Percentage of gross profits to gross sales.
• Amount collected.
• Gross profit on the amount collected.

Line 2. Cost of Goods Sold

See the instructions for Schedule A on page 18.

Line 4. Net Gain (Loss) From Form 4797

CAUTION *Include only ordinary gains or losses from the sale, exchange, or involuntary conversion of assets used in a trade or business activity. Ordinary gains or losses from the sale, exchange, or involuntary conversions of assets used in rental activities are reported separately on Schedule K as part of the net income (loss) from the rental activity in which the property was used.*

A corporation that is a partner in a partnership must include on Form 4797, Sales of Business Property, its share of ordinary gains (losses) from sales, exchanges, or involuntary or compulsory conversions (other than casualties or thefts) of the partnership's trade or business assets.

If the corporation sold or otherwise disposed of business property for which the corporation passed through a section 179 expense deduction to its shareholders, the disposition must be reported separately in box 17, code E, of Schedule K-1 instead of being reported on Form 4797.

Line 5. Other Income (Loss)

Enter on line 5 trade or business income (loss) that is not included on lines 1a through 4. List the type and amount of income on an attached schedule. If the corporation has only one item of other income, describe it in parentheses on line 5.

Examples of other income include:

• Interest income derived in the ordinary course of the corporation's trade or business, such as interest charged on receivable balances.

• Recoveries of bad debts deducted in prior years under the specific charge-off method.

• Taxable income from insurance proceeds.

• The amount of credit figured on Form 6478, Credit for Alcohol Used as Fuel.

• The amount of credit figured on Form 8864, Biodiesel Fuels Credit.

• Recapture amount under section 280F if the business use of listed property drops to 50% or less. To figure the recapture amount, the corporation must complete Part IV of Form 4797.

• Recapture of any deduction previously taken under section 179A. The S corporation may have to recapture part or all of the benefit of any allowable deduction for qualified clean-fuel vehicle property (or clean-fuel vehicle refueling property), if the property ceases to qualify for the deduction within 3 years after the date it was placed in service. See Pub. 535, Business Expenses, for details on how to figure the recapture.

• All section 481 income adjustments resulting from changes in accounting methods. Show the computation of the section 481 adjustments on an attached schedule.

Do not net any expense item (such as interest) with a similar income item. Report all trade or business expenses on lines 7 through 19.

Do not include items requiring separate computations by shareholders that must be reported on Schedules K and K-1. See the instructions for Schedules K and K-1 beginning on page 20.

Ordinary Business Income (Loss) From a Partnership, Estate, or Trust

Enter the ordinary trade or business income (loss) from a partnership shown on Schedule K-1 (Form 1065), from an estate or trust shown on Schedule K-1 (Form 1041), or from a foreign partnership, estate, or trust. Show the partnership's, estate's, or trust's name, address, and EIN (if any) on a separate statement attached to this return. If the amount entered is from more than one source, identify the amount from each source.

Do not include portfolio income or rental activity income (loss) from a partnership, estate, or trust on this line. Instead, report these amounts on the applicable lines or boxes of Schedules K and K-1, or on line 20a of Form 8825 if the amount is from a rental real estate activity.

Ordinary income or loss from a partnership that is a publicly traded partnership is not reported on this line. Instead, report the amount separately on line 10 of Schedule K and in box 10, code E, of Schedule K-1.

Treat shares of other items separately reported on Schedule K-1 issued by the other entity as if the items were directly realized or incurred by the S corporation.

If there is a loss from a partnership, the amount of the loss that may be claimed is subject to the at-risk and basis limitations as appropriate.

If the tax year of the S corporation does not coincide with the tax year of the partnership, estate, or trust, include the ordinary income (loss) from the other entity in the tax year in which the other entity's tax year ends.

Deductions

Report only trade or business activity expenses on lines 7 through 19.

Do not report rental activity expenses or deductions allocable to portfolio income on these lines. Report rental activity expenses on Form 8825 or line 3b of Schedule K (box 3 of Schedule K-1). Deductions allocable to portfolio income are separately reported on line 12b of Schedule K and in box 12, code G, H or J, of Schedule K-1. See *Passive Activity Limitations* beginning on page 8 for more information on rental activities and portfolio income.

Do not report any nondeductible amounts (such as expenses connected with the production of tax-exempt income) on lines 7 through 19. Instead, report nondeductible expenses on line 16c of Schedule K and in box 16, code C, of Schedule K-1. If an expense is connected with both taxable income and nontaxable income, allocate a reasonable part of the expense to each kind of income.

Limitations on Deductions

Section 263A uniform capitalization rules. The uniform capitalization rules of section 263A require corporations to capitalize or include in inventory certain costs incurred in connection with:

- The production of real and tangible personal property held in inventory or held for sale in the ordinary course of business.
- Real property or personal property (tangible and intangible) acquired for resale.
- The production of real property and tangible personal property by a corporation for use in its trade or business or in an activity engaged in for profit.

The costs required to be capitalized under section 263A are not deductible until the property to which the costs relate is sold, used, or otherwise disposed of by the corporation.

Exceptions. Section 263A does not apply to:

- Personal property acquired for resale if the taxpayer's average annual gross receipts for the 3 prior tax years are $10 million or less.
- Timber.
- Most property produced under a long-term contract.
- Certain property produced in a farming business. See *Special rules for certain corporations engaged in farming* below.

The corporation must report the following costs separately to the shareholders for purposes of determinations under section 59(e):

- Research and experimental costs under section 174.
- Intangible drilling costs for oil, gas, and geothermal property.
- Mining exploration and development costs.
- Inventoriable items accounted for in the same manner as materials and supplies that are not incidental. See *Schedule A. Cost of Goods Sold* on page 18 for details.

Tangible personal property produced by a corporation includes a film, sound recording, video tape, book, or similar property.

Indirect costs. Corporations subject to the uniform capitalization rules are required to capitalize not only direct costs but an allocable portion of most indirect costs (including taxes) that benefit the assets produced or acquired for resale or are incurred by reason of the performance of production or resale activities.

For inventory, some of the indirect costs that must be capitalized are:

- Administration expenses.
- Taxes.
- Depreciation.
- Insurance.
- Compensation paid to officers attributable to services.
- Rework labor.
- Contributions to pension, stock bonus, and certain profit-sharing, annuity, or deferred compensation plans.

Regulations section 1.263A-1(e)(3) specifies other indirect costs that relate to production or resale activities that must be capitalized and those that may be currently deducted.

Interest expense paid or incurred during the production period of designated property must be capitalized and is governed by special rules. For more details, see Regulations sections 1.263A-8 through 1.263A-15.

For more details on the uniform capitalization rules, see Regulations sections 1.263A-1 through 1.263A-3.

Special rules for certain corporations engaged in farming. For S corporations not required to use the accrual method of accounting, the rules of section 263A do not apply to expenses of raising any:

- Animal or
- Plant that has a preproductive period of 2 years or less.

Shareholders of S corporations not required to use the accrual method of accounting may elect to currently deduct the preproductive period expenses of certain plants that have a preproductive period of more than 2 years. Because each shareholder makes the election to deduct these expenses, the corporation should not capitalize them. Instead, the corporation should report the expenses separately on line 12e of Schedule K and report each shareholder's pro rata share in box 12, code M, of Schedule K-1.

See *Uniform Capitalization Rules* in chapter 6 of Publication 225, sections 263A(d) and (e), and Regulations section 1.263A-4 for definitions and other details.

Transactions between related taxpayers. Generally, an accrual basis S corporation may deduct business expenses and interest owed to a related party (including any shareholder) only in the tax year of the corporation that includes the day on which the payment is includible in the income of the related party. See section 267 for details.

Section 291 limitations. If the S corporation was a C corporation for any of the 3 immediately preceding years, the corporation may be required to adjust deductions allowed to the corporation for depletion of iron ore and coal, and the amortizable basis of pollution control facilities. See section 291 to determine the amount of the adjustment.

Business start-up and organizational costs. Business start-up and organizational costs must be capitalized unless an election is made to deduct or amortize them. For costs paid or incurred before October 23, 2004, the corporation must capitalize them unless it elects to amortize these costs over a period of 60 months or more. For costs paid or incurred after October 22, 2004, the following rules apply separately to each category of costs.

- The corporation can elect to deduct up to $5,000 of such costs for the year the corporation begins business operations.
- The $5,000 deduction is reduced (but not below zero) by the amount the total costs exceed $50,000. If the total costs are $55,000 or more, the deduction is reduced to zero.
- If the election is made, any costs that are not deductible must be amortized ratably over a 180-month period beginning with the month the corporation begins business operations.

For more details on the election for business start-up costs, see section 195. To make the election, attach the statement required by Regulations section 1.195-1(b). For more details on the election for organizational costs, see section 248. To make the election, attach the statement required by Regulations section 1.248-1(c). Report the deductible amount of these costs and any amortization on line 19. For amortization that begins during the tax year, complete and attach Form 4562.

Film and television expenses. The corporation can elect to deduct costs of certain qualified film and television productions that begin after October 22, 2004. See section 181 for details.

Reducing certain expenses for which credits are allowable. For each credit listed below, the corporation must reduce the otherwise allowable deduction for expenses used to figure the credit by the amount of the current year credit.

• The work opportunity credit,
• The welfare-to-work credit,
• The credit for increasing research activities,
• The enhanced oil recovery credit,
• The disabled access credit,
• The empowerment zone and renewal community employment credit,
• The Indian employment credit,
• The credit for employer social security and Medicare taxes paid on certain employee tips,
• The orphan drug credit,
• Credit for small employer pension plan start-up costs,
• Credit for employer-provided childcare facilities and services,
• The New York Liberty Zone business employee credit, and
• The low sulfur diesel fuel production credit.

If the corporation has any of these credits, be sure to determine each current year credit before figuring the deductions for expenses on which the credit is based.

Line 7. Compensation of Officers and Line 8. Salaries and Wages

Distributions and other payments by an S corporation to a corporate officer must be treated as wages to the extent the amounts are reasonable compensation for services rendered to the corporation.

Enter on line 7 the total compensation of all officers paid or incurred in the trade or business activities of the corporation. The corporation determines who is an officer under the laws of the state where it is incorporated.

Enter on line 8 the amount of salaries and wages paid or incurred to employees (other than officers) during the tax year.

Do not include amounts reported elsewhere on the return, such as salaries and wages included in cost of goods sold, elective contributions to a section 401(k) cash or deferred arrangement, or amounts contributed under a salary reduction SEP agreement or a SIMPLE IRA plan.

Reduce the amounts on lines 7 and 8 by any applicable employment credits from:
• Form 5884, Work Opportunity Credit,
• Form 8861, Welfare-to-Work Credit,
• Form 8844, Empowerment Zone and Renewal Community Employment Credit,
• Form 8845, Indian Employment Credit, and
• Form 8884, New York Liberty Zone Business Employee Credit.

See the instructions for these forms for more information.

Include fringe benefit expenditures made on behalf of officers and employees owning more than 2% of the corporation's stock. Also report these fringe benefits as wages in box 1 of Form W-2. Do not include amounts paid or incurred for fringe benefits of officers and employees owning 2% or less of the corporation's stock. These amounts are reported on line 18, page 1, of Form 1120S. See the instructions for that line for information on the types of expenditures that are treated as fringe benefits and for the stock ownership rules.

Report amounts paid for health insurance coverage for a more than 2% shareholder (including that shareholder's spouse and dependents) as an information item in box 14 of that shareholder's Form W-2. For 2004, a more-than-2% shareholder may be allowed to deduct up to 100% of such amounts on Form 1040, line 31.

If a shareholder or a member of the family of one or more shareholders of the corporation renders services or furnishes capital to the corporation for which reasonable compensation is not paid, the IRS may make adjustments in the items taken into account by such individuals to reflect the value of such services or capital. See section 1366(e).

Line 9. Repairs and Maintenance

Enter the costs of incidental repairs and maintenance, such as labor and supplies, that do not add to the value of the property or appreciably prolong its life. The corporation may deduct these repairs only to the extent they relate to a trade or business activity and are not claimed elsewhere on the return. New buildings, machinery, or permanent improvements that increase the value of the property are not currently deductible. They are chargeable to capital accounts and may be depreciated or amortized.

Line 10. Bad Debts

Enter the total debts that became worthless in whole or in part during the year, but only to the extent such debts relate to a trade or business activity. Report deductible nonbusiness bad debts as a short-term capital loss on Schedule D (Form 1120S).

Cash method corporations may not claim a bad debt deduction unless the amount was previously included in income.

Line 11. Rents

If the corporation rented or leased a vehicle, enter the total annual rent or lease expense paid or incurred in the trade or business activities of the corporation. Also complete Part V of Form 4562, Depreciation and Amortization. If the corporation leased a vehicle for a term of 30 days or more, the deduction for vehicle lease expense may have to be reduced by an amount called the inclusion amount. The corporation may have an inclusion amount if:

The lease term began:	And the vehicle's FMV on the first day of the lease exceeded:
After 12/31/03 and before 1/1/05	$17,500
After 12/31/02 and before 1/1/04	$18,000
After 12/31/98 and before 1/1/03	$15,500

If the lease term began before January 1, 1999, see Pub. 463, Travel, Entertainment, Gift, and Car Expenses, to find out if the corporation has an inclusion amount and how to figure it.

Line 12. Taxes and Licenses

Enter taxes and licenses paid or incurred in the trade or business activities of the corporation, unless they are reflected in cost of goods sold. Federal import duties and federal excise and stamp taxes are deductible only if paid or incurred in carrying on the trade or business of the corporation.

Do not deduct the following taxes on line 12:
• Federal income taxes (except for the portion of built-in gains tax allocable to ordinary income), or taxes reported elsewhere on the return.
• Section 901 foreign taxes. Report these taxes separately on line 14l and 14m of Schedule K and in box 14 of Schedule K-1, using codes L and M.
• Taxes allocable to a rental activity. Taxes allocable to a rental real estate activity are reported on Form 8825. Taxes allocable to a rental activity other than a rental real estate activity are reported on line 3b of Schedule K.
• Taxes allocable to portfolio income. Report these taxes separately on line 12b of Schedule K and in box 12, code G, of Schedule K-1.
• Taxes paid or incurred for the production or collection of income, or for the management, conservation, or maintenance of property held to produce income. Report these taxes separately on line 12e of Schedule K and in box 12, code P, of Schedule K-1.

See section 263A(a) for information on capitalization of allocable costs (including taxes) for any property.

• Taxes not imposed on the corporation.
• Taxes, including state or local sales taxes, that are paid or incurred in connection with an acquisition or disposition of property (these taxes must be treated as a part of the cost of the acquired property or, in the case of a disposition, as a reduction in the amount realized on the disposition).
• Taxes assessed against local benefits that increase the value of the property assessed (such as for paving, etc.).
• Taxes deducted elsewhere on the return, such as those reflected in cost of goods sold.

See section 164(d) for apportionment of taxes on real property between seller and purchaser.

Line 13. Interest

Report interest incurred in the trade or business activities of the corporation that is not claimed elsewhere on the return. Do not include interest expense:

- On debt used to purchase rental property or debt used in a rental activity. Interest allocable to a rental real estate activity is reported on Form 8825 and is used in arriving at net income (loss) from rental real estate activities on line or box 2 of Schedules K and K-1. Interest allocable to a rental activity other than a rental real estate activity is included on line 3b of Schedule K and is used in arriving at net income (loss) from a rental activity (other than a rental real estate activity). This net amount is reported on line 3c of Schedule K and in box 3 of Schedule K-1.
- Clearly and directly allocable to portfolio or investment income. This interest expense is reported separately on line 12c of Schedule K.
- On debt proceeds allocated to distributions made to shareholders during the tax year. Instead, report such interest on line 12e of Schedule K and in box 12, code P, of Schedule K-1. To determine the amount to allocate to distributions to shareholders, see Notice 89-35, 1989-1 C.B. 675.
- On debt required to be allocated to the production of designated property. Interest allocable to designated property produced by an S corporation for its own use or for sale must instead be capitalized. The corporation must also capitalize any interest on debt allocable to an asset used to produce designated property. A shareholder may have to capitalize interest that the shareholder incurs during the tax year for the production expenditures of the S corporation. Similarly, interest incurred by an S corporation may have to be capitalized by a shareholder for the shareholder's own production expenditures. The information required by the shareholder to properly capitalize interest for this purpose must be provided by the corporation on an attachment for box 17, code J, of Schedule K-1. See section 263A(f) and Regulations sections 1.263A-8 through 1.263A-15 for additional information, including the definition of "designated property."

Special rules apply to:

- Allocating interest expense among activities so that the limitations on passive activity losses, investment interest, and personal interest can be properly figured. Generally, interest expense is allocated in the same manner as debt is allocated. Debt is allocated by tracing disbursements of the debt proceeds to specific expenditures. Temporary Regulations section 1.163-8T gives rules for tracing debt proceeds to expenditures.
- Prepaid interest, which generally can only be deducted over the period to which the prepayment applies. See section 461(g) for details.
- Limit the interest deduction if the corporation is a policyholder or beneficiary with respect to a life insurance, endowment, or annuity contract issued after June 8, 1997. For details, see section 264(f). Attach a statement showing the computation of the deduction.

Line 14. Depreciation

Report only the depreciation claimed on assets used in a trade or business activity. See the Instructions for Form 4562 or Pub. 946, How To Depreciate Property, to figure the amount of depreciation to enter on this line.

Complete and attach Form 4562 only if the corporation placed property in service during the tax year, or claims depreciation on any car or other listed property.

Do not include any section 179 expense deduction on this line. This amount is not deductible by the corporation. Instead, it is reported and passed through to the shareholders in box 11 of Schedule K-1.

Line 15. Depletion

If the corporation claims a deduction for timber depletion, complete and attach Form T, Forest Activities Schedule.

Do not deduct depletion for oil and gas properties. Each shareholder figures depletion on these properties under section 613A(c)(11). See the instructions on page 31 for box 17, code L, for information on oil and gas depletion that must be supplied to the shareholders by the corporation.

Line 17. Pension, Profit-Sharing, etc., Plans

Report the deductible contributions not claimed elsewhere on the return made by the corporation for its employees under a qualified pension, profit-sharing, annuity, or simplified employee pension (SEP) or SIMPLE plan, and under any other deferred compensation plan.

If the corporation contributes to an individual retirement arrangement (IRA) for employees, include the contribution in salaries and wages on page 1, line 8, or Schedule A, line 3, and not on line 17.

Employers who maintain a pension, profit-sharing, or other funded deferred compensation plan, whether or not qualified under the Internal Revenue Code and whether or not a deduction is claimed for the current tax year, generally must file the applicable form listed below.

- Form 5500, Annual Return/Report of Employee Benefit Plan. File this form for a plan that is not a one-participant plan.
- Form 5500-EZ, Annual Return of One-Participant (Owners and Their Spouses) Retirement Plan. File this form for a plan that only covers the owner (or the owner and his or her spouse) but only if the owner (or the owner and his or her spouse) owns the entire business.

There are penalties for failure to file these forms on time and for overstating the pension plan deduction.

Line 18. Employee Benefit Programs

Report amounts for fringe benefits paid or incurred on behalf of employees owning 2% or less of the corporation's stock. These fringe benefits include (a) employer contributions to certain accident and health plans, (b) the cost of up to $50,000 of group-term life insurance on an employee's life, and (c) meals and lodging furnished for the employer's convenience.

Do not deduct amounts that are an incidental part of a pension, profit-sharing, etc., plan included on line 17 or amounts reported elsewhere on the return.

Report amounts paid on behalf of more than 2% shareholders on line 7 or 8, whichever applies. A shareholder is considered to own more than 2% of the corporation's stock if that person owns on any day during the tax year more than 2% of the outstanding stock of the corporation or stock possessing more than 2% of the combined voting power of all stock of the corporation. See section 318 for attribution rules.

Line 19. Other Deductions

Enter the total of all allowable trade or business deductions that are not deductible elsewhere on page 1 of Form 1120S. Attach a schedule listing by type and amount each deduction included on this line.

Examples of other deductions include:

- Amortization (except as noted below)—see the Instructions for Form 4562 for more information. Complete and attach Form 4562 if the corporation is claiming amortization of costs that began during the tax year.
- Insurance premiums.
- Legal and professional fees.
- Supplies used and consumed in the business.
- Utilities.

Also, see *Special Rules* below for limits on certain other deductions.

Do not deduct on line 19:

- Items that must be reported separately on Schedules K and K-1.
- Qualified expenditures to which an election under section 59(e) may apply. See the instructions on page 25 for lines 12d(1) and 12d(2) for details on the treatment of these items.
- Reforestation expenditures. The corporation must separately state the reforestation expense deduction for expenditures paid or incurred after October 22, 2004, and the amortizable basis of expenditures paid or incurred before October 23, 2004. See the instructions for *Reforestation expense deduction (code L)* on page 25 and *Amortization of reforestation costs (code M)* on page 31. Deduct on line 19 only the amortization of reforestation expenditures paid or incurred after October 22, 2004. The amount the corporation can amortize is only the portion of such expenditures in excess of the separately-stated reforestation expense deduction.

• Fines or penalties paid to a government for violating any law. Report these expenses on Schedule K, line 16c.
• Expenses allocable to tax-exempt income. Report these expenses on Schedule K, line 16c.

Special Rules

Commercial revitalization deduction. If the corporation constructs, purchases, or substantially rehabilitates a qualified building in a renewal community, it may qualify for a deduction of either (a) 50% of qualified capital expenditures in the year the building is placed in service or (b) amortization of 100% of the qualified capital expenditures over a 120-month period beginning with the month the building is placed in service. If the corporation elects to amortize these expenditures, it must complete and attach Form 4562. To qualify, the building must be nonresidential (as defined in section 168(e)(2)(B)) and placed in service by the corporation. The corporation must be the original user of the building unless it is substantially rehabilitated. The amount of the qualified expenditures cannot exceed the lesser of $10 million or the amount allocated to the building by the commercial revitalization agency of the state in which the building is located. Any remaining expenditures are depreciated over the regular depreciation recovery period. See Pub. 954, Tax Incentives for Distressed Communities, and section 1400I for details.

Rental real estate. The corporation cannot deduct commercial revitalization expenditures for a building placed in service as rental real estate. Instead, the commercial revitalization deduction for rental real estate is reported separately to shareholders in box 12 of Schedule K-1, using code N.

Travel, meals, and entertainment. Subject to limitations and restrictions discussed below, a corporation can deduct ordinary and necessary travel, meals, and entertainment expenses paid or incurred in its trade or business. Also, special rules apply to deductions for gifts, skybox rentals, luxury water travel, convention expenses, and entertainment tickets. See section 274 and Pub. 463 for more details.

Travel. The corporation cannot deduct travel expenses of any individual accompanying a corporate officer or employee, including a spouse or dependent of the officer or employee, unless:
• That individual is an employee of the corporation and
• His or her travel is for a bona fide business purpose and would otherwise be deductible by that individual.

Meals and entertainment. Generally, the corporation can deduct only 50% of the amount otherwise allowable for meals and entertainment expenses paid or incurred in its trade or business. In addition (subject to exceptions under section 274(k)(2)):
• Meals must not be lavish or extravagant;
• A bona fide business discussion must occur during, immediately before, or immediately after the meal; and
• An employee of the corporation must be present at the meal.

See section 274(n)(3) for a special rule that applies to expenses for meals consumed by individuals subject to the hours of service limits of the Department of Transportation.

Membership dues. The corporation may deduct amounts paid or incurred for membership dues in civic or public service organizations, professional organizations (such as bar and medical associations), business leagues, trade associations, chambers of commerce, boards of trade, and real estate boards. However, no deduction is allowed if a principal purpose of the organization is to entertain, or provide entertainment facilities for, members or their guests. In addition, corporations may not deduct membership dues in any club organized for business, pleasure, recreation, or other social purpose. This includes country clubs, golf and athletic clubs, airline and hotel clubs, and clubs operated to provide meals under conditions favorable to business discussion.

Entertainment facilities. Generally, the corporation cannot deduct an expense paid or incurred for a facility (such as a yacht or hunting lodge) used for an activity usually considered entertainment, amusement, or recreation.

Amounts treated as compensation. Generally, the corporation may be able to deduct otherwise nondeductible meals, travel, and entertainment expenses if the amounts are treated as compensation to the recipient and reported on Form W-2 for an employee or on Form 1099-MISC for an independent contractor.

However, if the recipient is an officer, director, or beneficial owner (directly or indirectly) of more than 10% of the corporation's stock, the deduction for otherwise nondeductible meals, travel, and entertainment expenses incurred after October 22, 2004, is limited to the amount treated as compensation. See section 274(e)(2).

Lobbying expenses. Do not deduct amounts paid or incurred to participate or intervene in any political campaign on behalf of a candidate for public office, or to influence the general public regarding legislative matters, elections, or referendums. In addition, corporations generally cannot deduct expenses paid or incurred to influence federal or state legislation, or to influence the actions or positions of certain federal executive branch officials. However, certain in-house lobbying expenditures that do not exceed $2,000 are deductible. See section 162(e) for more details.

Clean-fuel vehicles and certain refueling property. A deduction is allowed for part of the cost of qualified clean-fuel vehicle property and qualified clean-fuel vehicle refueling property placed in service during the tax year. For more details, see section 179A and Pub. 535.

Certain corporations engaged in farming. Section 464(f) limits the deduction for certain expenditures of S corporations engaged in farming if they use the cash method of accounting, and their prepaid farm supplies are more than 50% of other deductible farming expenses. Prepaid farm supplies include

---

Worksheet for Line 22a

1. Enter gross receipts for the tax year (see section 1362(d)(3)(B) for gross receipts from the sale of capital assets)* . . . . ______
2. Enter passive investment income as defined in section 1362(d)(3)(C)* . . ______
3. Enter 25% of line 1 (If line 2 is less than line 3, stop here. You are not liable for this tax.) . . . . ______
4. Excess passive investment income—Subtract line 3 from line 2 . . ______
5. Enter deductions directly connected with the production of income on line 2 (see section 1375(b)(2))* . . ______
6. Net passive income—Subtract line 5 from line 2 . . . . ______
7. Divide amount on line 4 by amount on line 2 . . . . ______ %
8. Excess net passive income—Multiply line 6 by line 7 . . . . . . ______
9. Enter taxable income (see instructions for taxable income below) . . . ______
10. Enter smaller of line 8 or line 9 . ______
11. Excess net passive income tax—Enter 35% of line 10. Enter here and on line 22a, page 1, Form 1120S . . . ______

*Income and deductions on lines 1, 2, and 5 are from total operations for the tax year. This includes applicable income and expenses from page 1, Form 1120S, as well as those reported separately on Schedule K. See section 1375(b)(4) for an exception regarding lines 2 and 5.

Line 9 of Worksheet—Taxable income

Line 9 taxable income is defined in Regulations section 1.1374-1A(d). Figure this income by completing lines 1 through 28 of **Form 1120,** U.S. Corporation Income Tax Return. Include the Form 1120 computation with the worksheet computation you attach to Form 1120S. You do not have to attach the schedules, etc., called for on Form 1120. However, you may want to complete certain Form 1120 schedules, such as Schedule D (Form 1120) if you have capital gains or losses.

expenses for feed, seed, fertilizer, and similar farm supplies not used or consumed during the year. They also include the cost of poultry that would be allowable as a deduction in a later tax year if the corporation were to (a) capitalize the cost of poultry bought for use in its farm business and deduct it ratably over the lesser of 12 months or the useful life of the poultry and (b) deduct the cost of poultry bought for resale in the year it sells or otherwise disposes of it. If the limit applies, the corporation can deduct prepaid farm supplies that do not exceed 50% of its other deductible farm expenses in the year of payment. The excess is deductible only in the year the corporation uses or consumes the supplies (other than poultry, which is deductible as explained above). For exceptions and more details on these rules, see Pub. 225, Farmer's Tax Guide.

Line 21. Ordinary Business Income (Loss)

Enter this income or loss on line 1 of Schedule K. Line 21 income is **not** used in figuring the tax on line 22a or 22b. See the instructions for line 22a for figuring taxable income for purposes of line 22a or 22b tax.

Tax and Payments

Line 22a. Excess Net Passive Income Tax

If the corporation has always been an S corporation, the excess net passive income tax does not apply.

If the corporation has accumulated earnings and profits (AE&P) at the close of its tax year, has passive investment income for the tax year that is in excess of 25% of gross receipts, and has taxable income at year-end, the corporation must pay a tax on the excess net passive income. Complete lines 1 through 3 and line 9 of the worksheet below to make this determination. If line 2 is greater than line 3 and the corporation has taxable income (see instructions for line 9 of worksheet), it must pay the tax. Complete a separate schedule using the format of lines 1 through 11 of the worksheet to figure the tax. Enter the tax on line 22a, page 1, Form 1120S, and attach the computation schedule to Form 1120S.

Reduce each item of passive income passed through to shareholders by its portion of tax on line 22a. See section 1366(f)(3).

Line 22b. Tax From Schedule D (Form 1120S)

Enter the built-in gains tax from line 21 of Part III of Schedule D. See the instructions for Part III of Schedule D to determine if the corporation is liable for the tax.

Line 22c

Include in the total for line 22c the following:

Investment credit recapture tax. The corporation is liable for investment credit recapture attributable to credits allowed for tax years for which the corporation was not an S corporation. Figure the corporation's investment credit recapture tax by completing Form 4255, Recapture of Investment Credit.

To the left of the line 22c total, enter the amount of recapture tax and "Tax From Form 4255." Attach Form 4255 to Form 1120S.

LIFO recapture tax. The corporation may be liable for the additional tax due to LIFO recapture under Regulations section 1.1363-2 if:

- The corporation used the LIFO inventory pricing method for its last tax year as a C corporation, or
- A C corporation transferred LIFO inventory to the corporation in a nonrecognition transaction in which those assets were transferred basis property.

The additional tax due to LIFO recapture is figured for the corporation's last tax year as a C corporation or for the tax year of the transfer, whichever applies. See the Instructions for Forms 1120 and 1120-A to figure the tax.

The tax is paid in four equal installments. The C corporation must pay the first installment by the due date (not including extensions) of Form 1120 for the corporation's last tax year as a C corporation or for the tax year of the transfer, whichever applies. The S corporation must pay each of the remaining installments by the due date (not including extensions) of Form 1120S for the 3 succeeding tax years. Include this year's installment in the total amount to be entered on line 22c. To the left of the total on line 22c, enter the installment amount and "LIFO tax."

Interest due under the look-back method for completed long-term contracts. If the corporation owes this interest, attach Form 8697. To the left of the total on line 22c, enter the amount owed and "From Form 8697."

Interest due under the look-back method for property depreciated under the income forecast method. If the corporation owes this interest, attach Form 8866. To the left of the total on line 22c, enter the amount owed and "From Form 8866."

Line 23d

If the S corporation is a beneficiary of a trust and the trust makes a section 643(g) election to credit its estimated tax payments to its beneficiaries, include the corporation's share of the payment (reported to the corporation on Schedule K-1 (Form 1041)) in the total amount entered on line 23d. Also, to the left of line 23d, enter "T" and the amount of the payment.

Line 24. Estimated Tax Penalty

A corporation that fails to make estimated tax payments when due may be subject to an underpayment penalty for the period of underpayment. Use Form 2220, Underpayment of Estimated Tax by Corporations, to see if the corporation owes a penalty and to figure the amount of the penalty. If you attach Form 2220 to Form 1120S, be sure to check the box on line 24 and enter the amount of any penalty on this line.

Line 27

Direct Deposit of Refund. If the corporation wants its refund directly deposited into its checking or savings account at any U.S. bank or other financial institution instead of having a check sent to the corporation, complete Form 8050 and attach it to the corporation's return. However, the corporation cannot have its refund from an amended return directly deposited.

Schedule A. Cost of Goods Sold

Generally, inventories are required at the beginning and end of each tax year if the production, purchase, or sale of merchandise is an income-producing factor. See Regulations section 1.471-1.

However, if the corporation is a qualifying taxpayer or a qualifying small business taxpayer, it may adopt or change its accounting method to account for inventoriable items in the same manner as materials and supplies that are not incidental (unless its business is a tax shelter (as defined in section 448(d)(3))).

A qualifying taxpayer is a taxpayer that, for each prior tax year ending after December 16, 1998, has average annual gross receipts of $1 million or less for the 3-tax-year period ending with that prior tax year. See Rev. Proc. 2001-10, 2001-2 I.R.B. 272 for details.

A qualifying small business taxpayer is a taxpayer (a) that, for each prior tax year ending on or after December 31, 2000, has average annual gross receipts of $10 million or less for the 3-tax-year period ending with that prior tax year and (b) whose principal business activity is not an ineligible activity. See Rev. Proc. 2002-28, 2002-18 I.R.B. 815 for details.

If the corporation elects to account for inventoriable items in the same manner as materials and supplies that are not incidental, then inventory costs for raw materials purchased for use in producing finished goods and merchandise purchased for resale are deductible in the year the finished goods or merchandise are sold (but not before the year the corporation paid for the raw materials or merchandise if it is also using the cash method). For additional guidance on this method of accounting for inventoriable items, see Pub. 538.

Enter amounts paid for all raw materials and merchandise during the tax year on line 2. The amount the corporation can deduct for the tax year is figured on line 8.

Section 263A Uniform Capitalization Rules. The uniform capitalization rules of section 263A are discussed under *Limitations on Deductions* on page 14.

See those instructions before completing Schedule A.

Line 1. Inventory at Beginning of Year

If the corporation changes its method of accounting to no longer account for inventories, it must refigure the prior year's closing inventory using its new method of accounting, and enter the result on line 1. If there is a difference between the prior year's closing inventory and the refigured amount, attach an explanation and take it into account when figuring the corporation's section 481(a) adjustment (explained on page 4).

Line 4. Additional Section 263A Costs

An entry is required on this line only for corporations that have elected a simplified method of accounting.

For corporations that have elected the simplified production method, additional section 263A costs are generally those costs, other than interest, that were not capitalized under the corporation's method of accounting immediately prior to the effective date of section 263A but that are required to be capitalized under section 263A. For new corporations, additional section 263A costs are the costs, other than interest, that must be capitalized under section 263A, but which the corporation would not have been required to capitalize if it had existed before the effective date of section 263A. For more details, see Regulations section 1.263A-2(b).

For corporations that have elected the simplified resale method, additional section 263A costs are generally those costs incurred with respect to the following categories.
- Off-site storage or warehousing.
- Purchasing.
- Handling, such as processing, assembly, repackaging, and transporting.
- General and administrative costs (mixed service costs).

For details, see Regulations section 1.263A-3(d).

Enter on line 4 the balance of section 263A costs paid or incurred during the tax year not includable on lines 2, 3, and 5.

Line 5. Other Costs

Enter on line 5 any other inventoriable costs paid or incurred during the tax year not entered on lines 2 through 4. Attach a schedule.

Line 7. Inventory at End of Year

See Regulations sections 1.263A-1 through 1.263A-3 for details on figuring the amount of additional section 263A costs to be included in ending inventory.

If the corporation accounts for inventoriable items in the same manner as materials and supplies that are not incidental, enter on line 7 the portion of its raw materials and merchandise purchased for resale that is included on line 6 and was not sold during the year.

Lines 9a Through 9e. Inventory Valuation Methods

Inventories can be valued at:
- Cost;
- Cost or market value (whichever is lower); or
- Any other method approved by the IRS that conforms to the requirements of the applicable regulations cited below.

However, if the corporation is using the cash method of accounting, it is required to use cost.

Corporations that account for inventoriable items in the same manner as materials and supplies that are not incidental may currently deduct expenditures for direct labor and all indirect costs that would otherwise be included in inventory costs.

The average cost (rolling average) method of valuing inventories generally does not conform to the requirements of the regulations. See Rev. Rul. 71-234, 1971-1 C.B. 148.

Corporations that use erroneous valuation methods must change to a method permitted for federal income tax purposes. To make this change, use Form 3115.

On line 9a, check the method(s) used for valuing inventories. Under "lower of cost or market," market (for normal goods) means the current bid price prevailing on the inventory valuation date for the particular merchandise in the volume usually purchased by the taxpayer. For a manufacturer, market applies to the basic elements of cost—raw materials, labor, and burden. If section 263A applies to the taxpayer, the basic elements of cost must reflect the current bid price of all direct costs and all indirect costs properly allocable to goods on hand at the inventory date.

Inventory may be valued below cost when the merchandise is unsalable at normal prices or unusable in the normal way because the goods are subnormal due to damage, imperfections, shopwear, etc., within the meaning of Regulations section 1.471-2(c). These goods may be valued at a current bona fide selling price, minus direct cost of disposition (but not less than scrap value) if such a price can be established.

If this is the first year the Last-in, First-out (LIFO) inventory method was either adopted or extended to inventory goods not previously valued under the LIFO method provided in section 472, attach Form 970, Application To Use LIFO Inventory Method, or a statement with the information required by Form 970. Also check the LIFO box on line 9c. On line 9d, enter the amount or the percent of total closing inventories covered under section 472. Estimates are acceptable.

If the corporation changed or extended its inventory method to LIFO and has had to write up its opening inventory to cost in the year of election, report the effect of this write-up as income (line 5, page 1) proportionately over a 3-year period that begins with the tax year of the LIFO election (section 472(d)).

See Pub. 538 for more information on inventory valuation methods.

Schedule B. Other Information

Be sure to answer all the questions in Schedule B.

Line 7

Complete line 7 if the corporation: (a) was a C corporation before it elected to be an S corporation or the corporation acquired an asset with a basis determined by reference to its basis (or the basis of any other property) in the hands of a C corporation and (b) has net unrealized built-in gain (defined below) in excess of the net recognized built-in gain from prior years.

The corporation is liable for section 1374 tax if (a) and (b) above apply and it has a net recognized built-in gain (section 1374(d)(2)) for its tax year.

The corporation's net unrealized built-in gain is the amount, if any, by which the fair market value of the assets of the corporation at the beginning of its first S corporation year (or as of the date the assets were acquired, for any asset with a basis determined by reference to its basis (or the basis of any other property) in the hands of a C corporation) exceeds the aggregate adjusted basis of such assets at that time.

Enter on line 7 the corporation's net unrealized built-in gain reduced by the net recognized built-in gain for prior years. See sections 1374(c)(2) and (d)(1).

Line 8

Check the box on line 8 if the corporation was a C corporation in a prior year and has accumulated earnings and profits (AE&P) at the close of its 2004 tax year. For details on figuring AE&P, see section 312. If the corporation has AE&P, it may be liable for tax imposed on excess net passive income. See the instructions for line 22a, page 1, of Form 1120S for details on this tax.

Line 9

Total receipts is the sum of the following amounts:
- Gross receipts or sales (page 1, line 1a).
- All other income (page 1, lines 4 and 5).
- Income reported on Schedule K, lines 3a, 4, 5a, and 6.
- Income or net gain reported on Schedule K, lines 7, 8a, 9, and 10.
- Income or net gain reported on Form 8825, lines 2, 19, and 20a.

General Instructions for Schedules K and K-1. Shareholders' Shares of Income, Credits, Deductions, etc.

Purpose of Schedules

The corporation is liable for taxes on lines 22a, 22b, and 22c, page 1 of Form 1120S. Shareholders are liable for income tax on their share of the corporation's income (reduced by any taxes paid by the corporation on income). Shareholders must include their share of the income on their tax return whether or not it is distributed to them. Unlike most partnership income, S corporation income is not self-employment income and is not subject to self-employment tax.

Schedule K is a summary schedule of all shareholders' shares of the corporation's income, deductions, credits, etc. Schedule K-1 shows each shareholder's individual share. Attach a copy of each shareholder's Schedule K-1 to the Form 1120S filed with the IRS. Keep a copy for the corporation's records and give each shareholder a copy.

Be sure to give each shareholder a copy of the Shareholder's Instructions for Schedule K-1 (Form 1120S).

Note. You may prepare and give to each shareholder only those Instructions that apply to items reported on Schedule K-1 instead of the instructions printed by the IRS.

Substitute Forms

The corporation does not need IRS approval to use a substitute Schedule K-1 if it is an exact copy of the IRS schedule. The substitute schedule must include the OMB number and either: (a) the Shareholder's Instructions for Schedule K-1 (Form 1120S) or (b) instructions that apply to the items reported on Schedule K-1 (Form 1120S).

The corporation must request IRS approval to use other substitute Schedules K-1. To request approval, write to Internal Revenue Service, Attention: Substitute Forms Program, SE:W:CAR:MP:T:T:SP, 1111 Constitution Avenue, NW, IR-6406, Washington, DC 20224.

The corporation may be subject to a penalty if it files a substitute Schedule K-1 that does not conform to the specifications of Rev. Proc. 2004-62, 2004-44 I.R.B. 728.

Shareholder's Pro Rata Share Items

General Rule

Items of income, loss, deductions, etc., are allocated to a shareholder on a daily basis, according to the number of shares of stock held by the shareholder on each day of the corporation's tax year. See the instructions for item H in *Part II. Information About the Shareholder*.

A shareholder who disposes of stock is treated as the shareholder for the day of disposition. A shareholder who dies is treated as the shareholder for the day of the shareholder's death.

Special Rules

Termination of shareholders interest. If a shareholder terminates his or her interest in a corporation during the tax year, the corporation, with the consent of all affected shareholders (including those whose interest is terminated), may elect to allocate income and expenses, etc., as if the corporation's tax year consisted of 2 separate tax years, the first of which ends on the date of the shareholders termination.

To make the election, the corporation must attach a statement to a timely filed original or amended Form 1120S for the tax year for which the election is made. In the statement the corporation must state that it is electing under section 1377(a)(2) and Regulations section 1.1377-1(b) to treat the tax year as if it consisted of 2 separate tax years. The statement must also explain how the shareholder's entire interest was terminated (e.g., sale or gift), and state that the corporation and each affected shareholder consent to the corporation making the election. A single statement may be filed for all terminating elections made for the tax year. If the election is made, write "Section 1377(a)(2) Election Made" at the top of each affected shareholders Schedule K-1.

For more details, see Temporary Regulations section 1.1377-1T(b).

Qualifying dispositions. If a qualifying disposition takes place during the tax year, the corporation may make an irrevocable election to allocate income and expenses, etc., as if the corporation's tax year consisted of 2 tax years, the first of which ends on the close of the day the qualifying disposition occurs.

A qualifying disposition is:

1. A disposition by a shareholder of at least 20% of the corporation's outstanding stock in one or more transactions in any 30-day period during the tax year,
2. A redemption treated as an exchange under section 302(a) or 303(a) of at least 20% of the corporation's outstanding stock in one or more transactions in any 30-day period during the tax year, or
3. An issuance of stock that equals at least 25% of the previously outstanding stock to one or more new shareholders in any 30-day period during the tax year.

To make the election the corporation must attach a statement to a timely filed original or amended Form 1120S for the tax year for which the election is made. In the statement the corporation must state that it is electing under Regulations section 1.1368-1(g)(2)(i) to treat the tax year as if it consisted of two separate tax years, give the facts relating to the qualifying disposition (e.g., sale, gift, stock issuance, or redemption), and state that each shareholder who held stock in the corporation during the tax year consents to the election. A single election statement may be filed for all elections made under this special rule for the tax year.

For more details, see Temporary Regulations section 1.1368-1T(g)(2).

Specific Instructions (Schedule K-1 Only)

General Reporting Information

On each Schedule K-1, enter the information about the corporation and the shareholder in Parts I and II of the schedule (items A through H). In Part III, enter the shareholder's pro rata share of each item of income, deduction, and credit and any other information the shareholder needs to prepare his or her tax return. If the return is for a fiscal year or a short tax year, fill in the tax year space at the top of each Schedule K-1.

Codes. In box 10 and boxes 12 through 17, identify each item by entering a code in the column to the left of the dollar amount entry space. These codes are identified on the back of Schedule K-1 and in the Shareholder's Instructions for Schedule K-1.

Attached statements. Enter an **asterisk (*)** after the code, if any, in the column to the left of the dollar amount entry space for each item for which you have attached a statement providing additional information. For those informational items that cannot be reported as a single dollar amount, enter the code and asterisk in the left column and write "STMT" in the dollar amount entry space to indicate the information is provided on an attached statement.

More than one attached statement can be placed on the same sheet of paper and should be identified in alphanumeric order by box number followed by the letter code (if any). For example: "Box 17, Code L— Information Needed to Figure Depletion—Oil and Gas" (followed by the information the shareholder needs).

Too few entry spaces on Schedule K-1? If the corporation has more coded items than the number of entry spaces in box 10, or boxes 12 through 17, do not enter a code or dollar amount in the last entry space of the box. In the last entry space, enter an asterisk in the left column and enter "STMT" in the entry space to the right. Report the additional items on an attached statement and provide the box number, the code, description, and dollar amount or information for each additional item. For example: "Box 13, Code J—Work Opportunity Credit— $1,000."

Due date for furnishing Schedule K-1. Schedule K-1 must be prepared and given to each shareholder on or before the day on which Form 1120S is required to be filed (including extensions).

Special Reporting Requirements for Corporations With Multiple Activities

If items of income, loss, deduction, or credit from more than one activity (determined for purposes of the passive activity loss and credit limitations) are reported on Schedule K-1, the corporation must provide information for each activity to its shareholders. See *Passive Activity Reporting Requirements* on page 11 for details on the reporting requirements.

Special Reporting Requirements for At-Risk Activities

If the corporation is involved in one or more at-risk activities for which a loss is reported on Schedule K-1, the corporation must report information separately for each at-risk activity. See section 465(c) for a definition of at-risk activities.

For each at-risk activity, the following information must be provided on an attachment to Schedule K-1:

1. A statement that the information is a breakdown of at-risk activity loss amounts.
2. The identity of the at-risk activity; the loss amount for the activity; other income and deductions; and any other information that relates to the activity.

Specific Items

Part I. Information About the Corporation

Item D. If the corporation is a registration-required tax shelter, it must enter its tax shelter registration number in item D.

Item E. A corporation that has invested in a registration-required tax shelter must furnish a copy of its Form 8271 to its shareholders. See Form 8271 for more details.

Part II. Information About the Shareholder

Items F and G. If a single member limited liability company (LLC) owns stock in the corporation, and the LLC is treated as a disregarded entity for federal income tax purposes, enter the owner's identifying number in Item F and the owner's name and address in Item G. The owner must be eligible to be an S corporation shareholder. An LLC that elects to be treated as a corporation for federal income tax purposes is not eligible to be an S corporation shareholder.

Item H. If there was no change in shareholders or in the relative interest in stock the shareholders owned during the tax year, enter the percentage of total stock owned by each shareholder during the tax year. For example, if shareholders X and Y each owned 50% for the entire tax year, enter 50% in item H for each shareholder. Each shareholder's pro rata share items (boxes 1 through 17 of Schedule K-1) are figured by multiplying the corresponding Schedule K amount by the percentage in item H.

If there was a change in shareholders or in the relative interest in stock the shareholders owned during the tax year:

- Each shareholder's percentage of ownership is weighted for the number of days in the tax year that stock was owned. For example, A and B each held 50% for half the tax year and A, B, and C held 40%, 40%, and 20%, respectively, for the remaining half of the tax year. The percentage of ownership for the year for A, B, and C is figured as presented in the illustration and is then entered in item H.

	a	b	c (a × b)	
	% of total stock owned	% of tax year held	% of ownership for the year	
A	50 40	50 50	25 +20	45
B	50 40	50 50	25 +20	45
C	20	50	10	10
Total				100%

- Each shareholder's pro rata share items generally are figured by multiplying the Schedule K amount by the percentage in item H. However, if a shareholder terminated his or her entire interest in the corporation during the year or a qualifying disposition took place, the corporation may elect to allocate income and expenses, etc., as if the tax year consisted of 2 tax years, the first of which ends on the day of the termination or qualifying disposition.

See *Special Rules* on page 20 for more details. Each shareholder's pro rata share items are figured separately for each period on a daily basis, based on the percentage of stock held by the shareholder on each day.

Specific Instructions (Schedules K and K-1, Part III)

Income (Loss)

Reminder: Before entering income items on Schedule K or K-1, be sure to reduce the items of income for the following:

- Built-in gains tax (Schedule D, Part III, line 21). Each recognized built-in gain item (within the meaning of section 1374(d)(3)) is reduced by its proportionate share of the built-in gains tax.
- Excess net passive income tax (line 22a, page 1, Form 1120S). Each item of passive investment income (within the meaning of section 1362(d)(3)(C)) is reduced by its proportionate share of the net passive income tax.

Line 1. Ordinary Business Income (Loss)

Enter the amount from line 21, page 1. Enter the income or loss without reference to:

- Shareholders' basis in the stock of the corporation and in any indebtedness of the corporation to the shareholders (section 1366(d)),
- Shareholders' at-risk limitations, and
- Shareholders' passive activity limitations.

These limitations, if applicable, are determined at the shareholder level.

Line 1 should not include rental activity income (loss) or portfolio income (loss).

Schedule K-1. Enter each shareholder's pro rata share of ordinary business income (loss) in box 1 of Schedule K-1. If the corporation has more than one trade or business activity, identify on an attachment to Schedule K-1 the amount from each separate activity. See *Passive Activity Reporting Requirements* on page 11.

Line 2. Net Rental Real Estate Income (Loss)

Enter the net income or loss of the corporation from rental real estate activities from Form 8825. Attach this form to Form 1120S.

Schedule K-1. Enter each shareholder's pro rata share of net rental real estate income (loss) in box 2 of Schedule K-1. If the corporation has more than one rental real estate activity, identify on an attachment to Schedule K-1 the amount from each separate activity. See *Passive Activity Reporting Requirements* on page 11.

Line 3. Other Net Rental Income (Loss)

Enter on line 3a the gross income from rental activities other than those reported on Form 8825. Include on line 3a the gain (loss) from line 17 of Form 4797 that is attributable to the sale, exchange, or involuntary conversion of an asset used in a rental activity other than a rental real estate activity.

Enter on line 3b the deductible expenses from these activities. Attach a schedule separately identifying these expenses.

Enter on line 3c the net rental income (loss). See page 9 of these instructions and Publication 925, Passive Activity and At-Risk Rules, for more information on rental activities.

Schedule K-1. Enter in box 3 of Schedule K-1 each shareholder's pro rata share of other net rental income (loss) reported on line 3c of Schedule K. If the corporation has more than one rental activity reported in box 3, identify on an attachment to Schedule K-1 the amount from each separate activity. See *Passive Activity Reporting Requirements* on page 11.

Portfolio Income

See *Portfolio Income* on page 10 for a comprehensive definition of portfolio income.

Do not reduce portfolio income by deductions allocated to it. Report such deductions (other than interest expense) on line 12b of Schedule K. Report each shareholder's pro rata share in box 12 of Schedule K-1 using codes G, H, and J.

Interest expense allocable to portfolio income is generally investment interest expense. It is reported on line 12c of Schedule K. Report each shareholder's pro rata share of interest expense allocable to portfolio income in box 12 of Schedule K-1 using code I.

Line 4. Interest Income

Enter only taxable portfolio interest on this line. Interest income derived in the ordinary course of the corporation's trade or business, such as interest charged on receivable balances, is reported on line 5, page 1, of Form 1120S. See Temporary Regulations section 1.469-2T(c)(3).

Schedule K-1. Enter each shareholder's pro rata share of interest income in box 4 of Schedule K-1.

Line 5a. Ordinary Dividends

Enter only taxable ordinary dividends on line 5a. Include any qualified dividends reported on line 5b.

Schedule K-1. Enter each shareholder's pro rata share of ordinary dividends in box 5a of Schedule K-1.

Line 5b. Qualified Dividends

Enter qualified dividends on line 5b. Except as provided below, qualified dividends are ordinary dividends received from domestic corporations and qualified foreign corporations.

Exceptions. The following dividends are not qualified dividends:

- Dividends the corporation received on any share of stock held for less than 61 days during the 121-day period that began 60 days before the ex-dividend date. When determining the number of days the corporation held the stock, it cannot count certain days during which the corporation's risk of loss was diminished. The ex-dividend date is the first date following the declaration of a dividend on which the purchaser of a stock is not entitled to receive the next dividend payment. When counting the number of days the corporation held the stock, include the day the corporation disposed of the stock but not the day the corporation acquired it.
- Dividends attributable to periods totaling more than 366 days that the corporation received on any share of preferred stock held for less than 91 days during the 181-day period that began 90 days before the ex-dividend date. When determining the number of days the corporation held the stock, do not count certain days during which the corporation's risk of loss was diminished. Preferred dividends attributable to periods totaling less than 367 days are subject to the 61-day holding period rule above.
- Dividends that relate to payments that the corporation is obligated to make with respect to short sales or positions in substantially similar or related property.
- Dividends paid by a regulated investment company that are not treated as qualified dividend income under section 854.
- Dividends paid by a real estate investment trust that are not treated as qualified dividend income under section 857(c).

See Pub. 550 for more details.

Qualified foreign corporation. A foreign corporation is a qualified foreign corporation if it is:

1. Incorporated in a possession of the United States or
2. Eligible for benefits of a comprehensive income tax treaty with the United States that the Secretary determines is satisfactory for this purpose and that includes an exchange of information program. See Notice 2003-69, 2003-42 I.R.B. 851 for details.

If the foreign corporation does not meet either 1 or 2 above, then it may be treated as a qualified foreign corporation for any dividend paid by the corporation if the stock associated with the dividend paid is readily tradable on an established securities market in the United States.

However, qualified dividends do not include dividends paid by the following foreign entities in either the tax year of the distribution or the preceding tax year:

- A foreign investment company (defined in section 1246(b)),
- A passive foreign investment company (defined in section 1297), or
- A foreign personal holding company (defined in section 552).

See Notice 2004-71, 2004-45 I.R.B. 793 for more details.

Schedule K-1. Enter each shareholder's pro rata share of qualified dividends in box 5b of Schedule K-1.

Line 6. Royalties

Enter the royalties received by the corporation.

Schedule K-1. Enter each shareholder's pro rata share of royalties in box 6 of Schedule K-1.

Line 7. Net Short-Term Capital Gain (Loss)

Enter the gain (loss) from line 6 of Schedule D (Form 1120S).

Schedule K-1. Enter each shareholder's pro rata share of net short-term capital gain (loss) in box 7 of Schedule K-1.

Line 8a. Net Long-Term Capital Gain (Loss)

Enter the gain or loss that is portfolio income (loss) from Schedule D (Form 1120S), line 13.

Schedule K-1. Enter each shareholder's pro rata share of net long-term capital gain (loss) in box 8a of Schedule K-1.

CAUTION *If any gain or loss from lines 6 or 13 of Schedule D is not portfolio income (e.g., gain or loss from the disposition of nondepreciable personal property used in a trade or business), do not report this income or loss on lines 7 or 8a. Instead, report it on line 10 (box 10, code E, of Schedule K-1).*

Line 8b. Collectibles (28%) Gain (Loss)

Figure the amount attributable to collectibles from the amount reported on Schedule D (Form 1120S) line 13. A collectibles gain (loss) is any long-term gain or deductible long-term loss from the sale or exchange of a collectible that is a capital asset.

Collectibles include works of art, rugs, antiques, metal (such as gold, silver, platinum bullion), gems, stamps, coins, alcoholic beverages, and certain other tangible property.

Also, include gain (but not loss) from the sale or exchange of an interest in a partnership or trust held for more than 1 year and attributable to unrealized appreciation of collectibles. For details, see Regulations section 1.1(h)-1. Also attach the statement required under Regulations section 1.1(h)-1(e).

Schedule K-1. Report each shareholder's pro rata share of the collectibles (28%) gain (loss) in box 8b of Schedule K-1.

Line 8c. Unrecaptured Section 1250 Gain

The three types of unrecaptured section 1250 gain must be reported separately on an attached statement to Form 1120S.

- **From the sale or exchange of the corporation's business assets.** Figure this amount for each section 1250 property in Part III of Form 4797 (except property for which gain is reported using the installment method on Form 6252) for which you had an entry in Part I of Form 4797 by subtracting line 26g of Form 4797 from the smaller of line 22 or line 24. Figure the total of these amounts for all section 1250 properties. Generally, the result is the corporation's unrecaptured section 1250 gain. However, if the corporation is reporting gain on the installment method for a section 1250 property held more than 1 year, see the next paragraph to figure the unrecaptured section 1250 gain on that property for this tax year.

The total unrecaptured section 1250 gain for an installment sale of section 1250 property held more than 1 year is figured in a manner similar to that used in the preceding paragraph. However, the total unrecaptured section 1250 gain must be allocated to the installment payments received from the sale. To do so, the corporation generally must treat the gain allocable to each installment payment as unrecaptured section 1250 gain until all such gain has been used in full. Figure the unrecaptured section 1250 gain for installment payments received during the tax year as the smaller of (a) the amount from line 26 or line 37 of Form 6252, Installment Sale Income, (whichever applies) or (b) the total unrecaptured section 1250 gain for the sale reduced by all gain reported in prior years (excluding section 1250 ordinary income recapture).

CAUTION *However, if the corporation chose not to treat all of the gain from payments received after May 6, 1997, and before August 24, 1999, as unrecaptured section 1250 gain, use only the amount the corporation chose to treat as unrecaptured section 1250 gain for* *those payments to reduce the total unrecaptured section 1250 gain remaining to be reported for the sale.*

• **From the sale or exchange of an interest in a partnership.** Also report as a separate amount any gain from the sale or exchange of an interest in a partnership attributable to unrecaptured section 1250 gain. See Regulations section 1.1(h)-1 and attach a statement required under Regulations section 1.1(h)-1(e).

• **From an estate, trust, RIC, or REIT.** If the corporation received a Schedule K-1 or Form 1099-DIV from an estate, a trust, a real estate investment trust (REIT), or a regulated investment company (RIC) reporting "unrecaptured section 1250 gain," do not add it to the corporation's own unrecaptured section 1250 gain. Instead, report it as a separate amount. For example, if the corporation received a Form 1099-DIV from a REIT with unrecaptured section 1250 gain, report it as "Unrecaptured section 1250 gain from a REIT."

Schedule K-1. Report each shareholder's pro rata share of unrecaptured section 1250 gain from the sale or exchange of the corporation's business assets in box 8c of Schedule K-1. If the corporation is reporting unrecaptured section 1250 gain from an estate, trust, REIT, or RIC or from the corporation's sale or exchange of an interest in a partnership (as explained above), enter "STMT" in box 8c and an asterisk (*) in the left column of the box and attach a statement that separately identifies the amount of unrecaptured section 1250 gain from:

• The sale or exchange of the corporations business assets.
• The sale or exchange of an interest in a partnership.
• An estate, trust, REIT, or RIC.

Line 9. Net Section 1231 Gain (Loss)

Enter the net section 1231 gain (loss) from Form 4797, line 7, column (g).

Do not include net gain or loss from involuntary conversions due to casualty or theft. Report net loss from involuntary conversions due to casualty or theft on line 10 of Schedule K (box 10, code B, of Schedule K-1). See the instructions for line 10 on how to report net gain from involuntary conversions.

Schedule K-1. Report each shareholder's pro rata share of net section 1231 gain (loss) in box 9 of Schedule K-1. If the corporation has more than one rental, trade, or business activity, identify on an attachment to Schedule K-1 the amount of section 1231 gain (loss) from each separate activity. See *Passive Activity Reporting Requirements* on page 11.

Line 10. Other Income (Loss)

Enter any other item of income or loss not included above. Attach a statement to Form 1120S that separately identifies each type and amount of income for each of the following five categories. The codes needed for Schedule K-1 reporting are provided for each category.

Other portfolio income (loss) (code A). Portfolio income not reported on lines 4 through 8.

If the corporation holds a residual interest in a REMIC, report on an attachment each shareholder's share of taxable income (net loss) from the REMIC (line 1b of Schedule Q (Form 1066)); excess inclusion (line 2c of Schedule Q (Form 1066)); and section 212 expenses (line 3b of Schedule Q (Form 1066)). Because Schedule Q (Form 1066) is a quarterly statement, the corporation must follow the Schedule Q (Form 1066) Instructions for Residual Interest Holder to figure the amounts to report to shareholders for the corporation's tax year.

Involuntary conversions (code B). Report net loss from involuntary conversions due to casualty or theft. The amount for this item is shown on Form 4684, Casualties and Thefts, line 38a or 38b. Each shareholder's pro rata share must be entered on Schedule K-1. Enter the net gain from involuntary conversions of property used in a trade or business (line 39 of Form 4684) on line 3 of Form 4797. If there was a gain (loss) from a casualty or theft to property not used in a trade or business or for income-producing purposes, notify the shareholder. The corporation should not complete Form 4684 for this type of casualty or theft. Instead, each shareholder will complete his or her own Form 4684.

1256 contracts and straddles (code C). Report any net gain or loss from section 1256 contracts from Form 6781, Gains and Losses From Section 1256 Contracts and Straddles.

Mining exploration costs recapture (code D). Provide the information shareholders will need to recapture certain mining exploration expenditures. See Regulations section 1.617-3.

Other income (loss) (code E). Include any other type of income, such as:

• Recoveries of tax benefit items (section 111).
• Gambling gains and losses subject to the limitations in section 165(d).
• Disposition of an interest in oil, gas, geothermal, or other mineral properties. Report the following information on an attached statement to Schedule K-1: (a) description of the property, (b) the shareholder's share of the amount realized on the sale, exchange, or involuntary conversion of each property (fair market value of the property for any other disposition, such as a distribution), (c) the shareholder's share of the corporation's adjusted basis in the property (except for oil or gas properties), and (d) total intangible drilling costs, development costs, and mining exploration costs (section 59(e) expenditures) passed through to shareholders for the property. See Regulations section 1.1254-4 for more information.
• Gain from the sale or exchange of qualified small business stock (as defined in the Instructions for Schedule D) that is eligible for the partial section 1202 exclusion. To be eligible for the section 1202 exclusion, the stock must have been held by the corporation for more than 5 years. Additional limitations apply at the shareholder level. Report each shareholder's share of section 1202 gain on Schedule K-1. Each shareholder will determine if he or she qualifies for the section 1202 exclusion. Report on an attachment to Schedule K-1 for each sale or exchange the name of the qualified small business that issued the stock, the shareholder's share of the corporation's adjusted basis and sales price of the stock, and the dates the stock was bought and sold.
• Gain eligible for section 1045 rollover (replacement stock purchased by the corporation). Include only gain from the sale or exchange of qualified small business stock (as defined in the Instructions for Schedule D) that was deferred by the corporation under section 1045 and reported on Schedule D. See the Instructions for Schedule D for more details. Additional limitations apply at the shareholder level. Report each shareholder's share of the gain eligible for section 1045 rollover on Schedule K-1. Each shareholder will determine if he or she qualifies for the rollover. Report on an attachment to Schedule K-1 for each sale or exchange the name of the qualified small business that issued the stock, the shareholder's share of the corporation's adjusted basis and sales price of the stock, and the dates the stock was bought and sold.
• Gain eligible for section 1045 rollover (replacement stock not purchased by the corporation). Include only gain from the sale or exchange of qualified small business stock (as defined in the Instructions for Schedule D) the corporation held for more than 6 months but that was not deferred by the corporation under section 1045. See the Instructions for Schedule D for more details. A shareholder may be eligible to defer his or her pro rata share of this gain under section 1045 if he or she purchases other qualified small business stock during the 60-day period that began on the date the stock was sold by the corporation. Additional limitations apply at the shareholder level. Report on an attachment to Schedule K-1 for each sale or exchange the name of the qualified small business that issued the stock, the shareholder's share of the corporation's adjusted basis and sales price of the stock, and the dates the stock was bought and sold.
• Net short-term capital gain or loss and net long-term capital gain or loss that is not portfolio income (e.g., gain or loss from the disposition of nondepreciable personal property used in a trade or business activity of the corporation). Report total net short-term gain or loss on Schedule D (Form 1040), line 5, column (f). Report the total net long-term gain or

loss on Schedule D (Form 1040), line 12, column (f).

Schedule K-1. Enter each shareholder's pro rata share of the five other income categories listed above in box 10 of Schedule K-1. Enter the applicable code A, B, C, D, or E (as shown above). If you are reporting each shareholder's pro rata share of only one type of income under Code E, enter the code with an asterisk (E*) and the dollar amount in the entry space in box 10 and attach a statement that shows the type of income. If you are reporting multiple types of income under code E, enter the code with an asterisk (E*) and enter "STMT" in the entry space in box 10 and attach a statement that shows the dollar amount of each type of income. If the corporation has more than one trade or business or rental activity (for codes B through E), identify on an attachment to Schedule K-1 the amount from each separate activity. See *Passive Activity Reporting Requirements* on page 11.

Deductions

Line 11. Section 179 Deduction

An S corporation may elect to expense part of the cost of certain property that the corporation purchased and placed in service this year for use in its trade or business or certain rental activities. See the Instructions for Form 4562 for more information.

Complete Part I of Form 4562 to figure the corporation's section 179 deduction. The corporation does not claim the deduction itself, but instead passes it through to the shareholders. Attach Form 4562 to Form 1120S and show the total section 179 deduction on Schedule K, line 11.

If the corporation is an enterprise zone business, also report on an attachment to Schedules K and K-1 the cost of section 179 property placed in service during the year that is qualified zone property.

See the instructions for line 17d of Schedule K for sales or other dispositions of property for which a section 179 deduction has passed through to shareholders and for the recapture rules if the business use of the property dropped to 50% or less.

Schedule K-1. Report each shareholder's pro rata share of the section 179 expense deduction in box 11 of Schedule K-1. If the corporation has more than one rental, trade, or business activity, identify on an attachment to Schedule K-1 the amount of section 179 deduction from each separate activity. See *Passive Activity Reporting Requirements* on page 11.

Do not complete box 11 of Schedule K-1 for any shareholder that is an estate or trust; estates and trusts are not eligible for the section 179 expense deduction.

Line 12a. Contributions

Generally, no deduction is allowed for any contribution of $250 or more unless the corporation obtains a written acknowledgment from the charitable organization that shows the amount of cash contributed, describes any property contributed, and gives an estimate of the value of any goods or services provided in return for the contribution. The acknowledgment must be obtained by the due date (including extensions) of the corporation's return, or if earlier, the date the corporation files its return. Do not attach the acknowledgment to the tax return, but keep it with the corporation's records. These rules apply in addition to the filing requirements for Form 8283 described below.

Enter the amount of charitable contributions made during the tax year. Attach a statement to Form 1120S that separately identifies the corporation's contributions for each of the following six categories.

See *Limits on Deductions* in Publication 526, Charitable Contributions, for information on adjusted gross income (AGI) limitations on deductions for charitable contributions.

The codes needed for Schedule K-1 reporting are provided for each category.

Cash contributions (50%) (code A). Enter the amount of cash contributions subject to the 50% AGI limitation.

Cash contributions (30%) (code B). Enter the amount of cash contributions subject to the 30% AGI limitation.

Noncash contributions (50%) (code C). Enter the amount of noncash contributions subject to the 50% AGI limitation.

Noncash contributions (30%) (code D). Enter the amount of noncash contributions subject to the 30% AGI limitation.

Capital gain property to a 50% organization (30%) (code E). Enter the amount of capital gain property contributions subject to the 30% AGI limitation.

Capital gain property (20%) (code F). Enter the amount of capital gain property contributions subject to the 20% AGI limitation.

Contributions of property. See *Noncash Contributions and Contributions of Property* in Pub. 526 for information on noncash contributions and on contributions of capital gain property. If the deduction claimed for noncash contributions exceeds $500, complete Form 8283, Noncash Charitable Contributions, and attach it to Form 1120S.

The corporation must attach a copy of its Form 8283 to the Schedule K-1 of each shareholder if the deduction for any item or group of similar items of contributed property exceeds $5,000, even if the amount allocated to any shareholder is $5,000 or less.

If the corporation made a qualified conservation contribution under section 170(h), also include the fair market value of the underlying property before and after the donation, as well as the type of legal interest contributed, and describe the conservation purpose furthered by the donation. Give a copy of this information to each shareholder.

Nondeductible contributions. Certain contributions made to an organization conducting lobbying activities are not deductible. See section 170(f)(9) for more details. Also, see *Contributions You Cannot Deduct* in Publication 526 for more examples of nondeductible contributions.

CAUTION *An accrual basis S corporation* ***may not*** *elect to treat a contribution as having been paid in the tax year the board of directors authorizes the payment if the contribution is not actually paid until the next tax year.*

Schedule K-1. Report each shareholder's pro rata share of charitable contributions in box 12 of Schedule K-1 using codes A through F for each of the six contribution categories shown above. See the above instructions for *Contributions of property* for information on a statement concerning qualified conservation contributions that you may be required to attach to Schedule K-1.

Line 12b. Deductions Related to Portfolio Income (Loss)

Enter on line 12b the deductions clearly and directly allocable to portfolio income (other than investment interest expense). Attach a statement to Form 1120S that separately identifies the corporation's deduction related to portfolio income for each of the following categories. The codes needed for Schedule K-1 reporting are provided for each category.

Deductions—royalty income (code J). Enter the deductions related to royalty income.

Deductions—portfolio (2% floor) (code G). Enter the deductions related to portfolio income that are subject to the 2% of AGI floor (see the instructions for Schedule A (Form 1040)).

Deductions—portfolio (other) (code H). Enter the amount of any other deductions related to portfolio income.

No deduction is allowed under section 212 for expenses allocable to a convention, seminar, or similar meeting. Because these expenses are not deductible by shareholders, the corporation does not report these expenses on line 12b of Schedule K. The expenses are nondeductible and are reported as such on line 16c of Schedule K (box 16, code C of Schedule K-1).

Schedule K-1. Report each shareholder's pro rata share of deductions related to portfolio income that are reported on line 12b of Schedule K using codes J (for deductions related to royalty income), G (for deductions related to portfolio income and subject to the 2% of AGI floor), or H (for other deductions related to portfolio income).

Line 12c. Investment Interest Expense

Include on this line the interest properly allocable to debt on property held for investment purposes. Property held for investment includes property that produces income (unless derived in the ordinary course of a trade or business) from interest, dividends, annuities, or royalties; and gains from the disposition of property that produces those types of income or is held for investment.

Investment interest expense does not include interest expense allocable to a passive activity.

Investment income and investment expenses other than interest are reported on lines 17a and 17b respectively. This information is needed by shareholders to determine the investment interest expense limitation (see Form 4952, Investment Interest Expense Deduction, for details).

Schedule K-1. Report each shareholder's pro rata share of investment interest expense in box 12 of Schedule K-1 using code I.

Lines 12d(1) and 12d(2). Section 59(e)(2) Expenditures

Generally, section 59(e) allows each shareholder to make an election to deduct their pro rata share of the corporation's otherwise deductible qualified expenditures ratably over 10 years (3 years for circulation expenditures), beginning with the tax year in which the expenditures were made (or for intangible drilling and development costs, over the 60-month period beginning with the month in which such costs were paid or incurred).

The term "qualified expenditures" includes only the following types of expenditures paid or incurred during the tax year:

- Circulation expenditures.
- Research and experimental expenditures.
- Intangible drilling and development costs.
- Mining exploration and development costs.

If a shareholder makes the election, the above items are not treated as tax preference items.

Because the shareholders are generally allowed to make this election, the corporation cannot deduct these amounts or include them as AMT items on Schedule K-1. Instead, the corporation passes through the information the shareholders need to figure their separate deductions.

On line 12d(1), enter the type of expenditures claimed on line 12d(2). Enter on line 12d(2) the qualified expenditures paid or incurred during the tax year to which an election under section 59(e) may apply. Enter this amount for all shareholders whether or not any shareholder makes an election under section 59(e).

On an attached statement, identify the property for which the expenditures were paid or incurred. If the expenditures were for intangible drilling costs or development costs for oil and gas properties, identify the month(s) in which the expenditures were paid or incurred. If there is more than one type of expenditure or more than one property, provide the amounts (and the months paid or incurred if required) for each type of expenditure separately for each property.

Schedule K-1. Report each shareholder's pro rata share of section 59(e) expenditures in box 12 of Schedule K-1 using code K. On an attached statement, identify (a) the type of expenditure, (b) the property for which the expenditures are paid or incurred, and (c) for oil and gas properties only, the month in which intangible drilling costs and development costs were paid or incurred. If there is more than one type of expenditure or the expenditures are for more than one property, provide each shareholder's pro rata share of the amounts (and the months paid or incurred for oil and gas properties) for each type of expenditure separately for each property.

Line 12e. Other Deductions

Enter deductions not included on lines 11, 12a, 12b, 12c, 12d(2), 14l, or 14m. Attach a statement to Form 1120S that separately identifies the type and amount of each deduction for the following five categories. The codes needed for Schedule K-1 reporting are provided for each category.

Reforestation expense deduction (code L). The corporation may elect to deduct a limited amount of its reforestation expenditures paid or incurred after October 22, 2004. The amount the corporation may elect to deduct is limited to $10,000 for each qualified timber property. See section 194(c) for a definition of reforestation expenditures and qualified timber property. Provide a description of the qualified timber property on an attached statement to Form 1120S and Schedule K-1. If the corporation is electing to deduct amounts for more than one qualified timber property, provide a description and the amount on the statement for each property . The corporation must amortize over 84 months any amount not deducted. See the instructions for line 19 on page 16.

Preproductive period expenses (code M). If the corporation is required to use an accrual method of accounting under section 447 or 448(a)(3), it must capitalize these expenses. If the corporation is permitted to use the cash method, enter the amount of preproductive period expenses that qualify under Regulations section 1.263–4(d). An election not to capitalize these expenses must be made at the shareholder level. See *Uniform Capitalization Rules* in Publication 225, Farmer's Tax Guide.

Commercial revitalization deduction from rental real estate activities (code N). Enter the commercial revitalization deduction on line 12e only if it is for a rental real estate activity. If the deduction is for a nonrental building, deduct it on line 19 of Form 1120S. See the instructions for line 19 on page 16 for more information.

Penalty on early withdrawal of savings (code O). Enter the amount of any penalty on early withdrawal of savings not reported on line 12b because the corporation withdrew funds from its time savings deposit before its maturity.

Other deductions (code P). Include any other deduction, such as:

- Amounts paid by the corporation that would be allowed as itemized deductions on any of the shareholders' income tax returns if they were paid directly by a shareholder for the same purpose. These amounts include, but are not limited to, expenses under section 212 for the production of income other than from the corporation's trade or business. However, do not enter expenses related to portfolio income or investment interest expense reported on line 12c of Schedule K on this line.
- Soil and water conservation expenditures (section 175).
- Expenditures paid or incurred for the removal of architectural and transportation barriers to the elderly and disabled that the corporation has elected to treat as a current expense. See section 190.
- Interest expense allocated to debt-financed distributions. See Notice 89-35, 1989-1 C.B. 675, or Publication 535, chapter 5, for more information.
- Contributions to a capital construction fund.

Schedule K-1. Enter each shareholder's pro rata share of the five deduction categories listed above in box 12 of Schedule K-1. Enter the applicable code L, M, N, O, or P (as shown above). If you are reporting each shareholder's pro rata share of only one type of deduction under Code P, enter the code with an asterisk (P*) and the dollar amount in the entry space in box 12 and attach a statement that shows the type of deduction. If you are reporting multiple types of deductions under code P, enter the code with an asterisk (P*) and enter "STMT" in the entry space in box 12 and attach a statement that shows the dollar amount of each type of deduction. If the corporation has more than one trade or business activity, identify on an attachment to Schedule K-1 the amount for each separate activity. See *Passive Activity Reporting Requirements* on page 11.

Credits & Credit Recapture

Note. Do not attach Form 3800, General Business Credit, to Form 1120S.

Low-Income Housing Credit

Section 42 provides for a credit that may be claimed by owners of low-income residential rental buildings. Complete Form 8586, Low-Income Housing Credit, and attach it to Form 1120S. Enter the credit figured by the corporation on Form 8586, and any low-income housing credit received from other entities on the applicable line as explained below. The corporation must also complete and attach Form 8609, Low-Income Housing Credit Allocation Certification, and Schedule A (Form 8609), Annual

Statement, to Form 1120S. See the Instructions for Form 8586 and Form 8609 for information on completing these forms.

Note. If part or all of the credit reported on lines 13a or 13b is attributable to additions to qualified basis of property placed in service before 1990, report on an attachment to Schedules K and K-1 the amount of the credit on each line that is attributable to property placed in service (a) before 1990 and (b) after 1989.

Line 13a. Low-Income Housing Credit (Section 42(j)(5))

If the corporation invested in a partnership to which the provisions of section 42(j)(5) apply, report on line 13a the credit the partnership reported to the corporation in box 15, code A, of Schedule K-1 (Form 1065).

Schedule K-1. Report in box 13 of Schedule K-1 each shareholder's pro rata share of the low income housing credit reported on line 13a of Schedule K using code A. If the corporation has credits from more than one rental activity, identify on an attachment to Schedule K-1 the amount for each separate activity. See *Passive Activity Reporting Requirements* on page 11.

Line 13b. Low-Income Housing Credit (Other)

Report on line 13b any low-income housing credit not reported on line 13a. This includes any credit from a partnership reported to the corporation in box 15, code B, of Schedule K-1 (Form 1065).

Schedule K-1. Report in box 13 of Schedule K-1 each shareholder's pro rata share of the low income housing credit reported on line 13b of Schedule K using code B. If the corporation has credits from more than one rental activity, identify on an attachment to Schedule K-1 the amount for each separate activity. See *Passive Activity Reporting Requirements* on page 11.

Line 13c. Qualified Rehabilitation Expenditures (Rental Real Estate)

Enter total qualified rehabilitation expenditures related to rental real estate activities of the corporation. Complete line 1 of Form 3468, Investment Credit, for property related to rental real estate activities of the corporation for which income or loss is reported on line 2 of Schedule K. See Form 3468 for details on qualified rehabilitation expenditures. Attach Form 3468 to Form 1120S.

Note. Report qualified rehabilitation expenditures not related to rental real estate activities on line 13g, Other Credits and Credit Recapture.

Schedule K-1. Report each shareholder's pro rata share of qualified rehabilitation expenditures related to rental real estate activities in box 13 of Schedule K-1 using code C. Attach a statement to Schedule K-1 that separately identifies the shareholder's share of expenditures from pre-1936 buildings and from certified historic structures (lines 1b and 1c of Form 3468 respectively). If the corporation has credits from more than one rental real estate activity, identify on an attachment to Schedule K-1 the amount for each separate activity. See *Passive Activity Reporting Requirements* on page 11.

Line 13d. Other Rental Real Estate Credits

Enter on line 13d any other credit (other than credits reported above) related to rental real estate activities. On the dotted line to the left of the entry space for line 13d, identify the type of credit. If there is more than one type of credit, attach a statement to Form 1120S that identifies the type and amount for each credit. These credits may include any type of credit listed in the instructions for line 13g.

Schedule K-1. Report in box 13 of Schedule K-1 each shareholder's pro rata share of other rental real estate credits reported on line 13d of Schedule K using code G. If you are reporting each shareholder's pro rata share of only one type of rental real estate credit under code G, enter the code with an asterisk (G*) and the dollar amount in the entry space in box 13 and attach a statement that shows the type of credit. If you are reporting multiple types of rental real estate credit under code G, enter the code with an asterisk (G*) and enter "STMT" in the entry space in box 13 and attach a statement that shows the dollar amount of each type of credit. If the corporation has credits from more than one rental real estate activity, identify on the attached statement the amount of each type of credit for each separate activity. See *Passive Activity Reporting Requirements* on page 11.

Line 13e. Other Rental Credits

Enter on line 13e any other credit (other than credits reported above) related to rental activities. On the dotted line to the left of the entry space for line 13e, identify the type of credit. If there is more than one type of credit, attach a statement to Form 1120S that identifies the type and amount for each credit. These credits may include any type of credit listed in the instructions for line 13g.

Schedule K-1. Report in box 13 of Schedule K-1 each shareholder's pro rata share of other rental credits using code H. If you are reporting each shareholder's pro rata share of only one type of rental credit under code H, enter the code with an asterisk (H*) and the dollar amount in the entry space in box 13 and attach a statement that shows the type of credit. If you are reporting multiple types of rental credit under code H, enter the code with an asterisk (H*) and enter "STMT" in the entry space in box 13 and attach a statement that shows the dollar amount of each type of credit. If the corporation has credits from more than one rental activity, identify on the attached statement the amount of each type of credit for each separate activity. See *Passive Activity Reporting Requirements* on page 11.

Line 13f. Credit for Alcohol Used as Fuel

Enter on line 13f the credit for alcohol used as fuel attributable to trade or business activities. Enter on line 13d or 13e the credit for alcohol used as fuel attributable to rental activities.

Figure this credit on Form 6478, Credit for Alcohol Used as Fuel, and attach it to Form 1120S. The credit must be included in income on page 1, line 5, of Form 1120S.

See section 40(f) for an election the corporation can make to have the credit not apply.

Schedule K-1. Report in box 13 of Schedule K-1 each shareholder's pro rata share of the credit for alcohol used as a fuel reported on line 13f using code R. If this credit includes the small ethanol producer credit, identify on a statement attached to each Schedule K-1 (a) the amount of the small producer credit included in the total credit allocated to the shareholder, (b) the number of gallons of qualified ethanol fuel production allocated to the shareholder, and (c) the shareholder's pro rata share, in gallons, of the corporation's productive capacity for alcohol. If the corporation has credits from more than one activity, identify on an attachment to Schedule K-1 the amount for each separate activity. See *Passive Activity Reporting Requirements* on page 11.

Line 13g. Other Credits and Credit Recapture

Enter on line 13g any other credit, except credits or expenditures shown or listed for lines 13a through 13f or the credit for federal tax paid on fuels (which is reported on line 23c of page 1). Do not include any credit recapture amounts on line 13g, but provide credit recapture information on an attached statement to Schedule K-1 as explained below. On the dotted line to the left of the entry space for line 13g, identify the type of credit. If there is more than one type of credit or if there are any credits subject to recapture, attach a statement to Form 1120S that separately identifies each type and amount of credit and credit recapture information for the following categories. The codes needed for Schedule K-1 reporting are provided for each category.

Qualified rehabilitation expenditures (other than rental real estate) (code D). Enter total qualified rehabilitation expenditures from activities other than rental real estate activities. Complete line 1 of Form 3468 for property related to rental real estate activities of the corporation for which income or loss is reported on line 1 of Schedule K. See Form 3468 for details on qualified rehabilitation expenditures. Attach Form 3468 to Form 1120S.

Note. Report qualified rehabilitation expenditures related to rental real estate activities on line 13c.

Schedule K-1. Report each shareholder's pro rata share of qualified rehabilitation expenditures related to other than rental real estate activities in box 13 of Schedule K-1 using code D. Attach a statement to Schedule K-1 that separately identifies the shareholder's share of expenditures from pre-1936 buildings and from certified historic structures (lines 1b and 1c of Form 3468 respectively). If the corporation has credits from more than one rental real estate activity, identify on an attachment to Schedule K-1 the amount for each separate activity. See *Passive Activity Reporting Requirements* on page 11.

Basis of energy property (code E). Enter the basis of energy property placed in service during the tax year that qualifies for the energy credit. See the instructions for Form 3468 for details. Complete line 2 of Form 3468; attach Form 3468 to Form 1120S.

Qualified timber property (code F). Enter the amortizable basis of timber property acquired before October 23, 2004, that qualifies for the reforestation credit. See the instructions for Form 3468 for details. Complete line 3 of Form 3468 and attach it to Form 1120S.

Undistributed capital gains credit (code I). This credit represents taxes paid on undistributed capital gains by a regulated investment company (RIC) or a real estate investment trust (REIT). As a shareholder of a RIC or REIT, the corporation will receive notice of the amount of tax paid on undistributed capital gains on Form 2439, Notice to Shareholder of Undistributed Long-Term Capital Gains.

Work opportunity credit (code J). Complete Form 5884 to determine the amount of the credit. Attach it to Form 1120S.

Welfare-to-work credit (code K). Complete Form 8861 to determine the amount of the credit. Attach it to Form 1120S.

Disabled access credit (code L). Complete Form 8826 to determine the amount of the credit. Attach it to Form 1120S.

Empowerment zone and renewal community employment credit (code M). Complete Form 8844 to determine the amount of the credit. Attach it to Form 1120S.

New York Liberty Zone business employee credit (code N). Complete Form 8884 to determine the amount of the credit. Attach it to Form 1120S.

New markets credit (code O). Complete Form 8874 to determine the amount of the credit. Attach it to Form 1120S.

Credit for employer social security and Medicare taxes (code P). Complete Form 8846 to determine the amount of the credit. Attach it to Form 1120S.

Backup withholding (code Q). This credit is for backup withholding on dividends, interest, and other types of income of the corporation.

Recapture of low-income housing credit (codes S and T). If recapture of part or all of the low-income housing credit is required because (a) prior year qualified basis of a building decreased or (b) the corporation disposed of a building or part of its interest in a building, see Form 8611, Recapture of Low-Income Housing Credit. Complete lines 1 through 7 of Form 8611 to determine the amount of credit to recapture. Use code S on Schedule K-1 to report recapture of the low-income housing credit from a section 42(j)(5) partnership. Use code T to report recapture of any other low-income housing credit. See the instructions for lines 13a and 13b above for more information.

Note. If a shareholder's ownership interest in a building decreased because of a transaction at the shareholder level, the corporation must provide the necessary information to the shareholder to enable the shareholder to figure the recapture.

CAUTION *If the corporation filed Form 8693, Low-Income Housing Credit Disposition Bond, to avoid recapture of the low-income housing credit, no entry should be made on Schedule K-1.*

See Form 8586, Form 8611, and section 42 for more information.

Recapture of investment credit (code U). Complete and attach Form 4255, Recapture of Investment Credit, when investment credit property is disposed of, or it no longer qualifies for the credit, before the end of the recapture period or the useful life applicable to the property. State the type of property at the top of Form 4255, and complete lines 2, 4, and 5, whether or not any shareholder is subject to recapture of the credit.

Attach to each Schedule K-1 a separate schedule providing the information the corporation is required to show on Form 4255, but list only the shareholder's pro rata share of the cost of the property subject to recapture. Also indicate the lines of Form 4255 on which the shareholders should report these amounts.

The corporation itself is liable for investment credit recapture in certain cases. See the instructions for line 22c, page 1, Form 1120S, for details.

Other credits (code V). Attach a statement to Form 1120S that identifies the type and amount of any other credits not reported elsewhere, such as:

- Nonconventional source fuel credit. Compute this credit on an attached statement and attach it to Form 1120S. See section 29 for rules on figuring the credit.
- Qualified electric vehicle credit. Complete Form 8834 to determine the amount of the credit and attach it to Form 1120S.
- Unused investment credit from cooperatives.
- Credit for increasing research activities. Complete Form 6765 to determine the amount of the credit and attach it to Form 1120S.
- Enhanced oil recovery credit. Complete Form 8830 to determine the amount of the credit and attach it to Form 1120S.
- Renewable electricity and refined coal production credit. Complete Form 8835 to determine the amount of the credit. Attach a statement to Form 1120S and Schedule K-1 showing separately the amount of the credit from Section A and from Section B of Form 8835. Attach Form 8835 to Form 1120S.
- Indian employment credit. Complete Form 8845 to determine the amount of the credit and attach it to Form 1120S.
- Orphan drug credit. Complete Form 8820 to determine the amount of the credit and attach it to Form 1120S.
- Credit for contributions to selected community development corporations. Complete Form 8847 to determine the amount of the credit and attach it to Form 1120S.
- Credit for small employer pension plan start-up costs. Complete Form 8881 to determine the amount of the credit and attach it to Form 1120S.
- Credit for employer-provided childcare facilities and services. Complete Form 8882 to determine the amount of the credit and attach it to Form 1120S.
- Biodiesel fuels credit. Complete Form 8864 to determine the amount of the credit and attach it to Form 1120S. The credit must be included in income on page 1, line 5 of Form 1120S.
- Low sulfur diesel fuel production credit. Complete Form 8896 to determine the amount of the credit and attach it to Form 1120S.
- General credits from an electing large partnership.
- Qualified zone academy bond credit. Complete Form 8860 to determine the amount of the credit and attach it to Form 1120S. Also, be sure to include the proper amount in income as explained in the instructions for Form 8860. Also, see the instructions for line 17d, code N.

Recapture of other credits (code W). On an attached statement to Schedule K-1, provide any information shareholders will need to report recapture of credits (other than recapture of low-income housing credit and investment credit reported on Schedule K-1 using codes S, T, and U). Examples of credit recapture information reported using code W include:

- Any information needed by a shareholder to compute recapture of the qualified electric vehicle credit. See Pub. 535 for more information.
- Any information needed by a shareholder to compute recapture of the new markets credit. See Form 8874 for details on recapture.
- Any information needed by a shareholder to compute recapture of the Indian employment credit. Generally, if the corporation terminates a qualified employee less than 1 year after the date of initial employment, any Indian employment credit allowed for a prior tax year by reason of wages paid or incurred

to that employee must be recaptured. For details, see section 45A(d).

- Any information needed by a shareholder to compute recapture of the credit for employer-provided child care facilities and services. See section 45F(d) for details on recapture.

Schedule K-1. Enter each shareholder's pro rata share of the credit and credit recapture categories listed above (for line 13g) in box 13 of Schedule K-1. See additional Schedule K-1 reporting information provided in the instructions above. Enter the applicable code, D through W, in the column to the left of the dollar amount entry space. If you are reporting each shareholder's pro rata share of only one type of credit under Code V, enter the code with an asterisk (V*) and the dollar amount in the entry space in box 13 and attach a statement that shows the type of credit. If you are reporting multiple credits under code V, enter the code with an asterisk (V*) and enter "STMT" in the entry space in box 13 and attach a statement that shows the dollar amount of each type of credit. If the corporation has credits or expenditures from more than one trade or business activity, identify on an attachment to Schedule K-1 the amount for each separate activity. See *Passive Activity Reporting Requirements* on page 11.

Foreign Transactions

Lines 14a through 14n must be completed if the corporation has foreign income, deductions, or losses, or has paid or accrued foreign taxes.

The codes A through N for box 14 of Schedule K-1 correspond with the line numbers 14a through 14n. Codes O, P, and Q for box 14 are reported on line 17d of Schedule K. On Schedule K-1 for the items coded C, E, J, L, M, and N, enter the code followed by an asterisk and the shareholder's pro rata share of the dollar amount. Attach a statement to Schedule K-1 for these coded items providing the information described below. If the corporation had income from, or paid or accrued taxes to, more than one country or U.S. possession, see the requirement for an attached statement in the instruction for line 14a below. See Pub. 514, Foreign Tax Credit for Individuals, and the Instructions for Form 1116, for more information.

Line 14a. Name of Country or U.S. Possession

Enter the name of the foreign country or U.S. possession from which the corporation had income or to which the corporation paid or accrued taxes. If the corporation had income from, or paid or accrued taxes to, more than one foreign country or U.S. possession, enter "See attached" and attach a schedule for each country for lines 14a through 14n (codes A through N of Schedule K-1). On Schedule K-1, if there is more than one country enter code A followed by an asterisk (A*), enter "STMT," and attach a statement to Schedule K-1 for each country for the information and amounts coded A through N and code Q.

Line 14b. Gross Income From all Sources

Enter the corporation's gross income from all sources (both U.S. and foreign).

Line 14c. Gross Income Sourced at Shareholder Level

Enter the total gross income of the corporation that is required to be sourced at the shareholder level. This includes income from the sale of most personal property, other than inventory, depreciable property, and certain intangible property. See Pub. 514 and section 865 for details. Attach a schedule showing the following information:

- The amount of this gross income (without regard to its source) in each category identified in the instructions for lines 14d, 14e, and 14f, including each of the listed categories.
- Specifically identify gains on the sale of personal property other than inventory, depreciable property, and certain intangible property on which a foreign tax of 10% or more was paid or accrued. Also list losses on the sale of such property if the foreign country would have imposed a 10% or higher tax had the sale resulted in a gain. See *Sales or Exchanges of Certain Personal Property* in Pub. 514 and section 865.
- Specify foreign source capital gains or losses within each separate limitation category. Also separately identify foreign source gains or losses within each separate limitation category that are collectibles (28%) gains and losses or unrecaptured section 1250 gains.

Lines 14d–14f. Foreign Gross Income Sourced at Corporate Level

Separately report gross income from sources outside the United States by category of income as identified under lines 14d, 14e and 14f. See Pub. 514 for more information on the categories of income.

Line 14d. Passive foreign source income.

Line 14e. Attach a schedule showing the amount of foreign source income included in each of the following listed categories:

- Financial services income;
- High withholding tax interest;
- Shipping income;
- Dividends from a domestic international sales corporation (DISC) or a former DISC;
- Distributions from a foreign sales corporation (FSC) or a former FSC;
- Section 901(j) income; and
- Certain income re-sourced by treaty.

Line 14f. General limitation foreign source income (all other foreign source income).

Lines 14g–14h. Deductions Allocated and Apportioned at Shareholder Level

Enter on line 14g the corporation's total interest expense (including interest equivalents under Temporary Regulations section 1.861-9T(b)). Do not include interest directly allocable under Temporary Regulations section 1.861-10T to income from a specific property. This type of interest is allocated and apportioned at the corporate level and is included on lines 14i through 14k.

On line 14h, enter the total of all other deductions or losses that are required to be allocated at the shareholder level. For example, include on line 14h research and experimental expenditures (see Regulations section 1.861-17(f)).

Lines 14i–14k. Deductions Allocated and Apportioned at Corporate Level to Foreign Source Income

Separately report corporate deductions that are apportioned at the corporate level to (a) passive foreign source income, (b) each of the listed foreign categories of income (14e), and (c) general limitation foreign source income (see the instructions for lines 14d-14f). Attach a schedule showing the amount of deductions allocated and apportioned at the corporate level to each of the listed categories from line 14e. See Pub. 514 for more information.

Lines 14l–14m. Total Foreign Taxes Paid or Accrued

Enter in U.S. dollars the total foreign taxes (described in section 901 or section 903) that were paid (on line 14l) or accrued (on line 14m) according to the corporation's method of accounting for such taxes. On Schedule K-1, report each shareholder's share of the line 14l taxes using code L and the line 14m taxes using code M. Translate these amounts into U.S. dollars by using the applicable exchange rate (see Pub. 514).

A corporation reporting foreign taxes using the cash method can make an irrevocable election to report the taxes using the accrual method for the year of the election and all future years. Make this election by reporting all foreign taxes using the accrual method on line 14m (see Regulations section 1.905-1).

Attach a schedule reporting the following information:

1. The total amount of foreign taxes (including foreign taxes on income sourced at the shareholder level) relating to each category of income (see instructions for lines 14d-14f).
2. The dates on which the taxes were paid or accrued, the exchange rates used, and the amounts in both foreign currency and U.S. dollars, for:

- Taxes withheld at source on interest.
- Taxes withheld at source on dividends.
- Taxes withheld at source on rents and royalties.
- Other foreign taxes paid or accrued.

Line 14n. Reduction in Taxes Available for Credit

Enter the total reductions in taxes available for credit. Attach a schedule showing the reductions for:

- Taxes on foreign mineral income (section 901(e)).
- Taxes on foreign oil and gas extraction income (section 907(a)).
- Taxes attributable to boycott operations (section 908).
- Failure to timely file (or furnish all of the information required on) Forms 5471 and 8865.
- Any other items (specify).

Alternative Minimum Tax (AMT) Items

Lines 15a through 15f must be completed for all shareholders.

Enter items of income and deductions that are adjustments or tax preference items for the alternative minimum tax (AMT). See Form 6251, Alternative Minimum Tax—Individuals, or Schedule I of Form 1041, U.S. Income Tax Return for Estates and Trusts, to determine the amounts to enter and for other information.

Do not include as a tax preference item any qualified expenditures to which an election under section 59(e) may apply. Because these expenditures are subject to an election by each shareholder, the corporation cannot figure the amount of any tax preference related to them. Instead, the corporation must pass through to each shareholder in box 12, code K, of Schedule K-1 the information needed to figure the deduction.

Schedule K-1. Report each shareholder's pro rata share of amounts reported on lines 15a through 15f (concerning alternative minimum tax items) in box 15 of Schedule K-1 using codes A through F respectively. If the corporation is reporting items of income or deduction for oil, gas, and geothermal properties, you may be required to identify these items on a statement attached to Schedule K-1 (see the instructions for lines 15d and 15e below for details). Also see the requirement for an attached statement in the instructions for line 15f.

Line 15a. Post-1986 Depreciation Adjustment

Figure the adjustment for line 15a based only on tangible property placed in service after 1986 (and tangible property placed in service after July 31, 1986, and before 1987 for which the corporation elected to use the general depreciation system). Do not make an adjustment for motion picture films, videotapes, sound recordings, certain public utility property (as defined in section 168(f)(2)), property depreciated under the unit-of-production method (or any other method not expressed in a term of years), qualified Indian reservation property, property eligible for a special depreciation allowance, qualified revitalization expenditures, or the section 179 expense deduction.

For property placed in service before 1999, refigure depreciation for the AMT as follows (using the same convention used for the regular tax):

- For section 1250 property (generally, residential rental and nonresidential real property), use the straight line method over 40 years.
- For tangible property (other than section 1250 property) depreciated using the straight line method for the regular tax, use the straight line method over the property's class life. Use 12 years if the property has no class life.
- For any other tangible property, use the 150% declining balance method, switching to the straight line method the first tax year it gives a larger deduction, over the property's AMT class life. Use 12 years if the property has no class life.

Note. See Pub. 946 for a table of class lives.

For property placed in service after 1998, refigure depreciation for the AMT only for property depreciated for the regular tax using the 200% declining balance method. For the AMT, use the 150% declining balance method, switching to the straight line method the first tax year it gives a larger deduction, and the same convention and recovery period used for the regular tax.

Figure the adjustment by subtracting the AMT deduction for depreciation from the regular tax deduction and enter the result on line 15a. If the AMT deduction is more than the regular tax deduction, enter the difference as a negative amount. Depreciation capitalized to inventory must also be refigured using the AMT rules. Include on this line the current year adjustment to income, if any, resulting from the difference.

Line 15b. Adjusted Gain or Loss

If the corporation disposed of any tangible property placed in service after 1986 (or after July 31, 1986, if an election was made to use the General Depreciation System), or if it disposed of a certified pollution control facility placed in service after 1986, refigure the gain or loss from the disposition using the adjusted basis for the AMT. The property's adjusted basis for the AMT is its cost or other basis minus all depreciation or amortization deductions allowed or allowable for the AMT during the current tax year and previous tax years. Enter on this line the difference between the regular tax gain (loss) and the AMT gain (loss). If the AMT gain is less than the regular tax gain, or the AMT loss is more than the regular tax loss, or there is an AMT loss and a regular tax gain, enter the difference as a negative amount.

If any part of the adjustment is allocable to net short-term capital gain (loss), net long-term capital gain (loss), or net section 1231 gain (loss), attach a schedule that identifies the amount of the adjustment allocable to each type of gain or loss.

For a net long-term capital gain (loss), also identify the amount of the adjustment that is collectibles (28%) gain (loss).

For a net section 1231 gain (loss), also identify the amount of adjustment that is unrecaptured section 1250 gain.

Line 15c. Depletion (Other Than Oil and Gas)

Do not include any depletion on oil and gas wells. The shareholders must figure their oil and gas depletion deductions and preference items separately under section 613A.

Refigure the depletion deduction under section 611 for mines, wells (other than oil and gas wells), and other natural deposits for the AMT. Percentage depletion is limited to 50% of the taxable income from the property as figured under section 613(a), using only income and deductions for the AMT. Also, the deduction is limited to the property's adjusted basis at the end of the year as figured for the AMT. Figure this limit separately for each property. When refiguring the property's adjusted basis, take into account any AMT adjustments made this year or in previous years that affect basis (other than the current year's depletion).

Enter the difference between the regular tax and AMT deduction. If the AMT deduction is greater, enter the difference as a negative amount.

Oil, Gas, and Geothermal Properties — Gross Income and Deductions

Generally, the amounts to be entered on lines 15d and 15e are only the income and deductions for oil, gas, and geothermal properties that are used to figure the corporation's ordinary business income (loss) on line 21, page 1, Form 1120S.

If there are any items of income or deductions for oil, gas, and geothermal properties included in the amounts that are required to be passed through separately to the shareholders on Schedule K-1, give each shareholder a schedule that shows, for the box in which the income or deduction is included, the amount of income or deductions included in the total amount for that box. Do not include any of these direct pass-through amounts on line 15d or 15e. The shareholder is told in the Shareholder's Instructions for Schedule K-1 (Form 1120S) to adjust the amounts in box 15, code D or E, for any other income or deductions from oil, gas, or geothermal properties included in boxes 2 through 12, 16 or 17 of Schedule K-1 in order to determine the total income and deductions from oil, gas, and geothermal properties for the corporation.

Figure the amounts for lines 15d and 15e separately for oil and gas properties that are not geothermal deposits and for all properties that are geothermal deposits.

Give each shareholder a schedule that shows the separate amounts included in the computation of the amounts on lines 15d and 15e of Schedule K.

Line 15d. Oil, Gas, and Geothermal Properties — Gross Income

Enter the total amount of gross income (within the meaning of section 613(a)) from all oil, gas, and geothermal properties received or accrued during the tax year and included on page 1, Form 1120S.

Line 15e. Oil, Gas, and Geothermal Properties — Deductions

Enter the amount of any deductions allowed for the AMT that are allocable to oil, gas, and geothermal properties.

Line 15f. Other AMT Items

Attach a schedule to Form 1120S and Schedule K-1 that shows other items not shown on lines 15a through 15e that are adjustments or tax preference items or that the shareholder needs to complete Form 6251 or Schedule I of Form 1041. See these forms and their instructions to determine the amount to enter.

Other AMT items include the following:

- Accelerated depreciation of real property under pre-1987 rules.
- Accelerated depreciation of leased personal property under pre-1987 rules.
- Long-term contracts entered into after February 28, 1986. Except for certain home construction contracts, the taxable income from these contracts must be figured using the percentage of completion method of accounting for the AMT.
- Losses from tax shelter farm activities. No loss from any tax shelter farm activity is allowed for the AMT.

Schedule K-1. If you are reporting each shareholder's pro rata share of only one type of AMT item under code F, enter the code with an asterisk (F*) and the dollar amount in the entry space in box 15 and attach a statement that shows the type of AMT item. If you are reporting multiple types of AMT items under code F, enter the code with an asterisk (F*) and enter "STMT" in the entry space in box 15 and attach a statement that shows the dollar amount of each type of AMT item.

Items Affecting Shareholder Basis

Line 16a. Tax-Exempt Interest Income

Enter on line 16a tax-exempt interest income, including any exempt-interest dividends received from a mutual fund or other regulated investment company. This information must be reported by individuals on line 8b of Form 1040. Generally, under section 1367(a)(1)(A), the basis of the shareholder's stock is increased by the amount shown on this line.

Line 16b. Other Tax-Exempt Income

Enter on line 16b all income of the corporation exempt from tax other than tax-exempt interest (e.g., life insurance proceeds). Generally, under section 1367(a)(1)(A), the basis of the shareholder's stock is increased by the amount shown on this line.

Line 16c. Nondeductible Expenses

Enter on line 16c nondeductible expenses paid or incurred by the corporation.

Do not include separately stated deductions shown elsewhere on Schedules K and K-1, capital expenditures, or items for which the deduction is deferred to a later tax year. Generally, under section 1367(a)(2)(D), the basis of the shareholder's stock is decreased by the amount shown on this line.

Line 16d. Property Distributions

Enter the total property distributions (including cash) made to each shareholder other than dividends reported on line 17c of Schedule K. Distributions of appreciated property are valued at fair market value. See *Distributions* on page 33 for the ordering rules.

Line 16e. Repayment of Loans From Shareholders

Enter any repayments made to shareholders during the current tax year.

Schedule K-1. Report each shareholder's pro rata share of amounts reported on lines 16a, 16b, and 16c (concerning items affecting shareholder basis) in box 16 of Schedule K-1 using codes A through C respectively. Report property distributions (line 16d) and repayment of loans from shareholders (line 16e) on the Schedule K-1 of the shareholder(s) that received the distributions or repayments (using codes D and E).

Other Information

Lines 17a and 17b. Investment Income and Expenses

Enter on line 17a the investment income included on lines 4, 5a, 6 and 10, of Schedule K. Do not include other portfolio gains or losses on this line.

Enter on line 17b the investment expense included on line 12b of Schedule K.

Investment income includes gross income from property held for investment, the excess of net gain attributable to the disposition of property held for investment over net capital gain from the disposition of property held for investment, and any net capital gain from the disposition of property held for investment that each shareholder elects to include in investment income under section 163(d)(4)(B)(iii). Generally, investment income and investment expenses do not include any income or expenses from a passive activity. See Regulations section 1.469-2(f)(10) for exceptions.

Property subject to a net lease is not treated as investment property because it is subject to the passive loss rules. Do not reduce investment income by losses from passive activities.

Investment expenses are deductible expenses (other than interest) directly connected with the production of investment income. See the Instructions for Form 4952 for more information.

Schedule K-1. Report each shareholder's pro rata share of amounts reported on lines 17a and 17b (investment income and expenses) in box 17 of Schedule K-1 using codes A and B respectively.

If there are other items of investment income or expense included in the amounts that are required to be passed through separately to the shareholders on Schedule K-1, such as net short-term capital gain or loss, net long-term capital gain or loss, and other portfolio gains or losses, give each shareholder a schedule identifying these amounts.

Line 17c. Dividend Distributions Paid From Accumulated Earnings and Profits (Schedule K Only)

Enter total dividends paid to shareholders from accumulated earnings and profits. Report these dividends to shareholders on Form 1099-DIV. Do not report them on Schedule K-1.

Line 17d. Other Items and Amounts

Report the following information on a statement attached to Form 1120S. In box 17 of Schedule K-1 enter the appropriate code for each information item followed by an asterisk in the left-hand column of the entry space (e.g., C*). In the right-hand column, enter "STMT". The codes are provided below.

Lookback interest—completed long-term contracts (code C). If the corporation is a closely held S corporation (defined in section 460(b)(4)(C)(iii)) and it entered into any long-term contracts after February 28, 1986, that are accounted for under either the percentage of completion-capitalized cost method or the percentage of completion method, it must attach a schedule to Form 1120S showing the information required in items (a) and (b) of the instructions for lines 1 and 3 of Part II of Form 8697. It must also report the amounts for Part II, lines 1 and 3, to its shareholders. See the Instructions for Form 8697 for more information.

Lookback interest—income forecast method (code D). If the corporation is a closely held S corporation (defined in section 460(b)(4)(C)(iii)) and it depreciated certain property placed in service after September 13, 1995, under the income forecast method, it must attach to Form 1120S the information specified in the instructions for Form 8866, line 2, for the 3rd and 10th tax years beginning after the tax year the property was placed in service. It must also report the line 2 amounts to its shareholders. See the Instructions for Form 8866 for more details.

Dispositions of property with section 179 deductions (code E). This represents gain or loss on the sale, exchange, or other disposition of property for which a section 179 deduction has been passed through to shareholders.

The corporation must provide all the following information with respect to such dispositions (see the instructions for line 4, page 1, on page 13).

- Date the property was acquired and placed in service.
- Date of the sale or other disposition of the property.
- The shareholder's pro rata share of the gross sales price or amount realized.
- The shareholder's pro rata share of the cost or other basis plus expense of sale (reduced as explained in the instructions for Form 4797, line 21).
- The shareholder's pro rata share of the depreciation allowed or allowable, determined as described in the instructions for Form 4797, line 22, but excluding the section 179 deduction.
- The shareholder's pro rata share of the section 179 deduction (if any) passed through for the property and the corporation's tax year(s) in which the amount was passed through.
- If the disposition is due to a casualty or theft, a statement indicating so, and any additional information needed by the shareholder.
- For an installment sale made during the corporation's tax year, any information needed to complete Form 6252. The corporation also must separately report the shareholder's pro rata share of all payments received for the property in future tax years. (Installment payments received for installment sales made in prior tax years should be reported in the same manner used in prior tax years.)

Recapture of section 179 deduction (code F). This amount represents recapture of section 179 deduction if business use of the property dropped to 50% or less. If the business use of any property (placed in service after 1986) for which a section 179 deduction was passed through to shareholders dropped to 50% or less (for a reason other than disposition), the corporation must provide all the following information.

- The shareholder's pro rata share of the original basis and depreciation allowed or allowable (not including the section 179 deduction).
- The shareholder's pro rata share of the section 179 deduction (if any) passed through for the property and the corporation's tax year(s) in which the amount was passed through.

Section 453(l)(3) information (code G). Supply any information needed by a shareholder to compute the interest due under section 453(l)(3). If the corporation elected to report the dispositions of certain timeshares and residential lots on the installment method, each shareholder's tax liability must be increased by the shareholder's pro rata share of the interest on tax attributable to the installment payments received during the tax year.

Section 453A(c) information (code H). Supply any information needed by a shareholder to compute the interest due under section 453A(c). If an obligation arising from the disposition of property to which section 453A applies is outstanding at the close of the year, each shareholder's tax liability must be increased by the tax due under section 453A(c) on the shareholder's pro rata share of the tax deferred under the installment method.

Section 1260(b) information (code I). Supply any information needed by a shareholder to figure the interest due under section 1260(b). If the corporation had gain from certain constructive ownership transactions, each shareholder's tax liability must be increased by the shareholder's pro rata share of interest due on any deferral of gain recognition. See section 1260(b) for details, including how to figure the interest.

Interest allocable to production expenditures (code J). Supply any information needed by a shareholder to properly capitalize interest as required by section 263A(f). See *Section 263A uniform capitalization rules* on page 14 for more information.

CCF nonqualified withdrawal (code K). Report nonqualified withdrawals by the corporation from a capital construction fund. Attach a statement to the shareholder's Schedule K-1 providing details of the withdrawal.

Information needed to figure depletion—oil and gas (code L). Report gross income and other information relating to oil and gas well properties to shareholders to allow them to figure the depletion deduction for oil and gas well properties. Allocate to each shareholder a proportionate share of the adjusted basis of each corporate oil or gas property. See section 613A(c)(11) for details. The corporation cannot deduct depletion on oil and gas wells. Each shareholder must determine the allowable amount to report on his or her return. See Pub. 535 for more information.

Amortization of reforestation costs (code M). Report the amortizable basis of reforestation expenditures paid or incurred before October 23, 2004, for which the corporation elected amortization, and the tax year the amortization began for the current tax year and the 7 preceding tax years. The amortizable basis cannot exceed $10,000 for each of those tax years.

Other information (code N). Report to each shareholder:

- Any information or statements the shareholders need to allow them to comply with the registration and disclosure requirements under sections 6111 and 6662(d)(2)(B)(ii) and the list keeping requirements of Regulations section 301.6112-1. See Form 8264 and Notice 2004-80, 2004-50 I.R.B. 963 for more information.
- If the corporation participates in a transaction that must be disclosed on Form 8886 (see page 7), both the corporation and its shareholders may be required to file Form 8886. The corporation must determine if any of its shareholders are required to disclose the transaction and provide those shareholders with information they will need to file Form 8886. This determination is based on the category(s) under which a transaction qualified for disclosures. See the instructions for Form 8886 for details.
- If the corporation is involved in farming or fishing activities, report the gross income from these activities.
- Any income or gain reported on lines 1 though 10 of Schedule K that qualify as inversion gain, if the corporation is an expatriated entity or is a partner in an expatriated entity. For details, see section 7874. Attach a statement to Form 1120S that shows the amount of each type of income or gain included in the inversion gain. The corporation must report each shareholder's pro rata share of the inversion gain in box 17 of Schedule K-1 using code N. Attach a statement to Schedule K-1 that shows the shareholder's pro rata share of the amount of each type of income or gain included in the inversion gain.
- Any other information the shareholders need to prepare their tax returns.

Other Foreign Transactions (Box 14 of Schedule K-1, Codes O, P, and Q)

Caution: Do not report these amounts in box 17 of Schedule K-1. Instead, report them in box 14 as explained below.

- **Foreign trading gross receipts (code O).** Report each shareholder's pro rata share of foreign trading gross receipts from line 15 of Form 8873 in box 14 using code O. See *Extraterritorial Income Exclusion* on page 12.
- **Extraterritorial income exclusion (code P).** If the corporation is not permitted to deduct the extraterritorial income exclusion as a non-separately stated item, attach a statement to Schedule K-1 showing the shareholder's pro rata share of the extraterritorial income exclusion reported on lines 52a and 52b of Form 8873. Also identify the activity to which the exclusion is related. See *Extraterritorial Income Exclusion* on page 12 for more information
- **Other foreign transactions (code Q).** Report any other foreign transaction information the shareholders need to prepare their tax returns.

Line 17e. Income/Loss Reconciliation (Schedule K only)

If the corporation has an amount on lines 14l and 14m of Schedule K (foreign taxes paid and accrued), add these amounts for purposes of computing the corporation's net income (loss). The amount reported on line 17e must be the same as the amount reported on line 8 of Schedule M-1.

Schedule L. Balance Sheets per Books

Schedules L and M-1 are not required to be completed if the corporation answered Yes to Question 9 of Schedule B.

Schedule M-2 Worksheet

	(a) Accumulated adjustments account	(b) Other adjustments account	(c) Shareholders' undistributed taxable income previously taxed
1 Balance at beginning of tax year . . .	-0-	-0-	
2 Ordinary income from page 1, line 21 .	10,000		
3 Other additions	20,000	5,000	
4 Loss from page 1, line 21	( )		
5 Other reductions	(36,000)	( )	
6 Combine lines 1 through 5	(6,000)	5,000	
7 Distributions other than dividend distributions	-0-	5,000	
8 Balance at end of tax year. Subtract line 7 from line 6	(6,000)	-0-	

The balance sheets should agree with the corporation's books and records. Include certificates of deposit as cash on line 1 of Schedule L. Attach a statement explaining any differences.

If the S election terminated during the tax year and the corporation reverted to a C corporation, the year-end balance sheet generally should agree with the books and records at the end of the C short year. However, if the corporation elected under section 1362(e)(3) to have items assigned to each short year under normal tax accounting rules, the year-end balance sheet should agree with the books and records at the end of the S short year.

Line 5. Tax-Exempt Securities

Include on this line:

- State and local government obligations, the interest on which is excludible from gross income under section 103(a), and
- Stock in a mutual fund or other regulated investment company that distributed exempt-interest dividends during the tax year of the corporation.

Line 24. Retained Earnings

If the corporation maintains separate accounts for appropriated and unappropriated retained earnings, it may want to continue such accounting for purposes of preparing its financial balance sheet. Also, if the corporation converts to C corporation status in a subsequent year, it will be required to report its appropriated and unappropriated retained earnings on separate lines of Schedule L of Form 1120.

Line 25. Adjustments to Shareholders' Equity

Some examples of adjustments to report on this line include:

- Unrealized gains and losses on securities held "available for sale."
- Foreign currency translation adjustments.
- The excess of additional pension liability over unrecognized prior service cost.
- Guarantees of employee stock (ESOP) debt.
- Compensation related to employee stock award plans.

If the total adjustment to be entered is a negative amount, enter the amount in parentheses.

Schedule M-1. Reconciliation of Income (Loss) per Books With Income (Loss) per Return

Line 2

Report on this line income included on Schedule K, lines 1, 2, 3c, 4, 5a, 6, 7, 8a, 9, and 10 not recorded on the books this year. Describe each such item of income. Attach a statement if necessary.

Line 3b. Travel and Entertainment

Include on this line:

- Meals and entertainment not allowed under section 274(n).
- Expenses for the use of an entertainment facility.
- The part of business gifts over $25.
- Expenses of an individual allocable to conventions on cruise ships over $2,000.
- Employee achievement awards over $400.
- The part of the cost of entertainment tickets that exceeds face value (also subject to 50% limit).
- The part of the cost of skyboxes that exceeds the face value of nonluxury box seat tickets.
- The part of the cost of luxury water travel not allowed under section 274(m).
- Expenses for travel as a form of education; nondeductible club dues.
- Other travel and entertainment expenses.

Note. If the corporation has an amount on lines 14l and 14m of Schedule K (foreign taxes paid and accrued), take both of these amounts into account for purposes of determining the amount of expenses and deductions to enter on lines 3 and 6.

Schedule M-2. Analysis of Accumulated Adjustments Account, Other Adjustments Account, and Shareholders' Undistributed Taxable Income Previously Taxed

Column (a). Accumulated Adjustments Account

The accumulated adjustments account (AAA) is an account of the S corporation that generally reflects the accumulated undistributed net income of the corporation for the corporation's post-1982 years. S corporations with accumulated E&P must maintain the AAA to determine the tax effect of distributions during S years and the post-termination transition period. An S corporation without accumulated E&P does not need to maintain the AAA in order to determine the tax effect of distributions. Nevertheless, if an S corporation without accumulated E&P engages in certain transactions to which section 381(a) applies, such as a merger into an S corporation with accumulated E&P, the S corporation must be able to calculate its AAA at the time of the merger for purposes of determining the tax effect of post-merger distributions. Therefore, it is recommended that the AAA be maintained by all S corporations.

On the first day of the corporation's first tax year as an S corporation, the balance of the AAA is zero. At the end of the tax year, adjust the AAA for the items as explained below and in the order listed.

1. Increase the AAA by income (other than tax-exempt income) and the excess of the deduction for depletion over the basis of the property subject to depletion (unless the property is an oil and gas property the basis of which has been allocated to shareholders).

2. Generally, decrease the AAA by deductible losses and expenses, nondeductible expenses (other than expenses related to tax-exempt income and federal taxes attributable to a C

corporation tax year), and the sum of the shareholders' deductions for depletion for any oil or gas property held by the corporation as described in section 1367(a)(2)(E). However, if the total decreases under 2 exceeds the total increases under 1 above, the excess is a "net negative adjustment." If the corporation has a net negative adjustment, do not take it into account under 2. Instead, take it into account only under 4 below.

3. Decrease AAA (but not below zero) by property distributions (other than dividend distributions from accumulated E&P), unless the corporation elects to reduce accumulated E&P first. See *Distributions* below for definitions and other details.

4. Decrease AAA by any net negative adjustment. For adjustments to the AAA for redemptions, reorganizations, and corporate separations, see Regulations section 1.1368-2(d).

Note. The AAA may have a negative balance at year end. See section 1368(e).

Column (b). Other Adjustments Account

The other adjustments account is adjusted for tax-exempt income (and related expenses) and federal taxes attributable to a C corporation tax year. After these adjustments are made, the account is reduced for any distributions made during the year. See *Distributions* below.

Column (c). Shareholders' Undistributed Taxable Income Previously Taxed

The shareholders' undistributed taxable income previously taxed account, also called previously taxed income (PTI), is maintained only if the corporation had a balance in this account at the start of its 2004 tax year. If there is a beginning balance for the 2004 tax year, no adjustments are made to the account except to reduce the account for distributions made under section 1375(d) (as in effect before the enactment of the Subchapter S Revision Act of 1982). See *Distributions* below for the order of distributions from the account.

Each shareholder's right to nontaxable distributions from PTI is personal and cannot be transferred to another person. The corporation is required to keep records of each shareholder's net share of PTI.

Distributions

General rule. Unless the corporation makes one of the elections described below, property distributions (including cash) are applied in the following order (to reduce accounts of the S corporation that are used to figure the tax effect of distributions made by the corporation to its shareholders):

1. Reduce the AAA determined without regard to any net negative adjustment for the tax year (but not below zero). If distributions during the tax year exceed the AAA at the close of the tax year determined without regard to any net negative adjustment for the tax year, the AAA is allocated pro rata to each distribution made during the tax year. See section 1368.

2. Reduce shareholders' PTI account for any section 1375(d) (as in effect before 1983) distributions. A distribution from the PTI account is tax free to the extent of a shareholder's basis in his or her stock in the corporation.

3. Reduce accumulated E&P. Generally, the S corporation has accumulated E&P only if it has not distributed E&P accumulated in prior years when the S corporation was a C corporation (section 1361(a)(2)). See section 312 for information on E&P. The only adjustments that can be made to the accumulated E&P of an S corporation are (a) reductions for dividend distributions; (b) adjustments for redemptions, liquidations, reorganizations, etc.; and (c) reductions for investment credit recapture tax for which the corporation is liable. See sections 1371(c) and (d)(3).

4. Reduce the other adjustments account (OAA).

5. Reduce any remaining shareholders' equity accounts.

Elections relating to source of distributions. The corporation may modify the above ordering rules by making one or more of the following elections:

Election to distribute accumulated E&P first. If the corporation has accumulated E&P and wants to distribute from this account before making distributions from the AAA, it may elect to do so with the consent of all its affected shareholders (section 1368(e)(3)(B)). This election is irrevocable and applies only for the tax year for which it is made. For details on making the election, see *Statement regarding elections* below.

Election to make a deemed dividend. If the corporation wants to distribute all or part of its accumulated E&P through a deemed dividend, it may elect to do so with the consent of all its affected shareholders (section 1368(e)(3)(B)). Under this election, the corporation will be treated as also having made the election to distribute accumulated E&P first. The amount of the deemed dividend cannot exceed the accumulated E&P at the end of the tax year, reduced by any actual distributions of accumulated E&P made during the tax year. A deemed dividend is treated as if it were a pro rata distribution of money to the shareholders, received by the shareholders, and immediately contributed back to the corporation, all on the last day of the tax year. This election is irrevocable and applies only for the tax year for which it is made. For details on making the election, see *Statement regarding elections* below.

Election to forego PTI. If the corporation wants to forego distributions of PTI, it may elect to do so with the consent of all its affected shareholders (section 1368(e)(3)(B)). Under this election, paragraph 2 under the *General rule* above does not apply to any distribution made during the tax year. This election is irrevocable and applies only for the tax year for which it is made. For details on making the election, see *Statement regarding elections* below.

Statement regarding elections. To make any of the above elections, the corporation must attach a statement to a timely filed original or amended Form 1120S for the tax year for which the election is made. In the statement, the corporation must identify the election it is making and must state that each shareholder consents to the election. The statement of election to make a deemed dividend must include the amount of the deemed dividend distributed to each shareholder. For more details on the election, see Temporary Regulations section 1.1368-1T(f)(5).

Example

The following example shows how the Schedule M-2 accounts are adjusted for items of income (loss), deductions, and distributions reported on Form 1120S. In this example, the corporation has no PTI or accumulated E&P.

Items per return are:

1. Page 1, line 21 income—$10,000
2. Schedule K, line 2 loss—($3,000)
3. Schedule K, line 4 income—$4,000
4. Schedule K, line 5a income—$16,000
5. Schedule K, line 12a deduction—$24,000
6. Schedule K, line 12e deduction—$3,000
7. Schedule K, line 13g work opportunity credit—$6,000
8. Schedule K, line 16a tax-exempt interest—$5,000
9. Schedule K, line 16c nondeductible expenses—$6,000 (reduction in salaries and wages for work opportunity credit), and
10. Schedule K, line 16d distributions—$65,000.

Based on items 1 through 10 above and starting balances of zero, the columns for the AAA and the other adjustments account are completed as shown in the Schedule M-2 Worksheet on page 32.

For the AAA, the worksheet line 3—$20,000 amount is the total of the Schedule K, lines 4 and 5a income of $4,000 and $16,000. The worksheet line 5—$36,000 amount is the total of the Schedule K, line 2 loss of ($3,000), line 12a (code A) deduction of $24,000, line 12e (code P) deduction of $3,000, and the line 16c nondeductible expenses of $6,000. The worksheet line 7 is zero. The AAA at the end of the tax year (figured without regard to distributions and the net negative adjustment of $6,000) is zero, and distributions cannot reduce the AAA below zero.

For the other adjustments account, the worksheet line 3 amount is the Schedule K, line 16a, tax-exempt interest income of $5,000. The worksheet line 7 amount is $5,000, reducing the other adjustments account to zero. The remaining $60,000 of distributions are not entered on Schedule M-2.

Privacy Act and Paperwork Reduction Act Notice. We ask for the information on this form to carry out the Internal Revenue laws of the United States. You are required to give us the information. We need it to ensure that you are complying with these laws and to allow us to figure and collect the right amount of tax. Section 6109 requires return preparers to provide their identifying numbers on the return.

You are not required to provide the information requested on a form that is subject to the Paperwork Reduction Act unless the form displays a valid OMB control number. Books or records relating to a form or its instructions must be retained as long as their contents may become material in the administration of any Internal Revenue law. Generally, tax returns and return information are confidential, as required by section 6103.

The time needed to complete and file this form and related schedules will vary depending on individual circumstances. The estimated average times are:

Form	Recordkeeping	Learning about the law or the form	Preparing the form	Copying, assembling, and sending the form to the IRS
1120S	65 hr., 45 min.	25 hr., 52 min.	48 hr., 27 min.	5 hr., 54 min.
Sch. D (1120S)	7 hr., 10 min.	4 hr., 37 min.	9 hr., 36 min.	1 hr., 20 min.
Sch. K-1 (1120S)	13 hr., 31 min.	11 hr., 24 min.	16 hr., 3 min.	1 hr., 4 min.

If you have comments concerning the accuracy of these time estimates or suggestions for making these forms simpler, we would be happy to hear from you. You can write to the Internal Revenue Service, Tax Products Coordinating Committee, SE:W:CAR:MP:T:T:SP, 1111 Constitution Avenue, NW, IR-6406, Washington, DC 20224. **Do not** send the tax form to this address. Instead, see *Where To File* on page 3.

Form 1120S

Codes for Principal Business Activity

This list of principal business activities and their associated codes is designed to classify an enterprise by the type of activity in which it is engaged to facilitate the administration of the Internal Revenue Code. These principal business activity codes are based on the North American Industry Classification System.

Using the list of activities and codes below, determine from which activity the company derives the largest percentage of its "total receipts." Total receipts is defined as the sum of gross receipts or sales (page 1, line 1a); all other income (page 1, lines 4 and 5); income reported on Schedule K, lines 4, 5a, and 6; income or net gain reported on Schedule K, lines 7, 8a, 9 and 10; and income or net gain reported on Form 8825, lines 2, 19 and 20a. If the company purchases raw materials and supplies them to a subcontractor to produce the finished product, but retains title to the product, the company is considered a manufacturer and must use one of the manufacturing codes (311110-339900).

Once the principal business activity is determined, enter the six-digit code from the list below on page 1, item B. Also enter a brief description of the business activity on page 2, Schedule B, line 2(a) and the principal product or service of the business on line 2(b).

Code

Agriculture, Forestry, Fishing and Hunting

Crop Production

111100 Oilseed & Grain Farming
111210 Vegetable & Melon Farming (including potatoes & yams)
111300 Fruit & Tree Nut Farming
111400 Greenhouse, Nursery, & Floriculture Production
111900 Other Crop Farming (including tobacco, cotton, sugarcane, hay, peanut, sugar beet & all other crop farming)

Animal Production

112111 Beef Cattle Ranching & Farming
112112 Cattle Feedlots
112120 Dairy Cattle & Milk Production
112210 Hog & Pig Farming
112300 Poultry & Egg Production
112400 Sheep & Goat Farming
112510 Animal Aquaculture (including shellfish & finfish farms & hatcheries)
112900 Other Animal Production

Forestry and Logging

113110 Timber Tract Operations
113210 Forest Nurseries & Gathering of Forest Products
113310 Logging

Fishing, Hunting and Trapping

114110 Fishing
114210 Hunting & Trapping

Support Activities for Agriculture and Forestry

115110 Support Activities for Crop Production (including cotton ginning, soil preparation, planting, & cultivating)
115210 Support Activities for Animal Production
115310 Support Activities For Forestry

Mining

211110 Oil & Gas Extraction
212110 Coal Mining
212200 Metal Ore Mining
212310 Stone Mining & Quarrying
212320 Sand, Gravel, Clay, & Ceramic & Refractory Minerals Mining & Quarrying
212390 Other Nonmetallic Mineral Mining & Quarrying
213110 Support Activities for Mining

Utilities

221100 Electric Power Generation, Transmission & Distribution
221210 Natural Gas Distribution
221300 Water, Sewage & Other Systems

Construction

Construction of Buildings

236110 Residential Building Construction
236200 Nonresidential Building Construction

Heavy and Civil Engineering Construction

237100 Utility System Construction
237210 Land Subdivision
237310 Highway, Street, & Bridge Construction

Code

237990 Other Heavy & Civil Engineering Construction

Specialty Trade Contractors

238100 Foundation, Structure, & Building Exterior Contractors (including framing carpentry, masonry, glass, roofing, & siding)
238210 Electrical Contractors
238220 Plumbing, Heating, & Air-Conditioning Contractors
238290 Other Building Equipment Contractors
238300 Building Finishing Contractors (including drywall, insulation, painting, wallcovering, flooring, tile, & finish carpentry)
238900 Other Specialty Trade Contractors (including site preparation)

Manufacturing

Food Manufacturing

311110 Animal Food Mfg
311200 Grain & Oilseed Milling
311300 Sugar & Confectionery Product Mfg
311400 Fruit & Vegetable Preserving & Specialty Food Mfg
311500 Dairy Product Mfg
311610 Animal Slaughtering and Processing
311710 Seafood Product Preparation & Packaging
311800 Bakeries & Tortilla Mfg
311900 Other Food Mfg (including coffee, tea, flavorings & seasonings)

Beverage and Tobacco Product Manufacturing

312110 Soft Drink & Ice Mfg
312120 Breweries
312130 Wineries
312140 Distilleries
312200 Tobacco Manufacturing

Textile Mills and Textile Product Mills

313000 Textile Mills
314000 Textile Product Mills

Apparel Manufacturing

315100 Apparel Knitting Mills
315210 Cut & Sew Apparel Contractors
315220 Men's & Boys' Cut & Sew Apparel Mfg
315230 Women's & Girls' Cut & Sew Apparel Mfg
315290 Other Cut & Sew Apparel Mfg
315990 Apparel Accessories & Other Apparel Mfg

Leather and Allied Product Manufacturing

316110 Leather & Hide Tanning & Finishing
316210 Footwear Mfg (including rubber & plastics)
316990 Other Leather & Allied Product Mfg

Wood Product Manufacturing

321110 Sawmills & Wood Preservation
321210 Veneer, Plywood, & Engineered Wood Product Mfg
321900 Other Wood Product Mfg

Paper Manufacturing

322100 Pulp, Paper, & Paperboard Mills

Code

322200 Converted Paper Product Mfg

Printing and Related Support Activities

323100 Printing & Related Support Activities

Petroleum and Coal Products Manufacturing

324110 Petroleum Refineries (including integrated)
324120 Asphalt Paving, Roofing, & Saturated Materials Mfg
324190 Other Petroleum & Coal Products Mfg

Chemical Manufacturing

325100 Basic Chemical Mfg
325200 Resin, Synthetic Rubber, & Artificial & Synthetic Fibers & Filaments Mfg
325300 Pesticide, Fertilizer, & Other Agricultural Chemical Mfg
325410 Pharmaceutical & Medicine Mfg
325500 Paint, Coating, & Adhesive Mfg
325600 Soap, Cleaning Compound, & Toilet Preparation Mfg
325900 Other Chemical Product & Preparation Mfg

Plastics and Rubber Products Manufacturing

326100 Plastics Product Mfg
326200 Rubber Product Mfg

Nonmetallic Mineral Product Manufacturing

327100 Clay Product & Refractory Mfg
327210 Glass & Glass Product Mfg
327300 Cement & Concrete Product Mfg
327400 Lime & Gypsum Product Mfg
327900 Other Nonmetallic Mineral Product Mfg

Primary Metal Manufacturing

331110 Iron & Steel Mills & Ferroalloy Mfg
331200 Steel Product Mfg from Purchased Steel
331310 Alumina & Aluminum Production & Processing
331400 Nonferrous Metal (except Aluminum) Production & Processing
331500 Foundries

Fabricated Metal Product Manufacturing

332110 Forging & Stamping
332210 Cutlery & Handtool Mfg
332300 Architectural & Structural Metals Mfg
332400 Boiler, Tank, & Shipping Container Mfg
332510 Hardware Mfg
332610 Spring & Wire Product Mfg
332700 Machine Shops; Turned Product; & Screw, Nut, & Bolt Mfg
332810 Coating, Engraving, Heat Treating, & Allied Activities
332900 Other Fabricated Metal Product Mfg

Machinery Manufacturing

333100 Agriculture, Construction, & Mining Machinery Mfg
333200 Industrial Machinery Mfg
333310 Commercial & Service Industry Machinery Mfg

Code

333410 Ventilation, Heating, Air-Conditioning, & Commercial Refrigeration Equipment Mfg
333510 Metalworking Machinery Mfg
333610 Engine, Turbine & Power Transmission Equipment Mfg
333900 Other General Purpose Machinery Mfg

Computer and Electronic Product Manufacturing

334110 Computer & Peripheral Equipment Mfg
334200 Communications Equipment Mfg
334310 Audio & Video Equipment Mfg
334410 Semiconductor & Other Electronic Component Mfg
334500 Navigational, Measuring, Electromedical, & Control Instruments Mfg
334610 Manufacturing & Reproducing Magnetic & Optical Media

Electrical Equipment, Appliance, and Component Manufacturing

335100 Electric Lighting Equipment Mfg
335200 Household Appliance Mfg
335310 Electrical Equipment Mfg
335900 Other Electrical Equipment & Component Mfg

Transportation Equipment Manufacturing

336100 Motor Vehicle Mfg
336210 Motor Vehicle Body & Trailer Mfg
336300 Motor Vehicle Parts Mfg
336410 Aerospace Product & Parts Mfg
336510 Railroad Rolling Stock Mfg
336610 Ship & Boat Building
336990 Other Transportation Equipment Mfg

Furniture and Related Product Manufacturing

337000 Furniture & Related Product Manufacturing

Miscellaneous Manufacturing

339110 Medical Equipment & Supplies Mfg
339900 Other Miscellaneous Manufacturing

Wholesale Trade

Merchant Wholesalers, Durable Goods

423100 Motor Vehicle & Motor Vehicle Parts & Supplies
423200 Furniture & Home Furnishings
423300 Lumber & Other Construction Materials
423400 Professional & Commercial Equipment & Supplies
423500 Metal & Mineral (except Petroleum)
423600 Electrical & Electronic Goods
423700 Hardware, & Plumbing & Heating Equipment & Supplies
423800 Machinery, Equipment, & Supplies
423910 Sporting & Recreational Goods & Supplies
423920 Toy & Hobby Goods & Supplies
423930 Recyclable Materials

Code

423940 Jewelry, Watch, Precious Stone, & Precious Metals
423990 Other Miscellaneous Durable Goods

Merchant Wholesalers, Nondurable Goods

424100 Paper & Paper Products
424210 Drugs & Druggists' Sundries
424300 Apparel, Piece Goods, & Notions
424400 Grocery & Related Products
424500 Farm Product Raw Materials
424600 Chemical & Allied Products
424700 Petroleum & Petroleum Products
424800 Beer, Wine, & Distilled Alcoholic Beverages
424910 Farm Supplies
424920 Book, Periodical, & Newspapers
424930 Flower, Nursery Stock, & Florists' Supplies
424940 Tobacco & Tobacco Products
424950 Paint, Varnish, & Supplies
424990 Other Miscellaneous Nondurable Goods

Wholesale Electronic Markets and Agents and Brokers

425110 Business to Business Electronic Markets
425120 Wholesale Trade Agents & Brokers

Retail Trade

Motor Vehicle and Parts Dealers

441110 New Car Dealers
441120 Used Car Dealers
441210 Recreational Vehicle Dealers
441221 Motorcycle Dealers
441222 Boat Dealers
441229 All Other Motor Vehicle Dealers
441300 Automotive Parts, Accessories, & Tire Stores

Furniture and Home Furnishings Stores

442110 Furniture Stores
442210 Floor Covering Stores
442291 Window Treatment Stores
442299 All Other Home Furnishings Stores

Electronics and Appliance Stores

443111 Household Appliance Stores
443112 Radio, Television, & Other Electronics Stores
443120 Computer & Software Stores
443130 Camera & Photographic Supplies Stores

Building Material and Garden Equipment and Supplies Dealers

444110 Home Centers
444120 Paint & Wallpaper Stores
444130 Hardware Stores
444190 Other Building Material Dealers
444200 Lawn & Garden Equipment & Supplies Stores

Food and Beverage Stores

445110 Supermarkets and Other Grocery (except Convenience) Stores
445120 Convenience Stores
445210 Meat Markets
445220 Fish & Seafood Markets
445230 Fruit & Vegetable Markets
445291 Baked Goods Stores
445292 Confectionery & Nut Stores
445299 All Other Specialty Food Stores
445310 Beer, Wine, & Liquor Stores

Health and Personal Care Stores

446110 Pharmacies & Drug Stores
446120 Cosmetics, Beauty Supplies, & Perfume Stores
446130 Optical Goods Stores

Code

446190 Other Health & Personal Care Stores

Gasoline Stations

447100 Gasoline Stations (including convenience stores with gas)

Clothing and Clothing Accessories Stores

448110 Men's Clothing Stores
448120 Women's Clothing Stores
448130 Children's & Infants' Clothing Stores
448140 Family Clothing Stores
448150 Clothing Accessories Stores
448190 Other Clothing Stores
448210 Shoe Stores
448310 Jewelry Stores
448320 Luggage & Leather Goods Stores

Sporting Goods, Hobby, Book, and Music Stores

451110 Sporting Goods Stores
451120 Hobby, Toy, & Game Stores
451130 Sewing, Needlework, & Piece Goods Stores
451140 Musical Instrument & Supplies Stores
451211 Book Stores
451212 News Dealers & Newsstands
451220 Prerecorded Tape, Compact Disc, & Record Stores

General Merchandise Stores

452110 Department Stores
452900 Other General Merchandise Stores

Miscellaneous Store Retailers

453110 Florists
453210 Office Supplies & Stationery Stores
453220 Gift, Novelty, & Souvenir Stores
453310 Used Merchandise Stores
453910 Pet & Pet Supplies Stores
453920 Art Dealers
453930 Manufactured (Mobile) Home Dealers
453990 All Other Miscellaneous Store Retailers (including tobacco, candle, & trophy shops)

Nonstore Retailers

454110 Electronic Shopping & Mail-Order Houses
454210 Vending Machine Operators
454311 Heating Oil Dealers
454312 Liquefied Petroleum Gas (Bottled Gas) Dealers
454319 Other Fuel Dealers
454390 Other Direct Selling Establishments (including door-to-door retailing, frozen food plan providers, party plan merchandisers, & coffee-break service providers)

Transportation and Warehousing

Air, Rail, and Water Transportation

481000 Air Transportation
482110 Rail Transportation
483000 Water Transportation

Truck Transportation

484110 General Freight Trucking, Local
484120 General Freight Trucking, Long-distance
484200 Specialized Freight Trucking

Transit and Ground Passenger Transportation

485110 Urban Transit Systems
485210 Interurban & Rural Bus Transportation
485310 Taxi Service
485320 Limousine Service
485410 School & Employee Bus Transportation
485510 Charter Bus Industry

Code

485990 Other Transit & Ground Passenger Transportation

Pipeline Transportation

486000 Pipeline Transportation

Scenic & Sightseeing Transportation

487000 Scenic & Sightseeing Transportation

Support Activities for Transportation

488100 Support Activities for Air Transportation
488210 Support Activities for Rail Transportation
488300 Support Activities for Water Transportation
488410 Motor Vehicle Towing
488490 Other Support Activities for Road Transportation
488510 Freight Transportation Arrangement
488990 Other Support Activities for Transportation

Couriers and Messengers

492110 Couriers
492210 Local Messengers & Local Delivery

Warehousing and Storage

493100 Warehousing & Storage (except lessors of miniwarehouses & self-storage units)

Information

Publishing Industries (except Internet)

511110 Newspaper Publishers
511120 Periodical Publishers
511130 Book Publishers
511140 Directory & Mailing List Publishers
511190 Other Publishers
511210 Software Publishers

Motion Picture and Sound Recording Industries

512100 Motion Picture & Video Industries (except video rental)
512200 Sound Recording Industries

Broadcasting (except Internet)

515100 Radio & Television Broadcasting
515210 Cable & Other Subscription Programming

Internet Publishing and Broadcasting

516110 Internet Publishing & Broadcasting

Telecommunications

517000 Telecommunications (including paging, cellular, satellite, cable & other program distribution, resellers, & other telecommunications)

Internet Service Providers, Web Search Portals, and Data Processing Services

518111 Internet Service Providers
518112 Web Search Portals
518210 Data Processing, Hosting, & Related Services

Other Information Services

519100 Other Information Services (including news syndicates & libraries)

Finance and Insurance

Depository Credit Intermediation

522110 Commercial Banking
522120 Savings Institutions
522130 Credit Unions
522190 Other Depository Credit Intermediation

Nondepository Credit Intermediation

522210 Credit Card Issuing
522220 Sales Financing
522291 Consumer Lending

Code

522292 Real Estate Credit (including mortgage bankers & originators)
522293 International Trade Financing
522294 Secondary Market Financing
522298 All Other Nondepository Credit Intermediation

Activities Related to Credit Intermediation

522300 Activities Related to Credit Intermediation (including loan brokers, check clearing, & money transmitting)

Securities, Commodity Contracts, and Other Financial Investments and Related Activities

523110 Investment Banking & Securities Dealing
523120 Securities Brokerage
523130 Commodity Contracts Dealing
523140 Commodity Contracts Brokerage
523210 Securities & Commodity Exchanges
523900 Other Financial Investment Activities (including portfolio management & investment advice)

Insurance Carriers and Related Activities

524140 Direct Life, Health, & Medical Insurance & Reinsurance Carriers
524150 Direct Insurance & Reinsurance (except Life, Health & Medical) Carriers
524210 Insurance Agencies & Brokerages
524290 Other Insurance Related Activities (including third-party administration of insurance and pension funds)

Funds, Trusts, and Other Financial Vehicles

525100 Insurance & Employee Benefit Funds
525910 Open-End Investment Funds (Form 1120-RIC)
525920 Trusts, Estates, & Agency Accounts
525930 Real Estate Investment Trusts (Form 1120-REIT)
525990 Other Financial Vehicles (including closed-end investment funds)

"Offices of Bank Holding Companies" and "Offices of Other Holding Companies" are located under **Management of Companies (Holding Companies)** on page 38.

Real Estate and Rental and Leasing

Real Estate

531110 Lessors of Residential Buildings & Dwellings
531114 Cooperative Housing
531120 Lessors of Nonresidential Buildings (except Miniwarehouses)
531130 Lessors of Miniwarehouses & Self-Storage Units
531190 Lessors of Other Real Estate Property
531210 Offices of Real Estate Agents & Brokers
531310 Real Estate Property Managers
531320 Offices of Real Estate Appraisers
531390 Other Activities Related to Real Estate

Rental and Leasing Services

532100 Automotive Equipment Rental & Leasing
532210 Consumer Electronics & Appliances Rental
532220 Formal Wear & Costume Rental

Code

532230 Video Tape & Disc Rental
532290 Other Consumer Goods Rental
532310 General Rental Centers
532400 Commercial & Industrial Machinery & Equipment Rental & Leasing

Lessors of Nonfinancial Intangible Assets (except copyrighted works)

533110 Lessors of Nonfinancial Intangible Assets (except copyrighted works)

Professional, Scientific, and Technical Services

Legal Services

541110 Offices of Lawyers
541190 Other Legal Services

Accounting, Tax Preparation, Bookkeeping, and Payroll Services

541211 Offices of Certified Public Accountants
541213 Tax Preparation Services
541214 Payroll Services
541219 Other Accounting Services

Architectural, Engineering, and Related Services

541310 Architectural Services
541320 Landscape Architecture Services
541330 Engineering Services
541340 Drafting Services
541350 Building Inspection Services
541360 Geophysical Surveying & Mapping Services
541370 Surveying & Mapping (except Geophysical) Services
541380 Testing Laboratories

Specialized Design Services

541400 Specialized Design Services (including interior, industrial, graphic, & fashion design)

Computer Systems Design and Related Services

541511 Custom Computer Programming Services
541512 Computer Systems Design Services
541513 Computer Facilities Management Services
541519 Other Computer Related Services

Other Professional, Scientific, and Technical Services

541600 Management, Scientific, & Technical Consulting Services
541700 Scientific Research & Development Services
541800 Advertising & Related Services
541910 Marketing Research & Public Opinion Polling
541920 Photographic Services
541930 Translation & Interpretation Services
541940 Veterinary Services
541990 All Other Professional, Scientific, & Technical Services

Management of Companies (Holding Companies)

551111 Offices of Bank Holding Companies
551112 Offices of Other Holding Companies

Code

Administrative and Support and Waste Management and Remediation Services

Administrative and Support Services

561110 Office Administrative Services
561210 Facilities Support Services
561300 Employment Services
561410 Document Preparation Services
561420 Telephone Call Centers
561430 Business Service Centers (including private mail centers & copy shops)
561440 Collection Agencies
561450 Credit Bureaus
561490 Other Business Support Services (including repossession services, court reporting, & stenotype services)
561500 Travel Arrangement & Reservation Services
561600 Investigation & Security Services
561710 Exterminating & Pest Control Services
561720 Janitorial Services
561730 Landscaping Services
561740 Carpet & Upholstery Cleaning Services
561790 Other Services to Buildings & Dwellings
561900 Other Support Services (including packaging & labeling services, & convention & trade show organizers)

Waste Management and Remediation Services

562000 Waste Management & Remediation Services

Educational Services

611000 Educational Services (including schools, colleges, & universities)

Health Care and Social Assistance

Offices of Physicians and Dentists

621111 Offices of Physicians (except mental health specialists)
621112 Offices of Physicians, Mental Health Specialists
621210 Offices of Dentists

Offices of Other Health Practitioners

621310 Offices of Chiropractors
621320 Offices of Optometrists
621330 Offices of Mental Health Practitioners (except Physicians)
621340 Offices of Physical, Occupational & Speech Therapists, & Audiologists
621391 Offices of Podiatrists
621399 Offices of All Other Miscellaneous Health Practitioners

Outpatient Care Centers

621410 Family Planning Centers
621420 Outpatient Mental Health & Substance Abuse Centers

Code

621491 HMO Medical Centers
621492 Kidney Dialysis Centers
621493 Freestanding Ambulatory Surgical & Emergency Centers
621498 All Other Outpatient Care Centers

Medical and Diagnostic Laboratories

621510 Medical & Diagnostic Laboratories

Home Health Care Services

621610 Home Health Care Services

Other Ambulatory Health Care Services

621900 Other Ambulatory Health Care Services (including ambulance services & blood & organ banks)

Hospitals

622000 Hospitals

Nursing and Residential Care Facilities

623000 Nursing & Residential Care Facilities

Social Assistance

624100 Individual & Family Services
624200 Community Food & Housing, & Emergency & Other Relief Services
624310 Vocational Rehabilitation Services
624410 Child Day Care Services

Arts, Entertainment, and Recreation

Performing Arts, Spectator Sports, and Related Industries

711100 Performing Arts Companies
711210 Spectator Sports (including sports clubs & racetracks)
711300 Promoters of Performing Arts, Sports, & Similar Events
711410 Agents & Managers for Artists, Athletes, Entertainers, & Other Public Figures
711510 Independent Artists, Writers, & Performers

Museums, Historical Sites, and Similar Institutions

712100 Museums, Historical Sites, & Similar Institutions

Amusement, Gambling, and Recreation Industries

713100 Amusement Parks & Arcades
713200 Gambling Industries
713900 Other Amusement & Recreation Industries (including golf courses, skiing facilities, marinas, fitness centers, & bowling centers)

Accommodation and Food Services

Accommodation

721110 Hotels (except Casino Hotels) & Motels
721120 Casino Hotels
721191 Bed & Breakfast Inns
721199 All Other Traveler Accommodation

Code

721210 RV (Recreational Vehicle) Parks & Recreational Camps
721310 Rooming & Boarding Houses

Food Services and Drinking Places

722110 Full-Service Restaurants
722210 Limited-Service Eating Places
722300 Special Food Services (including food service contractors & caterers)
722410 Drinking Places (Alcoholic Beverages)

Other Services

Repair and Maintenance

811110 Automotive Mechanical & Electrical Repair & Maintenance
811120 Automotive Body, Paint, Interior, & Glass Repair
811190 Other Automotive Repair & Maintenance (including oil change & lubrication shops & car washes)
811210 Electronic & Precision Equipment Repair & Maintenance
811310 Commercial & Industrial Machinery & Equipment (except Automotive & Electronic) Repair & Maintenance
811410 Home & Garden Equipment & Appliance Repair & Maintenance
811420 Reupholstery & Furniture Repair
811430 Footwear & Leather Goods Repair
811490 Other Personal & Household Goods Repair & Maintenance

Personal and Laundry Services

812111 Barber Shops
812112 Beauty Salons
812113 Nail Salons
812190 Other Personal Care Services (including diet & weight reducing centers)
812210 Funeral Homes & Funeral Services
812220 Cemeteries & Crematories
812310 Coin-Operated Laundries & Drycleaners
812320 Drycleaning & Laundry Services (except Coin-Operated)
812330 Linen & Uniform Supply
812910 Pet Care (except Veterinary) Services
812920 Photofinishing
812930 Parking Lots & Garages
812990 All Other Personal Services

Religious, Grantmaking, Civic, Professional, and Similar Organizations

813000 Religious, Grantmaking, Civic, Professional, & Similar Organizations (including condominium and homeowners associations)

Instructions for Schedule D (Form 1120S)

Capital Gains and Losses and Built-in Gains of an S Corporation

2004

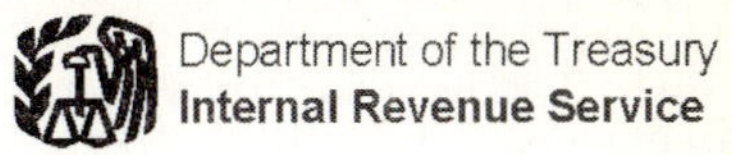

Instructions for Schedule D (Form 1120S)

Capital Gains and Losses and Built-In Gains

Section references are to the Internal Revenue Code unless otherwise noted.

General Instructions

Purpose of Schedule

Schedule D is used to report:

- Sales or exchanges of capital assets.
- Gains on distributions to shareholders of appreciated capital assets (referred to here as distributions).
- Nonbusiness bad debts.
- Net recognized built-in gain as defined in section 1374(d)(2). The built-in gains tax is figured in Part III of Schedule D.

Other Forms the Corporation May Have To File

Use Form 4797, Sales of Business Property, to report:

- Sales, exchanges, and distributions of property used in a trade or business.
- Sales, exchanges, and distributions of depreciable and amortizable property.
- Sales or other dispositions of securities or commodities held in connection with a trading business, if the corporation made a mark-to-market election (see page 4 of the Instructions for Form 1120S).
- Involuntary conversions (other than from casualties or thefts).
- The disposition of noncapital assets (other than inventory or property held primarily for sale to customers in the ordinary course of a trade or business).

Use Form 4684, Casualties and Thefts, to report involuntary conversions of property due to casualty or theft.

Use Form 6781, Gains and Losses From Section 1256 Contracts and Straddles, to report gains and losses from section 1256 contracts and straddles.

Use Form 8824, Like-Kind Exchanges, if the corporation made one or more like-kind exchange. A "like-kind exchange" occurs when business or investment property is exchanged for other business or investment property.

For exchanges of capital assets, enter the gain or loss from Form 8824, if any, on line 3 or line 9 in column (f) of Schedule D.

Capital Asset

Each item of property the corporation held (whether or not connected with its trade or business) is a capital asset except:

- Stock in trade or other property included in inventory or held mainly for sale to customers.
- Accounts or notes receivable acquired in the ordinary course of the trade or business for services rendered or from the sale of stock in trade or other property held mainly for sale to customers.
- Depreciable or real property used in the trade or business, even if it is fully depreciated.
- Certain copyrights; literary, musical, or artistic compositions; letters or memorandums; or similar property. See section 1221(a)(3).
- U.S. Government publications, including the Congressional Record, that the corporation received from the Government, other than by purchase at the normal sales price, or that the corporation got from another taxpayer who had received it in a similar way, if the corporation's basis is determined by reference to the previous owner.
- Certain commodities derivative financial instruments held by a dealer. See section 1221(a)(6).
- Certain hedging transactions entered into in the normal course of the trade or business. See section 1221(a)(7).
- Supplies regularly used in the trade or business.

Items for Special Treatment

Note: For more information, see Pub. 544, Sales and Other Dispositions of Assets.

Loss from a sale or exchange between the corporation and a related person. Except for distributions in complete liquidation of a corporation, no loss is allowed from the sale or exchange of property between the corporation and certain related persons. See section 267 for details.

Loss from a wash sale. The corporation cannot deduct a loss from a wash sale of stock or securities (including contracts or options to acquire or sell stock or securities) unless the corporation is a dealer in stock or securities and the loss was sustained in a transaction made in the ordinary course of the corporation's trade or business. A wash sale occurs if the corporation acquires (by purchase or exchange), or has a contract or option to acquire, substantially identical stock or securities within 30 days before or after the date of the sale or exchange. See section 1091 for more information.

Gain on distribution of appreciated property. Generally, gain (but not loss) is recognized on a nonliquidating distribution of appreciated property to the extent that the property's fair market value exceeds its adjusted basis. See section 311(b) for details.

Gain or loss on distribution of property in complete liquidation. Generally, gain or loss is recognized by a corporation upon the liquidating distribution of property as if it had sold the property at its fair market value. See section 336 for details and exceptions.

Gain or loss on certain short-term Federal, state, and municipal obligations. Such obligations are treated as capital assets in determining gain or loss. Gain realized is first treated as ordinary income; any balance remaining is considered short-term capital gain. See section 1271(a)(3).

Gain from installment sales. If the corporation sold property at a gain and will receive a payment in a tax year

Cat. No. 64419L

after the year of sale, it generally must report the sale on the installment method unless it elects not to. However, the installment method may not be used to report sales of stock or securities traded on an established securities market.

Use Form 6252, Installment Sale Income, to report the sale on the installment method. Also use Form 6252 to report any payment received during the tax year from a sale made in an earlier year that was reported on the installment method. To elect out of the installment method, report the full amount of the gain on Schedule D for the year of the sale on a return filed by the due date (including extensions). If the original return was filed on time, the corporation may make the election on an amended return filed no later than 6 months after the original due date (excluding extensions). Write "Filed pursuant to section 301.9100-2" at the top of the amended return.

Gain or loss on an option to buy or sell property. See sections 1032 and 1234 for the rules that apply to a purchaser or grantor of an option or a securities futures contract (as defined in section 1234B). For details, see Pub. 550, Investment Income and Expenses.

Gain or loss from a short sale of property. Report the gain or loss to the extent that the property used to close the short sale is considered a capital asset in the hands of the taxpayer.

Loss from securities that are capital assets that become worthless during the year. Except for securities held by a bank, treat the loss as a capital loss as of the last day of the tax year. See section 582 for the rules on the treatment of securities held by a bank.

Nonrecognition of gain on sale of stock to an employee stock ownership plan (ESOP) or an eligible cooperative. See section 1042 and Temporary Regulations section 1.1042-1T for rules under which a taxpayer may elect not to recognize gain from the sale of certain stock to an ESOP or an eligible cooperative.

Disposition of market discount bonds. See section 1276 for rules on the disposition of any market discount bonds. See Pub. 550 for more information.

Capital gain distributions. Report the total amount of capital gain distributions as long-term capital gain on line 10, column (f), regardless of how long the corporation held the investment.

Nonbusiness bad debts. A nonbusiness bad debt must be treated as a short-term capital loss and can be deducted only in the year the debt becomes totally worthless. For each bad debt, enter the name of the debtor and "schedule attached" in column (a) of line 1 and the amount of the bad debt as a loss in column (f). Also attach a statement of facts to support each bad debt deduction.

Real estate subdivided for sale. Certain lots or parcels that are part of a tract of real estate subdivided for sale may be treated as capital assets. See section 1237.

Sale of a partnership interest. A sale or other disposition of an interest in a partnership owning unrealized receivables or inventory items may result in ordinary gain or loss. See Pub. 541, Partnerships, for more details.

Special rules for traders in securities. Traders in securities are engaged in the business of buying and selling securities for their own account. To be engaged in a business as a trader in securities the corporation:

- Must seek to profit from daily market movements in the prices of securities and not from dividends, interest, or capital appreciation.
- Must be involved in a trading activity that is substantial.
- Must carry on the activity with continuity and regularity.

The following facts and circumstances should be considered in determining if a corporation's activity is a business:

- Typical holding periods for securities bought and sold.
- The frequency and dollar amount of the corporation's trades during the year.
- The extent to which the activity is pursued to produce income for a livelihood.
- The amount of time devoted to the activity.

Like an investor, a trader must report each sale of securities (taking into account commissions and any other costs of acquiring or disposing of the securities) on Schedule D or on an attached statement containing all the same information for each sale in a similar format. However, if a trader made the mark-to-market election (see page 4 of the Instructions for Form 1120S), each transaction is reported in Part II of Form 4797 instead of Schedule D.

The limitation on investment interest expense that applies to investors does not apply to interest paid or incurred in a trading business. A trader reports interest expense and other expenses (excluding commissions and other costs of acquiring and disposing of securities) from a trading business on page 1 of Form 1120S.

A trader also may hold securities for investment. The rules for investors generally will apply to those securities. Allocate interest and other expenses between a trading business and investment securities. Investment interest expense is reported on line 12c of Schedule K and in box 12, code I, of Schedule K-1.

Certain constructive ownership transactions. Gain in excess of the gain the corporation would have recognized if it had held a financial asset directly during the term of a derivative contract must be treated as ordinary income. See section 1260 for details.

Constructive sale treatment for certain appreciated positions. Generally, the corporation must recognize gain (but not loss) on the date it enters into a constructive sale of any appreciated interest in stock, a partnership interest, or certain debt instruments as if the position were disposed of at fair market value on that date.

The corporation is treated as making a constructive sale of an appreciated position if it (or a related person, in some cases) does one of the following:

- Enters into a short sale of the same or substantially identical property (i.e., a "short sale against the box").
- Enters into an offsetting notional principal contract relating to the same or substantially identical property.
- Enters into a futures or forward contract to deliver the same or substantially identical property.
- Acquires the same or substantially identical property (if the appreciated position is a short sale, offsetting notional principal contract, or a futures or forward contract).

Exception. Generally, constructive sale treatment does not apply if:

- The transaction was closed before the end of the 30th day after the end of the year in which it was entered into,
- The appreciated position to which the transaction relates was held throughout the 60-day period starting on the date the transaction was closed, **and**
- At no time during that 60-day period was the corporation's risk of loss reduced by holding certain other positions.

For details and other exceptions to these rules, see Pub. 550.

Gain from qualified stock. If the corporation sold qualified small business stock (defined below) that it held for more than 6 months, it may postpone gain if it purchased other qualified small business stock during the 60-day period that began on the date of the sale. The corporation must recognize gain to the extent the sale proceeds exceed the cost of the replacement stock.

Reduce the basis of the replacement stock by any postponed gain.

If the corporation chooses to postpone gain, report the entire gain realized on the sale on line 1 or 7. Directly below the line on which the corporation reported the gain, enter in column (a) "Section 1045 Rollover" and enter the amount of the postponed gain as a (loss) in column (f).

CAUTION *The corporation also must separately state the amount of the gain rolled over on qualified stock under section 1045 on Form 1120S, Schedule K, line 10, because each shareholder must determine if he or she qualifies for the rollover at the shareholder level. Also, the corporation must include on Schedule D, line 1 or 7 (and on Form 1120S, Schedule K, line 10), any gain that could qualify for the section 1045 rollover at the shareholder level instead of the corporate level (because a shareholder was entitled to purchase replacement stock). If the corporation had a gain on qualified stock that could qualify for the 50% exclusion under section 1202, report that gain on Schedule D, line 7 (and on Form 1120S, Schedule K, line 10).*

To be qualified small business stock, the stock must meet all of the following tests:

- It must be stock in a C corporation.
- It must have been originally issued after August 10, 1993.
- As of the date the stock was issued, the C corporation was a qualified small business. A qualified small business is a domestic C corporation with total gross assets of $50 million or less (a) at all times after August 9, 1993, and before the stock was issued, and (b) immediately after the stock was issued. Gross assets include those of any predecessor of the corporation. All corporations that are members of the same parent-subsidiary controlled group are treated as one corporation.
- The corporation must have acquired the stock at its original issue (either directly or through an underwriter), either in exchange for money or other property or as pay for services (other than as an underwriter) to the corporation. In certain cases, the corporation may meet the test if it acquired the stock from another person who met this test (such as by gift or inheritance) or through a conversion or exchange of qualified small business stock held by the corporation.
- During substantially all the time the corporation held the stock:

1. The issuer was a C corporation,
2. At least 80% of the value of the issuer's assets were used in the active conduct of one or more qualified businesses (defined below), and
3. The issuing corporation was not a foreign corporation, DISC, former DISC, corporation that has made (or that has a subsidiary that has made) a section 936 election, regulated investment company, real estate investment trust, REMIC, FASIT, or cooperative.

Note: A specialized small business investment company (SSBIC) is treated as having met test ***2*** above.

A qualified business is any business other than the following:

- One involving services performed in the fields of health, law, engineering, architecture, accounting, actuarial science, performing arts, consulting, athletics, financial services, or brokerage services.
- One whose principal asset is the reputation or skill of one or more employees.
- Any banking, insurance, financing, leasing, investing, or similar business.
- Any farming business (including the raising or harvesting of trees).
- Any business involving the production of products for which percentage depletion can be claimed.
- Any business of operating a hotel, motel, restaurant, or similar business.

Exclusion of Gain from DC Zone Assets. If the corporation sold or exchanged a District of Columbia Enterprise Zone (DC Zone) asset that it held for more than 5 years, it may be able to exclude the qualified capital gain. The sale or exchange of DC Zone capital assets reported on Schedule D include:

- Stock in a domestic corporation that was a DC Zone business.
- Interest in a partnership that was a DC Zone business.

Report the sale or exchange of property used in the corporation's DC Zone business on Form 4797.

Gains not qualified for exclusion. The following gains do not qualify for the exclusion of gain from DC Zone assets.

- Gain on the sale of an interest in a partnership, which is a DC Zone business, attributable to unrecaptured section 1250 gain. See the instructions for line 8c of Schedule K for information on how to report unrecaptured section 1250 gain.
- Gain on the sale of an interest in a partnership attributable to real property or an intangible asset which is not an integral part of the DC Zone business.
- Gain from a related-party transaction. See *Sales and Exchanges Between Related Persons* in chapter 2 of Pub. 544.

See Pub. 954, Tax Incentives for Distressed Communities, and section 1400B for more details on DC Zone assets and special rules.

How to report. Report the entire gain realized from the sale or exchange on Schedule D, Part II, line 7, as you otherwise would without regard to the exclusion. To report the exclusion, enter "DC Zone Asset Exclusion" as a separate entry on line 7, column (a) and enter as a (loss) in column (f) the amount of the exclusion.

Rollover of gain from empowerment zone investments. If the corporation sold a qualified empowerment zone asset it held for more than one year, it may be able to elect to postpone part or all of the gain. For details, see Pub. 954 and section 1397B.

Collectibles (28%) rate gain or (loss). Report any 28% gain or loss on line 8b of Schedule K (and each shareholder's share in box 8b of Schedule K-1). A collectibles gain or loss is any long-term gain or deductible long-term loss from the sale or exchange of a collectible that is a capital asset.

Collectibles include works of art, rugs, antiques, metals (such as gold, silver, and platinum bullion), gems, stamps, coins, alcoholic beverages, and certain other tangible property.

Also include gain (but not loss) from the sale or exchange of an interest in a partnership or trust held more than 1 year and attributable to unrealized appreciation of collectibles. For details, see Regulations section 1.1(h)-1. Also, attach the statement required under Regulations section 1.1(h)-1(e).

Specific Instructions

Parts I and II

Generally, report sales or exchanges (including like-kind exchanges) even if there is no gain or loss. In Part I, report the sale, exchange, or distribution of capital assets held 1 year or less. In Part II, report the sale, exchange, or distribution of capital assets held more than 1 year. Use the trade dates for the dates of acquisition and sale of stocks and bonds traded on an exchange or over-the-counter market.

Column (b)—Date acquired. The acquisition date for an asset the corporation held on January 1, 2001, for which it made an election to recognize any gain on a deemed sale, is the date of the deemed sale and reacquisition.

Column (e)—Cost or other basis. In determining gain or loss, the basis of property is generally its cost (see section 1012 and related regulations). These rules may apply to the corporation on the receipt of certain distributions with respect to stock (section 301), liquidation of another corporation (334), transfer to another corporation (358), transfer from a shareholder or reorganization (362), bequest (1014), contribution or gift (1015), tax-free exchange (1031), involuntary conversion (1033), certain asset acquisitions (1060), or wash sale of stock (1091). Attach an explanation if you use a basis other than actual cash cost of the property. See Pub. 551, Basis of Assets, for more details.

If the corporation is allowed a charitable contribution deduction because it sold property to a charitable organization for less than its fair market value (a "bargain sale"), figure the adjusted basis for determining gain from the sale by dividing the amount realized by the fair market value and multiplying that result by the adjusted basis.

If the corporation elected to recognize gain on an asset held on January 1, 2001, its basis in the asset is its closing market price or fair market value, whichever applies, on the date of the deemed sale and reacquisition, whether the deemed sale resulted in a gain or unallowed loss.

See section 852(f) for the treatment of certain load charges incurred in acquiring stock in a mutual fund with a reinvestment right.

Before making an entry in column (e), increase the cost or other basis by any expense of sale, such as broker's fees, commissions, option premiums, and state and local transfer taxes, unless the net sales price was reported in column (d).

Column (f)—Gain or (loss). Make a separate entry in this column for each transaction reported on lines 1 and 7 and any other line(s) that apply to the corporation. For lines 1 and 7, subtract the amount in column (e) from the amount in column (d). Enter negative amounts in parentheses.

Part III—Built-In Gains Tax

Section 1374 provides for a tax on built-in gains, without regard to when S corporation status was elected, if the corporation sold or exchanged an asset acquired from a C corporation with a basis determined by reference to its basis (or the basis of any other property) in the hands of a C corporation.

Line 14. Enter the amount that would be the taxable income of the corporation for the tax year if only recognized built-in gains (including any carryover of gain under section 1374(d)(2)(B)) and recognized built-in losses were taken into account.

Section 1374(d)(3) defines a recognized built-in gain as any gain recognized during the recognition period (the 10-year period beginning on the first day of the first tax year for which the corporation is an S corporation, or beginning the date the asset was acquired by the S corporation, for an asset with a basis determined by reference to its basis (or the basis of any other property) in the hands of a C corporation) on the sale or distribution (disposition) of any asset, except to the extent the corporation establishes that—

- The asset was not held by the corporation as of the beginning of the first tax year the corporation was an S corporation (except this does not apply to an asset acquired by the S corporation with a basis determined by reference to its basis (or the basis of any other property) in the hands of a C corporation), or
- The gain exceeds the excess of the fair market value of the asset as of the start of the first tax year (or as of the date the asset was acquired by the S corporation, for an asset with a basis determined by reference to its basis (or the basis of any other property) in the hands of a C corporation) over the adjusted basis of the asset at that time.

Certain transactions involving the disposal of timber, coal, or domestic iron ore under section 631 are not subject to the built-in gains tax. For details, see Rev. Rul. 2001-50, 2001-43 I.R.B. 343.

Section 1374(d)(4) defines a recognized built-in loss as any loss recognized during the recognition period (stated above) on the disposition of any asset to the extent the corporation establishes that—

- The asset was held by the corporation as of the beginning of the first tax year the corporation was an S corporation (except that this does not apply to an asset acquired by the S corporation with a basis determined by reference to its basis (or the basis of any other property) in the hands of a C corporation), and
- The loss does not exceed the excess of the adjusted basis of the asset as of the beginning of the first tax year (or as of the date the asset was acquired by the S corporation, for an asset with a basis determined by reference to its basis (or the basis of any other property) in the hands of a C corporation), over the fair market value of the asset as of that time.

The corporation must show on an attachment its total net recognized built-in gain and list separately any capital gain or loss and ordinary gain or loss.

Line 15. Figure taxable income by completing lines 1 through 28 of Form 1120. Follow the instructions for Form 1120. Enter the amount from line 28 of Form 1120 on line 15 of Schedule D. Attach to Schedule D the Form 1120 computation or other worksheet used to figure taxable income.

Note: Taxable income is defined in section 1375(b)(1)(B) and is generally figured in the same manner as taxable income for line 9 of the worksheet for line 22a of Form 1120S (see page 17 of the Instructions for Form 1120S).

Line 16. If for any tax year the amount on line 14 exceeds the taxable income on line 15, the excess is treated as a recognized built-in gain in the succeeding tax year. This carryover provision applies only in the case of an S corporation that made its election to be an S corporation after March 30, 1988. See section 1374(d)(2)(B).

Line 17. Enter the section 1374(b)(2) deduction. Generally, this is any net operating loss carryforward or capital loss carryforward (to the extent of net capital gain included in recognized built-in gain for the tax year) arising in tax years for which the corporation was a C corporation. See section 1374(b)(2) and Regulation 1.1374-5 for details.

Line 21. The built-in gains tax is treated as a loss sustained by the corporation during the same tax year. Deduct the tax attributable to:

- Ordinary gain as a deduction for taxes on Form 1120S, line 12.
- Short-term capital gain as short-term capital loss on Schedule D, line 5.
- Long-term capital gain as long-term capital loss on Schedule D, line 12.

Instructions for Schedule K-1 (Form 1120S)

Shareholder's Share of Income, Credits, Deductions, etc.

2004

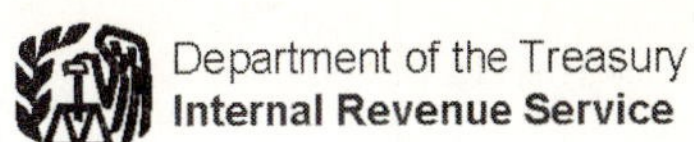

Department of the Treasury
Internal Revenue Service

Shareholder's Instructions for Schedule K-1 (Form 1120S)

Shareholder's Share of Income, Deductions, Credits, etc. (For Shareholder's Use Only)

Section references are to the Internal Revenue Code unless otherwise noted.

What's New

- Schedule K-1 has been redesigned. Codes are used to identify many of the items on the schedule and, if necessary, statements are attached to provide additional information. See the instructions for Part III on page 4 for more information on the codes and attached statements.
- You can use the new worksheet on page 2 to keep track of the basis of your stock.

General Instructions

Purpose of Schedule K-1

The corporation uses Schedule K-1 (Form 1120S) to report your pro rata share of the corporation's income (reduced by any tax the corporation paid on the income), deductions, credits, etc. Keep it for your records. Do not file it with your tax return. The corporation has filed a copy with the IRS.

Although the corporation may have to pay a built-in gains tax and an excess net passive income tax, you are liable for income tax on your share of the corporation's income, whether or not distributed, and you must include your share on your tax return if a return is required. Your pro rata share of S corporation income is not self-employment income and it is not subject to self-employment tax.

Schedule K-1 does not show the amount of actual dividend distributions the corporation made to you. The corporation must report such amounts totaling $10 or more for the calendar year on Form 1099-DIV, Dividends and Distributions.

Inconsistent Treatment of Items

Generally, you must report subchapter S items shown on your Schedule K-1 (and any attached schedules) the same way that the corporation treated the items on its return.

If the treatment on your original or amended return is inconsistent with the corporation's treatment, or if the corporation has not filed a return, you must file Form 8082, Notice of Inconsistent Treatment or Administrative Adjustment Request (AAR), with your original or amended return to identify and explain any inconsistency (or to note that a corporate return has not been filed).

If you are required to file Form 8082, but fail to do so, you may be subject to the accuracy-related penalty. This penalty is in addition to any tax that results from making your amount or treatment of the item consistent with that shown on the corporation's return. Any deficiency that results from making the amounts consistent may be assessed immediately.

Errors

If you believe the corporation has made an error on your Schedule K-1, notify the corporation and ask for a corrected Schedule K-1. Do not change any items on your copy of Schedule K-1. Be sure that the corporation sends a copy of the corrected Schedule K-1 to the IRS. If you are unable to reach agreement with the corporation regarding the inconsistency, you must file Form 8082.

International Boycotts

Every corporation that had operations in, or related to, a boycotting country, company, or national of a country, must file Form 5713, International Boycott Report.

If the corporation cooperated with an international boycott, it must give you a copy of its Form 5713. You must file your own Form 5713 to report the corporation's activities and any other boycott operations that you may have. You may lose certain tax benefits if the corporation participated in, or cooperated with, an international boycott. See Form 5713 and its instructions for more information.

Elections

Generally, the corporation decides how to figure taxable income from its operations. For example, it chooses the accounting method and depreciation methods it will use. However, certain elections are made by you separately on your income tax return and not by the corporation. These elections are made under the following code sections:

- Section 59(e) (deduction of certain qualified expenditures ratably over the period of time specified in that section). For more information, see the instructions for code K in box 12.
- Section 263A(d) (preproductive expenses). See the instructions for code M in box 12.
- Section 617 (deduction and recapture of certain mining exploration expenditures), and
- Section 901 (foreign tax credit).

If the corporation attaches a statement to Schedule K-1 indicating that it has changed its tax year and that you may elect to report your pro rata share of the income attributable to that change ratably over 4 tax years, see Rev. Proc. 2003-79, 2003-45 I.R.B. 1036 for details on making the election. To make the election, you must file Form 8082 with your income tax return for each of the 4 tax years. File Form 8082 for this purpose in accordance with Rev. Proc. 2003-79 instead of the Form 8082 instructions.

Additional Information

For more information on the treatment of S corporation income, deductions, credits, etc., see Pub. 535, Business Expenses; Pub. 550, Investment Income and Expenses; and Pub. 925, Passive Activity and At-Risk Rules.

To get forms and publications, see the instructions for your tax return.

Limitations on Losses, Deductions, and Credits

There are three separate potential limitations on the amount of losses passed to the shareholder that you may deduct on your return. These limitations and the order in which you must apply them are as follows: the basis rules, the at-risk limitations, and the passive activity limitations. Each of these limitations is discussed separately below.

Other limitations may apply to specific deductions (for example, the section 179 expense deduction). Generally, specific limitations apply before the basis, at-risk, and passive limitations.

Basis Rules

Generally, the deduction for your share of aggregate losses and deductions reported on Schedule K-1 is limited to the basis of your stock (determined with regard to distributions received during the tax year) and loans from you to the corporation. The basis of your stock is figured at year-end. Any losses and deductions not allowed this year because of the basis limit can be carried forward indefinitely and deducted in a later year subject to the basis limit for that year.

You are responsible for maintaining records to show the computation of the basis of your stock in the corporation. Schedule K-1 provides information to help you make the computation at the end of each corporate tax year. The basis of your stock (generally, its cost) is adjusted as follows and, except as noted, in the order listed. In addition, basis may be adjusted under other provisions of the Internal Revenue Code. You may use the worksheet on the next page to figure your aggregate stock basis.

1. Basis is increased by (a) all income (including tax-exempt income) reported on Schedule K-1 and (b) the excess of the deduction for depletion (other than oil and gas depletion) over the basis of the property subject to depletion.

Cat. No. 11521O

You must report the taxable income on your return (if you are required to file one) for it to increase your basis.

Basis is not increased by income from discharge of your indebtedness in the S corporation (nor by the amount included in income with respect to qualified zone academy bonds).

2. Basis is decreased by property distributions (including cash) made by the corporation (excluding dividend distributions reported on Form 1099-DIV and distributions in excess of basis) reported on Schedule K-1, box 16, code D.

3. Basis is decreased by (a) nondeductible expenses and (b) the depletion deduction for any oil and gas property held by the corporation, but only to the extent your pro rata share of the property's adjusted basis exceeds that deduction.

4. Basis is decreased by all deductible losses and deductions reported on Schedule K-1.

You may elect to decrease your basis under 4 above prior to decreasing your basis under 3 above. If you make this election, any amount described under 3 that exceeds the basis of your stock and debt owed to you by the corporation is treated as an amount described under 3 for the following tax year. To make the election, attach a statement to your timely filed original or amended return that states you agree to the carryover rule of Regulations section 1.1367-1(g) and the name of the S corporation to which the rule applies. Once made, the election applies to the year for which it is made and all future tax years for that S corporation, unless the IRS agrees to revoke your election.

The basis of each share of stock is increased or decreased (but not below zero) based on its pro rata share of the above adjustments. If the total decreases in basis attributable to a share exceed that share's basis, the excess reduces (but not below zero) the remaining bases of all other shares of stock in proportion to the remaining basis of each of those shares.

Basis of loans. The basis of your loans to the corporation is generally the balance the corporation owes you, adjusted for any reductions and restorations of loan basis (see the instructions for box 16, code E). Any amounts described in **3** and **4** above not used to offset amounts in **1** above, or reduce your stock basis, are used to reduce your loan basis (to the extent of such basis prior to such reduction).

When determining your basis in loans to the corporation, remember that:

- *Distributions do not reduce loan basis, and*
- *Loans that a shareholder guarantees or co-signs are not part of a shareholder's loan basis.*

See section 1367 and its regulations for more details.

Worksheet instructions. For lines 6 and 7, do not enter more than the aggregate sum of the preceding lines. Any excess of the amounts that would otherwise be entered on lines 6 and 7 without regard to this limit over the amounts actually entered on those lines is a reduction to your basis, if any, in loans you made to the corporation (to the extent of such basis). Any portion of the excess not used to reduce your basis in stock and loans is not deductible in the current year and is carried over to next year and subject to that year's basis limit. See the preceding instructions for more details.

At-Risk Limitations

Generally, you will have to complete Form 6198, At-Risk Limitations, to figure your allowable loss, if you have:

1. A loss or other deduction from any activity carried on by the corporation as a trade or business or for the production of income, and
2. Amounts in the activity for which you are not at risk.

The at-risk rules generally limit the amount of loss and other deductions that you can claim to the amount you could actually lose in the activity. These losses and deductions include a loss on the disposition of assets and the section 179 expense deduction. However, if you acquired your stock before 1987, the at-risk rules do not apply to losses from an activity of holding real property placed in service before 1987 by the corporation. The activity of holding mineral property does not qualify for this exception. The corporation should identify on an attachment to Schedule K-1 the amount of any losses that are not subject to the at-risk limitations.

Generally, you are not at risk for amounts such as the following:

- The basis of your stock in the corporation or basis of your loans to the corporation if the cash or other property used to purchase the stock or make the loans was from a source (a) covered by nonrecourse indebtedness (except for certain qualified nonrecourse financing, as defined in section 465(b)(6)); (b) protected against loss by a guarantee, stop-loss agreement, or other similar arrangement; or (c) that is covered by indebtedness from a person who has an interest in the activity or from a related person to a person (except you) having such an interest, other than a creditor.
- Any cash or property contributed to a corporate activity, or your interest in the corporate activity, that is (a) covered by nonrecourse indebtedness (except for certain qualified nonrecourse financing, as defined in section 465(b)(6)); (b) protected against loss by a guarantee, stop-loss agreement, or other similar arrangement; or (c) that is covered by indebtedness from a person who has an interest in such activity or from a related person to a person (except you) having such an interest, other than a creditor.

Any loss from a section 465 activity not allowed for this tax year will be treated as a deduction allocable to the activity in the next tax year.

You should get a separate statement of income, expenses, etc., for each activity from the corporation.

Passive Activity Limitations

Section 469 provides rules that limit the deduction of certain losses and credits. These rules apply to shareholders who:

- Are individuals, estates, or trusts and
- Have a passive activity loss or credit for the year.

Generally, passive activities include:

1. Trade or business activities in which you did not materially participate and
2. Activities that meet the definition of rental activities under Temporary Regulations section 1.469-1T(e)(3) and Regulations section 1.469-1(e)(3).

Passive activities do not include:

1. Trade or business activities in which you materially participated.
2. Rental real estate activities in which you materially participated if you were a "real estate professional" for the tax year. You were a real estate professional only if you met both of the following conditions:

a. More than half of the personal services you performed in trades or businesses were performed in real property trades or businesses in which you materially participated and

b. You performed more than 750 hours of services in real property trades or businesses in which you materially participated.

Worksheet for Determining a Shareholder's Stock Basis
(Keep for your records.)

1.	Your stock basis at the beginning of the year	**1.** ______
	Increases:	
2.	Money and your adjusted basis in property contributed to the corporation	**2.** ______
3.	Your share of the corporation's income, including tax-exempt income, (reduced by the amount included in income with respect to the qualified zone academy bonds)	**3.** ______
4.	Other increases to basis, including your share of the excess of the deductions for depletion (other than oil and gas depletion) over the basis of the property subject to depletion	**4.** ______
	Decreases:	
5.	Distributions of money and the fair market value of property (excluding dividend distributions reportable on Form 1099-DIV and distributions in excess of basis)	**5.** ( )
6.	Enter: **(a)** Your share of the corporation's nondeductible expenses and the depletion deduction for any oil and gas property held by the corporation (but only to the extent your pro rata share of the property's adjusted basis exceeds the depletion deduction) **or (b)** If the election under Regulations section 1.1367-1(g) applies, your share of the corporation's deductions and losses (include your entire share of the section 179 expense deduction even if your allowable section 179 expense deduction is smaller)	**6.** ( )
7.	If the election under Regulations section 1.1367-1(g) applies, enter the amount from (a) on line 6. Otherwise enter the amount from (b) on line 6	**7.** ( )
8.	Enter the smaller of **(a)** the excess of the amount you are owed for loans you made to the corporation over your basis in those loans **or (b)** the sum of lines 1 through 7. This amount increases your loan basis	**8.** ( )
9.	Your stock basis in the corporation at end of year. Combine lines 1 through 8	**9.** ______

For purposes of this rule, each interest in rental real estate is a separate activity, unless you elect to treat all interests in rental real estate as one activity. For details on making this election, see the Instructions for Schedule E (Form 1040).

If you are married filing jointly, either you or your spouse must separately meet both of the above conditions, without taking into account services performed by the other spouse.

A real property trade or business is any real property development, redevelopment, construction, reconstruction, acquisition, conversion, rental, operation, management, leasing, or brokerage trade or business. Services you performed as an employee are not treated as performed in a real property trade or business unless you owned more than 5% of the stock (or more than 5% of the capital or profits interest) in the employer.

3. The rental of a dwelling unit any shareholder used for personal purposes during the year for more than the greater of 14 days or 10% of the number of days that the residence was rented at fair rental value.

4. Activities of trading personal property for the account of owners of interests in the activities.

The corporation will identify separately each activity that may be passive to you. If the corporation had more than one activity it will attach a statement that (a) identifies each activity (trade or business activity, rental real estate activity, rental activity other than rental real estate, etc.); (b) specifies the income (loss), deductions, and credits from each activity; and (c) provides other details you may need to determine if an activity loss or credit is subject to the passive activity limitations.

If you have a passive activity loss or credit, see Form 8582, Passive Activity Loss Limitations, to figure your allowable passive losses, and Form 8582-CR, Passive Activity Credit Limitations, to figure your allowable passive credit. See the instructions for these forms for more information.

Material participation. You must determine if you materially participated (a) in each trade or business activity held through the corporation and (b), if you were a real estate professional (defined above), in each rental real estate activity held through the corporation. All determinations of material participation are made based on your participation during the corporation's tax year.

Material participation standards for shareholders who are individuals are listed below. Special rules apply to certain retired or disabled farmers and to the surviving spouses of farmers. See the Instructions for Form 8582 for details.

Individuals. If you are an individual, you materially participate in a trade or business activity only if one or more of the following apply:

1. You participated in the activity for more than 500 hours during the tax year.

2. Your participation in the activity for the tax year constituted substantially all of the participation in the activity of all individuals (including individuals who are not owners of interests in the activity).

3. You participated in the activity for more than 100 hours during the tax year, and your participation in the activity for the tax year was not less than the participation in the activity of any other individual (including individuals who were not owners of interests in the activity) for the tax year.

4. The activity was a significant participation activity for the tax year, and your aggregate participation in all significant participation activities (including those outside the corporation) during the tax year exceeded 500 hours. A significant participation activity is any trade or business activity in which you participated for more than 100 hours during the year and in which you did not materially participate under any of the material participation tests (other than this test 4).

5. You materially participated in the activity for any 5 tax years (whether or not consecutive) during the 10 tax years that immediately precede the tax year.

6. The activity was a personal service activity and you materially participated in the activity for any 3 tax years (whether or not consecutive) preceding the tax year. A personal service activity involves the performance of personal services in the fields of health, law, engineering, architecture, accounting, actuarial science, performing arts, consulting, or any other trade or business, in which capital is not a material income-producing factor.

7. Based on all of the facts and circumstances, you participated in the activity on a regular, continuous, and substantial basis during the tax year.

Work counted toward material participation. Generally, any work that you or your spouse does in connection with an activity held through an S corporation (in which you own stock at the time the work is done) is counted toward material participation. However, work in connection with an activity is not counted toward material participation if either of the following applies:

1. The work is not the type of work that owners of the activity would usually do and one of the principal purposes of the work that you or your spouse does is to avoid the passive loss or credit limitations.

2. You do the work in your capacity as an investor and you are not directly involved in the day-to-day operations of the activity. Examples of work done as an investor that would not count toward material participation include:

a. Studying and reviewing financial statements or reports on operations of the activity,

b. Preparing or compiling summaries or analyses of the finances or operations of the activity, and

c. Monitoring the finances or operations of the activity in a nonmanagerial capacity.

Effect of determination. If you determine that you (a) materially participated in a trade or business activity of the corporation or (b) were a real estate professional (defined on page 2) in a rental real estate activity of the corporation, the income (loss), deductions, and credits from the activity are nonpassive. See the specific instructions for each item for reporting information.

If you determine that you did not materially participate in a trade or business activity of the corporation, or you have income (loss), deductions, or credits from a rental activity of the corporation (other than a rental real estate activity in which you materially participated, if you were a real estate professional), the amounts from that activity are passive. Report passive income (losses), deductions, and credits as follows:

1. If you have an overall gain (the excess of income over deductions and losses, including any prior year unallowed loss) from a passive activity, report the income, deductions, and losses from the activity as indicated in these instructions.

2. If you have an overall loss (the excess of deductions and losses, including any prior year unallowed loss, over income) or credits from a passive activity, you must report the income, deductions, losses, and credits from all passive activities using the Instructions for Form 8582 or Form 8582-CR, to see if your deductions, losses, and credits are limited under the passive activity rules.

Special allowance for a rental real estate activity. If you actively participated in a rental real estate activity, you may be able to deduct up to $25,000 of the loss from the activity from nonpassive income. This special allowance is an exception to the general rule disallowing losses in excess of income from passive activities. The special allowance is not available if you were married, are filing a separate return for the year, and did not live apart from your spouse at all times during the year.

Only individuals and qualifying estates can actively participate in a rental real estate activity. Estates (other than qualifying estates) and trusts cannot actively participate.

You are not considered to actively participate in a rental real estate activity if, at any time during the tax year, your interest (including your spouse's interest) in the activity was less than 10% (by value) of all interests in the activity.

Active participation is a less stringent requirement than material participation. You may be treated as actively participating if you participated, for example, in making management decisions or arranging for others to provide services (such as repairs) in a significant and bona fide sense. Management decisions that can count as active participation include approving new tenants, deciding on rental terms, approving capital or repair expenditures, and other similar decisions.

An estate is a qualifying estate if the decedent would have satisfied the active participation requirement for the activity for the tax year the decedent died. A qualifying estate is treated as actively participating for tax years ending less than 2 years after the date of the decedent's death.

Modified adjusted gross income limitation. The maximum special allowance that single individuals and married individuals filing a joint return can qualify for is $25,000. The maximum is $12,500 for married individuals who file separate returns and who lived apart at all times during the year. The maximum special allowance for which an estate can qualify is $25,000 reduced by the special allowance for which the surviving spouse qualifies.

If your modified adjusted gross income (defined below) is $100,000 or less ($50,000 or less if married filing separately), your loss is deductible up to the amount of the maximum special allowance referred to in the preceding paragraph. If your modified adjusted gross income is more than $100,000 (more than $50,000 if married filing separately), the special allowance is limited to 50% of the difference between $150,000 ($75,000 if married filing separately) and your modified adjusted gross income. When modified adjusted gross income is $150,000 or more ($75,000 or more if married filing separately), there is no special allowance.

Modified adjusted gross income is your adjusted gross income figured without taking into account:

- Any passive activity loss.

• Any rental real estate loss allowed under section 469(c)(7) to real estate professionals (as defined on page 2).
• Any taxable social security or equivalent railroad retirement benefits.
• Any deductible contributions to an IRA or certain other qualified retirement plans under section 219.
• The student loan interest deduction.
• The tuition and fees deduction.
• The deduction for one-half of self-employment taxes.
• The exclusion from income of interest from Series EE or I U.S. Savings Bonds used to pay higher education expenses.
• The exclusion of amounts received under an employer's adoption assistance program.

Commercial revitalization deduction. The special $25,000 allowance for the commercial revitalization deduction from rental real estate activities is not subject to the active participation rules or modified adjusted gross income limits discussed above. See the instructions for box 12, code N, for more information.

Special rules for certain other activities. If you have net income (loss), deductions, or credits from any activity to which special rules apply, the corporation will identify the activity and all amounts relating to it on Schedule K-1 or on an attachment.

If you have net income subject to recharacterization under Temporary Regulations section 1.469-2T(f) and Regulations section 1.469-2(f), report such amounts according to the Instructions for Form 8582.

If you have net income (loss), deductions, or credits from either of the following activities, treat such amounts as nonpassive and report them as instructed in these instructions:

1. The rental of a dwelling unit any shareholder used for personal purposes during the year for more than the greater of 14 days or 10% of the number of days that the residence was rented at fair rental value.
2. Trading personal property for the account of owners of interests in the activity.

Self-charged interest. The corporation will report any "self-charged" interest income or expense that resulted from loans between you and the corporation (or between the corporation and other S corporation or partnership in which you have an interest). If there was more than one activity, the corporation will provide a statement allocating the interest income or expense with respect to each activity. The self-charged interest rules do not apply to your interest in the S corporation if the corporation made an election under Regulations section 1.469-7(g) to avoid the application of these rules. See the Instructions for Form 8582 for more information.

Specific Instructions

Part I. Information about the Corporation

Item D

If the corporation is a registration-required tax shelter, it should have completed Item D. Use the information on Schedule K-1 (name of corporation, corporation identifying number, and tax shelter registration number) to complete your Form 8271, Investor Reporting of Tax Shelter Registration Number.

Item E

If you claim or report any income, loss, deduction, or credit from a registration-required tax shelter, you must attach Form 8271 to your tax return. If the corporation has invested in a registration-required tax shelter, it will check item E and it must give you a copy of its Form 8271 with Schedule K-1. Use this information to complete your Form 8271.

Part III. Shareholder's Share of Current Year Income, Deductions, Credits, and Other Items

The amounts shown in boxes 1 through 17 reflect your share of income, loss, deductions, credits, and other information from all corporate activities without reference to limitations on losses, credits, or other items that may have to be adjusted because of:

1. The adjusted basis of your stock and debt in the corporation,
2. The at-risk limitations,
3. The passive activity limitations, or
4. Any other limitations that must be taken into account at the shareholder level in figuring taxable income (e.g., the section 179 expense limitation).

For information on these provisions, see *Limitations on Losses, Deductions, and Credits* beginning on page 1. The limitations for 4 are discussed throughout these instructions and in other referenced forms and instructions.

If you are an individual, and your pro rata share items are not affected by any of the limitations, take the amounts shown and enter them on the lines of your tax return as indicated in the summarized reporting information showing on the back of the Schedule K-1. If any of the limitations apply, adjust the amounts for the limitations before you enter them on your return. When applicable, the passive activity limitations on losses are applied after the limitations on losses for a shareholder's basis in stock and debt and the shareholder's at-risk amount.

Note: The line number references on page 2 of Schedule K-1 are to forms in use for tax years beginning in 2004. If you are a calendar year shareholder in a fiscal year 2004–2005 corporation, enter these amounts on the corresponding lines of the tax form in use for 2005.

If you have losses, deductions, credits, etc., from a prior year that were not deductible or usable because of certain limitations, such as the basis rules or the at-risk limitations, take them into account in determining your income, loss, etc., for this year. However, except for passive activity losses and credits, do not combine the prior-year amounts with any amounts shown on this Schedule K-1 to get a net figure to report on your return. Instead, report the amounts on your return on a year-by-year basis.

CAUTION *If you have amounts other than those shown on Schedule K-1 to report on Schedule E (Form 1040), enter each item separately on line 28 of Schedule E.*

Codes. In box 10 and boxes 12 through 17, the corporation will identify each item by entering a code in the column to the left of the dollar amount entry space. These codes are identified on the back of Schedule K-1 and in these instructions.

Attached statements. The corporation will enter an asterisk (*) after the code, if any, in the column to the left of the dollar amount entry space for each item for which it has attached a statement providing additional information. For those informational items that cannot be reported as a single dollar amount, the corporation will enter an asterisk in the left column and write "STMT" in the dollar amount entry space to indicate the information is provided on an attached statement.

Income (loss)

Box 1. Ordinary business income (loss)

The amount reported in box 1 is your share of the ordinary income (loss) from trade or business activities of the corporation. Generally, where you report this amount on Form 1040 depends on whether or not the amount is from an activity that is a passive activity to you. If you are an individual shareholder, find your situation below and report your box 1 income (loss) as instructed after applying the basis and at-risk limitations on losses. If the corporation had more than one trade or business activity, it will attach a statement identifying the amount of income or loss from each activity.

1. Report box 1 income (loss) from trade or business activities in which you materially participated on Schedule E (Form 1040), line 28, column (h) or (j).
2. Report box 1 income (loss) from trade or business activities in which you did not materially participate, as follows:

a. If income is reported in box 1, report the income on Schedule E, line 28, column (g).
b. If a loss is reported in box 1, follow the Instructions for Form 8582 to determine how much of the loss can be reported on Schedule E, line 28, column (f).

Box 2. Net rental real estate income (loss)

Generally, the income (loss) reported in box 2 is a passive activity amount for all shareholders. However, the income (loss) in box 2 is not from a passive activity if you were a real estate professional (defined on page 2) and you materially participated in the activity. If the corporation had more than one rental real estate activity, it will attach a statement identifying the amount of income or loss from each activity.

If you are filing a 2004 Form 1040, use the following instructions to determine where to enter a box 2 amount:

1. If you have a loss from a passive activity in box 2 and you meet all of the following conditions, enter the loss on Schedule E (Form 1040), line 28, column (f):

a. You actively participated in the corporate rental real estate activities. (See *Special allowance for a rental real estate activity* on page 3.)
b. Rental real estate activities with active participation were your only passive activities.
c. You have no prior year unallowed losses from these activities.
d. Your total loss from the rental real estate activities was not more than $25,000 (not more than $12,500 if married filing separately and you lived apart from your spouse all year).
e. If you are a married person filing separately, you lived apart from your spouse all year.
f. You have no current or prior year unallowed credits from a passive activity.
g. Your modified adjusted gross income was not more than $100,000 (not more than $50,000 if married filing separately and you lived apart from your spouse all year).

2. If you have a loss from a passive activity in box 2 and you do not meet all of the conditions in 1 above, follow the Instructions

for Form 8582 to determine how much of the loss can be reported on Schedule E (Form 1040), line 28, column (f).

3. If you have income from a passive activity in box 2, enter the income on Schedule E, line 28, column (g).

4. If you were a real estate professional and you materially participated in the activity, report box 2 income (loss) on Schedule E, line 28, column (h) or (j).

Box 3. Other net rental income (loss)

The amount in box 3 is a passive activity amount for all shareholders. If the corporation had more than one such rental activity, it will attach a statement identifying the amount of income or loss from each activity. Report the income or loss as follows:

1. If box 3 is a loss, follow the instructions for Form 8582 to figure how much of the loss can be reported on Schedule E, line 28, column (f).

2. If income is reported in box 3, report the income on Schedule E (Form 1040), line 28, column (g).

Portfolio income

Portfolio income or loss (shown in boxes 4 through 8b and in box 10, code A) is not subject to the passive activity limitations. Portfolio income includes income not derived in the ordinary course of a trade or business from interest, ordinary dividends, annuities, or royalties, and gain or loss on the sale of property that produces such income or is held for investment.

Box 4. Interest income.

Report taxable interest income on line 8a of Form 1040.

Box 5a. Ordinary dividends.

Report taxable ordinary dividends on line 9a of Form 1040.

Box 5b. Qualified dividends.

Report qualified dividends on line 9b of Form 1040.

Note: Qualified dividends are excluded from investment income, but you may elect to include part or all of these amounts in investment income. See the instructions for line 4g of Form 4952, Investment Interest Expense Deduction, for important information on making this election.

Box 6. Royalties.

Report royalties on Schedule E, Part I, line 4.

Box 7. Net short-term capital gain (loss).

Report the net short-term capital gain or (loss) on Schedule D, line 5, column (f).

Box 8a. Net long-term capital gain (loss)

Report the net long-term capital gain (loss) on Schedule D, line 12, column (f).

Box 8b. Collectibles (28%) gain (loss)

This is your share of collectibles gain or loss. Include this amount on line 4 of the 28% Rate Gain worksheet in the instructions for Schedule D (Form 1040), line 18.

Box 8c. Unrecaptured section 1250 gain.

There are three types of unrecaptured section 1250 gain. Report your share of this unrecaptured gain on the *Unrecaptured Section 1250 Gain Worksheet* in the instructions for Schedule D (Form 1040), as follows:

- Report unrecaptured section 1250 gain from the sale or exchange of the corporation's business assets on line 5.
- Report unrecaptured section 1250 gain from the sale or exchange of an interest in a partnership on line 10.
- Report unrecaptured section 1250 gain from an estate, trust, regulated investment company (RIC), or real estate investment trust (REIT) on line 11.

If the corporation reports only unrecaptured section 1250 gain from the sale or exchange of its business assets, it will enter a dollar amount in box 8c. If it reports the other two types of unrecaptured gain, it will provide an attached statement that shows the amount for each type of unrecaptured section 1250 gain.

Box 9. Net Section 1231 Gain (Loss)

The amount in box 9 is generally a passive activity amount if it is from a:

- Rental activity or
- Trade or business activity in which you did not materially participate.

However, an amount from a rental real estate activity is not from a passive activity if you were a real estate professional (defined on page 2) and you materially participated in the activity.

If the amount is either (a) a loss that is not from a passive activity or (b) a gain, report it on Form 4797, line 2, column (g). Do not complete columns (b) through (f) on line 2. Instead, write "From Schedule K-1 (Form 1120S)" across these columns.

If the amount is a loss from a passive activity, see *Passive loss limitations* in the Instructions for Form 4797. You will need to report the loss following the Instructions for Form 8582 to determine the amount to enter on Form 4797. If the corporation had net section 1231 gain (loss) from more than one activity, it will attach a statement that will identify the amount of section 1231 gain (loss) from each activity.

Box 10. Other income (loss)

Code A. Other portfolio income (loss). The corporation will attach a schedule to tell you what kind of portfolio income, other than interest, ordinary dividends, royalty and capital gain, is reported.

If the corporation held a residual interest in a real estate mortgage investment conduit (REMIC), it will report on a statement your share of REMIC taxable income or (net loss) that you report on Schedule E (Form 1040), line 38, column (d). The statement will also report your share of any "excess inclusion" that you report on Schedule E, line 38, column (c), and your share of section 212 expenses that you report on Schedule E, line 38, column (e). If you itemize your deductions on Schedule A (Form 1040), you may also deduct these section 212 expenses as a miscellaneous deduction subject to the 2% limit on Schedule A, line 22.

Code B. Involuntary conversions. This is your share of net loss from involuntary conversions due to casualty or theft. The corporation will give you a schedule that shows the amounts to be reported on Form 4684, Casualties and Thefts, line 34, columns (b)(i), (b)(ii) and (c).

If there was a gain (loss) from a casualty or theft to property not used in a trade or business or for income-producing purposes, the corporation will provide you with the information you need to complete Form 4684.

Code C. 1256 contracts & straddles. The corporation will report any net gain or loss from section 1256 contracts. Report this amount on line 1 of Form 6781, Gains and Losses From Section 1256 Contracts and Straddles.

Code D. Mining exploration costs recapture. The corporation will give you a schedule that shows the information needed to recapture certain mining exploration expenditures (section 617).

Code E. Other income (loss). Amounts with code E are other items of income, gain, or loss not included elsewhere on Schedule K-1. The corporation should give you a description and the amount of your pro rata share for each of these items.

Report loss items that are passive activity amounts to you using the Instructions for Form 8582.

Report income or gain items that are passive activity amounts to you as instructed below. The instructions given below also tell you where to report code E items if such items are not passive activity amounts.

Code E items may include:

- Income from recoveries of tax benefit items. A tax benefit item is an amount you deducted in a prior tax year that reduced your income tax. Report this amount on Form 1040, line 21, to the extent it reduced your tax.
- Gambling gains and losses subject to the limitations in section 165(d).
- Gain (loss) from the disposition of an interest in oil, gas, geothermal, or other mineral properties. The corporation will give you an attached statement that provides a description of the property, your share of the amount realized from the disposition, your share of the corporation's adjusted basis in the property (for other than oil or gas properties), and your share of the total intangible drilling costs, development costs, and mining exploration costs (section 59(e) expenditures) passed through for the property. You must determine the amount of gain or loss from the disposition by increasing your share of the adjusted basis by the amount of intangible drilling costs, development costs, or mine exploration costs for the property that you capitalized (i.e., costs that you did not elect to deduct under section 59(e)). Report a loss in Part I of Form 4797. Report a gain in Part III of Form 4797 in accordance with the instructions for line 28. See Regulations section 1.1254-4 for more information.
- Gain from the sale or exchange of qualified small business stock (as defined in the Instructions for Schedule D (Form 1040)) that is eligible for the partial section 1202 exclusion. The corporation should also give you the name of the corporation that issued the stock, your share of the corporation's adjusted basis and sales price of the stock, and the dates the stock was bought and sold. The following additional limitations apply at the shareholder level:

1. You must have held an interest in the corporation when the corporation acquired the qualified small business stock and at all times thereafter until the corporation disposed of the qualified small business stock.

2. Your pro rata share of the eligible section 1202 gain cannot exceed the amount that would have been allocated to you based on your interest in the corporation at the time the stock was acquired.

See the Instructions for Schedule D (Form 1040) for details on how to report the gain and the amount of the allowable exclusion.

- Gain eligible for section 1045 rollover (replacement stock purchased by the corporation). The corporation should also give you the name of the corporation that issued the stock, your share of the corporation's adjusted basis and sales price of the stock, and the dates the stock was bought and sold. To qualify for the section 1045 rollover:

1. You must have held an interest in the corporation during the entire period in which the corporation held the qualified small business stock (more than 6 months prior to the sale) and

2. Your pro rata share of the gain eligible for the section 1045 rollover cannot exceed the amount that would have been allocated to you based on your interest in the corporation at the time the stock was acquired.

See the Instructions for Schedule D (Form 1040) for details on how to report the gain and the amount of the allowable postponed gain.

• Gain eligible for section 1045 rollover (replacement stock not purchased by the corporation). The corporation should also give you the name of the corporation that issued the stock, your share of the corporation's adjusted basis and sales price of the stock, and the dates the stock was bought and sold. To qualify for the section 1045 rollover:

1. You must have held an interest in the corporation during the entire period in which the corporation held the qualified small business stock (more than 6 months prior to the sale).

2. Your pro rata share of the gain eligible for the section 1045 rollover cannot exceed the amount that would have been allocated to you based on your interest in the corporation at the time the stock was acquired, and

3. You must purchase other qualified small business stock (as defined in the Instructions for Schedule D (Form 1040)) during the 60-day period that began on the date the stock was sold by the corporation.

See the Instructions for Schedule D (Form 1040) for details on how to report the gain and the amount of the allowable postponed gain.

• Net short-term capital gain or loss and net long-term capital gain or loss that is not portfolio income (e.g., gain or loss from the disposition of nondepreciable personal property used in a trade or business activity of the corporation). Report total net short-term gain or loss on Schedule D (Form 1040), line 5, column (f). Report the total net long-term gain or loss on Schedule D (Form 1040), line 12, column (f).

Deductions

Box 11. Section 179 deduction

Use this amount, along with the total cost of section 179 property placed in service during the year from all other sources, to complete Part I of Form 4562, Depreciation and Amortization.

Use Part I of Form 4562 to figure your allowable section 179 deduction from all sources. Report the amount on line 12 of Form 4562 allocable to a passive activity using the Instructions for Form 8582. If the amount is not from a passive activity, report it on Schedule E (Form 1040), line 28, column (i).

Box 12. Other deductions

Contributions. Codes A through F. The corporation will give you a schedule that shows the amount of contributions subject to the 50%, 30%, and 20% adjusted gross income limitations. For more details, see Pub. 526, Charitable Contributions, and the Instructions for Schedule A (From 1040). If your contributions are subject to more than one of the AGI limitations, see the *Filled-in Worksheet for Limit on Deductions* in Pub. 526. Charitable contribution deductions are not taken into account in figuring your passive activity loss for the year. Do not enter them on Form 8582.

Code A. Cash contributions (50%). Enter this amount, subject to the 50% AGI limitation, on line 15 of Schedule A (Form 1040).

Code B. Cash contributions (30%). Report this amount, subject to the 30% AGI limitation, on line 15 of Schedule A (Form 1040).

Code C. Noncash contributions (50%). If property other than cash is contributed, and the claimed deduction for one item or group of similar items of property exceeds $5,000, the corporation must give you a copy of Form 8283, Noncash Charitable Contributions, to attach to your tax return. Do not deduct the amount shown on Form 8283. It is the corporation's contribution. Instead, deduct the amount identified by code C, box 12, subject to the 50% AGI limitation, on line 16 of Schedule A (Form 1040).

If the corporation provides you with information that the contribution was property other than cash and does not give you a Form 8283, see the Instructions for Form 8283 for filing requirements. Do not file Form 8283 unless the total claimed deduction of all contributed items of property exceeds $500.

Code D. Noncash contributions (30%). Report this amount, subject to the 30% AGI limitation, on line 16 of Schedule A (Form 1040).

Code E. Capital gain property to a 50% organization (30%). Report this amount, subject to the 30% AGI limitation, on line 16 of Schedule A (Form 1040). See *Special 30% Limit for Capital Gain Property* in Pub. 526.

Code F. Capital gain property (20%). Report this amount, subject to the 20% AGI limitation, on line 16 of Schedule A (Form 1040).

Code G. Deductions–portfolio (2% floor). Amounts with this code are deductions that are clearly and directly allocable to portfolio income (other than investment interest expense and section 212 expenses from a REMIC). Generally, you should enter these amounts on Schedule A (Form 1040), line 22. See the instructions for Schedule A, lines 22 and 27, for more information.

These deductions are not taken into account in figuring your passive activity loss for the year. Do not enter them on Form 8582.

Code H. Deductions—portfolio (other). Generally, you should enter these amounts on Schedule A (Form 1040), line 27. See the instructions for Schedule A, lines 22 and 27, for more information.

These deductions are not taken into account in figuring your passive activity loss for the year. Do not enter them on Form 8582.

Code I. Investment Interest Expense. Enter this amount on Form 4952, line 1.

If the corporation has investment income or other investment expense, it will report your share of these items in box 17 using codes A and B. You will need to include investment income and expenses from all other sources to determine how much of your total investment interest is deductible.

For more information on the special provisions that apply to investment interest expense, see Form 4952 and Pub. 550.

Code J. Deductions—royalty income. Enter deductions allocable to royalties on Schedule E (Form 1040), line 18. For this type of expense, write "From Schedule K-1 (Form 1120S)."

These deductions are not taken into account in figuring your passive activity loss for the year. Do not enter them on Form 8582.

Code K. Section 59(e)(2) Expenditures. On an attached statement, the corporation will show the type and the amount of qualified expenditures to which an election under section 59(e) may apply. The statement will also identify the property for which the expenditures were paid or incurred. If there is more than one type of expenditure, the amount of each type will be listed on an attachment.

Generally, section 59(e) allows each shareholder to elect to deduct certain expenses ratably over the number of years in the applicable period rather than deduct the full amount in the current year. Under the election, you may deduct circulation expenditures ratably over a 3-year period. Research and experimental expenditures and mining exploration and development costs qualify for a write-off period of 10 years. Intangible drilling and development costs may be deducted over a 60-month period, beginning with the month in which such costs were paid or incurred.

If you make this election, these items are not treated as adjustments or tax preference items for purposes of the alternative minimum tax. Make the election on Form 4562.

Because each shareholder decides whether to make the election under section 59(e), the corporation cannot provide you with the amount of the adjustment or tax preference item related to the expenses. You must decide how to claim the expenses on your return and how to figure the resulting adjustment or tax preference item.

Code L. Reforestation expense deduction. The corporation will provide a statement that describes the qualified timber property for these reforestation expenses. The expense deduction is limited to $10,000 ($5,000 if married filing separately) for each qualified timber property, including your pro rata share of the corporation's expense and any reforestation expenses you separately paid or incurred after October 22, 2004, for the property. Follow the instructions for Form 8582 to report a deduction allocable to a passive activity. If you materially participated in the reforestation activity, report the deduction on line 28, column (h), of Schedule E (Form 1040).

Code M. Preproductive period expenses. You may elect to deduct these expenses currently or capitalize them under section 263A. See Pub. 225, Farmer's Tax Guide, and Regulations section 1.263A-4 for more information.

Code N. Commercial revitalization deduction from rental real estate activities. Follow the instructions for Form 8582 to determine how much of this deduction can be reported on Schedule E, line 28, column (f).

Code O. Penalty on early withdrawal of savings. Report this amount on Form 1040, line 33.

Code P. Other deductions. Amounts with this code may include:

• Itemized deductions that Form 1040 filers enter on Schedule A (Form 1040).

• Soil and water conservation expenditures. See section 175(b) for limitations on the amount you are allowed to deduct.

• Expenditures for the removal of architectural and transportation barriers to the elderly and disabled that the corporation elected to treat as a current expense. The deductions are limited by section 190(c) to $15,000 per year from all sources.

• Interest expense allocated to debt-financed distributions. If the proceeds were used in a trade or business activity, report the interest on line 28 of Schedule E (From 1040). In column (a) enter the name of the corporation and "interest expense." If you materially participated in the trade or business activity, enter the amount of interest expense in column (h). If you did not materially participate in the activity, follow the instructions for Form 8582 to determine the amount of interest expense you can report in column (f). See page 3 for a definition of material participation. If the proceeds were used in an investment activity, enter the interest on Form 4952. If the proceeds are used for personal purposes the interest is generally not deductible.

- Contributions to a capital construction fund (CCF). The deduction for a CCF investment is not taken on Schedule E (Form 1040). Instead, you subtract the deduction from the amount that would normally be entered as taxable income on line 42 (Form 1040). In the margin to the left of line 42, write "CCF" and the amount of the deduction.

The corporation will give you a description and the amount of your share of each of these items.

Box 13. Credits & Credit Recapture

If you have credits that are passive activity credits to you, you must complete Form 8582-CR in addition to the credit forms identified below. See *Passive Activity Limitations* on page 2 and the Instructions for Form 8582-CR for more information.

Also, if you are entitled to claim more than one listed general business credit (investment credit, work opportunity credit, welfare-to-work credit, credit for alcohol used as fuel, research credit, low-income housing credit, enhanced oil recovery credit, disabled access credit, renewable electricity and refined coal production credit, Indian employment credit, credit for employer social security and Medicare taxes paid on certain employee tips, orphan drug credit, new markets credit, credit for small employer pension plan start-up costs, credit for employer-provided childcare facilities and services, biodiesel fuels credit, low sulfur diesel fuel production credit, and credit for contributions to selected community development corporations), you must complete Form 3800, General Business Credit, in addition to the credit forms identified. If you have more than one credit, see the Instructions for Form 3800.

Codes A and B. Low-income housing credit. The corporation will report your share of the low-income housing credit using code A if section 42(j)(5) applies. If section 42(j)(5) does not apply, your share of the credit will be reported using Code B. Any allowable low-income housing credit (reported as code A or code B) is entered on line 5 of Form 8586, Low-Income Housing Credit.

If the corporation invested in a partnership to which the provisions of section 42(j)(5) apply, it will attach a schedule to identify your share of the credit received from the partnership.

Keep a separate record of the low-income housing credits from each of these sources so that you will be able to correctly figure any recapture that may result from the disposition of all or part of your stock in the corporation. For more information, see the instructions for Form 8611, Recapture of Low-Income Housing Credit.

If part or all of the low-income housing credit reported using code A or B is attributable to additions to qualified basis property placed in service before 1990, the corporation will provide an attached statement that will separately identify these amounts. Amounts placed in service before 1990 are subject to different passive activity limitation rules. See *Passive Activity Limitations* and Form 8582-CR for more information.

Codes C and D. Qualified rehabilitation expenditures. The corporation will report your share of the qualified rehabilitation expenditures related to rental real estate activities using code C. Your share of qualified rehabilitation expenditures from property not related to rental real estate activities will be reported using code D. On an attached statement the corporation will indicate the line number on Form 3468, Investment Credit, to report these expenditures (line 1b for pre-1936 buildings or line 1c for certified historic structures). If the corporation is reporting expenditures from more than one activity, the attached statement will separately identify the amount of expenditures from each activity for lines 1b and 1c.

Combine the code C and code D expenditures on lines 1b and 1c of Form 3468. The expenditures related to rental real estate activities (code C) are reported on Schedule K-1 separately from other qualified rehabilitation expenditures (code D) because they are subject to different passive activity limitation rules. See the instructions for Form 8582-CR for details.

Code E. Basis of energy property. Report this amount on Form 3468, line 2.

Code F. Qualified timber property. Report this amount on Form 3468, line 3.

Code G. Other rental real estate credits. The corporation will identify the type of credit and any other information you need to compute credits from rental real estate activities (other than the low-income housing credit and qualified rehabilitation expenditures). These credits may be limited by the passive activity limitations. If the credits are from more than one activity, the corporation will identify the amount of credits from each activity on an attached statement. See *Passive Activity Limitations* on page 2 and Form 8582-CR for details.

Code H. Other rental credits. The corporation will identify the type of credit and any other information you need to compute these rental credits. These credits may be limited by the passive activity limitations. If the credits are from more than one activity, the corporation will identify the amount of credits from each activity on an attached statement. See *Passive Activity Limitations* on page 2 and Form 8582-CR for details.

Code I. Undistributed capital gains credit. Code I represents taxes paid on undistributed capital gains by a regulated investment company or real estate investment trust. Form 1040 filers, enter your share of these taxes on line 69 of Form 1040, check box 'a' for Form 2439, and add "Form 1120S." Also reduce the basis of your stock by this tax.

Code J. Work opportunity credit. Report this amount on line 3 of Form 5884, Work Opportunity Credit.

Code K. Welfare-to-work credit. Report this amount on line 3 of Form 8861, Welfare-to-Work Credit.

Code L. Disabled access credit. Report this amount on line 7 of Form 8826, Disabled Access Credit.

Code M. Empowerment zone and renewal community employment credit. Report this amount on line 3 of Form 8844, Empowerment Zone and Renewal Community Employment Credit.

Code N. New York Liberty Zone business employee credit. Report this amount on line 3 of Form 8884, New York Liberty Zone Business Employee Credit.

Code O. New markets credit. Report this amount on line 2 of Form 8874, New Markets Credit.

Code P. Employer social security and Medicare tax paid on certain employee tips. Report this amount on line 5 of Form 8846, Credit for Employer Social Security and Medicare Taxes Paid on Certain Employee Tips.

Code Q. Backup withholding. This is your share of the credit for backup withholding on dividends, interest income, and other types of income. Include the amount the corporation reports to you in the total that you enter on Form 1040, line 63.

Code R. Credit for alcohol used as fuel. This is your share of the corporation's credit for alcohol used as fuel from all trade or business activities. Enter this credit on Form 6478, Credit for Alcohol Used as Fuel, to determine your allowed credit for the year.

Codes S and T. Recapture of low-income housing credit. The corporation will identify by code S your share of any recapture of a low-income housing credit from its investment in partnerships to which the provisions of section 42(j)(5) apply. All other recapture of low-income housing credits will be identified by code T.

Keep a separate record of each type of recapture so that you will be able to correctly figure any credit recapture that may result from the disposition of all or part of your corporate stock. For more information, see Form 8611.

Code U. Recapture of investment credit. The corporation will provide any information you need to figure your recapture tax on Form 4255, Recapture of Investment Credit. See the Form 3468 on which you took the original credit for other information you need to complete Form 4255.

You may also need Form 4255 if you disposed of more than one-third of your stock in the corporation.

Code V. Other credits. The corporation will identify your pro rata share of any other credit by code V on an attached schedule. If more than one credit is reported, the credits will be identified on an attached schedule.

Credits that may be reported with code V (depending on the type of activity they relate to) include the following:

- Nonconventional source fuel credit. Attach a schedule to your return showing how you calculated the amount of credit you are allowed to take on your tax return. See section 29 for rules on how to figure the credit. Report this credit on Form 1040, line 54, box c.
- Qualified electric vehicle credit (Form 8834).
- Unused investment credit from cooperatives (Form 3468, line 4).
- Credit for increasing research activities (Form 6765).
- Enhanced oil recovery credit (Form 8830).
- Renewable electricity and refined coal production credit. The corporation will provide a statement showing separately the amount of credit from section A and section B of Form 8835.
- Indian employment credit (Form 8845).
- Orphan drug credit (Form 8820).
- Credit for contributions to selected community development corporations (Form 8847).
- Credit for small employer pension plan start-up costs (Form 8881).
- Credit for employer-provided childcare facilities and services (Form 8882).
- Qualified zone academy bond credit (Form 8860).
- Biodiesel fuels credit (Form 8864).

• Low sulfur diesel fuel production credit (Form 8896).
• General credits from an electing large partnership. Report these credits on Form 3800, line 1t.

Code W. Recapture of other credits. On an attachment to Schedule K-1, the corporation will report any information you need to figure the recapture of the new markets credit; qualified electric vehicle credit (see Pub. 535); Indian employment credit (see section 45A(d)); or any credit for employer-provided childcare facilities and services.

Box 14. Foreign Transactions

Codes A through N. Use the information identified by codes A through N and attached schedules to figure your foreign tax credit. For more information, see Form 1116, Foreign Tax Credit, and its instructions. Also see Pub. 514, Foreign Tax Credit for Individuals.

Codes O and P. Extraterritorial income exclusion.

1. *Corporation did not claim the exclusion.* If the corporation reports your pro rata share of foreign trading gross receipts (code O) and the extraterritorial income exclusion (code P), the corporation was not entitled to claim the exclusion because it did not meet the foreign economic process requirements. You may still qualify for your pro rata share of this exclusion if the corporation's foreign trading gross receipts for the tax year were $5 million or less. To qualify for this exclusion, your foreign trading gross receipts from all sources for the tax year also must have been $5 million or less. If you qualify for the exclusion, report the exclusion amount in accordance with the instructions beginning on page 4 for boxes 1, 2, or 3, whichever applies. See Form 8873, Extraterritorial Income Exclusion, for more information.

2. *Corporation claimed the exclusion.* If the corporation reports your pro rata share of foreign trading gross receipts but not the amount of the extraterritorial income exclusion, the corporation met the foreign economic process requirements and claimed the exclusion when figuring your pro rata share of corporate income. You also may need to know the amount of your pro rata share of foreign trading gross receipts from this corporation to determine if you met the $5 million or less exception discussed above for purposes of qualifying for an extraterritorial income exclusion from other sources.

Note: *Upon request, the corporation should furnish you a copy of the corporation's Form 8873 if there is a reduction for international boycott operations, illegal bribes, kickbacks, etc.*

Code Q. Other foreign transactions. On an attachment to Schedule K-1, the corporation will report any other information on foreign transactions that you may need using code Q.

Box 15. Alternative minimum tax (AMT) items

Use the information reported in box 15 (as well as adjustments and tax preference items from other sources) to prepare your Form 6251, Alternative Minimum Tax—Individuals, or Schedule I of Form 1041, U.S. Income Tax Return for Estates and Trusts.

Code A. This amount is your share of the corporation's post-1986 depreciation adjustment. If you are an individual shareholder, report this amount on line 17 of Form 6251.

Code B. This amount is your share of the corporation's adjusted gain or loss. If you are an individual shareholder, report this amount on line 16 of Form 6251.

Code C. This amount is your share of the corporation's depletion adjustment. If you are an individual shareholder, report this amount on line 9 of Form 6251.

Codes D and E. Oil, gas, & geothermal properties—gross income and deductions. The amounts reported on these lines include only the gross income from, and deductions allocable to, oil, gas, and geothermal properties included in box 1 of Schedule K-1. The corporation will report separately any income from or deductions allocable to such properties that are included in boxes 2 through 12, and 17. Use the amounts reported here and any other reported amounts to help you determine the net amount to enter on line 25 of Form 6251.

Code F. Other AMT items. Enter the information on the statement attached by the corporation, along with items from other sources, on the applicable lines of Form 6251.

Box 16. Items Affecting Shareholder Basis

Code A. Tax-exempt interest income. You must report on your return, as an item of information, your share of the tax-exempt interest received or accrued by the corporation during the year. Individual shareholders include this amount on Form 1040, line 8b. Generally, you must increase the basis of your stock by this amount.

Code B. Other tax-exempt income. Generally, you must increase the basis of your stock by the amount shown, but do not include it in income on your tax return.

Code C. Nondeductible expenses. The nondeductible expenses paid or incurred by the corporation are not deductible on your tax return. Generally, you must decrease the basis of your stock by this amount.

Code D. Property distributions. Reduce the basis of your stock (as explained on page 2) by these distributions. If these distributions exceed the basis of your stock, the excess is treated as capital gain from the sale or exchange of property and is reported on Schedule D (Form 1040).

Code E. Repayment of loans from shareholders. If these payments are made on a loan with a reduced basis, the repayments must be allocated in part to a return of your basis in the loan and in part to the receipt of income. See Regulations section 1.1367-2 for information on reduction in basis of a loan and restoration in basis of a loan with a reduced basis. See Rev. Rul. 64-162, 1964-1 (Part 1) C.B. 304 and Rev. Rul. 68-537, 1968-2 C.B. 372, for other information.

Box 17. Other Information

Code A. Investment income. Report this amount on line 4a of Form 4952.

Code B. Investment expenses. Report this amount on line 5 of Form 4952.

Code C. Look back interest—completed long-term contracts. The corporation will report any information you need to figure the interest due or to be refunded under the look-back method of section 460(b)(2) on certain long-term contracts. Use Form 8697, Interest Computation Under the Look-Back Method for Completed Long-Term Contracts, to report any such interest.

Code D. Look back interest—income forecast method. The corporation will report any information you need to figure the interest due or to be refunded under the look-back method of section 167(g)(2) for certain property placed in service after September 13, 1995, and depreciated under the income forecast method.

Use Form 8866, Interest Computation Under the Look-Back Method for Property Depreciated Under the Income Forecast Method, to report any such interest.

Code E. Dispositions of property with section 179 deductions. The corporation will report your pro rata share of gain or loss on the sale, exchange, or other disposition of property for which a section 179 expense deduction was passed through to shareholders. If the corporation passed through a section 179 deduction for the property, you must report the gain or loss and any recapture of the section 179 expense deduction for the property on your income tax return (see the instructions for Form 4797 for details). The corporation will provide all the following information with respect to a disposition of property for which a section 179 expense deduction was passed through to shareholders.

1. Description of the property.
2. Date the property was acquired and placed in service.
3. Date of the sale or other disposition of the property.
4. Your pro rata share of the gross sales price or amount realized.
5. Your pro rata share of the cost or other basis plus the expense of sale (reduced as explained in the instructions for Form 4797, line 21).
6. Your pro rata share of the depreciation allowed or allowable, determined as described in the instructions for Form 4797, line 22, but excluding the section 179 expense deduction.
7. Your pro rata share of the section 179 expense deduction (if any) passed through for the property and the corporation's tax year(s) in which the amount was passed through.

To compute the amount of depreciation allowed or allowable for Form 4797, line 22, add to the amount from item 6 above the amount of your pro rata share of the section 179 expense deduction, reduced by any unused carryover of the deduction for this property. This amount could be different than the amount of section 179 expense you deducted for the property if your interest in the corporation has changed.

8. If the disposition is due to a casualty or theft, a statement providing the information you need to complete Form 4684, Casualties and Thefts.
9. If the sale was an installment sale made during the corporation's tax year, a statement providing the information you need to complete Form 6252, Installment Sale Income. The corporation will separately report your share of all payments received from the property in the following tax years. See the instructions for Form 6252 for details.

Code F. Recapture of section 179 deduction. The corporation will report your pro rata share of any recapture of section 179 expense deduction if business use of any property dropped to 50 percent or less. If this occurs, the corporation must provide the following information.

1. Your pro rata share of the depreciation allowed or allowable (not including the section 179 expense deduction).
2. Your pro rata share of the section 179 expense deduction (if any) passed through for the property and the corporation's tax year(s) in which the amount was passed through. Reduce this amount by the portion, if any, of your unused (carryover) section 179 expense deduction for this property.

Code G. Section 453(l)(3) information. The corporation will report any information you need to figure the interest due under section 453(l)(3). If the corporation elected to report the dispositions of certain timeshares and residential lots on the installment method, your tax liability must be increased by the interest on tax attributable to your pro rata share of the installment payments received by the corporation during its tax year. If you are an individual, report the interest on Form 1040, line 62. Write "453(l)(3)" and the amount of the interest on the dotted line to the left of line 62.

Code H. Section 453A(c) information. The corporation will report any information you need to figure the interest due under section 453A(c). If you are an individual, report the interest on Form 1040, line 62. Write "453A(c)" and the amount of the interest on the dotted line to the left of line 62. See the instructions for Form 6252 for more information. Also see section 453A(c) for details on making the computation.

Code I. Section 1260(b) information. The corporation will report any information you need to figure the interest due under section 1260(b). If the corporation had gain from certain constructive ownership transactions, your tax liability must be increased by the interest charge on any deferral of gain recognition under section 1260(b). If you are an individual, report the interest on Form 1040, line 62. Write "1260(b)" and the amount of the interest on the dotted line to the left of line 62. See section 1260(b) for details, including how to figure the interest.

Code J. Interest allocable to production expenditures. To the extent certain production or construction expenditures of the corporation are made from proceeds associated with debt you incur as an owner-shareholder, you must capitalize the interest on this debt. Use the information the corporation gives you to determine the amount of interest you must capitalize. See Regulations sections 1.263A-8 through 1.263A-15 for more information.

Code K. CCF nonqualified withdrawal. The corporation will report your pro rata share of nonqualified withdrawals from a capital construction fund (CCF). These withdrawals are taxed separately from your other gross income at the highest marginal ordinary income or capital gains tax rate. Attach a statement to your Federal income tax return to show your computation of both the tax and interest for a nonqualified withdrawal. Include the tax and interest on Form 1040, line 62. To the left of line 62, write the amount of tax and interest and "CCF."

Code L. Information needed to figure depletion-oil and gas. This is your share of gross income from the property, share of production for the tax year, etc., needed to figure your depletion deduction for oil and gas wells. The corporation should also allocate to you a proportionate share of the adjusted basis of each corporate oil or gas property. The corporation should attach a schedule to report all applicable information. See Pub. 535 for how to figure your depletion deduction.

Reduce the basis of your stock by the amount of this deduction up to the extent of your adjusted basis in the property.

Code M. Amortization of reforestation costs. The corporation will provide a statement identifying your share of the amortizable basis of reforestation expenditures paid or incurred before October 23, 2004. The corporation will separately report your share of the amortizable basis of reforestation expenditures for the current tax year and the 7 preceding tax years. Your amortizable basis of reforestation expenditures for each tax year from all properties is limited to $10,000 ($5, 000 if married filing separately), including your pro rata share of the corporation's expenditures and any qualified reforestation expenditures you separately paid or incurred. To figure your allowable amortization, see section 194 and Pub. 535.

Follow the instructions for Form 8582 to report a deduction allocable to a passive activity. If you materially participated in the reforestation activity, report the deduction on line 28, column (h), of Schedule E (Form 1040).

Code N. Other information The corporation will report:

1. Any information or statements you need to comply with the registration and disclosure requirements under sections 6111 and 6662(d)(2)(B)(ii) and the list keeping requirements of Regulations section 301.6112-1. See Form 8264 and Notice 2004-80, 2004-50 I.R.B. 963 for more information.

2. Any information you need to complete a disclosure statement for reportable transactions in which the corporation participates. If the corporation participates in a transaction that must be disclosed on Form 8886, Reportable Transaction Disclosure Statement, both you and the corporation may be required to file Form 8886 for the transaction. The determination of whether you are required to disclose a transaction of the corporation is based on the category(s) under which the transaction qualifies for disclosure and is determined by the corporation. See the instructions for Form 8886 for details.

3. Gross farming and fishing income. If you are an individual shareholder, enter this income, as an item of information, on Schedule E (Form 1040), Part V, line 42. Do not report this income elsewhere on Form 1040.

For a shareholder that is an estate or trust, report this income to the beneficiaries, as an item of information, on Schedule K-1 (Form 1041). Do not report it elsewhere on Form 1041.

4. The amount the corporation included in gross income with respect to qualified zone academy bonds. This amount cannot be used to increase your stock basis. However, because this amount is already included in income elsewhere on Schedule K-1, you must reduce your stock basis by this amount.

5. Inversion gain. The corporation will provide a statement showing the amounts of each type of income or gain that is included in inversion gain. The corporation has included inversion gain in income elsewhere on Schedule K-1. Inversion gain is also reported under code N because your taxable income and alternative minimum taxable income cannot be less than the inversion gain. Also, your inversion gain **(a)** is not taken into account in figuring the amount of net operating loss (NOL) for the tax year or the amount of NOL that can be carried over to each tax year, **(b)** may limit the amount of your credits, and **(c)** is treated as income from sources within the U.S. for the foreign tax credit . See section 7874 for details.

6. Any other information you may need to file with your individual tax return that is not shown elsewhere on Schedule K-1.

INSTRUCTIONS FOR FORM 4562

Depreciation and Amortization

2004

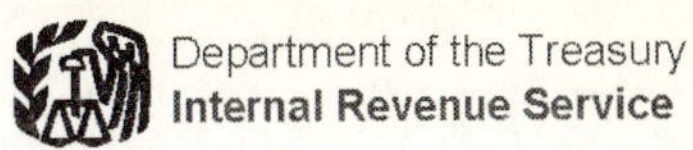

Instructions for Form 4562

Depreciation and Amortization (Including Information on Listed Property)

Section references are to the Internal Revenue Code unless otherwise noted.

General Instructions

What's New

- For tax years beginning in 2004, the maximum section 179 expense deduction is $102,000 ($137,000 for qualified enterprise zone, renewal community, and New York Liberty Zone (Liberty Zone) property). This limit is reduced by the amount by which the cost of section 179 property placed in service during the tax year exceeds $410,000. See page 2 of the instructions.
- The maximum section 179 expense deduction for certain sport utility and other vehicles placed in service after October 22, 2004, is $25,000. See the instructions for lines 26 and 27, column (i), on page 10.
- The 30% and 50% special depreciation allowances will not apply to most property placed in service after 2004. See the instructions for line 14 on page 3 (for listed property, see the instructions for line 25 on page 8).
- New regulations provide guidance for depreciating property acquired through a like-kind exchange or involuntary conversion and placed in service after February 27, 2004. See Temporary Regulations sections 1.168(i)-1T and 1.168(i)-6T and the instructions for Part III on page 5.
- Qualified leasehold improvement property and qualified restaurant property placed in service after October 22, 2004, are now treated as 15-year property under the Modified Accelerated Cost Recovery System (MACRS). See the instructions for line 19 on page 5.
- You can elect to deduct a limited amount of business start-up and organizational costs paid or incurred after October 22, 2004. Such costs that are not deducted currently can be amortized ratably over a 180-month period. See the instructions on page 11.
- You can elect to deduct a limited amount of reforestation costs paid or incurred after October 22, 2004. Such costs that are not deducted currently can be amortized over an 84-month period. See the instructions on page 11.

Purpose of Form

Use Form 4562 to:

- Claim your deduction for depreciation and amortization,
- Make the election under section 179 to expense certain property, and
- Provide information on the business/investment use of automobiles and other listed property.

Who Must File

Except as otherwise noted, complete and file Form 4562 if you are claiming any of the following.

- Depreciation for property placed in service during the 2004 tax year.
- A section 179 expense deduction (which may include a carryover from a previous year).
- Depreciation on any vehicle or other listed property (regardless of when it was placed in service).
- A deduction for any vehicle reported on a form other than Schedule C (Form 1040), Profit or Loss From Business, or Schedule C-EZ (Form 1040), Net Profit From Business.
- Any depreciation on a corporate income tax return (other than Form 1120S).
- Amortization of costs that begins during the 2004 tax year.

If you are an employee deducting job-related vehicle expenses using either the standard mileage rate or actual expenses, use Form 2106, Employee Business Expenses, or Form 2106-EZ, Unreimbursed Employee Business Expenses, for this purpose.

File a separate Form 4562 for each business or activity on your return for which Form 4562 is required. If you need more space, attach additional sheets. However, complete only one Part I in its entirety when computing your section 179 expense deduction. See the instructions for line 12 on page 3.

Additional Information

For more information about depreciation and amortization (including information on listed property) see the following.

- Pub. 463, Travel, Entertainment, Gift, and Car Expenses.
- Pub. 534, Depreciating Property Placed in Service Before 1987.
- Pub. 535, Business Expenses.
- Pub. 551, Basis of Assets.
- Pub. 946, How To Depreciate Property.

Definitions

Depreciation

Depreciation is the annual deduction that allows you to recover the cost or other basis of your business or investment property over a certain number of years. Depreciation starts when you first use the property in your business or for the production of income. It ends when you either take the property out of service, deduct all your depreciable cost or basis, or no longer use the property in your business or for the production of income.

Generally, you can depreciate:

- Tangible property such as buildings, machinery, vehicles, furniture, and equipment; and
- Intangible property such as patents, copyrights, and computer software.

Exception. You cannot depreciate land.

Section 179 Property

Section 179 property is property that you acquire by purchase for use in the active conduct of your trade or business, and is one of the following.

- Tangible personal property.
- Other tangible property (except buildings and their structural components) used as:

1. An integral part of manufacturing, production, or extraction or of furnishing transportation, communications, electricity, gas, water, or sewage disposal services;
2. A research facility used in connection with any of the activities in (1) above; or
3. A facility used in connection with any of the activities in (1) above for the bulk storage of fungible commodities.

- Single purpose agricultural (livestock) or horticultural structures.
- Storage facilities (except buildings and their structural components) used in connection with distributing petroleum or any primary product of petroleum.
- Off-the-shelf computer software.

For additional details and exceptions, see Pub. 946.

You can elect to expense part or all of the cost of section 179 property in the current tax year.

However, for taxpayers other than a corporation, this election does not apply to any section 179 property you purchased and leased to others unless:

Cat. No. 12907Y

• You manufactured or produced the property or
• The term of the lease is less than 50% of the property's class life and, for the first 12 months after the property is transferred to the lessee, the deductions related to the property allowed to you as trade or business expenses (except rents and reimbursed amounts) are more than 15% of the rental income from the property.

See the instructions for Part I below.

Amortization

Amortization is similar to the straight line method of depreciation in that an annual deduction is allowed to recover certain costs over a fixed time period. You can elect to amortize such items as the costs of starting a business, goodwill, and certain other intangibles. See the instructions for Part VI on page 11.

Listed Property

Listed property generally includes the following.
• Passenger automobiles weighing 6,000 pounds or less. See *Limits for passenger automobiles* on page 9.
• Any other property used for transportation if the nature of the property lends itself to personal use, such as motorcycles, pick-up trucks, sport utility vehicles, etc.
• Any property used for entertainment or recreational purposes (such as photographic, phonographic, communication, and video recording equipment).
• Cellular telephones (or other similar telecommunications equipment).
• Computers or peripheral equipment.

Exception. Listed property does not include:

1. Photographic, phonographic, communication, or video equipment used exclusively in a taxpayer's trade or business or at the taxpayer's regular business establishment;
2. Any computer or peripheral equipment used exclusively at a regular business establishment and owned or leased by the person operating the establishment; or
3. An ambulance, hearse, or vehicle used for transporting persons or property for hire.

For purposes of the exceptions above, a portion of the taxpayer's home is treated as a regular business establishment only if that portion meets the requirements for deducting expenses attributable to the business use of a home. However, for any property listed in (1) above, the regular business establishment of an employee is his or her employer's regular business establishment.

Commuting

Generally, commuting is travel between your home and a work location. However, travel that meets any of the following conditions is not commuting.
• You have at least one regular work location away from your home and the travel is to a temporary work location in the same trade or business, regardless of the distance. Generally, a temporary work location is one where your employment is expected to last 1 year or less. See Pub. 463 for details.
• The travel is to a temporary work location outside the metropolitan area where you live and normally work.
• Your home is your principal place of business for purposes of deducting expenses for business use of your home and the travel is to another work location in the same trade or business, regardless of whether that location is regular or temporary and regardless of distance.

Alternative Minimum Tax (AMT)

Depreciation may be an adjustment for the AMT. However, no adjustment applies for qualified property for which you claim a special depreciation allowance (if the depreciable basis of the qualified property for the AMT is the same as for the regular tax). See Form 4626, Alternative Minimum Tax—Corporations; Form 6251, Alternative Minimum Tax—Individuals; or Schedule I of Form 1041, U.S. Income Tax Return for Estates and Trusts.

Recordkeeping

Except for Part V (relating to listed property), the IRS does not require you to submit detailed information with your return on the depreciation of assets placed in service in previous tax years. However, the information needed to compute your depreciation deduction (basis, method, etc.) must be part of your permanent records.

You may use the depreciation worksheet on page 15 to assist you in maintaining depreciation records. However, the worksheet is designed only for federal income tax purposes. You may need to keep additional records for accounting and state income tax purposes.

Specific Instructions

Part I. Election To Expense Certain Property Under Section 179

Note. An estate or trust cannot make this election.

You can elect to expense part or all of the cost of section 179 property that you placed in service during the tax year and used predominantly (more than 50%) in your trade or business.

You must make the election on Form 4562 filed with either:
• The original return you file for the tax year the property was placed in service (whether or not you file your return on time) or
• An amended return filed within the time prescribed by law for the applicable tax year. The election made on an amended return must specify the item of section 179 property to which the election applies and the part of the cost of each such item to be taken into account. The amended return must also include any resulting adjustments to taxable income.

The election (and the selection of the property you elected to expense) can be revoked without IRS approval by filing an amended return. The amended return must be filed within the time prescribed by law for the applicable tax year. The amended return must also include any resulting adjustments to taxable income. Once made, the revocation is irrevocable.

Limitations. The amount of section 179 property for which you can make the election is limited to the maximum dollar amount on line 1. In most cases, this amount is reduced if the cost of all section 179 property placed in service during the year is more than $410,000. Your total section 179 expense deduction cannot exceed your business income (line 11).

For a partnership (other than an electing large partnership) these limitations apply to the partnership and each partner. For an electing large partnership, the limitations apply only to the partnership. For an S corporation, these limitations apply to the S corporation and each shareholder. For a controlled group, all component members are treated as one taxpayer.

If you elect to expense section 179 property, you must reduce the amount on which you figure your depreciation or amortization deduction (including any special depreciation allowance) by the section 179 expense deduction.

Line 1

For an enterprise zone business or a renewal community business, the maximum section 179 expense deduction of $102,000 is increased by the smaller of:
• $35,000 or
• The cost of section 179 property that is also qualified zone property or qualified renewal property (including such property placed in service by your spouse, even if you are filing a separate return).

For qualified Liberty Zone property, the maximum section 179 expense deduction is increased by the smaller of:
• $35,000 or
• The cost of section 179 property that is also qualified Liberty Zone property (including such property placed in service by your spouse, even if you are filing a separate return).

If applicable, cross out the preprinted entry on line 1 and enter in the right margin the larger amount. For more information, including definitions of qualified zone property, qualified renewal property, and qualified Liberty Zone property, see Pub. 954, Tax Incentives for Distressed Communities.

Recapture rule. If any qualified zone property (or qualified renewal property) placed in service during the current year ceases to be used in an empowerment zone (or a renewal community) by an enterprise zone business (or a renewal community business) in a later year, the benefit of the increased section 179 expense deduction must be reported as "other income" on your return. Similar rules apply to qualified Liberty Zone property that ceases to be used in the Liberty Zone.

Line 2

Enter the cost of all section 179 property placed in service during the tax year. Also include the cost of the following.

- Any listed property from Part V.
- Any property placed in service by your spouse, even if you are filing a separate return.
- 50% of the cost of section 179 property that is also qualified zone property, qualified renewal property, or qualified Liberty Zone property.

Line 5

If line 5 is zero, you cannot elect to expense any section 179 property. In this case, skip lines 6 through 11, enter zero on line 12, and enter the carryover of any disallowed deduction from 2003 on line 13.

If you are married filing separately, you and your spouse must allocate the dollar limitation for the tax year. To do so, multiply the total limitation that you would otherwise enter on line 5 by 50%, unless you both elect a different allocation. If you both elect a different allocation, multiply the total limitation by the percentage elected. The sum of the percentages you and your spouse elect must equal 100%.

Do not enter on line 5 more than your share of the total dollar limitation.

Line 6

Do not include any listed property on line 6. Enter the elected section 179 cost of listed property in column (i) of line 26.

Column (a) — Description of property. Enter a brief description of the property you elect to expense (e.g., truck, office furniture, etc.).

Column (b) — Cost (business use only). Enter the cost of the property. If you acquired the property through a trade-in, do not include any carryover basis of the property traded in. Include only the excess of the cost of the property over the value of the property traded in.

Column (c) — Elected cost. Enter the amount you elect to expense. You do not have to expense the entire cost of the property. You can depreciate the amount you do not expense. See the line 19 and line 20 instructions.

To report your share of a section 179 expense deduction from a partnership or an S corporation, write "from Schedule K-1 (Form 1065)" or "from Schedule K-1 (Form 1120S)" across columns (a) and (b).

Line 10

The carryover of disallowed deduction from 2003 is the amount of section 179 property, if any, you elected to expense in previous years that was not allowed as a deduction because of the business income limitation. If you filed Form 4562 for 2003, enter the amount from line 13 of your 2003 Form 4562.

Line 11

The total cost you can deduct is limited to your taxable income from the active conduct of a trade or business during the year. You are considered to actively conduct a trade or business only if you meaningfully participate in its management or operations. A mere passive investor is not considered to actively conduct a trade or business.

Note. If you have to apply another Code section that has a limitation based on taxable income, see Pub. 946 for rules on how to apply the business income limitation for the section 179 expense deduction.

Individuals. Enter the smaller of line 5 or the total taxable income from any trade or business you actively conducted, computed without regard to any section 179 expense deduction, the deduction for one-half of self-employment taxes under section 164(f), or any net operating loss deduction. Also include all wages, salaries, tips, and other compensation you earned as an employee (from Form 1040, line 7). Do not reduce this amount by unreimbursed employee business expenses. If you are married filing a joint return, combine the total taxable incomes for you and your spouse.

Partnerships. Enter the smaller of line 5 or the partnership's total items of income and expense described in section 702(a) from any trade or business the partnership actively conducted (other than credits, tax-exempt income, the section 179 expense deduction, and guaranteed payments under section 707(c)).

S corporations. Enter the smaller of line 5 or the corporation's total items of income and expense described in section 1366(a) from any trade or business the corporation actively conducted (other than credits, tax-exempt income, the section 179 expense deduction, and the deduction for compensation paid to the corporation's shareholder-employees).

Corporations other than S corporations. Enter the smaller of line 5 or the corporation's taxable income before the section 179 expense deduction, net operating loss deduction, and special deductions (excluding items not derived from a trade or business actively conducted by the corporation).

Line 12

The limitations on lines 5 and 11 apply to the taxpayer, and not to each separate business or activity. Therefore, if you have more than one business or activity, you may allocate your allowable section 179 expense deduction among them.

To do so, write "Summary" at the top of Part I of the separate Form 4562 you are completing for the total amounts from all businesses or activities. Do not complete the rest of that form. On line 12 of the Form 4562 you prepare for each separate business or activity, enter the amount allocated to the business or activity from the "Summary." No other entry is required in Part I of the separate Form 4562 prepared for each business or activity.

Part II. Special Depreciation Allowance and Other Depreciation

Line 14

For qualified property (defined below) placed in service during the tax year, you may be able to take an additional 50% (or 30%, if applicable) special depreciation allowance. The special allowance applies only to the first year the property is placed in service.

50% special allowance. To qualify for the 50% special allowance, you must have acquired the property after May 5, 2003, and before January 1, 2005. If a binding contract to acquire the property existed before May 6, 2003, the property does not qualify.

30% special allowance. This allowance applies to qualified property for which the 50% allowance does not apply (or for property for which you have elected to claim the 30% allowance for property that would otherwise qualify for the 50% allowance). You must have acquired the property after September 10, 2001, and before January 1, 2005. If a binding contract to acquire the property existed before September 11, 2001, the property does not qualify.

Qualified property. Qualified property is:

- Tangible property depreciated under MACRS with a recovery period of 20 years or less,
- Water utility property (see 25-year property on page 6),
- Computer software defined in and depreciated under section 167(f)(1), or
- Qualified leasehold improvement property.

For purposes of the additional 30% special allowance, qualified property is also qualified Liberty Zone property, other than qualified Liberty Zone leasehold improvement property, not otherwise treated as qualified property.

Qualified property also must meet the following rules.

• The property must be placed in service before January 1, 2005, unless it is:

1. Property with a long production period that meets the requirements of section 168(k)(2)(B) (but only to the extent of the property's pre-January 1, 2005 basis),

2. Noncommercial aircraft that meets the requirements of section 168(k)(2)(C), or

3. Qualified Liberty Zone property.

• The original use of the property (except for qualified Liberty Zone property) must begin with you. For qualified Liberty Zone property, only the original use of the property within the Liberty Zone must begin with you.

• For property you sold and leased back or for self-constructed property, special rules apply. See Temporary Regulations section 1.168(k)-1T(b).

Qualified property does not include:

• Listed property used 50% or less in a qualified business use (defined on page 8).

• Any property required to be depreciated under the alternative depreciation system (ADS) (that is, not property for which you elected to use ADS).

• Qualified Liberty Zone leasehold improvement property.

• Property placed in service and disposed of in the same year.

• Property converted from business or income-producing use to personal use in the same year it is acquired.

• Property for which you elected not to claim any special allowance.

Figure the special allowance by multiplying the depreciable basis of the property by 50% (or 30%, if applicable). To figure the depreciable basis, subtract from the business/investment portion of the cost or other basis of the property the total of the following amounts allocable to the property.

• Section 179 expense deduction.

• Deduction for removal of barriers to the disabled and the elderly.

• Disabled access credit.

• Enhanced oil recovery credit.

• Credit for employer-provided childcare facilities and services.

• Basis adjustment to investment credit property under section 50(c).

Note. If you acquired qualified property through a trade-in, the carryover basis and any excess basis of the acquired property is eligible for the special allowance. See Temporary Regulations section 1.168(k)-1T(f)(5).

CAUTION *If you take the 30% or 50% special allowance, you must reduce the amount on which you figure your regular depreciation or amortization deduction by the amount deducted. Also, you will not have any AMT adjustment for the property if the depreciable basis of the property for the AMT is the same as for the regular tax.*

Election out. You can elect, for any class of property, to either deduct the 30% special allowance, instead of the 50% special allowance, for all such property in such class placed in service during the tax year or not to claim any special allowance for all such property in such class placed in service during the tax year. If you elect not to have any special allowance apply, the property may be subject to an AMT adjustment for depreciation.

To make an election, attach a statement to your timely filed return (including extensions) indicating the class of property for which you are making the election and that, for such class you are either electing to claim the 30% special allowance instead of the 50% special allowance or you are electing not to claim any special allowance.

The election must be made separately by each person owning qualified property (for example, by the partnership, by the S corporation, or by the common parent of a consolidated group).

If you timely filed your return without making an election, you can still make the election by filing an amended return within 6 months of the due date of the return (excluding extensions). Write "Filed pursuant to section 301.9100-2 on the amended return."

Once made, the election cannot be revoked without IRS consent.

Line 15

Report on this line depreciation for property that you elect to depreciate under the unit-of-production method or any other method not based on a term of years (other than the retirement-replacement-betterment method).

Attach a separate sheet showing:

• A description of the property and the depreciation method you elect that excludes the property from MACRS or the Accelerated Cost Recovery System (ACRS) and

• The depreciable basis (cost or other basis reduced, if applicable, by salvage value, any section 179 expense deduction, deduction for removal of barriers to the disabled and the elderly, disabled access credit, enhanced oil recovery credit, credit for employer-provided childcare facilities and services, and any special depreciation allowance).

See section 50(c) to determine the basis adjustment for investment credit property.

Line 16

Enter the total depreciation you are claiming for the following types of property (except listed property and property subject to a section 168(f)(1) election).

• ACRS property (pre-1987 rules). See Pub. 534.

• Property placed in service before 1981.

• Certain public utility property which does not meet certain normalization requirements.

• Certain property acquired from related persons.

• Property acquired in certain nonrecognition transactions.

• Certain sound recordings, movies, and videotapes.

• Property depreciated under the income forecast method. The use of the income forecast method is limited to motion picture films, videotapes, sound recordings, copyrights, books, and patents. For property placed in service after October 22, 2004, you can either include certain participations and residuals in the adjusted basis of the property in the year the property is placed in service or deduct these amounts when paid. See section 167(g)(7). You cannot use this method to depreciate any amortizable section 197 intangible. See the instructions on page 11 for more details on section 197 intangibles.

If you use the income forecast method for any property placed in service after September 13, 1995, you may owe interest or be entitled to a refund for the 3rd and 10th tax years beginning after the tax year the property was placed in service. For details, see Form 8866, Interest Computation Under the Look-Back Method for Property Depreciated Under the Income Forecast Method.

• Intangible property, other than section 197 intangibles, including:

1. Computer software. Use the straight line method over 36 months. A longer period may apply to software leased under a lease agreement entered into after March 12, 2004, to a tax-exempt organization, governmental unit, or foreign person or entity (other than a partnership). See section 167(f)(1)(C).

CAUTION *If you elect the section 179 expense deduction or take the special depreciation allowance for computer software, you must reduce the amount on which you figure your regular depreciation deduction by the amount deducted.*

2. Any right to receive tangible property or services under a contract or granted by a governmental unit (not acquired as part of a business).

3. Any interest in a patent or copyright not acquired as part of a business.

4. Residential mortgage servicing rights. Use the straight line method over 108 months.

5. Other intangible assets with a limited useful life that cannot be estimated with reasonable accuracy. Generally, use the straight line method over 15 years. See Regulations section 1.167(a)-3(b) for details and exceptions.

See section 167(f) for more details.

Prior years' depreciation, plus current year's depreciation, can never exceed the depreciable basis of the property.

Part III. MACRS Depreciation

The term "Modified Accelerated Cost Recovery System" (MACRS) includes the General Depreciation System and the Alternative Depreciation System. Generally, MACRS is used to depreciate any tangible property placed in service after 1986. However, MACRS does not apply to films, videotapes, and sound recordings. For more details and exceptions, see Pub. 946.

Section A

Line 17

For tangible property placed in service in tax years beginning before 2004 and depreciated under MACRS, enter the deductions for the current year. To figure the deductions, see the instructions for line 19, column (g).

Line 18

To simplify the computation of MACRS depreciation, you can elect to group assets into one or more general asset accounts. The assets in each general asset account are depreciated as a single asset.

Each general asset account must include only assets that were placed in service during the same tax year with the same asset class (if any), depreciation method, recovery period, and convention. However, an asset cannot be included in a general asset account if the asset is used both for personal purposes and business/investment purposes.

When an asset in an account is disposed of, the amount realized generally must be recognized as ordinary income. The unadjusted depreciable basis and depreciation reserve of the general asset account are not affected as a result of a disposition.

Special rules apply to passenger automobiles, assets generating foreign source income, assets converted to personal use, certain asset dispositions, and like-kind exchanges or involuntary conversions of property in a general asset account. For more details, see Regulation sections 1.168(i)-1 and Temporary Regulations section 1.168(i)-1T. For more information on depreciating property in a general asset account, see Pub. 946.

To make the election, check the box on line 18. You must make the election on your return filed no later than the due date (including extensions) for the tax year in which the assets included in the general asset account were placed in service. Once made, the election is irrevocable and applies to the tax year for which the election is made and all later tax years.

Section B

Property acquired in a like-kind exchange or involuntary conversion. You generally must depreciate the carryover basis of property you acquire after February 27, 2004, in a like-kind exchange or involuntary conversion over the remaining recovery period of the property exchanged or involuntarily converted. Use the same depreciation method and convention that was used for the exchanged or involuntarily converted property. Treat any excess basis as newly placed in service property. Figure depreciation separately for the carryover basis and the excess basis, if any.

These rules apply only to acquired property with the same or a shorter recovery period or the same or a more accelerated depreciation method than the property exchanged or involuntarily converted. See Temporary Regulations section 1.168(i)-6T(c) and Pub. 946.

For a like-kind exchange or involuntary conversion for which the date of disposition, replacement, or both was before February 28, 2004, you may follow these rules or rely on prior IRS guidance using any reasonable, consistent method of figuring depreciation.

Election out. Instead of using the above rules, you can elect, for depreciation purposes, to treat the adjusted basis of the exchanged property as if it was disposed of at the time of the exchange or involuntary conversion. Treat the carryover basis and excess basis, if any, for the acquired property as if placed in service on the date you acquired it. The depreciable basis of the new property is the adjusted basis of the exchanged or involuntarily converted property plus any additional amount paid for it.

To make the election, figure the depreciation deduction for the new property in Part III. For listed property, use Part V. Attach a statement indicating "Election made under section 1.168(i)-6T(i)" for each property involved in the exchange or involuntary conversion. The election must be made separately by each person acquiring replacement property (for example, by the partnership, by the S corporation, or by the common parent of a consolidated group). The election must be made on your timely filed return (including extensions). Once made, the election cannot be revoked without IRS consent.

CAUTION *If you trade in a vehicle used for employee business use, complete* Form 2106, Part II, Section D, *instead of* Form 4562, *to "elect out" of Temporary Regulations section 1.168(i)-6T. If you do not "elect out," you must use* Form 4562 *instead of Form 2106. See the* Instructions for Form 2106.

Lines 19a Through 19i

Use lines 19a through 19i only for assets placed in service during the tax year beginning in 2004 and depreciated under the General Depreciation System (GDS), except for automobiles and other listed property (which are reported in Part V).

Column (a) — Classification of property. Determine which property you acquired and placed in service during the tax year beginning in 2004. Then, sort that property according to its classification (3-year property, 5-year property, etc.) as shown in column (a) of lines 19a through 19i. The classifications for some property are shown below. For property not shown, see *Determining the classification* on page 6.

3-year property includes:

- A race horse that is more than 2 years old at the time it is placed in service.
- Any horse (other than a race horse) that is more than 12 years old at the time it is placed in service.
- Any qualified rent-to-own property (as defined in section 168(i)(14)).

5-year property includes:

- Automobiles.
- Light general purpose trucks.
- Typewriters, calculators, copiers, and duplicating equipment.
- Any semi-conductor manufacturing equipment.
- Any computer or peripheral equipment.
- Any section 1245 property used in connection with research and experimentation.
- Certain energy property specified in section 168(e)(3)(B)(vi).
- Appliances, carpets, furniture, etc., used in a rental real estate activity.
- Any qualified Liberty Zone leasehold improvement property. However, you can elect not to treat the property as qualified Liberty Zone leasehold improvement property. If you make this election, the property will be depreciable under the rules for nonresidential real property if placed in service before October 23, 2004, and under the rules for qualified leasehold improvement property if placed in service after October 22, 2004. To make the election, attach a statement to your return indicating that you are making an election under section 1400L(c)(5). This election applies to all qualified Liberty Zone leasehold improvement property placed in service during the same year. Rules similar to the rules for electing out of the special depreciation allowance apply.

7-year property includes:

- Office furniture and equipment.
- Railroad track.
- Any property that does not have a class life and is not otherwise classified.
- Any motorsports entertainment complex (as defined in section 168(i)(15)) placed in service after October 22, 2004.

10-year property includes:

- Vessels, barges, tugs, and similar water transportation equipment.
- Any single purpose agricultural or horticultural structure (see section 168(i)(13)).

• Any tree or vine bearing fruit or nuts.

15-year property includes:

• Any municipal wastewater treatment plant.

• Any telephone distribution plant and comparable equipment used for 2-way exchange of voice and data communications.

• Any section 1250 property that is a retail motor fuels outlet (whether or not food or other convenience items are sold there).

• Any qualified leasehold improvement property (as defined in section 168(e)(6)) placed in service after October 22, 2004.

• Any qualified restaurant property (as defined in section 168(e)(7)) placed in service after October 22, 2004.

• Initial clearing and grading land improvements for gas utility property placed in service after October 22, 2004.

20-year property includes:

• Farm buildings (other than single purpose agricultural or horticultural structures).

• Municipal sewers not classified as 25-year property.

• Initial clearing and grading land improvements for electric utility transmission and distribution plants placed in service after October 22, 2004.

25-year property is water utility property, which is:

• Property that is an integral part of the gathering, treatment, or commercial distribution of water that, without regard to this classification, would be 20-year property.

• Municipal sewers. This classification does not apply to property placed in service under a binding contract in effect at all times since June 9, 1996.

Residential rental property is a building in which 80% or more of the total rent is from dwelling units.

Nonresidential real property is any real property that is neither residential rental property nor property with a class life of less than 27.5 years.

50-year property includes any improvements necessary to construct or improve a roadbed or right-of-way for railroad track that qualifies as a railroad grading or tunnel bore under section 168(e)(4).

There is no separate line to report 50-year property. Therefore, attach a statement showing the same information as required in columns (a) through (g). Include the deduction in the line 22 "Total" and write "See attachment" in the bottom margin of the form.

Determining the classification. If your depreciable property is not listed above, determine the classification as follows.

1. Find the property's class life. See the Table of Class Lives and Recovery Periods in Pub. 946.

2. Use the following table to find the classification in column (b) that corresponds to the class life of the property in column (a).

(a) Class life (in years) (See Pub. 946)	(b) Classification
4 or less	3-year property
More than 4 but less than 10	5-year property
10 or more but less than 16	7-year property
16 or more but less than 20	10-year property
20 or more but less than 25	15-year property
25 or more	20-year property

Column (b) — Month and year placed in service. For lines 19h and 19i, enter the month and year you placed the property in service. If you converted property held for personal use to use in a trade or business or for the production of income, treat the property as being placed in service on the conversion date.

Column (c) — Basis for depreciation (business/investment use only). To find the basis for depreciation, multiply the cost or other basis of the property by the percentage of business/investment use. From that result, subtract any section 179 expense deduction, deduction for removal of barriers to the disabled and the elderly, disabled access credit, enhanced oil recovery credit, credit for employer-provided childcare facilities and services, and any special depreciation allowance included on line 14. See section 50(c) to determine the basis adjustment for investment credit property.

Column (d) — Recovery period. Determine the recovery period from the table below, unless you acquired qualified Indian reservation property. Qualified Indian reservation property does not include property placed in service to conduct class I, II, or III gaming activities. See Pub. 946 for more information, including the table for qualified Indian reservation property.

Recovery Period for Most Property

Classification	Recovery period
3-year property	3 yrs.
5-year property	5 yrs.
7-year property	7 yrs.
10-year property	10 yrs.
15-year property	15 yrs.
20-year property	20 yrs.
25-year property	25 yrs.
Residential rental property	27.5 yrs.
Nonresidential real property	39 yrs.
Railroad gradings and tunnel bores	50 yrs.

Column (e) — Convention. The applicable convention determines the portion of the tax year for which depreciation is allowable during a year property is either placed in service or disposed of. There are three types of conventions. To select the correct convention, you must know the type of property and when you placed the property in service.

Half-year convention. This convention applies to all property reported on lines 19a through 19g, unless the mid-quarter convention applies. It does not apply to residential rental property, nonresidential real property, and railroad gradings and tunnel bores. It treats all property placed in service (or disposed of) during any tax year as placed in service (or disposed of) on the midpoint of that tax year. Enter "HY" in column (e).

Mid-quarter convention. If the total depreciable bases (before any special depreciation allowance) of MACRS property placed in service during the last 3 months of your tax year exceed 40% of the total depreciable bases of MACRS property placed in service during the entire tax year, the mid-quarter, instead of the half-year, convention generally applies.

In determining whether the mid-quarter convention applies, do not take into account the following.

• Property that is being depreciated under a method other than MACRS.

• Any residential rental property, nonresidential real property, or railroad gradings and tunnel bores.

• Property that is placed in service and disposed of within the same tax year.

The mid-quarter convention treats all property placed in service (or disposed of) during any quarter as placed in service (or disposed of) on the midpoint of that quarter. However, no depreciation is allowed under this convention for property that is placed in service and disposed of within the same tax year. Enter "MQ" in column (e).

Mid-month convention. This convention applies only to residential rental property (line 19h), nonresidential real property (line 19i), and railroad gradings and tunnel bores. It treats all property placed in service (or disposed of) during any month as placed in service (or disposed of) on the midpoint of that month. Enter "MM" in column (e).

Column (f) — Method. Applicable depreciation methods are prescribed for each classification of property as follows. However, you can make an irrevocable election to use the straight line method for all property within a classification that is placed in service during the tax year. Enter "200 DB" for 200% declining balance, "150 DB" for 150% declining balance, or "S/L" for straight line.

• **3-, 5-, 7-, and 10-year property.** Generally, the applicable method is the 200% declining balance method, switching to the straight line method in the first tax year that the straight line rate exceeds the declining balance rate.

Note. The straight line method is the only applicable method for trees and vines bearing fruit or nuts and qualified Liberty Zone leasehold improvement property.

For 3-, 5-, 7-, or 10-year property eligible for the 200% declining balance method, you can make an irrevocable election to use the 150% declining balance method, switching to the straight line method in the first tax year that the straight line rate exceeds the declining balance rate. The election applies to all property within the classification for which it is made and that was placed in service during the tax year. You will not have an AMT adjustment for any property included under this election.

• **15- and 20-year property and property used in a farming business.** The applicable method is the 150% declining balance method, switching to the straight line method in the first tax year that the straight line rate exceeds the declining balance rate.

• **Water utility property, residential rental property, nonresidential real property, any railroad grading or tunnel bore, or any qualified leasehold improvement or qualified restaurant property placed in service after October 22, 2004.** The only applicable method is the straight line method.

Column (g) — Depreciation deduction. To figure the depreciation deduction you may use optional Tables A through E, which begin on page 13. Multiply column (c) by the applicable rate from the appropriate table. See Pub. 946 for complete tables. If you disposed of the property during the current tax year, multiply the result by the applicable decimal amount from the tables in Step 3 below. Or, you may compute the deduction yourself by completing the following steps.

Step 1. Determine the depreciation rate as follows.

• If you are using the 200% or 150% declining balance method in column (f), divide the declining balance rate (use 2.00 for 200 DB or 1.50 for 150 DB) by the number of years in the recovery period in column (d). For example, for property depreciated using the 200 DB method over a recovery period of 5 years, divide 2.00 by 5 for a rate of 40%. You must switch to the straight line rate in the first year that the straight line rate exceeds the declining balance rate.

• If you are using the straight line method, divide 1.00 by the remaining number of years in the recovery period as of the beginning of the tax year (but not less than one). For example, if there are 6½ years remaining in the recovery period as of the beginning of the year, divide 1.00 by 6.5 for a rate of 15.38%.

Step 2. Multiply the percentage rate determined in Step 1 by the property's unrecovered basis (basis for depreciation (as defined in column (c)) reduced by all prior years' depreciation).

Step 3. For property placed in service or disposed of during the current tax year, multiply the result from Step 2 by the applicable decimal amount from the tables below (based on the convention shown in column (e)).

Half-year (HY) convention		0.5

Mid-quarter (MQ) convention

Placed in service (or disposed of) during the:	**Placed in service**	**Disposed of**
1st quarter	0.875	0.125
2nd quarter	0.625	0.375
3rd quarter	0.375	0.625
4th quarter	0.125	0.875

Mid-month (MM) convention

Placed in service (or disposed of) during the:	**Placed in service**	**Disposed of**
1st month	0.9583	0.0417
2nd month	0.8750	0.1250
3rd month	0.7917	0.2083
4th month	0.7083	0.2917
5th month	0.6250	0.3750
6th month	0.5417	0.4583
7th month	0.4583	0.5417
8th month	0.3750	0.6250
9th month	0.2917	0.7083
10th month	0.2083	0.7917
11th month	0.1250	0.8750
12th month	0.0417	0.9583

Short tax years. See Pub. 946 for rules on how to compute the depreciation deduction for property placed in service in a short tax year.

Section C

Lines 20a Through 20c

Complete lines 20a through 20c for assets, other than automobiles and other listed property, placed in service only during the tax year beginning in 2004 and depreciated under the Alternative Depreciation System (ADS). Report on line 17 MACRS depreciation on assets placed in service in prior years.

Under ADS, use the applicable depreciation method, the applicable recovery period, and the applicable convention to compute depreciation.

The following types of property must be depreciated under ADS.

• Tangible property used predominantly outside the United States.
• Tax-exempt use property.
• Tax-exempt bond financed property.
• Imported property covered by an executive order of the President of the United States.
• Property used predominantly in a farming business and placed in service during any tax year in which you made an election under section 263A(d)(3) not to have the uniform capitalization rules of section 263A apply.

Instead of depreciating property under GDS (line 19), you can make an irrevocable election with respect to any classification of property for any tax year to use ADS. For residential rental and nonresidential real property, you can make this election separately for each property.

Column (a) — Classification of property. Use the following rules to determine the classification of the property under ADS.

Under ADS, the depreciation deduction for most property is based on the property's class life. See section 168(g)(3) for special rules for determining the class life for certain property. See Pub. 946 for information on recovery periods for ADS and the Table of Class Lives and Recovery Periods.

Use line 20a for all property depreciated under ADS, except property that does not have a class life, residential rental and nonresidential real property, water utility property, and railroad gradings and tunnel bores. Use line 20b for property that does not have a class life. Use line 20c for residential rental and nonresidential real property.

Water utility property and railroad gradings and tunnel bores. These assets are 50-year property under ADS. There is no separate line to report 50-year property. Therefore, attach a statement showing the same information required in columns (a) through (g). Include the deduction in the line 22 "Total" and write "See attachment" in the bottom margin of the form.

Column (b) — Month and year placed in service. For 40-year property, enter the month and year placed in service or converted to use in a trade or business or for the production of income.

Column (c) — Basis for depreciation (business/investment use only). See the instructions for line 19, column (c).

Column (d) — Recovery period. On line 20a, enter the property's class life.

Column (e) — Convention. Under ADS, the applicable conventions are the same as those used under GDS. See the instructions for line 19, column (e).

Column (g) — Depreciation deduction. Figure the depreciation deduction in the same manner as under GDS, except use the straight line method over the ADS recovery period and use the applicable convention.

Recapture. When you dispose of property you depreciated using MACRS, any gain on the disposition is generally recaptured (included in income) as ordinary income up to the amount of the depreciation previously allowed or allowable for the property. Depreciation, for this purpose, includes any section 179 deduction claimed on the property, any special depreciation allowance available for the property (unless you elected not to claim it), and any deduction claimed for clean-fuel vehicles and clean-fuel vehicle refueling property. There is no recapture for residential rental and nonresidential real property, unless that property is qualified property for which you claimed a special depreciation allowance (discussed earlier). For more information on depreciation recapture, see Pub. 946.

Part IV. Summary

Line 22

A partnership (other than an electing large partnership) or S corporation does not include any section 179 expense deduction (line 12) on this line. Instead, any section 179 expense deduction is passed through separately to the partners and shareholders on the appropriate line of their Schedules K-1.

Line 23

If you are subject to the uniform capitalization rules of section 263A, enter the increase in basis from costs you must capitalize. For a detailed discussion of who is subject to these rules, which costs must be capitalized, and allocation of costs among activities, see Regulations section 1.263A-1.

Part V. Listed Property

If you claim the standard mileage rate, actual vehicle expenses (including depreciation), or depreciation on other listed property, you must provide the information requested in Part V, regardless of the tax year the property was placed in service. However, if you file Form 2106, 2106-EZ, or Schedule C-EZ (Form 1040), report this information on that form and not in Part V. Also, if you file Schedule C (Form 1040) and are claiming the standard mileage rate or actual vehicle expenses (except depreciation), and you are not required to file Form 4562 for any other reason, report vehicle information in Part IV of Schedule C and not on Form 4562.

Section A

The section 179 expense deduction should be computed before calculating any special depreciation allowance and/or regular depreciation deduction. See the instructions for line 26, column (i) on page 10.

Listed property used 50% or less in a qualified business use (defined below) does not qualify for the section 179 expense deduction or special depreciation allowance.

Line 25

If you acquired and placed qualified listed property in service during the tax year, you may be able to deduct an additional special depreciation allowance. See the instructions for line 14 for the definition of qualified property and how to figure the deduction. This special depreciation allowance is included in the overall limit on depreciation and section 179 expense deduction for passenger automobiles. However, the limit is increased for passenger automobiles (except for qualified Liberty Zone property) for which the special depreciation allowance is claimed. Enter on line 25 your total special depreciation allowance for all listed property.

Lines 26 and 27

Use line 26 to figure depreciation for property used more than 50% in a qualified business use. Use line 27 to figure the depreciation for property used 50% or less in a qualified business use. Also see *Limits for passenger automobiles* on page 9.

If you acquired the property through a trade-in, special rules apply for determining the basis, recovery period, depreciation method, and convention. For more details, see Property acquired in a like-kind exchange or involuntary conversion, *on page 5. Also, see Temporary Regulations section 1.168(i)-6T(d)(3).*

Qualified business use. To determine whether to use line 26 or line 27 to report your listed property, you must first determine the percentage of qualified business use for each property. Generally, a qualified business use is any use in your trade or business. However, it does not include any of the following.

- Investment use.
- Leasing the property to a 5% owner or related person.
- The use of the property as compensation for services performed by a 5% owner or related person.
- The use of the property as compensation for services performed by any person (who is not a 5% owner or related person), unless an amount is included in that person's income for the use of the property and, if required, income tax was withheld on that amount.

Determine your percentage of qualified business use similar to the method used to figure the business/investment use percentage in column (c). Your percentage of qualified business use may be smaller than the business/investment use percentage.

For more information, including the definition of 5% owner and related person and exceptions, see Pub. 946.

Recapture. If you used listed property more than 50% in a qualified business use in the year you placed the property in service, and used it 50% or less in a later year, you may have to include part of the depreciation deducted as income. Use Form 4797, Sales of Business Property, to figure the recapture amount.

Column (a) — Type of property. List on a property-by-property basis all your listed property (defined on page 2) in the following order.

1. Automobiles and other vehicles.
2. Other listed property (computers and peripheral equipment, etc.).

In column (a), list the make and model of automobiles, and give a general description of other listed property.

If you have more than five vehicles used 100% for business/investment purposes, you may group them by tax year. Otherwise, list each vehicle separately.

Column (b) — Date placed in service. Enter the date the property was placed in service. If property held for personal use is converted to business/investment use, treat the property as placed in service on the date of conversion.

Column (c) — Business/investment use percentage. Enter the percentage of business/investment use. For automobiles and other vehicles, determine this percentage by dividing the number of miles the vehicle is driven for trade or business purposes or for the production of income during the year (not to include any commuting mileage) by the total number of miles the vehicle is driven for all purposes. Treat vehicles used by employees as being used 100% for business/investment purposes if the value of personal use is included in the employees' gross income, or the employees reimburse the employer for the personal use.

Employers who report the amount of personal use of the vehicle in the employee's gross income, and withhold the appropriate taxes, should enter "100%" for the percentage of business/investment use. For more information, see Pub. 463.

For other listed property (such as computers or video equipment), allocate the use based on the most appropriate unit of time the property is actually used (rather than merely being available for use).

If during the tax year you convert property used solely for personal purposes to business/investment use (or vice versa), figure the percentage of business/investment use only for the number of months you use the property in your business or for the production of income. Multiply that percentage by the number of months you use the property in your business or for the production of income, and divide the result by 12.

Column (d) — Cost or other basis. Enter the property's actual cost (including sales tax) or other basis (unadjusted for prior years' depreciation). If you traded in old property, see *Property acquired in a like-kind exchange or involuntary conversion* on page 5.

For a vehicle, reduce your basis by any qualified electric vehicle credit or deduction for clean-fuel vehicles you claimed.

If you converted the property from personal use to business/investment use, your basis for depreciation is the smaller of the property's adjusted basis or its fair market value on the date of conversion.

Column (e) — Basis for depreciation (business/investment use only). Multiply column (d) by the percentage in column (c). From that result, subtract any section 179 expense deduction, any special depreciation allowance, any credit for employer-provided childcare facilities and services, and half of any investment credit taken before 1986 (unless you took the reduced credit). For automobiles and other listed property placed in service after 1985 (i.e., transition property), reduce the depreciable basis by the entire investment credit.

Column (f) — Recovery period. Enter the recovery period. For property placed in service after 1986 and used more than 50% in a qualified business use, use the table in the instructions for line 19, column (d). For property placed in service after 1986 and used 50% or less in a qualified business use, depreciate the property using the straight line method over its ADS recovery period. The ADS recovery period is 5 years for automobiles and computers.

Column (g) — Method/convention. Enter the method and convention used to figure your depreciation deduction. See the instructions for line 19, columns (e) and (f). Write "200 DB," "150 DB," or "S/L," for the depreciation method, and "HY," "MM," or "MQ," for half-year, mid-month, or mid-quarter conventions, respectively. For property placed in service before 1987, write "PRE" if you used the prescribed percentages under ACRS. If you elected an alternate percentage, enter "S/L."

Column (h) — Depreciation deduction. See *Limits for passenger automobiles* below before entering an amount in column (h).

For property used more than 50% in a qualified business use (line 26) and placed in service after 1986, figure column (h) by following the instructions for line 19, column (g). If placed in service before 1987, multiply column (e) by the applicable percentage given in Pub. 534 for ACRS property. If the recovery period for an automobile ended before your tax year beginning in 2004, enter your unrecovered basis, if any, in column (h).

For property used 50% or less in a qualified business use (line 27) and placed in service after 1986, figure column (h) by dividing the amount in column (e) by the amount in column (f). Use the same conventions as discussed in the instructions for line 19, column (e). The amount in column (h) cannot exceed the property's unrecovered basis. If the recovery period for an automobile ended before your tax year beginning in 2004, enter your unrecovered basis, if any, in column (h).

For property placed in service before 1987 that was disposed of during the year, enter zero.

Limits for passenger automobiles. The depreciation deduction, including any special depreciation allowance and section 179 expense deduction, for passenger automobiles is limited for any tax year.

For any passenger automobile (including an electric passenger automobile) you list on line 26 or line 27, the total of columns (h) and (i) on line 26 or 27 and column (h) on line 25 for that automobile cannot exceed the applicable limit shown in *Table 1, 2, 3,* or *4* below. If the business/investment use percentage in column (c) for the automobile is less than 100%, you must reduce the applicable limit to an amount equal to the limit multiplied by that percentage. For example, for an automobile (other than a truck or van or an electric automobile) placed in service in 2004 (for which you elect not to claim any special depreciation allowance) that is used 60% for business/investment, the limit is $1,776 ($2,960 x 60%).

Definitions. For purposes of the limits for passenger automobiles, the following apply.

- Passenger automobiles are 4-wheeled vehicles manufactured primarily for use on public roads that are rated at 6,000 pounds unloaded gross vehicle weight or less (for a truck or van, gross vehicle weight is substituted for unloaded gross vehicle weight).
- Trucks and vans placed in service after 2002 that are not qualified nonpersonal use vehicles (see *Exception* below) are passenger automobiles built on a truck chassis, including minivans and sport utility vehicles built on a truck chassis.
- Electric passenger automobiles are vehicles produced by an original equipment manufacturer and designed to run primarily on electricity.

Exception. The following vehicles are not considered passenger automobiles.

- An ambulance, hearse, or combination ambulance-hearse used in your trade or business.
- A vehicle used in your trade or business of transporting persons or property for compensation or hire.
- Any truck or van placed in service after July 6, 2003, that is a qualified nonpersonal use vehicle. A truck or van is a qualified nonpersonal use vehicle only if it has been specially modified with the result that it is not likely to be used more than a de minimis amount for personal purposes. For example, a van that has only a front bench for seating, in which permanent shelving has been installed, that constantly carries merchandise or equipment, and that has been specially painted with advertising or the company's name, is a vehicle not likely to be used more than a de minimis amount for personal purposes.

Exception for clean-fuel modifications. The limits for passenger automobiles placed in service after August 5, 1997, do not apply to the cost of any qualified clean fuel property (such as retrofit parts and components) installed on a vehicle to permit that vehicle to run on a clean-burning fuel.

Exception for leasehold property. The business use requirement and the limits for passenger automobiles generally do not apply to passenger automobiles leased or held by anyone regularly engaged in the business of leasing passenger automobiles.

For a detailed discussion on passenger automobiles, including leased automobiles, see Pub. 463.

Table 1—Limits for Passenger Automobiles Placed in Service Before 2002 (excluding electric passenger automobiles placed in service after August 5, 1997)

IF you placed your automobile in service:	THEN the limit on your depreciation and section 179 expense deduction is:
June 19—Dec. 31, 1984	$6,000
Jan. 1—Apr. 2, 1985	$6,200
Apr. 3, 1985—Dec. 31, 1986	$4,800
Jan. 1, 1987—Dec. 31, 1990	$1,475
Jan. 1, 1991—Dec. 31, 1992	$1,575
Jan. 1, 1993—Dec. 31, 1994	$1,675
Jan. 1, 1995—Dec. 31, 2001	$1,775

Table 2—Limits for Passenger Automobiles Placed in Service After 2001 (excluding trucks and vans placed in service after 2002 and electric passenger automobiles)

IF you placed your automobile in service:	AND the number of tax years in which this automobile has been in service is:	THEN the limit on your depreciation and section 179 expense deduction is:
Jan. 1 — Dec. 31, 2002	3	$2,950
	4	$1,775
Jan. 1 — Dec. 31, 2003	2	$4,900
	3	$2,950
Jan. 1 — Dec. 31, 2004	1	$10,610*
	2	$4,800

*If you elect **not** to claim any special depreciation allowance for the vehicle or the vehicle is not qualified property, or the vehicle is qualified Liberty Zone property, the limit is $2,960.

Table 3—Limits for Trucks and Vans Placed in Service After 2002

IF you placed your truck or van in service:	AND the number of tax years in which this truck or van has been in service is:	THEN the limit on your depreciation and section 179 expense deduction is:
Jan. 1 — Dec. 31, 2003	2	$5,400
	3	$3,250
Jan. 1 — Dec.31, 2004	1	$10,910*
	2	$5,300

*If you elect **not** to claim any special depreciation allowance for the vehicle or the vehicle is not qualified property, or the vehicle is qualified Liberty Zone property, the limit is $3,260.

Table 4—Limits for Electric Passenger Automobiles Placed in Service After August 5, 1997

IF you placed your electric automobile in service:	AND the number of tax years in which this automobile has been in service is:	THEN the limit on your depreciation and section 179 expense deduction is:
Aug. 6, 1997 — Dec. 31, 1998	4 or more	$5,425
Jan. 1, 1999 — Dec. 31, 2001	4 or more	$5,325
Jan. 1 — Dec. 31, 2002	3	$8,750
	4 or more	$5,325
Jan. 1 — Dec. 31, 2003	2	$14,600
	3	$8,750
Jan. 1 — Dec. 31, 2004	1	$31,830*
	2	$14,300

*If you elect **not** to claim any special depreciation allowance for the vehicle or the vehicle is not qualified property, or the vehicle is qualified Liberty Zone property, the limit is $8,880.

Note. The limit for automobiles (including trucks and vans and electric passenger automobiles) placed in service after December 31, 2004, will be published in the Internal Revenue Bulletin. These amounts were not available at the time these instructions were printed.

Column (i) — Elected section 179 cost. Enter the amount you elect to expense for section 179 property used more than 50% in a qualified business use (subject to the limits for passenger automobiles). Refer to the Part I instructions to determine if the property qualifies under section 179.

You cannot elect to expense more than $25,000 of the cost of any sport utility vehicle (SUV) and certain other vehicles placed in service after October 22, 2004. This rule applies to any 4-wheeled vehicle primarily designed or used to carry passengers over public streets, roads, or highways, that is not subject to the passenger automobile limits, and is rated at no more than 14,000 pounds gross vehicle weight. However, the $25,000 limit does not apply to any vehicle:

- Designed to have a seating capacity of more than 9 persons behind the driver's seat, or
- Equipped with a cargo area of at least 6 feet in interior length that is an open area or is designed for use as an open area but is enclosed by a cap and is not readily accessible directly from the passenger compartment, or
- That has an integral enclosure, fully enclosing the driver compartment and load carrying device, does not have seating rearward of the driver's seat, and has no body section protruding more than 30 inches ahead of the leading edge of the windshield.

Recapture of section 179 expense deduction. If you used listed property more than 50% in a qualified business use in the year you placed the property in service and used it 50% or less in a later year, you may have to recapture in the later year part of the section 179 expense deduction. Use Form 4797, Sales of Business Property, to figure the recapture amount.

Section B

Except as noted below, you must complete lines 30 through 36 for each vehicle identified in Section A. Employees must provide their employers with the information requested on lines 30 through 36 for each automobile or vehicle provided for their use.

Exception. Employers are not required to complete lines 30 through 36 for vehicles used by employees who are not more than 5% owners or related persons and for which the question on line 37, 38, 39, 40, or 41 is answered "Yes."

Section C

Employers providing vehicles to their employees satisfy the employer's substantiation requirements under section 274(d) by maintaining a written policy statement that:

- Prohibits personal use including commuting or
- Prohibits personal use except for commuting.

An employee does not need to keep a separate set of records for any vehicle that satisfies these written policy statement rules.

For both written policy statements, there must be evidence that would enable the IRS to determine whether use of the vehicle meets the conditions stated below.

Line 37

A policy statement that prohibits personal use (including commuting) must meet all of the following conditions.

- The employer owns or leases the vehicle and provides it to one or more employees for use in the employer's trade or business.
- When the vehicle is not used in the employer's trade or business, it is kept on the employer's business premises, unless it is temporarily located elsewhere (e.g., for maintenance or because of a mechanical failure).
- No employee using the vehicle lives at the employer's business premises.
- No employee may use the vehicle for personal purposes, other than de minimis personal use (e.g., a stop for lunch between two business deliveries).
- Except for de minimis use, the employer reasonably believes that no employee uses the vehicle for any personal purpose.

Line 38

A policy statement that prohibits personal use (except for commuting) is not available if the commuting employee is an officer, director, or 1% or more owner. This policy must meet all of the following conditions.

- The employer owns or leases the vehicle and provides it to one or more employees for use in the employer's trade or business, and it is used in the employer's trade or business.
- For bona fide noncompensatory business reasons, the employer requires the employee to commute to and/or from work in the vehicle.
- The employer establishes a written policy under which the employee may not use the vehicle for personal purposes, other than commuting or de minimis personal use (e.g., a stop for a personal errand between a business delivery and the employee's home).
- Except for de minimis use, the employer reasonably believes that the employee does not use the vehicle for any personal purpose other than commuting.
- The employer accounts for the commuting use by including an appropriate amount in the employee's gross income.

Line 40

An employer that provides more than five vehicles to its employees who are not 5% owners or related persons need not complete Section B for such vehicles. Instead, the employer must obtain the information from its employees and retain the information received.

Line 41

An automobile meets the requirements for qualified demonstration use if the employer maintains a written policy statement that:

- Prohibits its use by individuals other than full-time automobile salespersons,
- Prohibits its use for personal vacation trips,
- Prohibits storage of personal possessions in the automobile, and
- Limits the total mileage outside the salesperson's normal working hours.

Part VI. Amortization

Each year you can elect to deduct part of certain capital costs over a fixed period.

If you amortize property, the part you amortize does not qualify for the section 179 expense deduction or for depreciation.

Attach any information the Code and regulations may require to make a valid election. See the applicable Code section, regulations, and Pub. 535 for more information.

Line 42

Complete line 42 only for those costs you elect to amortize for which the amortization period begins during your tax year beginning in 2004.

Column (a) — Description of costs. Describe the costs you are amortizing. You can elect to amortize the following.

Pollution control facilities (section 169). You can elect to amortize the cost of a certified pollution control facility over a 60-month period. See section 169 and the related regulations for details and information required in making the election. Also see Pub. 535.

You can deduct a special depreciation allowance on a certified pollution control facility that is qualified property. However, you must reduce the amount on which you figure your amortization deduction by any special allowance that you claim.

Also, a corporation must reduce its amortizable basis of a pollution control facility by 20% before figuring the amortization deduction.

Certain bond premiums (section 171). For individuals reporting amortization of bond premium for bonds acquired before October 23, 1986, do not report the deduction here. See the instructions for Schedule A (Form 1040), line 27.

For taxpayers (other than corporations) claiming a deduction for amortization of bond premium for bonds acquired after October 22, 1986, but before January 1, 1988, the deduction is treated as interest expense and is subject to the investment interest limitations. Use Form 4952, Investment Interest Expense Deduction, to compute the allowable deduction.

For taxable bonds acquired after 1987, you can elect to amortize the bond premium over the life of the bond by reporting the amortization deduction on line 42 each year the election applies. The amortization deduction offsets the interest income from the bond. See Pub. 550, Investment Income and Expenses.

Research and experimental expenditures (section 174). You can elect to either amortize your research and experimental costs, deduct them as current business expenses, or write them off over a 10-year period. If you elect to amortize these costs, deduct them in equal amounts over 60 months or more. For more information, see Pub. 535.

The cost of acquiring a lease (section 178). Amortize these costs over the term of the lease. For more information, see Pub. 535.

Qualified forestation and reforestation costs (section 194). Generally, you can elect to amortize up to $10,000 ($5,000 if married filing separately) of reforestation costs paid or incurred before October 23, 2004, for qualified timber property over an 84-month period.

You can elect to deduct a limited amount of reforestation costs paid or incurred after October 22, 2004. You can elect to amortize costs that are not deducted currently over an 84-month period. There is no limit on the amount of your amortization deduction for reforestation costs paid or incurred after October 22, 2004.

See Pub. 535 for information on amortizing reforestation costs, including limitations and other requirements. Partnerships and S corporations, see the instructions for line 44.

Qualified revitalization expenditures (section 1400I). These amounts are certain capital expenditures that relate to a qualified revitalization building located in an area designated as a renewal community. The amount of qualified revitalization expenditures cannot exceed the commercial revitalization expenditure amount allocated to the qualified revitalization building by the commercial revitalization agency for the state in which the building is located.

You can elect to either (a) deduct one-half of the expenditures for the year the building is placed in service or (b) amortize all such expenditures ratably over the 120-month period beginning with the month the building is placed in service. Report any amortization on line 42. Report any deductions on the applicable "Other Deductions" or "Other Expenses" line of your return. This deduction is treated as depreciation for purposes of basis adjustments and ordinary income recapture upon disposition.

Optional write-off of certain tax preferences over the period specified in section 59(e). You can elect to amortize certain tax preference items over an optional period. If you make this election, there is no AMT adjustment. The applicable expenditures and the optional recovery periods are as follows:

- Circulation expenditures (section 173) — 3 years.
- Intangible drilling and development costs (section 263(c)) — 60 months.
- Research and experimental expenditures (section 174(a)), mining exploration and development costs (section 616(a) and 617(a)) — 10 years.

Certain section 197 intangibles. The following costs must be amortized over 15 years (180 months) starting with the later of (a) the month the intangibles were acquired or (b) the month the trade or business or activity engaged in for the production of income begins.

- Goodwill;
- Going concern value;
- Workforce in place;
- Business books and records, operating systems, or any other information base;
- A patent, copyright, formula, process, design, pattern, know-how, format, or similar item;
- A customer-based intangible (e.g., composition of market or market share);
- A supplier-based intangible;
- A license, permit, or other right granted by a governmental unit;
- A covenant not to compete entered into in connection with the acquisition of a business; and
- A franchise (including a sports franchise acquired after October 22, 2004), trademark, or trade name.

A longer period may apply to section 197 intangibles leased under a lease agreement entered into after March 12, 2004, to a tax-exempt organization, governmental unit, or foreign person or entity (other than a partnership). See section 197(f)(10).

For more details on section 197 intangibles, see Pub. 535.

Start-up and organizational costs. You can elect to amortize the following costs for setting up your business.

- Business start-up costs (section 195).
- Organizational costs for a corporation (section 248).
- Organizational costs for a partnership (section 709).

For costs paid or incurred before October 23, 2004, you can elect an amortization period of 60 months or more. For costs paid or incurred after October 22, 2004, you can elect to deduct a limited amount of start-up or organizational costs. The costs that are not deducted currently can be amortized ratably over a 180-month period. The amortization period starts with the month you begin business operations.

Attach the statement required by the appropriate Code section and related regulations. If you have both start-up and organizational costs, attach a separate statement for each type of cost. See Pub. 535 for more information.

The statements required to make the elections must be attached to Form 4562 and filed by the due date, including extensions, of your return for the year in which the active trade or business begins. If you timely filed that return without making the election, you can still make the election on an amended return filed within 6 months of the due date, excluding extensions, of that return. Write "Filed pursuant to section 301.9100-2" on the amended return.

Creative property costs. These are costs paid or incurred to acquire and develop screenplays, scripts, story outlines, motion picture production rights to books and plays, and other similar properties for purposes of potential future film development, production, and exploitation. You may be able to amortize creative property costs for properties not set for production within 3 years of the first capitalized transaction. These costs are amortized ratably over a 15-year period under the rules of Rev. Proc. 2004-36, 2004-24 I.R.B. 1063.

Column (b) — Date amortization begins. Enter the date the amortization period begins under the applicable Code section.

Column (c) — Amortizable amount. Enter the total amount you are amortizing. See the applicable Code section for limits on the amortizable amount.

Column (d) — Code section. Enter the Code section under which you amortize the costs.

Column (f) — Amortization for this year. Compute the amortization deduction by:

1. Dividing the amount in column (c) by the number of months over which the costs are to be amortized and multiplying the result by the number of months in the amortization period included in your tax year beginning in 2004 or

2. Multiplying the amount in column (c) by the percentage in column (e).

Line 43

If you are reporting the amortization of costs that began before your 2004 tax year and you are not required to file Form 4562 for any other reason, do not file Form 4562. Report the amortization directly on the "Other Deductions" or "Other Expenses" line of your return. See Pub. 535.

Line 44

Report the total amortization, including the allowable portion of forestation or reforestation amortization, on the applicable "Other Deductions" or "Other Expenses" line of your return. For more details, including limitations that apply, see Pub. 535. Partnerships (other than electing large partnerships) and S corporations, report the amortizable basis of any forestation or reforestation expenses for which amortization is elected and the year in which the amortization begins as a separately stated item on Schedules K and K-1 (Form 1065 or 1120S). See the instructions for Schedule K (Form 1065 or 1120S) for more details on how to report.

Paperwork Reduction Act Notice. We ask for the information on this form to carry out the Internal Revenue laws of the United States. You are required to give us the information. We need it to ensure that you are complying with these laws and to allow us to figure and collect the right amount of tax.

You are not required to provide the information requested on a form that is subject to the Paperwork Reduction Act unless the form displays a valid OMB control number. Books or records relating to a form or its instructions must be retained as long as their contents may become material in the administration of any Internal Revenue law. Generally, tax returns and return information are confidential, as required by section 6103.

The time needed to complete and file this form will vary depending on individual circumstances. The estimated average time is: **Recordkeeping,** 38 hr., 29 min.; **Learning about the law or the form,** 4 hr., 16 min.; **Preparing and sending the form to the IRS,** 5 hr., 5 min.

If you have comments concerning the accuracy of these time estimates or suggestions for making this form simpler, we would be happy to hear from you. See the instructions for the tax return with which this form is filed.

Table A—General Depreciation System

Method: 200% declining balance switching to straight line

Convention: Half-year

	If the recovery period is:			
Year	3 years	5 years	7 years	10 years
1	33.33%	20.00%	14.29%	10.00%
2	44.45%	32.00%	24.49%	18.00%
3	14.81%	19.20%	17.49%	14.40%
4	7.41%	11.52%	12.49%	11.52%
5		11.52%	8.93%	9.22%
6		5.76%	8.92%	7.37%
7			8.93%	6.55%
8			4.46%	6.55%
9				6.56%
10				6.55%
11				3.28%

Table B—General and Alternative Depreciation System

Method: 150% declining balance switching to straight line

Convention: Half-year

	If the recovery period is:					
Year	5 years	7 years	10 years	12 years	15 years	20 years
1	15.00%	10.71%	7.50%	6.25%	5.00%	3.750%
2	25.50%	19.13%	13.88%	11.72%	9.50%	7.219%
3	17.85%	15.03%	11.79%	10.25%	8.55%	6.677%
4	16.66%	12.25%	10.02%	8.97%	7.70%	6.177%
5	16.66%	12.25%	8.74%	7.85%	6.93%	5.713%
6	8.33%	12.25%	8.74%	7.33%	6.23%	5.285%
7		12.25%	8.74%	7.33%	5.90%	4.888%
8		6.13%	8.74%	7.33%	5.90%	4.522%
9			8.74%	7.33%	5.91%	4.462%
10			8.74%	7.33%	5.90%	4.461%
11			4.37%	7.32%	5.91%	4.462%
12				7.33%	5.90%	4.461%
13				3.66%	5.91%	4.462%
14					5.90%	4.461%
15					5.91%	4.462%
16					2.95%	4.461%
17						4.462%
18						4.461%
19						4.462%

Table C—General Depreciation System

Method: Straight line

Convention: Mid-month

Recovery period: 27.5 years

Year	The month in the 1st recovery year the property is placed in service:											
	1	2	3	4	5	6	7	8	9	10	11	12
1	3.485%	3.182%	2.879%	2.576%	2.273%	1.970%	1.667%	1.364%	1.061%	0.758%	0.455%	0.152%
2–9	3.636%	3.636%	3.636%	3.636%	3.636%	3.636%	3.636%	3.636%	3.636%	3.636%	3.636%	3.636%
10,12,14,16,18	3.637%	3.637%	3.637%	3.637%	3.637%	3.637%	3.636%	3.636%	3.636%	3.636%	3.636%	3.636%
11,13,15,17,19	3.636%	3.636%	3.636%	3.636%	3.636%	3.636%	3.637%	3.637%	3.637%	3.637%	3.637%	3.637%

Table D—General Depreciation System

Method: Straight line

Convention: Mid-month

Recovery period: 31.5 years

Year	The month in the 1st recovery year the property is placed in service:											
	1	2	3	4	5	6	7	8	9	10	11	12
13,15,17,19	3.174%	3.175%	3.174%	3.175%	3.174%	3.175%	3.174%	3.175%	3.174%	3.175%	3.174%	3.175%
12,14,16,18	3.175%	3.174%	3.175%	3.174%	3.175%	3.174%	3.175%	3.174%	3.175%	3.174%	3.175%	3.174%

Table E—General Depreciation System

Method: Straight line

Convention: Mid-month

Recovery period: 39 years

Year	The month in the 1st recovery year the property is placed in service:											
	1	2	3	4	5	6	7	8	9	10	11	12
1	2.461%	2.247%	2.033%	1.819%	1.605%	1.391%	1.177%	0.963%	0.749%	0.535%	0.321%	0.107%
2–39	2.564%	2.564%	2.564%	2.564%	2.564%	2.564%	2.564%	2.564%	2.564%	2.564%	2.564%	2.564%

INSTRUCTIONS FOR FORM 4626

Alternative Minimum Tax—Corporations

2004

Department of the Treasury
Internal Revenue Service

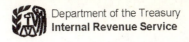

Instructions for Form 4626

Alternative Minimum Tax—Corporations

Section references are to the Internal Revenue Code unless otherwise noted.

General Instructions

Purpose of Form

Use Form 4626 to figure the alternative minimum tax (AMT) under section 55 for a corporation that is not exempt from the AMT.

Consolidated returns. For an affiliated group filing a consolidated return under the rules of section 1501, AMT must be figured on a consolidated basis.

Who Must File

If the corporation is a "small corporation" exempt from the AMT (as explained below), do not file Form 4626.

Generally, file Form 4626 if either of the following apply.

- The corporation's taxable income or (loss) before the net operating loss (NOL) deduction plus its adjustments and preferences total more than $40,000 or, if smaller, its allowable exemption amount.
- The corporation claims any general business credit, the qualified electric vehicle credit, the nonconventional source fuel credit, or the credit for prior year minimum tax.

Exemption for Small Corporations

A corporation is treated as a small corporation exempt from the AMT for its current tax year beginning in 2004 if:

1. The current year is the corporation's first tax year in existence (regardless of its gross receipts for the year), or
2. Both of the following apply.

a. It was treated as a small corporation exempt from the AMT for all prior tax years beginning after 1997.

b. Its average annual gross receipts for the 3-tax-year period (or portion thereof during which the corporation was in existence) ending before its tax year beginning in 2004 did not exceed $7.5 million ($5 million if the corporation had only 1 prior tax year).

The following rules apply when figuring gross receipts under 2b above.

- Gross receipts must be figured using the corporation's tax accounting method and include total sales (net of returns and allowances), amounts received for services, and income from investments and other sources. See Temporary Regulations section 1.448-1T(f)(2)(iv) for more details.
- Gross receipts include those of any predecessor of the corporation, including non-corporate entities.
- For a short tax year, gross receipts must be annualized by multiplying them by 12 and dividing the result by the number of months in the tax year.
- The gross receipts of all persons treated as a single employer under section 52(a), 52(b), 414(m), or 414(o) must be aggregated.

Loss of small corporation status. If the corporation qualified as a small corporation exempt from the AMT for its previous tax year, but does not meet the gross receipts test for its tax year beginning in 2004, it loses its AMT exemption status. Special rules apply in figuring AMT for the tax year beginning in 2004 and all later years based on the "change date." The change date is the first day of the corporation's tax year beginning in 2004. Where this applies, complete Form 4626 taking into account the following modifications.

- The adjustments for depreciation and amortization of pollution control facilities apply only to property placed in service on or after the change date.
- The adjustment for mining exploration and development costs applies only to amounts paid or incurred on or after the change date.
- The adjustment for long-term contracts applies only to contracts entered into on or after the change date.
- When figuring the amount to enter on line 6, for any loss year beginning before the change date, use the corporation's regular tax NOL for that year.
- Figure the limitation on line 4d only for prior tax years beginning on or after the change date.
- Enter zero on line 2c of the Adjusted Current Earnings (ACE) Worksheet on page 11. When completing line 5 of the ACE Worksheet, take into account only amounts from tax years beginning on or after the change date. Also, for line 8 of the ACE Worksheet, take into account only property placed in service on or after the change date.

See section 55(e)(3) for exceptions related to any item acquired in a corporate acquisition or to any substituted basis property, if an AMT provision applied to the item or property while it was held by the transferor.

Once the corporation loses its small corporation status, it cannot qualify for any subsequent tax year.

Credit for Prior Year Minimum Tax

A corporation may be able to take a minimum tax credit against the regular tax for AMT incurred in prior years. See Form 8827, Credit for Prior Year Minimum Tax—Corporations, for details.

Recordkeeping

Certain items of income, deductions, credits, etc., receive different tax treatment for the AMT than for the regular tax. Therefore, the corporation should keep adequate records to support items refigured for the AMT. Examples include:

- Tax forms completed a second time to refigure the AMT;
- The computation of a carryback or carryforward to other tax years of certain deductions or credits (for example, net operating loss, capital loss, and foreign tax credit) if the AMT amount is different from the regular tax amount;
- The computation of a carryforward of a passive loss or tax shelter farm activity loss if the AMT amount is different from the regular tax amount; and
- A "running balance" of the excess of the corporation's total increases in

Cat. No. 64443L

alternative minimum taxable income (AMTI) from prior year adjusted current earnings (ACE) adjustments over the total reductions in AMTI from prior year ACE adjustments (see the instructions for line 4d on page 6).

Short Period Return

If the corporation is filing for a period of less than 12 months, AMTI must be annualized and the tentative minimum tax prorated based on the number of months in the short period. Complete Form 4626 as follows.

1. Complete lines 1 through 6 in the normal manner. Subtract line 6 from line 5 to figure AMTI for the short period, but do not enter it on line 7.
2. Multiply AMTI for the short period by 12. Divide the result by the number of months in the short period. Enter this result on line 7 and write "Sec. 443(d)(1)" on the dotted line to the left of the entry space.
3. Complete lines 8 through 11.
4. Subtract line 11 from line 10. Multiply the result by the number of months in the short period and divide that result by 12. Enter the final result on line 12 and write "Sec. 443(d)(2)" on the dotted line to the left of the entry space.
5. Complete the rest of the form in the normal manner.

Allocating Differently Treated Items Between Certain Entities and Their Investors

For a regulated investment company, a real estate investment trust, or a common trust fund, see section 59(d) for details on allocating certain differently treated items between the entity and its investors.

Optional Write-Off for Certain Expenditures

There is no AMT adjustment for the following items if the corporation elects to deduct them ratably over the period of time shown for the regular tax.

- Circulation expenditures (personal holding companies only)—3 years.
- Mining exploration and development costs—10 years.
- Intangible drilling costs—60 months.

See section 59(e) for more details.

Specific Instructions

Line 1. Taxable Income or (Loss) Before Net Operating Loss Deduction

Enter the corporation's taxable income or (loss) before the NOL deduction, after the special deductions, and without regard to any excess inclusion (for example, if filing Form 1120, subtract line 29b from line 28 of that form).

Line 2. Adjustments and Preferences

To avoid duplication, do not include any AMT adjustment or preference taken into account on line 2i, 2j, 2k, or 2o in the amounts to be entered on any other line of this form.

Line 2a. Depreciation of Post-1986 Property

What Adjustments Are Not Included As Depreciation Adjustments?

Do not make a depreciation adjustment on line 2a for:

- A tax shelter farm activity. Take this adjustment into account on line 2i.
- Passive activities. Take this adjustment into account on line 2j.
- An activity for which the corporation is not at risk or income or loss from a partnership interest or stock in an S corporation if the basis limitations apply. Take this adjustment into account on line 2k.

What Depreciation Must Be Refigured for the AMT?

Generally, the corporation must refigure depreciation for the AMT, including depreciation allocable to inventory costs, for:

- Property placed in service after 1998 depreciated for the regular tax using the 200% declining balance method (generally 3-, 5-, 7-, or 10-year property under the modified accelerated cost recovery system (MACRS));
- Section 1250 property placed in service after 1998 that is not depreciated for the regular tax using the straight line method; and
- Tangible property placed in service after 1986 and before 1999. (If the transitional election was made under section 203(a)(1)(B) of the Tax Reform Act of 1986, this rule applies to property placed in service after July 31, 1986.)

What Depreciation Is Not Refigured for the AMT?

Do not refigure depreciation for the AMT for the following.

- Residential rental property placed in service after 1998.
- Nonresidential real property with a class life of 27.5 years or more (generally, a building and its structural components) placed in service after 1998 that is depreciated for the regular tax using the straight line method.
- Other section 1250 property placed in service after 1998 that is depreciated for the regular tax using the straight line method.
- Property (other than section 1250 property) placed in service after 1998 that is depreciated for the regular tax using the 150% declining balance method or the straight line method.
- Property for which the corporation elected to use the alternative depreciation system (ADS) of section 168(g) for the regular tax.
- Qualified property eligible for the special depreciation allowance under section 168(k) if the depreciable basis of the property for the AMT is the same as for the regular tax. The special allowance is deductible for the AMT. And, there also is no adjustment required for any depreciation figured on the remaining basis of the qualified property if the depreciable basis of the property for the AMT is the same as for the regular tax. Property for which an election is in effect to not have the special allowance apply is not qualified property. See the Instructions for Form 4562 for the definition of qualified property.
- Any part of the cost of any property that the corporation elected to expense under section 179. The reduction to the depreciable basis of section 179 property by the amount of the section 179 expense deduction is the same for the regular tax and the AMT.
- Certain public utility property (if a normalization method of accounting is not used), motion picture films and video tape, sound recordings, and property that the corporation elects to exclude from MACRS by using a depreciation method based on a term of years, such as the unit-of-production method.
- Qualified Indian reservation property.
- Qualified revitalization expenditures for a building for which the corporation elected to claim the commercial

revitalization deduction under section 1400I.

How Is Depreciation Refigured for the AMT?

Property placed in service after 1998. Use the same convention and recovery period used for the regular tax. Use the straight line method for section 1250 property. Use the 150% declining balance method, switching to the straight line method the first tax year it gives a larger deduction, for other property.

Property placed in service before 1999. Refigure depreciation for the AMT using ADS, with the same convention used for the regular tax. See the table below for the method and recovery period to use.

Property Placed in Service Before 1999

IF the property is	THEN use the . . .
Section 1250 property.	Straight line method over 40 years.
Tangible property (other than section 1250 property) depreciated using straight line method for the regular tax.	Straight line method over the property's AMT class life.
Any other tangible property.	150% declining balance method, switching to straight line method the first tax year it gives a larger deduction, over the property's AMT class life.

How is the AMT class life determined? For property placed in service before 1999, the class life used for the AMT is not necessarily the same as the recovery period used for the regular tax.

The class lives are listed in Rev. Proc. 87-56, 1987-2 C.B. 674, and in Pub. 946, How To Depreciate Property.

See Pub. 946 for tables that may be used to figure AMT depreciation. Rev. Proc. 89-15, 1989-1 C.B. 816, has special rules for short tax years and for property disposed of before the end of the recovery period.

How Is the Line 2a Adjustment Figured?

Subtract the AMT deduction for depreciation from the regular tax deduction and enter the result on line 2a. If the AMT deduction is more than the regular tax deduction, enter the difference as a negative amount.

In addition to the AMT adjustment to the deduction for depreciation, also adjust the amount of depreciation that was capitalized, if any, to account for the difference between the rules for the regular tax and the AMT. Include on this line the current year adjustment to taxable income, if any, resulting from the difference.

Line 2b. Amortization of Certified Pollution Control Facilities

For facilities placed in service before 1999, figure the amortization deduction for the AMT using ADS (that is, the straight line method over the facility's class life). For facilities placed in service after 1998, figure the amortization deduction for the AMT under MACRS using the straight line method. Figure the AMT deduction using 100% of the asset's amortizable basis. Do not reduce the corporation's AMT basis by the 20% section 291 adjustment that applied for the regular tax.

Enter the difference between the AMT deduction and the regular tax deduction on line 2b. If the AMT deduction is more than the regular tax deduction, enter the difference as a negative amount.

Line 2c. Amortization of Mining Exploration and Development Costs

This adjustment applies only to costs for which the corporation did not elect the optional 10-year write-off under section 59(e) for the regular tax.

For the AMT, the regular tax deductions under sections 616(a) and 617(a) are not allowed. Instead, capitalize these costs and amortize them ratably over a 10-year period beginning with the tax year in which the corporation paid or incurred them. The 10-year amortization applies to 100% of the mining development and exploration costs paid or incurred during the tax year. Do not reduce the corporation's AMT basis by the 30% section 291 adjustment that applied for the regular tax.

If the corporation had a loss on property for which mining exploration and development costs have not been fully amortized for the AMT, the AMT deduction is the smaller of (a) the loss allowable for the costs had they remained capitalized or (b) the remaining costs to be amortized for the AMT.

Subtract the AMT deduction from the regular tax deduction. Enter the result on line 2c. If the AMT deduction is more than the regular tax deduction, enter the difference as a negative amount.

Line 2d. Amortization of Circulation Expenditures

This adjustment applies only to expenditures of a personal holding company for which the company did not elect the optional 3-year write-off under section 59(e) for the regular tax.

For the regular tax, circulation expenditures may be deducted in full when paid or incurred. For the AMT, these expenditures must be capitalized and amortized over 3 years beginning with the tax year in which the expenditures were made.

If the corporation had a loss on property for which circulation expenditures have not been fully amortized for the AMT, the AMT deduction is the smaller of (a) the loss allowable for the expenditures had they remained capitalized or (b) the remaining expenditures to be amortized for the AMT.

Subtract the AMT deduction from the regular tax deduction. Enter the result on line 2d. If the AMT deduction is more than the regular tax deduction, enter the difference as a negative amount.

Line 2e. Adjusted Gain or Loss

If, during the tax year, the corporation disposed of property for which it is making (or previously made) any of the adjustments described on lines 2a through 2d above, refigure the property's adjusted basis for the AMT. Then refigure the gain or loss on the disposition.

The property's adjusted basis for the AMT is its cost minus all applicable depreciation or amortization deductions allowed for the AMT during the current tax year and previous tax years. Subtract this AMT basis from the sales price to get the AMT gain or loss.

Dispositions for which line 2i, 2j, and 2k adjustments are made. The corporation may also have gains or losses from lines 2i, 2j, and 2k that must be considered on line 2e. For example, if for the regular tax the corporation reports a loss from the disposition of an asset used in a passive activity, include the loss in the computations for line 2j to determine if any passive activity loss is limited for the AMT. Then, include the AMT passive activity loss allowed that relates to the disposition of the asset on line 2e in determining the corporation's AMT basis adjustment. It may be helpful to refigure the following for the AMT: Form 8810 and related worksheets, Schedule D (Form 1120), Form 4684 (Section B), or Form 4797.

Enter on line 2e the difference between the regular tax gain or loss and the AMT gain or loss. Enter the difference as a negative amount if any of the following apply.

- The AMT gain is less than the regular tax gain.
- The AMT loss exceeds the regular tax loss.
- The corporation has an AMT loss and a regular tax gain.

Line 2f. Long-Term Contracts

For the AMT, the corporation generally must use the percentage-of-completion method described in section 460(b) to determine the taxable income from any long-term contract (defined in section 460(f)). However, this rule does not apply to any home construction contract (as defined in section 460(e)(6)).

For contracts excepted from the percentage-of-completion method for the regular tax by section 460(e)(1), determine the percentage of completion using the simplified procedures for allocating costs outlined in section 460(b)(3).

Subtract the regular tax income from the AMT income. Enter the difference on line 2f. If the AMT income is less than the regular tax income, enter the difference as a negative amount.

Line 2g. Merchant Marine Capital Construction Funds

Amounts deposited in these funds are not deductible for the AMT. Earnings on these funds must be included in gross income for the AMT. If the corporation deducted these amounts or excluded them from income for the regular tax, add them back on line 2g.

Line 2h. Section 833(b) Deduction

This deduction is not allowed for the AMT. If the corporation took this deduction for the regular tax, add it back on line 2h.

Line 2i. Tax Shelter Farm Activities

Complete this line only if the corporation is a personal service corporation and it has a gain or loss from a tax shelter farm activity that is not a passive activity. If the tax shelter farm activity is a passive activity, include the gain or loss in the computations for line 2j.

Refigure all gains and losses reported for the regular tax from tax shelter farm activities by taking into account any AMT adjustments and preferences. Determine the AMT gain or loss using the rules for the regular tax with the following modifications.

- No loss is allowed except to the extent the personal service corporation is insolvent.
- Do not use a loss in the current tax year to offset gains from other tax shelter farm activities. Instead, suspend any loss and carry it forward indefinitely until the corporation has a gain in a subsequent tax year from that same tax shelter farm activity or it disposes of the activity.

Keep adequate records for losses that are not deductible (and therefore carried forward) for both the AMT and regular tax.

Enter on line 2i the difference between the AMT gain or loss and the regular tax gain or loss. Enter the difference as a negative amount if the corporation had:

- An AMT loss and a regular tax gain,
- An AMT loss that exceeds the regular tax loss, or
- A regular tax gain that exceeds the AMT gain.

Line 2j. Passive Activities

This adjustment applies only to closely held corporations and personal service corporations.

Refigure all passive activity gains and losses reported for the regular tax by taking into account the corporation's AMT adjustments and preferences and AMT prior year unallowed losses.

Determine the corporation's AMT passive activity gain or loss using the same rules used for the regular tax. Generally, no loss is allowed. However, if the corporation is insolvent, losses are allowed to the extent the corporation is insolvent (see section 58(c)).

Disallowed losses of a personal service corporation are suspended until the corporation has income from that (or any other) passive activity or until the passive activity is disposed of (that is, its passive losses cannot offset "net active income" (defined in section 469(e)(2)(B) or "portfolio income")). Disallowed losses of a closely held corporation that is not a personal service corporation are treated the same except that, in addition, they may be used to offset "net active income."

Keep adequate records for losses that are not deductible (and therefore carried forward) for both the AMT and regular tax.

Enter on line 2j the difference between the AMT gain or loss and the regular tax gain or loss. Enter the difference as a negative amount if the corporation had:

- An AMT loss and a regular tax gain,
- An AMT loss that exceeds the regular tax loss, or
- A regular tax gain that exceeds the AMT gain.

Tax Shelter Farm Activities That Are Passive Activities

Refigure all gains and losses reported for the regular tax by taking into account the corporation's AMT adjustments and preferences and AMT prior year unallowed losses.

Use the same rules as outlined above for other passive activities, with the following modifications.

- AMT gains from tax shelter farm activities that are passive activities may be used to offset AMT losses from other passive activities.
- AMT losses from tax shelter farm activities that are passive activities may not be used to offset AMT gains from other passive activities. These losses must be suspended and carried forward indefinitely until the corporation has a gain in a subsequent year from that same activity or it disposes of the activity.

Line 2k. Loss Limitations

Refigure gains and losses reported for the regular tax from at-risk activities and partnerships by taking into account the corporation's AMT adjustments and preferences. If the corporation has recomputed losses that must be limited for the AMT by section 465 or section 704(d) or the corporation reported losses for the regular tax from at-risk activities or partnerships that were limited by those sections, figure the difference between the loss limited for the AMT and the loss limited for the regular tax for each applicable at-risk activity or partnership. "Loss limited" means the amount of loss that is not allowable for the year because of the limitations above.

Enter on line 2k the excess of the loss limited for the AMT over the loss limited for the regular tax. If the loss limited for the regular tax is more than the loss limited for the AMT, enter the difference as a negative amount.

Line 2l. Depletion

Refigure depletion using only income and deductions allowed for the AMT when refiguring the limit based on taxable income from the property under section 613(a) and the limit based on taxable income, with certain adjustments, under section 613A(d)(1). Also, the depletion deduction for mines, wells, and other natural deposits is limited to the property's adjusted basis at the end of the year, as refigured for the AMT, unless the corporation is an independent producer or royalty owner claiming percentage depletion for oil and gas wells. Figure this limit separately for each property. When refiguring the property's adjusted basis, take into account any AMT adjustments the corporation made this year or in previous years that affect basis (other than the current year's depletion). Do not include in the property's adjusted basis any unrecovered costs of depreciable tangible property used to exploit the deposits (for example, machinery, tools, pipes, etc.).

For iron ore and coal (including lignite), apply the section 291 adjustment before figuring this preference.

Enter on line 2l the difference between the regular tax and the AMT deduction. If the AMT deduction is more than the regular tax deduction, enter the difference as a negative amount.

Line 2m. Tax-Exempt Interest Income From Specified Private Activity Bonds

Enter interest income from specified private activity bonds, reduced by any deduction that would have been allowable if the interest were includible in gross income for the regular tax. Generally, a specified private activity bond is any private activity bond (as defined in section 141) issued after August 7, 1986, on which the interest is not includible in gross income for the regular tax. See section 57(a)(5) for exceptions and details.

Line 2n. Intangible Drilling Costs

This preference applies only to costs for which the corporation did not elect the optional 60-month write-off for the regular tax.

Intangible drilling costs (IDCs) from oil, gas, and geothermal properties are a preference to the extent excess IDCs exceed 65% of the net income from the properties. Figure the preference for all geothermal deposits separately from the preference for all oil and gas properties that are not geothermal deposits.

Excess IDCs are the excess of:

- The amount of IDCs the corporation paid or incurred for oil, gas, or geothermal properties that it elected to expense for the regular tax (not including any deduction for nonproductive wells) reduced by the section 291(b)(1) adjustment for integrated oil companies and increased by any amortization of IDCs allowed under section 291(b)(2) over
- The amount that would have been allowed if the corporation had amortized that amount over a 120-month period starting with the month the well was placed in production or, alternatively, had elected any method that is permissible in determining cost depletion.

Net income is the gross income the corporation received or accrued from all oil, gas, and geothermal wells minus the deductions allocable to these properties (reduced by the excess IDCs). When refiguring net income, use only income and deductions allowed for the AMT.

Exception. The preference for IDCs from oil and gas wells does not apply to corporations that are independent producers (that is, not integrated oil companies as defined in section 291(b)(4)). However, this benefit may be limited. First, figure the IDC preference as if this exception did not apply. Then, for purposes of this exception, complete a second Form 4626 through line 5, including the IDC preference. If the amount of the IDC preference exceeds 40% of the amount figured for line 5, enter the excess on line 2n (the benefit of this exception is limited). If the amount of the IDC preference is equal to or less than 40% of the amount figured for line 5, do not include an amount on line 2n for oil and gas wells (the benefit of this exception is not limited).

Line 2o. Other Adjustments And Preferences

Enter the net amount of any other adjustments and preferences, including the following.

Income eligible for the possessions tax credit. If this income was included in the corporation's taxable income for the regular tax, include this amount on line 2o as a negative amount.

Income from the alcohol fuel credit. If this income was included in the corporation's income for the regular tax, include this amount on line 2o as a negative amount.

Income as the beneficiary of an estate or trust. If the corporation is the beneficiary of an estate or trust, include on line 2o the minimum tax adjustment from Schedule K-1 (Form 1041), line 9.

Net AMT adjustment from an electing large partnership. If the corporation is a partner in an electing large partnership, include on line 2o the amount from Schedule K-1 (Form 1065-B), box 6. Also include on line 2o any amount from Schedule K-1 (Form 1065-B), box 5, unless the corporation is a closely held or personal service corporation. Closely held and personal service corporations should take any amount from box 5 into account when figuring the amount to enter on line 2j.

Patron's AMT adjustment. Distributions the corporation received from a cooperative may be includible in income. Unless the distributions are nontaxable, include on line 2o the total AMT patronage dividend adjustment reported to the corporation from the cooperative.

Cooperative's AMT adjustment. If the corporation is a cooperative, refigure the cooperative's deduction for patronage dividends by taking into account the cooperative's AMT adjustments and preferences. Subtract the cooperative's AMT deduction for patronage dividends from its regular tax deduction for patronage dividends and include the result on line 2o. If the AMT deduction is more than the regular tax deduction, include the result as a negative amount.

Installment sales. The installment method does not apply for the AMT to any nondealer disposition of property that occurred after August 16, 1986, but before the first day of the corporation's tax year that began in 1987, if an installment obligation to which the proportionate disallowance rule applied arose from the disposition. Include as a negative adjustment on line 2o the amount of installment sale income reported for the regular tax.

Accelerated depreciation of real property and certain leased personal property (pre-1987).

This preference generally applies only to property placed in service after 1987, but depreciated using pre-1987 rules due to transition provisions of the Tax Reform Act of 1986.

Refigure depreciation for the AMT using the straight line method for real property for which accelerated depreciation was determined for the regular tax using pre-1987 rules. Use a recovery period of 19 years for 19-year real property and 15 years for low-income housing property. Figure the excess of the regular tax depreciation over the AMT depreciation separately for each property and include only positive adjustments on line 2o.

The adjustment for leased personal property only applies to personal holding companies. For leased personal property other than recovery property, enter the excess of the depreciation claimed for the property for the regular tax using pre-1987 rules over the depreciation allowable for the AMT as refigured using the straight line method.

For leased 10-year recovery property and leased 15-year public utility property, enter the excess of the regular tax depreciation over the depreciation allowable using the straight line method with a half-year convention, no salvage value, and a recovery period of 15 years (22 years for 15-year public utility property).

Figure this amount separately for each property and include only positive adjustments on line 2o.

Related adjustments. AMT adjustments and preferences may affect deductions that are based on an income limit (for example, charitable contributions). Refigure these deductions using the income limit as modified for the AMT. Include on line 2o an adjustment for the difference between the regular tax and AMT amounts for all such deductions. If the AMT deduction is more than the regular tax deduction, include the difference as a negative amount.

Line 4. Adjusted Current Earnings (ACE) Adjustment

The ACE adjustment does not apply to a regulated investment company or a real estate investment trust. Also, for an affiliated group filing a consolidated return under the rules of section 1501, figure line 4b on a consolidated basis.

Line 4b. The following examples illustrate the manner in which line 3 is subtracted from line 4a to get the amount to enter on line 4b.

Example 1. Corporation A has line 4a ACE of $25,000. If Corporation A has line 3 pre-adjustment AMTI in the amounts shown below, its line 3 and line 4a amounts would be combined as follows to determine the amount to enter on line 4b.

Line 4a ACE	$25,000	$25,000	$25,000
Line 3 pre-adj. AMTI	10,000	30,000	(50,000)
Amount to enter on line 4b	$15,000	$(5,000)	$75,000

Example 2. Corporation B has line 4a ACE of $(25,000). If Corporation B has line 3 pre-adjustment AMTI in the amounts shown below, its line 3 and line 4a amounts would be combined as follows to determine the amount to enter on line 4b.

Line 4a ACE	$(25,000)	$(25,000)	$(25,000)
Line 3 pre-adj. AMTI	(10,000)	(30,000)	50,000
Amount to enter on line 4b	$(15,000)	$5,000	$(75,000)

Line 4d. A potential negative ACE adjustment (that is, a negative amount on line 4b multiplied by 75%) is allowed as a negative ACE adjustment on line 4e only if the corporation's total increases in AMTI from prior year ACE adjustments exceed its total reductions in AMTI from prior year ACE adjustments (line 4d). The purpose of line 4d is to provide a "running balance" of this limitation amount. As such, the corporation must keep adequate records (for example, a copy of Form 4626 completed at least through line 5) from year to year (even in years in which it does not owe any AMT).

Any potential negative ACE adjustment that is not allowed as a negative ACE adjustment in a tax year because of the line 4d limitation cannot be used to reduce a positive ACE adjustment in any other tax year. Combine lines 4d and 4e of the 2003 Form 4626 and enter the result on line 4d of the 2004 form, but do not enter less than zero.

Example. Corporation C, a calendar-year corporation, was incorporated January 1, 2000. Its ACE and pre-adjustment AMTI for 2000 through 2004 were as follows.

Year	ACE	Pre-adjustment AMTI
2000	$700,000	$800,000
2001	900,000	600,000
2002	400,000	500,000
2003	(100,000)	300,000
2004	250,000	100,000

Corporation C subtracts its pre-adjustment AMTI from its ACE in each of the years and then multiplies the result by 75% to get the following potential ACE adjustments for 2000 through 2004.

Year	ACE minus pre-adjustment AMTI	Potential ACE adjustment
2000	$(100,000)	$ (75,000)
2001	300,000	225,000
2002	(100,000)	(75,000)
2003	(400,000)	(300,000)
2004	150,000	112,500

Under these facts, Corporation C has the following increases or reductions in AMTI for 2000 through 2004.

Year	Increase or (reduction) in AMTI from ACE adjustment
2000	$0
2001	225,000
2002	(75,000)
2003	(150,000)
2004	112,500

In 2000, Corporation C was not allowed to reduce its AMTI by any part of the potential negative ACE adjustment because it had no increases in AMTI from prior year ACE adjustments.

In 2001, Corporation C had to increase its AMTI by the full amount of its potential ACE adjustment. It was not allowed to use any part of its 2000 unallowed potential negative ACE adjustment of $75,000 to reduce its 2001 positive ACE adjustment of $225,000.

In 2002, Corporation C was allowed to reduce its AMTI by the full amount of its potential negative ACE adjustment because that amount is less than its line 4d limit of $225,000.

In 2003, Corporation C was allowed to reduce its AMTI by only $150,000. Its potential negative ACE adjustment of $300,000 was limited to its 2001 increase in AMTI of $225,000 minus its 2002 reduction in AMTI of $75,000.

In 2004, Corporation C must increase its AMTI by the full amount of its potential ACE adjustment. It cannot use any part of its 2003 unallowed potential negative ACE adjustment of $150,000 to reduce its 2004 positive ACE adjustment of $112,500. Corporation C would complete the relevant portion of its 2004 Form 4626 as follows.

Line	Amount
4a	$250,000
4b	150,000
4c	112,500
4d	-0-
4e	112,500

Line 6. Alternative Tax Net Operating Loss Deduction (ATNOLD)

The ATNOLD is the sum of the ATNOL carrybacks and carryforwards to the tax year, subject to the limitation explained below. For a corporation that held a residual interest in a real estate mortgage investment conduit (REMIC), figure the ATNOLD without regard to any excess inclusion.

NOLs arising in tax years beginning before August 6, 1997, may be carried forward no more than 15 years. Therefore, the corporation may not carry forward an NOL to this tax year from a loss year beginning before 1989.

The ATNOL for a loss year is the excess of the deductions allowed in figuring AMTI (excluding the ATNOLD) over the income included in AMTI. This excess is figured with the modifications in section 172(d), taking into account the adjustments in sections 56 and 58 and preferences in section 57 (that is, the section 172(d) modifications must be separately figured for the ATNOL).

In applying the rules relating to the determination of the amount of carrybacks and carryforwards, use the modification to those rules described in section 56(d)(1)(B)(ii).

The ATNOLD is limited to 90% of AMTI determined without regard to the ATNOLD. To figure AMTI without regard to the ATNOLD, use a second Form 4626 as a worksheet. Complete the second Form 4626 through line 5, but when figuring lines 2l and 2o, treat line 6 as if it were zero. The amount figured on line 5 of the second Form 4626 is the corporation's AMTI determined without regard to the ATNOLD.

The ATNOL may be carried back or forward using the rules outlined in section 172(b). An election under section 172(b)(3) to forego the carryback period for the regular tax also applies for the AMT.

The ATNOL carried back or forward may differ from the NOL (if any) that is carried back or forward for the regular tax. Keep adequate records for both the AMT and the regular tax.

Line 7. Alternative Minimum Taxable Income

For a corporation that held a residual interest in a REMIC and is not a thrift institution, line 7 may not be less than the total of the amounts shown on Schedule(s) Q (Form 1066), Quarterly Notice to Residual Interest Holder of REMIC Taxable Income or Net Loss Allocation, line 2c, for the periods included in the corporation's tax year. If the total of the line 2c amounts is larger than the amount the corporation would otherwise enter on line 7, enter that total and write "Sch. Q" on the dotted line next to line 7.

Line 8. Exemption Phase-Out Computation

Line 8a. If this Form 4626 is for a member of a controlled group of corporations, subtract $150,000 from the combined AMTI of all members of the controlled group. Divide the result among the members of the group in the same manner as the $40,000 tentative exemption is divided among the members. Enter this member's share on line 8a. The tentative exemption must be divided equally among the members, unless all members consent to a different allocation. See section 1561 for details.

Line 8c. If this Form 4626 is for a member of a controlled group of corporations, reduce the member's share of the $40,000 tentative exemption by the amount entered on line 8b.

Line 11. Alternative Minimum Tax Foreign Tax Credit (AMTFTC)

The AMTFTC is the foreign tax credit refigured as follows.

1. Complete a separate AMT Form 1118, Foreign Tax Credit—Corporations, for each separate limitation category specified at the top of Form 1118. Include as a separate limitation category dividends received from a corporation that qualifies for the possessions tax credit if the dividends-received deduction for those dividends is disallowed under the ACE rules.

   In determining if any income is "high-taxed" in applying the separate limitation categories, use the AMT rate (20%) instead of the regular tax rate.

2. For each separate AMT Form 1118, if the corporation previously made or is making the simplified limitation election (discussed on page 8), skip Schedule A and enter on Schedule B, Part II, line 6, the same amount you entered on that line for the regular tax. Otherwise, complete Schedule A using only income and deductions that are allowed for the AMT and attributable to sources outside the United States.

3. For each separate AMT Form 1118, complete Schedule B, Part II. Enter any AMTFTC carryover on Schedule B, Part II, line 4. Enter the AMTI from Form 4626, line 7, on Schedule B, Part II, line 7a. Enter the amount from Form 4626, line 10, on Schedule B, Part II, line 9.

   When completing Schedule B, treat as a tax paid to a foreign country 75% of any withholding or income tax paid to a U.S. possession on dividends received from a corporation that qualifies for the possessions tax credit (if the dividends-received deduction for those dividends is disallowed under the ACE rules).

4. For the AMT Form 1118, complete Schedule B, Part III, Summary of Separate Credits. The total foreign tax credit on line 13 is limited to the tax on Form 4626, line 10, minus 10% of the tax that would be on that line if Form 4626 were refigured using zero on line 6 and without regard to the exception for intangible drilling costs (IDCs) under section 57(a)(2)(E).

If there is no entry on Form 4626, line 6, and no IDCs (or the exception does not apply to the corporation), enter on Form 4626, line 11, the smaller of:

- 90% of Form 4626, line 10, or
- The amount from the AMT Form 1118, Schedule B, Part III, line 13.

If Form 4626, line 6, has an amount entered or the exception for IDCs applies to the corporation, complete the following steps.

1. Refigure what the tax on line 10 would have been if line 6 were zero and the exception did not apply.
2. Multiply that amount by 10%.
3. Subtract the result from the tax on line 10.
4. Enter on Form 4626, line 11, the smaller of that amount or the amount from the AMT Form 1118, Schedule B, Part III, line 13.

The corporation can use any reasonable method, consistently applied, to apportion the disallowed amount among the separate limitation categories (including the general limitation income category). Any AMT foreign tax credit for each separate limitation category that the corporation cannot claim (because of the limitation fraction and/or the 90% limit) is treated as a credit carryback or carryforward for that limitation category under section 904(c). (Because these amounts may differ from the amounts that are carried back or forward for the regular tax, keep adequate records for both the AMT and regular tax.) When carried back or forward, the credit is reported on Schedule B, Part II, line 4, of the carryover year's AMT Form 1118 for that separate limitation category.

Simplified Limitation Election

The corporation may elect to use a simplified section 904 limitation to figure its AMTFTC. The corporation must make the election for its first tax year beginning after 1997 for which it claims an AMTFTC. If it does not make the election for that tax year, it may not make the election for a later tax year. Once made, the election applies to all later tax years and may only be revoked with IRS consent.

If the corporation made the election for each of its AMT separate limitations, the corporation uses its separate limitation income or loss that it determined for the regular tax (instead of refiguring the separate limitation income or loss for the AMT, as described earlier).

Line 13

Enter the corporation's regular tax liability (as defined in section 26(b)) minus any foreign tax credit and possessions tax credit (for example, for Form 1120: Schedule J, line 3, minus the sum of Schedule J, lines 6a and 6b). Do not include any:

- Tax on nondeductible portion of qualifying dividends from a controlled foreign corporation reported on Form 8895,
- Tax on accumulation distribution of trusts from Form 4970,
- Recapture of investment credit (under section 49(b) or 50(a)) from Form 4255,
- Recapture of low-income housing credit (under section 42(j) or (k)) from Form 8611, or
- Recapture of any other credit.

ACE Worksheet Instructions

Treatment of Certain Ownership Changes

If a corporation with a net unrealized built-in loss (within the meaning of section 382(h)) undergoes an ownership change (within the meaning of Regulations section 1.56(g)-1(k)(2)), refigure the adjusted basis of each asset of the corporation (immediately after the ownership change). The new adjusted basis of each asset is its proportionate share (based on respective fair market values) of the fair market value of the corporation's assets (determined under section 382(h)) immediately before the ownership change.

To determine if the corporation has a net unrealized built-in loss immediately before an ownership change, use the aggregate adjusted basis of its assets used for figuring its ACE. Also, use these new adjusted bases for all future ACE calculations (such as depreciation and gain or loss on disposition of an asset).

Line 2. ACE Depreciation Adjustment

Line 2a. AMTdepreciation. Generally, the amount entered on this line is the depreciation the corporation claimed for the regular tax (Form 4562, line 22), modified by the AMT depreciation adjustments reported on lines 2a and 2o of Form 4626.

Line 2b(1). Post-1993 property. For property placed in service after 1993, the ACE depreciation is the same as the AMT depreciation. Therefore, enter on line 2b(1) the same depreciation expense you included on line 2a of this worksheet for such property.

Line 2b(2). Post-1989, pre-1994 property. For property placed in service in a tax year that began after 1989 and before 1994, use the ADS depreciation described in section 168(g). However, for property (a) placed in service in a tax year that began after 1989 and (b) described in sections 168(f)(1) through (4), use the same depreciation claimed for the regular tax and enter it on line 2b(5).

Line 2b(3). Pre-1990 MACRS property. For property placed in service after 1986 (after July 1, 1986, if an election to apply MACRS was made) and in a tax year that began before 1990 (MACRS property), use the straight line method over the remainder of the recovery period for the property under the ADS of section 168(g). In doing so, use the convention that would have applied to the property under section 168(d). For more information (including an example that illustrates the application of these rules), see Regulations section 1.56(g)-1(b)(2).

Line 2b(4). Pre-1990 original ACRS property. For property generally placed in service in a tax year that began after 1980 and before 1987 (to which the original ACRS applies), use the straight line method over the remainder of the recovery period for the property under ADS. In doing so, use the convention that would have applied to the property under section 168(d) (without regard to section 168(d)(3)). For more information (including an example that illustrates the application of these rules), see Regulations section 1.56(g)-1(b)(3).

Line 2b(5). Property described in sections 168(f)(1) through (4). For property described in sections 168(f)(1) through (4), use the regular tax depreciation, regardless of when the property was placed in service.

CAUTION *Line 2b(5) takes priority over lines 2b(1), 2b(2), 2b(3), and 2b(4) (that is, for property that is described in sections 168(f)(1) through (4), use line 2b(5) instead of the line 2b(1), 2b(2), 2b(3), or 2b(4) that would otherwise apply).*

Line 2b(6). Other property. Use the regular tax depreciation for (a) property placed in service before 1981 and (b) property placed in service after 1980, in a tax year that began before 1990, that is excluded from MACRS by section

168(f)(5)(A)(i) or original ACRS by section 168(e)(4), as in effect before the Tax Reform Act of 1986.

Line 2c. Total ACE depreciation. Subtract line 2b(7) from line 2a and enter the result on line 2c. If line 2b(7) exceeds line 2a, enter the difference as a negative amount.

Line 3. Inclusion in ACE of Items Included in Earnings and Profits (E&P)

In general, any income item that is not taken into account (see below) in determining the corporation's pre-adjustment AMTI but that is taken into account in determining its E&P must be included in ACE. Any such income item may be reduced by all items related to that income item and that would be deductible when figuring pre-adjustment AMTI if the income items to which they relate were included in the corporation's pre-adjustment AMTI for the tax year. Examples of adjustments for these income items include:

- Interest income from tax-exempt obligations excluded under section 103 minus any costs incurred in carrying these tax-exempt obligations and
- Proceeds of life insurance contracts excluded under section 101 minus the basis in the contract for purposes of ACE.

An income item is considered taken into account without regard to the timing of its inclusion in a corporation's pre-adjustment AMTI or its E&P. Only income items that are permanently excluded from pre-adjustment AMTI are included in ACE. An income item will not be considered taken into account merely because the proceeds from that item might eventually be reflected in the pre-adjustment AMTI of another taxpayer (for example, that of a shareholder) on the liquidation or disposal of a business.

Exceptions. Do not make an adjustment for the following.

- Any income from discharge of indebtedness excluded from gross income under section 108 (or the corresponding provision of prior law).
- Any extraterritorial income excluded from gross income under section 114.
- For an insurance company taxed under section 831(b), any amount not included in gross investment income (as defined in section 834(b)).
- Any special subsidy payment for prescription drug plans excluded from gross income under section 139A.
- Any qualified shipping income excluded under section 1357.

Line 3d. Include in ACE the income on life insurance contracts (as determined under section 7702(g)) for the tax year minus the part of any premium attributable to insurance coverage.

Line 3e. Do not include any adjustment related to the E&P effects of any charitable contribution.

Line 4. Disallowance of Items Not Deductible From E&P

Generally, no deduction is allowed when figuring ACE for items not taken into account (see below) in figuring E&P for the tax year. These amounts increase ACE if they are deductible in figuring pre-adjustment AMTI (that is, they would be positive adjustments).

However, there are exceptions. Do not add back:

- Any deduction allowable under section 243 or 245 for any dividend that qualifies for a 100% dividends-received deduction under section 243(a), 245(b), or 245(c) and
- Any dividend received from a 20%-owned corporation (see section 243(c)(2)), but only if the dividend is from income of the paying corporation that is subject to Federal income tax.

Special rules apply to the following.

- Dividends from section 936 corporations (including section 30A corporations) (section 56(g)(4)(C)(iii)).
- Certain dividends received by certain cooperatives (section 56(g)(4)(C)(iv)).
- Certain distributions from controlled foreign corporations under section 965 (section 56(g)(4)(C)(vi)).

An item is considered taken into account without regard to the timing of its deductibility in figuring pre-adjustment AMTI or E&P. Therefore, only deduction items that are permanently disallowed in figuring E&P are disallowed in figuring ACE.

Items for which no adjustment is necessary. Generally, no deduction is allowed for an item in figuring ACE if the item is not deductible in figuring pre-adjustment AMTI (even if the item is deductible in figuring E&P). The only exceptions to this general rule are the related reductions to an income item described in the second sentence of the instructions for line 3 above. Deductions that are not allowed in figuring ACE include:

- Capital losses that exceed capital gains;
- Bribes, fines, and penalties disallowed under section 162;
- Charitable contributions that exceed the limitations of section 170;
- Meals and entertainment expenses that exceed the limitations of section 274;
- Federal taxes disallowed under section 275; and
- Golden parachute payments that exceed the limitation of section 280G.

Line 4e. Do not include any adjustment related to the E&P effects of any charitable contribution.

Line 5. Other Adjustments

Line 5a. Except as noted below, in figuring ACE, determine the deduction for intangible drilling costs under section 312(n)(2)(A).

Subtract the ACE expense (if any) from the AMT expense (used to figure line 2n of Form 4626) and enter the result on line 5a. If the ACE expense exceeds the AMT amount, enter the result as a negative amount.

Exception. The above rule does not apply to amounts paid or incurred for any oil or gas well by corporations that are independent producers (that is, not integrated oil companies as defined in section 291(b)(4)). If this exception applies, do not enter an amount on line 5a for oil and gas wells.

Line 5b. When figuring ACE, the current year deduction for circulation expenditures under section 173 does not apply. Therefore, treat circulation expenditures for ACE using the case law that existed before section 173 was enacted.

Subtract the ACE expense (if any) from the regular tax expense (for a personal holding company, from the AMT expense used to figure line 2d of Form 4626) and enter the result on line 5b. If the ACE expense exceeds the regular tax amount (for a personal holding company, the AMT amount), enter the result as a negative amount.

Do not make this adjustment for expenditures for which the corporation elected the optional 3-year write-off under section 59(e) for the regular tax.

Line 5c. When figuring ACE, the amortization provisions of section 248 do not apply. Therefore, charge all organizational expenditures to a capital account and do not take them into account when figuring ACE until the corporation is sold or otherwise disposed of. Enter on line 5c all amortization deductions for organizational expenditures that were taken for the regular tax during the tax year.

Line 5d. The adjustments provided in section 312(n)(4) apply in figuring ACE. See Regulations section 1.56(g)-1(f)(3).

Line 5e. For any installment sale in a tax year that began after 1989, a corporation generally cannot use the installment method to figure ACE. However, it may use the installment method for the applicable percentage (as determined under section 453A) of the gain from any installment sale to which section 453A(a)(1) applies.

Subtract the installment sale income reported for AMT from the ACE income from the sales and enter the result on line 5e. If the ACE income from the sales is less than the AMT amount, enter the difference as a negative amount.

Line 6. Disallowance of Loss on Exchange of Debt Pools

When figuring ACE, a corporation may not recognize any loss on the exchange of any pool of debt obligations for any other pool of debt obligations having substantially the same effective interest rates and maturities. Add back (that is, enter as a positive adjustment) on line 6 any such loss to the extent recognized for the regular tax.

Line 7. Acquisition Expenses of Life Insurance Companies for Qualified Foreign Contracts

For ACE, acquisition expenses of life insurance companies for qualified foreign contracts (as defined in section 807(e)(4) without regard to the treatment of reinsurance contract rules of section 848(e)(5)) must be capitalized and amortized by applying the treatment generally required under generally accepted accounting principles (and as if this rule applied to such contracts for all applicable tax years).

Subtract the ACE expense (if any) from the regular tax expense and enter the result on line 7. If the ACE expense is more than the regular tax expense, enter the result as a negative amount.

Line 8. Depletion

When figuring ACE, the allowance for depletion for any property placed in service in a tax year that began after 1989 generally must be determined under the cost depletion method.

Subtract the ACE expense (if any) from the AMT expense (used to figure line 2l of Form 4626) and enter the result on line 8 of the worksheet. If the ACE expense is more than the AMT amount, enter the result as a negative amount.

Exception. Independent oil and gas producers and royalty owners that figured their regular tax depletion deduction under section 613A(c) do not have an adjustment for ACE purposes.

Line 9. Basis Adjustments in Determining Gain or Loss From Sale or Exchange of Pre-1994 Property

If, during the tax year, the corporation disposed of property for which it is making (or previously made) any of the ACE adjustments, refigure the property's adjusted basis for ACE. Then refigure the property's gain or loss.

Enter the difference between the AMT gain or loss (used to figure line 2e of Form 4626) and the ACE gain or loss. Enter the difference as a negative amount if any of the following apply.

- The ACE gain is less than the AMT gain.
- The ACE loss is more than the AMT loss.
- The corporation had an ACE loss and an AMT gain.

Paperwork Reduction Act Notice. We ask for the information on this form to carry out the Internal Revenue laws of the United States. You are required to give us the information. We need it to ensure that you are complying with these laws and to allow us to figure and collect the right amount of tax.

You are not required to provide the information requested on a form that is subject to the Paperwork Reduction Act unless the form displays a valid OMB control number. Books or records relating to a form or its instructions must be retained as long as their contents may become material in the administration of any Internal Revenue law. Generally, tax returns and return information are confidential, as required by section 6103.

The time needed to complete and file this form will vary depending on individual circumstances. The estimated average time is:

Recordkeeping	17 hr., 13 min.
Learning about the law or the form	12 hr., 36 min.
Preparing and sending the form to the IRS	13 hr., 27 min.

If you have comments concerning the accuracy of these time estimates or suggestions for making this form simpler, we would be happy to hear from you. See the instructions for the tax return with which this form is filed.

Adjusted Current Earnings (ACE) Worksheet

► See ACE Worksheet Instructions (which begin on page 8).

1	Pre-adjustment AMTI. Enter the amount from line 3 of Form 4626		**1**
2	ACE depreciation adjustment:		
a	AMT depreciation	**2a**	
b	ACE depreciation:		
	(1) Post-1993 property — **2b(1)**		
	(2) Post-1989, pre-1994 property — **2b(2)**		
	(3) Pre-1990 MACRS property — **2b(3)**		
	(4) Pre-1990 original ACRS property — **2b(4)**		
	(5) Property described in sections 168(f)(1) through (4) — **2b(5)**		
	(6) Other property — **2b(6)**		
	(7) Total ACE depreciation. Add lines 2b(1) through 2b(6)	**2b(7)**	
c	ACE depreciation adjustment. Subtract line 2b(7) from line 2a		**2c**
3	Inclusion in ACE of items included in earnings and profits (E&P):		
a	Tax-exempt interest income	**3a**	
b	Death benefits from life insurance contracts	**3b**	
c	All other distributions from life insurance contracts (including surrenders)	**3c**	
d	Inside buildup of undistributed income in life insurance contracts	**3d**	
e	Other items (see Regulations sections 1.56(g)-1(c)(6)(iii) through (ix) for a partial list)	**3e**	
f	Total increase to ACE from inclusion in ACE of items included in E&P. Add lines 3a through 3e		**3f**
4	Disallowance of items not deductible from E&P:		
a	Certain dividends received	**4a**	
b	Dividends paid on certain preferred stock of public utilities that are deductible under section 247	**4b**	
c	Dividends paid to an ESOP that are deductible under section 404(k)	**4c**	
d	Nonpatronage dividends that are paid and deductible under section 1382(c)	**4d**	
e	Other items (see Regulations sections 1.56(g)-1(d)(3)(i) and (ii) for a partial list)	**4e**	
f	Total increase to ACE because of disallowance of items not deductible from E&P. Add lines 4a through 4e		**4f**
5	Other adjustments based on rules for figuring E&P:		
a	Intangible drilling costs	**5a**	
b	Circulation expenditures	**5b**	
c	Organizational expenditures	**5c**	
d	LIFO inventory adjustments	**5d**	
e	Installment sales	**5e**	
f	Total other E&P adjustments. Combine lines 5a through 5e		**5f**
6	Disallowance of loss on exchange of debt pools		**6**
7	Acquisition expenses of life insurance companies for qualified foreign contracts		**7**
8	Depletion		**8**
9	Basis adjustments in determining gain or loss from sale or exchange of pre-1994 property		**9**
10	**Adjusted current earnings.** Combine lines 1, 2c, 3f, 4f, and 5f through 9. Enter the result here and on line 4a of Form 4626		**10**

INSTRUCTIONS FOR FORM 4797

Sales of Business Property

2004

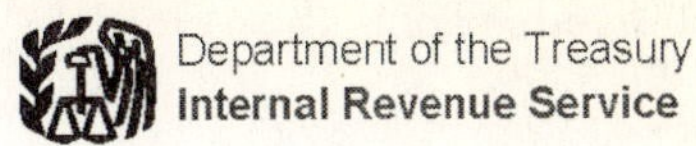

Department of the Treasury
Internal Revenue Service

Instructions for Form 4797

Sales of Business Property (Also Involuntary Conversions and Recapture Amounts Under Sections 179 and 280F(b)(2))

Section references are to the Internal Revenue Code unless otherwise noted.

General Instructions

What's New

• Partnerships and S corporations, and their partners and shareholders, must follow new procedures for reporting all sales (or other dispositions) by the partnership or S corporation of property for which the section 179 expense deduction was claimed. See *Disposition by a Partnership or S Corporation of Section 179 Property* on page 3 for details.

• If you sold or exchanged a District of Columbia Enterprise Zone (DC Zone) asset that you held for more than 5 years, you may be able to exclude the "qualified capital gain." For more information, see *Exclusion of Gain From Sale of DC Zone Assets* on page 3.

• New rules apply for certain weather-related sales or exchanges of livestock used for draft, breeding, or dairy purposes, in tax years with a return due date after 2002. See Pub. 225, Farmer's Tax Guide, for additional information.

Purpose of Form

Use Form 4797 to report:

• The sale or exchange of:

1. Property used in your trade or business;
2. Depreciable and amortizable property;
3. Oil, gas, geothermal, or other mineral properties; and
4. Section 126 property.

• The involuntary conversion (from other than casualty or theft) of property used in your trade or business and capital assets held in connection with a trade or business or a transaction entered into for profit.

• The disposition of noncapital assets (other than inventory or property held primarily for sale to customers in the ordinary course of your trade or business).

• The disposition of capital assets not reported on Schedule D.

• The gain or loss (including any related recapture) for partners and S corporation shareholders from certain section 179 property dispositions by partnerships (other than electing large partnerships) and S corporations.

• The computation of recapture amounts under sections 179 and 280F(b)(2) when the business use of section 179 or listed property decreases to 50% or less.

Other Forms To Use

• Use Form 4684, Casualties and Thefts, to report involuntary conversions from casualties and thefts.

• Use Form 6252, Installment Sale Income, to report the sale of property under the installment method.

• Use Form 8824, Like-Kind Exchanges, to report exchanges of qualifying business or investment property for property of a like kind. For exchanges of property used in a trade or business (and other noncapital assets), enter the gain or (loss) from Form 8824, if any, on line 5 or 16.

• If you sold property on which you claimed investment credit, see Form 4255, Recapture of Investment Credit, to find out if you must recapture some or all of the credit.

Special Rules

At-Risk Rules

If you report a loss on an asset used in an activity for which you are not at risk, in whole or in part, see the instructions for Form 6198, At-Risk Limitations. Also, see Pub. 925, Passive Activity and At-Risk Rules. Losses from passive activities are subject first to the at-risk rules and then to the passive activity rules.

Where To Make First Entry for Certain Items Reported on This Form

	(a) Type of property	(b) Held 1 year or less	(c) Held more than 1 year
1	Depreciable trade or business property		
a	Sold or exchanged at a gain	Part II	Part III (1245, 1250)
b	Sold or exchanged at a loss	Part II	Part I
2	Depreciable residential rental property:		
a	Sold or exchanged at a gain	Part II	Part III (1250)
b	Sold or exchanged at a loss	Part II	Part I
3	Farmland held less than 10 years upon which soil, water, or land clearing expenses were deducted:		
a	Sold at a gain	Part II	Part III (1252)
b	Sold at a loss	Part II	Part I
4	All other farmland	Part II	Part I
5	Disposition of cost-sharing payment property described in section 126	Part II	Part III (1255)
6	Cattle and horses used in a trade or business for draft, breeding, dairy, or sporting purposes:	**Held less than 24 months**	**Held 24 months or more**
a	Sold at a gain	Part II	Part III (1245)
b	Sold at a loss	Part II	Part I
c	Raised cattle and horses sold at a gain	Part II	Part I
7	Livestock other than cattle and horses used in a trade or business for draft, breeding, dairy, or sporting purposes:	**Held less than 12 months**	**Held 12 months or more**
a	Sold at a gain	Part II	Part III (1245)
b	Sold at a loss	Part II	Part I
c	Raised livestock sold at a gain	Part II	Part I

Cat. No. 13087T

Depreciable Property and Other Property Disposed of in the Same Transaction

If you disposed of both depreciable property and other property (for example, a building and land) in the same transaction and realized a gain, you must allocate the amount realized between the two types of property based on their respective fair market values (FMVs) to figure the part of the gain to be recaptured as ordinary income because of depreciation. The disposition of each type of property is reported separately in the appropriate part of Form 4797 (for example, for property held more than 1 year, report the sale of a building in Part III and land in Part I).

Disposition of Assets That Constitute a Trade or Business

If you sell a group of assets that makes up a trade or business, both you and the buyer generally must allocate the total sales price to the assets transferred and file Form 8594, Asset Acquisition Statement. Pub. 544, Sales and Other Dispositions of Assets, discusses the sale of business assets in chapter 2 under *Other Dispositions*.

Installment Sales

If you sold property at a gain and you will receive a payment in a tax year after the year of sale, you generally must report the sale on the installment method unless you elect not to do so.

Use Form 6252 to report the sale on the installment method. Also use Form 6252 to report any payment received during your 2004 tax year from a sale made in an earlier year that you reported on the installment method.

To elect out of the installment method, report the full amount of the gain on a timely filed return (including extensions). If you timely filed your tax return without making the election, you can still make the election by filing an amended return within 6 months of the due date of your return (excluding extensions). Write "Filed pursuant to section 301.9100-2" at the top of the amended return.

See Pub. 537, Installment Sales, for more details.

Traders Who Made a Mark-To-Market Election

A trader in securities or commodities may elect under section 475(f) to use the mark-to-market method to account for securities or commodities held in connection with a trading business. Under this method of accounting, any security or commodity held at the end of the tax year is treated as sold (and reacquired) at its FMV on the last business day of that year.

Unless you are a new taxpayer, the election must be made by the due date (not including extensions) of the tax return for the year prior to the year for which the election becomes effective.

If you are a trader in securities or commodities with a mark-to-market election under section 475(f) in effect for the tax year, the following special rules apply.

- Gains and losses from all securities or commodities held in connection with your trading business (including those marked to market) are treated as ordinary income and losses, instead of capital gains and losses. As a result, the lower capital gain tax rates and the limitation on capital losses do not apply.
- The gain or loss from each security or commodity held in connection with your trading business (including those marked to market) is reported on Form 4797, line 10 (see the instructions for line 10 on page 5).
- The wash sale rule does not apply to securities or commodities held in connection with your trading business.

For details on the mark-to-market election and how to make it, see Pub. 550, Investment Income and Expenses; sections 475(e) and 475(f); and Rev. Proc. 99-17, 1999-1 C.B. 503. You can find Rev. Proc. 99-17 on page 52 of Internal Revenue Bulletin 1999-7 at *www.irs.gov/pub/irs-irbs/irb99-07.pdf*

Involuntary Conversion of Property

You may not have to pay tax on a gain from an involuntary or compulsory conversion of property. See Pub. 544 for details.

Exclusion of Gain on Sale of a Home Used for Business

If the property sold was used for business or to produce rental income and was also owned and used as your home during the 5-year period ending on the date of the sale, you may be able to exclude part or all of the gain figured on Form 4797. For details on the exclusion (including how to figure the amount of the exclusion), see Pub. 523, Selling Your Home.

If the property was held more than 1 year, complete Part III to figure the amount of the gain. Do not take the exclusion into account when figuring the gain on line 24. If line 22 includes depreciation for periods after May 6, 1997, you cannot exclude gain to the extent of that depreciation. On line 2 of Form 4797, write "Section 121 exclusion," and enter the amount of the exclusion as a (loss) in column (g).

If the property was held for 1 year or less, report the sale and the amount of the exclusion, if any, in a similar manner on line 10 of Form 4797.

Passive Loss Limitations

If you have an overall loss from passive activities and you report a loss on an asset used in a passive activity, use Form 8582, Passive Activity Loss Limitations, or Form 8810, Corporate Passive Activity Loss and Credit Limitations, to see how much loss is allowed before entering it on Form 4797.

You cannot claim unused passive activity credits when you dispose of your interest in an activity. However, if you dispose of your entire interest in an activity, you may elect to increase the basis of the credit property by the original basis reduction of the property to the extent that the credit has not been allowed because of the passive activity rules. Make the election on Form 8582-CR, Passive Activity Credit Limitations, or Form 8810. No basis adjustment may be elected on a partial disposition of your interest in an activity.

Recapture of Preproductive Expenses

If you elected out of the uniform capitalization rules of section 263A, any plant that you produce is treated as section 1245 property. For dispositions of plants reportable on Form 4797, enter the recapture amount taxed as ordinary income on line 22 of Form 4797. See Pub. 225, Farmer's Tax Guide, for details.

Section 197(f)(9)(B)(ii) Election

If you elected under section 197(f)(9)(B)(ii) to recognize gain on the disposition of a section 197 intangible and to pay a tax on that gain at the highest tax rate, include the additional tax on Form 1040, line 43 (or the appropriate line of other income tax returns). On the dotted line next to that line, enter "197" and the amount. The additional tax is the amount that, when added to any other income tax on the gain, equals the gain multiplied by the highest tax rate.

Rollover of Gain From Sale of Empowerment Zone Assets

If you sold a qualified empowerment zone asset that you held for more than 1 year, you may be able to elect to postpone part or all of the gain that you would otherwise include on Form 4797, Part I. If you make the election, the gain on the sale generally is recognized only to the extent, if any, that the amount realized on the sale exceeds the cost of qualified empowerment zone assets (replacement property) you purchased during the 60-day period beginning on the date of the sale. The following rules apply.

- No portion of the cost of the replacement property may be taken into account to the extent the cost is taken into account to exclude gain on a different empowerment zone asset.
- The replacement property must qualify as an empowerment zone asset with respect to the same empowerment zone as the asset sold.
- You must reduce the basis of the replacement property by the amount of postponed gain.
- This election does not apply to any gain (a) treated as ordinary income or (b) attributable to real property, or an intangible asset, which is not an integral part of an enterprise zone business.
- The District of Columbia enterprise zone is not treated as an empowerment zone for this purpose.

• The election is irrevocable without IRS consent.

See Pub. 954, Tax Incentives for Distressed Communities, for the definition of empowerment zone and enterprise zone business. You can find out if your business is located within an empowerment zone by using the RC/EZ/EC Address Locator at *www.hud.gov/crlocator*.

Qualified empowerment zone assets are:

• Tangible property, if:

1. You acquired the property after December 21, 2000,

2. The original use of the property in the empowerment zone began with you, and

3. Substantially all of the use of the property, during substantially all of the time that you held it, was in your enterprise zone business; and

• Stock in a domestic corporation or a capital or profits interest in a domestic partnership, if:

1. You acquired the stock or partnership interest after December 21, 2000, solely in exchange for cash, from the corporation at its original issue (directly or through an underwriter) or from the partnership;

2. The business was an enterprise zone business (or a new business being organized as an enterprise zone business) as of the time you acquired the stock or partnership interest; and

3. The business qualified as an enterprise zone business during substantially all of the time during which you held the stock or partnership interest.

How to report. Report the entire gain realized from the sale as you otherwise would without regard to the election. On Form 4797, line 2, enter "Section 1397B Rollover" in column (a) and enter as a (loss) in column (g) the amount of gain included on Form 4797 that you are electing to postpone. If you are reporting the sale directly on Form 4797, line 2, use the line directly below the line on which you reported the sale.

See section 1397B for more details.

Exclusion of Gain From Sale of DC Zone Assets

If you sold or exchanged a District of Columbia Enterprise Zone (DC Zone) asset that you held for more than 5 years, you may be able to exclude the "qualified capital gain." The qualified gain is, generally, any gain recognized in a trade or business that you would otherwise include on Form 4797, Part I. This exclusion also applies to an interest in, or property of, certain businesses operating in the District of Columbia.

DC Zone asset. A DC Zone asset is any of the following:

• DC Zone business stock.
• DC Zone partnership interest.
• DC Zone business property.

Qualified capital gain. The qualified capital gain is any gain recognized on the sale or exchange of a DC Zone asset that is a capital asset or property used in a trade or business. It does not include any of the following gains.

• Gain treated as ordinary income under section 1245;
• Gain treated as unrecaptured section 1250 gain. The section 1250 gain must be figured as if it applied to **all** depreciation rather than the additional depreciation;
• Gain attributable to real property, or an intangible asset, which is not an integral part of a DC Zone business; and
• Gain from a related-party transaction. See *Sales and Exchanges Between Related Persons* in chapter 2 of Pub. 544.

See Pub. 954, Tax Incentives for Distressed Communities, and section 1400B for more details on DC Zone assets and special rules.

How to report. Report the entire gain realized from the sale or exchange as you otherwise would without regard to the exclusion. To report the exclusion, enter "DC Zone Asset Exclusion" on Form 4797, line 2, column (a) and enter as a (loss) in column (g) the amount of the exclusion that offsets the gain reported in Part I, line 6.

Any unrecaptured section 1250 gain is not qualified capital gain. Identify the amount of gain that is unrecaptured section 1250 gain and report it on the Schedule D for the form you are filing.

Election To Defer Gain From Certain Dispositions of Electric Transmission Property

If you sold or exchanged qualifying electric transmission property after October 22, 2004, you may elect to defer part of the realized gain. The sale or disposition must be made to an independent transmission company. If you make the election, part or all of the realized gain is recognized ratably over the 8-year period that begins with the tax year that includes the date of the disposition. The amount of gain that is not eligible to be recognized over the 8-year period is the excess, if any, of the amount realized from the disposition over the cost of the exempt utility property purchased during the 4-year period beginning on the date of the disposition.

To make the election, you must attach a statement to your tax return for the tax year in which the transaction takes place that states you are making an election under section 451(i). The statement should also provide a description and the cost of any exempt utility property purchased to defer gain as of the date of the filing of the election. See section 451(i) for more details.

How to report. Report the sale or disposition of the qualifying electric transmission property in Part III of the Form 4797 without regard to any deferred gain. Enter the amounts from lines 31 and 32 on lines 13 and 6, respectively, of Form 4797.

Figure the gain eligible for deferral and enter it as a loss in column (g) of line 2, but only to the extent of the gain from the transaction included on line 6. Enter "Deferred gain under section 451(i)" in column (a) of line 2. Enter any remaining gain eligible for deferral as a loss in column (g) of line 10. Enter "Deferred gain under section 451(i)" in column (a) of line 10. The recognized gain for the tax year of the disposition must equal the gain, if any, not eligible for deferral plus $^1/_8$ of the deferred gain.

Specific Instructions

To show losses, enclose figures in (parentheses).

If you disposed of property you acquired by inheritance, enter "INHERITED" in column (b) instead of the date you acquired the property.

Disposition by a Partnership or S Corporation of Section 179 Property

Partnerships (other than electing large partnerships) and S corporations that sell or otherwise dispose of property for which the section 179 expense deduction was previously claimed and passed through to the partners or shareholders must follow these instructions to report the transaction. Partners and shareholders who receive a Schedule K-1 showing such a disposition must also follow these instructions to report the transaction.

Partnerships and S corporations. Partnerships and S corporations do not report these transactions on Form 4797, 4684, 6252, or 8824. Instead, all details of the sale or other disposition must be separately reported on Schedule K-1, including:

• Description of the property.
• Date the property was acquired and placed in service.
• Date of the sale or other disposition of the property.
• The partner's or shareholder's share of the gross sales price or amount realized.
• The partner's or shareholder's share of the cost or other basis plus the expense of sale (reduced as explained in the instructions for Form 4797, line 21).
• The partner's or shareholder's share of the depreciation allowed or allowable, determined as described in the instructions for Form 4797, line 22, but excluding the section 179 expense deduction.
• The partner's or shareholder's share of the section 179 expense deduction (if any) passed through for the property and the partnership's tax year(s) in which the amount was passed through.
• If the disposition is due to a casualty or theft, a statement indicating so, and any additional information needed by the partner or shareholder to complete Form 4684.

Worksheet for Partners and S Corporation Shareholders to Figure Gain or Loss on Dispositions of Property for Which a Section 179 Deduction Was Claimed

(Keep for Your Records)

Caution: See the instructions after line 5 before starting this worksheet.

1. Gross sales price . . . . 1. ______
2. Cost or other basis . . . . 2. ______
3. a Depreciation (excluding section 179 expense deduction) . . . . . 3a. ______
   b Section 179 expense deduction . . . . . 3b. ______
   c Unused carryover of section 179 expense deduction . . . 3c. ______
   d Subtract line 3c from line 3b . . . . . 3d. ______
   e Add lines 3a and 3d . . . . . 3e. ______
4. **Adjusted basis.** Subtract line 3e from line 2 . . . . . 4. ______
5. **Gain or loss.** Subtract line 4 from line 1 (see *Where To Report Amounts From Worksheet*, below) . . . . . 5. ______

Worksheet Instructions

Caution: *For a disposition due to casualty or theft, skip lines 1 and 5 and enter the amount from line 4 on Form 4684, line 20, and complete the rest of Form 4684.*

Lines 1, 2, 3a, and 3b. Enter these amounts from Schedule K-1 (Form 1065 or 1120S).

Line 3c. If you were unable to claim all of the section 179 expense deduction previously passed through to you for the property (if any), enter the smaller of line 3b or the portion of your unused carryover of section 179 expense deduction attributable to the property. Make sure you reduce your carryover of disallowed section 179 expense deduction shown on Form 4562 by the amount on line 3c.

Where To Report Amounts From Worksheet

Generally, the information from the above worksheet is reported on the lines specified below for Form 4797, Part III. However, for a disposition under the installment method, complete the lines shown below for Form 6252. For dispositions of property given up in an exchange involving like-kind property, complete the lines shown below for Form 8824.

▶ If line 5 is a gain and the property was held more than 1 year, report the disposition as follows.
- Complete Form 4797, line 19, columns (a), (b), and (c); Form 6252, lines 1 through 4; or Form 8824, Parts I and II.
- Report the amount from line 1 above on Form 4797, line 20; Form 6252, line 5; or Form 8824, line 12 or 16.
- Report the amount from line 2 above on Form 4797, line 21; or Form 6252, line 8.
- Report the amount from line 3e above on Form 4797, line 22; or Form 6252, line 9.
- Report the amount from line 4 above on Form 4797, line 23; Form 6252, line 10; or Form 8824, line 13 or 18.
- Complete the rest of the applicable form.

▶ If line 5 is zero or a loss and the property was held more than 1 year, report the disposition as follows. Do not report a loss on Form 6252; instead, report the disposition on the lines shown for Form 4797.
- Complete Form 4797, line 2, columns (a), (b), and (c); or Form 8824, Parts I and II.
- Report the amount from line 1 above on Form 4797, line 2, column (d); or Form 8824, line 12 or 16.
- Report the amount from line 2 above on Form 4797, line 2, column (f).
- Report the amount from line 3e above on Form 4797, line 2, column (e).
- Report the amount from line 4 above on Form 8824, line 13 or 18.
- Complete the rest of the applicable form.

▶ If the property was held one year or less, report the gain or loss on the disposition as shown below. Do not report a loss on Form 6252; instead, report the disposition on the lines shown for Form 4797.
- Complete Form 4797, line 10, columns (a), (b), and (c); Form 6252, lines 1 through 4; or Form 8824, Parts I and II.
- Report the amount from line 1 above on Form 4797, line 10, column (d); Form 6252, line 5; or Form 8824, line 12 or 16.
- Report the amount from line 2 above on Form 4797, line 10, column (f); or Form 6252, line 8.
- Report the amount from line 3e above on Form 4797, line 10, column (e); or Form 6252, line 9.
- Report the amount from line 4 above on Form 6252, line 10; or Form 8824, line 13 or 18.
- Complete the rest of the applicable form.

- If the disposition was an installment sale made during the partnership's or S corporation's tax year reported using the installment method, any information needed by the partner or shareholder to complete Form 6252. The partnership or S corporation also must separately report the partner's or shareholder's share of all payments received for the property in the following tax years. (Installment payments received for sales made in prior tax years should be reported in the same manner used in the prior tax years.) See the instructions for Form 6252 for details.
- If the disposition was a disposition of property given up in an exchange involving like-kind property made during the partnership's or S corporations's tax year, any information needed by the partner or shareholder to complete Form 8824.

See the instructions for Schedule K (Form 1065 or 1120S) for more details.

Partners and S corporation shareholders. If you receive a Schedule K-1 reporting such a transaction, you must report your share of the transaction on Form 4797, 4684, 6252, or 8824 (whether or not you were a partner or shareholder at the time the section 179 expense deduction was claimed). If you have a carryforward of unused section 179 expense deduction that includes section 179 expense deduction previously passed through to you for the disposed asset, you must reduce your carryforward by your share of the section 179 expense deduction shown on Schedule K-1 (or the amount attributable to that property included in your carryforward amount). See the worksheet on the next page to figure the amounts to report on Form 4797, 4684, 6252, or 8824, and to figure any reduction in your carryforward of unused section 179 expense deduction.

Line 1

Enter on line 1 the total gross proceeds from:

- Sales or exchanges of real estate reported to you for 2004 on Form(s) 1099-S (or substitute statement) that you are including on line 2, 10, or 20 and
- Sales of securities or commodities reported to you for 2004 on Forms 1099-B (or substitute statements) that you are including on line 10 because you are a trader with a mark-to-market election under section 475(f) in effect for the tax year. See *Traders Who Made a Mark-To-Market Election* on page 2 and the instructions for line 10 on page 5.

Part I

Use Part I to report section 1231 transactions that are not required to be reported in Part III.

Section 1231 transactions. The following are section 1231 transactions.

- Sales or exchanges of real or depreciable property used in a trade or business and held for more than 1 year. To figure the holding period, begin counting on the day after you received the property and include the day you disposed of it.
- Cutting of timber that the taxpayer elects to treat as a sale or exchange under section 631(a).
- Disposal of timber with a retained economic interest that is treated as a sale under section 631(b).
- Disposal of coal (including lignite) or domestic iron ore with a retained economic interest that is treated as a sale under section 631(c).
- Sales or exchanges of cattle and horses, regardless of age, used in a trade or business for draft, breeding, dairy, or sporting purposes and held for 24 months or more from acquisition date.
- Sales or exchanges of livestock other than cattle and horses, regardless of age, used in a trade or business for draft, breeding, dairy, or sporting purposes and held for 12 months or more from acquisition date.

Note. Livestock does not include poultry, chickens, turkeys, pigeons, geese, other birds, fish, frogs, reptiles, etc.

- Sales or exchanges of unharvested crops. See section 1231(b)(4).
- Involuntary conversions of trade or business property or capital assets held more than 1 year in connection with a trade or business or a transaction entered into for profit. These conversions may result from (a) part or total destruction, (b) theft or seizure, or (c) requisition or condemnation (whether threatened or carried out). If any recognized losses were from involuntary conversions from fire, storm, shipwreck, or other casualty or from theft and the losses exceed the recognized gains from the conversions, do not include any gains or losses from such conversions when figuring your net section 1231 losses.

Transactions to which section 1231 does not apply. Section 1231 transactions do not include sales or exchanges of:

- Inventory or property held primarily for sale to customers;
- Copyrights, literary, musical, or artistic compositions, letters or memoranda, or similar property (a) created by your personal efforts, (b) prepared or produced for you (in the case of letters, memoranda, or similar property), or (c) received from someone who created them or for whom they were created, as mentioned in (a) or (b), in a way that entitled you to the basis of the previous owner (such as by gift); or
- U.S. Government publications, including the Congressional Record, that you received from the Government other than by purchase at the normal sales price or that you got from someone who had received it in a similar way, if your basis is determined by reference to the previous owner's basis.

Line 8

Your net section 1231 gain on line 7 is treated as ordinary income to the extent of your "nonrecaptured section 1231 losses." Your nonrecaptured section 1231 losses are your net section 1231 losses deducted during the 5 preceding tax years that have not yet been applied against any net section 1231 gain to determine how much net section 1231 gain is treated as ordinary income under this rule.

Example. You had net section 1231 losses of $4,000 and $6,000 in 1999 and 2000, respectively, and net section 1231 gains of $3,000 and $2,000 in 2003 and 2004, respectively. The 2004 net section 1231 gain of $2,000 is entered on line 7 and the nonrecaptured net section 1231 losses of $7,000 ($10,000 net section 1231 losses minus the $3,000 that was applied against the 2003 net section 1231 gain) are entered on line 8. The entire $2,000 net section 1231 gain on line 7 is treated as ordinary income and is entered on line 12 of Form 4797. For recordkeeping purposes, the $4,000 loss from 1999 is all recaptured ($3,000 in 2003 and $1,000 in 2004), and you have $5,000 of section 1231 losses from 2000 left to recapture ($6,000 minus the $1,000 recaptured this year).

Figuring the Prior Year Losses

You had a net section 1231 loss if section 1231 losses exceeded section 1231 gains. Gains are included only to the extent taken into account in figuring gross income. Losses are included only to the extent taken into account in figuring taxable income except that the limitation on capital losses does not apply.

Line 9

For recordkeeping purposes, if line 9 is zero, the amount on line 7 is the amount of net section 1231 loss recaptured in 2004. If line 9 is more than zero, you have recaptured all of your net section 1231 losses from prior years.

Part II

If a transaction is not reportable in Part I or Part III and the property is not a capital asset reportable on Schedule D, report the transaction in Part II.

If you received ordinary income from a sale or other disposition of your interest in a partnership, see Pub. 541, Partnerships.

Line 10

Report other ordinary gains and losses, including gains and losses from property held 1 year or less, on this line.

Deduct the loss from a qualifying abandonment of business or investment property on line 10. See *Abandonments* in Pub. 544 for more information.

Securities or Commodities Held by a Trader Who Made a Mark-To-Market Election

Report on line 10 all gains and losses from sales and dispositions of securities or commodities held in connection with your trading business, including gains and losses from marking to market securities and commodities held at the end of the tax year (see *Traders Who Made a Mark-To-Market Election* on page 2). Attach to your tax return a statement, using the same format as line 10, showing the details of each transaction. Separately show and identify securities or commodities held and marked to market at the end of the year. On line 10, enter "Trader—see attached" in column (a) and the totals from the statement in columns (d), (f), and (g). Also, see the instructions for line 1 on page 5.

Small Business Investment Company Stock

Report on line 10 ordinary losses from the sale or exchange (including worthlessness) of stock in a small business investment company operating under the Small Business Investment Act of 1958. See section 1242.

Also attach a statement that includes the name and address of the small business investment company and, if applicable, the reason the stock is worthless and the approximate date it became worthless.

Section 1244 (Small Business) Stock

Individuals report ordinary losses from the sale or exchange (including worthlessness) of section 1244 (small business) stock on line 10.

To qualify as section 1244 stock, all six of the following requirements must be met.

1. You acquired the stock after June 30, 1958, upon original issuance of the shares from a domestic corporation (or the stock was acquired by a partnership in which you were a partner continuously from the date the stock was issued until the time of the loss).
2. If the stock was issued before November 7, 1978, it was issued under a written plan that met the requirements of Regulations section 1.1244(c)-1(f), and when that plan was adopted, the corporation was treated as a small business corporation under Regulations section 1.1244(c)-2(c).
3. If the stock was issued after November 6, 1978, the corporation was treated as a small business corporation at the time the stock was issued under Regulations section 1.1244(c)-2(b). To be treated as a small business corporation, the total amount of money and other property received by the corporation for its stock as a contribution to capital and paid-in surplus generally may not exceed $1 million.
4. The stock was issued for money or other property (excluding stock or securities).
5. The corporation, for its 5 most recent tax years ending before the date of the loss, derived more than 50% of its gross receipts from sources other than royalties, rents, dividends, interest, annuities, and gains from sales and exchanges of stocks or securities. (If the corporation was in existence for at least 1 tax year but fewer than 5 tax years ending before the date of the loss, the 50% test applies for the tax years ending before that date. If the corporation was not in existence for at least 1 tax year ending before the date of the loss, the 50% test applies for the entire period ending before that date.) The 50% test does not apply if the corporation's deductions (other than the net operating loss and dividends-received deductions) exceeded its gross income during the applicable period. But this exception to the 50% test applies only if the corporation was largely an operating company within the 5 most recent tax years ending before the date of the loss (or, if less, the entire period the corporation was in existence).
6. If the stock was issued before July 19, 1984, it must have been common stock.

The maximum amount that may be treated as an ordinary loss is $50,000 ($100,000 if married filing jointly). Special rules may limit the amount of your ordinary loss if (a) you received section 1244 stock in exchange for property with a basis in excess of its FMV or (b) your stock basis increased because of contributions to capital or otherwise. See Pub. 550 for more details. Report on Schedule D losses in excess of the maximum amount that may be treated as an ordinary loss (and all gains) from the sale or exchange of section 1244 stock.

Keep adequate records to distinguish section 1244 stock from any other stock owned in the same corporation.

Line 18a

You must complete this line if there is a gain on Form 4797, line 3; a loss on Form 4797, line 11; and a loss on Form 4684, line 35, column (b)(ii). Enter on this line the smaller of the loss on Form 4797, line 11, or the loss on Form 4684, line 35, column (b)(ii). To figure which loss is smaller, treat both losses as positive numbers. Enter the part of the loss from income-producing property on Schedule A (Form 1040), line 27, and the part of the loss from property used as an employee on Schedule A (Form 1040), line 22.

Part III

TIP *Partnerships and S corporations, see* Partnerships and S corporations *at the beginning of the* Specific Instructions. *Partners and shareholders reporting a disposition of section 179 property which was separately reported to you on Schedule K-1 (Form 1065 or 1120S), see* Partners and S corporation shareholders *at the beginning of the* Specific Instructions.

Generally, for property held 1 year or less, do not complete Part III; instead use Part II. For exceptions, see the chart on page 1.

Use Part III to figure recapture of depreciation and certain other items that must be reported as ordinary income on the disposition of property. Fill out lines 19 through 24 to determine the gain on the disposition of the property. If you have more than four properties to report, use additional forms. For more details on depreciation recapture, see Pub. 544.

Note. If the property was sold on the installment sale basis, see the Instructions for Form 6252 before completing Part III. Also, if you have both installment sales and noninstallment sales, you may want to use separate Forms 4797, Part III, for the installment sales and the noninstallment sales.

Line 20

The gross sales price includes money, the FMV of other property received, and any existing mortgage or other debt the buyer assumes or takes the property subject to. For casualty or theft gains, include insurance or other reimbursement you received or expect to receive for each item. Include on this line your insurance coverage, whether or not you are submitting a claim for reimbursement.

For section 1255 property disposed of in a sale, exchange, or involuntary conversion, enter the amount realized. For section 1255 property disposed of in any other way, enter the FMV.

Line 21

Reduce the cost or other basis of the property by the amount of any diesel-powered highway vehicle credit, enhanced oil recovery credit, or disabled access credit. However, do not adjust the cost or other basis for any of the items taken into account on line 22.

Line 22

Complete the following steps to figure the amount to enter on line 22.

Step 1. Add the following amounts.

- Deductions allowed or allowable for depreciation (including the 30% or 50% special depreciation allowance), amortization, depletion, or preproductive expenses.
- The section 179 expense deduction.
- The commercial revitalization deduction.
- The downward basis adjustment under section 50(c) (or the corresponding provision of prior law).
- The deduction for qualified clean-fuel vehicle property or refueling property.
- Deductions claimed under section 190, 193, or 1253(d)(2) or (3) (as in effect before the enactment of P.L. 103-66).
- The basis reduction for the qualified electric vehicle credit.
- The basis reduction for the employer-provided childcare facility credit.

Step 2. From the Step 1 total, subtract the following amounts.

- Any investment credit recapture amount if the basis of the property was reduced in the tax year the property was placed in service under section 50(c)(1) (or the corresponding provision of prior law). See section 50(c)(2) (or the corresponding provision of prior law).
- Any section 179 or 280F(b)(2) recapture amount included in gross income in a prior tax year because the business use of the property decreased to 50% or less.
- Any qualified clean-fuel vehicle property or refueling property deduction you were required to recapture because the property ceased to be eligible for the deduction.
- Any basis increase for qualified electric vehicle credit recapture.
- Any basis increase for recapture of the employer-provided childcare facility credit.

You may have to include depreciation allowed or allowable on another asset (and refigure the basis amount for line 21) if you use its adjusted basis in determining the adjusted basis of the property described on line 19. An example is property acquired by a trade-in. See Regulations section 1.1245-2(a)(4). Also, see *Like-Kind*

Exchanges under *Nontaxable Exchanges* in chapter 1 of Pub. 544.

Line 23

For section 1255 property, enter the adjusted basis of the section 126 property disposed of.

Line 25

Section 1245 property is property that is depreciable (or amortizable under section 185 (repealed), 197, or 1253(d)(2) or (3) (as in effect before the enactment of P.L. 103-66)) and is one of the following.

- Personal property.
- Elevators and escalators placed in service before 1987.
- Real property (other than property described under tangible real property below) subject to amortization or deductions under section 169, 179, 179A, 185 (repealed), 188 (repealed), 190, 193, or 194.
- Tangible real property (except buildings and their structural components) if it is used in any of the following ways.

1. As an integral part of manufacturing, production, or extraction or of furnishing transportation, communications, or certain public utility services.
2. As a research facility in these activities.
3. For the bulk storage of fungible commodities (including commodities in a liquid or gaseous state) used in these activities.

- A single purpose agricultural or horticultural structure (as defined in section 168(i)(13)).
- A storage facility (not including a building or its structural components) used in connection with the distribution of petroleum or any primary petroleum product.
- Any railroad grading or tunnel bore (as defined in section 168(e)(4)).

Exceptions and limits. See section 1245(b) for exceptions and limits involving the following.

- Gifts.
- Transfers at death.
- Certain tax-free transactions.
- Certain like-kind exchanges, involuntary conversions, etc.
- Exchanges to comply with SEC orders.
- Property distributed by a partnership to a partner.
- Transfers to tax-exempt organizations where the property will be used in an unrelated business.
- Timber property.

Special rules. See the following sections for special rules.

- Section 1245(a)(4) for player contracts and section 1056(c) for information required from the transferor of a franchise of any sports enterprise, for sales or exchanges before October 23, 2004, involving the transfer of player contracts.
- Section 1245(a)(5) (repealed) for property placed in service before 1987, if only a portion of a building is section 1245 recovery property.
- Section 1245(a)(6) (repealed) for qualified leased property placed in service before 1987.

Line 26

Section 1250 property is depreciable real property (other than section 1245 property). Section 1250 recapture applies if you used an accelerated depreciation method or you claimed the 30% or 50% special depreciation allowance, or the commercial revitalization deduction. Section 1250 recapture does not apply to dispositions of the following property placed in service after 1986 (or after July 31, 1986, if elected).

- 27.5-year (or 40-year, if elected) residential rental property (except for 27.5 year qualified New York Liberty Zone property acquired after September 10, 2001).
- 22-, 31.5-, or 39-year (or 40-year, if elected) nonresidential real property (except for 39-year qualified New York Liberty Zone property acquired after September 10, 2001, and property for which you elected to claim a commercial revitalization deduction).

Real property depreciable under ACRS (pre-1987 rules) is subject to recapture under section 1245, except for the following, which are treated as section 1250 property.

- 15-, 18-, or 19-year real property and low-income housing that is residential rental property.
- 15-, 18-, or 19-year real property and low-income housing that is used mostly outside the United States.
- 15-, 18-, or 19-year real property and low-income housing for which a straight line election was made.
- Low-income rental housing described in clause (i), (ii), (iii), or (iv) of section 1250(a)(1)(B). See the instructions for line 26b.

Exceptions and limits. See section 1250(d) for exceptions and limits involving the following.

- Gifts.
- Transfers at death.
- Certain tax-free transactions.
- Certain like-kind exchanges, involuntary conversions, etc.
- Exchanges to comply with SEC orders.
- Property distributed by a partnership to a partner.
- Disposition of qualified low-income housing.
- Transfers of property to tax-exempt organizations if the property will be used in an unrelated business.
- Dispositions of property as a result of foreclosure proceedings.

Special rules. Special rules apply in the following cases.

- For additional depreciation attributable to rehabilitation expenditures, see section 1250(b)(4).
- If substantial improvements have been made, see section 1250(f).

Line 26a

Enter the additional depreciation for the period after 1975. Additional depreciation is the excess of actual depreciation (including any 30% or 50% special depreciation allowance, or commercial revitalization deduction) over depreciation figured using the straight line method. For this purpose, do not reduce the basis under section 50(c)(1) (or the corresponding provision of prior law) to figure straight line depreciation. Also, if you claimed a commercial revitalization deduction, figure straight-line depreciation using the property's applicable recovery period under section 168.

Line 26b

Generally, use 100% as the percentage for this line. However, for low-income rental housing described in clause (i), (ii), (iii), or (iv) of section 1250(a)(1)(B), see that section for the percentage to use.

Line 26d

Enter the additional depreciation after 1969 and before 1976. If straight line depreciation exceeds the actual depreciation for the period after 1975, reduce line 26d by the excess. Do not enter less than zero on line 26d.

Line 26f

The amount the corporation treats as ordinary income under section 291 is 20% of the excess, if any, of the amount that would be treated as ordinary income if such property were section 1245 property, over the amount treated as ordinary income under section 1250. If the corporation used the straight line method of depreciation, the ordinary income under section 291 is 20% of the amount figured under section 1245.

Line 27

Partnerships (other than electing large partnerships) skip this section. Partners must enter on the applicable lines of Part III amounts subject to section 1252 according to instructions from the partnership.

You may have ordinary income on the disposition of certain farmland held more than 1 year but less than 10 years.

Refer to section 1252 to determine if there is ordinary income on the disposition of certain farmland for which deductions were allowed under sections 175 (soil and water conservation) and 182 (land clearing) (repealed). Skip line 27 if you dispose of such farmland during the 10th or later year after you acquired it.

Gain from disposition of certain farmland is subject to ordinary income rules under section 1252 before the application of section 1231 (Part I).

Enter 100% of line 27a on line 27b except as follows.

- 80% if the farmland was disposed of within the 6th year after it was acquired.
- 60% if disposed of within the 7th year.
- 40% if disposed of within the 8th year.
- 20% if disposed of within the 9th year.

Line 28

If you had a gain on the disposition of oil, gas, or geothermal property placed in service before 1987, treat all or part of the gain as ordinary income. Include on line 22 of Form 4797 any depletion allowed (or allowable) in determining the adjusted basis of the property.

If you had a gain on the disposition of oil, gas, geothermal, or other mineral properties (section 1254 property) placed in service after 1986, you must recapture all expenses that were deducted as intangible drilling costs, depletion, mine exploration costs, and development costs under sections 263, 616, and 617.

Exception. Property placed in service after 1986 and acquired under a written contract entered into before September 26, 1985, and binding at all times thereafter is treated as placed in service before 1987.

Note. A corporation that is an integrated oil company completes line 28a by treating amounts amortized under section 291(b)(2) as deductions under section 263(c).

Line 28a

If the property was placed in service before 1987, enter the total expenses after 1975 that:

- Were deducted by the taxpayer or any other person as intangible drilling and development costs under section 263(c) (except previously expensed mining costs that were included in income upon reaching the producing state) and
- Would have been reflected in the adjusted basis of the property if they had not been deducted.

If the property was placed in service after 1986, enter the total expenses that:

- Were deducted under section 263, 616, or 617 by the taxpayer or any other person; and
- But for such deduction, would have been included in the basis of the property, plus
- The deduction under section 611 that reduced the adjusted basis of such property.

If you disposed of a portion of section 1254 property or an undivided interest in it, see section 1254(a)(2).

Line 29a

Use 100% if the property is disposed of less than 10 years after receipt of payments excluded from income. Use 100% minus 10% for each year, or part of a year, that the property was held over 10 years after receipt of the excluded payments. Use zero if 20 years or more.

Line 29b

If any part of the gain shown on line 24 is treated as ordinary income under sections 1231 through 1254 (for example, section 1252), enter the smaller of (a) line 24 reduced by the part of the gain treated as ordinary income under the other provision or (b) line 29a.

Part IV

Column (a)

If you took a section 179 expense deduction for property placed in service after 1986 (other than listed property, as defined in section 280F(d)(4)) and the business use of the property decreased to 50% or less this year, complete column (a) of lines 33 through 35 to figure the recapture amount.

Column (b)

If you have listed property that you placed in service in a prior year and the business use decreased to 50% or less this year, figure the amount to be recaptured under section 280F(b)(2). Complete column (b), lines 33 through 35. See Pub. 463, Travel, Entertainment, Gift, and Car Expenses, for more details on recapture of excess depreciation.

Note. If you have more than one property subject to the recapture rules, figure the recapture amounts separately for each property. Show these calculations on a separate statement and attach it to your tax return.

Line 33

In column (a), enter the section 179 expense deduction you claimed when the property was placed in service. In column (b), enter the depreciation allowable on the property in prior tax years (plus any section 179 expense deduction you claimed when the property was placed in service).

Line 34

In column (a), enter the depreciation that would have been allowable on the section 179 property from the year the property was placed in service through (and including) the current year. See Pub. 946, How To Depreciate Property.

In column (b), enter the depreciation that would have been allowable if the property had not been used more than 50% in a qualified business. Figure the depreciation from the year it was placed in service up to (but not including) the current year. See Pub. 463 and Pub. 946.

Line 35

Subtract line 34 from line 33 and enter the recapture amount as "other income" on the same form or schedule on which you took the deduction. For example, if you took the deduction on Schedule C (Form 1040), report the recapture amount as other income on Schedule C (Form 1040).

Note. If you filed Schedule C or F (Form 1040) and the property was used in both your trade or business and for the production of income, the portion of the recapture amount attributable to your trade or business is subject to self-employment tax. Allocate the amount on line 35 to the appropriate schedules.

Be sure to increase your basis in the property by the recapture amount.

Paperwork Reduction Act Notice. We ask for the information on this form to carry out the Internal Revenue laws of the United States. You are required to give us the information. We need it to ensure that you are complying with these laws and to allow us to figure and collect the right amount of tax.

You are not required to provide the information requested on a form that is subject to the Paperwork Reduction Act unless the form displays a valid OMB control number. Books or records relating to a form or its instructions must be retained as long as their contents may become material in the administration of any Internal Revenue law. Generally, tax returns and return information are confidential, as required by section 6103.

The time needed to complete and file this form will vary depending on individual circumstances. The estimated average time is:

Recordkeeping	35 hr., 23 min.
Learning about the law or the form	8 hr., 20 min.
Preparing, copying, assembling, and sending the form to the IRS	9 hr., 17 min.

If you have comments concerning the accuracy of these time estimates or suggestions for making this form simpler, we would be happy to hear from you. See the instructions for the tax return with which this form is filed.